The Transformation of
British Politics
1860-1995

# ONE WEEK LOAN

# The Transformation of British Politics 1860–1995

BRIAN HARRISON

OXFORD UNIVERSITY PRESS

1996

Oxford University Press, Walton Street, Oxford OX2 6DP

Oxford New York
Athens Auckland Bangkok Bombay
Calcutta Cape Town Dar es Salaam Delhi
Florence Hong Kong Istanbul Karachi
Kuala Lumpur Madras Madrid Melbourne
Mexico City Nairobi Paris Singapore
Taipei Tokyo Toronto
and associated companies in
Berlin Ibadan

Oxford is a trade mark of Oxford University Press

Published in the United States
by Oxford University Press Inc., New York

British Library Cataloguing in Publication Data
Data available

Library of Congress Cataloging in Publication Data
Harrison, Brian Howard.
The transformation of British politics, 1860–1995 /
Brian Harrison.
p. cm.
Includes bibliographical references and indexes.
1. Great Britain—Politics and government—19th century. 2. Great
Britain—Politics and government—20th century. I. Title.
JN216.H335  1996     320.441′09′04—dc20      95–44970
ISBN 0–19–873122–1
ISBN 0–19–873121–3 (pbk)

1 3 5 7 9 10 8 6 4 2

Typeset by Graphicraft Typesetters Ltd., Hong Kong
Printed in Great Britain
on acid-free paper by
Bookcraft Ltd., Midsomer Norton
Nr Bath, Avon

For Vicky

# Contents

2-2 23rd

0-0

# Introduction

'THE British constitution, which used to be treated like an exhibit in a museum, too precious to touch, is now more like a target on a shooting-range.'[1] This remark from one of the more sophisticated marksmen in 1979 highlights a national tendency since the 1960s to grumble about the British political system that reached a peak in the early 1990s. In his widely read book *The State We're In* (1995), for example, Will Hutton claimed that 'the country needs and must have a modern constitutional settlement'[2] without feeling the need for facts or reasoning to back up his argument's political dimension; mere assertion seemed sufficient. Yet the British once prided themselves on their talent for devising, and still more for operating, political institutions. In politics as in manufacture, they needed few imports and had much to export. As recently as 1950 the American Political Science Association, through its committee on political parties *Towards a more Responsible Two-Party System*, could still see the British system as a model. But Britain's dramatic decline in world status has subsequently prompted a hunt for scapegoats, and many critics have homed in on the British political system. Already by 1965 two political scientists could alight upon the tendency: 'particular British institutions had been criticised before,' wrote Butler and King; 'Now Britain herself—her past and her future, and her characteristic values—all seemed to be called in question.'[3] Politicians have sometimes themselves been the accusers. Indeed, the promise of constitutional reform had become the most conspicuous distinguishing feature of two of the four leading political parties in the 1980s and of two of the three in the 1990s. Today it is fashionable to feel cross about British political institutions; to view them sympathetically is to be dismissed as bland or blind.

Yet if Walter Bagehot were with us now, he would warn us against projects for improvement, especially if foreign-inspired. Pressure for constitutional reform has grown remarkably. In 1991 the Institute for Public Policy Research published a constitution for Britain consisting of 129 articles and six schedules 'in the conviction that an example would advance the public argument more effectively than further general discussion of the problems which it raises and attempts to resolve'.[4] The foreword to *Common Sense* (1993) by Tony Benn and Andrew Hood claims that 'over the last forty years Britain has been increasingly seen as a comic and antiquated Ruritania', and that 'the time has come to refound our public institutions upon the principles of the common weal, democracy and an internationalism more in tune with the needs of the 21st century'.[5] After a substantial discussion, there follows the complete draft of Benn's 'Commonwealth of Britain Bill'. Charter 88 is a pressure group entirely concerned with constitutional change. Most of the reformers are no doubt keen to help the nation in its difficulties and are open-mindedly unsentimental and cosmopolitan in searching for remedies. Some have understandably reacted against an uncritical adulation of British political institutions that was once widespread. Herbert Morrison's formerly influential *Government and Parliament* (1954), for instance, breathes an unfamiliar air of chauvinist complacency, whereas his successors accompany their analyses with a string of reforming proposals, many of them foreign imports. The reformers include many academic students of politics; constitutional reform offers them the hope of bringing them as near as they are likely to get to the natural scientist's controlled experiment, together with a welcome discovery that their expertise can in some circumstances be thought useful. Others in the reforming camp have axes to grind, interests to promote, and frustrations to relieve. For if their campaign had been primarily inspired by concern that the political system was functioning badly, their full-blown and much-publicized conference on monarchy would have shown itself better informed and more resourceful on constitutional matters, more constructive in mood, and less prone to populist mud-slinging.[6] Their movement would also have been more preoccupied with the locality where the British political system has undeniably been functioning worst of all in recent years: Northern Ireland.

In a political system so dominated by political party, party interests are never far below the surface, especially those of parties in opposition. The reforming impulse began with disquiet in the late 1950s that Britain was slipping in the world's economic league, and with the related upsurge of radical enthusiasm for institutional change that helped Labour into power in 1964. The general elections of 1974 provided a second boost for reform because in that year the simple-majority electoral system penalized the third (Liberal) party even more severely than usual. Then came the notion that the union could be preserved only through concessions to Welsh and Scottish nationalism, whose impulse owed much to Scottish oil. It also gained from the threat to the nation state posed by the EEC, which Britain had joined in 1973. Constitutional debate in Britain now owes much to an enhanced knowledge of European electoral and judicial systems and federal structures. After 1974 some Conservatives—most notably Lords Blake, Hailsham, and Home—worried about Britain's 'elective dictatorship': devolution and reforms in the electoral system and House of Lords were needed, they thought, to curb socialist pretensions. But then came Thatcher, contemptuous of the institutional tinkering that had occurred under Wilson and Heath; for her, as for Lord Beloff, this was 'an escape route for those unwilling to tackle real problems'.[7] In summer 1983, when setting up party policy-groups to identify tasks for the rest of the decade, she says she dropped any idea of a group on 'constitutional reform' 'because I felt that there was really nothing of note to say on that subject'.[8]

Her ruthless exploitation of executive power caused constitutional reformers to gather on the left, for Liberals and Labour were alarmed at their electoral failure and at being thrown so severely on to the defensive. The reformers, though mostly anti-Conservative, did not form an integrated movement. Divided by political party, they also disagree on important details. Tony Benn, for one, thinks that 'to undermine the House of Commons by subordinating it to judges, commissioners and bankers and paralysing it with endless coalitions through proportional representation would be to . . . inflict a grave defeat upon the very idea of democracy'. With Tom Paine he objects to entrenching civil rights because it involves the dead controlling the living.[9] The reformers do, however, broadly agree on the need for more democracy, and think it would be enhanced by a written constitution, electoral reform, bills of rights, and devolution. The bicentenary celebrations in 1988 edged things forward, with the publication of the Constitutional Reform Centre's *1688–1988: Time for a New Constitution*. Charter 88 is, in its co-ordinator's words, 'an anti-establishment campaign dedicated to becoming a full-scale citizens' movement'.[10] From the late 1980s the left's think-tanks transferred to political and constitutional reform the structures that the right created in the 1970s to promote economic reform. Charter 88, the Institute for Public Policy Research (founded in 1989), the Social Market Foundation (founded in 1992), and DEMOS (founded in 1993) are the non-Conservative riposte to the Institute of Economic Affairs, the Centre for Policy Studies, and the Adam Smith Institute. The scale of the present-day liberal advance over socialism is nowhere clearer than in this repositioning of middle-class rationalistic tidy-mindedness. The Webbs' measurement and publicity are now directed, not at capitalist inefficiencies, but at constitutional anomalies.

The reforming case has not so far been politically or intellectually powerful enough to call out its opponents' full strength. Only when there is some chance of action will the counter-arguments come into focus and make converts, though the wilting of Labour's regional assemblies early in 1995 whets the sceptic's appetite for what is to come. Self-interest, traditionalist instinct, and an opportunistic diversion from difficulties elsewhere make it likely that Conservatives will sharpen the opposition. They have never had much taste for written constitutions, for these involve 'setting out the machinery of government in a document that can be altered only by exceptionally difficult procedures', as Lord Beloff put it, contemptuously dismissing Charter 88's 'constitutional convention' in 1991. 'In reality, such documents are circumvented by judicial interpretation, political manœuvres or emergency provisions, or there is a revolution and a new constitution emerges to undergo the fate of its predecessor.'[11]

This book's purpose is not to criticize the reformers' proposals. Its only partisan commitment is to the civilizing art of politics: to the belief that the much-depreciated skills of the politician are even more important in a democracy than they are in societies which pretend they have no politics; and to the belief that those skills are therefore eminently worth studying. The book's aim is historical, not prescriptive. It seeks to demonstrate in historical detail what was once widely known and also widely appreciated: that the British political system operates under what Bagehot once called 'a living constitution'. Sidney Low pointed out in 1904 that 'other constitutions have been built; that of England has been allowed to grow . . . Its development has been biological rather than mechanical' and its essence is that it 'is in a state of constant development'.[12] When one bears in mind the scale of the social, political, economic, international, and intellectual changes that have occurred since Bagehot's day, the system has proved remarkably adaptable. The two leading sources of change are discussed in Chapter 2: the rise and fall of empire, and the concomitant growth of state intervention to promote economic growth and public welfare—developments that were focused and enhanced by two devastating world wars. For it is important to judge the British political system not against some impracticably abstract standard, but in the context of the formidable problems it confronted. Any political system that can survive changes of this order must have as its foundation something more substantial than inertia, insularity, party self-interest, or lack of imagination. But this book does not intend to massage the prejudices of the British political system's admirers. It aims to provide ideas and ammunition to people of many diverse views. It does not implicitly set up a model for other countries to follow, as did the ambitious studies of the British political system that used to be compiled before the 1950s, though it plunders those studies for raw material. Nor does it seek to portray a heroic story for domestic consumption in which everything points towards present perfection, for that would indeed be futile.

Yet it does not allow present-day problems to conceal the British political system's past achievement or continuing virtues. Take the system's flexibility and adaptability. These are in themselves virtues. Still more so are the political continuity and wealth of accumulated political experience that longevity in a political system allows. One authoritative commentator has recently dismissed the idea of British institutional flexibility as 'fantastic', arguing that 'the . . . claim of flexibility is a myth long overdue for explosion'.[13] If by this he means that there has been little enthusiasm at any time since 1789 in Britain for fundamental constitutional change, he is of course right. But a flexible political system adapts to circumstances without needing to change its formal structures, as long as its politicians respond to external pressure and 'trim' them resourcefully to perform new roles or old roles in a new context. Adaptation can perhaps better gain acceptance, and so prove lasting, if it is unobtrusive and continuous. It is in this way that the British political system has for centuries shown itself flexible. The complaint is often made that the British constitution is unwritten. Less stress tends to be laid on the consequence: that it is, in Sidney Low's words, 'unfixed and flexible, where others are rigid'. He went on to say that he was not concerned 'with a solid building, to which a room may be added here, or a wing there; but with a living organism, in a condition of perpetual growth and change'.[14]

Opinions will differ on the merits of how political continuity in Britain has been achieved. Some will relish the shrewdness the system has nourished in its governing élite, the humanitarian impulse behind its responsiveness to opinion and distaste for histrionic politics, and its assiduity at initiating each set of newcomers to power. The dissatisfied, on the other hand, will resent being dragged back to what for them may seem a distasteful subject: to the 'establishment' that has been so central to the concerns of British government's critics since the 1950s. For, as Jeremy Paxman writes, half admiringly, 'the Establishment has an infinite capacity to absorb people and ideas, is endlessly adaptable'.[15] The dissatisfied will include those whose humanitarian compassion focuses on the element of continuous exploitation that gradualism entails, and those who relish the drama of revolutionary events. Among them will also be many who deplore the British political system's elevation of the dull and the practical over the intellectually sparkling and the flamboyant, and who regret the absence (except in parliament) of sharpened polarities, the scarcity of irresponsibly exhilarating political satire. Yet Britain's marked decline in world status does nothing to deny the interest of its political institutions. Those who wish to continue painstakingly adapting them to meet new challenges (for there still are such people) will want to know how their predecessors set about the task. As for those who yearn for something more, they have become so energetic in recent years that constitutional reform may soon occur more as a result of deliberate intention than has ever been the case during the past century. Unless such reforms harmonize with their context, they may well produce surprising (and perhaps unintended) results. Effective change can proceed only on the basis of full knowledge and understanding.

Yet anyone who wants to know how the British political system has evolved since the 1860s is at present in trouble. One institution, the monarchy, has received ample attention, but less from historians than from biographers. They are more concerned with individual personality than with monarchy's institutional evolution or its role within the political system. Indeed, the 1930s have the edge over us here. In 1938 Harold Laski complained that 'on no element in the Constitution is our knowledge so inexact' as on constitutional monarchy,[16] yet its student could at least then draw upon the famous series of Queen Victoria's letters. Its final volume came up to 1901 and was published in 1932, so Laski's analysis could be well informed up to the years of his childhood. Nobody can do that now, for there have been no successor volumes, whereas on inter-war precedent the published royal correspondence would now have taken us up to the Labour government of 1964. True, Queen Victoria's letters were assiduously bowdlerized by Princess Beatrice, who dedicated twenty years of her life to the task.[17] But bowdlerized letters and diaries are better than none at all. Now that daylight has been shed upon magic, the monarchy can only gain from getting its less headline-catching but more important day-to-day workings properly understood. There is no study, for instance, of the administrative structure which services the royal family. Shutting out serious writers does not prevent comment; it ensures only that comment is trivial and scurrilous. Reticence means tittle-tattle. The problem feeds upon itself because the subject then seems unrespectable to academic students of politics. In 1993 Tony Benn was fully justified in regretting that 'the aura which surrounds our system of monarchical government . . . is sustained by lack of any serious analysis of how it really works'.[18] Ferdinand Mount refers to this neglect as 'a bizarre truncation in almost all modern writings on the British Constitution'.[19] For John Cannon, neglect 'is too mild a word. There seems to have been almost a conspiracy *not* to discuss the matter.'[20] There is a short section on 'royalty' in David Butler's *British Political Facts*, but that much-used handbook on recent changes in the political system *Developments in British Politics* (now in its fourth recension) has no such section, and refers to the institution only cursorily.

The neglect of the British political system's history goes further. In 1926 Laski complained that 'the three outstanding institutions of our own day still await adequate treatment. We have no history, at least worth the name, of the Cabinet; we have none upon local government in the nineteenth century; we have no satisfactory treatment of the civil service.'[21] John Mackintosh filled one of these three gaps in 1962 with his fine history of the cabinet, but even its third edition (1977) badly needs updating. Furthermore, Anthony King complained even in 1969 that 'the academic literature on the prime ministership is thin', causing discussions of the office to be rather primitive.[22] The need for updating is still greater in local government, whose history tends to be studied only as context for some current emergency. As for the civil service, we have no 'satisfactory treatment' for either nineteenth or twentieth centuries. Anti-government, too, suffers from neglect. Introducing his study of civil liberties during the Second World War, Neil Stammers says he 'failed to uncover a single volume which tries to make a systematic study of government practice towards civil liberties'.[23] The historian of legal aid sees his subject as 'falling . . . between the two great disciplines of history and law' and so is ignored by both.[24] Other important British political institutions have been still more seriously neglected—most notably, pressure groups and parliament.[25] 'Extraordinarily little of lasting value', wrote Janet Morgan in 1975, 'has been published on the House of Lords.'[26] Andrew Adonis has handsomely dispatched that problem for the late-Victorian period, but other periods need similar treatment, and there is no Adonis for any period in the history of the House of Commons since the eighteenth century. Furthermore, Adonis rightly regrets historians' neglect of 'the minutiae of parliamentary procedure and the legislative process', and urges attention to 'what might perhaps be called the "low politics of high politics", the operation of the national legislature and its impact on the wider polity'.[27]

Politicians cannot always be relied upon to fill the gap. Given the myriad pressures, distractions, and emergencies of their life, their frequent lack of historical perspective is understandable. So short is their historical memory, indeed, that the politicians of the 1980s often ignored historical precedents that could have been helpful.[28] Perhaps the most striking instance is Thatcher's failure to learn from the defeat of the poll tax levied in 1380, whose fate so closely resembles that of its successor in 1990.[29] The problem is not new. 'It requires a great deal of time to have opinions,' wrote Bagehot. Explaining in 1885 why politicians pondered so little about politics, Lord Randolph Churchill claimed that 'railways and telegraphs, the steam printing machine, and shorthand-writing have done their best to kill political thought'. As a result, 'an English politician of the present day lives in such a giddy hurly-burly of events . . . and he has at the same time to deal with such a complexity, such a heterogeneous mass of business, that as for sitting down quietly to think out . . . any grave political situation . . . such a process is out of the question'.[30] None the less, three politicians since 1975 have made an important and unprecedented contribution—not through interpreting the past, but through closely observing their own time. R. H. S. Crossman seems to have been prompted to merge his projected study of present-day government with his memoirs after reading Robert Blake's *Disraeli*, which in his view suffered from not providing any account of Disraeli's daily life as a minister.[31] Tony Benn records that he had 'great fun' addressing a seminar at Nuffield College in 1966 'on becoming a minister', where he pointed out that 'no book I had ever read on the British constitution had been any help or had given me any indication of what to expect'.[32] Thanks to him, Crossman, and Barbara Castle, nobody can say that now.

Crossman was surely right to think that historical writing should be integrated with recent experience of what political life is like. 'The events for which one generation cares most are often those of which the next knows least,' said Bagehot, who in later life wanted a book written on the history of recent politics that drew upon knowledge of English politicians' personal relationships.[33] The integration of past with present in the history of British political institutions has been rendered urgent by the remarkable developments (not as yet illuminated by cabinet diaries, though substantially illuminated by memoirs) that occurred after 1979. Despite her conservatism on constitutional reform Thatcher exploited, some thought dangerously, the British political system's potential for strengthening executive power. She 'has so strained the conventional limits of the British constitution', wrote Vernon Bogdanor in 1989, 'that the constitution itself has become a part of party politics, rather than a set of rules lying above politics'.[34] She unintentionally fuelled the debate that had begun in the

1960s about the defects of the British constitution. 'Mrs Thatcher's greatest service to the nation', it has been claimed, 'may yet be the institutional reforms that take place on her departure.'[35] Besides, her handling of the cabinet was unusual enough to constitute an important moment in its history, and dangerous enough to accelerate her downfall. So it is now specially important to map out the no man's land between journalism and history. Now is a good time to draw historical analysis closer to recent writings (mainly by people who would call themselves students of 'politics') on how the major British political institutions have evolved since Bagehot's day.

This is not a task historians seem to have relished. A gap seems to have opened up between their diminishingly political preoccupations and the increasingly present- or future-orientated preoccupations of those who study or write about 'politics'. To help bridge this hiatus since the 1970s I have occasionally given a series of lectures in Oxford on the history of British political institutions since the 1860s. The span in both time and range of institutions discussed is intimidating, and the monograph literature is correspondingly formidable. For some years I hoped that somebody else would produce the necessary synthesis. My lectures seemed no more than an interim expedient before something better appeared. Yet the need has still not been met, so here I make the lectures more widely available in substantially revised form. So tenacious are political traditions and attitudes in Britain that it would have been good to begin at the beginning, a task historians in earlier and bolder generations would not have shirked. I take up here the less ambitious task of launching the discussion only at the 1860s. It is a good starting-point for several reasons. It was the decade when discussion among Liberals on the British political system was particularly vigorous and resourceful. Mill in 1861 and Bagehot in 1867 published important books about the British political system which equipped us with much of the political vocabulary we now use. Furthermore, in 1867 the second Reform Act launched the transition towards the mass politics in which we now live, and prepared the ground for the mass parties and national election campaigns which are now familiar. Yet in the 1860s the two major forces subverting individualist Liberal values—imperialism and the welfare state—were only beginning to impinge on the political system, and civil service, local government, and monarchy faced formidable problems of adjustment. So the years since the 1860s offer both the quantity of raw material and the time-span needed to discuss an important and continuing theme: the adaptability and flexibility of British government.

How should the material be arranged? The historian might prefer a chronologically 'cross-sectional' approach: to demonstrate long-term change by showing how the entire political system worked at, say, the mid-Victorian, Edwardian, inter-war, and post-war periods. This would be the best way to illuminate interaction between the system's constituent parts, but it would obscure the continuity in the internal history of each, so I opted for a 'segmental' approach. After a survey in Chapter 1 of the system as it worked in Bagehot's day, I analyse in Chapter 2 the challenges it faced from two striking and formidable developments whose impact Bagehot could scarcely have predicted: the growth of empire and the welfare state. In Chapters 3 to 6 I emphasize four dimensions of the pluralism that lies behind British political institutions. The first of these sketches out how the constituent nations of what we now know as the United Kingdom were held together during the period, and the next three discuss local self-government, freedom of the individual, and voluntarism. With the basis of Britain's 'civil society' established, the later chapters can survey changes in central government. Chapters 7 to 12 are concerned with, respectively, political parties, elections, parliament, cabinet, civil service, and monarchy. My aim throughout has been to rescue present-day discussion from parochialism in time. So I include a chapter (13) on the changes in the system that are now being debated. In Chapter 14 I try to rescue the book from parochialism in space by setting it into some sort of international framework. And to reflect the book's emphasis on the importance of cultural rather than institutional influences on British political life, the concluding chapter (15) refrains from espousing any of Chapter 13's causes, and instead discusses selected cultural obstacles to the system's continued effectiveness.

Although I have provided a 'political calendar' of essential political events, I have not sought to lay out the basic facts about British political institutions because several textbooks and handbooks already do that quite adequately. Instead, this book plunders such books mercilessly, for it aims to be a commentary on the facts. There is little original research in this book. Chapter 8 depends heavily, for instance, on the Nuffield election studies, and Chapter 10 on John Mackintosh's *The British Cabinet*. Rather than pushing forward the frontiers, I aim primarily to synthesize the research that has already been done and to relate it to more recent developments. In attempting this, I have tried to avoid merely reverting to old-style constitutional history, and to capture something of the broadened perspective that historians now bring to bear on their subject-matter. History can never be narrowly political because politicians can survive only by responding to wider social, economic, and intellectual developments. To quote

Butler and Rose on the general election of 1959, 'electoral trends cannot be understood without reference to social trends'.[36]

I end with two acknowledgements. The first is to an anonymous but most conscientious publisher's reader, whose suggestions improved the text considerably, though I fear not sufficiently to satisfy him. Secondly, I acknowledge the consistent understanding, patience, and loyalty my wife, Vicky, has shown while I was writing not only this book but all its predecessors. It is the first book that I have dedicated to her, and for several reasons it is perhaps the most appropriate. Her career leads her to move widely, for practical purposes, among the institutions I describe, and with far more skill than I could ever do. It was she who persuaded me to overcome my initial reluctance and publish on such a subject. She has given me every encouragement while I have been trying to write it. I wish the book could have done better justice to all that I owe to her.

# 1

## Bagehot's System

WALTER BAGEHOT was a brilliant essayist—epigrammatic, worldly-wise, deeply suspicious of the intellectual and the doctrinaire. His direct, fresh, unpompous, down-to-earth style of writing carries the reader along with his zest for life and affairs, and is often refreshingly forthright in uncovering the reality that lies behind appearances. He takes his reader into his confidence, conducts a conversation with him, sets him puzzles, and then shows him how to solve them in a commonsensical but shrewd and highly readable way. He is a master at setting the career of a public figure into its political context, and at explaining how the world works. He does this without sentiment, yet also with a broad human sympathy. In his three famous books—*The English Constitution* (1865–7), *Physics and Politics* (1867–72), and *Lombard Street* (1873)—he brought a new liveliness of tone to the discussion of serious subjects. *The English Constitution* shows him at his best. When confronted by British society, he somehow unites the intelligent outsider's puzzled curiosity and quick insight with the insider's knowing yet tolerant affection for his subject-matter. *The English Constitution* is the inevitable starting-point for any account of how British government has come to be what it now is.

Yet it is not infallible as an account of how the British political system worked even in the 1860s, let alone subsequently, if only because Bagehot's background gave him a rather unusual perspective on politics. Born in 1826, he took a degree in economics from University College London. Lacking a classical education and distant from Oxford and Cambridge, those nurseries of Britain's political élite, he was always in some sense an outsider, even when dining with Gladstone or week-ending at Highclere. Furthermore, as a well-known journalist in the 1850s, and as editor of *The Economist* from 1860 until he died in 1877, he was a member of a profession which then enjoyed less prestige, and therefore less access to the decision-makers, than it enjoys now. 'The knowledge of public men, so freely given by newspapers', he wrote, 'is a knowledge of masks rather than realities.'[1] Bagehot failed in his two attempts to get into parliament as a Liberal candidate, and as a middle-class journalist and banker he could have no direct experience of political decision-making.

Nor could reading do much to repair the gap, for little had then been published on how the British political system worked. Queen Victoria's letters were not published until the 1920s, and published diaries of cabinet discussions would have been inconceivable in Bagehot's day. 'Politics' had hardly yet emerged as a distinct subject of study. Even within the political élite, understanding of the subject was not usually acquired through an academic route. The conversation which overflowed in the 1860s and 1870s at the breakfast-table of the third Marquis of Salisbury, for instance, was spiced with political argument, laced with readings aloud from the newspapers, and disciplined by his recurrent question, when words were being used loosely: 'Would you mind defining?'[2] Where the route to political knowledge did lie through the university, it was usually circuitous, by way of history and the classics. So Bagehot had to pick up what he could from conversations, at which he excelled, and from the occasional unintended leak. 'He studied Life through contact with Life', said his sister-in-law, 'rather than from books. Ideas, he felt, must be taken in, first hand; they must be inspired by contact with living creatures, living interests.'[3]

Bagehot was limited, too, in his sympathies. As a Liberal, his serious-minded rationality led him to dismiss Disraeli as 'a political adventurer'.[4] He underestimated, and could not fully comprehend, the forces the Conservative leader was attempting to harness. But as a moderate Liberal, Bagehot also lacked affinity with his Party's left: 'I hate the Liberal enthusiasts,' he once told a friend. 'I feel inclined to say "go home, Sir, and take a dose of salts, and see if it won't clear it all out of you".'[5] As a Somerset man, far removed from the new industrial cities, who valued above all things a balanced judgement, he was out of tune with the passions of 'mass politics': with the new popular structures that Gladstone was harnessing as Liberal leader. 'At no former time', Bagehot wrote in 1859, 'was there such a difference as there now is between Lancashire and Devonshire.'[6] His premature death in 1877 denied him the opportunity he would surely have taken of gravitating in the 1880s towards the Conservative Party, no doubt via Liberal Unionism.

Hence Bagehot's unobtrusive conflict with J. S. Mill, a radical and rationalistic reformer on the Liberal Party's left. Bagehot in his obituary of Mill made 'no claim to belong' to the inner circle of Mill's followers.[7]

But he was an admirer, was thoroughly acquainted with Mill's writings, and devoted one of his earliest reviews to Mill's *Principles of Political Economy* ('this admirable work').[8] In his view of 'the lower orders' whose structures were soon to become politically so important, Bagehot diverged markedly from Mill, claiming that 'the working classes contribute almost nothing to our corporate public opinion'.[9] He criticized Mill's *Political Economy* for treating them 'as if they were beings of pure intellect', whereas 'great towns are depots of temptation'.[10] Mill was already arguing in 1848 that 'the working classes are now part of the public; in all discussions on matters of general interest they, or a portion of them, are now partakers'.[11] Bagehot was preoccupied in the 1860s with 'the dangers of democracy in great industrial cities, where the majority live by wages, where they have no fixed property, where they have scarcely a fixed home, where they may be excited by agitators'.[12] John Ruskin's *Unto this Last*, which so profoundly moved them, attracted his scorn in *The Economist*, and Bagehot's apprehensive comments on the likely effects of a mass franchise became prize exhibits a century later in Tony Benn's diary.[13] When commenting on the lower orders, Bagehot's frankness was at its most robust, and resembles what the future prime minister Lord Salisbury was writing in the *Quarterly Review* at the time.[14] Arguing for constitutional monarchy as an effective safeguard for public order, Bagehot pointed out in 1870 that 'society in England without a queen would have to treat evil-doers much more sternly, and control roughs by a much more unmistakable display of its power, if necessary, to shoot them down'.[15] To modern eyes, Bagehot seems complacent on the virtues of the British political system, unperceptive about its long-term potential for adjustment, and patronizing towards the foreigners who were denied its benefits.

So although he is always worth listening to, he cannot be our sole guide at the outset of our journey through the British political system. This chapter will survey the operation of the entire system at the time he was writing, highlighting the debate about it with Mill that Bagehot unobtrusively conducted. It will take us in turn to each of the starting-points from which Chapters 4 to 12 set out. It will not, however, take us to the starting-points from which Chapters 2 and 3 set out because Bagehot had little to say about the two great threats to the political system he knew: the growth and decline of empire and the advance of public welfare. Nor was he greatly concerned about threats to the union of the United Kingdom. His book was entitled 'The *English* Constitution', and it did not discuss the special problems of Ireland, Scotland, and Wales. In the 1860s the United Kingdom's nations still seemed to be drawing together, and progressive people then favoured amalgamating smaller states into larger. Bagehot strongly opposed Irish home rule, and (with more prescience than Gladstone) denied that Ireland's inhabitants were united by nationality. The fact that the United Kingdom was made up from nations each with its own traditions was the first of four reasons why a governmental structure that to all appearances seemed authoritarian turned out to be much less so in practice. The three others, covered in Chapters 4 to 6, were local self-government, a libertarian tradition, and a voluntarist culture. All three seemed secure and familiar enough not to demand Bagehot's overt attention, but he knew well enough how firmly they moulded British government in practice.

*

In Bagehot's day, as now, the British political system was unitary in nature, and because government had inherited the monarch's prerogative powers, its writ ran throughout the nation. Yet governmental reality is moulded as much by cultural attitudes as by political structure, and these ensured fragmentation at the centre. Britain has long possessed an independent judiciary, a politically neutral civil service, and a parliament which accommodates opposition as well as government. Central-government pluralism was complemented by pluralism within the community at large— so much so that until August 1914, according to A. J. P. Taylor, 'a sensible, law-abiding Englishman could pass through life and hardly notice the existence of the state, beyond the post office and the policeman'.[16] This was partly because in a regionally variegated economy where agriculture is salient, as in nineteenth-century Britain, it was not administratively sensible to centralize: local people knew more than central government about local needs. But there was more to it than this. Popular fears of government spies and excisemen ran deep, and in Britain before 1914 interested parties (especially nonconformist radicals and Whig politicians) stored up the distasteful folk memory of a centralizing Stuart autocracy in the seventeenth century. The periodic upheavals of government in nineteenth-century France revived such memories. Early-Victorian educational, housing, and health reformers like Chadwick and Shaftesbury were unusual in taking France's relatively centralized government as their model, for in Britain libertarian traditions and *laissez-faire* economic philosophy favoured decentralization. Industrialization also had the effect of strengthening anti-metropolitan attitudes. As viewed by the new large and self-confident provincial commercial communities, London was a centre of aristocratic extravagance, moral decay, political backwardness, and social instability.

In endorsing local self-government, Mill was very much working with the early-Victorian grain. As late as 1919 C. B. Fawcett, delimiting his 'provinces of England', claimed that patriotism must begin at home, and that local patriotism reinforced 'national patriotism', whereas over-centralization inflated the capital city's political influence.[17] For him the French Revolution showed how dangerous it was to ignore geography in the pursuit of uniform administrative boundaries. 'A strong local patriotism is essential to good provincial government under democratic conditions,' he wrote, 'and this can be developed only if the provinces are closely related to natural divisions of the country.'[18] Hence British nineteenth-century central government aimed to do little more than inform and guide local authorities in taking their own initiatives. Much nineteenth-century interventionist legislation took a permissive form, leaving the localities to decide whether to act. Politicians were slow to use national revenue to meet what were seen as predominantly local responsibilities. The Local Government Board, central government's link with the local authorities, was reactive in its responses, negative in its view of its own function, and preoccupied largely with ensuring correct accounting procedure.[19] It was 'a Board of controls', said Redlich in 1903, 'but not a Board of control. It enjoys no general abstract delegated authority.'[20] It was assumed that initiatives on such things as housing, transport, welfare, police, and health would come largely from the localities.

The simple-majority electoral system rooted Liberal and Conservative parties in the constituencies and therefore in local government. The few party officials at the centre intruded only reluctantly upon local political relationships. Although both parties had originated at Westminster, their MPs at least until the 1880s usually owed their seats to local influence. If they were landowners, they were usually keen to get back to their estates for much of the year. Nineteenth-century Conservatives were strong in the countryside and welcomed decentralization for ensuring that London was no Paris. It would both limit the damage that any London-based coup could do, and train up the people in the realities of government, thus insulating them against what Lord Salisbury described as 'wild teachers'.[21] For Salisbury in 1885, decentralized government was 'a special Tory doctrine which we have held through good report and evil report for many and many a generation'.[22] Given their influence with the land and established Church, Conservatives were well entrenched in the entire system of rural local government. The county in Bagehot's England evoked powerful loyalties, and had its own ecclesiastical structure, its own law-courts, its own social functions, and even its own foxhounds. In the lords-lieutenant, county administration retains its feudal flavour still. As the Queen's representatives in the county, they have direct access to her, and are recruited from the well-to-do. Of the forty-six male English lords-lieutenant in 1990, thirty had been educated at Eton.[23]

Until 1888 the county was not seen as a mere rural equivalent of the municipal authority, with an overall administrative responsibility for the area. Still less was it required to respond to its inhabitants at elections. Instead, rural administration was carried on by *ad hoc* bodies (elected administrative structures created for a specific purpose, each with its own boundary) supplemented by more ancient and unelected institutions. A strong sense of public duty led landowners to spend much time acting as local poor-law guardians, officers in the militia, and magistrates at Quarter Sessions. They were entrenched, too, at the parish level. 'The unity between church and state is typified in the administration of an English village at every turn,' wrote T. H. S. Escott in 1885. 'The squire is a magistrate; not improbably the rector is a magistrate too. The clergyman and the congregation have each their churchwarden. The parish clerk, beadle, and sexton have all of them a legal and civil status.'[24] Dissenters, pressure groups, and socialists might send out their missionaries, confident in their urban values, but such values made their way only slowly in the countryside. The landowners' high social standing often ensured that politically they lived on into the era of the new local-government franchise, as the local-government elections of 1889 were to show.

Liberals, too, believed in local self-government, and diverged from Conservatives only on how democratic it should be. The Liberal ideal was ultimately in the strict sense anarchist: that is, its policies aimed to minimize central-government authority and to remove coercive authority altogether. Richard Cobden, for instance, thought that central government's role was inflated by war and protection, and that under free trade 'we should see, at a far distant period, the governing system of this world revert to something like the municipal system'.[25] Liberals at every level thought local self-government best for mobilizing local expertise and initiative, for, as Mill put it, 'all the facilities which a government enjoys of access to information . . . are not an equivalent for the one great disadvantage of an inferior interest in the result'.[26] The growth of large provincial cities after the industrial revolution evoked a combination of middle-class self-confidence and dissenting (mainly Unitarian and Quaker) idealism which eventually brought major gains to the Liberal Party and major achievement in nineteenth-century urban government.[27] Belief in local self-government was not confined to those with (to use the contemporary phrase) 'a stake in the country': it attracted working people too. The reformed poor law in 1834 had after all demonstrated how central government could neglect working people's sensibilities. For many working men, central government was in enemy hands, and must be warded off. 'Chartism and local self-government, stand in the relation of cause and effect,' wrote *The Charter* in 1839.[28] The paper argued that instead of magistrates there should be a local authority elected annually by adult male suffrage, by districts subdivided into wards, each sending one member to form a district board. 'In domestic policy', said the Chartist leader Ernest Jones in his election address at Nottingham in 1857, 'I strenuously advocate increased liberty of municipal action, as opposed to those centralising tendencies which have become so marked of late.'[29] At local government elections the humbler voters struggled to keep the rates down by resisting imaginative schemes for improvement.[30]

All this helps to explain why British local government was anything but uniform in Bagehot's day. Indeed, its lack of system explains why the phrase 'local government' did not emerge till the 1850s.[31] Scotland had its own distinct machinery. In England in the 1860s there were quite separate systems of local government in town and country. The Municipal Reform Act of 1835, which reformed 178 boroughs, sharpened that contrast with a boundary revision which aimed to separate out rural areas and include in boroughs only 'a population having a community of interest'.[32] And the Act, by entrusting elected town councils with the administrative responsibilities hitherto carried out in the towns by justices of the peace, again accentuated the contrast with rural areas, where the justices continued to combine their judicial and administrative roles. The Act placed municipal government on so secure a foundation that it was able to take up the regulatory role industrialization demanded in areas like health, housing, and transport. The City of London was exempt from the Act, and cleverly upheld its independence throughout the nineteenth century. Co-ordinated local government of London outside the City began in 1855 when the Metropolitan Board of Works was set up to gather representatives from London's vestries or district boards.

The success of early-Victorian municipal government made it the model for local-government reform in the countryside, where the new pressures for regulation were inevitably also felt. The justices of the peace could not long continue to combine the judicial and administrative roles which in boroughs had already become distinct. In the mid-Victorian period the pressures began building up for more democracy in rural local government too.[33] Complexity in rural administration was compounded after 1834 by the Poor Law Amendment Act. Its poor-law boards involved superimposing an *ad hoc* body on the existing local-government system throughout England and Wales. Furthermore, the poor-law boards, unlike other local-government bodies, were centrally supervised by a specially designated government department, a situation its critics viewed as decidedly 'un-English'. The *ad hoc* body later diversified into separate boards concerned with public health (from 1848) and education (from 1870). Complexity was particularly enhanced in rural areas, where no local authority existed to assume these new functions. Poor-law unions, boards of health, and school boards all held sway within areas that did not coincide with the borough or county boundaries. As for the smallest of the local-government units, the parish, it took three forms, each with differing boundaries: the civil, the ecclesiastical, and the poor-law.[34] As between all the units of mid-Victorian local government there were contrasts in area, population, timing and method of election, and qualification of voters and candidates.[35] By 1861 J. S. Mill understandably thought it time to concentrate all local-government responsibilities on a single local parliament with a wide brief.[36]

   In bringing order into this local confusion, central government could move only cautiously. Its most powerful weapon was money: the grant-in-aid, which could be earmarked and made to a local authority only on conditions. These would naturally include safeguards for efficiency, including arrangements for the central audit of local-authority accounts. The process had begun well before the 1860s, especially with the aim of improving provision for police and prisons. Grants contributed 3 per cent of total local-authority income in England and Wales in 1842/3, rising to 6 per cent by 1872/3;[37] and whereas the total received from rates doubled between 1830 and 1870, the total from central-government grants rose twelvefold.[38] 'No subject except, perhaps, war, so annoyed Mr Gladstone as that of grants-in-aid . . .', said Sidney Webb in 1899: 'what he did not realise is that sometimes it is desirable to encourage expenditure.'[39] Whatever Gladstone might say, central government found grants-in-aid invaluable for guiding local authorities in desired directions.[40] At the same time, central government's auditing procedure was becoming more elaborate. Administered after 1871 by the Local Government Board, it opened out from the poor-law structure, becoming increasingly comprehensive and stringent. It was complemented by mounting central-government supervision of the valuation process for local-government rates.[41] So local government in Bagehot's day was already moving towards that integration of central and local administration which lies behind the centralized 'welfare state' that we now know.

Despite or even because of its anomalies, nineteenth-century British local-government machinery had its overseas admirers. Josef Redlich in 1903 admired the way in which British government, in its administrative counties, had taken care to preserve 'local traditions and historical associations at the expense of scientific geography and, to a certain extent, of administrative convenience'. There was, he said something 'un-English' about a central state ruling over 'subjects'. Mounting a major reform of rural local government in 1888 with minimum boundary changes was 'only an expression of the English idea of the State as an association or federation of self-governing communities'. He saw Englishmen as having 'wisely set limits to that centralised omnipotence which the Continent too often admires as the zenith of statesmanship'.[42]

\*

Bagehot's *English Constitution* has no chapter on the third important constituent of civil society in Britain: a concern for the defence of rights and liberties. This was because his main aim was to explain how British government worked, and he took its libertarian context largely for granted. He knew well enough how firmly this hedged in what politicians in the 1860s could achieve. In England, he wrote, 'the natural impulse of the English people is to resist authority', so that 'we love independent "local authorities", little centres of outlying authority'.[43] But he would probably have preferred to discuss duties rather than rights, and he would not have shared Mill's enthusiasm for democratic structures at every level. For Mill, 'a democratic constitution, not supported by democratic institutions in detail, but confined to the central government, not only is not political freedom, but often creates a spirit precisely the reverse, carrying down to the lowest grade in society the desire and ambition of political domination'.[44] This much needed saying, if only because some Liberals failed to apply their liberal principles below the level of the state: that is, in family, pressure group, chapel, and factory. Conservatives were unlikely to use the language of rights, but they were enthusiastic for its reality—entrenched defensively as they were in their provincial estates, their established interests, their traditionalist trades and professions. So in the 1860s there was all-party agreement on the need to uphold not only local self-government, but also individual liberty.

It was in their concern for religious liberty that the Liberals overtook the Conservatives. The Reformation had introduced a pluralism into religious structures that was carried further by parliament's triumph in the seventeenth-century civil war and by the defeat of James II in 1688. Constitutional monarchy then grew up in a context of decentralized government and increasing religious pluralism. This in turn fostered governmental pluralism and created in the United Kingdom a religious grouping that was highly sympathetic to protest groups: organized dissent. Memories of the puritan triumph over Charles I helped to restrain the authoritarian instincts of British Conservatives, and also to foster the concessionary instincts of British Whigs and Liberals when confronted by popular pressure. Religious pluralism was carried still further during the nineteenth century when toleration spread to Unitarians, Roman Catholics, Jews, and ultimately even to atheists. Mid-Victorian Liberals showed a real passion for liberty, conceived somewhat abstractly. Of her father, John Grey of Dilston, Josephine Butler recalled that 'he would speak of the imposition of social disabilities of any kind, by one class of persons on another, with kindling eyes and breath which came quickly'.[45] Their enthusiasm reflects how recently justice had been done to individuals—nonconformists, Catholics, and any group unpopular with the Anglicans and aristocrats who ran the state. Many of their descendants were active within the Victorian Liberal Party. It assumed that, with Protestant help, British society was struggling slowly out of medieval interventionist obscurantism under the guidance of the urban middle classes. 'He taught me to take the strongest interest in the Reformation', J. S. Mill recalled of the education he had received from his father, 'as the great and decisive contest against priestly tyranny for liberty of thought.'[46] The discovery of printing, declared the former Chartist Henry Vincent in 1850, 'settled the question between light and darkness, liberty and slavery', for the printing-press 'refused to be the vassal of Government or of priestcraft'.[47] Magna Carta, the Reformation, the seventeenth-century puritans and Covenanters, the anti-slavery movement, and a whole series of subsequent crusades were central to this Liberal interpretation of history.

Liberalism in the 1860s was at its most powerful. It owed much to the long battle Protestant England had earlier fought against what were seen as French authoritarianism and Romish superstition. Bagehot claimed in 1863 that 'all sound thinkers are bound to prefer, and to say that they prefer, the liberty of England to the equality of France'.[48] An unobtrusive impulse that prompted Bagehot to write his *English Constitution* was disagreement with what J. S. Mill had written in *Representative Government* (1861); but on the essentials of Mill's *Liberty* (1859), the classic mid-Victorian defence, the two men would have been at one. For Mill the major threat to liberty came not from the state but from the tyranny of social opinion. 'Over himself, over his own body and mind, the individual is sovereign,' he wrote;[49] the individual must be free to decide how best to promote his own good, and the state should restrain him only to prevent him from interfering with the freedom of others to do the same. Hence the need for free speech, free association, free thought. The tyranny of fashionable opinion was something of which Bagehot, too, was well aware. 'There is much quiet intellectual persecution among "reasonable" men,' he wrote; 'a cautious person hesitates before he tells them anything new, for if he gets a name for such things he will be called "flighty" and in times of decision he will not be attended to.'[50] In his famous second chapter on 'liberty of thought and discussion', Mill argued that the entire race suffers if opinion cannot be freely expressed. First, the opinion may be true. Second, the opinion may be partly true. Perhaps, said Mill, it is not possible for any one individual to carry the whole truth in his mind. Perhaps the truth can be attained only through the free conflict in society between opposites—for example, between the forces of order and progress. Third, even if the opinion is untrue, its restatement will provoke those who hold the true ideas into vigorously restating them. In this way, true ideas in danger of being lost can, through free debate, actually be revived. Mill claimed that he who knows only his own side of the case knows little even of that. Here again Bagehot was in complete sympathy with Mill, for both saw the political system as a gigantic classroom, resonating with energetic self-instruction.

In his third chapter ('of individuality, as one of the elements of well-being'), Mill argued that a society should tolerate not only diversity of ideas but also 'different experiments of living',[51] so long as they respect the freedom of others. Different life-styles might suit different individuals. Mill had Victorian puritanism in his sights here; personal austerity may be a virtue, he thought, but so also is individual spontaneity. Mill's defence of spontaneity extended even to championing the eccentric, and like many Liberals later mobilized in the Lunacy Laws Amendment Association he worried about lunacy law's threat to the property and liberty of eccentrics.[52] In *Representative Government* he referred to 'the antagonism of influences which is the only real security for continued progress'.[53] Only this, he thought, could ward off the continuous tendency towards mediocrity in society. He feared the onset of middle-class mediocrity—a sort of 'stationary state' such as had once held back progress in China. Here again Mill was at one with Bagehot, who knew well enough how free argument was needed 'to break the thick crust of custom'.[54] Mill's argument concluded by discussing applications of his ideas, and by emphasizing that the state should do nothing that can be better done by individuals.

Mill's *Liberty* was written in the context of what he saw as mounting encroachments on liberty. He argued that in some areas the individual citizen rather than the state should act, not because the job would be done better, but because the citizen would benefit from the act of choice. Individualist Liberalism (as in Herbert Spencer) was keener to promote moral than material progress, if only because it thought that material progress would spontaneously occur within a morally disciplined society. Some degree of suffering was, it thought, unavoidable, but the state's hasty attempt to remove it might in the long term make the suffering worse. Through encouraging choice, popular government, said Mill, 'promotes a better and higher form of national character, than any other polity whatsoever'.[55] So progressive mid-Victorian Liberals favoured franchise extension, devolution, limited government, and participation at every turn. These were desirable for their own sake, but they also fostered political stability. The French and English revolutions showed what happens when citizens entrust too much to government, and when government loses touch with the citizen. Freedom of expression and association, by keeping government in touch with opinion, made opinion easier to handle. Subversive language was more destabilizing when secret than when open. Procession, public meeting, and petition seemed the alternatives to riot and revolution.

Liberals claimed that political stability in turn produced prosperity for Great Britain, whereas Catholic obscurantism and an over-mighty state caused Spain, Portugal, and Ireland to languish. H. T. Buckle provided historical endorsement with his influential but highly tendentious comparative analysis of national histories, the *Introduction to the History of Civilization in England* (1857–61). Liberty was thought to foster intelligence, initiative, and enterprise. It had indeed long been fertilizing British society with a rich infusion of talented immigrants, one of whom was Karl Marx, and among the Englishman's reasons for rejecting Marx's ideas in the 1880s was the belief that British prosperity resulted directly from the freedom of the individual. This belief 'was not just Victorian cant; it was one of the most deeply held intellectual convictions of late Victorian Englishmen'.[56] Reading Mill's *Liberty* was a major formative experience for Victorian Liberals. Charles Kingsley picked it up in Parker's bookshop in Oxford and became so entranced that he sat down, read it through without stopping, and departed 'clearer-headed, braver-minded'.[57] Mill had

many disciples among the intellectuals whom the Liberal Party mobilized
on the British left. Among them Henry Fawcett, James Bryce, John Morley,
and Herbert Spencer were perhaps the most distinguished. Mill's book was
radical enough to have implications for social arrangements more than a
century later. For all the Labour Party's debt to its Liberal predecessor, the
defence of liberty against the state has never been as central to its outlook.

*

Voluntarism was a constituent of civil society that grew out of, and in
turn accentuated, its self-governing and libertarian constituents. Used in
the sense of 'the principle of relying on voluntary action rather than
compulsion', its first citation in the *Oxford English Dictionary* dates from
1924,[58] but the practice of voluntarism in Britain is as old as the hills.
The nineteenth-century labels for it were 'self-help', 'self-improvement',
charity, or philanthropy. Voluntarism was built into the very structure of
nineteenth-century government, much of which was carried out by unpaid
local functionaries. A. J. P. Taylor says that even in the 1920s 'the most
influential figures in public life were ... voluntary workers ... The public
life of England was sustained by a great army of busybodies, and anyone could enlist in this army who felt inclined to ... These were the active people of England and provided the ground swell of her history.'[59]
Voluntarism was central to the activities of the pressure group, and still
more to the type of pressure group that united reformers round a 'cause',
and got them to crusade for it. Bagehot claimed in 1867 that 'there is no
worse trade than agitation at this time', and that 'a man can hardly get an
audience if he wishes to complain of anything'.[60] It was not one of his
more perceptive remarks, for during the 1860s the cause group was preparing itself for the Gladstonian Liberal leap forward in political participation.
The Reform League, the trade unions, the Liberation Society, the attack
on state-regulated prostitution, the temperance and feminist movements—
all these and more were beginning to flex their political muscles.

Of the two broad types of pressure group, the 'cause group'—predominantly Liberal in mood, and campaigning to change opinion—was complemented by the relatively conservative 'interest group', which was more to
Bagehot's taste. Whereas the cause group saw itself as promoting the
general interest through change, the interest group aimed at protecting
particular interests through conservation. Whereas the cause group sought
to transcend local interests in pursuing high-flown ideals, the interest

group sought to mobilize local interests in promoting earthbound priorities. Early-Victorian free traders, organized into that most famous of cause groups the Anti-Corn Law League, wanted to push the interest group to the sidelines, thus clearing the way for the cause group's free trade in ideas. The League's assault on the interest group was direct, for it thought that with free trade the economy would become self-acting, and that business interests would no longer need to lobby government about tariffs. A preference for cause over interest group was one reason why J. S. Mill backed proportional representation. 'I cannot see why the feelings and interests which arrange mankind according to localities, should be the only ones thought worthy of being represented', he wrote, 'or why people who have other feelings and interests, which they value more than they do their geographical ones, should be restricted to these as the sole principle of their political classification.'[61]

A predominantly rural society tends to regard change as cyclical rather than linear, sees much of man's fate as lying beyond his control, and defers to age and experience. In challenging the agricultural interest, nineteenth-century cause groups contested such assumptions. Allied with aristocracy and established Church, land was at first well able to defend itself against middle-class newcomers. Prudent reformers had to present their case in terms of restoring lost rights or returning to a lost utopia, for this was a society profoundly conscious of history. Besides, in any society possession is nine-tenths of the law, and Mill pointed out that if superior intelligence, wealth, and numbers are to enjoy power, they 'must be organized; and the advantage in organization is necessarily with those who are in possession of the government'.[62] Not only do those already in power know the ropes; their influence gains from the inertia of people who have other things to do, or who simply want to be left alone. Recurring public rituals—weddings, anniversaries, layings of foundation-stones—strengthen and sanctify existing institutions.

A further obstacle lay in the early nineteenth century's strong sense of the dignity of government and parliament. George Eliot was accustomed to hearing her father 'utter the word "Government" in a tone that charged it with awe . . . in contrast with the word "rebel" which seemed to carry the stamp of evil in its syllables'.[63] She knew that for different reasons his attitude was shared lower down in society. For an early-Victorian agricultural labourer whose 'solar system was the parish', culturally and geographically far removed from London at a time when travel was expensive and slow and education was restricted, 'that mysterious distant system of things called "Gover'ment"' was remote indeed.[64] Only slowly did voluntarist pressure come to seem legitimate. Major legal as well as conventional restraints limited its freedom to organize: taxes on and censorship of the press, restricted access to meeting-places, laws against conspiracy and corresponding societies, and so on. In overseas, economic, and poor-law policy it seemed specially necessary to protect government from undue popular pressure—most notably in the Bank Charter Act's complex machinery of 1844 for warding off pressure on the politicians to expand the issue of notes in a financial crisis. Peel in his budget speech of 1845 repeatedly denied that popular pressure had influenced his decisions, for 'it is the duty of the Executive Government to take those articles which, whether there has been any clamour for a reduction of duty on them or not, are articles in respect of which any duty at all is open to the greatest objection'.[65]

Yet the reformers were gaining strength, if only because nonconformist voluntarism was on the march. The United Kingdom, the USA, and Scandinavia were the pioneers of the cause group. The British dissenting tradition nourished the ideal of the active citizen, who is prepared when necessary to resist the state, and who knows that the individual can by his own actions change things. Mill and other mid-Victorian Liberals prized the uncontented characters and the active type of personality who alone was thought to secure human progress.[66] Although Mill did not share the religious ideas of the nonconformists, he shared their belief in the power of ideas to mould conduct. Slavery had been destroyed, he thought, not by structural or economic influences, but by 'the spread of moral convictions', for 'one person with a belief, is a social power equal to ninety-nine who have only interests'.[67] Nonconformists, wary of governments which had so recently oppressed their ancestors, had no fear of standing out against prevailing opinion, and tended to people the world with heroes and villains. It was a cast of mind which George Orwell thought 'belongs to the nursery',[68] yet out of these simplicities came forth courage, energy, and even arrogance, and so a political impact was made. Secularization gradually eroded the religious impulse behind cause groups, but even in the 1950s the Campaign for Nuclear Disarmament owed much to Christians who disliked the churches' links with the establishment.

The religious impulse to voluntarism had regional implications. Nonconformists were deeply involved in promoting industrialization, and were relatively strong in the industrial areas because the established church had responded only slowly to the late-eighteenth-century redistribution in population. Industrialization reinforced voluntarism and Liberalism by complementing religious and political pluralism with social diversity. Not only did it rear up huge cities distant from London; it also generated a mood of independence from government, whose Anglican and aristocratic flavour provincials disliked. In Victorian Britain so much economic progress seemed to stem from individual initiative, so little from state direction, that provincial England, South Wales, and the Lowlands of Scotland gained a new self-confidence by comparison with London. Commercial and manufacturing people readily chimed in with Bentham and the utilitarians, and applied the idea of inventions and machinery to politics. They came to view the political system as itself a piece of machinery which intelligence could continuously refine, and the public agitation was implicitly likened to an engine 'getting up steam'. There was also a real Liberal enthusiasm, almost mystical in nature, for that great Liberal mechanism the free press, which greatly expanded after the 1850s. Voluntarist ideas spread gradually out into the countryside. The late eighteenth century saw the start of a process which by the mid-nineteenth century had covered the countryside with societies for agricultural improvement. A network of associations offering prizes for agricultural innovation developed at national, regional, and local level. By the mid-Victorian period the cause group had come to be seen more as safeguarding than as threatening the security of the state, and a certain pride was taken in it. By linking government to governed, it seemed to ward off more violent approaches to change. 'Public meetings are the safety valves of society,' the former Chartist Henry Vincent declared in 1850, cocking an eye at French alternatives: 'they let off the steam.'[69]

Industrialization occurred primarily north and west of the Trent, and except in its earliest stages occurred in the towns. Flowing from this was the fact that nineteenth-century British Liberalism, unlike its European counterpart, was town-based. Cause groups began in the towns, and exploited civic rivalries: between Manchester and Birmingham, Leeds and Bradford, Edinburgh and Glasgow. Towns like these were large enough to render feasible large meetings of the like-minded, but not so large as to have lost their sense of community and civic identity. Liberalism simultaneously reinforced its urban base with forays into the countryside, where it found new worlds to conquer. So two nineteenth-century polarities developed: between apathetic London and the great radical northern provincial cities; and between all urban areas and a countryside that, in England at least, was relatively quiescent. 'Deep under the superficial controversies of English society', wrote Bagehot, 'there is a struggle between what we may call the Northern and business element of English society, and the Southern and aristocratic element.'[70] His distinction between the 'quiet saving districts of the country and the active employing districts', between the agricultural south and the manufacturing north, reappeared in the contrast between 'Producer's England' and 'Consumer's England' that J. A. Hobson drew when discussing the general election of January 1910.[71] Provincial incorruptibles thought London-based governments needed to be continuously stirred up. The agitation against Bulgarian atrocities in 1876, for example, was strong in the north, south-west, and in Wales, but relatively weak in Scotland and elsewhere in England, and non-existent in Ireland. A similar pattern can be found in many late-Victorian Liberal movements, from Josephine Butler's attack on state-regulated prostitution to the campaign for disestablishment. The polarity between north-west and south-east persists into our own time, but provincial prosperity and self-confidence have now declined so far that what Manchester thinks today the world no longer thinks tomorrow.

Voluntarism also gained from shifts in class relationships. Cause groups were hardly congenial to aristocrats and gentry, but Mill claimed in 1859 that 'those whose opinions go by the name of public opinion' were by then 'chiefly the middle class'.[72] Bagehot claimed that 'the aristocracy live in the fear of the middle classes—of the grocer and the merchant. They dare not frame a society of enjoyment as the French aristocracy once formed it.'[73] A sequence of provincial humanitarian movements vented middle-class indignation against Anglican and aristocratic government, carrying forward into a very different age much of the traditional contempt felt by 'country' for 'court'. When the radical Charles Gilpin became parliamentary secretary to the Poor Law Board in 1859, for example, John Bright's response was uncompromising: 'so thou's got thy snout in the trough, Charles'.[74] These humanitarian movements—from anti-slavery through the Anti-Corn Law League and on to internationalism and feminism—mark an important episode in the 'making' of the English middle class. Richard Cobden, leading figure in the Anti-Corn Law League, described their basis in 1843: 'I have faith in the middle classes, backed by the more intelligent of the working classes, and led by the more honest section of the aristocracy.'[75] His social map rejected any Marxian polarity between bourgeoisie and proletariat for a self-confident middle grouping which recruited both upwards and downwards. He and Bagehot, however, wanted the working class kept in middle-class leading-strings. Bagehot was decidedly apprehensive in 1859 at the idea that trade unions could be co-ordinated round a central London structure.[76] He wanted the franchise weighted towards property, which 'has not only a certain connection with general intelligence, but . . . has a peculiar connection with *political* intelligence'. It was, he thought, 'a great guide to a good judgment to have much to lose by a bad judgment'.[77] Many Victorian Liberals were bolder and, when worsted in the short term, tended to place their long-term hopes in a wider franchise: for women or for working men, who might show themselves more enlightened than the present electors. Franchise reform profited by cause-group disappointments, and came to seem the ultimate Liberal remedy for all things.

For many Victorian Liberal reformers, the journey was at least as important as the arrival, for agitation trained the activist to be politically alert. Against selfish men, corrupt officials, ambitious bureaucrats, haughty aristocrats, backward-looking warmongers, arrogant and obscurantist clerics, Liberals saw themselves as raising up a rival army powered by Liberal ideals: humane, self-regulating, self-educating, progressive, rational, and free. The hope was to propagate this type of personality through crusades to enfranchise and extend citizenship to ever wider groups (middle class, working men, subordinate nationalities, women, nonconformists, Catholics) both at home and overseas. There was a concomitant distrust of the state, especially when in enemy hands: a fear of officialism, and of creeping bureaucracy, nourished by a reading of Alexis de Tocqueville, together with a fear of power's corrupting influence. The cause groups were interlinked. Personnel and technique readily moved between them[78] to ensure that the reforming engine was kept continuously ticking over, though the reform crisis of 1832 shows that it was difficult to keep up the pressure. Organizational power steadily accumulated within each individual movement, and at any one time there were several such structures in existence, so that agitation never ceased. Wyvill's reform movement of the 1780s was the earliest of these proliferating and interacting causes. By the 1860s their competing demands were beginning to clog up the political system, and new ways of assigning priorities were needed.

\*

It is the political party which nowadays co-ordinates opinion, but parties in Bagehot's day were only beginning to take responsibility for formulating policy; they had only begun to interact with the pressure group, and were deeply rooted in the localities. So much so, that voters' changes of political allegiance tended to be collective rather than individual, responding to some prior change by landlord or employer. Even in the Lancashire manufacturing town, the employer's allegiance powerfully influenced employees' voting habits. In Portadown, Northern Ireland, even within living memory, 'you were known as a Metal Box man. In other places, you were a Mackie's man or a Shorts' man. Sons followed fathers into the job.'[79] The MP and his agent aimed to tune into this network of community relationships. The opinion poll, which did not then exist, would have been redundant for this purpose, for significant and relevant opinion was discovered through links with important local families and institutions, in communities where open voting made electors' opinions widely known. For long after Bagehot's day, the canvass by local political structures was designed to discover what relationships would determine a voter's behaviour, and then to get known supporters to the poll. Right up to 1914 a good party agent could estimate quite accurately the balance of political opinion in a constituency.[80]

The idea of 'converting' opponents through argument would have seemed inappropriate, even impertinent, and at the local and even higher levels the parties were much less preoccupied with propaganda than one would now expect. Liberal theorists believed in allowing people to reach their own opinions through reason and reflection; Conservatives suspected opinions that stemmed from anything other than personal interest and connection, and feared that campaigning would merely stir the other side into action. Interference from outside the constituency, let alone from London, was likely to be counter-productive, and could achieve little against an MP who was self-financed and who owed his seat to a largely local following. A party's local agent was usually appointed by the candidate, perhaps with help from a registration society funded by local subscribers; he was not appointed by any central party machine, for no such machine existed. Nor was he a crusader or counter-crusader in continuous partisan activity. He was a solicitor with the relatively mundane and part-time duty of ensuring that his candidate's supporters were registered to vote, and he sprang into political life only when elections were in the offing. None the less, the competition between the parties for local advantage was fierce and continuous. The Conservatives may have been relatively fertile in the 1830s with registration associations, but radicals within the Anti-Corn Law League in the 1840s soon outpaced the Conservatives at that game. Less easy for radicals to subvert were the symbols of traditional authority: crown, mace, and open Bible, paraded in Tory processions.[81] Instead, Whigs and radicals argued that authority could be secure only if more broadly based, and if political maturity was fostered among the groups who would soon demand the franchise. This in turn led them to mount moralistic and supposedly non-party movements that threw traditionalists on to the defensive.

Because they were community events, elections in Bagehot's day were much more exciting than they are now, with large gatherings during the hustings when the candidates were nominated. The poll itself offered all the drama involved in seeing how a voter defined himself through his vote in relation to his neighbours. MPs were then much more likely to represent an entire community. Of the 401 constituencies at the general elections from 1832 to 1865, no less than 240 were double-member, seven were three-member, and one (City of London) was four-member; nor did franchise extension in 1867 alter this picture greatly.[82] So there was much preoccupation with tactics: should one divide one's vote between the candidates, for example, or 'plump' for one of them? Add to this the suspense involved in a cumulative electoral build-up, because a vote became public when cast. The later voters could be influenced by what the earlier voters had done, hence more scope for the constituency tactician. Should one muster friendly forces early or late? How could the enemy be deterred from mustering theirs at all? In this local saturnalia, well-known 'characters' performed, crowds gathered, exhilarating repartee was exchanged, and drink (then strong and cheap) flowed freely, followed by fights and threats to property. Polling, though limited by the Reform Act of 1832 to two days in any one constituency, occurred on different days in different constituencies until 1918, and so the results could cumulate over a period of up to a month.[83] Hence a double cumulation of votes: within the constituency during polling, and across the nation as each constituency separately went to the poll. Not surprisingly, some authorities warded off such excitements by informally dividing up a multi-member constituency between the parties, or by withdrawing candidates the canvassers thought likely to fail. In two-fifths of the seats between 1832 and 1880 no contest occurred.[84] The average number of constituencies contested was, however, increasing, and doubled in the five general elections after the Reform Act of 1832 by comparison with the five general elections before it.[85]

'Many a time at elections I fancied myself more at the Derby,' wrote Ostrogorski. 'To the women and children the polling-day brings all the excitement of a fair.'[86] The sporting analogy was appropriate, for British electors both during and since Bagehot's day have embraced one of two 'sides', and discuss political questions in terms of rival 'teams'. Pioneer socialists looked on sadly as impoverished voters fiercely identified with Liberal or Conservative parties, from neither of which they had anything to gain.[87] In most communities there was enough shared ground between the two sides to make this periodic electoral settling of scores cathartic and ultimately unifying in its effect on the community. Only in Northern Ireland have the dangers of social polarization seemed serious enough for the single transferable vote to replace simple-majority voting—in 1921–9 and since 1973.[88] The two 'sides' carried their game up from the constituency

to the national arena. Late-Victorian oratorical sparring matches oc
between leading stars who challenged one another from rival platform
before a fascinated national audience which had no cinema or television
screens to watch. There was Lord Randolph Churchill versus Gladstone
in the 1880s, for example. For Lord Rosebery, Churchill evoked 'something of the adoration with which famous pugilists were regarded in the
palmy days of the Ring: the people loved to see the young David hurling
his stones . . . at the giant whom they also loved.'[89]

In Bagehot's time, there was as yet little need to articulate party structures in any formal way, given that the electorate was small and MPs well
informed on significant constituency opinion. In 1880 less than 4 per cent
of the entire returned election expenditure came from the central party
organizations.[90] Mid-Victorian Britain was not swept by rival political
creeds, each clamouring for supporters. The registration society was created
after 1832 by subscribers for specific purposes, and was not a club in search
of a large membership. Such political clubs as did exist during Bagehot's
time sprang up spontaneously to meet some local need: the desire felt by
beleaguered Conservatives in progressive towns, for example, for a place
where they could meet friends and enjoy shared recreations. The parties
had neither the funds nor the personnel to do anything more than encourage such local developments, and in the countryside any central interference would have been much resented. In 1874 there were Conservative
associations in only forty-four of the eighty-two English county divisions.[91]
The localism of the parties in Bagehot's time both reflected and accentuated what we would now see as their unconcern with precise legislative
commitment. The voter might be individually bribed locally, but he was
not yet collectively bribed nationally. A government's supposed duty to
introduce a set of measures and carry them through parliament was, said
Lord John Russell in 1848, 'a duty which was hardly known and recognised
by the Governments and Ministers of this country at a former period'.[92]
None the less, the sporting combat between two sides was carried up to
the national level. The successful candidate, whether his election had been
contested or uncontested, found himself in an assembly bifurcated between government and opposition. 'We in this country have got the games
instinct', said Labour's former prime minister Clement Attlee in 1958, 'and
there are only two teams in a game . . . The electorate puts one party in;
after some time they decide they want a change so they put the other
chaps in. That reflects the strong sporting instinct of this country . . . it is
better to look on politics as a game than as a fight.'[93]

The history of British political parties is often compartmentalized and published within blue or red covers, partly because neither party likes to acknowledge its plunderings of policies and personnel from the other. Each party likes to think of its history as involving a clear-eyed and single-minded progress towards a somewhat high-minded goal. Bagehot was on his own account 'between sizes in politics', a man of the left-centre who 'will neither drive so slow as to miss the train, or so fast as to meet with an accident'.[94] He was well placed to take a detached view of this structure, and as a practical man was unlikely to make Mill's mistake of underestimating party's permanent importance. Yet his vision was inevitably limited by the party situation at the time of writing. He could not perceive, as we now can, how tenacious is the British two-party system. Its tenacity at the national and local level can be demonstrated through outlining a long pulsating sequence whereby on six occasions since 1789 the two-party system has been almost disrupted by splits and recombinations, but has in each case gradually recouped itself before its next disruption. Bagehot was writing mid-way between the second disruption (in 1846) and the third (in 1886), at a time when restoration of the two-party system was not yet complete. In his book he generalized too readily from the fluid and fragmented party situation then prevailing.

Since the seventeenth century the parties have diverged in psychological tendency. For many Victorians, the seventeenth-century Civil War had never ended, and for every Tory high-churchman who saw himself as a latter-day cavalier there was a Liberal dissenter who saw himself as a latter-day puritan. Conservatives, like the seventeenth-century royalists, have a taste for leadership, which for them was until recently often buttressed by traditionalist and even mystical arguments. Liberals, by contrast—together with their heirs, the Labour Party—have an affinity with dissent, and are prone to distrust authority and place their hopes in reason and debate. The parties' institutional connection with seventeenth-century alignments is weak, and their continuous story is best launched with the French Revolution's disruption of British political alignments after 1789. Until the early nineteenth century the influence and patronage which the monarch brought to his governments denied them a narrowly party image. Governments of whatever inclination still formed a sort of 'King's party', backed when in difficulties by the 'independent' country gentlemen, especially those who sat for county seats. So the early nineteenth-century House of Commons was polarized less between political parties than between those who were in government and those who were not: that is, between 'court' and 'country'. The phrases applied to eighteenth-century parliamentary groupings referred to 'sides' of the House, to 'the administration' and 'the opposition' or to 'the majority' and 'the minority', whereas the party terms 'Whig' and 'Tory' tended to denote only the views of individuals.[95]

Still, there is a direct line of institutional and emotional continuity between the Younger Pitt and modern Conservatism on the one hand, and between Fox and the modern parties of the left on the other—though like so many profound long-term shifts in history, this long-term destiny was not perceived by contemporaries. The liberalized Tory Party of Lord Liverpool that lasted until 1827 still thought of itself primarily as the King's government, though some of his ministers, especially Canning, were beginning to broaden out the government's contacts in the country. By the 1820s the notion of 'loyal opposition' was getting established, the labels 'Whig' and 'Tory' were becoming widely used. The term 'His Majesty's Opposition' was first used facetiously—by the Whig J. C. Hobhouse in 1826, when welcoming the Liverpool government's acceptance of an important part of Whig policy—but the phrase caught on. Partly from self-imposed necessity, Disraeli became the first party leader in the House of Commons to cultivate the art of leading a loyal opposition—in his capacity as Conservative leader in the Commons from 1848 to 1874, spent mostly in opposition. The term 'Liberal' was applied to the Whigs' more popular and libertarian adherents. Between 1828 and 1830 the Whigs at last shed their long-term distaste for office, and became readier to reach out into the community for support. Something akin to the modern two-party system was coming into existence.

Yet at the very end of this first phase in modern party history a major split among Tories over Roman Catholic emancipation in 1829 disrupted the new pattern, and had the effect of letting the Whigs into office in 1830. Whig reforms immediately began to disappoint their more radical followers, and the fragility of the Whig–Liberal–radical consortium was exposed. Would the Whigs be able to create a solid governmental party of the left, running all the way from Whigs through the Liberals to the radicals? Would the Tories be able to reunite so as to re-create the Liberal Toryism of Lord Liverpool? Neither question could readily be answered in the fluid and unpredictable situation politicians faced after franchise reform in 1832. The outcome in modern party history's second phase, running from 1832 to 1846, was the gradual crystallization of the two-party system on both right and left. The monarchy was by now gradually lifting itself above party politics. The Whigs in the 1830s slowly gained ground at the expense of the radicals, and in 1835 brought off a formal alliance with the Irish MPs. At the same time Peel was painstakingly re-creating and extending Liverpool's governmental party by getting supporters organized more widely within the country, and by reaching out towards moderate and middle-class opinion. Hence his adoption of the label 'Conservative' for his Party in 1834.

Extension of the franchise and the attack on royal patronage weakened the monarch without providing any new way of getting parliamentary opinion to cohere. So inconvenient a situation could not persist, and partly as a result the court–country polarity was gradually replaced by a new polarity: that between rival political parties, each competing for access to governmental power. Furthermore, although general elections were still dominated by local issues and personalities, the great sequence of national cause groups was beginning to convert them into national debates on policy. At first such debates were promoted by the reformers alone, acting largely in criticism of the party leaders. But gradually the reformers (marshalled in cause groups) began coalescing with the party of the left, while their opponents (often marshalled into interest groups) gravitated rightwards. Slavery produced the first such polarization on policy, with the attack on the slave-trade moving from the 1780s to victory in 1807. There followed the attack on slavery, mounted in the 1820s, which prevailed in 1833. The Anti-Corn Law League (1839–46) was the most brilliantly organized and immediately successful cause group in the second phase of modern party history—a phase terminated by its disruption of the two-party system. Peel's powerful ministry of 1841 was returned on a broad base and a practical programme, and up till about 1844 it looked as though Lord Liverpool's party of government was restored. But in 1846 the split between Protectionists and Peelites introduced a long period of one-party dominance by the Whig–Liberal–radical combination.

During the third phase in modern party history, from 1846 to 1886, the Conservatives won no parliamentary majority till 1874. Yet this could not have been predicted in 1846, because the Peelites postponed the decision on whether to align with Conservatives or Liberals, and caused much confusion thereby. Disraeli, who repeatedly at this time praised party for forcing politicians to answer to the electors, could still complain in 1859 that 'under present circumstances there is no reason why there should not be a dissolution, or a Ministerial crisis, every February'.[96] Pressure from constituency organizations and personal ambition, however, caused most Peelites quite quickly to plump for one side or the other. When Gladstone joined Palmerston's Liberal government in 1859, the Peelite episode came to an end. The two-party system was well on the way to restoration at the time Bagehot was writing, but the complexities of franchise reform and the shift of political generations after Palmerston's death in 1865 concealed this fact from his view. His vision in 1867 was inevitably moulded, not by John Bright's entering Gladstone's cabinet in 1868, but by Richard Cobden's refusal to enter Palmerston's cabinet in 1859.

We now know that both parties survived splits during the reform crisis of 1866–7. Shortly after Bagehot published his book, the parties' local and national leaders began to annexe and integrate both reformer and interest group. By accumulating loyalties to a national party structure and leadership, and even by edging towards the idea of a national party programme, they disciplined both causes and interests. The threat to the Liberal Party came from the semi-autonomous cause groups modelled on the Anti-Corn Law League: free traders, disestablishers, temperance reformers, feminists, trade unionists. Gladstone as Liberal leader sought to outflank them by appropriating their techniques. His address to 25,000 people for two hours at Greenwich marked, as Bagehot realized, 'a new era in English politics', whereby 'it will be one of the most important qualifications of a prime minister to exert a direct control over the masses'.[97] Disraeli, somewhat less flamboyantly, could now broaden out his Party beyond the protectionists, the planters, and the established church to embrace the middle classes whom his defeat of Peel in 1845–6 had earlier repelled. In 1859 Bagehot had described 'a *capitalist conservatism*' as 'the great political want of our day', for if wealth could unite with intelligence and property, 'we should have almost secured the stability of our Constitution; we should have pacified its most dangerous assailants'.[98] This powerful combination Disraeli in Bagehot's later years was in the process of re-creating.

\*

Skill in assessing and responding to public opinion was less central to the politician's art in mid-Victorian Britain than it was soon to become. This was partly because those in authority liked to distinguish between public opinion and the public interest. 'I hate the whole tribe of news-writers', Wellington told Peel in 1827, 'and I prefer to suffer from their falsehoods to dirtying my fingers with communications with them.'[99] For Peel, 'public opinion was something to scrutinise rather than to follow'.[100] But because British politicians had no standing army, no effective police force, and nothing resembling the locally based information service that the prefecture supplied to French governments, they needed to work with the grain of significant public opinion, and had long experience of doing so. A government which ignored opinion risked humiliation, as with the failed attempt in 1816 to retain the income tax. Yet there were then no sophisticated devices for measuring opinion. A casual conversation between aristocrats at a race-meeting or county ball often had to suffice, reinforced by the landowner's close knowledge of his locality. But as change speeded up, as the electorate grew larger and as the pressure for political participation extended, skill at handling public opinion became essential. Whig fears that Wellington lacked such skill eased them into office in 1830, and by the 1840s a politician like Sir James Graham who neglected to cultivate opinion was in difficulties. Far from criticizing Peel for changing his mind when Conservative leader, Bagehot praised him for it, claiming that 'the calling of a constitutional statesman is very much that of a political advocate; he receives a new brief with the changing circumstances of each successive day'.[101]

The mid-Victorian electoral system was not entirely helpful as a guide to opinion, and some wanted to minimize social pressures on voters by introducing secret voting. Yet the ballot was not an unequivocally progressive cause, if only because it threatened to shield voters from the moral pressure that other progressive causes could bring to bear, and both Bagehot and Mill marshalled several powerful arguments against it.[102] The ballot threatened the vitality of general elections as community events; it seemed conspiratorial, reminiscent even of the Catholic confessional; and it undermined the idea of the vote as a public responsibility, cast unashamedly by the upstanding Englishman in full public view. None the less the reform was introduced in 1872, though its impact on voting behaviour was neither universal nor immediate. Meanwhile, new guides to public opinion were emerging. Mid-Victorian cause groups and political parties measured opinion in a rough-and-ready way, hoping thereby to guide or coerce the politicians. Petitions, canvasses, pledges, public meetings, and processions were central to their routine. Interacting with these was the press, seen by Mill as 'the real equivalent . . . of the Pnyx and the Forum' in political communities that were now too large to conduct their politics face to face. The newspapers and railways were, he said, 'solving the problem of bringing the democracy of England to vote, like that of Athens, simultaneously in one *agora*', and the masses were taking their opinions not from leaders in church or state, but from 'men much like themselves, addressing them or speaking in their name, on the spur of the moment, through the newspapers'.[103]

The utilitarians were well aware that the press could be used as a political weapon. Indeed, Roebuck claimed that the first Earl of Durham's 'whole life was regulated by leading articles'.[104] In promoting their radical causes, Cobden and Bright made shrewd use of newspapers, some of which they helped to found. Even a politician like Lord John Russell, who made a point of having nothing to do with newspaper editors, saw the printing-press as a corrective to corrupt governments.[105] Bagehot went so far as to claim that '*The Times* has made many ministries.'[106] It was even arguable that a press so efficient at ventilating opinion made a broader franchise less urgent.[107] None the less, Bagehot feared that these trends would subvert the impartial and balanced judgement that he so prized in the politician. Among his many objections to Mill's idea of proportional representation was the risk that it would so mobilize earnest opinion as to create 'a church with tenets', a powerfully organized group that would coerce the MP.[108] Four months before he died, Bagehot reported with some apprehension that 'there is already, in many places, a committee which often telegraphs to London hoping that their member will vote this way or that'.[109] He admired the English constitution largely because there flourished at its heart a parliament which, far from deferring unduly to opinion, was well placed to educate it.

*

Articulating opinion was still, in Bagehot's time, the speciality of West-minster. Strictly speaking, the term 'parliament' denotes the monarch sit-ting with the Lords spiritual and temporal, and with the Commons standing at the Bar,[110] but for practical purposes by the nineteenth century it in-creasingly denoted the House of Commons, as monitored by the House of Lords. Searching for creeds and institutions characteristic of the Vic-torians, the historian G. M. Young came up with only two: the family, and representative institutions,[111] and it was the Victorians who built the striking complex of buildings that parliament now occupies. Parliament derived prestige from having survived centuries of dramatic social and political change, and from the nation's unprecedented prosperity and world power. The Victorians were confident enough about the 'British model' of representative government to manufacture it for export. Parliamentary institutions provoked an interesting divergence between Bagehot and Mill, and this will be briefly considered in the next few paragraphs. It was with the Commons that Bagehot and Mill were primarily concerned—Mill primarily with what parliament ought to do, Bagehot with what it actually did. Though Bagehot in his *English Constitution* rather coyly avoids plac-ing Mill centrally in his sights, his book does in fact challenge much of what Mill said in his *Representative Government* (1861).

Bagehot ascribed five functions to parliament: the elective, the expressive, the teaching, the informing, and the legislating.[112] By 'elective function' he meant parliament's election of the executive: that is, of those responsible for running the country's affairs. He saw the cabinet as a committee of parliament, and welcomed the fact (and in this was echoed by the distinguished political analyst J. R. Seeley[113]) that parliament could in theory dismiss the executive at will. Such built-in unpredictability rendered parliament's debates more exciting than those of Congress, whose members and whose executive (the president) enjoy a fixed term. There was some wishful thinking here because the Queen's role in choosing a government was larger than Bagehot supposed;[114] furthermore, the growing role of the electorate was soon to supplant it. Such power as the House possessed over choosing the cabinet in the 1860s reflected a situation whose transitional nature Bagehot did not perceive, and which reflected the party instability stemming from the disruption of 1846. As far as the electors' role is concerned, Bagehot knew that the cabinet 'though appointed by one parliament . . . can appeal if it chooses to the next'[115]—that is, present its case to the electorate and hope to prevail. But he did not then fully grasp, though he showed some signs of doing so a few years later,[116] that the price of such freedom lay in the cabinet's mounting dependence on extra-parliamentary structures.

Bagehot saw parliament's second function, the 'expressive', as to express 'the mind of the English people on all matters which come before it'[117]— that is, to articulate existing opinions efficiently. Whereas administration and drafting legislation required expertise, the legislature's role was to talk, to criticize, to monitor. On this function, Bagehot and Mill largely agreed, and Mill wanted the legislature made up, not from 'the greatest political minds in the country', but from 'a fair sample of every grade of intellect among the people which is at all entitled to a voice in public affairs'.[118] The House of Commons in the 1860s was indeed an effective megaphone for opinions widely held, for as Disraeli pointed out, a good report of a speech 'is better than 10,000 articles'.[119] Its role, structure, and procedure generated several varieties of oratory. 'The essence of good House of Commons speaking is the conversational style,' Winston Churchill pointed out, 'the facility for quick, informal interruptions and interchanges,' and this required the sense of intimacy created by an assembly too small to seat all its members. This also helped to produce 'a sense of crowd and urgency' on great occasions. Parliament's hold on the electors, Churchill continued, 'depends to no small extent upon its episodes and great moments, even upon its scenes and rows, which, as everyone will agree, are better conducted at close quarters'.[120] The polarity between government and opposition, and the absence of any fixed term for the government, ensured that 'great moments' could occur at any time.

On parliament's 'teaching' function Bagehot and Mill diverged. Both agreed that parliament should not only reflect existing opinion but also 'teach the nation what it does not know'. Both were, after all, mid-Victorian Liberals who thought no political community healthy without continuous and vigorous debate. For Bagehot, parliament should propagate true ideas from the nation's 'highest minds', for the House of Commons was 'the great engine of popular instruction'.[121] He and Mill agreed that the MP, although bound to listen to constituents' views, should not become their mere delegate; he should be pledged to constituents' views only on fundamentals, and should normally remain free to exercise his judgement. Where they disagreed was over Mill's elevation of intellectuals in the teaching process. In tune with the rationalistic traditions of his Party, which lent a special prominence to sympathetic authors and thinkers, Mill made several suggestions for increasing their parliamentary influence: proportional representation to safeguard them against mass opinion, educational qualifications for electors, special representation in the second chamber, and so on. Partly in reaction against Mill, Bagehot championed 'common sense' in politics. He was not at all sure that intellectuals possessed enough of it, and referred disparagingly to 'the "too clever by half" people who live in "Bohemia"'.[122]

Mill and Bagehot agreed that government should be decentralized, and that many grievances should be handled locally rather than nationally. But they also thought parliament had a role here through its 'informing' function, a fourth role whereby it alerted the executive to the people's grievances. Mill thought parliament should be a 'Committee of Grievances, and ... Congress of Opinions',[123] and both thought there should be working-class MPs to articulate working-class opinion. 'Every class knows some things not so well known to other people ...', said Mill in a franchise debate. 'Is there, I wonder, a single Member of this House who thoroughly knows the working men's views of trades unions, or of strikes ... ?'[124] Yet their agreement on this point was superficial. Mill could never have said, with Bagehot, that 'a political combination of the lower classes, as such and for their own objects, is an evil of the first magnitude'.[125] Nor would he ever have advocated Bagehot's safeguard: a drawing together of middle class and aristocracy, symbolized and consolidated through drawing upper and lower house closer together. Far from attacking the aristocratic assembly, Bagehot wanted to rejuvenate it by introducing life peerages, abolishing proxies, and admitting distinguished civil servants so as to increase its representative and intellectual power. He thought a strengthened House of Lords would reduce friction within the propertied classes and strengthen them to confront 'the ignorant multitude of the new constituencies' he so greatly feared. 'The main interest of both these classes is now identical,' he wrote in 1872, of aristocracy and plutocracy: '. . . to prevent or to mitigate the rule of uneducated numbers'.[126] But so untidy and irrational a second chamber was obnoxious to Mill, the arch-opponent of aristocratic values. Because it would carry weight only if it rivalled the House of Commons in its popular support, Mill thought any limits on democracy 'must act in and through the democratic House'.[127]

On the fifth and final function, the legislative, Mill and Bagehot agreed that no assembly of more than 600 people could legislate or administer, but they diverged in at least three respects. Mill's criticism of the House of Commons as legislature was radical. He wanted legislation formulated by a Commission of Legislation, whose members parliament elected for a fixed term. He thought the Commission should speak but not vote, and should also act as a Commission of Codification to ensure the overall coherence of the law. Parliament should be free to enact or reject the laws presented to it, but should not draft laws or alter drafts made by others. Bagehot too thought legislation by parliamentary committee untidy, and in 1874 welcomed the French idea for submitting all laws passed by the legislature to the Council of State for revision, with the legislature voting later on its proposed amendments.[128] Bagehot wanted British legislation, however, to come from the cabinet, which he saw as a body elected by parliament and responsive to it. He also favoured enhancing an existing remedy that was anathema to Mill: the revising powers of the House of Lords. Bagehot was on the whole content with the second chamber's aristocratic composition, perhaps leavened by a few life peers; 'sensible men of substantial means are what we wish to be ruled by', he wrote, 'and a peerage of genius would not compare with it in power'.[129]

Mill and Bagehot also diverged on party's role within parliament. For Bagehot, party was 'bone of its bone, and breath of its breath';[130] by causing opinion to cohere, it was essential to parliament's functioning. Mill, by contrast, wrote almost as though party was redundant—as though MPs, if sufficiently intelligent and unconstrained by distorting loyalties and pledges to constituents, would eventually discuss themselves into agreement. An incidental (and probably illusory) benefit of proportional representation for him was that it would diminish the influence of party,[131] whereas Bagehot thought this a recipe for instability; it would give the government 'no security against repeated and continuous defeats'.[132] Their positions on political party reflect a third divergence: over the need for compromise in politics. Bagehot welcomed the fact that MPs reach agreement through compromise, and relished the consequential downgrading of the doctrinaire. The only type of leader popular in the House of Commons, he pointed out, was the sort of person who affects 'a studied and illogical moderation':[133] an Althorp, a Palmerston, a W. H. Smith. Mill too yearned for compromise, 'one of the most indispensable requisites in the practical conduct of politics'.[134] He too valued debate over public policy: 'in all human affairs, conflicting influences are required, to keep one another alive and efficient even for their own proper uses'.[135] Yet Mill's type of compromise did not emerge from the clash between government and opposition parties, and in his *Representative Government* he did not analyse, let alone relish, that clash. Mill's type of compromise involved skill at synthesis, and in another context Bagehot praised his writings for displaying it.[136] Compromise for Mill involved a rationalistic reconciliation of contrary views, not the day-to-day pragmatic and often illogical 'deal' between adversaries such as the British parliamentary system fosters and Bagehot relished.[137] Mill even thought that 'as mankind improve, the number of doctrines which are no longer disputed or doubted will be constantly on the increase'.[138]

*

Synthesis in quite another area made Bagehot famous, for it was he who first publicized the idea of the cabinet as the '*hyphen* which joins, a *buckle* which fastens, the legislative part of the state to the executive part of the state'.[139] Power and decision lay with the cabinet, said Bagehot, yet 'the most curious point about the cabinet is that so very little is known about it'.[140] Until Canning spoke publicly about it in the early nineteenth century, the cabinet's very existence was secret, and in 1851 the House of Commons rejected a proposal to give precedence to cabinet ministers in its ceremonial on the ground that the cabinet was unknown to the constitution.[141] This reticence reflected the cabinet's informality. The early-Victorian cabinet was somewhat smaller than modern cabinets, averaging fourteen between 1832 and 1868. It did not even meet at a fixed location (10 Downing Street) until 1856, and did not sit round a single table until then. It did not need to meet more than once a week (on Saturdays) during the parliamentary session to arrange the next week's business. Until 1852 ministers took it in turns to act as host to a cabinet dinner every Wednesday. There was then no firm distinction between social and political life, given that cabinet ministers also met frequently in country houses and clubs. So there was little need for formality or paperwork. In the 1820s civil servants assisting the cabinet had to write out any duplicates of documents they wanted. It was then so difficult to copy documents quickly that cabinet ministers in 1826 who wanted to see documents had to inspect them in a special room. So the cabinet was a group of aristocrats settling the affairs of the nation informally, rather as they would settle the business of their estates. So few were their administrative duties that they could afford to disperse to their estates from August to late October when parliament was not sitting.

The cabinet was in relatively firm control of the entire political system, and Bagehot's account of it somewhat underestimated how far it had already captured the legislative initiative from parliament. The aristocracy dominated both cabinet and House of Lords, was powerful in the House of Commons, and dominated the post of foreign secretary well into the twentieth century. So it helped to draw together the constitution's three major constituents. The cabinet was not very busy, partly because business then was relatively uncomplicated. Government was not expected to do much, if only because *laissez-faire* domestic policy ensured that the major governmental issues involved foreign affairs, Ireland and the empire. Yet in these areas, governmental decision-making was devolved either to local authorities within the United Kingdom, or to ambassadors and imperial proconsuls overseas. Such cabinet decisions as were required in these areas could largely take the form of executive acts, and did not require minutes or a secretariat. No legislative package was yet expected from a government, and standing committees of cabinet were not required. Detailed questions could be settled by appointing *ad hoc* subcommittees, for example on the Reform Bill of 1831. The cabinet's leading historian, John Mackintosh, discovered twenty-six cabinet committees on miscellaneous subjects between 1832 and 1868.[142]

Though the monarch did not attend, the cabinet was still in some sense the monarch's personal group of advisers; party was only in the process of solidifying it against outsiders. It was still not necessary for a cabinet minister to attend all meetings, and by staying away he could indicate his dissent. In relation to the cabinet, the monarch possessed the power that stems from access to valuable information, especially on foreign policy, and from influence and patronage within both houses of parliament. The monarch still had agents within the cabinet, especially the Lord Chancellor. Lord Granville was the last such agent, though mounting party pressures made his role very awkward by the 1880s. The last formal minute of dissent sent up from a cabinet minority to the monarch occurred in 1840, in opposition to Palmerston's foreign policy, and monarchs were gradually and politely squeezed out from knowing what were the alignments and arguments being used within the cabinet. All this prepared the way for a rise in the power of the prime minister, who was as yet little more than the cabinet's instrument for communicating with the monarch. The prime minister's rise was slow, if only because his own status did not necessarily match that of cabinet colleagues in what was still an aristocratic society. Not until 1878 was his office formally mentioned in any public document.[143]

\*

Bagehot's prime concern was to identify where power lay, so he was more interested in the cabinet than in the civil service, more preoccupied with how the machinery of government was set in motion than with what happened after that. So neither central nor local government featured prominently in his book. He thought that a department's civil servants needed firm control from a minister whose role was to combat the bureaucrat's tendency to routine. So he should not stay in one post for too long; he must be 'an outsider to his office', and 'bring a representative of outside sense and outside animation in contact with the inside world'.[144] Bagehot did not share the 'kind of admiration for bureaucracy' that Prussian successes temporarily produced among some 'writers and talkers' in the mid-1860s.[145] Yet the civil service deserved attention, because its calibre was high by the standards of its time. In 1867 Karl Marx contrasted it favourably with its German equivalent: German social evils were not exposed, he said, because Germany lacked 'men as competent, as free from partisanship and respect of persons as are the English factory-inspectors, her medical reporters on public health, her commissioners of inquiry into the exploitation of women and children, into housing and food'.[146]

In Bagehot's time the civil service was only in the process of welding itself together into a co-ordinated machine with corporate morale and standardized recruitment and procedures. The modern civil service has very disparate origins: in the civilians who organized supply and accounting for the armed services; in the separate staffs of the Post Office and boards of customs and inland revenue; and in the senior clerks who assisted individual ministers. The term 'civil servant' was first employed in its modern usage in 1816, and the phrase 'civil service' did not come into general use until after 1855.[147] Bagehot was impressed by 'the unsystematic and casual arrangement of our public offices', and pointed out that 'there are almost no two offices which are exactly alike in the defined relations of the permanent official to the Parliamentary chief'.[148] The three patterns of departmental organization then prevailing were for the office to be headed by a secretary of state with a seat in the cabinet; by a working board acting under the direction of a cabinet minister; or by a phantom board that was in practice directed by a minister with the title of president or vice-president.[149]

Integration was fostered by the mid-Victorian standardization of entrance examinations. Meritocratic recruitment of the British civil service began before the political system was democratized, so British politicians were not tempted to introduce party nominees into civil-service posts—a development which democratization produced in the USA. The mid-Victorian attack on patronage reflected a bid for middle-class emancipation from the aristocracy. Bagehot was sceptical: he thought that the recruits most needed were usually 'those in whom judgement predominates over mere cleverness—those of steady habits, of plodding diligence, of strict honesty, and proper feeling'.[150] None the less, in 1855 entrance examinations were introduced into parts of the civil service, and thereafter recruitment by examination steadily encroached on patronage. From 1870 it was universal throughout the civil service except at the Foreign Office. Standardization later gradually extended to hours, holidays, sick leave, and so on. The Treasury was in the vanguard of change, though given the initial autonomy of government departments it could advance only cautiously and gradually, with help from its control over finance and its responsibility for civil-service entry examinations.

A clear distinction between politician and civil servant emerged only during Bagehot's lifetime, and in 1876 he regretted the fact that by then a prominent modern civil servant no more thought of becoming a politician 'than a Hindoo thinks of becoming an Englishman'.[151] He thought that if life peerages could sometimes be given to retired civil servants, 'that semi-hostility between the civil service and the legislature which we so often now see' would be curbed.[152] So he welcomed Gladstone's promotion of Frederic Rogers, Permanent Under-Secretary of State for the Colonies, to the Lords in 1871. Three other civil servants followed Rogers: Hammond (1874), Lingen (1885), and Farrer (1893). This could not in itself arrest the long-term separation between politics and administration, which after Bagehot's time was intensified by the increasing integration of departments and standardization of civil-service grades. From the late 1980s, however, the 'Next Steps' reforms began to reintroduce into the civil service some features that Bagehot would have found familiar.

\*

A society that in Bagehot's day was so diverse in its governmental structures, so fragmented in its regional traditions, so lacking in powerful central institutions, needed the monarchy as focus and unifying symbol. Besides, monarchy epitomized the hereditary principle that governed so many aspects of British society at the time, for the middle-class voters had by no means unhorsed the aristocracy in 1832. So it was to the monarchy that Bagehot in his *English Constitution* gave his most memorable attention. His knowing account must have seemed almost pert in the climate of the time. Yet it was influential not just on students of monarchy but also on the conduct of Queen Victoria's successors. The future George V painstakingly studied Bagehot's book as a young man in 1894, as did his son Albert, the future George VI, many years later. 'To all Bagehot's principles of Monarchy', writes George VI's biographer, '—its necessary dignity, its social value and its essential morality—Prince Albert dedicated himself with a solemn rectitude and an upright probity.'[153]

Bagehot's view of monarchy must be seen in the context of its time: in relation to his belief that 'we have in a great community like England crowds of people scarcely more civilised than the majority of two thousand years ago'.[154] It was to these people that the politicians were now conceding electoral power, and like many of his contemporaries Bagehot worried about the consequences. Mill put his faith in reason, and set about educating the masses and reforming the political system on rational principles. Bagehot had much less faith in reason, and, since the British public were less affluent and worse educated than Americans or Canadians, thought that education alone would not suffice. Indeed, he thought the political system could survive the apparent advent of democracy only through recognizing, perpetuating, and even welcoming the persistence of unreason in human affairs. With characteristic anti-intellectual and down-to-earth paradox, he argued that in Britain only the irrational would enable the rational ultimately to prevail in politics; that is, the practical institutions of government (which he saw as in some sense rational) would be workable only if reinforced by mystery and disguise. Stable government needed the traditionalism, the deference, and the ceremonial display that monarchy could provide. Bagehot saw the cabinet as the practical or 'efficient' section of the political system. He thought that sovereignty rested with the House

of Commons; monarchy was no longer essential to parliamentary government, which in many new countries could operate without any monarchy
at all. After 1834 no monarch could prudently dismiss a government on his
own initiative, and if the monarch could still create peers, he could no
longer do much to promote his cause in the lower house should Lords and
Commons conflict. So Bagehot thought that the role of the 'dignified'
institutions—monarchy and the aristocratic trappings of the House of Lords
—was to create the climate within which the cabinet and other 'efficient'
political institutions could work satisfactorily.

Bagehot welcomed the fact that Britain in 1867 was already a disguised
republic. Outlining the role of monarchy in 1867, he pointed out that
though in theory the Queen could do many things without consulting
parliament, no politician could in practice risk his career by advising her
to do them. Her role was, in reality, fourfold. First, she diverted from the
politicians, already powerful enough, some of the prestige that might otherwise have given them delusions of grandeur; she helped to divert the
trappings of power from those who possessed its reality. She lacked real
power but retained the prestige that so often accompanies power, so Britain enjoyed some of the republic's advantages without its drawbacks.
Bagehot thought that monarchy, secondly, rendered government 'intelligible', not in the sense of clarifying the workings of government for the
multitude to see, but in the sense of making government's authority seem
clear and justifiable. Britain's political system must in the 1860s have seemed
even less comprehensible than it does now. Europe's norm was then still
absolute monarchy, and constitutional monarchy was a bridge between
traditional and modern forms of government. The British monarchy, said
Bagehot, 'acts as a *disguise*. It enables our real rulers to change without
heedless people knowing it.'[155] By concealing the political system's apparent defects, monarchy enabled the system to work smoothly and acceptably. Bagehot thought it fortunate that 'the excitement of choosing our
rulers is prevented by the apparent existence of an unchosen ruler. The
poorer and more ignorant classes . . . really believe that the Queen gov-
erns'. So monarchy was 'an intelligible government. The mass of mankind
understand it.'[156]

Monarchy could achieve this only because it rose above party, and
mobilized religious sentiments of reverence behind the existing political
structure. So its third role was to provide a unifying symbol for a nation
whose real rulers were 'secreted in second-rate carriages'.[157] An executive
must be able to enforce its decisions, and Bagehot emphasized that this
was easier for the British executive because it could annexe the prestige of

monarchy and aristocracy. He thought that most English people deferred 'to what we may call the *theatrical show* of society . . . Philosophers may deride this superstition, but its results are inestimable. By the spectacle of this august society, countless ignorant men and women are induced to obey the few nominal electors.'[158] Furthermore, the ordinary person could identify with a family that seemed to rule. A royal family 'sweetens politics by the seasonable addition of nice and pretty events'.[159] From this flowed naturally the monarchy's fourth major function, newly acquired: acting as exemplar to the nation in personal conduct and family values.

In these passages, Bagehot almost caricatured himself in the convolutions of his paradoxes. He claimed of monarchy that 'its mystery is its life. We must not let in daylight upon magic,'[160] and yet that is precisely what he set about doing. He must have assumed that those who were so easily duped would not read his book and thus be undeceived. He made dismissive asides about the profound ignorance to be found among servants about the workings of the English constitution,[161] yet seemed content deliberately to perpetuate that ignorance. In 1866 the positivist E. S. Beesly was already citing Bagehot's approach as illustrating how 'some kinds of education seem to be worse than none at all'. 'A clever writer in the *Fortnightly Review*', he pointed out, 'has lately been picking out for special eulogy all the most contemptible tricks and hypocrisies of the British Constitution. To cheat the masses . . . is in this gentleman's eyes the crowning proof of political sagacity.'[162] Bagehot was running full tilt against the progressive Liberal's high-minded programme for national self-education, and seemed to envisage the infinite postponement of an enlightened democracy. If he sought to educate the masses at all, he set about it in a strangely ironic and surreptitious manner. Fearing the political influence of the masses as he undoubtedly did, he was rashly free with his exposure of the deceits which held it in check.[163] His biographers have not thought it important to resolve the puzzle. The solution perhaps lies partly in the fact that Bagehot had committed himself to his overall position at the time when his first articles were published in 1865, and could not thereafter retreat from it amidst the quite unexpected major franchise reform two years later. However this may be, his subsequent criticism of Dilke for 'placing the sovereign under a microscope, beneath which no majesty . . . can possibly endure'[164] seems a decided case of the pot calling the kettle black.

Bagehot's view of monarchy's practical working in the 1860s was incorrect, and more appropriate for describing the monarch's domestic role under George V. To begin with, until the First World War international relations were conducted in such a way as to give the monarchy far more power than Bagehot imagined. On 6 February 1886 the Queen urged her new Foreign Secretary Lord Rosebery 'not to bring too many matters before the Cabinet, as nothing was decided there, and it would be far better to discuss everything with me and Mr Gladstone'.[165] The Queen could speak so confidently because of at least two contrasts between the situation then and now. Most foreign governments were not then parliamentary in nature, and so foreign policy even under a parliamentary regime like the British had to be more secret than now. Britain could not normally afford to put herself diplomatically at a disadvantage by risking a public debate on foreign relations which would embarrass potential allies or inflame enmities. Furthermore, these overseas governments were communicating with the British government at least partly through the monarch herself. Her authority in foreign policy stemmed partly from receiving confidential information on foreign affairs in her own right from her many European relatives. She had abundant information and experience to bestow as well as to receive. She knew many of the key personalities involved, and by the 1860s was building up unrivalled experience at working with their governments. Already by 1869 she was describing herself to her eldest daughter as 'the *doyenne* of the Sovereigns' with 'much experience which public men nowadays . . . do not even possess'.[166] Still more was this so in 1886, the year in which she told Lord Rosebery she was 'ready to see him often, and to help him', and that she 'frequently had intelligence of a secret nature, which it would be useful and interesting for him to hear, and which came from a reliable source'.[167] It was sometimes more convenient for a foreign secretary to communicate with foreign governments through the Queen's personal correspondence rather than through the Foreign Office's more formal channels. In this situation, much of parliament's influence over foreign policy could be only retrospective. In her approach to the monarchy's formal powers, as in her approach to British overseas possessions, the Queen did not believe in giving away what she held.

Another source of royal power in the 1860s lay in the Queen's arbitrating role between conflicting sections of the political system. While it is true that no monarch after 1834 could risk being humiliated by the electorate through getting committed to the return of any single politician or party, governments still originated through 'an independent process beginning with the Monarch and carried on by the Prime Minister'.[168] Under scrutiny from the monarch, the prime minister chose the members of his cabinet; parliament had no direct influence on the matter. Some

Conservative leaders (Disraeli in 1868 and Salisbury in 1886) emphasized the Queen's persisting right to dissolve parliament if she did not like the policy of her government. Leading Conservatives were still making the same point in 1912–13, claiming that George V should dissolve parliament rather than agree to Irish home rule. Disraeli and Salisbury wisely did not urge the Queen to exercise this aspect of her power, but the very fact that in theory it still existed did something to enhance her bargaining position. With his view of the executive as elected by the legislature, Bagehot did not appreciate how much discretion this left to the monarch. In conflicts, for instance, between Lords and Commons there was much room for royal influence and intervention, as witness episodes during 1869, 1884–5, and 1910–11. Even in party conflict the electorate did not always settle the matter beyond doubt. Besides, the monarch could do much to mould the choices which the electors faced. In the 1880s, for example, the Queen feared the directions in which Gladstone was taking the Liberal Party. So she helped build up the centre grouping which (through the Liberal Unionist secession) defeated home rule in 1886. Not until George V did a monarch aim to act on Bagehot's prescription of complete political neutrality, and even his influence could be considerable when party disputes required him to arbitrate. Such situations were more likely to arise in the three-party situation created by Labour's gradual supplanting of the Liberals in the 1920s. Events in 1931 showed how the politician's shifting alliances could still produce a crisis requiring the King's arbitration. George V's influence was crucial in getting Ramsay MacDonald to form a National Government in 1931, an event which determined the entire shape of British party politics for many years to come.[169]

Nor should the monarch's power be viewed purely in institutional terms: it also comes from knowledge and experience, and monarchs after the 1860s had plenty of access to both. After fifty years on the throne Queen Victoria felt confident enough to put Campbell-Bannerman, her Secretary of State for War, firmly in his place: 'I remember Lord Melbourne using the same arguments many years ago, but it was not true then and it is not true now.'[170] The influence of any individual monarch varies with the combination of personality and circumstance, and trends in royal power are by no means institutional or linear. Queen Victoria reinforced herself with influential and well-informed advisers in several areas of policy—religious, military, and imperial. She might be geographically isolated in Balmoral, but she made it her business to avoid isolation from opinion by vigorously cross-questioning all and sundry, even when old and blind towards the end of her life. The future Queen Mary found it easier than most to get on with her, but even she told her husband in 1895 that Balmoral was rather an ordeal, 'as the everlasting questions and the carefulness of one's replies is extremely fatiguing in the long run'.[171] Reinforcing such informal advice was the Queen's non-party, patriotic, and robust temperament. It kept her views in closer accord with those of the general public than outsiders recognized. 'She had an extraordinary knowledge of what her people would think,' Lord Salisbury recalled, '—extraordinary, because it could not come from any personal intercourse.'[172] Though her letters of the 1880s inevitably reflect the political concerns of her ministers, they also reflect the diverse preoccupations and commonsensical but unconstrained responses of a person who, like her subjects, had not made politics her profession. Through direct links to generals in the field, with whom she instinctively sympathized, and through her deep knowledge of church patronage, a forceful personality could make a considerable impact on busy ministers. By contrast, a weak or short-tenured monarch inevitably carried less weight. Attlee could not recall a single instance during his premiership of 1945–51 when George VI's views had any effect on appointments or policies, imperial or domestic.[173]

The British monarchy up to 1901, then, cannot be pigeon-holed into Bagehot's 'dignified' category. It was simultaneously dignified and efficient. How could Bagehot so misunderstand the Queen's powers, as at 1867? The answer has already been provided. Government was then much less public than it now is. The press was either ill-informed or deferential, and there were no other media apart from public speaking; nobody then earned his living under the label of 'political scientist'; and there was no widespread belief in open government. Besides, Bagehot had the two special disabilities of not being inside the political élite and of lacking inside political knowledge. None the less, he was prescient: the British monarchy did eventually conform largely to his pattern, partly because his own writings were so influential. R. H. S. Crossman, rereading Bagehot after holding the post of Lord President, where he was in charge of the Privy Council's meetings with the Queen, 'found no point of *The English Constitution* more completely truthful to real life today than the chapter on the monarchy'.[174]

*

If Bagehot was not an entirely reliable guide to the English constitution even in his own day, we should certainly not assume, in carrying forward the discussion of British political institutions from then until now, that he

captured their workings for all time. Yet in some areas his analys
more accurate as time passed, and in all areas he offers arresting
Changes in each of the areas so far discussed—in local governm
liberties, pressure groups, political parties, elections, parliament, cabinet,
civil service, and monarchy—must be followed up in later chapters. But
first it is necessary in Chapter 2 to explain how constitutional evolution
was being accelerated by change in two major areas of policy, empire and
welfare, and then in Chapter 3 to clarify how the geographical area within
which British political institutions operated came to be delimited.

# 2

# *Empire and Welfare*

BAGEHOT'S system could not last. He acknowledged as much in 1872 when discussing what had happened since Palmerston died: 'in so short a period there have rarely been more changes'.[1] Neither he nor Mill could have known that within a generation mid-Victorian Liberal political attitudes and institutions would encounter two hostile, powerful, and interacting tendencies: the growth of empire and the advance of public welfare. They threatened many mid-Victorian Liberal rationalistic, voluntarist, and libertarian assumptions: the negative concept of liberty, the philosophy of free trade, the belief in the rational elector, and faith in local self-government. Both also severely tested parliamentary government. Both were accentuated by the two world wars which shattered so many Liberal hopes. Imperialism even reinvigorated the 'dignified' aspects of the British constitution: the aristocracy and monarchy which Bagehot had viewed in so utilitarian a fashion.

This book will show how these changes affected each dimension of the British political system. But this chapter must first describe the dynamic behind these changes in some detail, focusing on their implications for British government, and taking first the empire, then public welfare. Already in 1867 Bagehot knew that British governments were overstretched and under-resourced. He pointed out that whereas the European monarchies had only compact territories to defend and could deploy conscript armies, Britain's volunteer army had to defend 'territories far surpassing all Europe in magnitude, and situated all over the habitable globe', not to mention Britain's naval commitments. Yet British government lacked executive control over local authorities which foreign countries had long abolished.[2] In grappling with these two problems, British politicians transformed the political system that Bagehot knew.

In the 1860s the political parties were already beginning to strengthen their central machinery, and in Gladstone the Liberal Party had acquired a leader whose charisma and energy were soon to accumulate great power over the electorate. Gladstone did not use his influence to promote either empire or public welfare. Yet he was unintentional midwife to both, because as Chancellor of the Exchequer in 1852–3 and 1861–6 he had helped to create an efficient Whitehall machine and a prosperous economy. These could later assume heavier burdens which he would have thought inappropriate. His contribution towards strengthening British government did not stop there. By pushing Irish Church disestablishment to the fore in the general election of 1868, he reinstated the two-party system. This helped to restore the cabinet's control over parliament which Liverpool and Peel had wielded, but which the fragmentation of parties in 1846 had undermined. By the late 1870s Britain's mounting imperial responsibilities were undermining Gladstone's austerely economical financial system. The adventures of Disraeli's government on imperial frontiers in South Africa and India made new demands on the taxpayer and also on the British governmental machine. And by the 1890s the pressures of domestic expenditure were reinforcing such developments. Organized labour, progressive Liberal intellectuals and politicians, and Bismarckian Conservatives were all beginning to press for more public welfare. Indeed, imperialism and social reform reinforced one another, if only because an imperial nation needed more and healthier children for its emigrants and soldiers.

\*

The consequences of all this for Whitehall were at first surprisingly small. In the 1830s Palmerston depended on a staff of only thirty-nine, and wrote the drafts of important dispatches himself.[3] How could this be? To begin with, communication with colonial territories was difficult. There was no cable beneath the English Channel till 1850, no Atlantic cable in effective use till 1866.[4] When trying to control events in South Africa in 1878–9, Disraeli's government was constrained by the fact that the fastest recorded telegram from South Africa to that date (by mixed cable–mail route) took sixteen days; letters took at least three weeks. An all-British cable to link Canada and Australia was not achieved until December 1902.[5] So colonial administration and the execution of foreign policy had to be highly decentralized to the ambassadors, proconsuls, and military men on the spot. A civil servant in an outlying part of India was like an intendant under Louis XIV and XV: 'he had exactly the same sort of duties: magisterial, executive, and financial, and held his province *en tutelle* exactly as a civilian holds his district, interfering in every sort of affair from the highest to the lowest'.[6]

With British government so remote, British settlers often justifiably felt insecure, and often pressed the administrators into committing the government at home beyond its intentions. No doubt Gladstone's explanation of the government's difficulties in the Sudan seemed lame to the Queen in 1884, yet it encapsulates well the situation on the imperial frontier. He referred to 'the very imperfect knowledge with which the Government are required at the shortest notice to form conclusions in respect to a peculiar, remote, and more than half-barbarous region, with which they have but a very slight and indirect connection in the ordinary sense'.[7] Such difficulties transcended political party. It was the fate of British governments, Lord Salisbury told the Queen in August 1886, 'to be always making bricks without straw'. As land forces go in these days, he told her, 'we have no army capable of meeting even a second-class continental power', and British governments 'without money, without any strong land force, with an insecure tenure of power, and with an ineffective agency . . . have to counterwork the efforts of three Empires, who labour under none of these disadvantages'.[8] British influence could often be upheld only through a form of bluff. In India, where the mutiny of 1857 was an ever-present memory, a government of 250,000 whites ruled 250 million Indians, and continued British control 'rested almost entirely on its *morale* and prestige'.[9] British rule there, said Lord Randolph Churchill in 1885, was 'a sheet of oil spread over a surface of, and keeping calm and quiet and unruffled by storms, an immense and profound ocean of humanity'.[10] In this situation, 'character' was more important for the British administrator than technical expertise or bureaucratic skill: he had to be decisive and dignified in difficult circumstances with minimal resources. 'My whole life', George Orwell recalled, 'every white man's life in the East, was one long struggle not to be laughed at.'[11]

Within the colonies of white settlement, devolution soon took the form of local self-government on the model that operated at home, with the difference that devolution was expected eventually to lead, given the American precedent, to independence—a second reason why the empire's initial impact on Whitehall was so small. Even leading mid-Victorian officials in the Colonial Office assumed that separation was inevitable.[12] Meanwhile, devolution was a cheap and congenial expedient. The Durham report claimed that in the colonies of white settlement, 'the colonists may not always know what laws are best for them, or which of their countrymen are the fittest for conducting their affairs; but, at least, they have a greater interest in coming to a right judgement on these points, and will take greater pains to do so, than those whose welfare is very remotely and slightly affected by the good or bad legislation of these portions of the Empire'.[13] Devolution within the empire could take the form of indirect rule, or could involve devolving responsibility first to governors and then to local representative assemblies. Some even hoped that this might ward off the American precedent and draw Britain and its remaining colonies together, for no obvious alternative route to union lay to hand. Gladstone drew heavily on colonial precedents when preparing his Home Rule Bill for Ireland in 1886.[14]

Distance and devolution caused Britain's foreign and colonial problems in Bagehot's time to seem less complex, so less in need of civil servants to disentangle them, than they later became. Britain's twentieth-century bureaucratic growth in its overseas dimension sprang more from weakness than from strength. For much of the nineteenth century, this 'satisfied' power—secure in its island fortress—did not need allies, let alone any entanglement with a European *Zollverein*. And until the 1880s there were sufficient empty spaces in the world for colonial expansion to act as shock-absorber for potential international rivalry. So Lord Salisbury could view British foreign policy as involving little more than floating lazily down-stream, 'occasionally putting out a diplomatic boat-hook to avoid colli-sions'.[15] The Colonial Office was preoccupied more with finding ways of avoiding trouble and expense in particular colonies than with strategic planning for the empire as a whole. Its consistent enthusiasm for federat-ing colonial territories and for devolving power to them stemmed more from a desire (never discouraged by the Treasury) to offload sources of trouble and expense than from any liberal vision of a self-governing Com-monwealth. In 1825 its staff numbered only thirty-one, including two porters and a housekeeper,[16] and was organized regionally rather than function-ally. It was a somewhat unimaginative department, with no clear policy to propagate, no taste for publicity.

It did not encounter much pressure from publicity, given the existence until 1914 of a closed national and international monarchical and aristo-cratic élite. Secrecy gave ministers and civil servants at home the same free discretion which poor communications gave their agents overseas. After eight years in the Office, Henry Taylor had by his own account 'from the first year . . . been employed not in the business of a clerk but in that of a statesman'.[17] In 1840 Charles Buller thought such a system had 'all the faults of an essentially arbitrary government, in the hands of persons who have little personal interest in the welfare of those over whom they rule'.[18]

He claimed that 'in nine cases out of ten' parliament 'merely registers the edicts of the Colonial Office'. Such claims seem to have been exaggerated; about 8 per cent of parliament's time went on colonial affairs between 1830 and 1850, and much more in the 1860s.[19] Nonetheless, in 1845 an MP told parliament that it was 'the essence of our colonial system' that the Colonial Secretary should be 'in his administration supreme. What he does, he does unchecked by public opinion'.[20] Decisions on foreign and colonial policy tended to be reached outside the cabinet, in consultations between prime minister, foreign secretary, and monarch.[21]

The advance of democracy actually enhanced secrecy,[22] and led diplomats and foreign secretaries to present their craft as a mystique that passed all public understanding. As long as Britain's main diplomatic dealings were with undemocratic powers, diplomats' instinctive response was to react defensively in the face of democratic tendencies at home. Hazards seemed to lurk in participatory political parties with unpredictable policies, as well as in indiscreet and inexperienced newcomers to parliament and the cabinet. Less and less material on diplomatic activity was published, and in 1876 Disraeli, Lord Salisbury, and the Queen were horrified when agitation over the Bulgarian atrocities complicated diplomacy by mobilizing an ignorant and emotional public behind heated party alignments.[23] Britain, confronting powers with no party system, now seemed at risk of having to change its foreign policy as one party succeeded another in power. Something like this happened when the Liberals succeeded the Conservatives in power in 1880, and the Queen wanted no repeat performance. In 1886, in a similar situation, no such diplomatic overturn occurred. It became generally accepted that foreign secretaries should operate from the House of Lords, relatively secure from the pressures of opinion. Even there, Lord Salisbury admitted in 1887, 'we do not usually discuss what goes on in the Foreign Office'.[24] A grim concern pervaded his outlook on foreign policy, which he saw as striving to defend the nation's precarious assets amidst its self-created hazards of democracy. He once warned an audience, eager for a diplomatic achievement that they could applaud, that 'it is a subject about which we must all think a great deal and speak very little'.[25]

One final reason for the empire's small impact on Whitehall was that British governments did not then need to promote British overseas trade directly. For reasons of doctrine and convenience, trade could be left to look after itself. International relations then took the form more of contact between traders than between governments. Not till 1865 did the Foreign Office create a department specially responsible for commercial affairs, and it was slow to grow in size and status.[26] Even at the level of collecting statistical information, Foreign Office mechanisms long remained somewhat rudimentary.[27] British manufactured goods, backed by British shipping resources, were good enough to make their own way. Liberals widely assumed that the 'hidden hand' operated in foreign as in economic policy. 'Man, were he not corrupted by governments, is naturally the friend of man,' Tom Paine had written,[28] in a message that Cobden and Bright courageously carried forward from the 1830s to the 1880s. Peace, for them, would come through enhanced communication between peoples rather than between governments. For Cobden, 'the progress of freedom depends more upon the maintenance of peace, the spread of commerce, and the diffusion of education, than upon the labours of Cabinets or Foreign-offices'.[29]

In Bagehot's later years, however, all this was beginning to change. 'It is always the highest class which travels most,' he wrote, 'knows most of foreign nations, has the least of the territorial sectarianism which calls itself patriotism, and is often thought to be so.'[30] Throughout his time as Foreign Secretary Salisbury viewed jingoistic pressure with aristocratic disdain, as a dangerous distraction from the delicate task of preserving peace in a dangerous world. None the less, by the 1870s the public was getting more interested in imperial annexation. By August 1899 Salisbury regarded the annexationist outlook of Alfred Milner, High Commissioner for South Africa, as 'too heated'. But he recognized that 'we have to act upon a moral field prepared for us by him and his jingo supporters', making efforts 'for people whom we despise, and for territory which will bring no profit and no power to England'.[31] The cabinet had to be taken into closer consultation about international relations, otherwise two dangers would result: foreign secretaries would be placed in false positions, and governments would be denied the public support that diplomatic success ultimately required. A delaying action was played out within the Liberal government of 1906,[32] whose cabinet breathed (according to Lloyd George) 'an air of "hush hush" about every allusion to our relations with France, Russia and Germany'.[33] But when in 1914 such reticence seemed to have led to disaster, the line could no longer be held.

For some time an alternative approach had been developing, whereby the public could be taken broadly into the government's confidence, however necessary it might still be to keep the details under wraps. If public opinion could be harnessed behind British government policy, democracy could be converted into a diplomatic asset. George Canning perceived the opportunity from inside government.[34] Radicals led by Cobden and Bright later enlisted public opinion on overseas issues in directions less sympathetic to government. Through Joseph Chamberlain, much of their approach was carried (via Liberal Unionism) into the heart of the late-Victorian Conservative Party. 'There is no longer any room for the mysteries and the reticence of the diplomacy of fifty years ago,' Chamberlain declared at Birmingham in 1898. 'You must tell the people what you mean, and where you are going, if you want them to follow.'[35] Imperialist populism prompted imitation from anti-imperialists, now better informed as a result of improved communications. By the 1860s parliament was beginning to supervise colonial administrators more closely, whether sympathetically or otherwise. Colonists, ex-settlers, and journalists began working with backbenchers to generate an interest in empire.[36] Radical and later Labour MPs established links with the overseas critics of colonial regimes. John Bright became spokesman for India, and from 1867 was complemented by Henry Fawcett, the self-appointed parliamentary scrutineer of Indian government finance.[37] He in turn was succeeded by Charles Bradlaugh, at whose funeral an unknown 21-year-old law student was present: Mohandas K. Gandhi.[38] During the 1880s the Irish MPs detected in Indian administration a sore point which they could profitably inflame.[39]

Colonial administrators encountered mounting difficulties from governments at home. The problem lay partly in the lack of co-ordination at Whitehall. After four years spent in running Egyptian administration, Cromer told Goschen in 1887 that the British governmental machine was 'singularly ill-adapted' for its purposes, with 'no cohesion among the London Departments. Each seems to work independently, with the result that I hear sometimes the voice of the Foreign Office, sometimes that of the Treasury, sometimes that of the War Office, speaking to me in words that are by no means always identic.' Added to this, there was continual trouble from parliament.[40] 'The Government of India cannot retain the confidence of the House of Commons unless it keeps up its character as a progressive and reforming Government,' Sir John Gorst warned India's new Viceroy, Lord Lansdowne, in 1888.[41] 'One of the great problems you and I have to try to solve', Selborne told Curzon in 1907, 'is how to develop the constitution so as to remove things really imperial from the control of the House of Commons.'[42] Milner's private correspondence is peppered with scorching comment on the problems resulting from 'this rotten assembly in Westminster' where 'the whole future of the Empire may turn upon the whims of men who have been elected for their competence in dealing with Metropolitan tramways or country pubs'. Imperial proconsuls like Milner and Lloyd saw British parliamentary government as seriously obstructing

their long-term plans for constructive imperial achievement; serious difficulties were experienced even by the more prudent and liberal-minded
Egyptian proconsul Lord Cromer.[43]

The pressure to involve the public in formulating overseas policy was by
no means confined to colonial questions. The Union of Democratic Control after 1914 carried pressure-group politics into the heart of discussion
on foreign policy. Its London-based intellectual and radical support amply
reinforced the Labour Party's provincial and working-class base.[44] One of
Labour's major attractions for inter-war Liberals was its promise of a
new, internationalist, and more open diplomacy. Foreign policy could
then cease to be a mystique and become the theme of adult education in
its broadest sense; enhanced public understanding might then erode the
passions and prejudices that nourished conflict. In 1924 the Labour government included fifteen of the Union's members, nine of them in the
cabinet,[45] and launched the practice of laying treaties on the table of both
houses of parliament for twenty-one days before ratification.

We can now see that a political system incorporating conflict between
government and opposition parties was compatible only with the sort of
empire whose links with Britain were voluntary. First in Ireland, then in
India and later elsewhere, British rule ultimately succumbed before local
pressures for independence. Throughout the twentieth century Labour
MPs and intellectuals—from Harold Laski to Kingsley Martin, from Keir
Hardie to Fenner Brockway—aligned themselves with leading Indian and
African opponents of empire. Given the two-party system, their strategies
could plausibly assume that a government of the left was, at least in theory,
always in the offing.[46] 'I think no one in this Chamber will deny, we are
all Members for India,'[47] said Fred Pethick-Lawrence, the Labour MP, in
November 1943. Less than four years later, when Secretary of State for
India, he was to announce Britain's impending departure. After 1945 the
growing powers in the world, America and the USSR, were both anti-
imperialist and egalitarian, at least in theory, and both were alert to what
was going on beyond their frontiers. In the 1950s, having done its work in
Asia, the alliance of anti-imperialists at home and nationalists overseas
turned to Africa, with equal effect.[48]

To mounting publicity was added improved communications. At least
until 1895 the Colonial Office had no co-ordinated policy for the empire
as a whole, and not until 1903 did the idea of integrating the empire
through tariffs move centre-stage. But fear of Russian ambitions first produced a committee of civil servants and service personnel to co-ordinate
imperial defence in 1878, and from 1885 the line of continuity between such

committees was continuous; the committee became a subcommittee of the Committee of Imperial Defence in 1902.[49] By 1895 the Colonial Office seemed significant enough to attract a politician as ambitious as Joseph Chamberlain. As Colonial Secretary, he could dream of reproducing within the late Victorian empire as a whole the tightening links between centre and periphery that were occurring within British government at home. At the colonial conference of 1897 he envisaged 'a great council of the Empire', representative in nature, 'as our ultimate ideal'.[50] His South African tour of 1903 symbolized the new approach, for some thought improved communications could unify the empire. This was the first time that the British government had reached out directly to the colonies.[51] The first imperial conference in 1911 heard the Prime Minister of New Zealand advocating an 'Imperial Parliament of Defence' to co-ordinate imperial defence effort,[52] and collaboration during the First World War drew the colonial links tighter still. 'It has been, perhaps, a tragedy for the development of the British Commonwealth', Julian Amery reflected many years later, 'that the aeroplane was not invented and developed fifty years earlier.'[53]

Imperial proconsuls could increasingly be controlled from Westminster and Whitehall, and the complexities of international entanglement mounted with improved communications. The last of the semi-autonomous British ambassadors overseas was Lord Stratford de Redcliffe, the influential and long-standing British ambassador at Constantinople who retired in 1858.[54] By the 1880s decisions in any one colonial area increasingly carried implications for other areas. The number of telegrams and dispatches at the Foreign Office rose markedly—from 9,059 in 1825 to 91,433 in 1895—as did registered papers at the Colonial Office.[55] The number of papers handled by the Colonial Office doubled between 1868 and 1888. Its telegraph bill rose more than twelvefold between 1870 and 1900–1,[56] and the number of telegrams it dispatched rose sevenfold between 1907 and 1915.[57] The Edwardian Foreign Office was beginning to transform itself into a full-scale administrative department, taking its own decisions.[58] The numbers involved in Whitehall's machinery for running overseas policy rose during the twentieth century, regardless of governments' party complexion.[59] Colonial Office employees grew from 109 in 1900–1 to 1,286 in April 1950. Separate machinery for the dominions was growing up in parallel, with the Dominions Office supporting fifty-two civil servants in April 1930 and 904 twenty years later. And if in some respects Britain's involvement with the Commonwealth was declining, elsewhere within the empire (most notably on aid for underdeveloped countries) its commitments were growing. A minister was assigned to this area from 1964, and the Overseas Development Administration had 2,449 employees by April 1971. The Foreign Office, with only 142 employees in 1900–1 had 902 by April 1938 and 6,195 by April 1950.[60] And as Britain's military capability declined, the number of non-industrial civil servants in defence departments rose: from 10,000 in 1914 to 23,040 in 1935 to 135,270 in 1956.[61]

Ideas of buttressing colonial conferences with a permanent secretariat became current during the Edwardian period,[62] and all this culminated in what was misleadingly called the 'imperial war cabinet': fourteen meetings from March to May 1917 between the British cabinet, dominions premiers, and the representatives of India. The colonies had become involved in formulating imperial defence policy from 1911, when their prime ministers attended meetings of the Committee of Imperial Defence. In 1917 colonial representatives also attended a concurrent committee concerned with imperial matters, again chaired by Lloyd George, and again serviced by the new secretariat he had created in 1916. In 1919 colonial representatives met daily with Lloyd George in the same body before going to Versailles for the peace settlement. The years 1920–2 have been described as a 'period of tentative centralization', exciting for imperialists, when many assumed that an integrated imperial foreign policy could be founded on an 'imperial peace cabinet'.[63]

The movement for tariff reform, collaboration between British and dominions forces in the two world wars, the meetings of the imperial cabinet in 1917, and the introduction of the 10 per cent tariff in 1932 were all developments that made the empire–Commonwealth seem viable as a twentieth-century military, political, and economic entity. By 1938 the United Kingdom was sending 47 per cent of her exports to the empire, whereas in 1913 the equivalent figure had been only 22 per cent.[64] In its manifesto of 1945 the Conservative Party was still claiming that 'imperial ties should be knit together by closer personal contact and understanding'.[65] It was not until the 1950s that the option of tighter union with the former colonies, reinforced by protection, finally wilted under American and anti-imperialist pressure. To interpret Britain's move from empire to Europe as foreseen before the 1960s, let alone as predestined, would indeed be hindsighted. The administrative consequences for Whitehall of Britain's world role persisted well into the 1960s and were wound down less from inclination or design than in response to economic crises.

We now know that a unified British empire was an impossible dream, if only because the same changes in communications that drew colonies towards the 'mother country' were also converting their constituent populations into viable economies and lending them some sort of national identity. But here was one further reason why more public employees were needed. The empire in decline made greater bureaucratic demands than in its days of prosperity. Self-government, followed by independence, meant that relationships which for Britain had hitherto been executive now gradually became diplomatic. In 1879 Canada, now self-governing, felt the need for a new type of official in London: a high commissioner whose role would be 'quasi-diplomatic'[66] in nature. This was the first step in what eventually became the removal of any significant distinction between colonies and foreign countries for British diplomatic purposes. High commissioners were appointed for New Zealand in 1905, Australia in 1910, and South Africa in 1911. According to an internal memorandum of 1888, colonial self-government was lending Colonial Office responsibilities 'a still more anxious character, particularly as regards . . . international arrangements'.[67] It might as yet be impossible to allow colonies to negotiate treaties for themselves, but British foreign policy was increasingly being conducted with colonial feeling in mind, whatever the legal technicalities of the relationship might be. The imperial war conference of 1917 was unanimous in thinking that post-war relations among the dominions (including India) should assume that they were 'autonomous nations', consulting mutually on matters of common concern.[68] To the Paris peace conference of 1919 the dominions sent their own delegates. Canada appointed its own diplomatic representative to Washington in 1920, the Irish Free State a full-blown embassy there in 1924. It was generally admitted that dominion status was difficult to define, but what was the point of definition, asked W. M. Hughes, Prime Minister of Australia, if 'in effect, we have all the rights of self-government enjoyed by independent nations'? 'We are like so many Alexanders,' he told the imperial conference of 1921. 'What other worlds have we to conquer?'[69]

Definition was, however, eventually forced on the Commonwealth by members less reconciled than Australia to the British connection, and by world-wide changes which increasingly distanced even Australia from the United Kingdom. Within the year, the Chanak crisis was to expose the dominions as divided on an important international issue. When the Labour government in 1924 recognized the USSR without consulting the dominions, Canada pointedly issued her own formal recognition some weeks later. In the discussions leading up to the Locarno pact of 1925, Britain did no more than inform the dominions during the negotiations, and pursued her own local interests.[70] The breakdown of Lloyd George's vision of an integrated imperial foreign policy was formalized in the negotiations at the

imperial conference in the following year. From 1928 Britain began appointing its own high commissioners in the dominions, thus creating
a new colonial diplomatic service outside the Foreign Office. The high
commissioners' standing rose steadily as they grew more like ambassadors.
All this, together with enhanced colonial autonomy, tightening communications, and mounting publicity for the actions of government, enlarged
the central-government machinery for overseas relations still further. Britain's post-war mandates in the Middle East ensured that the rapid growth
in Colonial Office staff continued in the early 1920s.[71] Functional specialization within the Office was bound to accompany growth of this order,
and already by 1867 its structure acknowledged the distinctive administrative needs of self-governing and crown colonies.[72] There was talk during the
Edwardian period of creating a distinct dominions department within
the Office, and when a Colonial Secretary keen on the idea arrived in 1924
the change was made. Special training arrangements were soon required
to build up a co-ordinated colonial service, and the Dominions Office
increasingly saw its role as a diplomatic one: ensuring that the dominions'
aspirations were fully understood in Britain. Far from being jingoistic in
mood, the Office infuriated imperialists with its tactful failure to back
moves for imperial unification.[73]

Friction between the Dominions and Foreign Offices in the 1930s and
1940s reflected their increasingly similar roles, and three overseas ministries became increasingly difficult to justify. 'Dominion' turned out to be
only a transit lounge from colony to autonomy. Canadian ministers from
1857 and Australians from 1866 had begun to make the long journey to
London for direct conversations, and in 1860 the Duke of Newcastle was
the first colonial secretary to go to a dominion while in office.[74] Between
the wars it became common for foreign secretaries to bypass their ambassadors and converse directly, and on a memorable occasion in 1938 the
heads of the British and German governments did the same. Lulu Harcourt
as Colonial Secretary (1910–15) began the practice of meeting the high
commissioners regularly every month, and by the Second World War
there was a complex network of contacts between Britain and the empire
involving the Commonwealth high commissioners in London and the
British high commissioners overseas, as well as exchange visits by ministers, government missions, civil servants, and experts. So the twentieth
century witnessed the paradox that as Britain's international role declined,
its bureaucratic provision for relations with foreign and Commonwealth
powers and for national self-defence increased.

After 1945 the early twentieth-century growth in the Whitehall administration which managed the empire's devolutionary phase now at last began to level off. The Dominions Office absorbed the India Office in 1947, became the Commonwealth Relations Office, and moved out of the Colonial Office into its own premises. Thereafter its prestige mounted in relation to both the Foreign Office and the Colonial Office, and the logical consequence followed: union between all three in the 1960s. The Commonwealth Relations Office first absorbed the Colonial Office (in 1966) and then merged with the Foreign Office in 1968. Yet central government machinery for handling overseas matters did not thereafter decline as fast or as far as might have been expected. This was partly because large European empires gave way to numerous small autonomous governments, all requiring diplomatic representatives, as the recent collapse of the Russian empire illustrates. It was at first hoped that British colonial territories could be federated into larger units, or that the temperate dominions could absorb Britain's smaller tropical outposts to complement their own economies,[75] but these hopes were disappointed. And to these causes of mounting colonial and Commonwealth business should be added the mounting workload flowing from new international institutions, new international questions (space, pollution), and a new complexity of issues. Anthony Eden thought the Foreign Secretary's burden had doubled between 1945 and 1951.[76] It became still more complex when, from the early 1960s, Britain tried to ride two horses simultaneously: the weakening 'special relationship' with the USA and the growing relationship with the EEC. There was no full merger between the overseas and home sections of the civil service in the 1960s, but their continued separation was becoming unreal, given that civil servants from other government departments were increasingly engaged in diplomatic work, though more often now in Brussels and Strasbourg than in Bombay and Sydney.

\*

It is time now to turn to the second long-term reason why Bagehot's political system came under statist challenge: the growth of public welfare. The two spheres, empire and welfare, interacted. Edwardians increasingly recognized the need for a healthy and expanding population to populate and defend the empire, and the Liberal imperialist policy of 'national efficiency' showed signs of capturing Edwardian centrist opinion. Slum-based disease threatened the calibre of army recruits at a time when Britain seemed threatened by nations with larger rural populations, and when her empire thirsted for settlers. Emigration was seen as a palliative for domestic problems which could postpone the need for a direct attack on poverty at home. Empire was also seen as an opportunity for realizing world-wide the recurrent British dreams of domestic rural resettlement. Some even saw overseas adventurism as a diversion from socialism and as reinforcing social discipline. When confronted by Liberalism, imperialism and social reform had much in common, and their attack on *laissez-faire* in one sphere could readily spill over into other spheres. With welfare reforms at the centre of political debate, rival parties were bound to argue about how to fund them. Joseph Chamberlain saw protection not as an alternative to welfare reforms, but a way to fund them without redistribution.

Imperialism and welfare reinforced one another in many other ways. Imperialism and war were closely linked, and in wartime good morale on the home front was essential. During the two world wars the ideals of liberty and equality, advertised as being for export to populations oppressed by a German enemy, could scarcely be fended off at home. A good democratic example needed to be set to the foreigner, and a democratic justification provided for wars embarked upon for less elevated reasons. Wartime interventionism created structures and precedents needed for implementing more ambitious concepts of welfare in peacetime. In standardizing and inspecting fire services and hospital facilities, for instance, the Second World War prepared the ground for further collectivist advance. The memory of interventionism in the First World War stayed with Harold Macmillan for long enough to influence the entire tone of his *The Middle Way* (1938), and twenty years later his attitude to economic management when Prime Minister. War's 'inspection effect'—through recruitment procedures, welfare remedies for disrupted family life, and evacuation of inner-city populations—exposed welfare requirements. War nourished specific interventionist schemes that persisted in peacetime: works canteens in the First World War; nutritional guidance, food subsidies, and family allowances in the Second. There were also benefits in both wars for women separated from their bread-winners and for war workers required to move away from home. War prepared public opinion for the personal sacrifices involved in funding public welfare, given that both world wars raised the threshold of what had hitherto been regarded as the highest possible tolerable level of taxation. Referring to the need for improved nutrition, Macmillan pointed out that 'all these things that are denounced as impossible in the cause of peaceful progress immediately become possible for the purposes of war'.[77] Wartime rationing of consumer goods and labour won recruits for the general principle of equality, a change which long outlasted any short-term emergency. 'Now, when the war is abolishing landmarks of every kind,' said the Beveridge report in 1942, 'is the opportunity for using experience in a clear field. A revolutionary moment in the world's history is a time for revolutions, not for patching.'[78] In peacetime a reduced level of domestic service, high levels of taxation, and 'fair shares for all' came to seem permanently practicable and even desirable objectives.

Commonwealth precedents were important as influences on British social policy. Chamberlain himself was seeking information in January 1906 about New Zealand's legislation on old-age pensions and compulsory industrial arbitration.[79] Asquith saw New Zealand as 'a laboratory in which political and social experiments are every day made for the information and instruction of the older countries of the world'.[80] Citing egalitarian trends in New Zealand's social policy, Philip Snowden in 1908 dismissed the claim that Britain's heavier commitments invalidated such precedents: 'we as an old established country should be able to do what is impossible for a new country with growing expenditure and taxation to undertake'.[81] Municipal enterprise, nationalization, compulsory industrial arbitration, family allowances, and the attack on sweated labour were all aspects of an interventionist state for which Commonwealth precedents were cited in twentieth-century British domestic discussions on welfare.[82] Beveridge found in New Zealand an excellent precedent for the idea of a transition period to adequate contributory pensions,[83] and in the second-reading debate on the Family Allowances Bill on 8 March 1945, James Griffiths referred to 'the fine pioneering work done in this matter, as in every other kind of social security matter, by the Labour Government in New Zealand', whose success 'has had a very great influence on opinion in this country'.[84]

The empire was not the only overseas source of ideas on welfare. We have already seen the role of France in the British public-health movement of the 1840s.[85] In 1907 and 1909 Beveridge visited Germany to see their labour exchanges, and it was a visit to Germany that made Lloyd George enthusiastic for unemployment insurance.[86] Winston Churchill at the Board of Trade wanted to 'thrust a big slice of Bismarckianism over the whole underside of our industrial system', and took care to visit the labour bureaux at Strasbourg and Frankfurt-on-Main when observing German army manoeuvres in autumn 1909.[87] In his autobiography Beveridge thought it 'safe to say that Britain would not have had compulsory health insurance as early as 1911 if Germany had not shown the way'.[88]

The main impulse to the growth of public welfare, however, was domestic. The phrase 'welfare state' seems to have emerged only in the late 1930s, long after its build-up had begun. A complex interaction of influences, cumulatively powerful, produced this outcome. Welfare interventionism advanced pragmatically and unobtrusively. In 1889 *Fabian Essays* argued that socialism had arrived almost unnoticed as the result of cumulated empirical responses to practical situations by people who often disliked the very idea of socialism. Likewise Beveridge in his report of 1942; surveying the history of government welfare, he noted that 'in all this change and development, each problem has been dealt with separately, with little or no reference to allied problems'.[89] Pressure from the professional classes, including the Fabians, was important. By the 1880s, with Joseph Chamberlain as pioneer among the politicians, the radical section of the middle class was losing its early-Victorian fear of the state, which now seemed in increasingly friendly hands. Welfare interventionism helped to assuage middle-class discomfort at the contrasts in wealth they saw all around them, a discomfort reinforced by religion. Evangelical Christians wanted to render Christian belief feasible for slum-dwellers. T. H. Green encouraged Christians losing their faith to recover it by forsaking theological and liturgical controversy for 'good works' among the poor. From the 1880s such movements as the university settlement, the Salvation Army, and Christian Socialism ensured that at least some influential middle-class people identified politically with classes below their own. Many of the precedents for interventionist welfare reform were set by legislative attempts to promote moral reform.[90] Middle-class people whose faith was irredeemably lost included some who 'converted' to socialism as a sort of secular gospel.

Reason supplied a further impulse. State intervention attracted the rationalist who sought organization, tidiness, and 'planning': the irreligious person who forsook what he saw as religion's obscurantism or obtuseness for planned social reconstruction. Furthermore, the growing number of professional people felt concern about the consequences of gross contrasts in wealth: the doctor could not cure his patients till their daily living conditions were improved, the teacher could not educate his pupils till they were properly fed. Ruskin and Morris prompted the artist to feel uncomfortable in his middle-class suburb if beset by the ugliness of poverty. Both artists and Christians sought converts at lower levels in society. Forceful propagandists—Carlyle, Arnold, Green—stressed how interdependent the classes inevitably were in modern life. 'Individual perfection', wrote Matthew Arnold, 'is impossible so long as the rest of mankind are not perfected along with us.'[91] Poverty's evils did not respect social-class barriers. Diseases such as cholera spread outside the slum to other social classes, if only because there were enough domestic servants to plant a working-class person inside every middle-class home. 'Would it not have been *economy* to help this poor Widow?' asked Carlyle of the Edinburgh charitable bodies who had turned her away. 'She took typhus-fever, and killed seventeen of you!'[92]

Public welfare does not benefit only the deprived; other things being equal, it will also benefit the self-confident and the articulate, whether opera-goers at Covent Garden or parents of children at university. If Britain was to compete in international markets, she needed to compensate for poor material resources by fully exploiting her intellectual resources through improved education. So public welfare enlisted middle-class self-interest as well as altruism. Public welfare offered ample scope for the professions. The sorts of people who became Fabians—manager, artist, scientist, expert—had much to gain from it. The rational reorganization of society promised new roles for doctors, social workers, architects, teachers, civil servants, and administrators, not to mention sympathetic and ambitious politicians. As welfare advanced over empire among twentieth-century government's responsibilities, tutors in universities increasingly advised their more ambitious pupils to forsake ideas of the Indian or colonial services for a career in Whitehall.[93]

The working-class contribution to public welfare was substantial, but somewhat less direct. Many working-class people were wary of state intervention.[94] Their experience of the workhouse system introduced after 1834 did not warm them to state interference of any kind. They had good reason to dislike slum-clearance schemes which failed to replace the condemned accommodation with alternative cheap housing. Compulsory education burdened families which needed the wages or services of older children in order to support the younger as they passed through the worst phase in Seebohm Rowntree's poverty cycle. Even when well intentioned, the type of state interference working-class people experienced was often fussy, sectarian, and intrusive: in humanitarian, temperance, and sabbatarian activity, for example. Working people often saw the state as run by the enemy, or at the very least by people blind to the realities of life near the poverty-line and unduly influenced by a property-biased legal system. Some important welfare reforms were unpopular with working people until, or even after, they had been enacted: national insurance, for example. Nor is there strong evidence of working-class electoral pressure for public welfare, which was not prominent as an election issue between 1885 and 1914. Major welfare reforms such as old-age pensions did not result from popular pressure. Interventionist ideas were not prevalent in working-class organizations. It was the socialist intellectual, not the Lib-Lab MP, who first espoused socialism. It made headway only slowly within trade unions, friendly societies, and co-ops.

There was a conflict between the state route to public welfare and the ideal of self-help that so powerfully influenced the most articulate type of working man. Many who led working-class organizations were economical by temperament and outlook: Chartists elected to local authorities in the 1840s, for example; the former dockers' leader John Burns at the LCC and Local Government Board; Philip Snowden as Chancellor of the Exchequer; Ramsay MacDonald as Prime Minister in 1929–31. Such men rose in public life through personal economy and integrity. Aiming to propagate their own kind, they readily accepted the analogy between the private and the public purse.[95] So the mutuality of their trade unions, co-ops, and friendly societies did not readily transfer from community to national level. Working-class organizations for thrift, self-improvement, and self-insurance hindered middle-class reformers trying to introduce the Old-Age Pensions Bill in 1908, labour exchanges in 1909, or the Bill for national insurance in 1911. To the trade unionist who saw his trade union as his miniature welfare state, public welfare seemed a threatening form of nationalization, and he 'preferred *laissez-faire* collectivism to State Socialism'.[96]

Among the welfare state's intended beneficiaries lower down in the social system, new ideas on public welfare seemed still less congenial. For the very poor, the first priority was to scrape together a living in the short term; there was little energy left even for political activity, let alone for new ideas from alien quarters. Change of any kind, however well intentioned in the long term, risked producing an uncertainty that might push the poor below the poverty-line in the short term. Here, as later with nuclear disarmament, apathy prevailed because people were 'totally absorbed with their own day by day problems of survival'.[97] Here, traditionalist prejudice against middle- or upper-class London-based investigation and inspection was near the surface. Factory inspection, for instance, may have set the pace for government regulation, and (as Marx himself pointed out) for rejecting middle-class political economy. Yet it was opposed by the mass-based ten-hours movement in the 1830s, and the idea of factory hours inspection seems to have come from the middle-class administrator Edwin Chadwick. Employer and employee frequently collaborated to frustrate the intentions of the inspectors once appointed. Working people opposed factory hours restriction and compulsory education for the same reason: both denied the family much-needed income at a crucial phase in the poverty cycle.

None the less, public welfare does owe much to working-class influence.

To begin with, leaders of working-class organizations were pragmatic on the role of the state. They were well able to back collectivism when it seemed most likely to uphold respectable values. Working-class respectability's individualist face was foremost in the Victorian period only when the major threat to respectability appeared to come from an aristocratic and Anglican state. At times when the free market seemed the most serious threat, respectability could readily invoke state aid. Unemployed handloom weavers in the 1830s, for instance, were quite prepared to use under-consumptionist (rather than *laissez-faire*) arguments for boosting their trade. Likewise, in the 1920s the labour movement's modest approach to collectivism was designed to fend off the poverty for which governments rather than the failings of the individual were now increasingly blamed. For Labour's Minister of Labour Margaret Bondfield, one aim of national insurance was 'to preserve the self-respect of the worker who, through no fault of his own, is out of employment'.[98]

Nor was middle-class interventionism formulated in a social vacuum. The study, the library, and the discussion group which nourished the new interventionist fashion were responding to actual or potential pressure from without. There was the hope, for instance, of political allies. When pioneer British collectivists could not get support within the middle class, they often turned to working people for support. Tom Paine—the pioneer advocate of tax-funded maternity allowances, public works, and old-age pensions—won more support from working people than from elsewhere. Robert Owen, proposing state provision for the unemployed, sought working-class support after all else had failed, and won it. Collectivists such as Carlyle, Ruskin, and Morris who challenged mid-Victorian political economy found support among working men when they could get it nowhere else. The middle-class challenge to *laissez-faire* ideas was the more self-confident for knowing that it had at least some following lower down in society.

Fear of revolution reinforced the incentives to concern. At its crudest, this fear could consist simply of the knowledge that the poverty-stricken mob could emerge at any time from the back streets. In Germany in the 1880s Bismarck introduced welfare benefits partly to forestall and undermine the appeal of Marxism, and similar motives inspired Joseph Chamberlain's collectivism in that period. In March 1886 he told Balfour of his dilemma: state public works were 'absurd' and the alternative—paying people to do no work—was harmful. Yet something had to be done because if distress persisted for three more years 'we may find ourselves *en pleine révolution*'.[99] Likewise, after 1911 actuarial considerations did not prevent the extension of national insurance benefits, and once conceded they could not be withdrawn for fear of working-class resistance; unemployment insurance covered some 4 million by 1916, 11 million by 1920, and 15 million by 1938. The taxpayer had increasingly to fund all this because between 1911 and 1920 the government abandoned its original idea of keeping the national insurance fund solvent. Such developments reflect the salience after 1914 of the moral challenge offered to the other parties by the labour movement, whether in government or in opposition. In its early days the Labour Party was significant less for what it achieved when in power, more for what it extracted from governments run by rival parties; 'it would hardly be a paradox to say that socialism won its greatest victories before it came to power'.[100] The creativeness in public welfare of a Lloyd George, a Neville Chamberlain, or a Harold Macmillan derived much of its driving force from elsewhere.

Yet public welfare did not come solely from socialists enthusiastic for collectivism. It arose from the continuous interaction between a collectivism and an individualism that were in practice more compatible than might at first be supposed. The dynamic which eventually led to state intervention originated with the volunteer who recognized the existence of a problem. Typically, he tackled it first through voluntary methods and resorted to the state only when these failed. For example, the humane factory employer began with voluntary collaboration as a way of getting working hours restrained. When the less scrupulous (often smaller) factory owner round the corner would not co-operate, he pressed for legislation. The temperance reformer, unable since the 1830s to persuade people voluntarily to give up drink, turned in the 1850s to the idea of prohibition—that is, to the idea of getting local ratepayers empowered to ban the sale of drink from their locality.[101] The educational reformer in Birmingham in the 1860s wanted to get working-class children into school, but when voluntary methods failed he formed the National Education League to promote education that was unsectarian as well as compulsory and free. Between the wars the volunteer even set out with the aim of invoking state aid, as the Family Planning Association's history shows. The volunteer skirmished on the welfare state's frontiers, continuously extending them. His efforts in the twentieth century have merely been redirected, not superseded, for 'the ascertainment of the actual need of the individuals cannot be done by government officials taking time off from the desk'.[102]

State aid was invoked as much to prop up individualist values as to undermine them. Where the self-disciplined and rational citizen did not already exist, and where the free market could not effectively operate, the

individualist legislator invoked the state to bring both into existence—
through legislation promoting sobriety, education, thrift, and respectable
values. Such legislation might at first aim to be temporary, but it readily
became permanent. In 1881, for example, the Liberal government recognized that intimidation by landlords rendered the market in Irish land
only theoretically free. So its Irish Land Act aimed to create a genuinely
free market by getting the government to mediate between landlord and
tenant and fix fair rents. Likewise the Conservative Charles Booth advocated labour colonies and public welfare because he wanted to remove class
B (incapacitated or shiftless casual labourers) from the labour market;
individualism could then be more vigorously applied among the rest. 'Our
Individualism fails', he wrote, 'because our Socialism is incomplete.'[103]
Old-age pensions aimed in 1908 to empty the workhouse of respectable
working people too old to work; individualist values could then be fostered
among the younger and more able-bodied occupants who remained. Hence
also the moralistic restrictions on eligibility for early state benefits. Old-
age pensions when first introduced were denied to any old person who had
accepted poor-law relief in 1908–9, who had been imprisoned within the
previous ten years, or had failed to work to maintain himself and family.
The labour exchanges set up in 1909 aimed to render the free market in
labour more efficient. National insurance legislation in 1911 was framed so
as to encourage personal thrift by protecting the interests of the friendly
societies and trade unions. But the exceptions to the free market's operation eventually became numerous enough to reveal the individualist as
unconscious parent of collectivism.

Even the welfare interventionism of the 1940s was only very weakly
socialist. The leading campaigner for family allowances was that decidedly
unsocialist politician Eleanor Rathbone. Governments adopted her reform
in 1945 because they saw in family allowances a cheap way to relieve the
worst of the poverty then prevailing; they would make it unnecessary to
concede universal benefits which might undermine the incentive to work.
Middle-class individualist assumptions have at every stage been built into
the growth of the welfare state, at whose heart its founders placed the
insurance principle. The Beveridge report wanted the recipient to receive
later in life only benefits towards which he had contributed earlier; it did
not envisage government subsidizing the unemployment insurance fund. 'I
am a man of the middle classes . . .', Beveridge told de Jouvenel soon after
the war; 'I am the adversary of the Socialism which is throttling them and,
in throttling them, is throttling all that is most vigorous and most progressive in Society.'[104] Beveridge never liked the phrase 'welfare state', and

disclaimed its paternity. In his later career he acted as critic of government welfare policy, and preferred the term 'social service state', which implied that citizens have duties as well as rights.[105]

Labour's welfare policy was in truth more Liberal, and twentieth-century Liberalism more socialist, than it was in either party's interest to reveal. The middle-class conscience, the nonconformist social gospel, and the pursuit of respectable values within the working class caused Liberals to break with *laissez-faire* ideas progressively from the 1860s onwards, most notably in Ireland, but later elsewhere. Liberal theorists of collectivism— T. H. Green, Arnold Toynbee, Seebohm Rowntree, W. H. Beveridge, L. T. Hobhouse, J. A. Hobson—were all important in the history of the British welfare state, and Labour's inter-war welfarism owed much to its bid for ex-Liberal votes. Yet a Labour Party that sought to oust the Liberals as leading party of the left in the 1920s had no interest in publicizing the welfare state's non-Labour pedigree, or in pointing out that the Liberals before 1914 had never envisaged becoming separated politically from organized labour. Still less could Labour stress how much the welfare impulse owed to a powerful Edwardian Liberal alliance between working-class spokesmen and middle-class intellectuals, an alliance which it could never quite replicate.

The Labour Party's Liberal origins and inter-war pursuit of Liberal voters help to explain why Labour turned out to be rather less socialist in practice than its rhetoric and constitution might lead one to expect. Socialists had always inherited much of the radical's suspicion of the state, which was still for them largely in enemy hands. Much early British socialism was primarily local in its ambitions. With the Fabians and others, it sought to promote socialism through municipal machinery, or it set up alternative socialist communities. These could either be Owenite communitarian in form, or they could involve the less formalized type of community that emerged from the labour movement's local connections: socialist society, WEA branch, co-op society, Women's Co-operative Guild, or Labour Party branch. A Labour Party which by the 1930s was well entrenched at the local-government level in places like South Wales or Jarrow was reluctant to entrust public works to national authorities that were less securely within its control. Herbert Morrison, for example, in 1929–30 opposed Mosley on road-building because he wanted local-government powers upheld. Philip Snowden never envisaged a massive state machine as the vehicle for socialism, which for him 'meant the public ownership of the means of production, not arbitrary interference in the working of the law of supply and demand'. The stimulus of competition in the old world would be replaced by 'the selfless and co-operative spirit which would appear in an eventual Socialist community . . . The idea that Socialism would entail massive State planning and direction of industry had not occurred to him or to anybody else'. Elie Halévy describes inter-war labour leaders as 'men whose doctrine requires them to make the state stronger, and whose good British instinct is to make the state as weak as possible'.[106] Pioneer socialists never envisaged the impersonal and centralized welfare state that eventually came about, funded by contributions, rather than by redistributing wealth from the rich. When, after the 1940s, inflation caused public welfare to draw upon subsidies from taxation, liability to income tax moved steadily lower in society, so redistribution moved still further off the agenda. And far from superseding capitalism, the effect of public welfare was to free investor and entrepreneur to concentrate even more exclusively on money-making. Both could now expect the taxpayer to shoulder the burden of nationalized non-profit-making concerns, as well as to keep the work-force healthy, educated, and (when unemployed) maintained.

All this helps to explain why public welfare advanced in Britain continuously, whichever political party was in power. The Beveridge report described its welfare proposals as 'in some ways a revolution, but in more important ways it is a natural development from the past. It is a British revolution.'[107] The years between 1900 and 1938, which saw no majority Labour governments, saw total social security expenditure rise from 0.2 per cent of the United Kingdom's gross national product to 5.1 per cent.[108] During the period of Conservative government from 1951 to 1964, welfare expenditure almost doubled in real terms.[109] Welfare issues did not normally provoke controversy between the nineteenth-century parties. Since the 1830s welfare reforms have been non-party in flavour, and owed much to non-party figures like Beveridge and Rathbone. A major inter-war influence was the non-political enthusiast for planning: the scientist, the doctor, the nutritionist, the economist, the expert generally. It was the non-party mood of coalition that helped to make war the midwife of public welfare. The twentieth-century parties have fought more over means than ends. Even the Conservative Party was subject to welfare pressures from its supporters. Its rural base made urban welfare reforms more congenial than they could ever be for Liberals. Conservative rural aristocratic paternalism readily responded to urban grievances, especially when impelled by the Party's Anglican, evangelical, and philanthropic connections. Throughout the nineteenth century the Party's pragmatic mood insulated it more effectively than the Liberals from the doctrinaires of political economy or charity organization. Once urban welfare reforms had been conceded, Conservatives could plausibly argue that rural people should not be left out. Furthermore, the Party's preoccupation with national defence made welfare more than a matter of mere political calculation. There was an element of conviction in its concern for the health of the urban populations who must furnish a conscripted army, and in its support for allotting pensions to war widows and old soldiers. Here was a peace-time analogue of the classless bond between the officer and his men which so influenced Conservative leaders in wartime.

So whereas in overseas matters Britain's two-party system made for a subversive discontinuity, in public welfare it generated a political dynamic that was strong and cumulative. Each party when in power tried to implement reforms that seemed inevitable, so as to give it control over their scope and direction, and thereby limit the damage to its own supporters that the other party might do when it won office in its turn. It was largely for defensive reasons, for instance, that late-Victorian Conservatives involved the state more deeply in elementary education. In 1876 Disraeli's government tried to prop up the voluntarily funded denominational schools by boosting attendance-based subsidies to them. This would weaken the incentive for Liberals to introduce publicly provided non-denominational board schools (a radical influence) in rural areas, thereby leaving Conservatism intact in its rural strongholds.[110] Again in 1891 a Conservative government introduced universal free schooling in the hope that this would prevent the Liberals from making it free only in the board schools, thereby hopelessly disadvantaging the church schools.[111]

In the late-Victorian and Edwardian competition for votes, a public auction of welfare benefits entailed (according to its critics) replacing the earlier private corruption of individuals by the public corruption of a class.[112] Moderate Liberals like Bagehot had long ago feared such an outcome. 'In plain English,' he wrote in 1872, 'what I fear is that both our political parties will bid for the support of the working man; that both of them will promise to do as he likes if he will only tell them what it is; that, as he now holds the casting vote in our affairs, both parties will beg and pray him to give that vote to them.'[113] During the 1880s Lord Randolph Churchill speeded up the whole process by pushing his Conservative colleagues towards radical reform. In 1894 Joseph Chamberlain's partisan zeal led him privately even to recommend an auction between the two houses of parliament on social questions, with Unionists taking the initiative in the House of Lords. Lord Salisbury dismissed the idea, pointing out that the second chamber's role was primarily to be 'a good drag chain',[114] but this did not deter Chamberlain from promoting the auction elsewhere. Privately pressing Sir Henry James in 1896 for a good measure that would compensate workers for accidents, Chamberlain told him that 'it would be fatal to us if our first social reform were clearly less favourable to the working-classes than Asquith's proposal'.[115] A similar motive inspired the Conservative Party's long-drawn-out twentieth-century protectionist assault on free trade, which Chamberlain launched in 1903. Only by finding new sources of revenue could the Conservatives hope to combine upholding property with promoting social reform. 'The Conservative Party has become definitely protectionist,' wrote Beatrice Webb in her diary in 1906; '. . . In so far as it commits the most *laisser-faire* party to the policy of state control and increase of taxation, we rejoice in it.'[116] Chamberlain had, 'in effect, done more for true Radicalism than ever he did in his own Radical days'.[117]

A benefit once conceded could rarely be withdrawn, even when the situation which originally inspired the concession had disappeared. Reinforcing this political ratchet effect was the establishment by the 1950s of rising expectations, not just of annual increases of real wealth, but of better standards of welfare. Far from the health service gradually draining a fixed pool of ill health, as Beveridge envisaged, the pool seemed merely to grow larger with every new facility. 1.4 per cent of gross national product was spent on public health facilities in 1938, 3.8 per cent by 1951, and 4.7 per cent by 1969. Equivalent figures for social service expenditure as a whole at these three dates were 10.7, 16.2, and 23.7.[118] Although at first sight it might seem sensible to channel benefits only to those who really needed them, benefits ineluctably became universal. Discrimination risked humiliating the beneficiary; parents or their children disliked being singled out for benefits denied to others, so the most deserving often failed to claim or receive benefits that were only selective. For example, free school meals needed to become universal, otherwise accepting them seemed a humiliation.[119] There was also the sheer administrative difficulty, intrusiveness, and political embarrassment involved in applying the hated 'means test', and in administering anything other than a universal benefit. While the original intention might be to charge school fees, for instance, they were in practice difficult to collect, and exemptions from fees still more difficult to organize. In her *Disinherited Family*, Rathbone did not even propose selectivity in family allowances because at the margin it would be difficult to decide who should pay and who should not.[120]

Universality of benefit even seemed in some sense democratic, all citizens being equally eligible for it. The welfare state has been as much the outcrop of political ideas (liberalism) as of economic ideas (socialism). Indeed, Sidney Webb defined socialism as 'the economic side of the democratic ideal'.[121] So public welfare makes its appearance in all developed societies, whether social-democratic in flavour or not. The Republic of Ireland's twentieth-century progress towards social security, for instance, was achieved without any strong pressure from a labour movement. The best predictor of the percentage of gross national product devoted to social security is not the political flavour of the society, but its level of affluence.[122] This affluence stems from the society's level of economic growth, which eventually brings birth control and longevity, and so raises the percentage of old people (the main claimants on welfare) in the population.

A bureaucratic dynamic complemented the political, for government officials can be both cause and consequence of welfare interventionism. In 1967/8 analysis of twenty-two countries that spent 5 per cent or more of their national income on social security revealed that the best predictor of the share of its income that a nation would spend on social security was how long the country had been operating a system of social security. In other words, social insurance systems 'mature'.[123] Volunteers first expose an evil, and having failed to tackle it by voluntary methods force governments to legislate. The legislation fails because founded on insufficient information about the evil in question. The information is then acquired through appointing inspectors to enforce the legislation. With the information and expertise they accumulate, government gets more closely to grips with the evil and legislates again, perhaps simultaneously appointing more inspectors. In this pragmatic way legislation grapples ever more closely with the problem in hand. The state thus becomes continuously involved in legislation and enforcement, instead of making a once-for-all intervention, and the government machine extends with 'amoeba-like self-reproduction'.[124] Factory legislation illustrates the process well. Karl Marx in 1864 saw it as 'the first time that in broad daylight the political economy of the middle class succumbed to the political economy of the working class'.[125] Yet in reality it illustrates still more vividly something in which Marx showed too little interest: the growth of a state machine that transcended class rivalry. Inspection began in factories in 1833 and extended thereafter in all directions. Factories were the workplaces most accessible to inspection, but inspection soon reached other types of premises, other occupations. There was extension also in the type of regulation applied—

moving on from factory hours to the fencing of machinery, and from there to questions of pollution and public health. All the time the inspectors grew in number, so that by the 1890s they were beginning to specialize by type of factory, and were beginning to include women among their number. By 1867 subinspectors were doing all the actual visiting—so that by 1888 instead of the four inspectors of 1833, there were a chief inspector, five superintending inspectors, thirty-nine district inspectors, and ten other inspectors.[126]

Central government was not alone in intervening. In the nineteenth century there was much less opposition to intervention at the local than at the national level—so even in the supposed age of *laissez-faire*, local municipal management was quite common. In *Fabian Essays* Sidney Webb noted that public gasworks were supplying nearly half the gas consumers in the country and that local authorities owned more than a quarter of tramway mileage.[127] The analogy with the amoeba applies here too, so that eventually 'the English administration was made by administrators throwing out their lines until they met and formed a system'.[128] Central government could use its subsidies to local government as a way of controlling local-government policy. The percentage of local-government expenditure in England and Wales met by central government rose from 25 per cent in 1890 to 31 per cent in 1910 to 47 per cent in 1930 to 51 per cent in 1949.[129] From 1856 the exchequer-grant was being used to influence the local administration of police, education, and other services, as was the compulsory publication of local death-rates.

Information (accumulated through inspectors' annual reports, public inquiries, research work by academics, and civil-service documentation) buttressed the state's advance at every stage. Pioneer socialists from Robert Owen to Ramsay MacDonald urged the collection of statistics on unemployment as 'the first essential to the treatment of the unemployed problem'.[130] But the impulse was as much practical as ideological. The factory inspectors increasingly involved the doctors in collecting statistics on the factory children, and even a free-lance investigator like Charles Booth could use Board of Trade statistics on wages for London trades in the 1880s, or get questions inserted into the census in 1891. Booth's battery of statistics could buttress his case for old-age pensions, and by the Edwardian period the publications of his disciple Seebohm Rowntree were being recommended among politicians and waved by Lloyd George in front of his audiences during political speeches. Rowntree's belief in orientating social research towards a legislative remedy made him useful to politicians and administrators, and enabled him to establish a close working relationship with both Beveridge and Lloyd George. Beveridge read Rowntree's books and corresponded with him while compiling his report on social insurance, telling him on 29 December 1941: 'I have been studying both *Poverty and Progress* and *The Human Needs of Labour* with extreme interest and I hope profit during Christmas.' Likewise, Eleanor Rathbone exploited twentieth-century sociological research when arguing for family allowances in her *Disinherited Family* and in parliament. Meanwhile Conservative policies of protection were paradoxically accumulating the data on trade and industry that socialist planners yearned for. And once the planners had superseded the price mechanism in so many areas, the market researcher and the official inquiry stepped in to supply guidance on what the public wanted. Under the interventionist and increasingly egalitarian governments after 1945, statistics poured out copiously from official periodicals: from *Economic Trends* (1953– ) to the *Abstract of Regional Statistics* (1965– ) to *Trends in Education* (1966– ) to *Social Trends* (1970– ). Not till Thatcher's counter-revolution of 1979 against both planning and egalitarian policy did this escalating process of government-sponsored inquiry cease.

But the demographic impulse to mounting welfare expenditure persisted after 1979. Demographic trends in developed societies extend the cost of welfare provision without any need for legislation, simply because more people become eligible for the benefits that have already been conceded in principle. Such trends were very much Beveridge's preoccupation in his report of 1942. Between 1871 and 1947 the percentage of old people in the population rose from 4.8 to 10.4; once a system of old-age pensions had been set up, its overall real cost inevitably escalated as the numbers eligible for them rose.[131] A further demographic impulse came from birth control, which changed patterns of women's work. Because there were fewer women available to meet family emergencies, the state had to assume many of the functions formerly undertaken by the family. The old people's home had a threefold origin: in a longer life-span, in extended birth control, and in the wife-at-work. By 1972 a social commentator could note that 'a higher proportion of the total population is now in institutions than in any of the years . . . since 1910'.[132] The demographic impulse to welfare also began to operate at the other end of life in the 1940s, when concern at the falling birth-rate boosted the idea of family allowances as an encouragement to larger families.

This chapter has shown how empire and public welfare combined with non-political changes, such as improvements in transport and communications, to give mid-twentieth-century Britain a governmental machine whose size and impact on political attitudes would have astonished Bagehot. It was a development that inevitably impinged on all other aspects of a political system that was unconstrained by any written constitution. Quite how this worked out in detail is the theme of Chapters 4 to 12. But first we must clarify what determined the geographical area within which these influences operated.

# 3

# *Fragmentation and Union*

THE USSR's sudden dissolution has reminded us all of the power of national loyalties, which were tenacious enough there to prevail over decades of class-preoccupied propaganda. They were operating in Ireland well before the 1860s, and since then their influence in Wales and Scotland has grown. Yet within the United Kingdom an undivided civil service and a single parliament have persisted. The only unitary states with larger populations in 1971 were China, Indonesia, Pakistan, and Japan[1]—by no means all of them models of democracy. So before we discuss changes since the 1860s in British political institutions, their area of operation should not be taken for granted. Besides, nationalism impinged on the United Kingdom in an unusual way. The country has been held together, not by propagating a composite United Kingdom nationality, but by a somewhat informal and untrumpeted acquiescence in national diversity. This has led some to describe it as a 'union' rather than 'unitary' state. Although the United Kingdom's inhabitants are all 'British', this fact does not normally excite them. The terms 'British' and 'Briton' seem inappropriately strident and have never caught on; and the term 'Britisher' is applied by Americans to describe a group that subjectively hardly exists. Although the Victorians often used the term 'England' and 'the English' to denote the area and inhabitants of the entire British Isles,[2] this usage has gradually and unobtrusively succumbed before what is in effect dual nationality. We now think of ourselves as 'English', 'Welsh', or 'Scottish'. So we find it difficult to comprehend Ulster Unionists' enthusiasm for the union; their concept of the United Kingdom seems curiously abstract. All the more paradoxical, then, that between 1920 and 1972 this most self-consciously unionist area within the United Kingdom should alone have experienced a devolved political structure.

Like many mid-Victorian Liberals, Bagehot was not uncritical of nationalism, welcoming it only if it generated the larger political units that seemed likely to bring peace and prosperity. He did not favour the nationalism that would break off 'alien fragments of old races' from the larger units they had joined,[3] and he thought the Anglo-Irish union mutually beneficial, so he would have regretted southern Ireland's secession. In winning its independence, southern Ireland did not prompt the sort of overarching federal constitutional settlement that success for a Gladstonian 'home rule' scheme would have entailed, and Northern Ireland's autonomy after 1922 stemmed from accident and convenience rather than from any strong local desire for autonomy. If, other things being equal, the large political unit is seen as culturally, economically, and socially beneficial, southern Ireland's departure represents a major failure of the British political system. And because the politician is bound by profession to seek peaceful ways of settling disputes, Northern Ireland's history since the late 1960s represents major failure too. Yet it is also important sometimes to ask why things did not happen. Nationalist feeling was by no means absent from nineteenth-century Wales and Scotland; indeed, by the 1880s the phrase 'North Britain' was sufficiently unacceptable for Campbell-Bannerman to remove it from his letter-heading.[4] Twentieth-century British politicians have undoubtedly been worried that where southern Ireland led, Wales and Scotland might follow. In her dealings with Northern Ireland in the 1980s, for example, Thatcher was wary of setting devolutionary precedents for Scotland and Wales.[5] So why was southern Ireland alone in the path it took?

Part of the answer lies in reversing the question, and asking why nationalist feeling in Wales and Scotland was so weak. This is too large a question for a book on political institutions to answer. Suffice it to say that whereas Ireland, Wales, and Scotland were all geographically divided between areas sympathetic to the English connection (South Wales, Lothian, and Ulster) and areas less sympathetic (North Wales, the Highlands, and Southern Ireland), only in southern Ireland after the Reformation did a religious contrast accentuate those divisions. Only in southern Ireland did Roman Catholicism remain the religion of the mass of the people. The gulf was accentuated when threats from France and Spain made anti-Catholicism seem patriotic elsewhere in the United Kingdom. On the mainland, the union was cemented by a vigorously popular and patriotic Protestant culture, reinforced by Wesley in the eighteenth century. When, also in the eighteenth century, industrialization increasingly pervaded the Anglicized parts of Wales, Ireland, and Scotland, Protestantism seemed identified with progress and prosperity, whereas southern

Ireland could be labelled superstitious, disloyal, and backward. Southern Ireland seemed alien to many Victorians. 'If we are to be guided by experience in legislating for Ireland', J. S. Mill emphasized, 'it is Continental rather than English experience that we ought to consider.'[6] When the southern Irish, distant from established British forms of pressure, pioneered the guerrilla form of resistance that has since become more common, their intimidation, rick-burning, and maiming of cattle confirmed the stereotype, and received help from fashionable racial theories. The battle for British control in southern Ireland took on the guise of a battle for civilization, with all its accoutrements of spies, special policing arrangements, and suspensions of ordinary law. 'The state of society in Ireland . . .', Wellington told Peel in 1846, 'is in fact worse than it is in any of the wildest parts of Asia, Africa, or America.'[7] Lord Salisbury in 1886 even drew an analogy between the Irish and the Hottentots.[8] Irishmen who settled in England did not always improve the image. 'One may depend upon seeing mainly Celtic faces', wrote Engels, 'if ever one penetrates into a district which is particularly noted for its filth and decay.'[9]

In earlier centuries, the sea could unite peoples more than it divided them, but all this changed in Britain with the advent of an efficient road system during the eighteenth century and a railway system during the nineteenth. Both drew together the lines of cultural influence between England, Wales, and Scotland much more tightly than between England and Ireland. Wales and Scotland might have their rich and absentee English landlords, but socially and geographically they seemed far less distant from their tenants than those of southern Ireland. Improved communications increased the attraction of the journey to London for Welshmen and Scotsmen in pursuit of the great career. Given that respect for education was integral to the Welsh and Scottish identities,[10] these two nations generated much talent for export to England—talent which, particularly in Scotland, the English public-school and university system was well able to harness through establishing an Anglo-Scottish educational network. Scotland contributed four of Britain's eighteen prime ministers between 1815 and 1914. Lloyd George, T. B. Macaulay, James Mill, Thomas Carlyle, Ramsay MacDonald, Aneurin Bevan, and John Smith were all non-English talents given wider scope by the move to England. Irishmen too were of course attracted to the mainland, but mainly to low-status jobs, many of them temporary, and southern Irishmen who stayed at home lacked the expanding industrial areas which elsewhere absorbed a growing population. From this imbalance arose the great famine of 1845–6, with its lasting legacy of Anglo-Irish bitterness. Many of the survivors emigrated to the United States, where memories and resentments were stored up, with lasting damage to Anglo-American relations.

From a mixture of convenience and tradition, Welsh and Scottish nationalist feeling took a more cultural than political shape. To the Welsh identity, language and education were integral, and the Eisteddfod became a major national festival. The nonconformist repudiation of Anglican landlords focused nineteenth-century Welsh national feeling on promoting causes like temperance and disestablishment. In Scotland, by contrast, the established church could not be represented as foreign, and nonconformity was less integral to nationality. To the Scottish identity the Scottish legal system and the Kirk were central, and the Edinburgh Festival is no Scottish Eisteddfod. The union with Scotland was seen by its creators as a partnership of equals, and was reinforced when both nations collaborated in nineteenth-century industry and empire. Scottish highlanders, missionaries, sailors, and traders were if anything more closely identified than the English with empire. Rapid economic growth in the more Anglicized parts of Scotland and Wales ensured that by 1914 they were manifestly part of the United Kingdom's industrial success story. Shortly before the First World War the growth of heavy industry brought Scotland to the peak of her economic performance relative to the other British regions, with a gross national product per head almost equalling that of the United Kingdom as a whole,[11] and late-Victorian Cardiff was the largest coal-exporting port in the world. All three peoples were also drawn together by the experience of shared danger in the Napoleonic wars and in the twentieth century (together with Northern Ireland) in two world wars. As long as the United Kingdom seemed a successful collaborative venture, as it did until the 1960s, there seemed no Welsh or Scottish reason for fragmenting it. So in place of the literature of nationalism which developed elsewhere in Europe, but which would have been divisive in Britain, there arose the unifying literature of empire.[12] All too few of these integrating factors influenced southern Ireland, whose spokesmen frequently aligned themselves with the critics of empire, and many of whose leaders exploited Great Britain's vulnerability in both world wars. The critics of empire were prominent of course also in Wales, but there were so many economic, geographical, and religious countervailing influences tying Wales to England that such points of political disagreement had far less impact. Besides, as we have already seen, the premiership of the best known of all Welsh politicians coincided with the apogee of British imperial integration from 1918 to 1922.

*

To emphasize the cultural and economic contrasts between southern Ireland and the other non-English constituents of the British Isles is to scale down the importance of political and institutional hindrances to Anglo-Irish union. None the less, these were important, and of the three that deserve extended discussion—monarchy, party, and parliament—the first was the most visible instrument for holding the United Kingdom together. The British monarchy's peculiar constitutional position reflects the absence of any 'British' nationalism. The United Kingdom is united only through intermediate loyalties: to Protestant culture among the majority in Northern Ireland, and predominantly to Welshness, Scottishness, and Englishness elsewhere. Accordingly, the British royal family has a distinct relationship with each of the United Kingdom's constituent nations. It does not blur their distinctness with a shared appeal, but rests its authority on a fragmented attraction. Not so, though, in southern Ireland. Repudiation of its predominant religion lay at the very foundations of the British throne, whose nineteenth-century occupants made matters worse. 'The more one does for the Irish the more unruly and ungrateful they seem to be,' Queen Victoria told Earl Cowper in 1880.[13] She discouraged visits and residence there by members of the royal family in 1872, 1885, 1893, and 1897; she staunchly backed responding to nationalism by force; and she forsook political neutrality in promoting the coalition that defeated Gladstone's proposals for home rule. She seems never to have perceived that he was sacrificing much to achieve what she herself desired—the preservation of the union—by the one method then likely to succeed. Her failure to build on incipient Irish loyalty was, says G. M. Young, 'the gravest error of her life'.[14] Bagehot thought that the viceroyalty, 'as costly as it is useless',[15] did nothing to improve matters. A mere party appointment reminded the Irish of their distinctness, without epitomizing tradition or inspiring reverence.

George V had none of his grandmother's anti-Irish prejudice, and his visit to Ireland in 1900 was his own idea, but the Anglo-Irish gulf was by then too wide for any individual monarch to make much impact. George V was active in seeking a peaceful settlement in Ireland during 1914, and in June 1921 against the advice of many in his entourage visited Belfast to make an important conciliatory speech to the parliament of Northern Ireland. Since the King was, according to a private letter written by his prime minister the year before, 'frightened to death'[16] at the possibility of being assassinated by Irish nationalists, this was creditable. Likewise with his intervention in the private negotiations with de Valera in August and September 1921, which seems to have helped render the Anglo-Irish treaty feasible.[17] Thereafter monarchs could do little personally to improve

Anglo-Irish relations, given that the monarchy's status was itself in dispute between the two countries. As a somewhat melancholy testimony to monarchy's well-intentioned but ineffectual role, the exchange between George VI and the Irish minister John Dulanty in October 1948 at a party in Buckingham Palace deserves mention. The King had hoped one day to visit Dublin, and was distressed that Eire intended to sever its last links with the British monarchy. 'Was it any personal fault in himself?' he asked. No, Dulanty replied: 'even the archangel Gabriel' could not have prevented it.[18]

Since then, Irish politicians have more than once tentatively suggested that their country might find it politic to rejoin the Commonwealth.[19] Others have even proposed some form of confederal Anglo-Irish union,[20] yet the tragedy of Anglo-Irish fragmentation remains. As for Northern Ireland, the monarchy is divisive there. During the Queen's visit in 1977, the contrast between the well-decorated Protestant districts and the noticeably bare Catholic ones was striking.[21] 'Your Royal Family helps keep all this going', a foreign employer noted in 1986, explaining the recurrence of symbolic episodes in the work-force. 'They have a wedding. Then a baby. Then another wedding. The Protestants put up some banners and we take them down.'[22] Even the occasional state visits to Northern Ireland made by George V and George VI risked embarrassing Anglo-Irish relations.[23] Terrorism, and the need to enlist the Republic's support in curbing terrorism, have doubly threatened such visits since the 1960s. Terrorists in search of symbolic targets deter monarchy from exploiting its most powerful asset: ceremonial and symbolism. Bagehot's 'magic' can scarcely survive threats to the monarch's life and dignity. So royal visits to Northern Ireland in the 1970s and 1980s were few, furtive, and heavily guarded,[24] and to that extent hardly helpful.

Monarchs had more success in helping to integrate Scotland and Wales within the United Kingdom. The strength of the Anglo-Scottish connection was symbolized by George IV's state visit to Scotland in 1822, and Queen Victoria's acquisition of Balmoral in 1855 was preceded by state visits in 1842 and 1844. A Queen who spent a total of only five weeks in Ireland spent seven years in Scotland.[25] There has been a strong affinity between Scotland and the British monarchy ever since. For the Queen in 1869 the Scots were a 'high-spirited, intelligent and determined people, whose loyalty to herself, is exceeded by *none*—if it is *equalled* by *any* of her subjects'. She urged her Home Secretary not to tinker with their educational arrangements, for there was enough trouble with one kingdom without experimenting 'with the most loyal and most intelligent other

Kingdom'.[26] In 1977 Scottish nationalists made it quite clear that independence for Scotland would not entail a Scottish republic.[27] As for Wales, the Tudor monarchy was an important integrating factor in itself, and many Welshmen followed their King to London to pursue their careers there. When a fellow MP Sam Evans refused to rise to the toast of the Queen at a Mansion House banquet in 1892, Lloyd George (then still in his nationalist phase) strongly disapproved.[28] Twentieth-century governments have assiduously fostered links between the monarchy and Wales, most notably in the ceremonial of 1911 and 1969 involving the Prince of Wales.

*

The party system was a far more powerful integrating influence than monarchy, if only because political parties survive only by cultivating constituency opinion. In 1934 British parliamentary government was thought to require the interaction of four factors: 'the principle of majority rule; the willingness of the minority for the time being to accept the decisions of the majority; the existence of great political parties divided by broad issues of policy, rather than by sectional interests; and . . . the existence of a mobile body of political opinion, owing no permanent allegiance to any party and therefore able, by its instinctive reaction against extravagant movements on one side or the other, to keep the vessel on an even keel'.[29] These conditions have prevailed continuously in Wales and, at least until recently, in Scotland too. Up to 1914 they also prevailed somewhat precariously in Ireland, largely because of the Liberal Party's peculiar philosophy, structure, and leadership. Liberals did for nationality what their Labour successors did for social class: they simultaneously catered for and tamed a new self-consciousness. Party self-interest and political conviction kept them alert to the separate interests of the nations within the United Kingdom. Unlike Labour in the 1970s, nineteenth-century Liberals espoused devolution from conviction, not from expediency. Theirs was the party of liberty. It recognized the corrupting influence of power; it emphasized the educational importance of political structures; and it included national self-determination among its major overseas achievements and aims. Stretching out from its secure mid-Victorian base, late-Victorian Liberalism could spread its limbs into the countryside to mobilize agricultural labourer, rural craftsman and village nonconformist and Catholic against the tyranny of squire and parson. Right up to the First World War, devolution and local self-government was a growing cause.

Either through direct evangelism or through alliance with indigenous opinion groups, the Liberals tightened their hold on what was called the 'Celtic fringe'. John Bright, attacking the landlords and the established church in Ireland, was a pioneer here, stoutly and cleverly reinforced from 1868 by Gladstone. People saw Gladstone's sudden declaration for home rule in 1885 as inconsistent, even opportunist, yet this was only his latest move in a long-term strategy that aimed consistently to keep Ireland within the union. It was a strategy born in conviction and nourished by a sensitivity to European opinion that was unusual in an English politician. From 1868 to 1885 he set about tackling Ireland's practical grievances: educational, religious, political, and economic. He also favoured devolving wide powers to local authorities in Ireland. As he told Granville in 1879, 'it has always been my opinion that the question of *Local* Government opened a road for giving a considerable amount of satisfaction to persons in any way amenable to reason'.[30] His weapon against Irish nationalism was the same as the Fabian weapon against class consciousness: inveigling potential malcontents into the intricacies of local self-government. Gladstone of course aimed to remove genuine grievances, but his Irish strategy was many-layered. If the union was to be preserved, pressures for reform must above all things be pre-empted. Irishmen must be found who could take responsibility for managing Irish matters, and extremists must be denied credibility—though without risking government's dignity through confronting them directly.

As the third party in Ireland, the Liberals during the 1880s were squeezed out by the Conservatives and Home Rulers, more than sixty of whom were returned for Irish seats at the general election of 1880. The Liberal position could be recouped either by eroding their number or by annexing them. Gladstone first tried erosion, and told the Queen in February 1882 of his success in breaking up the group who might unite behind home rule; a year later he thought he had 'broken down to 35 or 40 what would have been a party . . . of 65 Home Rulers'.[31] The more ardent Home Rulers at Westminster must be given no excuse for removing themselves to Ireland, where they would be much harder to control. 'If there are wild ideas abroad', said Gladstone in 1871, 'depend upon it the place where they can most safely be promulgated is within the walls of the House of Commons.' As he told Grosvenor in January 1886, 'I should regard the withdrawal *en bloc* as by far the most formidable thing that can happen.'[32]

Like his predecessors, Gladstone wanted links cultivated with people in Ireland who could eventually themselves take partial responsibility for painful governmental decisions, and he prepared the ground for this by practical reforms. He hoped that these would free mainland governments from repeatedly having to suspend the usual operation of the law in Ireland. 'Legislation which introduces exceptional provisions into the law . . .', he said in 1886, 'has become for us not exceptional, but habitual.'[33] Such legislation was particularly embarrassing for Liberal governments; the Irish leaders must themselves be enlisted in the cause of order. After 1880 he began at the top with Parnell, eventually deciding that if tactfully handled he was better placed to curb Irish extremism than any mainland government. Already by May 1882 Gladstone was trying to educate the Queen (a slow learner) into this view.[34] This helped to ensure that the Irish MPs cautiously backed away from the revolutionary option of seceding from parliament[35] and unobtrusively scaled down their demands from independence to self-government through a provincial parliament under Westminster's ultimate authority.

Gladstone's strategy had to be negotiated not only past Queen and Liberal Party, but also through the two-party system. The Conservatives, who formed a government with Parnell's backing in June 1885, breached the two-party line by abandoning the Liberal government's coercive strategy in Ireland. Gladstone now had good reason to hope for a non-party Irish solution, rather as Peel and Wellington had settled Roman Catholic emancipation in 1829. After the general election of 1885, eighty-five nationalists represented Catholic Ireland. This strengthening of Parnell's position, reinforced by world opinion, demanded a settlement. 'Now there is an Irish nation in the United States . . .', said Harcourt in December, 'hostile with plenty of money, absolutely beyond our reach, and yet within ten days' sail of our shores.'[36] It was time for Gladstone to switch from his eroding to his annexing tactic, and draw the home rulers into formal alliance with the Liberals. Herbert Gladstone's revelation that his father now favoured home rule caused Parnell to switch his support to the Liberals, who now took power with a commitment to prepare a home rule proposal.

Public opinion, too, had to be won over. Yet here, as so often later, Irish nationalist tactics greatly complicated matters. The early 1880s saw many Fenian bombs exploding or failing to explode, mostly in London; two, on the London underground on 30 October 1883, injured seventy-two people. Such escapades did not win friends on the mainland, and the bombing campaign was prudently allowed to peter out after 1885 for fear that it would hinder home rule's parliamentary campaign.[37] The assassination in Dublin of Lord Frederick Cavendish and Thomas Burke with long surgical knives in May 1882 made a particularly powerful enemy: Lord

Frederick's brother, Lord Hartington, was a key figure in launching Liberal Unionism in 1886. The home rule MPs had already alienated English radicals, most notably John Bright and Joseph Chamberlain, when they obstructed House of Commons proceedings, played one party off against another, and failed to repudiate energetically nationalist violence and intimidation. 'The Irish members have acted as if their object were to disgust, embitter and prejudice all English opinion' against their cause, Chamberlain told Gladstone in 1882.[38] Far more was involved here than the wounded pride of radical leaders. British political institutions and methods in those days carried some prestige with public opinion. Furthermore, the Irish seemed to be putting at risk the humanitarian achievement, which had prevailed only recently over slavery, cruelty to animals, the duel, and public hanging, and was much prized by radicals and non-conformists. 'I believe the anti-Irish feeling is very strong with our best friends—the respectable artisans and the non-Conformists,' wrote Chamberlain in January 1886.[39]

Home rule in 1885–6 was one of those controversies which send party politics in an entirely unexpected direction. In the long term it brought the Conservatives a major accession of electoral and parliamentary strength which remained almost intact for twenty years, and which benefits them still. As soon as Gladstone went for home rule, Lord Randolph Churchill realized that 'the Orange card would be the one to play', and in a speech in Belfast declared 'Ulster will fight, and Ulster will be right.' The violence should, he said, be kept in reserve: 'we are essentially a party of law and order', and premature violence would risk alienating 'forces whose assistance would be beyond all price'.[40] At no stage between 1885 and 1920 did the Ulstermen resort to violence of the 'stunt' variety. They knew they must conciliate mainland opinion, but also that their variant of violence was of such potential that it did not need to be deployed. It was a potential for the sort of violence that toppled regime after regime in Eastern Europe in the late 1980s: a dignified violence that bided its time but rested upon support so widespread that governments dared not confront it. Liberal Unionism was strong in Scotland; 7 per cent of the Scottish population in 1861 had been born in Ireland, 6 per cent in 1881. Reacting against this, Scottish anti-Catholic sympathy with the Ulster presbyterians grew.[41] Churchill wanted to exploit the situation by calling the Conservatives 'Unionists'. Yet the Ulstermen were almost as remote from the British governmental mind as any nationalist. Gladstone seems to have paid little attention to Ulster in drafting his first Home Rule Bill, and it is not clear that Ulster would then have strongly opposed its introduction.[42] In discussions with Ulster's leaders in May 1916, Asquith found their hatred for the Catholics in the south 'very curious', and reflected that 'you never get to the bottom of this most perplexing and damnable country'. Perhaps more surprising is the fact that, except in the case of Bonar Law, Conservative leaders gave the Ulstermen little instinctive sympathy either.[43] The Conservative alliance with the Ulster Unionists has never been a love-match.

Gladstone now mounted a remarkable crusade to boost support for home rule throughout the British Isles, and after 1886 could rely on the Irish MPs' firm backing. All this sharpened the tone of political debate and tightened discipline among both government and opposition MPs. Henceforth frontbenchers and backbenchers on each side drew together, and frontbenchers on the two sides became less prone to conspire.[44] The focus here is on the role of political parties in integrating the United Kingdom, so there is no need to discuss the details of how the first and second home rule bills of 1886 and 1893 were framed and defeated. They may well have been impracticable in important details,[45] and likely to inflame Anglo-Irish relations by setting up conflicts between rival legislatures. This problem had led Bagehot in 1871 to argue that 'the Home Rule party would . . . be far more logical, if they were to raise a cry at once for an independent Irish Republic'.[46] Yet Gladstone was not dissatisfied: 'I am much more disposed to be thankful for what we then and afterwards accomplished', he recalled ten years later, 'than to murmur or to wonder at what we did not.'[47] His satisfaction stemmed less from the legislative detail than from his transformation of the party-political scene. His long-term concern was no doubt to do justice in Ireland and thereby to improve Britain's reputation overseas, but it was his immediate aim that triumphed. He had domesticated the Irish nationalist MPs, whose illiberal attitudes on many questions did not prevent them from remaining loyal to the Liberal Party for a generation. Perhaps their domestication at Westminster was too successful, for in 1914 when the Liberal government enacted home rule and then suspended its implementation for the duration of the war, the nationalists at Westminster were bereft of a programme, and soon lost their hold on opinion within Ireland itself.

If the two-party system tied Catholic Ireland to one party until 1916, it also tied the Ulstermen somewhat precariously to the other for much longer. Bagehot had dismissed the nationalist case for home rule with vigour in 1867. Pointing out that 'Ireland contains *two* peoples—one Irish . . . and another . . . substantially Scotch,' he claimed that 'not only is there no unity between these races, but there is no possibility of any' since they 'differ radically in race, creed, and civilisation'.[48] After 1886 Bagehot's two Irish nations aligned themselves behind the two rival British parties, so that henceforth it would be difficult to reach any Irish settlement without dividing the island. Complete victories can be won, at least in the short term, only in single-party systems; competitive party systems compel compromise. At first the Conservatives hoped to prevent home rule in any form, and 'the Ulster card' was worth playing more as a means than as an end. Unionists could conveniently embarrass Liberals by claiming that their arguments for self-determination could not stop short at the Irish Catholic minority within the British Isles; they must advance to protect the Protestant minority within Ireland. With the continuing growth of nationalist feeling in the south, however, and with the Liberal revival after the Boer War, Conservative hopes gradually and unobtrusively dwindled into defending Northern Ireland against rule from Dublin. Once the war had inflamed the situation, Unionists in southern Ireland could no longer be protected. 'Without a generation of resolute government', wrote Samuel Hoare in 1918, 'the Union is impossible and I am convinced that in the quick changes of English politics there is never going to be any resolute government of Ireland for any considerable time.'[49] Once dominion status for southern Ireland had been conceded, the remaining Irish MPs at Westminster overwhelmingly reinforced the right, whereas on balance they had earlier reinforced the left. And so, by a strange irony, Unionist Northern Ireland from 1920 to 1972 witnessed the British government's one attempt to act upon the Liberal belief in devolution. Its House of Commons of fifty-two members, who elected twenty-four of the Senate's twenty-six members, could legislate on all matters except those excluded by the Act of 1920, and produced a government to run the Province's eight departments.

These dramatic events inevitably had implications for nationalism in Wales and Scotland, for Gladstone had pointed out as early as 1871 that if home rule were conceded to Ireland, Scotland 'will be just as well entitled to it', and Wales likewise.[50] The early socialists sometimes saw the Liberal responsiveness to nationalist pressure as an invented diversion from socialist remedies for social problems.[51] Yet nationalism grew spontaneously, and impinged on the mid-Victorian Liberal Party from without. Cultural and educational in its origins, Welsh national feeling crystallized into organizing the first single national Eisteddfod eleven years before the first leading Liberal politician sought to stir the Welsh out of their political quietism: John Bright, with his address at Liverpool in June 1868. Thereafter consciousness grew quickly, fuelled by landlords' evictions of tenants for voting unsatisfactorily at the general election of 1868. Yet for the next few decades the Welsh national movement's Liberal allegiance was always somewhat precarious. Given the Liberal leaders' governmental priorities, the cultural issues which meant so much to Welshmen—temperance, disestablishment, and education—produced much friction within the Party.

None the less, Gladstone was adept at the flattering symbolic gesture that stirred emotions yet committed him to nothing legislatively precise. His speech at the Mold Eisteddfod of 1873, his declaration at Swansea in June 1887 that Wales was a nation, his address on a hillside in Snowdonia in 1892 to a meeting of hymn-singing miners—all three were important moments in the growth of Welsh consciousness. And by doing more than most to broaden the rural franchise in 1884, he more than trebled the Welsh county electorate and so prepared the ground that his home rule crusade was soon to cultivate. In 1868 he had described how in forcing disestablishment of the Church of Ireland to the forefront 'our three *corps d'armée* . . . have been Scotch presbyterians, English and Welsh nonconformists and Irish Roman Catholics',[52] and in 1883 he claimed that 'the back-bone of the Liberal party lies in the Nonconformists of England and Wales, and the Presbyterians of Scotland'.[53] In his pamphlet *The Irish Question* (1886), he claimed that the general election of 1886 had given 'a new place to nationality as an element of our political thought'. Scotland and Wales had assisted Ireland on home rule, and Ireland might now help them promote their special interests. He even floated vague ideas of subordinate parliaments for Wales and Scotland. 'The desire for Federation' had found 'an unexpected ally in the Irish policy of 1886' and might well go further.[54]

Given the low social status of Irish immigrants on the mainland and the prevalence of anti-Catholic feeling, Irish home rule was not necessarily a vote-winner. Nor was an alliance between the non-English nations easy to sustain. Nationalisms are almost by definition incapable of constituting a unifying principle. Besides, the demand for self-government was far weaker in England, Scotland, and Wales than in Ireland. Still, Gladstone's home rule crusade did strike some chords. The Welsh MPs being returned at by-elections in the late 1880s were all young, Welsh-born, nonconformist, and in some sense nationalist, and they included Lloyd George. Stuart Rendel was elected chairman of a new 'Welsh parliamentary party' in December 1888, with its own whips and joint balloting for private members' bills.[55] In 1889 the local-government elections ended landlord domination in that sphere, and one might then have expected Welsh nationalism to take an Irish direction. Yet devolution had never been uppermost among Welsh political aspirations, and any notion of Welsh nationalism eventually foundered on the jealousies among Welsh MPs and on the cultural contrasts between north and south. The main lines of communication in Wales lay from west to east, and ambitious Welshmen continued to make their fortunes in London. Lloyd George's horizons had never been confined to Wales, and Welsh concerns faded among his priorities once he became President of the Board of Trade in 1905.

Scottish nationalism was an even frailer plant. We have seen how Liberal Unionism was the answer offered by much of Scotland to home rule after 1886, and during the 1890s Glasgow (where Orange influences were strong) became the capital of Scottish Conservatism. Scottish national feeling, like Welsh, tended to take the form of pushing for more influence within the Liberal Party rather than of breaking free from British party politics altogether.[56] This in itself ensured Conservative hostility. A Scottish Home Rule Association was founded in Edinburgh in 1886, and home rule measures for Scotland were brought before the House of Commons on thirteen occasions before 1914. They won the support of a majority of Scottish MPs on eleven, and were accepted in principle by the House on eight, but no bill reached the committee stage.[57] As for England, its sense of nationhood could not be prised apart from the idea of the United Kingdom as a viable political entity, or from the sense of shared imperial achievement. Nor was it any more possible then than now to generate the sort of regional loyalties within England that would make it possible to build up a United Kingdom federation from regions rather than from nations.

Apparently more promising was the idea of 'home rule all round', for which there were practical as well as nationalist arguments. Ireland's special resentments could perhaps be eased more readily if catered for within a general devolutionary measure whose impulse was more than merely Irish. When Sir James Graham suggested a federal solution to the Irish problem in 1844, Peel objected that 'if Ireland must have Federalism so must Scotland. Why not Wales? Why not Wessex?—and the kingdoms of the Heptarchy?' For Lord John Russell in 1872 Peel's rejoinder had not foreclosed reform along these lines, if only because general devolution might relieve the pressure of business on parliament. He recommended setting up subordinate assemblies for the four Irish provinces and two in Scotland (one for the Lowlands, one for the Highlands).[58] In a speech of 1880 Gladstone expressed concern at the fact that 'we have got an over-weighted Parliament', and five years later noted that Norway, Finland, and

Austria all provided precedents for successful devolution.[59] By the Edwardian period the 'parliamentary overload' argument for 'home rule all round', moving forward from devolution towards federation, had become widely current, and attracted statesmen as prominent as Winston Churchill, Dilke, and Loreburn.[60] Federal institutions had, after all, successfully held together large units of population within the empire; could they not also hold together potentially fragmenting groups within the United Kingdom? The idea had wide appeal, but its supporters never united behind a viable scheme, and 'home rule all round' never became really popular either with leading politicians or with the general public. If the federation consisted of only four units, England would overbalance the rest. Yet if England were subdivided, its subdivisions were not obvious or popular. It was partly because he wanted to delimit viable regions of England as a basis for federalism that C. B. Fawcett set out to define the provinces of England in his famous book of 1919.[61] 'Home rule all round' also faced powerful enemies: most notably, Irishmen and Liberals afraid that it constituted a new hindrance to Ireland's special measure.[62]

One might have expected the devolutionary idea, embodied in Northern Ireland's own parliament after 1920, to boost the cause of 'home rule all round' between the wars. Not so, for at least two reasons. When southern Ireland won dominion status in 1922, the major impetus to devolution elsewhere in Britain was removed. And once electoral alignments on the Irish issue had vanished, together with the religious issues which in a secularizing society were waning, class politics could take their place. Prominent Irishmen on the mainland after 1922, notably the Clydesiders and Catholic trade unionists, were free either to retreat into the sectarian home-rule socialism of the Independent Labour or Communist parties (particularly active in Scotland) or into a Labour Party that forsook localism for central planning. With Lloyd George unwilling in the 1920s to take up devolution as a Liberal cause, with Liberals dwindling as a major national force, and with Conservatives lacking any taste for fragmentation or any incentive to take the matter up, devolutionary pressure diminished still further. All this meant that from the 1920s to the 1960s on the mainland, in contrast to Ireland before 1922, the British party system cut across national loyalties instead of reinforcing them. The depression enabled inter-war Marxism and socialism to mount a class-based crusade against injustice beside which Scottish and Welsh nationalism seemed a petty and backward-looking irrelevance—or, worse, a form of 'false consciousness'. The socialist ideal of equality, as relevant between regions as between social classes, required central direction of the economy. The idea of a

'Welsh day' of parliamentary debate in 1944 was, for Aneurin Bevan, a 'farce'. The Miners' Federation, he pointed out, 'have no special Welsh solution for the Welsh coal industry which is not a solution for the whole of the mining industry of Great Britain. There is no Welsh problem.'[63] So the inter-war Labour Party forgot that Keir Hardie had been a keen Scottish home ruler and that his Party's reconstruction programme of 1918 had favoured 'separate statutory legislative assemblies for England, Scotland, and Wales'.[64] Nor did Labour's triumph over the Liberals cause the Conservative Party, which had relabelled itself 'Unionist' in reaction to home rule, immediately to lose its unionist label, still less its unionist instincts. After 1918 the idea of a 'United Kingdom', defended against the fragmenting Liberal and Labour priorities of class and sectionalism, remained as powerful a Conservative asset as ever. Devolution, denied its Liberal foundation, retreated to the margins of British politics.

Party-political developments helped to perpetuate this for a generation and more. The formation of the national government in 1931, by splitting the Liberals three ways, helped to restore the two-party system, and between 1931 and 1945 the Labour Party gradually recovered lost ground. The years between 1945 and 1959 saw the two-party system in full operation. Given victory in war and the apparent successes of wartime consensus in British domestic policy, there was little demand for any new party structure. By 1959, however, the share of the total vote won at general elections by Conservatives and Labour combined (90 per cent in 1950) had begun to fall. The Liberal revival ensured that by February 1974 it had reached its lowest point up till that time (75 per cent),[65] though the simple-majority electoral system ensured that this shift was not mirrored in the percentage of seats won. A Liberal revival meant the resurgence of devolution, but the nationalist movements in Wales and Scotland (less disadvantaged by the simple-majority system) had less reason than the Liberals to espouse electoral reform. Besides, Plaid Cymru's aims were still predominantly cultural. It had been founded during Eisteddfod week in 1925 at a meeting of intellectuals, ministers, and others mostly from North Wales. It was at first more a pressure group for the Welsh language than a full-blown political party,[66] and did not at first make much electoral impact. Three years later, Scottish nationalist groups united to form the National Party of Scotland, which after another merger in 1934 became the Scottish National Party. Before they could make inroads on support for the other two parties, Scottish and Welsh nationalists needed to transcend their eccentric and sometimes racist or pacifist connections. By the 1960s, like the Liberals in England, they were able to capitalize on disappointment with the failures of Conservative and Labour governments. With nationalist by-election victories at Carmarthen in 1966 and at Hamilton in 1967 nationalism had at last gained a voice at Westminster.

The climate there was not congenial. The Conservative Party's unionist instincts remained strong, and many interests now clustered around Labour's zest for centralized planning, with its commitment to redistributing wealth between the regions. In 1964 Northern Ireland, Wales, and Scotland were major beneficiaries when the regional balance was struck between taxes and government subsidy.[67] As late as 1966 the Labour Party's election manifesto saw Britain's economic well-being 'as indivisible', with Scotland and Wales benefiting through the so-called National Plan.[68] By the late 1960s Scotland surpassed all European countries, including Russia, in the proportion of its housing being built in the public sector.[69] As Chancellor of the Exchequer, Jenkins challenged the economic case for an independent Scotland in 1969 by having a Scottish budget prepared in Whitehall. It showed the substantial sums Scotland would have to raise from its own resources if denied English subsidies.[70] The SNP leaders were practical and rational in outlook, and in its composition their Party was by now more representative of the Scottish population than either Labour or the Conservatives. Its vote in Scotland rose from 12 per cent in 1970 to 30 per cent in October 1974, at which election Scotland took a direction entirely different from the rest of Britain. The oil discoveries off the Scottish coast did much to dispel doubts about whether an independent Scottish economy would be viable. Plaid Cymru's instincts were more romantic and it advanced more slowly than its Scottish counterpart, but both parties in the 1970s were trenching deep into Labour territory. At the municipal elections of May 1976, Plaid Cymru ended fifty years of Labour rule at Merthyr.

Nationalism after the 1960s found Labour consistently unenthusiastic and the Conservatives enthusiastically inconsistent. Not till the late 1960s were the Conservatives prepared to make terms with Welsh and Scottish nationalism. In 1968 Heath proposed that a Scottish legislature should handle legislation relating to Scotland.[71] His government had other priorities between 1970 and 1974, but Heath supported the Labour government's devolution Bill in 1976. He saw it as 'the best way of maintaining the Union', given that neither Welsh nor Scots wanted separation. To refuse Scotland its assembly would be counter-productive because refusal would merely strengthen the nationalists. But Thatcher supplanted Heath's strand of devolutionary Conservatism with her conviction that a Scottish assembly would lead to confusion, waste, and increased friction.[72] Conservatives also disagreed about whether benevolent interventionism in Wales and Scotland was the best way to proceed. For Heath in the 1980s, the Scottish Development Agency (established in 1975) exemplified government's potential for a constructive economic role. As Secretary of State for Wales in 1987–90, Peter Walker could have said of Wales what James Prior, the Heathite Secretary of State for Northern Ireland, used to say of his fiefdom: 'we are all Keynesians here'.[73] On the other hand, in the late 1980s ministers such as Lawson and Rifkind, more Thatcherite in their tastes, began attacking Scotland's 'dependency culture', and arguing that privatization would restore the local economy to Scottish control.[74] Thatcher told the Scottish Conservative Party in 1988 that privatization involved 'devolution to the people'; whereas 'nationalisation took companies out of Scottish hands and into Whitehall', privatization would 'hand them back to Scotland'.[75]

Labour's response to mounting nationalist pressure was slow, calculating, and reluctant.[76] In September 1974 Healey and Prentice were highly sceptical, and even Castle, who took a different line, showed no enthusiasm: 'if devolution was inevitable we had better relax and at least look as though we enjoyed it . . . the worst of all worlds would be to publish policies grudgingly and reluctantly'.[77] Wilson later pronounced devolution 'a boring word, a boring and soporific subject so far as legislation is concerned',[78] but his government felt obliged to prepare devolutionary measures. Parliamentary necessity pushed the Callaghan government into devolutionary proposals, but the cabinet was lukewarm. When these came before parliament, the Party's distaste came out of the closet. Leo Abse thought 'the task of a Labour movement' was to 'teach people not to admire xenophobia but to be ashamed of it. Our task is to smudge boundaries.' 'We shall serve the cause of unity of the kingdom . . . ,' said Neil Kinnock in the parliamentary debate of 1977 on the Welsh devolution Bill, 'by exposing and destroying those who for petty political ends and antediluvian national purposes seek to profiteer out of the economic resentment of the people.'[79] The government responded to Labour dissidents by legislating for referenda of the Welsh and Scottish electorates before implementing a devolution bill. Pushed on at Westminster by an alliance between Liberals and Labour, in what had almost become a three-party system there, devolution promised to introduce in Scotland and Wales subordinate legislatures where multi-party politics were even more firmly entrenched. So much so, that House of Lords amendments to the Scottish Bill (later rejected by the Commons) introduced proportional representation. Supporting the proposal, Lord Home argued against saddling a

Scottish assembly with an electoral system that would replicate the draw-backs of the British system: governments elected on a minority vote which sought to impose policies for which the people had not voted.[80] All these labours were rendered fruitless, however, by the results of the referenda: 52 per cent yes in Scotland, 20 per cent in Wales. To implement devolution in Scotland, a yes vote from 40 per cent of the registered electorate was required; the figure obtained (33 per cent) was well short of the mark, and in Wales it reached only 12 per cent.

Though lukewarm about devolution, British politicians took Welsh and Scottish nationalism seriously in the 1970s for at least three reasons. The Labour government of 1974–9 came to depend on nationalist support for its parliamentary majority. Liberals and some Conservatives genuinely favoured curbing central-government power by boosting local self-government. And all parties knew that English public opinion would never tolerate resisting Welsh and Scottish aspirations by force. Terrorism has not complicated England's relations with Wales and Scotland in the same way as in Ireland, but British governments have been concerned lest the Irish model should prove contagious. Welsh nationalists have occasionally used violent tactics. The Penrhos aerodrome hutments were burned in 1936, the Free Wales Army caused explosions in public buildings during the mid-1960s, and English holiday homes in Wales have been set on fire. Fear of violence seems to have influenced the decision in September 1980 to allow an all-Welsh-language fourth television channel in Wales. Unable to win over middle opinion on the issue in Wales, the government did not feel it had isolated the extremists sufficiently to refuse. 'Violence is latent in all civil societies,' wrote *The Times*. 'It is the task of statesmen to deprive it of, and most certainly not to present it with, an effective cause.'[81] The SNP repudiated violent tactics in the 1960s,[82] but Michael Foot claimed in 1976 that if devolution for Scotland were rejected, violence of the Irish type might result. One MP thought this 'a most unusual and . . . a very irresponsible argument' that was 'wildly out of touch with feelings in Scotland and Wales', but it is significant that Foot thought the claim worth making.[83]

It is in Northern Ireland that the party system's failure to prevent violence has been most serious. The simple-majority electoral system drew in only the Unionist section of a divided community towards parliamentary politics, and both the leading mainland parties refrain from fighting elections there. Despite Northern Ireland's major contribution to defeating Hitler,[84] a contrast with Eire that was striking, the Ulster Unionist alliance with mainland Conservatives remained cool, and in retrospect it seems surprising that Lloyd George's settlement of 1920 lasted so long. There was some truth in the view of the Democratic Unionists' leader Ian Paisley that Ulster Unionism 'was not English Toryism grafted on to Ireland', but grew out of the peculiarities of Irish history. Its Protestant fervour had long departed from British Conservatism, and was paralleled on the mainland only by sects like the Jehovah's Witnesses or Seventh-day Adventists.[85] It was a Conservative government that disbanded the Stormont parliament in 1972.

As for the Labour Party, its mainland Roman Catholic connections did not ensure the full incorporation of the few non-Unionist MPs from Northern Ireland. The Province was the pioneer of, and the leading gainer from, central government's redistribution of wealth between the regions,[86] and yet this generated none of the entrenched labourist structures there that developed among the welfare state's mainland beneficiaries. A class-based and somewhat rationalistic mainland labour movement remained puzzled by a society whose driving passions cut across social class, and in the 1970s Wilson was at least as clumsy as Heath in handling Ulster Unionism. In November 1971 he returned from Dublin endorsing a remarkable scheme for unifying Ireland within fifteen years, whereby the Republic would recognize the Queen and rejoin the Commonwealth,[87] and at the climacteric of May 1974 his mishandling of Unionist opinion was disastrous. The irrelevantly class-based preoccupations of Len Murray, General Secretary of the TUC, led him on that occasion to try to help the Labour government in quite the wrong way. His bid to lead working-class resistance in Northern Ireland to the loyalist strike against the Sunningdale power-sharing agreement ended with his heading a 'pitifully small procession of 200 men and women' pelted by loyalist stones and eggs.[88]

Northern Ireland's distance from Westminster was by no means complete. Turn-out at general elections seldom fell far below the mainland; at four elections between 1922 and 1992 it was higher.[89] None the less, the bitterness of local conflict reflected the failure of the party system, and caused politicians who sought what is called a 'political solution' to pursue it by other routes. Well before referenda were held on the mainland, they were held in November 1972 to discover opinion on the border issue, and in March 1973 on whether the Province should remain within the United Kingdom. Proportional representation was another device pioneered in Northern Ireland. At the elections for the Northern Ireland assembly in 1921 and 1925 it broke up polarized politics and created an opening for the Northern Ireland Labour Party. This led the Unionists to supplant it with the simple-majority system in 1929.[90] The single transferable vote has, however, been reintroduced for all elections in Northern Ireland since 1973 and in direct elections for the EEC.

What ultimately put Northern Ireland out of gear with the mainland parties was the colonial analogy that many republicans apply to the situation there. They see Northern Ireland as involved in the last stages of decolonization. 'There are those who tell us that the British government will not be moved by armed struggle,' said Gerry Adams, Sinn Féin's leader, in November 1983. 'The history of Ireland and of British colonial involvement throughout the world tells us that they will not be moved by anything else.' Benn made the point more succinctly when sharing a platform with Adams in 1989: 'the history of Britain is a terrorist ending up having tea with the Queen at Buckingham Palace as a world statesman'.[91] British troops in Northern Ireland themselves implicitly accepted the colonial analogy, given the term 'bogwogs' that they often applied to Belfast Catholics, not to mention the order-keeping methods they applied in inner-city Belfast which they had learned in colonial situations.[92] Yet the analogy is seriously misleading, and it is surprising that British politicians and Commonwealth historians have not scrutinized it more closely. They could have pointed out that the oft-cited parallels with India, Palestine, and Cyprus in reality buttress the case for partition.[93] They could have questioned how useful are simple colonial parallels for understanding a 'colony' so close to the mother country, and whose Protestant majority have lived there for so many centuries. They might even have drawn attention to de Valera's offer in 1958, reiterated by Garret FitzGerald in 1979, for the Republic to rejoin the Commonwealth if this would secure a united Ireland.[94] After a quarter-century of terrorism, British governments would now require a better offer before doing business: abandonment by the Republic of any claim to Northern Ireland, certainly; the re-entry of Southern Ireland into some form of federal union with the mainland, perhaps.[95]

The IRA, however, small and introverted as always, convinced that it had the future on its side, urged on by its carefully nurtured memories of heroes on 'active service' who had gone before, moved in the 1970s and 1980s ever further out of touch with the real world. But despite being blessed with Unionist opponents peculiarly inept at winning friends, republicans motivated primarily by hatred, a minority even within their own locality, could anticipate sympathy only among sectarian groups in northern and southern Ireland and among Irish settlers in America who had learned nothing and forgotten nothing. They had no hope of the sort of mass support that eventually won the peoples of eastern Europe freedom from Communist rule. Only about 43 per cent of Northern Ireland's population were Roman Catholic in 1981, and two years earlier only half even of those supported the idea of Irish unity.[96] Instead, a tiny minority of them contented themselves with the 'stunt violence' that the Fenians had pioneered. 'It is the most messy kind of civil war one has ever seen,' wrote Crossman in August 1969, expressing a view that still has resonance: '... it doesn't give a sense of stirring, epic tragedy but is just awful and depressing.'[97]

As far as the mainland was concerned, the IRA seemed keen rather to make enemies than friends, and among the Protestants in Northern Ireland its violence evoked an equal and opposite reaction which was if anything more brutal and less discriminating than its own. It did not seem to see that its actions would be interpreted not just as nationalist but as antipolitical: as repudiating the claim of politicians in northern and southern Ireland to speak for opinion, and even as questioning the legitimacy of their profession. Concession could never emerge from such a 'solution'; equal and opposite reaction from the Protestants could and did. Nor is there any permanent solution to be found through re-drawing boundaries within Ireland, whatever their origins in 1920–2, and whatever the majorities for or against union in referenda held within whatever units of opinion. The essential point is that no modern democratic state could even contemplate coercing within its boundaries a group as numerous and determined as the Ulster Unionists, let alone bring it off.

Yet mistaken IRA tactics should not delude its critics into underestimating its capacity for disrupting a complex urban society. Indeed, the British government had itself adapted IRA guerrilla tactics with considerable effect when mounting European resistance movements to Hitler in the 1940s.[98] The image cultivated by the IRA for cold, cynical, ruthless, and manipulative violence was epitomized in its chilling comment on the failure of the Brighton bomb to kill Thatcher in 1984: 'today we were unlucky. But remember, we have only to be lucky once; you will have to be lucky always.'[99] The political economy of terrorism requires the stage-managing of unpredictable and varied types of incident by a tiny group of zealots in order to get maximum terror and propagandist advantage for effort expended. To quote an earlier and somewhat more scrupulous practitioner in the art, the suffragette Christabel Pankhurst: 'much depended, in militancy ... upon timing and placing, upon the dramatic arrangement and sequence of acts and events'.[100] The more brutal the actions, the more high-toned is the idealism required to justify them in the minds of their perpetrators. As Edmund Burke had long ago written: 'the worst of these politics of revolution is this; they temper and harden the breast, in order to prepare it for the desperate strokes which are sometimes used in extreme occasions'.[101] A high-flown nationalist and decidedly hermetic secular idealism, half religious in tone and imagery, was generated. Under its impulse terrorism became in a peculiar sense 'rational'; to speak of 'mindlessness', let alone of derangement or psychopathic motive, is to run away from a more complex reality. It also does nothing to explain why new generations of terrorist spring up to volunteer for very dangerous types of activity, and misleads the authorities into underestimating the IRA's skill at manipulating the media, remarkable when one considers how repugnant their tactics have been. Time and again the IRA outclassed the British government, and still more the Protestant terrorists, on the public-relations front.

This prompted repeated pleas on the mainland for 'a political solution'. In November 1975 Merlyn Rees, Secretary of State for Northern Ireland, made in cabinet a remark that Tony Benn thought shrewd: that 'the English disease is looking for a constitutional solution to the Irish problem'.[102] Enoch Powell's words for this English trait four years later were rather stronger. Those who unintentionally promote violence by failing to defend the union resolutely, he said, 'include the thoughtless, the woolly-minded, the men and women of so-called "good will", the open-mouthed and empty-headed in all walks of life'.[103] If the plea for a 'political solution' meant that politicians as well as the police must be involved in any final settlement, it was a mere truism. But if it meant buying off with concessions Protestant or Catholic groups who thought 'stunt' violence by a tiny minority on behalf of a larger minority or even majority could supplant democratic procedures, it was a 'solution' which no politician could endorse without betraying his profession. The plea for a 'political solution' could even make matters worse for two reasons. First, it posed a false antithesis between politics and policing, whereas in reality the two continuously interact; if the terrorist is under pressure from the forces of law and order he will be more likely to make terms with the politicians. Secondly, well-intentioned proposals for what Unionists saw as a sell-out raised false nationalist hopes, thereby inflating Unionist fears. Each well-intentioned plea gave the IRA the impression that one last terrorist push might at last achieve the desired result. As Labour's spokesman on Northern Ireland pointed out in 1989, 'in Great Britain careless talk only costs votes. In Northern Ireland, careless talk costs lives.'[104] Political solutions were sought through the brief experiment of 1974 in 'power-sharing' through the Sunningdale agreement, the attempt at a constitutional convention in 1975–6, Prior's attempt at 'rolling devolution' in 1982–6, the Anglo-Irish agreement of 1985, and the Anglo-Irish declaration of 1993 and its aftermath—not to mention numerous talks, and talks about talks.

The IRA claimed descent from the creators of the Irish Republic, but the Republic's real creators, democratic in their basis, soon found themselves in conflict with the terrorists, who were later to turn their attention to Northern Ireland. Cross-border collaboration between the British and Irish governments in pacifying the Province was an obvious expedient. In September 1973 Heath implicitly acknowledged the Republic's potential contribution by becoming the first British prime minister officially to visit the country since 1922. But the most ambitious attempt to enlist the Republic's help came, rather surprisingly, from a Conservative leader more unionist in her instincts, Margaret Thatcher, who at the Conservative Party conference of 1979 had pledged herself to all the people of Northern Ireland: 'we don't forget you, and we won't abandon you'.[105] The Anglo-Irish agreement of 1985 seems to stem from her good relations with the Republic's Prime Minister Dr Garret FitzGerald.[106] Both governments had an interest in stabilizing the situation, and their collaboration against terrorism involved compromise on both sides. But the agreement aroused so much Unionist hostility that Prior's scheme for 'rolling devolution' foundered in the following year. The effect of political violence in Northern Ireland has been, if anything, to postpone Irish unification into a still more distant future. By inflaming Protestant and Catholic hatreds there, and thus by adding the more localized and reactive violence of the Ulster Defence Association to its own, the IRA slowed down the gradual process of assimilation between north and south in a rapidly secularizing society that joint membership of the EEC might otherwise have made possible. Nor did it make any progress in shifting mainland opinion. Continuing themes there remained the all-party solidarity on a policy of reconciliation in Northern Ireland, a low salience for the Province at general elections, and a majority in opinion polls for 'troops out' which never represented feelings strong enough to push British governments into action.[107] The IRA's 'ceasefire' of 1994 represented a decision—unexpected, but most welcome—to pursue the same objective by a more civilized route to a destination that can at best end only in compromise.

*

Parliament made some contribution towards holding the United Kingdom together. The House of Lords—drawing together church, state, and legal system—reinforced the social integration of the British élite that the aristocratic London 'season' provided. By assembling landowners formidable in their localities, it could focus the entire country on a single political dialogue. But it was a dialogue dominated by England, for both assemblies were overwhelmingly English in their composition. In most decades after 1801 English MPs held three-quarters of the seats in the House of Commons. Ireland in the nineteenth century held more than a sixth but fell to a tiny proportion after 1922. Scotland's contribution oscillated around a tenth and Wales around a twentieth.[108] Any MP who had made a name outside parliament was scrutinized closely on becoming a member, and was assessed not at the valuation of himself or others, but on the basis of qualities displayed within the House. In the House of Commons, Wales and Scotland were not necessarily at a disadvantage as long as the landed aristocracy and gentry were dominant there, because aristocracy transcended regional difference. Early-Victorian English MPs customarily left their Scottish colleagues to manage their own bills,[109] and the first Scottish standing committee was not appointed till 1894. Nor did the Welsh representatives feel at a disadvantage until the social revolution in Welsh representation after 1868.

With Ireland, things were very different. Up to 1830 the government could always rely on support from about seventy Irish MPs,[110] but O'Connell's campaign for Roman Catholic emancipation required Peel and Wellington in 1829 to strike a balance of risks: to sacrifice this source of security for the gain involved in tempting O'Connell and his following of Irish repealers towards parliament, where they could be more closely monitored. In his 'National Political Union', O'Connell pioneered modern party organization—with elected members, annual subscriptions, and centralized information about registration and candidates. In 1832 he could rely on thirty-nine in his own grouping, together with extensive support from Irish Whigs and from English and Scottish radicals.[111] Though set apart from the rest by manners, accent, and appearance, their numbers dwindled as individuals were recruited to 'the ranks of Order and the British Connexion' by Whig leaders as shrewd as Lord John Russell.[112] We have seen how Gladstone pursued the same strategy in the early 1880s. None the less, opposition to the Arms Bill in 1843 shows the Irish MPs already prepared to anticipate Parnellite disruption of parliamentary conventions. Three years later Peel told Wellington that some Irish MPs aimed 'to disgust England with Irish business and with Irish Members', so that the union would be repealed in order to purge the House 'of a set of troublesome and factious members'.[113]

All this distanced Irish from other MPs. Gladstone devised his remedies for Irish problems in the 1870s and 1880s without consulting them,
and did not mix socially with them even at the height of the home rule
crisis.[114] Though Parnell's home rule MPs were men of substance, their
social and educational grade was on average lower than their predecessors',
and some were 'dynamically, noisily, plebeian'.[115] This made it easier for
them to disrupt Westminster's aristocratic club and subvert the Victorian
debating ideal with a contemptuous and sometimes deliberately obstruc-
tive oratory. Matters came to a head in 1881 when Speaker Brand closed
the debate on the Coercion Bill on 2 February and put the motion after
forty-one hours of obstruction. In November 1882 the Speaker was empowered to move the closure of any debate if the specified majority of
support for doing so was obtained. Home rule MPs specialized, too, in
disrupting solemn moments by challenging pious English orthodoxies with
their pert observations. Such incidents helped drive the country gentlemen
out of the House of Commons for good.[116] Indeed, one attraction of home
rule, for opponents and supporters alike, was that it held out the chance
that Irish colleagues would be tempted or devolved away to Dublin.[117] The
Irish strategies of Liberal leaders after 1886, however, assumed that Irish
nationalist MPs would remain at Westminster. In 1886 Joseph Chamberlain recommended consulting them and even promoting them into government posts.[118] In 1915 Redmond, then nationalist leader, was offered
office in the coalition government, but he thought 'the principles and history of the party he represented made the acceptance of the offer impossible'.[119] Redmond's Party was by then getting the worst of both worlds:
not seizing its chance to become a party of government, yet losing its hold
on Irish opinion by persisting with Parnell's strategy into a world very
different from his. With suspended implementation of home rule during
the First World War, with the shift in Irish opinion towards direct action
in the Easter rising of 1916, and with the consequent growth of Sinn Féin,
southern Ireland eventually rejected Westminster altogether.

Broadly based in its constituencies, with MPs drawn from a social grade
below the average and tightly disciplined through pledges that were not
broken, keeping itself to itself, meritocratic and unsnobbish in tone, irreverent towards House of Commons conventions, playing one English party
irreverently off against the other—the Home Rule Party inevitably set
precedents for other groups challenging the system: for the young Lloyd
George as well as for the early socialists.[120] Asquith was socially as distant
from the Welsh MPs as Gladstone from the Irish. Publicly 'among my
most faithful and loyal supporters' whose 'confidence and affection I prize

almost more than I can express', the Welsh MPs were for him privately (to Venetia Stanley) 'as touchy as they are stupid'.[121] In the parliamentary dimension, as in others, Labour's advent smoothed out such snobbish ways of distancing the non-English MPs. The importance of the Scots and Welsh contributions to Labour's inter-war impact ensured that no Labour leader could nourish such prejudices. And when nationalist feeling revived in the 1940s, parliament tried to meet its special needs. Megan Lloyd-George got her special Welsh debating day on 17 October 1944 as 'a recognition of the distinctive problems and needs of Wales, not as an area, not as a part of England, but as a nation with a living language of its own ... and with its own culture', and in 1982 the Scottish Grand Committee sat for the first time in Edinburgh.[122]

Ulster Unionist MPs could still be regarded in 1971 as 'the poor whites of the Conservative Party',[123] but this was less because of snobbery, more because their cultural background was so different and because they did not seek office. To these distancing influences were soon added their deliberate disruption of long-standing Conservative ties, together with occasional withdrawals from Westminster. But with newcomers from both warring camps within Northern Ireland after the 1960s, as with so many earlier newcomers to the House, parliament's scrutiny of new members, followed by acceptance or rejection, persisted. Two individual instances illustrate the limits of parliament's tolerance. Bernadette Devlin, elected in 1969 as Independent Unity candidate, made a good beginning with her maiden speech. Crossman thought 'the crowded House was spellbound by a tremendous performance' from 'this black, dark, tiny thing standing up in the third row back'. But when Prior, sitting immediately behind Heath, praised her speech, he replied 'yes, but it's the only speech she's got in her, she can't make another one'. As an MP she was soon found wanting by an assimilative assembly that values breadth of outlook in its members.[124] The same could be said of a leading Unionist, whose opportunities for learning how to impress the House have lasted for much longer: Ian Paisley. In 1970 a Unionist colleague claimed that he would find membership instructive, 'for he will see, and perhaps through him others will see, the mood and temper of the British Parliament'. He would 'come to learn that the disdain of this Parliament and of the British people as a whole for bigotry and intolerance is not just a fiction of my imagination but is hard fact'.[125] Though respected by MPs for preserving his integrity and even for preserving some dignity amidst widespread incomprehension of his ideals, Paisley as yet shows no sign of learning this lesson. Yet by his very presence at Westminster, he does at least witness to the unionist values which pervade his career, and to the faint possibility that one day parliament may perform its reconciling function there too.

*

The administrative structure's impact in holding the United Kingdom together deserves less attention than monarchy, party, and parliament because the civil service's impact on the constituent nations has been less sustained and less uniform. Northern Ireland had a separate administration from 1920 to 1972, whereas Wales and Scotland have only slowly built up an approach to one. Rather than clamping the nations together, the administration has responded to national susceptibilities, admittedly rather tentatively in the case of Wales and Scotland, through decentralization. Since Stormont's disbandment, the Northern Ireland Office has increasingly come to resemble the structures set up for other nationalities, most notably the Scottish Office.[126] Scotland acquired its own Secretary in 1885. He entered the cabinet in 1892, and became a Secretary of State in 1926. More and more powers have been transferred to the Scottish Office since the 1880s, and in 1939 what John Buchan called 'a visible proof of our nationhood' was provided when St Andrew's House was opened to house the Office's local departments.[127] Scottish business in parliament has been handled since 1907 by the Scottish Grand Committee,[128] to which a Welsh Grand Committee was added in 1960. Politically inspired administrative devolution to Wales began with education in 1907 and soon moved on to agriculture and health. By the Edwardian period, Wales had its county councils, its Welsh Council of Agriculture, and its Welsh commission to administer the National Health Insurance Act. By the 1950s all governments treated Wales as a single region, even though this was administratively inconvenient. In 1951 a Minister for Welsh Affairs was appointed, and in 1964 he became a Secretary of State with a Welsh Office which soon acquired extensive administrative responsibilities.[129] Twentieth-century Welsh and Scottish administrative decentralization, however, has been inspired by more than response to nationalist pressure; much of it reflects the convenience of British central government, especially given the existence of separate judicial and legal systems in Scotland.[130]

In conclusion, monarchy, political parties, and parliament since the 1860s have helped politically to hold together the geographical unit whose 'English' constitution Bagehot described. Their influence was not, however, powerful enough to prevent the loss of southern Ireland in 1922, or to prevent the union from running into difficulties elsewhere since the 1960s. In one way, these developments reflect the decline since Bagehot's day of Liberal internationalist optimism, for they reflect the persistence of national resentments and the tenacity of traditional and even irrational loyalties. These tendencies may even lead—paradoxically with help from the European Union, that embodiment of Liberal internationalism—to the break-up of the United Kingdom. Yet the flexibility of the British political system and the responsiveness of those who manage it may yet enable us to retain the cultural, economic, and other benefits of a multi-nation state by the only means feasible in a liberal society: through combining curbs on central government with a genuine belief in local self-government. It is to localism within the British political system that we must now turn, in the second of this book's four chapters on the pluralist dimensions of British political culture. Only this cultural background can explain how since the 1860s a political structure with such authoritarian potential could work out so differently in practice.

# 4

## County and Borough

ALTHOUGH British central government grew out of monarchical institutions, it operated within a 'civil society' that was and still is full of vitality. Parliament's sovereignty was in theory untrammelled within a unitary political system which left no autonomy to local authorities; yet in practice they enjoyed much freedom of action. Indeed, some see English local government as attaining its golden age between the 1860s and the 1930s, culminating in the Local Government Act of 1933.[1] This growth was possible partly because those who were active in local government saw, and had reason to see, central government less as an enemy than as a potential ally. The local authorities reached out towards the centre and the central authorities reached out towards the localities. So, in practice, central government was restrained by regional loyalties operating at the level not only of nationality but also of locality. This chapter and the next two will highlight the restraints on such authoritarian and centralized tendencies as British government might possess: the vitality of local self-government, a libertarian political tradition, and an associated voluntarist tradition that fuelled ideas on policy.

Rural government during Bagehot's day was carried out by an intricate network of unintegrated local authorities. 'The simple English villager is the creature of a highly complex economy,' wrote T. H. S. Escott in 1891. 'He may be defined as one who lives in a parish, in a union, in a highway district, or in a county, according to the point of view which is taken, while in three of these he always is.' He might also be subject to JPs and to a school board, local board, vestry, highway board, and poor-law board.[2] The rational solution might perhaps have been to supersede borough and county administration by the sort of uniform and utilitarian nation-wide structure that had run the poor law since 1834. But French precedents were not encouraging, and such a reform would have clashed with a host of vested interests. The boroughs had already received their reform in 1835, and it was not until 1888 that the countryside received its equivalent: a nation-wide structure that in an increasingly democratic society could command respect.

The County Councils Act (1888) did not eliminate the multi-layered aspect of English local government or the administrative contrast between town and country, nor did it set up standardized administrative areas. Still, it did at least give the English countryside the elected authorities and the separation of judicial from administrative procedures that the boroughs had won in 1835. It also gave county status to the area of London covered since 1855 by the Metropolitan Board of Works. The new edifice was completed at two levels below the county by the Local Government Act of 1894, whose boundary reforms eliminated duplications and set up an integrated three-tier local administrative structure. Beneath the county, the old sanitary boards in county and borough became urban and rural district councils; elected intermediate units for general purposes. Below them came the parish, which carried the ratepayer-democracy principles of 1835 down to the smallest units: the parish meeting, for communities with less than 300 inhabitants; and the parish council, for larger communities. Under the Act 6,880 parish councils were set up.[3] So the entire local-government system, rural and urban, was now equipped to assume new functions, most notably those of the *ad hoc* bodies. In 1902 the school boards were abolished, and in 1929 the poor-law boards.

Those who launched the reform of 1888 were decentralizers who wanted new responsibilities devolved to the revalidated local authorities. But the conflicting interests of county and borough, a theme that recurs in the discussion of British local government, helped to ensure that the outcome was just the reverse. The boroughs feared being enveloped by the rural authorities which surrounded them, and helped to dilute the decentralizing flavour of the original Bill.[4] So central government continued to take on more and more commitments, confident in the knowledge that the local authorities were now strong enough to implement its instructions. This was not how it seemed at the time, however, particularly as so many initiatives were still coming up from below, and nowhere more than from Joseph Chamberlain's Birmingham, where the local middle-class élite set the pace. Under Chamberlain's reign as radical mayor, they saw their city as a modern equivalent of the late-medieval Italian city state, and designed its buildings accordingly.[5] Civic pride required town halls with high towers and splendid façades. 'There is one eternal refrain in a Chamberlain–Kenrick household,' wrote Beatrice Webb: 'Birmingham society is superior in earnestness, sincerity and natural intelligence, to any society in the United Kingdom!'[6] Chamberlain in Birmingham, like Revd John Percival in Bristol and T. H. Green in Oxford, imbued local government with a 'civic gospel': a co-ordinated and secularized form of 'good works' which carried the work of local philanthropists and volunteers to a higher power. The Chamberlains and the T. H. Greens assumed that they spoke not only for their own class but also for working people, or at least for the best among them. The industrious Liberal middle and working classes worked together against idle aristocracy. Chamberlain showed how much the state could achieve when it intervened at the local level with slum clearance and public ownership. 'The politics of the future are social politics,' he wrote in 1882. 'Unless I can secure for the nation results similar to these which have followed the adoption of my policy in Birmingham', he told John Morley in 1883, 'it will have been a sorry exchange to give up the Town Council for the Cabinet.'[7]

The Chamberlains, the Percivals, and the Greens were battling against the nineteenth century's small ratepayers—shopkeepers, craftsmen, Chartists, and radicals—who were keen to pare down the rates and cut the cost of poor relief.[8] But local-government expenditure rose faster than national for most of the nineteenth century, and before 1914 revenue rose faster from local rates than from national taxation. From 1870 to 1908 the numbers relieved through the poor law were declining in England, Wales, and Scotland (though not in Ireland), but the real cost of relief in England and Wales was steadily rising,[9] and all this fell on the poor-law boards, funded from the rates. Worries about central government's apparently open-ended commitment to local authorities through the system of grants-in-aid prompted the attempt by G. J. Goschen as Chancellor of the Exchequer in 1888 to halt the process; his plan was to assign specific revenues to local authorities, within which they would thereafter be expected to balance their budgets. Restraint from the centre was reinforced by the Local Government Board, wielding that great Victorian invention: centralized inspection. Instead of presiding over a vast bureaucratic structure with local ramifications, the Board's central audit was, said Redlich, 'designed to obtain the advantages of efficiency without the incubus of bureaucracy'.[10] With its rising late-Victorian status within Whitehall, the Board was reinforced by an increasingly centralized supervision of rating valuation, for which the Inland Revenue took responsibility after 1909.

In such circumstances, local government required relatively few full-time employees. We have seen how the centralized system of specialized *ad hoc* bodies, pioneered with the poor-law reform of 1834, eventually gave way before the pattern set by the Municipal Reform Act of the following year—that is, to decentralized administration by non-specialist assembly. 'Englishmen have no liking and no need for the Continental conception of an official as a superior being,' wrote Redlich; rarely is it necessary for the committee, wrote Laski, 'to teach the official that he is the servant, and not the master, of his committee'.[11] The city or county council, which represented the electors, remained the sovereign body. It delegated day-to-day business to numerous specialist committees, each of whose chairmen wielded considerable power, and each of which worked closely with the relevant permanent officials—but it retained its oversight of committee decisions. 'The Council', wrote Redlich in 1903, 'may be described as the deliberative organ, the committees as the specialised organs of administration, the permanent staff as the executive which carries out the actual work of government.'[12] Redlich felt none of the scepticism about British arrangements that is now so fashionable. He admired a structure which he saw as 'perfectly elastic', adjusting the number of its committees and staff flexibly in the face of contrasting local situations. In country areas, for instance, the county council tended to sit rarely, its role being merely to co-ordinate its committees and represent the county 'in what may be called its "foreign" relations'.[13] Councils' power to delegate has been extended during the twentieth century, and council committees interact continuously with the paid officials. Yet Laski in 1935 was still enthusiastic about the British system: its success was 'built, not upon the separation of powers, but upon a confusion of them, half deliberate, half unconscious', with each committee legislating as well as administering, and even performing quasi-judicial roles.[14]

Edwardian town and county clerks tended to be qualified solicitors whose role was to advise the council on legal matters. They usually supervised the local-government officials, and in council sessions customarily spoke only when invited. E. D. Simon in 1926 was restive under such a system. A big city like Manchester, he thought, needed 'vision and imagination, the long and courageous view'; this was hardly likely to come from someone with a legal background whose 'whole instinct is to see and magnify the difficulties'.[15] For him, local government's biggest problem was to ensure that the council should be 'continually on the look-out for new opportunities of extending and adapting its services to the growing needs of the city'.[16] Simon complained of big-city government that 'it is nobody's business to think about the big things', and recommended dividing the mayor's ceremonial and administrative duties between two people.[17] Critics sometimes yearned for the firmness of direction given by the American directly elected mayor or by the Prussian burgomaster, a trained and paid administrator entrenched within a substantial term of office. 'It is needless to stress the contrast between the cleanness and beauty of a typical German city and the dirt and ugliness of a corresponding city in this country,' wrote Simon in 1926. 'It is a subject almost too painful for an Englishman to dwell upon.'[18]

Between the wars the local authorities were losing much of their Victorian impetus. This was not because their activities dwindled. Quite the reverse. But they took on their expanded functions in the context of mounting central control, and social justice seemed increasingly to demand larger administrative units. Central government intervened with subsidies, and local authorities drifted towards merely implementing its policies. Inevitably central government was called upon for grants-in-aid. The share contributed by these grants to total local-authority expenditure in England and Wales rose steadily with every twentieth-century decade— from 12 per cent in 1900 to 26 per cent in 1930 to 38 per cent in 1960 to 63 per cent in 1980.[19] The grants also accounted for a rising percentage of local-government income: 14 in 1887/8, 25 in 1913/14, 35 in 1927/8.[20] The values of the Local Government Board at its apogee were threatened by the twin contemporary justifications for mounting central-government expenditure: egalitarian redistribution and national defence. Its austere outlook fell increasingly out of fashion, and it was outflanked under John Burns's presidency by more imaginative and energetic ministers operating from rival power-bases. Goschen's scheme of 1888 soon broke down, and an attempt to attain the same result by a new route—through awarding block grants to local authorities—was adopted in 1929. Yet the attempt to preserve distinct spheres and funds for local and central government was doomed: central-government management of the economy and of welfare gradually edged out local initiative and local self-help. Central-government subsidies were directed to local authorities with diminishing discrimination. Local authorities in turn felt less pressure to fund new responsibilities with local revenue, and local accountability lost its edge.

Twentieth-century urban problems seemed increasingly to demand centralized remedy for several reasons. Larger administrative units had the double advantage of spreading risks and making the resources available that would produce fairness as between regions, most obviously in public welfare. Joseph Chamberlain wanted poor-law administration transferred to the new county councils in 1888,[21] but in the end it was central government that took on the responsibility. This transfer occurred through the sequence of welfare reforms running from old-age pensions (1908) through national insurance (1911) to the Unemployment Assistance Board's assumption in 1934 of local authorities' responsibilities to the unemployed, and the story ended with the abolition of the poor law in 1948. In the welfare sphere the local authorities found themselves increasingly implementing a centrally decided, taxpayer-funded policy. If better road transport segregated the social classes increasingly into distinct localities, they could hardly be expected to lift themselves up by their own local bootstraps.[22] Funds had to come from the centre if regional pockets of poverty and unemployment were to be removed. Traditional boundaries were further overridden by the need in two world wars to maximize production and minimize casualties from fire and bombing. Rent control during the First World War, complemented by promises of post-war 'homes for heroes', forced the local authorities into a new role: providing municipal housing on a large scale. Legislation of 1930 linked government subsidy to the numbers displaced and rehoused in a nation-wide slum-clearance programme, and by 1939 about half the housing which the government categorized as slums had been cleared.[23]

Transport changes helped to enlarge what was regarded as the viable community—a second impulse to twentieth-century centralization. The treaty for specific purposes between autonomous local-government authorities was an intermediate route towards a larger administrative unit for some purposes, and was popular in the late-Victorian period,[24] but the longer-term trend was towards the regional authority. Convinced in 1919, partly by the growth of regional sports groupings, that county patriotism was on the wane, C. B. Fawcett sought to establish viable 'provinces' of England that would help to 'reverse the disastrous separation of town and country in local government'.[25] The geographers' new concept of the 'conurbation', employed to describe a grouping of adjacent urban areas and endorsed by government statisticians in 1951, took regionalism a stage further. Planning needs in health, recreation, economic management, energy, and water coincided with such pressures. These culminated in the concept of the 'city region' which influenced the Maud Commission on local government (appointed in 1969), and which led to the creation of so-called 'metropolitan areas' under the Local Government Act of 1972.

But geographical broadening meant, in some sense, dilution of local commitment, and this lies behind the salience of 'planning' from the 1930s to the 1970s. It was by no means an inevitable trend; indeed, its advent constitutes a third reason why local government was in decline. With motor traffic came massive population shifts that demanded co-ordination at the regional level. Socialism had by no means at first envisaged a centralized state. Fabians, pursuing the right mix of efficiency and participation, pinned their collectivist hopes on municipalization. But in a pungent paper to the Fabian Society in 1903, H. G. Wells pointed out that this could succeed only on the basis of the much larger local-government units that alone could revive municipal pride. Whereas communities of five miles' radius had been appropriate in earlier transport conditions, the railway had created much larger economic units, and this must have a political consequence: regional authorities of 100 miles' radius to replace the cluster of petty bodies dating from an earlier age. 'Political efficiency', he believed, 'must precede Socialism.'[26] Partly because this political transformation could never be secured at the local level, and because Guild Socialism's alternative decentralized option came to nought, centralized socialism came to seem more attractive to the inter-war Labour Party.[27]

   'Planning' thenceforth tended to push decision-making upwards from smaller local authorities to larger, from local to regional authority, and from regional authority to central government. This happened in 1974 with personal health services, water supply, and sewerage, for instance. Again, the 'special areas' set up by the national government in the 1930s came to be seen as ancestors of the Wilson governments' 'development areas' which by 1966 covered a fifth of the working population.[28] In the 1980s terrorism and nationally co-ordinated trade-union tactics eroded local autonomy even in policing, at the same time as concern for educational standards produced a *dirigiste* scheme which would have shocked the Victorians: a national school curriculum. So a long twentieth-century list could be compiled of functions transferred to national government from local authorities which found no new worlds to conquer.[29] The economies of scale that were thought to result from nationalization and public welfare carried these trends further after 1945, supplanting the municipal provision that had earlier been so influential on the labour movement. The decision to municipalize a utility had not correlated in the early days with a local authority's party-political flavour;[30] indeed, some late-Victorian collectivists saw municipalization as an intermediate concept half-way between private enterprise and state socialism. Between 1913 and 1925 the percentage of total tramway passengers carried in municipal trams rose from 80 to 87. By the early 1920s nearly two-thirds of the electricity units sold came from a municipal supply. In the early 1930s municipal authorities in England and Wales owned more than a third of authorized gas undertakings and an eighth of the motor-buses.[31]

   None the less, early Fabian socialists were keen to exploit the opportunities local government presented.[32] It was at the local level that the

Labour Party first gained experience of power.[33] In the long term we can see that statist tendencies within the British labour movement were dominant, though libertarian and localist tendencies and offshoots kept budding out or breaking off—from the Guild Socialists to Morrison's inter-war London County Council to the Social Democratic Party of the 1980s. By 1945 Labour's statist tendency was at its apogee. Many municipal airports were taken over by the Ministry of Civil Aviation at the end of the Second World War, and the Electricity (1946) and Gas (1948) Acts transferred power from the local authorities to regional or central authorities.[34] Bevan rejected any idea of basing his national health service on joint boards of local authorities: these would, he thought, be too parochial in outlook, too fragmented by local jealousies and interests.[35] A Labour government now in command at the national level no longer needed to revere local autonomy, and both nationalization and public welfare meant centralization. After 1945 the local authorities were diminishingly preoccupied with utilities and trading services, more and more taken up with welfare activity. But whereas the earlier responsibilities had left much room for local autonomy, and were carried out on behalf of the entire local community, the new welfare responsibilities were centrally directed and aimed to provide benefits differentially between segments of it.[36] Local government employment went on growing: by December 1956, 1,510,000 people were employed by local authorities, a third of them in education, a tenth in health and welfare, and a tenth in catering and recreation.[37] But these larger numbers were becoming mere executants of decisions reached at the centre.

Fuelling all this centralization was a Labour Party which not only helped to shape policy at the national level, but which also accelerated the advance of party within local government. Party had pervaded nineteenth-century local government, especially in the boroughs. But politics then centred upon local personalities and interests rather than upon national policy, whereas the inter-war Labour Party linked local politics to the programme of a national party and provided a new discipline for its local councillors.[38] Few Labour councillors were rich enough to take their own line on any policy issue, and most instinctively preferred the trade-union tradition of collective action.[39] By the 1920s party committees were quite regularly communing privately before council committee meetings. The Conservative response was often to promote non-party front organizations, and put up candidates who posed as 'independent' or ratepayer candidates, especially in rural areas.[40] In 1955 independents still contributed the majority of county councillors in as many as half the county councils, and in 1969 there were over thirty boroughs with councils wholly composed of independents, and nearly fifty more where the independents outnumbered those with a party label.[41] Yet only party allegiance could mobilize enough volunteers for a local-government role that was becoming increasingly demanding. The Liberal collapse made it easier for Conservatives to jettison their supposedly non-party stance and appear in their true colours. By 1951 the party system prevailed in about 90 per cent of the counties and large towns, in about half the urban districts, and in a quarter of rural districts.[42] Likewise, only party could mobilize opinion among the electors and channel it towards local government. Nor was there any other way to get the coherence of policy and discipline that could render permanent officials accountable to the electors.

One final twentieth-century centralizing pressure lay in local government employees' growing professionalism. The mounting pressure and complexity of business in twentieth-century local government was coped with in rather the same way as at the national level: through a continued separation between the politicians and the administrators; through subordinating the paid administrators and experts to less expert but elected and unpaid politicians; through increasing the number of administrators organized ever more tightly in their professional structures; and through dispersing the politicians into proliferating committees. Whereas nineteenth-century provincial cities could enlist the business expertise and local pride of leading local entrepreneurs, many communities later became too large to evoke such pride, business life became more demanding, and volunteers dried up. Yet the system of government by part-time local councillors was still expected to suffice. Herman Finer's tone, in the edition of *English Local Government* that he published in 1946, was far more gloomy than Laski's in the celebratory volume of 1935. He doubted whether a fragmented system of council committees filled by part-time volunteer councillors could provide at the local level the co-ordination that the cabinet provided nationally.[43] Similar worries led the Maud Committee of 1967 to favour a small 'management board' in each council with extensive delegated powers, together with other changes to concentrate decision-making.[44]

Inevitably the full-time officials stepped in to fill the power vacuum.[45] Some effort was made between the wars to raise their status. Simon and Laski were particularly keen on the idea,[46] but in 1935 about 90 per cent of local-government officials were still being recruited as juniors between the ages of 15 and 18.[47] Oxford responded in the following year with a new two-year diploma and a one-year certificate in public and social administration, both designed for people active in local or national public administration, and in 1938 the diploma attracted fourteen candidates.[48] No such postgraduate project could begin to rival the strong career-line that ran from the undergraduate humanities degrees direct to the accelerated promotion offered in Whitehall, the place in a unitary system of government where power most conspicuously lay. None the less, with increasingly diverse responsibilities, local authorities were forced to structure their administration functionally. Each specialist department attracted its own full-time professionals, whose professional bodies helped members to raise their sights beyond the immediate locality.[49] Local-government employees at lower levels were organizing themselves nationally too. In 1937 NALGO persuaded parliament to establish a unified pension scheme, and after 1945 was very successful in organizing itself for national pay-bargaining, securing a national agreement on wages and conditions of service in 1946.[50]

To the full-time local-government official, the committee of councillors seemed distinctly amateur. 'Meetings were more of club evenings than anything else,' one chief officer complained in the mid-1960s, 'and members were often visibly disappointed if they did not drag on long enough.' Yet when asked what qualities their job required, the councillors tended to cite the more sociable virtues: broadmindedness, patience, impartiality, a sense of humour, and being a good communicator.[51] It was a tension inherent in the problem of operating democratic structures within a complex society. In local as in national government, British government needed to retain what Laski had called 'that curious combination of amateur and expert which is characteristic of English self-government', and which demanded skill at compromise 'at pivotal points'.[52] Officials were recruited for their technical training and skills, whereas the councillor was the generalist, the expert on the arts of politics and assessing public opinion.

Against this fivefold centralizing impetus—from public welfare, from larger units of community, from the growth of planning, from the onward march of party, and from professionalized public employees—the values associated with local self-government were weak indeed. Furthermore, the fragmentation of local authorities muted any collective national impact they might have made. In 1888 the government aimed at subordinating all but the largest county boroughs to the new county authorities, but parliament let far more of these boroughs through the net than had at first been intended. Urbanization—which accounted for 10 per cent of the acreage in England and Wales in 1901, 15 per cent in 1981—caused the number of county boroughs to grow further: from 61 in 1888 to 83 in 1974. Their size also grew as they filched adjacent territory from the counties.[53] Changes in road transport and in the media were breaking down the political and social divide between town and country, yet the economics were slow to determine the politics. In 1936 Winifred Holtby's *South Riding* could still portray Carne, the local landowner, as fighting a rearguard paternalist action against the democratic methods used by rising businessmen and Methodist lay preachers in South Riding's local-government elections; at the level of local government, battles between land and business, town and country, long persisted. County boroughs sought to enhance their status, with more and more smaller but growing towns seeking to join them; county councils resisted any urban poaching of their lucrative outer-suburban ratepayers. So until 1974 there persisted what the Maud Commission called a 'pock-marked administrative pattern', with county councils' authority limited by the autonomous county boroughs in their midst.[54]

Helping to perpetuate them, and further hindering local government's interests from being represented in any co-ordinated way, were the associations of local authorities. The Maud Commission referred to five of them—representing county councils, municipal corporations, urban districts, rural districts, and parish councils—as 'seldom able to present a united front in dealings with central government or to take a collective initiative in national policies'.[55] The complaint was not new. Referring to the lawyer-dominated Association of Municipal Corporations, E. D. Simon in 1926 grumbled that 'a committee of lawyers is never likely to take a bold or imaginative line'.[56] The interest groups were all entrenched behind segments of the established structures, and no group had an interest in campaigning powerfully for something new. Nor did the reforms following the Maud Commission realize its hope that a single representative body for local government would emerge. The administrative and other pressures towards larger administrative units have never been welcomed by the smaller, as Rutland's tenacity in defending its autonomy shows. They were doubly damaging to local government's national influence because they forced government, with its ever-extending responsibilities, to bypass them by setting up new regional structures.

The persisting complexity of traditional local-government boundaries helps to explain what might otherwise be puzzling about the poll tax that was introduced in 1990: the failure of the Department of the Environment to consult relevant local-government officials before committing itself to the tax, and their subsequent failure to mobilize effectively against it.[57] The complexity also helps to explain why, as the Maud Commission put it, 'there is both ignorance of and indifference to local government on the part of the public', so that 'it is not uncommon to hear contempt expressed'. The ordinary citizen 'will often find two "town halls" next door to each other, one being the county borough, borough or urban district office, the other the rural district office; and the county office may be somewhere else in the same town. There is no correspondence between this welter of authorities and the realities of people's lives.'[58] The Commission's diagnosis led to the reforms of 1972 in England and Wales which brought to an end the long-standing administrative distinction between town and country, and substituted for the eighty-three county boroughs and fifty-eight county councils a new system of six metropolitan county councils and forty-seven county councils. This reform, implemented in 1974, may partly have solved the problem of irrelevant boundaries, but many thought that by adding a third layer to local government authorities and by laying such stress on managerial skills it made management more difficult and raised costs still higher. Add to this the restiveness caused by restructuring and the complexity of the new system, and one can see why these reforms were among the least popular among several unpopular measures stemming from an unpopular government.

The fact that apathy persisted after the early 1970s, though, shows that the Commission had by no means entirely scotched the problem. The vitality of local government was in decline partly because of earlier reforms that had in themselves been highly desirable. Local councils increasingly accessible to women and working men could not bestow the social cachet that had tempted so many able businessmen into Victorian civic politics. Likewise, a broadened local-government franchise seemed to devalue the vote and weaken its impact, as did the spreading belief in centralized planning and welfare that reflects Labour's supersession of the Liberals. In the early 1970s it looked as though a new enthusiasm for participation in local government might emerge as an indirect legacy of the Campaign for Nuclear Disarmament (CND) from the late 1950s, reinforced by disappointments on the left with the Wilson governments of the 1960s. 'Community action' and 'community politics' became vogue phrases on the left, and lent much energy to the Liberal revival in the 1960s and 1970s.[59] But the newly fashionable pressure groups and single-issue causes probably channelled more enthusiasm away from local-government institutions than they brought to them. Much more important causes of apathy must be the diminished sense of local community that stems from the wider social and economic changes discussed in Chapter 8—most notably, changed methods of communication and styles of recreation, and the growing size of towns. Loyalty to locality declined as interest and commitment bifurcated either to the newly emergent national political community or to the newly affluent and home-based nuclear family.

Hints of a way out from this impasse were thrown up in the course of the Thatcher governments' uncoordinated but innovative attempts at local-government reform. They were drawn into this area only gradually and unexpectedly.[60] Their interest in the subject owed little to public inquiries of a reflective kind, somewhat more to ideology, and much to party interest. The initial impulse, however, came from the need to curb inflation through reducing government expenditure. Not only was there a long-term tendency for local-authority expenditure to rise; the proportion of local-government revenue contributed by central-government grants was rising too: from 27 per cent in 1933 to 45 per cent in 1973. And because the proportion of households' disposable income spent on rates had remained static during the same period, the ratepayer's incentive to reduce expenditure was diminished.[61] So the local authorities were spending a rising proportion of national wealth[62] and absorbing a rising proportion of the national work-force (8.5 per cent of it by 1979[63]), at a time when the government wished to reduce both. Cuts in local spending were pursued the more vigorously because, like the privatization of state-run concerns, they advanced the government's overall strategy of promoting choice by preventing the cumulation of economic and political power.

The most direct way to cut local-authority expenditure was to expose its services to market competition. The pioneer and ideologist was Nicholas Ridley, convinced that 'inside every fat and bloated local authority there is a slim one struggling to get out'.[64] Thatcher's rejection of incomes policies and government wage regulation freed managers to respond to local conditions in all their diversity, and Ridley envisaged confining local authorities to enabling and monitoring contracted-out services rather than providing them directly. Compulsory competitive tendering was first introduced in 1980, and similar procedures were introduced into the National Health Service in 1983. The Local Government Act of 1987 required councils from July 1988 to invite tenders for (among other things) school meals, refuse collection, street-cleaning, and grounds and vehicle maintenance.[65] These reforms helped to ensure that Ridley was backed up at local level by what Conservatives saw as model local authorities—most notably in two London boroughs: Westminster (under the multi-millionairess daughter of the founder of Tesco, Shirley Porter) and Wandsworth, whose good management was frequently contrasted with alleged mismanagement in Labour's nearby Lambeth. Between 1979, when the Conservatives won control in

Wandsworth, and 1985, the Council's staff numbers fell by a third.[66] In 1987 Paul Beresford boasted that 'it is possible, by using ordinary commonsense, to produce high quality services at relatively low cost'.[67] Among local authorities by 1992, more than a quarter of contracts in refuse collection and street-cleaning had gone to the private sector, and almost a fifth of the market in vehicle maintenance.[68] Considerable savings had been made both through contracting out and when a council's own labour force had won the contract against outside competition. Perhaps more prominent among the government's motives than was publicly avowed was the consequential decline in the big public-sector trade unions.

The Thatcher governments' second approach to curbing local-authority expenditure was by regulating it from the centre. This immediately involved them in paradox, for their entrepreneurial values chimed in with Conservative instinct to curb central government. The new regime had after all begun in 1979 by sweeping away numerous Whitehall controls over local authorities, arrested the long-term decline in the proportion of local-government revenue raised from the rates,[69] and kept reform of the rating system itself in reserve. And any central regulation of local-government expenditure would embroil the Conservative government with the Labour-controlled and largely urban local authorities hostile to such curbs. Battle was joined, and the high points of this struggle were rate-capping for high-spending authorities in 1984 and abolition of the metropolitan county councils, including the Greater London Council in 1986. The struggle nourished a more direct Conservative interest in local-government reform, especially in the inner cities, and the conduct of Derek Hatton's socialists in Liverpool and Ken Livingstone's in London lent enough justification to the phrase 'loony left' for an attack on them to seem electorally worth while. Thatcher wanted to replicate Michael Edwardes's earlier achievement in the motor industry: to reach across unrepresentative intermediate bodies (including trade unions in both cases) to the individual. This meant establishing a direct relationship with the ratepayer, the parent, and the owner-occupier whose entrepreneurial and individual instincts Conservatives thought Labour-controlled authorities were repressing. If these could only be released, more Conservative votes could be purloined from Labour's natural supporters. Conventional wisdom was being turned on its head: just as trade unions were blamed for low pay and unemployment, so the Labour authority was blamed for decayed inner-city housing estates and shoddy welfare standards.[70]

This Conservative search for popular backing increased preoccupation with three areas of policy: education, housing, and reform of the rating system. On education and housing, Conservatives found themselves working with the grain of respectable working-class opinion and ineluctably drawn into unexpected reforms. The scandals at William Tyndale School, Islington in 1975 seemed to arise out of the progressive educational attitudes of the 1960s. Pioneered by Sir Keith Joseph's path-breaking speeches of 1974 and accelerated by Rhodes Boyson and Norman Tebbit, a Conservative onslaught on local-authority discretion gradually built up. 'A new battle for Britain is under way in our schools,' Thatcher declared. 'Labour's tattered flag is there for all to see, limp in the stale breeze of Sixties ideology.'[71] The combination of a campaign for discipline and higher standards with efforts to 'empower' the parents was formidable. Kenneth Baker said that in the balance of power between 'hub' and 'rim' in his reforms of state schooling after 1986, 'some favoured the LEAs being the rim, but for me the rim consisted of the individual schools and colleges', whereby 'real influence' would go to parents and children, 'the consumers of education'.[72] In further-education colleges, too, Baker's policy was to erode local-authority control.[73] As for the funding of universities, Baker's model was 'the pattern of American higher education, responsive to the market and to young people's demands, and growing from the bottom up rather than being imposed from the top down . . . Diversification and differentiation were the ways forward.'[74]

More powerful as an influence on attitudes to local government, because so obvious to all, were the mounting social problems resulting from the local-authority high-rise housing schemes of the 1950s and 1960s. The local-authority scandals of the 1970s worsened local government's image still further, for John Poulson's bankruptcy case in 1972 exposed the corrupt regime of Newcastle council leader T. Dan Smith and shed some discredit on local authorities' ambitious welfare schemes.[75] A shift in architectural fashion away from modernism accompanied this populist reaction against the planning schemes that had once seemed so high-minded. 'The schemes won a number of architectural awards,' Thatcher recalled in 1987. 'They were a nightmare for the people . . . they made people entirely dependent on the local authorities.'[76] The demand remained buoyant for privately built housing—low-rise, suburban, and owner-occupied—whereas from the late 1970s high-rise blocks only 21 years old were being blown up. Symbolic of the change was the destruction of Ronan Point in Canning Town, whose partial collapse in 1968 had first highlighted the problems of high-rise local-authority housing.[77] 'We talked of building units rather than homes,' said one MP.[78] In 1980 council tenants won the right to buy their homes, and their rights were extended later; in 1988 they were also given the right to choose a new landlord in place of the local housing authority. Another Conservative device was to bypass the local authorities with 'urban development corporations', the first of which were set up in 1981 for London's decaying docklands and for Merseyside. Centrally appointed and funded, these seemed successful enough for two more groups of development corporations to be set up in 1987–9.[79] Heseltine's second term at the Department of the Environment after 1990 carried the partnership between local government and industry into new and fruitful areas with the aid of the successful 'city challenge' scheme for government funding of inner-city development projects.[80]

Rating reform was something that governments had postponed tackling for many years, and to Thatcher it offered the double attraction of promoting economy and encouraging participation. Legislation of 1988 introduced the community charge (popularly known as the poll tax) which was imposed two years later. It was a tax upon people rather than upon property. Unfair in its incidence, impracticable in its administration, inept in its presentation, this reform was none the less concerned with a serious and continuing problem that transcended the mere raising of money. It sought to rejuvenate local government by diffusing the load of local expenditure throughout the local electorate, thereby encouraging electors to take more interest in what their local authorities were doing. There would be many rebates for those on low incomes, but even the net beneficiaries of local-government expenditure were required to pay something. Thatcher claimed that 'a whole class of people—an "underclass" if you will—had been dragged back into the ranks of responsible society and asked to become not just dependants but citizens'.[81] Ridley saw the poll tax as 'a logical step towards greater local authority freedom. It should allow us to stand much further back from local government because the electors will stand much closer'.[82] The ultimate objective was the informed voter, who in local-government elections would have both the information and the incentive to participate more fully. 'The whole system of local government finance worked to obscure the performance of individual authorities,' Thatcher recalled, whereas one of the 'inestimable benefits' of her reform would be to create a 'ready reckoner' which would expose high-spending authorities for what they were. The 'principle of accountability underlay the whole reform'.[83] Here, as elsewhere, Thatcherism in the 1980s wielded what the Webbs saw as 'the essential instruments of Democracy, Measurement and Publicity'[84] on behalf of policies the Webbs would hardly have approved. The medicine was ill concocted, the patient spurned the remedy, and Thatcher's power-base was eroded further.

We saw in Chapter 3 that in Scotland and Wales after the 1860s, and in Northern Ireland between 1920 and 1972, nationality as a cultural restraint on British central government was enhanced. Although direct rule was imposed in Northern Ireland thereafter, the change was made reluctantly and (in the eyes of the mainland government) temporarily. In local government, however, this Chapter has revealed a very different trend since the 1860s. While local-government authorities in Britain have never enjoyed autonomy, in Bagehot's day the presumption in the distribution of power lay in their favour. Long-term socio-economic change has subsequently eroded that presumption, while at the same time markedly extending the scope and volume of local-government responsibilities. This trend in policy ceased in 1979, after which a retreat from nationalization, from incomes policies and from centralized planning aimed to fragment and decentralize governmental power. The overriding short-term need to curb inflation, however, made temporary extensions of central financial control over local-authority expenditure seem necessary. Yet this did not mean that cultural pressures in Britain towards localism had disappeared, for the Thatcher governments then embarked on a search for ways of restraining local-authority expenditure which could accommodate such pressures. Among the 'Victorian values' Thatcher championed were those of the city fathers who did so much to embellish Victorian cities: 'there was a complete, almost a city state, a complete ideal—"This is our city",' she enthused, outlining her plans for the inner cities in November 1987.[85] What she did not explain was how the Chamberlain family's local commitment could re-emerge in the more secular and specialized Britain of the 1980s. It is no accident that her quest for it led her ultimately into the pulpit.

Her governments none the less tried more boldly to extend choice within the community than any of their twentieth-century predecessors. For their aim was not to ignore local opinion, but to give better effect to it in two ways that were eminently compatible with Conservative property-owning and privatized values. First, through bypassing allegedly unrepresentative Labour-dominated local authorities elected on a low turnout by extending the area of informed choice enjoyed by parents, trade unionists, householders, consumers, patients, ratepayers, doctors, teachers, and even university students. Then, somewhat late in the day, there followed an ambitious attempt to reinvigorate self-acting and ratepayer-driven curbs on local-authority expenditure; if the poll tax could secure better informed and less apathetic voters in local elections, central regulation could be relaxed. The attempt, in which much thought and political capital were invested, failed disastrously, but an unfinished agenda should not be allowed to mould any final assessment of Thatcher's attitude to British localism. Furthermore, the rightward direction Thatcher lent to British government in the 1980s had if anything the (unintended) effect of nourishing nationality as a cultural curb on what central government could do, and also the (perhaps intended) effect of reviving in the Labour Party the localism that Morrison, Bevin, and Bevan had subordinated after the 1930s. For all her anti-inflationary activism at the centre, reinforced by her impatience with opponents, Thatcher in local government had as her long-term aim the revival of the British libertarian tradition, whose further ramifications must now be discussed.

# 5

## *Rights and Liberties*

BRITAIN'S libertarian political culture owes much to the historical traditions and religious pluralism touched upon in Chapter 1, but also something to the ethnic and regional diversity discussed in Chapters 3 and 4.
Britain's civil society flourished the more for the fact that the established
church possessed no monopoly. Nor was the nation's voluntarist culture
threatened by urgent need for centralized defence against enemies without.
The monarchy had no patriotic excuse for aggrandizing itself. Restraints
on central government were strengthened further by the voluntary nature
of the union between England and Scotland in 1707. Less voluntary was
the union with Ireland in 1800, but the Irish grievance if anything helped
reinforce traditions of resistance to central government, and was later joined
by a growth in Welsh and Scottish national consciousness. Mill thought
it difficult to operate free institutions in a multinational state, whose government could so easily divide and rule.[1] Yet nineteenth-century Britain's
consortium of nations came close to realizing the balance between fragmentation and union which Bagehot thought necessary to progress. Such
a balance was 'only possible in those happy cases where the force of legal-
ity has gone far enough to bind the nation together, but not far enough
to kill out all varieties and destroy nature's perpetual tendency to change'.[2]
Twentieth-century Britain's continuing ethnic diversity has provided many
more tests of, and occasions for reaffirming, libertarian values.

The amount of liberty citizens in practice enjoy owes much more to
context, and much less to legislation, than it is fashionable to suppose.
Indeed, it is worth beginning with the truism that large areas of personal
liberty are beyond human control. 'If I say that I am unable to jump more
than ten feet in the air . . .', writes Sir Isaiah Berlin, 'it would be eccentric
to say that I am to that degree enslaved or coerced.'[3] Even where liberty
does depend on human agency, its advances are often unplanned and come

from unexpected directions. The creation of the Equal Opportunities Commission in 1975 was more the consequence than the cause of women's advance. And if childbearing is 'equivalent to a fifteen-year sentence of partial house arrest, without remission for good behaviour',[4] the spread of birth control entirely through individual voluntary choice, not planned by the state, has been a major twentieth-century advance for the freedom of women.

Shifts in residential patterns profoundly affect the incidence of liberty. Whereas nineteenth-century town life seemed dangerously anonymous for some, for others anonymity meant freedom. There was safety in numbers. 'London life', said Charles Booth, 'secures for all men the maximum freedom of conduct . . . To ask no questions is commonly regarded as the highest form of neighbourliness.'[5] Patterns of residence within the town were also of course relevant here: less privacy was enjoyed in the 1950s in overcrowded Bethnal Green, for instance, than in suburban Woodford.[6] For the liberty of some groups, the larger the city the better: those whose shared tastes were officially disapproved, for example. 'In the solitude of great modern cities', wrote Havelock Ellis, 'it is possible for small homosexual coteries to form, in a certain sense, an environment of their own, favorable to their abnormality.'[7] The city's size also brought emancipation from a single employer. In a small and friendly Lancashire town in the 1950s Mrs Glass thought her husband enjoyed less economic freedom than in London, where 'if he has words with the boss . . . he can walk out and get into another firm. In Lancashire there was only one firm in his trade.'[8] On the other hand, the move from country to town sometimes involved changing bad masters for worse. The Chartist Ernest Jones pointed out in 1852 that migrants from country to town sometimes mistakenly assumed that the great cotton lords would be their friends 'because they are not known, and happen to be enemies of the special tyrants of the rural population— the parsons, the nobles, and the squires'.[9]

Liberty was distributed differentially by social class, and changing class distribution affected its incidence. There was not necessarily more freedom higher up than lower down. For example, twentieth-century technology invaded the privacy of those in the public eye. Recalling his childhood in 1951, the Duke of Windsor said that 'one of the most inconvenient developments since the days of my boyhood has been the disappearance of privacy . . . Because our likenesses seldom appeared in the Press, we were not often recognized in the street; when we were, the salutation would be a friendly wave of the hand or, in the case of a courtier or family friend, a polite lifting of the hat.'[10] Until quite recent times, a shared reticence within the élite and a collusive reticence from the media gave much protection.

They enabled Harold Macmillan's career, for instance, to survive his wife's infidelities, though they could not free his (really Robert Boothby's) daughter Sarah from being pressed into an abortion in the early 1950s.[11] Nor did the Duke of Windsor's sequence of mistresses, an open secret within the élite, prevent his accession from being endorsed by those who later found moral grounds for demanding his abdication. All such reticence has now departed. There were perhaps too many hand-wringings in the Prince of Wales's televised documentary in June 1994, but it would be callous not to endorse his regrets that 'where ever you are there's somebody hiding behind something, somewhere' with their 'immense cameras . . . with these huge lenses and magnification'.[12] The middle-class child, too, suffered relative confinement in the nineteenth-century city. 'He went by with tousled hair and dirty face, a glorious figure of freedom in the rain,' wrote Compton Mackenzie of the working-class boy, 'walking jauntily' while Michael Fane watched him from the window when confined indoors on a rainy day. 'Michael envied him passionately, this untrammelled fence-banging whistling spirit . . . He watched the boy disappear round the farther corner, and wished that he could disappear in such company round corner after corner of the world beyond the grey housebacks.'[13] And while domestic service might bring many freedoms for the privileged classes, its decline in other respects enhanced the freedom and privacy of both employer and employee. 'There were many things we might not do,' Gwen Raverat recalled of her late-Victorian Cambridge household, 'not because they were wrong in themselves, but "because of the maids".'[14]

Occupational balance, by no means static since the 1860s, also affects the incidence of liberty. Some people sign away their freedom: soldiers subject themselves voluntarily to military law, civil servants and public employees sacrifice their political rights. In the 1870s there were about 5,000 desertions from the British army per year,[15] and flogging was not abolished till 1881—long after it had been abolished in France, Prussia, and the USA.[16] By the Police Act of 1919, special representation of police grievances through the Police Federation accompanied a no-strike agreement.[17] Since the mid-Victorian period, restraints on civil servants' political rights have been gradually relaxed, most notably in 1953, when 450,000 civil servants gained more freedom of political activity. Thenceforward 62 per cent of civil servants were free to engage in all forms of political activity short of blatantly violating public trust.[18] Politicians, too, however, were increasingly disciplined by party. Introducing his *Modern Democracies* in 1921, the Liberal politician James Bryce welcomed the new-found freedom that accompanied his transition from politics to scholarship: 'a man must have

profited little by his experience of political life if he is not heartily glad to
be rid of the reticences which a party system imposes and free to state with
equal candour both sides of every case'.[19]

Freedom of speech and association are particularly vulnerable in occupations where it is important to be discreet or conformist. Rejecting Western
libertarian criticism of Communist society, the Webbs in 1935 cited the
unfreedom in Britain of, say, farm labourers in country areas, shopkeepers
in small communities, and domestic servants in all circumstances.[20] But
the Webbs could just as well have cited the penalties of indiscretion in
professional people. The Queen brought up Professor Freeman's celebrated
phrase 'perish India' against him when candidate for the Oxford chair in
1884, and indiscreet anti-imperialist comments in a sermon in 1889 caused
Revd John Llewelyn Davies to be consigned for twenty years to the remote
living of Kirkby Lonsdale.[21] The scientist's freedom has long been curbed
by colleagues' pressures towards orthodoxy. In his *Origin of Species* Darwin
expressed confidence in the younger generation of naturalists, and urged
those who accepted the idea of mutability of species to help remove prejudice by saying so openly.[22] None the less, 'many are so fearful of speaking
out . . .', he told Fawcett in 1861; 'the naturalists seem as timid as young
ladies should be, about their scientific reputation'.[23] Since the 1860s scientists have also been monitored by uncomprehending laymen mobilized in
emotional campaigns: against the contagious diseases acts, vaccination, or
vivisection. A professor of psychology told the British Association in 1986
that in deploring terrorism organized by animal liberationists he had 'taken
a calculated risk in coming here, but I have a wife and children to consider
and there are some public meetings that I and other colleagues now refuse
to attend'.[24]

More powerful still in their implications for freedom (as Orwell often
stressed[25]) are the pressures towards orthodoxy among the intelligentsia.
Virginia Woolf in 1939 felt that 'all books now seem to me surrounded by
a circle of invisible censors', inducing self-consciousness in the writer, who
continually asks whether 'If I say this So & So will think me sentimental.
If that . . . will think me Bourgeois'.[26] Within universities, academic fashions can be more restrictive than any number of formal restraints on free
publication. William Cunningham, noting Marshall's dominance over
English economics in 1894, pointed out that nonconformists 'must expect
to be ostracized, and the tyranny of intellectual fashions is even more
supercilious than that of Bond Street and Savile Row'. Graham Hough,
criticizing logical positivism in 1947 for ousting philosophical preoccupation with ethics, noted that 'there are many methods of suppressing free

discussion, and to shoulder a certain class of arguments out of the accepted range of discussable subjects is one of them'.[27] More overtly intimidating were threats to free speech among university students during the 'student troubles' of the 1970s and 1980s. Some students so lacked confidence in their contemporaries that they tried to prevent them from hearing intelligent but uncongenial speakers such as Keith Joseph and Enoch Powell, whereas (as Orwell had pointed out) 'if liberty means anything at all it means the right to tell people what they do not want to hear'.[28]

Turning from liberty's broad socio-economic to its narrower political context, there is a certain circularity. Where methods of pressure are customarily non-violent, the right of public meeting is more secure. Where traditions of public argument are restrained and 'responsible', governments will be less tempted to censor. The Bishop of Down and Connor pointed out at the funerals of two Catholic victims of loyalist terrorism in 1993 that 'there is such a thing as verbal terrorism'; local leaders should remember that 'words can be violent . . . Words can kill.'[29] The advent of terrorism usually has the effect of enhancing police powers. Legislation on civil liberties often merely crystallizes and legitimizes social developments that have already occurred, and the role of formal libertarian documents in defending them is small. It would be quite wrong to assume that bills of rights are the only, or even the most important, influences upon civil liberties. The only area of the United Kingdom which has ever had civil rights entrenched—Northern Ireland after 1920—is the only area in which discrimination was widespread.[30]

Even if attention is narrowed to the political sphere, the incidence of liberty is moulded as much by political attitudes as by legislation. The Victorians assumed that a continuous stream of ideas and initiatives would be generated from outside government. 'We look on state action, not as our own action, but as alien action,' wrote Bagehot: 'as an imposed tyranny from without, not as the consummated result of our own organised wishes.'[31] Self-regulation—of the press, of universities, of the professions—often seemed preferable to state regulation, and barriers were continuously erected against officials, the police, and civil servants. This tradition still holds the British state at bay. As Lord Stow Hill put it in 1970, in a debate on the idea of a bill of rights, the defence of freedom is to be found 'with the protestors against almost everything: the firm-voiced male and female in Trafalgar Square, in the Albert Hall, in Hyde Park, or carrying heavy banners along draughty streets in any of our great cities . . . I think it resides in the Nonconformist conscience. I think it resides in the long-haired student, in the lunatic fringe in all Parties.'[32] He stressed the

importance of parliament as defender of British liberties: 'I have complete
confidence in the Back Bench Member rising in his fury from his place
and . . . "raising hell" if a Minister on the Front Bench seeks to offend
against the basic freedoms.'[33]

Of all the political institutions moulding the incidence of liberty, political parties are the most pervasive and have encouraged the most notable
shifts in attitude since Bagehot's day. Liberty was more central to the
Liberal Party than to either Conservatives or Labour. Victorian Liberal individualism was a powerful philosophy, with ample potential for twentieth-
century growth. Liberals were especially concerned with religious freedom.
In Bagehot's day the Church of England provided a framework for cultural and social life, especially in the countryside. Catholics, Jews, dissenters, and secularists needed defence against its privileges, and non-Anglican
MPs remained overwhelmingly Liberal at least till the home rule crisis
of 1886, when Liberal Unionism enabled some nonconformists eventually
to join the Conservatives. Mid-Victorian Liberal concern with religious
freedom opened up large rural opportunities for the Party. 'The growth of
cities has . . . been a main cause of the decline of ecclesiastical power,'
wrote that ardent libertarian H. T. Buckle.[34] Liberalism could readily base
itself on the relative freedom of the 'open' village, whence it could undermine the Conservative hold on the 'closed' village where squire and parson
were dominant. It was in rural areas, too, that subordinate nationalities
could be championed, with landlord dominance to be thrown off in Wales,
in the Highlands of Scotland, and throughout southern Ireland. It was a
characteristically Liberal beginning to a career when Lloyd George in 1888
took up the case of a nonconformist whose local rector refused him the
right to bury his daughter in the village churchyard. By then disestablishment was waning as a Liberal asset, but secularization involved transfer-
ring a religious fervour to many other progressive causes. There was much
Liberal mileage in defending the unbeliever, for instance. J. S. Mill, who
had been urged by his father not to weaken his influence by publicizing
his lack of faith, pointed out that in the 1850s 'real belief in any religious
doctrine is feeble and precarious, but the opinion of its necessity for moral
and social purposes almost universal'.[35] Progressive Liberals wanted social
stability founded upon reason rather than religion, and put their trust in
the positivist and ethical movements that were so prominent in Victorian
intellectual life. These substitute faiths often turned out to be agnosticism
in disguise, with the additional attraction of Malthusian, humanitarian,
and feminist accoutrements.

At the heart of Liberalism lay an almost anarchist distrust of government and the belief that a properly educated society would be almost self-directing. Many of its activists—nonconformists distant from government, temperance reformers careless of social convention, autodidacts indifferent to wealth and status—pursued their freedom not by advancing into the political arena but by staging a half-retreat from it and reducing their wants. Liberal feminism, for example, saw men voluntarily divesting themselves of power in response to rational and libertarian ideas. 'The whole mode of thought of the modern world', Mill wrote, 'is, with increasing emphasis, pronouncing against the claim of society to decide for individuals what they are and are not fit for.'[36] It was through Josephine Butler's attack between 1869 and 1886 on state-regulated prostitution (involving compulsory inspection and sometimes hospitalization) that Victorian Liberals most vigorously championed women's liberties. But legislation could do little to remove what Florence Nightingale described as 'the petty grinding tyranny of a good English family',[37] nor can legislators be credited with the liberation that Edwardian middle-class women discovered in open-air sport and the teashop. The campaign to give women the vote did, however, have implications for women's status—though A. V. Dicey rightly warned the public against the sentimental implication of labelling votes for women as women's 'enfranchisement' or even 'emancipation': that women had hitherto been in bondage.[38] Owing much to the anti-slavery movement, the campaign began among Liberals, and especially with Mill. For him, in 1848, 'the domestic life of domestic tyrants is one of the things which it is the most imperative on the law to interfere with'.[39] He later published the foundation document of British feminism, *The Subjection of Women* (1869), and the leading late-Victorian parliamentary spokesmen for women's suffrage were all Liberals: Courtney, Fawcett, and Dilke.[40] Some Liberals, including Asquith, opposed women's suffrage of course, but their number was declining, and they were not the main reason for the Liberal governments' conflict with the suffragists between 1905 and 1914. That conflict stemmed rather from the fact that progressive Liberals preferred enfranchising women in virtue of their status as human beings—that is, through adult suffrage—rather than through duplicating the anomalies of the property franchise, which was in effect what the suffragists were proposing.[41] Nor could a consistent Liberal allow a violent minority to coerce an elected government, which in effect was what the militant sub-group of the suffragist movement was trying to secure.

Liberal individualism was continually finding new beneficiaries. Deprived minority groups were and are continually discovering themselves or being discovered: children, lunatics, homosexuals, prostitutes, and oppressed groups that are yet to make themselves manifest. Bentham even envisaged animals as one day acquiring rights.[42] Further worlds for Liberals to conquer spread out within the empire. For the colonies of white settlement, devolution was a means of self-education and of drawing dependent communities into a sense of responsibility. As for the colonies of non-white settlement, true Liberals denied that any community had the right to force 'civilization' on another. They thought that if there must be a choice, self-government was in the long term preferable to good government; devolution was itself a way of 'civilizing' subordinate peoples. We now know that the long-term price of civilization was the dissolution of empire, accelerated by that other powerful Liberal cause, Irish home rule. 'What fools we were not to have accepted Gladstone's Home Rule Bill,' George V told Ramsay MacDonald in 1930. 'The Empire now would not have had the Irish Free State giving us so much trouble and pulling us to pieces.'[43] Racial equality, closely linked to the Liberal belief in the free movement of peoples, also needed to be defended within the empire and, after its twentieth-century disruption had dispatched Commonwealth immigrants to the United Kingdom, at home as well.

One might at first sight suppose that the move from individualism to collectivism was the same thing as the move from Liberal to Labour. Mid-Victorian libertarians now seem curiously indifferent to the economic dimension of their subject, for example. Bagehot was quite unconcerned in 1863 at the fact that 'the propertied class . . . influences the press'. He thought that because 'its weight is always in favour of the order and decency without which political life soon becomes a mad strife of factions, it is well that it should'.[44] In 1921 James Bryce saw himself, in his preoccupation with political institutions rather than social reconstruction, as writing a book 'addressed rather to the last than to the present generation. That generation busied itself with institutions; this generation is bent rather upon the purposes which institutions may be made to serve.'[45] Yet the principles of Victorian Liberals, even as enunciated by Mill, did not preclude collectivism. Liberals had much more potential for collectivism, Labour more continuity with Liberalism, than is often realized. Many mid-Victorians, impatient with the cruelty, oppression, and poverty they saw around them, wanted a quick remedy, and T. H. Green (alarmed at the incidence of drunkenness[46]) was among them. Their half-way house on the road to collectivism took the form of promoting the moral collectivism of philanthropy and the civic virtues—of carrying into national politics the puritan values of the nonconformist chapel. This variant of collectivism gradually lost its moralism, but a Liberal like Green was tempted into thinking that state intervention—at least as a short-term and emergency measure—might actually help to create the type of self-directing, prudent personality that the high-minded Liberal admired. Especially as, after the Reform Acts of 1832 and 1867, and after Catholics, Jews, and dissenters had been emancipated, the state no longer seemed in enemy hands, and could be trusted with an enhanced role.

Green's argument in his *Liberal Legislation and Freedom of Contract* (1881) had three stages. He began by pointing out that Liberals had first concentrated on removing obstacles to the free flow of trade and talent, whereas after 1868 the Party had embarked on interventionism with compulsory education and health regulation—that is, on a 'positive' concept of liberty. Secondly, Green justified this shift by lending priority to the citizen's moral growth. A society's progress should be measured 'by the greater power on the part of the citizens as a body to make the most and best of themselves'.[47] Whereas in the ideal world it might be desirable for men to look after themselves, 'we must take men as we find them', and at present the 'degraded population' was perpetuating itself and even expanding. So no contract should be valid which prevented the individual from contributing to the common good—contracts, for example, which required him to damage his health. And although the state might not be able to promote moral goodness directly, it could at least create the conditions within which genuinely free choices could be made. In the third stage of his argument, Green tried to apply his conclusions. He cited early-Victorian factory legislation as a precedent for intervening in the free contract between individual citizens. Each generation of 'new Liberals' (including Gladstone, who had a talent for perpetual personal self-renewal) applied this insight to widening spheres. Green wanted the state to modify the free contract between landlord and tenant so as to encourage the tenant (especially in Ireland) to improve his land. He wanted the tenant protected against the landlord's game-birds, so that a peasant class could grow. And the state should curb drunkenness (harmful not only to the drunkard but also to his family and neighbours) by enabling ratepayers to reduce the number of pubs in their localities.

To us this argument for the advance of the state seems timid, too preoccupied with arresting an inevitable drift from the land, and impracticably enthusiastic for the direct promotion of morality. But Green and many late-Victorian Liberals expected a moralized and therefore law-abiding population to reduce its demands on the state. 'Manners are of more importance than laws,' said Burke. 'Upon them, in a great measure, the laws depend.'[48] Once intervention was embarked upon for whatever reason, however, its potential for extension was endless, and by the 1880s liberty's political location was beginning to become unclear. The number of prosecutions for offending against recent legislation—on education, vaccination, and health regulations, for example—was mounting,[49] and to restrain it the more conservative type of late-Victorian libertarian formed the Liberty and Property Defence League. 'The function of Liberalism in the past was that of putting a limit to the powers of kings,' wrote the prominent radical Herbert Spencer. 'The function of true Liberalism in the future will be that of putting a limit to the powers of Parliaments.' Yet as soon as a public figure prefixes the word 'true' to his party label, one can be sure that he is preparing to decamp. Presciently, Spencer complained that 'if the present drift of things continues, it may by and by really happen that the Tories will be defenders of liberties which the Liberals, in pursuit of what they think popular welfare, trample under foot'.[50] Green's significance for the future lay in the fact that late-Victorian and Edwardian Liberals applied his collectivist insights very much more widely than he. As we have seen in Chapter 4, even late-Victorian Liberals were ready to interfere with the free market provided that this was done at the local level. Edwardian Liberals moved further, and took their welfare interventionism to the national level, though as we saw in Chapter 2 they accompanied it with moral safeguards. Behind the Edwardian Liberal welfare reforms lay the idea of denying the 'unemployable' their citizen rights, including civil freedom and the vote—though such moralistic interpretations of poverty were abandoned when the First World War showed that no such class of citizen really existed. Under Lloyd George's leadership in the 1920s it was the Liberal Party which took the initiative in applying the doctrines of Keynes and in proposing the use of state machinery to redress random fluctuations in the economy. The worlds of morality and welfare were gradually drifting apart, though Liberals never entirely ceased to hope that a welfare-protected environment would eventually generate the individualist type of personality they so greatly valued.

So in libertarian and welfare matters, the gulf between Liberals and Labour is less clear than might at first sight be supposed. Besides, Labour gained much from the civil liberties which Victorian Liberals pioneered. The early British socialists were free to recruit far more openly than socialists under more authoritarian regimes. In challenging powerful economic orthodoxies they inevitably drifted into championing traditional liberal freedoms like the right of public meeting and freedom of association. After a struggle with police to hold the 'bloody Sunday' meeting in Trafalgar Square in November 1887, W. T. Stead organized a 'law and liberty league' to help the victims.[51] Labour harboured many of those spiky and independent critics of authority who had earlier called themselves Liberals. The early Labour Party had at least as much reason as any Liberal to cultivate the self-disciplined, self-denying type of spokesman for working people who could be relied upon to stand up to authority: the respectable, teetotal, independent-minded artisan.

So from the USSR's point of view the British labour movement's instincts were far too libertarian. The anti-Liberal rhetoric of Marx and Engels had been mounted in the 1840s, when the Liberal Party was in its most individualist phase. 'A fine freedom indeed', wrote Engels, 'when the worker has no choice but to accept the terms offered by the middle classes or go hungry and naked like the wild beasts.'[52] In a letter strongly criticizing British labour leaders' enthusiasm for democracy, civil liberties, and peace, Lenin pointed out that 'the freedom of the Press and assembly in a *bourgeois* democracy is tantamount to the freedom of the well-to-do to plot against the working people. It means freedom of bribing and buying up newspapers by the capitalists.'[53] Anti-Liberal rhetoric was taken up after 1917 by the Labour Party, but it was by then a party with an interest in caricaturing the position of its predecessor on the left as Gladstonian and backward-looking. In reality, organized labour before 1914 had been happily united with the Liberal Party in a progressive alliance. Victorian Liberals had never had to confront such things as Communism and Fascism. As one of their last survivors, Bertrand Russell, wrote gloomily in the postscript to his autobiography, Communism and Fascism had 'successively challenged all that I thought good, and in defeating them much of what their opponents have sought to preserve is being lost. Freedom has come to be thought weakness, and tolerance has been compelled to wear the garb of treachery.'[54]

The Labour Party was a vehicle for integrating class-conscious working people into the British political system, and in its earlier years was narrower than the Liberal Party. It put more stress on material issues, less on issues that were moral, religious, and strictly libertarian in nature. It had less room for the rationalist type of middle-class radical intellectual, with his somewhat ascetic and abstract zeal for liberty. And although it may have alerted the legal profession to the importance of justice to working people in questions such as legal aid,[55] it was wary of the judges, whose concern was to defend the individual against the group.[56] Trade-union history and watered-down Marxian ideas made Labour less ready than the Liberals to accept that neutrality was feasible, especially from judges, and less keen on arbitration in industrial disputes. 'If the freedom of the people of this country . . . had been left to the good sense and the fairmindedness of judges', said Michael Foot in 1977, 'we would have precious few freedoms in this country.' For Foot, as for many Labour leaders, freedom's defence lay only with voluntary action, reinforced by parliament,[57] so that 'the dialectic between hostile judicial decisions and protective statutes is the basis of our collective labour law'.[58] In the 1970s and 1980s a labour movement steeped in its own history repeatedly cited precedents for refusal to obey unjust laws,[59] and analogies with Tolpuddle were readily drawn when dockers were at risk of imprisonment for resisting the Conservatives' industrial relations legislation.[60] Labour was as much concerned with collective as with individual liberty, and was happy to mobilize its influence in parliament against the judges. Indeed, Labour's class loyalty seemed to offer a mounting threat to liberty, and Liberals were apprehensive of trade unions' sectionalism and capacity for intimidating minorities. The desire simultaneously to uphold liberty through group action and to defend the individual against the group is perennial, and was controversial enough in the area of industrial relations to help split the National Council for Civil Liberties wide apart in 1985.[61]

The Labour Party's economic perspective made it more alert than the Liberals to the threat to press freedom that stemmed from patterns of ownership and advertising policy. 'Especially during the stage of transition from a predominantly capitalist to a predominantly Socialist society', wrote the Webbs in 1920, 'it may be necessary to prohibit the publication of newspapers with the object of private profit, or under individual ownership, as positively dangerous to the community.'[62] Conservative libertarians were given some ammunition in 1972, 1974, 1977, and 1982 when trade unionists in press and Post Office used their strike weapon to restrict what newspapers could print, to insist on a right of reply, or to disrupt free telephone communication.[63] Michael Meacher claimed in 1982 that 'it took "blacking" action by Aslef members at Kings Cross to secure a right of reply to *The Sun*'s front-page and uncorroborated and indiscriminate allegations' about railmen.[64] In 1986 the attempt of Labour-controlled public libraries to ban Murdoch's newspapers, then in dispute with the printers' unions, led to defeat in a lawsuit during which Lord Justice Watkins pronounced the Labour councils' conduct 'a glaring example of abuse of power'.[65]

The Labour Party was, in truth, a strange amalgam of collectivism and individualism. Collectivism was welcome in nationalization but not in conscription.[66] Labour believed in 'planning', yet inherited much of the Liberals' wariness of authority. In Chapter 2 we have already observed this tension within British inter-war Labour leaders between statist socialist theory and libertarian instinct.[67] Their dilemma reflected the substantial impact made by non-statist variants of socialism—municipal, communitarian, and co-operative—on the early Labour Party. William Morris thought the phrase 'state socialism' self-contradictory, for it was 'the business of Socialism to destroy the State and put Free Society in its place'.[68] Whereas for many nineteenth-century nonconformists the state represented the denominational enemy, for many twentieth-century working people it represented the class enemy. Reinforcing such ideas were more practical considerations: Labour was better entrenched at local than at national level, and so tended to ward off central government. Not until it joined the Second World War coalition government did Labour fully appropriate the Liberals' collectivist legacy; only then did wartime experience show what wonders the state machine could perform. Thereafter, Labour's statism was unembarrassed, and its corporatist programme from the 1960s to the mid-1980s threatened freedom at some points, even the freedom of trade unions. Criticizing Conservative freedom as freedom only for the few, Labour's manifesto of 1987 echoed T. H. Green with its aim 'to broaden and deepen the liberty of all individuals in our community to free people from poverty, exploitation and fear; to free them to realise their full potential'.[69]

Yet in appropriating Liberal collectivism, Labour did not neglect those aspects of individualist Liberalism with potential for growth. Between the wars Labour was bidding for the votes of left-wing Liberals, and empire and foreign policy provided what seemed, at least in the short term, electorally more fertile ways of doing this than domestic reforms—let alone domestic reforms of a statist type. So in 1916 the Labour MPs joined many Liberals in opposing conscription, just as in the 1920s both held out against protection. Labour also took up much of the Liberals' democratic and humanitarian mission, and defended subordinate peoples within the empire against their masters. Thereafter Labour MPs carried forward the Liberal defence of women against male domination, of employees against the less progressive type of employer, and of subordinate ethnic groups against race prejudice. Labour carries forward to this day the Victorian radical's alertness to infringements of liberty by the police and his preoccupation with the rights of minorities.

Labour's middle-class recruits after 1945 encouraged it cautiously to take up Mill's project for encouraging 'different experiments of living'.[70] While economic collectivism during the twentieth century has advanced, moral collectivism has retired. In extending personal liberty, middle-class intellectuals have been prominent: authors, psychologists, and artists like Havelock Ellis, Bertrand Russell, and Edward Carpenter. Many were active in the early socialist societies, but their ideas by no means always attracted Labour's working-class following. Until the 1950s the latter was large enough, and its economic priorities urgent enough, to subordinate this subversive middle-class element. But Tony Crosland in 1956 and Roy Jenkins in the 1960s lent it more influence. The law on divorce, licensing, abortion, censorship, and sex, wrote Crosland, 'should be highly offensive to socialists, in whose blood there should always run a trace of the anarchist and the libertarian, and not too much of the prig and the prude'.[71] With Jenkins championing the permissive society in the mid-1960s, Labour's identification with moral individualism grew closer. The removal of taboos, the challenge to formality and etiquette, the advance of sexual freedom, the assertion that we have a right to control over our own bodies— all were Liberal causes that from the 1960s onwards were taken up somewhat nervously by individual Labour MPs, if not always by the Labour Party.

In 1964 Bernard Crick noted that the very concept of 'civil liberties', which 'until quite recently seemed somewhat un-British', was now 'on everyone's lips'.[72] At that time it was Labour which profited from the new climate. Lord Gardiner when Labour Lord Chancellor pointed out that 'if you look at the bodies which are really concerned with civil liberties, bodies like the National Council for Civil Liberties, the people who are doing all the work are nearly all Liberal and Labour. You do not find the Conservatives doing the work.'[73] During the 1970s, however, the Conservatives began to poach on this part of Labour's ground. Alert to this by 1972, Shirley Williams insisted that 'we should not allow the Conservative Party to claim that it is the party of individual liberty, for indeed its record is much less impressive than our own'.[74] Labour did not listen, which helps to explain why she and others decided to secede nine years later into the Social Democratic Party. The intrusiveness of Labour government planning, especially through incomes policies, made individualism a growing electoral asset to Conservatives in the 1960s and 1970s, for belief in individual liberty has never been confined to the privileged. As Orwell pointed out in 1941, liberty in England means 'the liberty to have a home of your own, to do what you like in your spare time . . . The most hateful of all names in an English ear is Nosey Parker.'[75] The extraordinarily ambitious attempt to plan the nation's wage structure stirred up enemies for Labour in its own trade-union camp, and Heath's backbenchers branded the two-year Conservative experiment along the same lines in 1972–4 as an aberration. Nigel Lawson complained in February 1978 that Labour's incomes policy was leading secret cabinet committees arbitrarily to infringe the liberty of citizens. 'We censure the Government . . .', said James Prior in December, 'because they are using arbitrary and discriminatory powers without Parliamentary authority and the demands of common justice. We can win the fight against inflation but not at the expense of freedom and democracy itself.'[76] Prior's worries had already been anticipated at the heart of the Labour government, for a week earlier the Prime Minister had admitted in cabinet that 'the use of powers without parliamentary authority is weighing on my conscience a little'.[77] The long-term effect of the SDP's secession was to force Labour back towards a more libertarian centre, but this resumed quest for centre opinion was not evident till after the general election of 1987, and meanwhile the Conservatives had espoused liberty from a quite different direction.

Conservatives rarely defend liberty in the abstract, for their instincts are pragmatic. Citizens' liberties, said Burke, 'vary with times and circumstances, and admit of infinite modifications, they cannot be settled upon any abstract rule; and nothing is so foolish as to discuss them upon that principle.'[78] Besides, many Conservatives share Oakeshott's view that 'the major part of mankind has nothing to say; the lives of most men do not revolve round a felt necessity to speak'[79]—a view which echoed Bryce's remark to Dicey in 1920 that 'the root error of Democracy lies in the assumption that every citizen has an opinion'.[80] Any defence of liberty in the abstract would also offend against the Conservative's belief that human nature requires monitoring by authority's watchful eye. Conservatives know that liberty can be enjoyed only in conjunction with public order and morality. They are more inclined than Liberals and Labour to see the police and the army as aids rather than threats to liberty; their eye rests more alertly on the dope-peddler and the man with the bomb than on the corrupt policeman and the soldier who exceeds his instructions. Hence the banning of media interviews with the IRA between 1988 and 1994. At the Guildhall in November 1988, Thatcher quoted from a letter sent her by the mother of a young serviceman killed by the IRA. 'Where is the freedom of the press? I hear them cry. Where is my son's freedom?'.[81] In 1989 all Thatcher's hackles rose when the French in their bicentennial celebrations emphasized their revolution's role in upholding liberty. Human rights 'did not begin with the French Revolution,' she told *Le Monde*; they stem 'from a mixture of Judaism and Christianity'. Britain's 'quiet revolution' of 1688 was very different from the French Revolution, which, she thought, 'forgot obligations and duties'.[82] For her nineteenth-century predecessors, social discipline had rested on the established church and the firm stamp of governmental authority, but Thatcher's resources in a democratic and secularized society were more limited. In 1990 she was still countering Labour's preoccupation with the material environment by stressing the need for the right 'environment of values'.[83]

None the less, Thatcher's Conservatism owes much to Liberalism, if only because statist socialism alerted her Party to the dangers of over-mighty government. Much of the impetus behind twentieth-century Conservative individualism comes from recruiting rightward-moving individualists like Alderman Roberts, her father. Conservative individualism became prominent in the 1920s when the Party was bidding for the Liberals' individualist legacy and standing out against the collectivism of Lloyd George. But this individualism interacted continuously with the Party's older and more paternalist traditions to provide it with a convenient ambiguity and flexibility. Individualist Conservatism tends to surface only at moments when the Party thinks it compatible with winning elections, most notably in 1970–2 and in 1981–90. Not that Conservative paternalism was ever strongly statist in tone. Disraeli's Conservatism, for instance, was wary of centralization, both because of the early-Victorian Party's strongly rural base, and because the Party's traditionalism led it to distrust 'improving' officials. The interventionism of his social-reform measures was never ambitious. Victorian Conservatives also feared the corruptions of big-city life, and the instability that would be imported into the political system by making a Paris out of London. The Liberals' devolutionary safeguard against government power was less to Conservatives' taste. They were keener on the Liberals' complementary approach: separating economic from political power. The Liberals' famous policy statement of 1928 known as the yellow book described the Liberal goal as one 'in which everybody will be a capitalist, and everybody a worker, as everybody is a citizen'.[84] Twentieth-century Conservative individualists did not disagree, and showed a Liberal zeal for the idea of everyone acquiring 'a stake in the country'. The 'property-owning democracy' ideal, prominent in the Party's appeal by the 1950s, was also thought likely to bring moral benefits by extending choice and cultivating independence. 'I very much want every man and woman to be a capitalist', said Thatcher in May 1977, 'because then they will have the means to support their own decisions, the means to stand up to someone in authority.'[85]

In the 1980s Thatcher carried her Party into the most vigorous promotion of Conservative individualism to date, at the same time as conducting a less obtrusive attack on the Party's traditionalist patrician image. This new-style liberalized Conservatism saw individual enterprise as enfranchising the consumer against monopolistic firm and feather-bedded trade unionist, and aimed to leave as much wealth as possible fructifying in the pockets of the people. A Liberal moralism also returned with a vengeance, for the retreat of the state was linked to the encouragement of initiative and respectability through the citizen's continuous exercise of choice. 'Individualism and responsibility', said Thatcher in 1981, 'are the springs of our prosperity, as well as the foundations of our moral order.'[86] Powell had already taken this position to extremes in his view of traffic issues. In 1973 he opposed compelling motor-cyclists to wear crash-helmets: 'the maintenance of individual responsibility is more important than the loss of lives as the result of the individual decision of the person who is lost'.[87] He took a similar line in 1976 on proposals to enforce the wearing of seat-belts. If this principle were conceded, he predicted 'an increasingly irresistible pressure' discouraging people from taking care for their own safety, so that 'one area of personal decision after another' would be brought within the criminal law.[88] The tangible evidence in the short term gave Powell little support: seat-belts became compulsory on 31 January 1983, and during the rest of the year saved 700 lives and prevented between 5,000 and 7,000 serious injuries.[89] The long-term drawbacks of the change he opposed are impossible to measure.

For theoretical underpinning, Conservatives in the 1970s went to a European Liberal: F. A. von Hayek. As an Austrian refugee to Britain from Fascism, and a devotee of Liberal classical economics, Hayek did what Conservatives rarely do: he wrote a book outlining his philosophy. Until the 1970s nobody thought of him as an important influence on modern Conservatism. His *The Road to Serfdom* (1944) was dedicated 'to the socialists of all parties', and was written because he was alarmed at the way socialist ideas were spreading even within the Conservative Party. The book caused 'fury' in certain circles in Britain when first published, and he 'was made to feel by most of my fellow social scientists that I had used my abilities on the wrong side'.[90] Hayek deplored the fall from fashion of the great Victorian Liberal thinkers such as Dicey, Morley, and Acton: 'it is scarcely an exaggeration to say that the more typically English a writer on political or social problems then appeared to the world, the more is he to-day forgotten in his own country'.[91] Libertarian ideas, he claimed, had probably travelled their furthest eastward by 1870; thereafter British liberalism began retreating before westward-pushing illiberal ideas from Germany. 'England lost her intellectual leadership in the political and social sphere and became an importer of ideas.'[92] Hayek wrote in 1944 as a beleaguered author who felt profoundly unpopular with the intelligentsia because he retained the classical economists' suspicion of state planning. His book gained a sense of urgency because he felt he was witnessing for the second time in his life developments which on the first occasion, when he was a young man in Austria in the 1920s, had led to the rise of Fascism.

The interventionists under attack were of course well-intentioned, but as Milton Friedman later pointed out, 'concentrated power is not rendered harmless by the good intentions of those who create it'.[93] In *The Road to Serfdom* Hayek argued that those whose benevolence invokes the aid of the state soon find themselves riding a tiger. He fully conceded that the state must help to create the conditions within which commerce can freely operate (by establishing public order and a legal framework, for instance) and must also promote welfare measures to help those who cannot to defend their own interests. But a certain amount of personal security must be sacrificed to ensure that the free market operates in the industrial and commercial sector. He feared that the state, once it tried to manipulate the market, would be ineluctably drawn into further and further regulation. And such intervention, by combining political with economic power, threatened liberty because it involved 'the substitution of power from which there is no escape for a power which is always limited'.[94] Joseph took up this theme in 1976, when he argued that only in a society where property ownership is dispersed can the dissident writer (Marx, for example) find a patron.[95]

Such ideas provided points of Conservative access to the working-class voter: to customers starved of choice and service; to budding entrepreneurs regulated out of existence; to trade unionists deterred by incomes policies from preserving their differentials. As early as 1965 Powell had embraced the enfranchisement of the consumer, arguing that 'everyone who goes into a shop and chooses one article instead of another is casting a vote in the economic ballot box'.[96] Whereas the voter can vote only at intervals for a package not all of which is acceptable, wrote Friedman, the consumer can daily choose exactly what he wants: 'the ballot box produces conformity without unanimity; the marketplace, unanimity without conformity'.[97] Robert Carr took up the message when attacking the Prices and Incomes Board in July 1970, declaring that 'competition . . . is the most effective means of safeguarding the consumer'.[98] As for trade unionists, according to Friedman, 'the most reliable and effective protection for most workers is provided by the existence of many employers',[99] for in the free market they can always push up wages (other things being equal) by threatening to take their labour elsewhere. Given their traditional Labour sympathies, such individualism could not be corporately espoused by trade unionists, but it lay deeply buried within their structure and nobody could stop individual trade unionists from endorsing it in the voting booth.

Hayek claimed that in a free-enterprise state economic power is not in government hands, is never complete, and never controls the entire life of the individual. For him, the encouragement of economic growth was intimately linked to the defence of liberty: the two ran together. In this Hayek was later echoed by Friedman, whose *Capitalism and Freedom* pointed out how free competition makes it plain to employers that it is too expensive to discriminate against particular groups in the community: the competitive firm needs talent wherever it can be found. 'It is a striking historical fact that the development of capitalism has been accompanied by a major reduction in the extent to which particular religious, racial, or social groups have operated under special handicaps in respect of their economic activities.'[100] This approach, too, was taken up by Conservatives after 1975, sceptical as many of them were about legislating in the area. The Labour government had set up the Race Relations Board in 1966 and the Community Relations Commission in 1968, and there were advocates of positive discrimination and 'black sections' within the Labour Party. By contrast, the official view[101] of Conservatives under Thatcher, with some Jewish support,[102] was that of Lord Scarman: that positive discrimination was 'very dangerous ground'[103] because it risked fomenting resentment. Conservatives emphasized instead the integrating impact of entrepreneurial values. Their approach was somewhat crudely expressed in the advertisement placed in the ethnic-minority press during the general election campaign of 1983. It showed a well-dressed black man with the caption 'To Labour he's black, to Conservatives he's British'.[104]

Hayek went on to argue that state intervention threatens democracy because it inflates electors' expectations of government. Socialist governments' efforts to meet the electors' expectations lead them ineluctably towards increasingly desperate and diminishingly humane ways of enforcing their policies. Their long-term humane objectives are increasingly held to justify the ruthless short cut, and the good of the individual succumbs before 'the good of the whole'.[105] This corrupts individual morality, at the level of both citizen and government, and disillusionment with democracy follows. So Hayek concluded that democratic and humanitarian values can survive only through the fragmented sovereignty which a free-enterprise economy makes possible. Stressing the limits to human capacity, he pointed out that amid the complexities of modern civilization, no one person or group of people can survey all the facts necessary to co-ordinate the economy through central planning. Only the free market and the price system, as indicators of demand and supply, can achieve this feat. There can be no such thing as 'the general interest' as a guide to government policy.[106]

The political climate of the mid-1940s was not at all favourable to Hayek's ideas. The fashion then was for employing in peacetime the interventionist methods that seemed to have been so successful in the Second World War. The Conservative Party, defeated at the general election of 1945, then sought to shake off the hard-line image it had acquired between the wars. Having jettisoned appeasement in foreign policy, the Conservative governments between 1951 and 1964 embraced appeasement at home. Only when intervention seemed, in the 1960s and 1970s, to create at least as many problems as it solved, did Hayek's ideas gain ground. There had always been a certain Conservative backbench restiveness at the Butskellite ideas that prevailed from 1945 to the late 1960s. In a brief foretaste of what was to come, the Heath government in its first two years espoused individualism, but only selectively, as Jenkins pointed out in 1972. Their economic individualism did not prevent them from having 'bitterly resisted the growth of greater legal tolerance in the field of personal conduct', or from 'instinctively regard[ing] a young man with long hair as a greater enemy of society than a factory owner who pollutes a river'.[107] In the peculiar circumstances of 1974–5 Conservative backbench restiveness at last erupted. In words that could have been Hayek's, Tebbit told the Conservative Party conference in October 1984 that the government's denationalization programme was 'driven by a belief that to combine economic power and political power in the same hands constitutes a needless and unacceptable risk'.[108] Looking back over her career in 1993, Thatcher felt that 'all my reading, thinking and experience has taught me that once the state plays fast and loose with economic freedom, political freedom risks being the next casualty'.[109]

It will now be clear that all three major political parties since the 1860s have been continuously involved in defending the individual against the state. Liberals were at first preoccupied with the need to ward off the state, later to exploit its potential for making liberty feasible for the deprived individual. Labour inherited much of the Liberal Party's libertarian outlook, but in the 1940s became more statist in strategy, thereby making it easier for Conservatives to steal the Liberals' more individualist clothes. Conservative Party history since then has largely involved a dialogue between its long-standing benevolent interventionist tradition and its newer Liberal entrepreneurial inheritance—a dialogue that persists. Interaction between these three parties has kept liberty high on the political agenda in Britain since the 1860s, and has ensured that its dimensions have been fully explored. But how far does the two-party system deny the smaller parties a fair hearing? The simple-majority electoral system ensures that if they are regionally concentrated in their support, they can win seats broadly proportional to their votes. As for parties that are more dispersed, inter-party competition for the centre ground ensures that where their ideas are popular and compatible with parliamentary government they will be seized upon by other parties. If their ideas are for some reason unacceptable, the small party's plight is indeed difficult, especially given that media time is assigned according to existing party strength. 'I had no resource except the spoken word,' wrote Mosley of British Fascism between the wars; 'public meetings were our only way of putting over our case.'[110] Politicians who grumble about National Front marches and demonstrations, wrote its chairman in 1977, fail to appreciate that these 'are one of the few ways we have to gain a hearing'.[111]

As far as the actions of the state are concerned, no linear move away from liberty can be detected since the 1860s: there has been both increased regulation and increased freedom. 'We cannot have too much of either of them . . . ,' wrote Havelock Ellis of collectivism and individualism; 'the field of each is distinct. No one needs individualism in his water supply, and no one needs Socialism in his religion.'[112] We seem to have acted upon Ellis's view that 'true individuality . . . is impossible until a social state is attained in which the whole of what was called the material side of life . . . is automatically supplied'.[113] Hence mounting regulation, at least till 1979, in the economic sphere; mounting deregulation, at least since the mid-1960s, of personal conduct and news reporting. The regulation aimed to promote liberty for the beneficiaries of public welfare but limited free-dom of manœuvre for managers and entrepreneurs. The deregulation, promoted largely on a non-party basis, went with the grain of major social changes, especially in personal conduct. These changes have meant emancipation for many, but have drawbacks sufficient to tempt some Conservatives—Tebbit, Thatcher in some of her moods—to consider fomenting an anti-permissive reaction. So since Bagehot's day all parties in their interaction have continuously pursued that fair balance between freedom and control which the democratic politician continuously seeks but seldom securely finds.

At this point, a theme must be brought out which will recur in this book: the distaste for precise definition that runs throughout the British political system. For it is this that has hitherto discouraged its formal definition of rights and liberties. The trait is deeply rooted in the national culture. 'The English are not sufficiently interested in intellectual matters to be intolerant about them...,' wrote Orwell in 1944; 'An ordinary Englishman... almost never grasps the full logical implications of the creed he professes: almost always he utters heresies without noticing it.'[114] Some would describe this as anti-intellectualism. But a dismissive labelling is no route to understanding. The anti-intellectualism that Bagehot and many other shrewd observers of the British (and especially English) scene have noted and relished has institutional explanations and perhaps real justifications.

To begin with, British anti-intellectualism interacts continuously with party. The British two-party system requires people of very diverse opinions to work together, and so discourages disputes on party 'theology' and even discourages consistency of policy over time. Where two parties continuously compete for governmental power, the winner is the party which adapts most quickly to shifts in opinion and attracts the widest range of opinion. The need for compromise and the unimportance of logic is central to the working even of party constitutions. The Conservative Party has long prospered with no party constitution, no clear policy stance, and no precise definition of what constitutes membership.[115] In its comprehensive review of Conservative Party organization in 1949, the Maxwell-Fyfe committee rejected any pursuit of 'a Constitution which seems tidy to the student of political history or logical in all respects', preferring instead 'an organization which is an educative political force and a machine for winning elections'.[116] When Gaitskell raised the Clause 4 issue after the Labour Party's electoral defeat in 1959, Attlee pointed out that 'the Party's passion for definition must always be resisted. Gaitskell stimulated it. He should have sedated it.'[117] Michael Foot preached the same message in 1974, when he discouraged a joint meeting of cabinet and Labour Party National Executive Committee from delimiting too clearly the respective powers of party conference and parliamentary party. 'The remarkable thing about our constitution is that it is unworkable—but it works...', he pointed out. 'The constitution embodied the concept of two paramount powers which in theory could not be reconciled but in practice were. The fact was that neither paramountcy must be pressed too far.'[118]

Parliament, too, prefers procedural informality. Discussing the rights of minorities in the House of Commons, Ivor Jennings pointed out that these 'depend not upon express rules but upon the custom of the House'. He thought lawyers too prone to assume that rules are obeyed because there is a policeman nearby, whereas rules of the House are followed 'because they are part of the tradition, because they are reasonable, and because they are essential to the working of a democratic system'.[119] Janet Morgan in 1975, when discussing the House of Lords in the 1960s, makes much of the 'self-restraint, hidden sanctions, and agreed conventions' that enable so anomalous an institution to survive; 'caution and self-control are second nature to a House accustomed to managing itself without a Speaker'.[120] John Patten's major argument, when dismissing proposals for constitutional reform in 1991, was that the libertarian flavour of British life rendered reform unnecessary: 'when rights are infringed, there is no resort to grand abstract principles or detached constitutional structures, but instead a reliance on the people themselves to make their voices heard'.[121] Among the advantages of a constitution largely unwritten, said Chief Justice Cockburn in 1868, is the fact that 'its elasticity enables those who administer it to adapt it to the varying conditions of society, and to the requirements and habits of the age in which we live, so as to avoid the inconsistencies and injustice which arise when the law is no longer in harmony with the wants and usages and interests of the generation to which it is immediately applied'. Or as Lord Simon put it in 1950, 'its proper working can always be adjusted to the public interest and to common sense'.[122]

Something similar could be said about most of the institutions discussed in this book. 'There are three main controlling forces in our system,' wrote the prominent Liberal Ramsay Muir in 1930, 'all of which are entirely unrecognised by the law of the constitution': a bureaucracy 'very able and omnipresent' with largely uncontrolled power; 'an all-but-omnipotent Cabinet' unable to carry out its huge responsibilities; and highly organized parties often under secret influence.[123] British political practice operates according to rules that are enforceable in the courts, but also depends heavily on acceptance of conventions: usages which acquire authority, not from the courts, but from sustained application. Parliamentary procedure exemplifies how such conventions can sometimes be written down with great precision. There is nothing new about objecting to these peculiarities of the British system. 'There ought to be some limit to the ignorance about the realities of life in which our legal system pretends to exist,' wrote Muir. 'The law pretends that there is no such person as the Prime Minister. It knows nothing of the Cabinet. It has never heard of bureaucracy. It pretends that Parliament is really responsible for legislation and taxation. It is unaware of the existence of political parties. If we are to maintain this astounding refusal to recognise real facts, we debar ourselves from taking the most direct means of remedying evils.'[124] Claiming in 1992 that 'today our constitution is not "unwritten" but hidden and difficult to find', Lord

Scarman regretted the fact that the British citizen lacks 'a constitution which he can read and understand and which enables him, if need be, to claim a right which he can enforce'.[125]

Yet Scarman's yearning to get everything clearly laid out on paper is not less controversial than Muir's sixty-two years before. A political system is not necessarily better for being easily grasped and memorized like an alphabet. The select committee on the Official Secrets Acts in 1939 cited Blackstone in support of the view that freedom might in practice suffer from defining too precisely the extent of immunity from prosecution under the Acts. 'If all the privileges of parliament were set down and ascertained, and no privilege to be allowed but what was so defined and determined, it were easy for the executive power to devise some new case, not within the line of privilege, and under pretence thereof to harass any refractory member and violate the freedom of parliament.'[126] Besides, all constitutions, whether written or not, are working systems whose every procedural wrinkle cannot possibly be written down, let alone be enforced in the courts. Precise definition is not always desirable in a pluralistic system where decisions must emerge from discussion between semi-autonomous institutions, where powers are in dispute, or where it may be desirable to let down the defeated party lightly. In such situations the system becomes workable through compromise rather than through the logic and precision that involving a host of lawyers would entail. Perhaps this British aptitude reached its apogee in the transition from empire to Commonwealth, where the studied vagueness of the integrators counteracted the determined precision of the fragmenters (notably the Irish). 'What does "Dominion status" mean?' asked Lloyd George, discussing the treaty with Ireland in parliament in 1921: 'It is difficult and dangerous to give a definition'; rigid definition 'is not the way of the British constitution'.[127] The silences of the British constitution, far from being regrettable, may denote a salutary decision, more or less deliberate, to restrict the involvement of lawyers, to avoid inflaming areas of controversy, and to make the system work.

# 6

## *Interests and Pressures*

THE local and libertarian flavour of British political culture has a fourth constituent: voluntarism. J. B. Priestley in 1959 went so far as to find the clue to English greatness in the habit of meeting 'in a thousand places to consider Alpine plants, migrant geese, or sixteenth century madrigals'.[1] Voluntarism is the more powerful for not requiring formal political structures. It lies behind the mutual exchange of services within family or neighbourhood, for instance. But volunteers often organize themselves to promote the interests of themselves and/or of others, and the structures they create are often now labelled with the catch-all term 'pressure group'. Its members join voluntarily, but often seek to coerce others: first, the politicians from whom they extract legislation; and then the general public who are expected to obey it. A pressure group has been defined as 'any organization which seeks to influence government policy without at the same time being willing to accept the responsibility of public office'.[2] This definition perhaps exaggerates the importance for pressure groups of influencing government policy. Organizations like anglers' associations are pressure groups even though their main purpose is not (at least, at present) to bring pressure to bear on government. Perhaps the beginning of the definition should be rephrased as 'any organization which seeks to influence public opinion and/or government policy . . .'. Unlike governments, pressure groups specialize, and feel no obligation to cover the entire range of policy. Again unlike governments, they do not necessarily seek wide appeal; they may claim to benefit society as a whole, but they will be recruited from a relatively narrow base; sometimes their formal objectives will be narrow as well. They leave the business of co-ordinating and integrating opinion to the politicians and civil servants.

Even the amended definition of 'pressure group' is in one way misleading, in that it exaggerates the pressure group's distance from government.

In its day-to-day operation the pressure group impinges on government from without, but governments none the less often find it useful. Indeed, governments may well find it convenient sometimes (notably in wartime) to set up a pressure group as a way of making contact with relevant opinion. Government established the Council of Industrial Design in 1944, for instance, and the British Travel and Holidays Association in 1947.[3] Where pressure groups are fragmented, government may seek to amalgamate them through forming 'umbrella' structures such as the Women's National Commission of 1969, or through getting schismatic structures to reunite. In 1978, for example, John Silkin as Minister for Agriculture was impatient with the bitter feud between the National Farmers' Union and the Farmers' Union of Wales. He told the latter's annual meeting that he must conserve his officials' time and the taxpayer's funds, and was 'not prepared to tolerate indefinitely the prospect of holding separate meetings in Whitehall with each of the two agricultural unions serving Wales'.[4] Just as government in the 1950s and 1960s found it administratively convenient to aggregate its former colonies into federations, so it built up the TUC and CBI as guides to opinions relevant for economic policy. There are economies of scale in domestic politics as well as in the international and industrial spheres.

The term 'pressure group' includes at least two types of institution which differ both in the extent of their altruism and in how they operate. There is first the 'interest group', which may operate in public, but which quite often functions only behind the scenes. It champions the sort of earth-bound freedom that welcomes being left alone, unmolested by trouble-makers or by the high-minded. Its aims primarily to promote the interests of its members—through employers' associations or trade unions, for example. But its own interest may well coincide with the interests of others, and it will certainly advertise and even exaggerate any such coincidence, as professional bodies often do. More altruistic and more likely to operate in public is the 'cause' or 'opinion' group. Its overt purpose is primarily altruistic, though on closer inspection its motives often turn out to be mixed. These two types of pressure group were both fully compatible with Victorian ideals of self-help and are by no means always clearly distinct. Sometimes they conflict, sometimes one turns into the other. Industrialization merely perpetuated (sometimes even curtailed) the activities of the interest groups which had long been familiar, whereas its impact on the cause group was more dramatic. For this reason, because it impinged more overtly on the political system, and because its importance within the political system has significantly changed since Bagehot's day, the cause group will be this Chapter's major concern. Still, the continuous and often unadvertised activities of the interest group must not be forgotten. Indeed, for the Victorians, interest groups probably seemed more legitimate than cause groups, whereas the opposite would now be the case.[5]

Industrialization occurred in Britain with relatively little prompting from the state. Where the state did intervene, interests sprang up in self-defence. Bodies such as the National Association of Factory Occupiers or the Liberty and Property Defence League mobilized against legislation (regulating factory conditions, for instance) that they disliked. Furthermore, increasingly diverse interests found it both useful and (in an urbanizing society) easier to associate voluntarily for their own purposes. Groups of tradesmen came together in 1860 to form the Associated British Chambers of Commerce with the aim of lobbying government. And with the advent of collective bargaining, employers felt the need to match the trade-union movement's growing structures.[6] At the same time, industrialization helped to create the outlook which challenged interests, together with the structures and techniques necessary to promote that challenge. The cause group saw self-organization and spontaneity as necessary for progress and enlightenment. Richard Cobden, the cause group's most distinguished nineteenth-century practitioner, was rather shocked by the experience of canvassing in Salisbury in 1843: 'I found that the experienced canvassers on the Free-Trade side there did not ask themselves so much what the opinions of the electors were, but who were their customers; who were their rich neighbours, whom they owed money to—whom they banked with—whether the neighbouring squire or neighbouring lord came in and dealt at his shop.'[7] Through the cause group, Cobden sought to promote less parochial and more idealistic attitudes.

Because the pressure group can survive only by successfully influencing opinion, it tries to ensure that its techniques move with the times. This is the first dimension of change in pressure-group history since the 1860s that deserves discussion. The Webbs claimed in 1920 that 'the reality of Democracy is . . . dependent to a vastly greater extent on the adoption of Measurement and Publicity than on any choice between one method of voting and another'.[8] Measurement and publicity lay at the heart of the cause group which operated in public. It aimed to force the authorities on to the defensive, so that they must explain themselves. Governments found this difficult where their case was (as so often) subtle or complex. 'The trouble is', wrote Samuel Hoare discussing the government of India in the early 1930s, 'that our case is a complicated case of detail, whilst the attack is an attack of headlines and platform slogans.'[9] The Webbs' phrase is somewhat rationalistic in laying such stress on the influence that facts in themselves enjoy. In practice, the cause group aiming to influence government adopts at least three broad types of approach towards public opinion: it collects information, it diffuses information, and it intimidates.

Nineteenth-century cause groups often saw their role as educational. Their public meetings were classrooms for adults. To quote Cobden, attacking the corn laws: 'knowledge is the power—knowledge alone— by which we shall bring this foul system to the dust'.[10] Two types of knowledge were being supplied to the public: opinion about the facts, and opinion about opinion. Taking the facts first, a free-trading, non-interventionist nineteenth-century government lacked machinery to gather the facts for itself. Cause groups plunged in to meet the need, and were often helped by fact-gathering agencies semi-independent from government: royal commissions, parliamentary committees, statistical societies, or free-lance social investigators like Henry Mayhew or Charles Booth. Like its successors, the anti-slavery movement exploited the parliamentary select committee between 1789 and 1791, and later cause groups exploited the royal commission, an institution which suffered seriously after 1979 from Thatcher's hostility to pressure groups. Finding the civil service unable to provide trade statistics, the Tariff Reform League even appointed a tariff commission of its own in 1904 to collect the facts about trade patterns on which alone an effective tariff policy could rest.[11] Yet the cause group was not objective in collecting information. It had a love–hate relationship with inquiry, if only because it usually thought it already knew the answer.

The information, once collected, had to be diffused. In the nineteenth century there were three major ways of doing this: through literature, the public meeting, and the petition. There was a widespread early-Victorian belief in the almost mystical power of the press, and cause groups distributed an abundance of tracts, periodicals, publications, and posters of all kinds. The costs of printing and postage were falling fast, and printing technique was becoming more sophisticated. During the twentieth century, press advertisements and (more recently) computerized direct mailing have carried this process much further. And as the spoken or televised word has become more important, cause groups (especially charities) have become adept at exploiting the new media. At the start of the nineteenth century there were severe restraints on public meetings. The normal outlet was the county meeting, controlled by the local hierarchy, and at which only freeholders were allowed to speak. Wyvill used county meetings a lot, but nineteenth-century reformers could not be sure of winning support there, and abandoned them for general meetings of the local inhabitants. The Chartists promoted huge public meetings—for example, the one at Kersal Moor near Manchester on 24 September 1838. Twentieth-century electronic innovation reared up a rival to the public meeting in the form of the fireside circle addressed from radio or (later) from television. Indeed, by the 1930s the public meeting and political oratory flourished mainly among those extreme groups which the BBC refused to broadcast—among Communists and Fascists, and with Maxton and Mosley.

By the late eighteenth century the petition as a way of diffusing information was growing more forceful in tone and more tightly organized. The campaign against the slave-trade perfected the petition's parliamentary timing as early as 1792. Opponents depreciated petitions, ascribing them to dragooned women and Sunday-school children; but as long as the franchise remained restricted, government could not ignore this guide to unenfranchised opinion. Petitions also had the great virtue, from the cause group's point of view, of giving its rank and file something to do, for collecting signatures was a laborious task that anyone could undertake. Even after the franchise had become universal, petitions could provide rough-and-ready guidance to opinion between elections, and on issues not raised in election manifestos. So in 1968 there were 1,086,590 signatures for a petition to save the Argyll and Sutherland Highlanders and in 1973, 1,350,000 signatures to a petition against pornography.[12] In the early 1980s there was 'a great upsurge' of petitions on subjects such as contraception, abortion, capital punishment, embryo research, and proportional representation.[13] In 1989 the Speaker failed to limit the number of boxes brought in when a petition with 4,500,000 signatures was presented in support of the ambulance workers' strike, Tony Benn declaring a restriction to four to be an affront to parliamentary democracy.[14]

Pressure groups, especially cause groups, know that the politician can be intimidated if they advertise the sheer numbers they can deploy. The smaller the electorate, the more impressed he is likely to be by intimidation of the electoral type. Cause groups are particularly active at by-elections, for then they can be sure of capturing headlines, as pacifists realized in the famous by-election at East Fulham in 1933. It also became more common in early-Victorian general elections to press MPs into making pledges—on parliamentary reform in 1831, for instance, on repeal of the Irish union in 1832, and so on. The 'test question' such as the trade-union lobby employed at the general election of 1874 was a powerful variant of this, especially when the pressure group reinforced it with the threat to put up independent candidates against party candidates whose answers failed to satisfy. Such tactics always carried the risk, though, that a divided progressive vote would let in the unprogressive candidate, as mid-Victorian nonconformist and temperance dissidents from the Liberal Party sometimes discovered. The politicians could regain control of the situation only through the ballot (which made it more difficult for cause groups to intimidate the voter and was secured in 1872); through extending the franchise (which weakened pressure-group influence at elections and eroded the mass movement's moral standing); and through the party programme (which shielded the MP against minority opinion). Politicians needed to regain control because cause groups' outlook on violence was always somewhat equivocal. Some of their apparently peaceable strategies were readily turned to more violent purposes—the procession, for example. Often reinforced by bands and banners, it was regularly used by the more popular causes in the nineteenth century, and was not clearly distinct from the techniques already discussed. When it reached its destination it turned itself into a public meeting, and when (as with Chartism) it paraded a petition through the streets it simultaneously promoted petitioning. The women's suffrage movement carried the procession to the peak of perfection in 1908, 1910, 1911, and 1913, and the hunger marches of the 1930s from north to south effectively advertised in prosperous areas the sheer scale of unemployment elsewhere. The Easter procession was integral to the Campaign for Nuclear Disarmament in the 1950s, the first one to Aldermaston, but the later ones from there to London.

The essence of the politician's trade is to uphold order in society without provoking violence and if possible without initiating it. From this point of view the procession is an ambivalent device, for it readily degenerates into the riot. Indeed, it is sometimes intended to do so, as with the Edwardian suffragette processions from Caxton Hall to parliament, the processions of the National Front into areas of immigrant settlement in the 1970s, or some of the processions that are so prominent in Northern Ireland. Cause groups, often humanitarian in objective, risked incongruity if they exploited violence directly. Indeed, a certain mid-Victorian pride was taken in the cause group as Britain's alternative to French revolutionary change. Still, the distinction between mass pressure and mass intimidation is not clear-cut; the cause-group leader simultaneously warns the authorities of the danger and tries to hold back his followers. But if he holds them back too vigorously he risks losing his influence over them, thereby losing his influence with the authorities. The delicacy of the relationship between pressure and intimidation was well displayed in the complex relations between the Whig government and the Birmingham

Political Union during the reform crisis of 1831–2. If government failed to respond to non-violent pressure there was always the temptation for the reformer to repudiate the existing government and fight for a better. If the opposition party seemed unpromising, there was the revolutionary option, certainly real for some Chartists in the 1840s. Also real, however, was the authorities' determination to resist, as the Chartists very soon discovered. Irish nationalist pressure on the British government throughout the nineteenth century continuously verged on the tactically violent and met sustained resistance. After 1916, however, it culminated in violence of the revolutionary sort, and by 1920–1 it was clear that the British authorities were losing their desire to resist.

The most striking instance of a cause group deliberately exploiting violence was Emmeline Pankhurst's Women's Social and Political Union between 1903 and 1914. The suffragettes used violence, not with any genuine revolutionary intent, but to simulate the popular pressure which seemed to have helped men to get the vote in 1832, 1867, and 1884. For Pankhurst 'the argument of the broken pane' was the most valuable in modern politics.[15] It was carefully timed to catch the headlines and was associated with the escalation of militancy in other dimensions: breaches of decorum, disruptions of etiquette, and so on. As with CND later, 'stunt violence' of this kind was organized in parallel with non-violent pressure, but the authorities had every interest in treating the violent activity as a prize diversion from the non-violent. In the case of the suffragettes and CND the violence was counter-productive,[16] but this is not to say that cause groups always lose by using violence. In political systems which offer no outlet for non-violent pressure, violent protest acquires a certain moral stature. Even in democratic political systems, violence can sometimes be effective. Simply by pushing up the insurance costs of stores selling furs, animal-lovers in the 1980s seem to have discouraged their sale. Similar tactics may well eventually be applied to the sale of meat, and the efforts of animal liberation movements have certainly accelerated hard thinking about the need for experiments on animals. In these instances, though, the apparent successes of violence seem merely to reflect the fact that the protesters are working with the grain of public opinion. Where this has not been so, as with the IRA in Northern Ireland since the late 1960s, violent tactics have been counter-productive. Besides, violence is so equivocal a tactic that any particular incident may suddenly turn public opinion in the wrong direction.

*

Pressure groups do not necessarily work through political parties. They have no reason to risk dividing their members by doing so, provided that they want nothing from parliament, and political neutrality brings legal and sometimes financial advantages. Their leaders are often driven by contempt for all existing parties. John Tyme, for example, the Sheffield Polytechnic lecturer who became well known at planning inquiries in the mid-1970s for vigorously resisting the planners and the 'road lobby', had once been a Communist but by then had repudiated all political parties.[17] A non-party pressure group can recruit from members of all parties and of none, and can play off one party against another, as the trade unions did in the 1870s. It can enjoy continuous access to government, whichever party is in power, and has no need to dilute its members' enthusiasm by any continuous preoccupation with the practicable. So pressure groups are especially active in the all-party groups of MPs (some of which they service secretarially) which meet periodically to promote a particular cause. In the early 1990s there were just over 100 of these to promote links with particular countries and just under 100 subject-groups.[18] The League of Nations Union followed a non-party strategy between the wars,[19] and by the early 1990s some thought the trade-union movement should do the same.[20] A non-party stance was more important for a pressure group in the early nineteenth century than later, especially where issues of domestic reform were concerned. This was because, in the absence of programmatic parties, a sympathetic backbencher was needed to push legislation through, for legislative initiatives then by no means came only from government. Much of parliament's time was taken up with private bill legislation, and backbenchers became increasingly professional in dealing with it.[21]

On non-party issues, pressure groups remain content to work through backbenchers outside the party structures. Both sides have much to gain from the relationship: the MP acquires technical know-how and potential votes, the pressure group gains political know-how and parliamentary support. On some controversial issues—the reforms concerning sexual issues in the 1960s, for example—the parties, too, have an interest in getting an issue settled in this way. Harold Wilson in 1961 thought the Labour Party would lose 6 million votes if it committed itself publicly to legislate for homosexual law reform, and as Leader of the House Crossman seven years later admitted using the private member's bill as a way of getting rid of difficult issues.[22] But on major matters of policy the backbencher during the nineteenth century became a waning asset. Government was absorbing more and more of parliament's time, legislation was becoming more and more complex, and party discipline was tightening. So pressure groups gradually realized that they had no option other than to capture a party which had some chance of forming a government.[23]

There is no clear distinction between pressure group and party, and each can transform itself into the other. The Labour Party originated essentially as the parliamentary instrument of trade-union pressure groups and has sometimes shown signs of reverting to its pressure-group status. The Green 'Party' is still more equivocal: it fought 133 constituencies in the general election of 1987, but fell back after 1989 when beset by an internal argument about how far it should remain a pressure group and how far it should aim to be a party.[24] An electoral system which replaces two parties (government and opposition) by many has the effect of blurring the distinction between pressure group and political party still further. For parties in that situation are not compelled, like parties of government and opposition in a two-party system, to offer alternative programmes for government, each internally coherent and each capable of winning sizeable support within the community. The formation of centre coalitions against the extremes, which such electoral systems often encourage, can have the effect of pushing the left and right extremes out of governmental politics. Dissatisfaction with the Lloyd George coalition, for instance, drove many Unionists into pressure groups like the Middle Class Union (founded 1920) and the Anti-Waste League (founded 1921) until two-party politics returned in 1922.[25]

A twentieth-century pressure group whose ideas are important and which needs legislation will not normally get very far at Westminster without party links. The movement for women's suffrage was greatly hindered by the non-party stance it assumed throughout its history.[26] Likewise the League of Nations Union: 'with everyone for it', says its historian, the League 'did not count. Party leaders had defused the League as a political issue.'[27] Party links will not of course guarantee complete success for a pressure group. If, as in Britain, political parties are committed to clear policies, their discipline and programmes can shield the politician against undue pressure, and the pressure group must show that it has enough electoral support to bring in new voters. Otherwise the party leader (Bonar Law after 1922, for example, or Thatcher after 1979) may feel that there is more to be gained by resistance. This is particularly likely to happen when the pressure group, for all its pretensions, seems unduly self-interested. Many electors came to feel this about the trade-union movement in the late 1970s. 'In all my many dealings with the NUT', wrote Bernard Donoughue, head of the Policy Unit in Downing Street from 1974 to 1979, 'I never once heard mention of education or children. The union's prime objective appeared to be to secure ever decreasing responsibilities and hours of work for its members.'[28] Where political parties are not identified clearly by policy, as in the United States, pressure groups can make more direct impact, particularly if the legislature is fragmented into numerous small but powerful all-party committees which can be captured with relative ease. In Britain, by contrast, the pressure group must normally capture a political party, unless party conflict is for some reason in abeyance, as during the two world wars.

A party without spontaneous organized support within the community is in trouble, as the Liberal Party discovered between the wars,[29] but political parties can sometimes win votes by resisting pressure groups, or at least by introducing legislation which dilutes their demands. They can sometimes gain from appearing to speak for the entire nation against sectional interests. Conservative leaders from Peel onwards laboured to broaden out their Party's support beyond the agricultural interest, just as Labour leaders from Ramsay MacDonald onwards sought to transcend organized labour. The Liberal and Social Democratic parties after 1970 felt they had much to gain, in what seemed like a class-polarizing society, from appearing free from control by any one class or pressure group.[30] 'Because we are not tied to employer interests or the unions', said Jeremy Thorpe the Liberal leader in the general election campaign of February 1974, 'we are in the strongest position to bring about peace and an understanding between the two.' At the same election Heath sought to turn Labour's trade-union ties to his own advantage: 'we are the trade union for the pensioners and children, the trade union for the disabled and sick. . . . We are the trade union for the nation as a whole.'[31] Ten years later his successor told journalists that she wanted her governments to be remembered for attacking 'vested interests'.[32]

The three major political parties in Britain relate differently to pressure groups. Whereas members of the Liberal and Labour parties typically see hope in change, the Conservative typically sees only danger. Still less does he relish the advocates of change. Their influence seems fragmenting, disgruntled, disruptive, irresponsible, factious, and even immature. 'A spirit of innovation', wrote Burke, 'is generally the result of a selfish temper and confined views.'[33] Enjoy what you have, says the Conservative, however little, and do not expect too much from change, and still less from change that is politically inspired. Yet the Conservative does not neglect politics. On the contrary: his belief that opponents' political meddling can do harm leads him to keep his political skills and machinery in trim. Gladstone in 1882, explaining why Conservatives were politically so much more powerful than their support in the country seemed to justify, pointed to 'the impossibility of keeping the *public* mind always lively and intent upon great national interests, while the opposite sentiment of class never slumbers'. He went on to stress 'the concentration of the higher social influences . . . at the fixed seat of government, and their ready and immediate influence from day to day on the action of the legislature'.[34]

Conservatives fear that cause groups will complicate the political process by introducing outsiders with exaggerated expectations. Cause groups seemed intimidatory, dangerously responsive to mass spontaneity, and then incapable of curbing the violence they had released. Concessionary governments risked finding that concession had not only failed to quell the agitation but had inserted thin ends of dangerous wedges. The IRA's unexpected re-emergence from civil rights movements in Northern Ireland in the late 1960s illustrates the danger. Many nineteenth-century Conservatives combined a very elevated notion of government's standing with an acute awareness of its fragility. They feared that authority would lose its prestige if it trafficked with agitators—hence their distaste for Whig dealings in 1831–2 with the Birmingham Political Union or for Gladstone's handling of Parnell before 1886. 'For twenty years he has held a season-ticket on the line of least resistance', complained Amery in July 1914 of Asquith's position on the Irish question, 'and has gone wherever the train of events has carried him, lucidly justifying his position at whatever point he has happened to find himself.'[35] Conservative suspicion of cause groups persisted until surprisingly recently: as Anthony Hurd pointed out in 1954, 'we do not have pressure groups on this side of the House'.[36]

Still, the term 'pressure group' cannot now be used as Hurd used it, as though synonymous with cause group; its ample embrace includes the interest group, where the Conservative Party has always been strong. The contest between left and right is, broadly speaking, a contest between pressure groups of contrasting types. A conservative party naturally champions interests that are already entrenched, usually at the local level within the constituency: the established church, the army, the agricultural interest, the slave traffic, the drink-trade, the property owner—groups which have something to lose, however little, by change. An eloquent witness to the power of such groups within the constituency was Lord Robert Cecil, writing in 1858—eloquent because he was later to act as their formidable champion when Conservative Prime Minister. 'No one can have watched the utter impotence of Parliament to raise its hand against the attorneys or the licensed victuallers, or the extreme difficulty with which even so small a body as the ecclesiastical lawyers have been dealt with', without realizing how their control over a minority of the electors 'wields the power of the whole constituency'.[37] Late-Victorian Conservatism gained much from its skill in drawing away from the left several interests which seemed threatened by the opinion groups that had become so active there: the drink and agricultural interests, the established church, and interests threatened by Liberal movements concerned with class and nationality. Gladstone's explanations of 1882 for Conservative success included 'the existence of powerful professional classes more or less sustained by privilege or by artfully constructed monopoly: the army, the law, the clergy'.[38] When Labour superseded the Liberals as leading party of the left, twentieth-century Conservatives had a good chance of attracting industrial and commercial interests rightwards. The entire Conservative economic strategy between the wars rested on the Gladstonian assumption that if government confined itself to 'holding the ring' through sound money, cutting costs, and avoiding war, self-organized economic groups would spontaneously cause the economy to flourish. But neither then nor later did the Party necessarily prefer the views of employers' organizations to the instinctive responses of the individual entrepreneur and investor. Protective tariffs might be desirable for imperial or short-term economic restructuring, but the inter-war Party never envisaged developing government machinery on any ambitious scale to 'manage' the economy. Civil servants under inter-war Conservative or Conservative-dominated governments sought to do no more than mediate between autonomous groups within the community and encourage them to collaborate.

None the less, in a rapidly changing society which inscribed democracy and publicity on its banners, Conservatives could not risk remaining entirely within their interest-group closet. Peel knew that after the 1830s Conservatives could not rely solely on an authoritarian response to popular pressure. According to John Morley, after 1832 'schemes of political improvement were henceforth to spring up outside of Parliament, instead of in the creative mind of the parliamentary leader; and official statesmanship has ever since consisted less in working out principles, than in measuring the force and direction of the popular gale'. Peel's responsiveness to outside pressure was so great, said Disraeli, that he 'was the unconscious parent of political agitation. He literally forced the people out of doors to become statesmen.'[39] Despite his sympathy with the protectionists, Disraeli in 1849 was inclined to take a high line with them. 'If the Party is to be managed by the Protection Society . . .', he told Stanley, 'I think that Society ought to have apprised the members of the House of Commons of their plan of campaign.' Stanley, on the other hand, was more receptive, pointing out that 'that body may be useful in keeping alive the spirit of the party'.[40] Still more did Conservatives need to show themselves responsive to outside pressure when further extensions of the franchise took place—extensions which gave them some hope of attracting new recruits from the left. Disraeli's handling of the franchise issue in 1866–7 and Baldwin's inter-war approach to socialism provide evidence of this. The Conservatives were learning from the Whigs the art of judicious and timely concession to initiatives which had begun elsewhere, and were ultimately denying the Whigs any reason for remaining on the left. Better still was to pre-empt outside pressure by catering more fully for political participation within the Party itself. By the early 1890s the Party's National Union and Primrose League were undermining a Conservative pressure group like the Church Defence Institution by draining off its local supporters and its more ambitious professional agents.[41]

When in serious trouble, the Conservative has always been ready to shed his distaste for public agitation and mobilize the latent sympathetic opinion that he knows is there. He can do this by mimicking opponents' methods through mounting conservative cause groups, somewhat neglected by historians,[42] such as the Church Defence Institution or the Tariff Reform League. Yet for the Conservative this is a risky strategy. Agitation does not come naturally to him, its tone and impulse are reactive and defensive, and so it is unlikely to be done well. At the same time as offending quietist supporters it may also rouse the enemy. By 1906 the Tariff Reform League was creating immense bad feeling by forcing its views on Conservative constituency parties with rogue parliamentary candidates who threatened to split the anti-Liberal vote;[43] it seemed all too reminiscent of what Chamberlain's radical colleagues had done to the Liberal Party in the 1870s. Besides, in the arena of public agitation Conservatives do not always find it easy to compete; contentment is less easily mobilized than discontent. 'Over the past few years', said a Labour MP in 1982, 'I have been on many demonstrations, but I have never heard of a demonstration in favour of the independent nuclear deterrent . . . What stops the Government is the fact that no one would turn up.'[44] There was a further danger: Conservative supporters once mobilized might acquire a dangerous taste for progressive styles of politics, as happened with some supporters of the Anti-League of 1844–6 and the National League for Opposing Women's Suffrage of 1908–18.[45] From the Conservative point of view it was better, perhaps, to compete on other territory with other tactics: obfuscation, diversion, stolid resistance, and playing for delay.

Yet when such congenial tactics have failed to suffice, Conservatives have more than once shown themselves well able to beat the enemy at his own game—as witness the Association Movement of the 1790s, the crusade against home rule after 1886, the handling of the general election in 1931, the recovery from electoral defeat in 1945, and the rise of Thatcherism after 1975. 'We must agitate', the Queen told Cranbrook in February 1886; '—I do not like agitation but we must agitate every place small as well as large and make people understand.'[46] During the 1920s the trade-union movement's mounting pretensions seemed dangerous enough to Baldwin for reluctant confrontation in 1926, during which his delicate handling of public opinion would have done credit to any nineteenth-century Whig. By 1935 (the year when Walter Citrine, General Secretary of the TUC, was knighted) Baldwin felt able publicly to acknowledge the stabilizing influence the trade-union movement was by then exerting on British society. 'The spirit of Trade Unionism', he told the Party conference in that year, 'is the bulwark of popular liberty. If Trade Unionism was destroyed, you would be on the road to Communism and from Communism to Fascism.'[47] During the 1970s trade-union pretensions once more seemed excessive: for many Conservatives, the cause groups of the left seemed to have become in effect conservative interest groups, though of course without the Conservative label. So in one of the most remarkable episodes in its history, the Party converted itself into a crusade for containment. Energized by small opinion-forming pressure groups of a rationalistic and cerebral kind—the Centre for Policy Studies, the Institute of Economic Affairs, Aims of Industry, and so on—the Party mobilized against the self-interest of the trade-union movement and of its middle-class equivalents: the professions.[48] Little help was forthcoming from the academic establishment. Looking back in 1994, John Redwood expressed surprise at the shortage of practical guidance politicians received from the universities on such subjects as morality, criminology, economics, and international relations.[49] Thatcher aimed to recover for politicians responsible to the electorate a control over policy that had seemed under consensus corporatist policies to be slipping into the hands of pressure-group leaders elected only by their more activist members.

Much more receptive to cause groups were the two parties of the left. Their importance in Liberal Party history is somewhat masked by the fact that the cause-group leaders tended to present their movements as non-party, and even thought of them as such. Yet however critical they might be of Liberal (and still more, of Whig) party leaders, in practice these groups brought the Liberal Party new ideas, idealism, personnel, energy, and cash. So much so, that Liberals before 1914 did not need to establish a nation-wide branch structure.[50] Radicals saw the very process of agitation as beneficial, and their Whig–Liberal leaders cultivated the art of at least appearing receptive to outside agitation. This ensured contact with the leaders of radical movements, often in the hope of ultimately co-opting them into a broadened establishment. As the Liberal Party annexed more and more radicals, and as the franchise extended, Liberal leaders found themselves pushed into adopting styles of leadership that seemed ever more adventurous. After the 1860s they developed two conflicting strategies for handling public opinion, of which the first was the Gladstonian single issue. Gladstone, like his Whig predecessors, was 'always listening for the gathering of the waters and the rising of the tide',[51] but always with a view to himself embarking on a crusade. The four occasions of his life when he thought he had formed 'a public opinion' were 1853, 1868, 1886, and 1894, and some would say there is a good case also for 1876.[52] By the 1880s, with his faith in the judgement of the aroused 'masses' confronting the privilege of the 'classes', he was even alarming the Queen by promoting agitation himself. Thereby he helped to rouse and unify a potentially fissile Party. The single issue at least had the advantage of assigning priority between reforms and reconciling conflicts between them, for by the 1880s the problem was serious even as regards access to parliamentary time. As John Bright pointed out in 1881, 'you cannot get six or 12 omnibuses abreast through Temple Bar'.[53]

Yet there were difficulties. By no means all Liberal leaders could conjure unifying causes like rabbits out of a hat; still less could they be relied upon to handle the crusade in such a way as to benefit the Party. Nor did such an Olympian style of leadership accord well with the Party's participatory instincts. So an alternative strategy, the Chamberlainite programme, gained much ground in the 1870s and 1880s. The aim was to identify the reforms to which the Party felt most committed, and to face the electorate only after ranking and reconciling them. Chamberlain thought interest groups ever watchful for their own advantage, so that it was essential to organize the forces of progress if they were not to become a mere 'mob that disperses before the steady tread of a few policemen, or before the charge of a handful of cavalry'.[54] This was the aim of the National Liberal Federation in 1877 and Chamberlain's 'unauthorized programme' in 1885. In the same year Gladstone's espousal of home rule pushed Chamberlain's programme into the background, but in 1891 Gladstone espoused a sort of halfway house between the two strategies: the Newcastle Programme, which aggregated into a Liberal package the separate demands of several cause groups, with home rule transcending its rivals in importance. In the longer term, the failure of home rule and the disappointments of Gladstone's fourth and final period of office assisted Chamberlain's programmatic alternative—though only under a degree of control from the leadership that Chamberlain had never envisaged. This was the strategy that the Liberal leaders were pursuing during the great period of Liberal welfare legislation from 1906 to 1914, and at the general elections of 1910 the two major cause groups mobilized behind the tariff issue—the Tariff Reform League and the Free Trade Union—each reinforced, rather than cut across, the two major political parties.

In its relationship with cause groups, the Labour Party resembled the Liberals more closely than it liked to pretend. Both parties were much more sympathetic to the cause group than to the interest group. Their support for free trade reflected this, because free trade directly subverted the interest group. When Snowden framed the first Labour budget in 1924 he set about repealing the McKenna duties, a policy opposed by the interests Conservative protectionism had brought into existence. The opposition reminded him of 'what I had always regarded as one of the greatest dangers of a tariff system, namely its corrupting influence on politics. The lobbies at the House of Commons were crowded out with representatives of vested interests bringing pressure to bear upon Members of Parliament to oppose the repeal of these duties.'[55] The Labour Party's socialist wing originated as a cause group, and in collaborating after 1900 with the trade unions it aligned itself with groups which combined elements of both cause and interest group. The Party's overall tone remained very much that of a cause group, though its leaders inherited the Whigs' assimilative and digestive 'handling' function in relation to extra-parliamentary pressure. So in the 1960s it ignored R. T. McKenzie's advice,[56] and continued giving the appearance of deferring to the party conference, thereby perpetuating ambiguity about the party's internal distribution of power. Labour knew that politicians of the left could not afford to lose contact with extra-parliamentary activists, and that the image presented by intra-party democracy would help in the process. Michael Foot in November 1980 was as keen as any nineteenth-century Whig to channel political discontent (in this instance, over high unemployment) into parliament. 'When it will explode I do not know. But I want it to explode in a way which will make it possible to maintain democratic institutions in this country, and that means that the agitation outside this place [sc. Westminster] has got to have its representation here. People outside have got to have some faith in what happens here.'[57]

Yet there were significant differences between Liberals and Labour. To begin with, the Liberal mind was relatively fragmented. 'Multitudinousness has always been the Liberal characteristic,' wrote H. G. Wells; 'it is the party against the predominating interests. It is at once the party of the failing and of the untried . . . Essentially it is the party of criticism, the "Anti" party.'[58] Labour's structure and outlook were more focused. The Party's 'socialism', however vague, constituted a relatively integrated philosophy, and led Labour to reject the individualistic outlook of the isolated and *ad hoc* crusade. While it inherited many of the Liberal Party's libertarian and humanitarian instincts, Labour's main priority from the 1940s became 'planning': the use of the state machine to create or redistribute wealth in the interests of the underprivileged. Labour was wary of the volunteer as a person likely to display patronizing and even self-interested class attitudes. 'One of the things I do not like about Socialists', wrote Harold Nicolson in 1949, 'is their distrust of gratuitous public service.'[59] So the types of cause group associated with Labour were different. Yet the volunteer was not to be so easily pushed aside. As we saw in Chapter 2 he skirmished at the fringes even of the welfare state, probing its defects and suggesting improvements. From the mid-1950s the term 'voluntarism' acquired a new usage to reflect this development: 'denoting the involvement of voluntary organizations in social welfare'.[60]

Because Labour flourished at a later and more secularized period than the Liberals, the types of pressure to which it responds are more secular and materialist. It had to respond to the new causes that had taken hold of the public imagination. The Child Poverty Action Group, Shelter, and the National Council for Civil Liberties had all appeared since Lloyd George's prime, and all inclined towards Labour. In the 1950s Gaitskell encouraged consumerism just as Wilson in the 1960s encouraged the environmentalist and feminist lobbies. In 1971 Tony Benn went further, and argued that kindred cause groups should be affiliated formally to the Labour Party through being given 'consultative status'. In 1979–80 he was pushing for affiliation of black, environmentalist, and feminist groups, telling a group of black leaders in 1980 that 'we go down separately or we win together'.[61] There followed in the 1980s a debate on whether blacks would be better integrated through creating 'black sections' in the Party, an option overwhelmingly rejected at the conference in 1985 and 1987.

One pressure group, or set of pressure groups, predominated with Labour: the trade-union movement. The Gladstonian Liberal Party was responsive to the trade unions, but they were only one among its several pressures. Trade unions had not given birth to the Liberal Party, which was too broad a church to be moulded by their class consciousness. Between the wars many in the Labour Party thought that their Party's hold on workers by hand and brain would eventually place it permanently in power. Perhaps this is why the Webbs in 1920 envisaged the demise of the existing party system in favour of 'more or less sporadic propagandist organisations, seeking to influence the electorate and the national assemblies on particular subjects'. Party would, in short, be supplanted by pressure group. By the 1960s the trade unions had moved towards a dangerously close identification with Labour government policies. In the 1950s they had refused to operate incomes policies in conjunction with the Conservative government. When Macmillan indicated as Chancellor of the Exchequer that he would like to be invited to the TUC, Frank Cousins received thunderous applause when he asked 'What does he think it is—A Film Festival? We will welcome a Chancellor of the Exchequer, but . . . we will wait for a Labour Chancellor of the Exchequer.'[62] So it was through the trade-union movement that Labour governments sought in the 1960s and 1970s to carry out the Whigs' traditional role of 'handling' potentially disruptive opinion through cultivating its leading spokesmen.

The trade unions founded and largely funded the Labour Party, but their policies by no means dominated Labour governments, all of which have disappointed the trade-union movement in important ways; some have conflicted frontally with it. Labour leaders deployed their governmental status and their claims on trade-union loyalty to draw trade-union leaders into uncongenial policies, especially incomes policies. Wilson and Callaghan repeatedly played the loyalty card in squeezing trade-union acquiescence. 'It is now Labour's Prime Minister, your Prime Minister,' Wilson told the National Union of Mineworkers' conference when urging wage restraint in July 1975, 'at a critical hour in the nation's history, enjoining this community, once again, to assert this loyalty for the nation.'[63] Even after the disappointments of the 1970s, no prominent trade-union leader seceded with the SDP in 1981. The maverick electricians' leaders Frank Chapple and Eric Hammond kept within the fold, and when John Lyons became the first trade-union general secretary to join in 1985, he described his decision as 'an entirely private and personal matter'.[64] Ties so long-standing and emotional in nature could prevail despite the fiercest disagreements on policy.

\*

Whether it captures a political party or not, the pressure group which wants legislation must ultimately come before parliament. 'What *ought* to be done can often be sufficiently seen by persons not in Parliament,' wrote Bagehot, 'but . . . what *can* be done, is not often fully seen except by those who are there.'[65] Parliament is an arena where the interest group feels happier than the cause group, for it is a pragmatic place where bargains are struck, and where there is no expectation of political, let alone non-political, transformation. When the cause group's spokesman addresses parliament he faces an audience that is inattentive and sceptical. A reforming speech in parliament gains valuable publicity, yet it must be delivered while facing opponents not friends, and in an assembly which is sceptical of the MP with an extra-parliamentary reputation. Some reforming leaders in the late eighteenth and early nineteenth centuries contented themselves with retreating into anti-parliaments, with forming rival assemblies stuffed with unelected sympathizers. Early-Victorian pressure groups, however, increasingly orientated themselves towards parliament, and bore the parliamentary timetable in mind when preparing their petitions and public meetings. As we have seen, late-Victorian politicians in search of wider support increasingly took the initiative in making contact with cause groups, and during the twentieth century the need to handle complex policy issues and (in wartime) mobilize the population and boost morale gave them an additional motive for doing so.

The need to curb Edwardian industrial unrest, and actually to eliminate it during the First World War, forced the politicians to move towards corporatist management of the economy, and to negotiate directly with the trade unions and employers. Lloyd George as Chancellor of the Exchequer in 1915 seized the chance of getting labour leaders to concede dilution of the work-force in the Treasury agreement of 11 March. In exchange for helping to discipline shop-floor dissidents, labour leaders (most notably Arthur Henderson) gained political influence. Employers, too, were mobilizing in the First World War. The Federation of British Industries was founded, with government encouragement, in 1916. From that year onwards, Lloyd George's coalition drew business organizations into a new style of 'managerial' government. For the time being, the strains this imposed on trade-union structures were too great, and in 1917 the brief experiment in tripartite collaboration between employers, trade unions, and government came to an end, though it briefly resumed under Lloyd George's coalition government of 1918. By then the trade unions were becoming large, centralized, bureaucratic structures, and were turning to the Labour Party as their political vehicle. Tripartism revived during the rearmament of the late 1930s and triumphed during the Second World War, when Bevin (former General Secretary of the TGWU) wielded immense power as Minister of Labour. Thereafter it became normal for governments of either party to pursue tripartite discussion in the hope of improving industrial relations and national economic performance. By 1976 the process had gone so far that Denis Healey as Chancellor of the Exchequer framed his budget in such a way as to offer the trade unions nation-wide tax-reductions in exchange for restraining their members' wage-claims.[66] The practitioners of tripartism genuinely believed in working through a pluralist structure that enlisted business and trade-union leaders in forming public policy, if only because it seemed likely to diffuse aware-ness of governmental priorities more widely.

As we now know, the interventionist consequences overstrained both Conservative backbench patience and union leaders' influence over their rank and file. Besides, Conservatives under Thatcher came to feel that the price of corporatist collaboration with pressure groups was too high both for the economy and for the Party. It was forcing special interests forward, thereby hindering governments from directly representing public opinion and promoting the national interest. It was also putting the Conservative Party (which lacked trade-union links) continuously at a disadvantage by comparison with Labour. Reassertion of the politician's primacy spread out from the central area of economic management during the 1980s to other areas of government. Kenneth Baker, for example, describes how, when he became Secretary of State for Education in 1986, he encountered a body of civil servants who epitomized 'producer capture'. The Depart-ment, the teacher unions, the university departments of education, and local authorities were wedded to teacher-training theories and practices of the 1960s. 'One of the things I soon discovered was how close, and indeed cosy, was the relationship between the teacher unions and the Education Department. The unions seemed to come in almost daily, and even had rooms at the Department designated for their use. This was all part and parcel of the culture of the education establishment which had reigned since the 1960s.' He 'made it clear that I had an agenda which I expected officials to deliver. There was only room for one boss in my Departments.'[67]

So Thatcherism distanced pressure groups from government and threw them back towards parliament, where the politician's control is inherent in the practicalities of the situation. The pressure group focuses so much on campaigning that it has little time (and perhaps also little inclination) for thinking out precise solutions. As late as 1885 the Parnellite home rulers (who resembled a pressure group more than a political party) had given remarkably little thought to formulating a precise scheme for Irish home rule, despite the fact that this was the unifying principle lying behind their party.[68] Likewise, Victorian temperance reformers, full of zeal for their reform, were remarkably cavalier about what sort of measure would meet their need, so late-Victorian cabinet ministers found them unhelpful at the denouement.[69] Yet in a parliamentary democracy the pressure group's demand must ultimately be sold to the electorate, and for this the politician's expertise is essential. Politicians, whether frontbenchers or back-benchers, cannot display the reformer's single-mindedness, or his frequent indifference to practical outcomes and the interests likely to be affected. Politicians exist to balance interests, and to devise administrative expedients in a situation which the reformer (at the last stages of his crusade) cannot entirely control. Furthermore, the politician must legislate, and this requires a precise scheme. In 1969 Antony Grey, Secretary of the Homosexual Law Reform Society, eloquently described the situation. Once the bill 'is in Parliament's maw, the most significant pressures which are exerted do not come from the "pressure groups", however well informed . . . they are apt to feel like helpless spectators . . . aware of all the backstage manœuvring and often hastily concocted compromises which are taking place between sponsors, opponents and interested Government departments, but powerless to affect the timing, details or final shape of what they have laboured for years to achieve'.[70]

The politician retains control not only because he possesses political skills, but because in a democratic society he needs to retain it, given that the public interest may be neglected if the only opinions mobilized are those of competing pressure groups. To take a controversy of recent interest: Sunday trading. There the two sides were, on the one hand, the retailers, on the other hand, the shopworkers' trade unions in alliance with the sabbatarians. Neither side represented the interests of the general public, so the politician had to meet the need. John Major's suggestion in 1990 that the two sides should get together to settle the matter in agreed legislation was, as the *Observer* pointed out, 'futile. There is no conceivable common ground between the two groups . . . It is for Ministers to hammer out a solution which will be acceptable to Parliament.'[71] In the much more difficult conflict of interests over transport policy (consisting broadly of environmentalists and motorists), the Major approach is more appropriate because the groups affected constitute so large a proportion of the population. So in 1995 the Transport Minister Brian Mawhinney, before himself making a move, promoted a public debate between the interested parties in the hope of discovering shared ground between them. Shirley Williams had attempted something similar in the 'great debate' on educational policy in 1976.

It will not now be surprising to say that few cause groups get all that they want, and many partly or completely fail, though one would not guess as much from the histories their leaders tend to write in their old age. Energy, idealism, and strength of conviction are not in themselves enough. With their contradictory demands and refusals to compromise, cause groups may well complicate the business of getting a reform. Operating on a misleading analogy with the Anti-Corn Law League, some nineteenth-century reformers wrongly assumed that if only you organize enough, and persist with sufficient courage, you are bound to succeed. On the other hand, without the enterprise, the impatience, the energy, and the dedication cause groups evoke, democracies would lose much of their vitality, and might not survive at all. And whether the cause groups succeed or fail, they help by their very existence to curb the manipulative ambitions of politicians and civil servants. Chapters 3, 4, 5, and 6 have shown that all three political parties have their links and affinities with the national, local, libertarian, and voluntarist flavour of political culture in the British multi-national state. Only this can explain what would otherwise seem the surprising nervousness and even timidity shown by even the strongest twentieth-century British governments when dealing with public opinion. This applies as much to coalition governments with huge majorities (in 1918–22 or in 1931–5) as to single-party governments led by a powerful personality (in 1979–90)—not to mention governments with smaller majorities and less assertive leaders. It also explains the recognition by governments on right and left that legislation can succeed only if it rests on the basis of consent. In a voluntarist society, it is counter-productive to ride roughshod over opinion.

If governments temporarily forget the dangers of intervention, the relevant sections of British opinion will be well organized to apply the necessary corrective. The abolition of the income tax in 1816, the resistance to the new poor law after 1834, the failure of prohibition ever to get implemented in Britain, the pressure for decontrol after the temporary interventionism of the two world wars, the rejection of the poll tax in 1990—all these curbs on governmental ambition reflected a groundswell of popular resistance that was not normally allowed to get as far as rioting in the street. The prejudices of the 'little man'—epitomized in the cartoons of Strube or Giles—firmly reined in the pretensions of 'the man from Whitehall'. The accountants under the Attlee government no more saw themselves as aides to the taxman than did businessmen to the planners.[72] In the nineteenth century such sentiments were linked to the thrusting entrepreneurial culture which Thatcher in the 1980s tried to revive. But if it worked with the entrepreneurial grain, voluntarism was by no means identical with it, and persisted throughout the period of corporatist government from 1940 to 1979. Throughout that period voluntarism limited what 'planning' and nationalization could achieve, and ultimately brought an end to incomes policies. The fourfold pluralist context—involving nationality, localism, liberty, and voluntarism—has now prepared us to grasp why the political institutions discussed in Chapters 7–12 are so much less authoritarian in practice than their formal structures might lead us to expect.

# 7

## Co-ordinating Opinion

'THERE are nations', wrote Bagehot, 'which *have* no public opinion. The having it requires . . . the *co-ordination of judgements*.'[1] In the last four chapters we have seen how opinion in Britain, despite the substantial executive powers government derived from a centralized and unitary monarchical political system, wells up spontaneously from below. Already in Bagehot's day changes in communications were drawing opinion further towards the centre, with political party as the vehicle. Party will be the first of the political institutions operating from the centre to be discussed in the next six chapters. Given what has been said in Chapters 3–6, this chapter will work up to Westminster from the constituencies, and show how the resilience of the two-party system among the politicians reflects a similar resilience among their constituents, with each party continuously seeking to steal a march on the other.

An early-Victorian MP was likely to have some personal link with his constituency. In 1841–7 two-thirds either lived there or lived within the county of the borough they represented. This had already become less common by 1900–10, and became still less common thereafter.[2] Extension of the mass franchise to the countryside in 1884–5 entailed redistributing seats on a scale that almost destroyed the close identification between representation and the traditional units of community: county and borough. Only twenty-seven double-member constituencies survived; the remaining 616 were all single-member constituencies, many of them mere fragments of once proudly distinctive political units. With the demise in 1950 of the sole three-member and the eighteen two-member constituencies, the single-member constituency's triumph was complete.[3] 'Great commercial and manufacturing towns have each a brain and nervous centre, and a real unity of organic life,' wrote the experienced Liverpool Liberal Samuel Smith. 'You cannot cut them into separate organisms without a kind of atrophy.'[4] Among the more plausible weapons of the electoral reformer, past and present, is the claim that only the multi-member constituency can restore the ancient principle of community representation.[5] Yet with political parties, as with other British political institutions, an authoritarian and centralizing appearance is belied by a mild and decentralized governmental reality. For British parties, whether on right or left, have been remarkably responsive since the 1860s to constituency pressure, sometimes prodding one another along in that direction. In redrawing the constituency map in 1884–5, care was taken to preserve the distinction between urban and rural constituencies, 'to respect the ancient divisions of the country, and to make no unnecessary changes'.[6] As late as 1927 there was no uniform Conservative Party national colour, with more than half the constituencies favouring blue but about ninety still preferring red,[7] and even within a Labour Party that embraced centralized planning, local autonomy was tenacious.

Chapter 1 discussed the ingenuity of early-Victorian parties in competing for new electors at the local level, a process which took another leap forward in the 1860s. The Conservatives were relatively strong in the English countryside, over large tracts of which the great Conservative families presided right up to 1914 almost as though over personal fiefdoms. In the towns the single-member constituencies of 1884–5 at last freed urban Conservative minorities from being swamped by local Liberal majorities. The basis for a national Conservative network was laid by two independent developments: the spontaneous growth of Conservative registration societies, funded by middle-class subscribers; and the spread of Conservative clubs for working men. Conservatives were temperamentally more alert to the recreational needs of their humbler supporters, and less inhibited by puritan or temperance connections from catering for them. The nonconformist chapel, the reforming association, and the trade-union branch might cater for the Liberal high mind, but the Tory working man wanted billiards and refreshments. 'All work and no play makes Jack a dull boy,' as one club president told the Conservatives' annual conference in 1874.[8] The Corrupt Practices Act (1883), by restraining election expenditure at just the time when candidates needed more help, made it necessary to recruit volunteers. Given that British elections are unpredictable in their timing, volunteers had to be kept in continuous readiness, and this meant local associations of a more structured and participatory kind. Women proved particularly adept at the work, and Conservative women had a double advantage: they were less divided by feminist disputes, and more likely to offer the magnetism of social standing.

By contrast, the Liberal strength lay in conviction politics. As we have seen, it was the hope of mobilizing electors on the basis of opinion rather than of interest or locality that had inspired much of Mill's enthusiasm for proportional representation. These progressive political passions stemmed from a diversion of religious energies to secular purposes, and owed little to Liberal leaders, who responded as best they could to a sequence of movements mounted by wayward but energetic moral and spiritual entrepreneurs. London radical working men's clubs and provincial debating societies stirred up discussion, nonconformist chapels and popular pressure groups brought out the vote, so no overtly Liberal party organization needed to be set up at the local level. And as long as two-member constituencies survived, pragmatists and idealists could be profitably yoked together in Whig–radical and later Liberal–Labour harness. Class politics need pose no serious threat, given the Asquith government's substantial welfare legislation and Lloyd George's anti-aristocratic and redistributive rhetoric.[9] Up to 1914 there seemed every electoral and even ideological reason why the Liberal–Labour alliance should persist. The labour movement might indeed be a 'movement' to which one 'belonged', but its political aspirations could be well catered for with help from the politically experienced, more rationalistic, and less classbound allies who gathered within the broader Liberal consortium. For Liberalism, too, was a creed in which one could 'believe', and its doctrine of mutual tolerance and spontaneity united anti-Conservatives into a powerful, if diverse, alliance.

The First World War's unexpected impact on the Liberal Party meant goodbye to all that. The strong sense of community and the class-conscious loyalties in single-industry towns, hitherto valuable ingredients of a broad alliance on the left, now became constraints upon the outlook and policies of an entire opposition party. Labour now needed to repudiate Liberalism and win converts for socialism, at least in its dilute labourist form. The pioneer socialists' street-corner meetings, adult education classes, co-ops, summer schools, and banner-laden processions must now be geared behind a governmental party. Payment of MPs from taxation had relieved the Labour Party since 1911 of its heaviest burden, and the Reform Act of 1918 reduced the cost of elections and gave women over 30 every encouragement to join the men in their crusade. The nation-wide network of party branches which the Liberals had never required must now be set up, with trade-union branches and co-ops at their foundation. Branch secretaries could get the names of local trade unionists paying the political levy, and could invite these 'indirect' members of the Party to pay a full subscription and become 'direct'. Within the rich diversity of sympathetic institutions in Labour's heartland constituencies, a whole life could be lived: from Young Labour League branch to co-op, from socialist Sunday school to Women's Co-operative Guild, from trade-union branch to WEA class, all pinned together by the local-authority structures where the Party was gaining ground. In constituencies where the trade unions were strong, Liberals found themselves almost naked in the face of their new rivals, and so in local government hovered between joining the Conservatives in an anti-socialist alliance and joining Labour in a progressive coalition. Given the trade unions' secession from the Liberals and the decline of nonconformity, together with its associated moralistic pressure groups, there was no new regional or occupational interest group that Liberals could call their own. Their distinguished but ageing politicians were no substitute. After the Party had split three ways at the national level in 1931–2 its influence in local government, already declining, turned into something like a rout.[10]

There was a danger, though, that easily acquired trade-union affiliation fees would encourage Labour into undue dependence and deter it from building up a nation-wide constituency party structure, especially as trade unions liked seeing their money go to their own kind.[11] Partly for this reason, the Labour Party had difficulty in breaking out of its heartland and into the many non-industrial areas where Liberals had usually enjoyed a sporting chance.[12] So the Labour Party's regional reach never quite matched that of the Liberals in their heyday, and the outcome was either a Conservative gain or a divided anti-Conservative vote. For the Conservative Party's counter-attack was formidable, though it seems inevitable only in retrospect. At the time, many Conservatives must have shared Labour's view that its permanent triumph was only a matter of time, given the spread of political awareness among workers, who constituted a majority of the electorate.[13] After all, in mobilizing working-class support the Conservatives had no equivalent of the trade-union movement to launch out from. Conservative success in creating a mass party which could outpace Labour's machine reflects a huge effort, at all levels in the Party, to accumulate and consolidate individual supporters.

The part-time Conservative agent had for some years been spending less time on registering the voters, and in 1918 the state assumed responsibility for this, so legal expertise was no longer integral to his role. Instead, he became full-time manager of a constituency association, and needed to combine qualities rarely found in one person: to be a good organizer, sociable, energetic, committed, and cautious. His association was thirsty for members and money, so he also needed to be good at winning friends

and prising wallets open. Since 1880 expenditure on constituency campaigning has massively declined in real terms; party expenditure (central or
local) per voter has also declined.[14] Because Conservative Central Office
could not afford to subsidize constituency associations extensively, their
funds had to come from the candidate, from rich subscribers, or from
fund-raising by individual members. Decades before the Maxwell-Fyfe
reforms of 1949 formalized the process, Conservative constituency associations began democratizing themselves, and already by the 1930s between
a quarter and a third of them were self-supporting.[15] The need to raise
funds, far from damaging Conservative vitality, gave the members something to do and hence a sense of belonging. Working in the same direction
was the Party's increasing, though somewhat reluctant, overt involvement
in local government elections, given the need to respond to Labour's activism. All this enhanced constituency power within the system. Labour
was raising money from individual members as well, but more through
trade-union affiliation fees than through individual members' direct donations to constituency parties. Besides, both in trade-union structure and in
Party policy, the tendencies were all towards the centre. So much so, that
Labour's inter-war constituency parties felt the need to mount a Constituency Parties Association in self-defence. Their success was far from complete, and there were proposals in 1937 and 1955 to hold a separate Party
conference of their own.[16]

So by the 1930s the two-party contest, which as we saw in Chapter
1 has long been integral to British party politics, was re-established at
the constituency level on a Labour–Conservative rather than Liberal–
Conservative footing, and Conservative precedents were set for funding
arrangements that enhanced the power of constituency parties. The 1940s
once more saw the parties leap-frogging over one another in competing for
support. The war gave a final boost to the single-industry communities
and heavy-industry localities where Labour was strong, and produced a
marked shift to the left in opinion at the national level. What with this
and the growth of Conservative constituency parties, organized political
participation at the local level in the late 1940s was carried to a height
attained neither before nor since. The Conservatives had a good base for
recovery after their electoral defeat in 1945. Puzzled as usual at losing the
governmental power which they saw as their birthright, they immediately
set about reorganizing themselves to recoup the situation. Their individual
membership rose from 1,200,000 in 1947 to a peak of 2,800,000 in 1952.[17]
The Young Conservatives, designed for people under 30, grew out of

earlier Conservative youth organizations and during the Second World War were tied more closely into the Party's structure.[18] With 160,000 members by 1949, they brought the Party a long-term asset of the greatest value, more numerous and far less troublesome than its equivalents on the left. In addition, Lord Woolton and R. A. Butler between them added a salutary reappraisal of national policy and Party structure and generated a wealth of publicity and propaganda. The Maxwell-Fyfe reforms, by requiring the constituency associations to meet both election costs and contribute towards the Party's central expenses, prepared the way for democratizing the choice of candidates.

The Maxwell-Fyfe committee knew well enough that a tight national structure, deploying resources where most needed, would in some ways be more efficient. But it also knew that Conservative constituency associations would not stand for it, and that local autonomy would in the long run release more energy and commitment than centralized direction. Throughout the 1950s and 1960s, energy and initiative bubbled up from below, giving Conservatives the edge over their opponents, especially in getting out the postal vote and organizing mutual aid among constituency associations in Labour-held marginal seats. Even in the 1970s, long after their membership peak had passed, the constituency associations—through fund-raising activities such as coffee mornings, raffles, jumble sales, fêtes, and dances—raised four times as much for Conservative Central Office through quota payments than Labour's constituency parties could rustle up for Transport House.[19] The general election's analysts echoed several of their predecessors in saying that 'by every measure the Conservative organisation at the outset of the 1970 campaign was superior to Labour's'.[20] At the general election of October 1974, 875,000 postal votes were cast, and in almost every close contest the Conservatives won more of them than Labour; in thirty-six seats the postal vote exceeded the Conservative majority.[21] Conservative associations were better, too, at bringing volunteers to areas of weakness from areas where they were strong.[22] Perhaps the most powerful testimony to the Conservatives' constituency associations came from the enemy, for the Labour Party's inquiry of 1955 into its own organization, chaired by Harold Wilson, kept looking enviously over its shoulder at what the Conservatives were doing. With their full-time organizers and their card-indexes of voters marked up by visiting teams of paid 'missioners' or canvassers, the Conservative structure was decentralized to the polling district and even the street, 'with polling district and street captains, on the model of the Air Raid Warden service'.[23]

In their local organization the Conservatives had, in short, once more leap-frogged over their rivals. The Wilson committee confronted a painful truth: 'there is a dangerous tendency in our own ranks to exaggerate the importance of money', whereas in truth Conservative success stemmed from 'the efficiency of the voluntary organisation'.[24] Labour's constituency parties in comparable areas showed marked contrasts in their number of members; in safe Labour seats there was complacency and in marginals there was too little help from outside; too much of Labour's effort was confined to election periods, registers were not efficiently marked up, and there were far fewer young volunteers on the left than on the right. Compared with the Conservatives, 'we are still at the penny-farthing stage in a jet-propelled era'.[25] In retrospect, the committee's predominantly organizational remedies seem short-sighted. Claiming that organization should be restored 'to its rightful standing and prestige' by comparison with debate over policy, it felt that 'a disproportionate amount of the time available during an election is still devoted to conversion, at the expense of the priority task of identifying the Labour voters and creating a machine to get them to the polls'.[26] Even at the organizational level, the committee seems to have achieved little. Crossman's diaries in the 1950s and 1960s are peppered with affectionate but despairing references to the Party branches' inward-looking and traditionalist attitudes. 'Oh dear, defunct Derby', he wrote in 1965 after a visit there: '—that soulless industrial Victorian town with its pathetically ingrained Labour administration terrified of any change.' Of the six councillors selected to receive him, all were over 62 and two were over 80.[27] Traditionalism in Labour Party branches was particularly rife in heavy-industry areas, and in the same year Crossman noted how unsophisticated were the Party's Scottish branches by comparison with Coventry.[28] When Tony Benn visited Carlisle Labour Party supporters in 1976 he was at once reminded of the 1930s: 'there were the working men with their raincoats and cloth caps and the women in scarves, just like the Thirties'. He 'was stirred by the absolutely basic, solid loyalty of it', which reminded him 'how little the postwar capitalist recovery in Britain had reached beyond the South and the Midlands'.[29] Yet these communities were in decline, whereas the Conservative areas (the prosperous, suburban, home-owning areas of the south-east) were growing fast.

Organization alone could not enable Labour effectively to compete, and at this point the two-party system's long-standing syncopation in refining party structures gradually slowed down, leaving the Conservatives with what seemed a permanent advantage. The central funds of both parties came from major national institutions (trade unions and business firms), but on the Conservative side these were supplemented by levies raised from constituency parties. The latter contributed about a fifth of the Party's central income by the 1970s.[30] Labour's difficulties in trying to respond were many-layered. Its funds came primarily from the trade unions, which were so well entrenched in the Party's power structure that Labour's leaders did not even contemplate building up constituency structure and funding as a counterbalance. Yet from the late 1950s the trade unions were increasingly unpopular, and after the 1970s, given the contraction of heavy industry, they were losing members fast. Meanwhile, the constituency branches were also losing members and becoming cliquish in their management.[31] Often meeting in gloomy halls and unpainted premises, they resembled the nearby decaying churches and chapels in providing facilities that failed to match the country's rising expectations. Comments were now being made on the prominence in the Party's conference of 'well-fed, ageing white males', with no brown or black faces, few women, and few men under 30.[32] When the Party was in opposition it was thrown back into depending on a dwindling heartland which in office it alienated with its incomes policies, industrial rationalization, European aspirations, and even (in 1969) attempts at trade-union reform. Wilson was assiduous in attending the Durham miners' gala, yet in addressing the conference of the National Union of Mineworkers in July 1975 he knew that the miners' strong sense of community 'would become a weakness if ever the mining community were to become isolated from the national community—if the mining industry ever said "Whatever the state of the economy, whatever the nation's crisis, we will protect ourselves from its effects".'[33]

With the real costs of fighting elections rising fast in the 1970s,[34] Labour's only resort seemed to be increased dependence on the trade unions or the funding of political parties by the taxpayer, as recommended by the Labour majority on the Houghton committee in 1976. Constituency autonomy remained so great that the committee found it difficult to get firm figures on their members and funds.[35] None the less, its majority favoured subsidizing the parties from taxation on the basis of five pence per vote cast at the preceding general election, as well as meeting half the candidates' permitted expenses in parliamentary and local-government elections. To some well-informed commentators, it seemed that this might free the Labour Party from dependence on the trade unions and boost the funds of a Conservative Party whose increasingly corporatist business donors were moving towards political neutrality.[36] Yet the Conservatives opposed the scheme, and we now know that they were moving in anything but corporatist directions. Besides, voluntary funding gave the politicians every incentive to extend their contacts within the community, enhanced political participation, and prevented party officials from arrogantly distancing themselves from the voters.[37]

There was no escape-route for Labour through bypassing ill-attended constituency meetings by organizing Soviet-style work-place politics; in 1979 Vauxhall car workers at Luton and Dunstable voted to ban speeches in their canteens at lunch-time, claiming that their digestion would suffer thereby.[38] Labour's constituency parties were now small enough to be at risk of take-over by well-organized 'parties within a party'. The Trotskyist Militant Tendency's so-called 'entryism' was already seen as a problem by 1975.[39] Reselection of MPs, compulsory from 1981, exacerbated relations between constituency parties and right-wing Labour MPs: at Newham North-East Reg Prentice, who joined the Conservatives in 1977, for example; and at Knowsley North Robert Kilroy-Silk, who decided to leave politics for television in 1986. Even Tony Benn, who did not want the Tendency pushed out from the Party, was wearied by its tactics within Bristol constituency meetings in 1979. 'They moved endless resolutions. . . . they do go on interminably in their speeches. They have a certain pleading manner which just infuriates the others. "Comrades, surely we must understand that the neo-colonialism in Zimbabwe is a threat to the very standards to which the movement belongs", and so on.'[40] For Callaghan in 1981 the Tendency's members were 'like the ivy that is a parasite on the oak', deriving their strength from the Labour Party, without which 'they would be a small contemptible fraction'.[41] Party conference voted in 1982 to re-establish the register of non-affiliated organizations that had been abolished in 1973, and in 1983 after internal inquiry and much difficulty, conference confirmed the Party's expulsion of the Tendency's five leading members. Kinnock's firmness as Labour leader in dealing with the Tendency was thought to be an electoral asset in 1987, when a much-praised Labour party-political broadcast centred on his confrontation at the Party conference in 1985 with the Liverpool Militant activist Derek Hatton. 'It made my blood run cold,' wrote Benn in his diary.[42] None the less, Kinnock did at least halt the headlong decline of 1983—when Labour's total vote had fallen back almost to its level of 1935, and when its vote per opposed candidate had plumbed lower depths than at any election since 1900.[43] Egged on by yet another Conservative victory, Labour played the same card again at its conference in 1991, voting overwhelmingly to expel Dave Nellist and Terry Fields as suspected Tendency supporters.

In some ways more threatening to Labour's constituency parties was the mounting challenge from the Liberals. Their share of the votes cast at general elections and their vote per opposed candidate rose at the three general elections of 1955, 1959, and 1964, and in the late 1960s some Young Liberals favoured making a virtue of the Party's weakness at Westminster by embracing 'community politics', involving a street-based populist crusade concerned with local issues. This was to evade all the complexities of devising a practicable programme relevant to the nation as a whole, but at least it represented an attempt at opening out the political process to new talent and wider concerns.[44] When Liberals allied with disaffected social democrats in the early 1980s, their challenge to Labour was much more formidable because aligned with a sizeable group of MPs who insisted that their constituents had chosen them 'to exercise . . . conscience and judgment', rather than be 'rubber stamps for a party caucus'.[45] Eric Ogden, who had represented Liverpool (West Derby) for seventeen years, left Labour for the SDP in 1981, saying 'I will do much to remain a Member of Parliament but the only crawling I ever did in my working life was in a two-foot seam of coal at Bradford colliery, and I have no intention of crawling to any man on the surface.'[46]

In retrospect we can see that the SDP's challenge was pioneered by Dick Taverne, the Labour MP for Lincoln whose European loyalties led his constituency party in 1973 to reject him as its candidate for the forthcoming general election. He resigned and successfully fought a by-election as Democratic Labour candidate, though was defeated at the general election of October 1974 and later became prominent in the SDP. Bruce Douglas-Mann, the one Labour MP who joined the SDP and then risked exposing himself to a by-election, was defeated by the Conservative candidate in 1982. Vulnerable to the simple-majority electoral system at the national level, the SDP seceders from the Labour Party lacked the strength at the constituency level that had enabled the Liberals to survive for so long. The SDP at its peak had only 65,000 members in 1982, and by January 1984 this had fallen to about 50,000, whereas the Liberals then had 175,000 and Labour 280,000 individual members.[47] Liberal candidates were understandably reluctant to stand down in favour of SDP candidates, and tension at the local level between the SDP's governmental priorities and Liberal protest-mindedness was exacerbated by friction between national personalities. So the number of MPs in the SDP fell from a peak of thirty in 1982 to six in 1983 and five in 1987. Thereafter part of the Party merged with the Liberals and the rest faded away.

The story cannot be left there because for all their mistakes the SDP and Liberals did at least help to transcend unrepresentative intermediate bodies, achieving on the centre-left a sort of mirror image of what Thatcher was achieving from the right. In 1976 the Liberals had enfranchised individual members through the constituency party in choosing the leader, and the founders of the SDP, though never active campaigners for direct democracy when still in the Labour Party, were quick to devise a party structure more democratic than the one they had left. Unlike the other parties, the SDP collected subscriptions from the centre and retained them there. One member one vote was the method for choosing both the SDP's leader and (through the area parties) its parliamentary candidates. Despite the SDP's subsequent demise, the idea of one member one vote, backed forlornly by Kinnock at the Labour Party conference in 1984,[48] gradually gained ground and ultimately triumphed at the Party conference of 1993, though it might well have triumphed much earlier if the SDP's founders had remained with Labour.

The SDP was ambiguous in its legacy as in so much else, for it signposted two possible routes towards reviving party-political involvement in Britain. Despite its decentralizing policy stance, it was firmly driven from the centre in both origins and structure. One might see centralism as both the major parties' way out of the decline which by the 1980s had hit Conservative as well as Labour constituency associations. In the 1960s and 1970s the Conservatives had far more party agents than Labour, and deployed them more effectively towards the constituencies where effort was most needed, but by then agents' numbers were dwindling in both parties.[49] As for the volunteers, the Conservative associations had done little to respond to 'Project '67', the scheme to broaden out local membership in line with the constituency's demographic composition,[50] and by the 1980s the Conservative constituency parties' members were ageing. Much of the work was done by women, so that women's growing pursuit of paid employment, together with the mounting pressures of middle-class life, constituted a major threat. Even a party based on prosperous areas was vulnerable to the many distractions from community involvement that affluence offered: travel, single-issue causes, and home-based recreations such as television. By 1990 there was a decline not only in Conservative membership, but also in degree of commitment and willingness to give active help.[51] As for Labour, its trade unions were now too centralized to bring much impetus at the local level, and a meritocratic educational system together with automation and mechanization had spirited away the educated but socially unambitious artisan who had once been so important among Labour's volunteers. The retired, the unemployed, and the ethnic minorities are hardly likely to possess the self-confidence, energy, or unanimity to take his place.

So perhaps the future lies with the centralizing aspect of the SDP

legacy. Whereas in the 1860s it would have seemed intrusive for an outsider to contest a hopeless seat, in the twentieth century this was the way
to gain credit with one's party.[52] We have already seen in Chapter 4 how
the vitality of local government has declined, and in Chapter 8 we will see
how centralized general election campaigns have become. Faster transport
and the growth of the mass media help to explain the decline since 1945
in civic pride and consciousness of community. Speculating about radio's
long-term significance for the shape of campaigns, the analysts of the
general election in 1945 saw the 'sense of constituency' as 'already growing
dim in those amorphous city divisions whose boundaries do not corres-
pond with those of any genuine local community', and went on to note
that 'this constituency sense is the foundation of the British representative
system of Parliamentary government'.[53] Commentators on politics from
R. T. McKenzie onwards have stressed the declining importance of local
activists by comparison with the national campaign in getting the voters
out. It was noticed in 1975 that despite the lack of conventional party
electioneering, the overall turn-out in the EEC referendum was only 8 per
cent lower than at the preceding general election.[54] 'Perhaps in retrospect',
McKenzie wrote in 1963, 'it will be evident that the mass party saw its
heyday during the period when the extension of the franchise had created
a mass electorate, but there was as yet no effective means of reaching the
voters in their own homes.'[55]

In the 1980s information technology carried this centralizing trend further. The centre's powerful computers reinforced the opinion poll and
survey information and accumulated political expertise that had already
begun to fertilize the constituencies with richer data. Cecil Parkinson as
Conservative Party Chairman (1981–3) set about identifying the marginal
seats and the seats where organizational weakness had rendered the Conservatives vulnerable, and established a by-election team with special expertise which could move into a constituency as the occasion arose. 'Fighting
by-elections is a specialized business', he recalled, 'and it seemed pointless
to me that we should reinvent the wheel on each occasion.'[56] Such an
attitude to the constituency would have been inconceivable in Bagehot's
England. Computers made it easier to target literature on selected voters.
Parkinson set up a marketing department influenced by American campaigning methods. A computer was installed in December 1982 to record
the names of key voters in critical constituencies, and word-processors
were used to send personal letters and appeals to potential donors for
funds. 1983 saw the first general election when the parties made serious use
of computers, and the Conservatives' central computer sent personal letters

to half a million people whom their canvassers in sixty marginal constituencies had identified as potential Conservative voters.[57] The SDP too was enthusiastic for direct mailing from the centre, and by 1986 the Labour Party was targeting potential supporters by using lists of trade-union members and subscribers to sympathetic periodicals.[58] A special effort was made at the general election of 1987 to target the individual voter as distinct from individual constituencies,[59] and in what Tebbit describes as 'the most successful direct mail campaign in British politics' more than a million shareholders in the newly privatized British Telecom proved a fertile source of donations to his Party.[60] The Conservative aim was not always accurate: Benn took pleasure in telling Tebbit in November 1987 that he had received three letters asking him to contribute to the Conservative Party, and that his mother had received two as well.[61] Accurate enough, though, for Major and Kinnock at the general election in 1992 to think it worth targeting one and a half and one million potential supporters, respectively, in marginal seats.[62]

Yet there was another aspect to the SDP legacy, for together with the Liberals it pioneered the more direct involvement of party members in deciding upon candidates, leaders, and policy. In the late 1960s the decision on who should be MP was in effect settled in three-quarters of the constituencies by the parties' selection conference and not by the electorate at all, given that seats had changed hands in only 160 of the 630 constituencies at elections and by-elections since 1955.[63] The Hansard Commission on electoral reform argued in 1976 that choice of candidates for parliament by selection committees was 'democracy at second hand', and thought that candidates should be chosen by all members in secret ballot.[64] In the Labour Party the block vote's 'indirect democracy' ensured that both conference policy and (after 1981) the selection of the Party leader, were unduly dominated by activist leaders. The SDP and still more the Liberals offered a way out of all this: more power for the ordinary member might get more people to join their local party associations. Given that the jealousy of central control is as lively as ever in Conservative associations,[65] reluctant in some cases even to provide Parkinson as Party Chairman with information about party organization for fear that it might be used against them,[66] such a decentralized and participatory direction for party organization would certainly be working with the Conservative grain. Tebbit even argued in 1983 that if trade unionists were required to contract in for Labour Party contributions instead of contracting out, the Labour Party would be forced into making the effort required to build up a mass individual membership; reliance on easily acquired trade-union funds, he argued, rendered such effort unnecessary, thereby opening the way to subversion by 'bedsit Trotskyites' of Labour's constituency parties.[67]

Furthermore, by the early 1990s the national political climate seemed more participatory than centralizing in mood. The continuing vitality of Welsh and Scottish nationalism, and the reaction against Thatcher's attacks in the 1980s on local authorities, made a less centralized variant of socialism popular on the left, where 'community' had become a vogue-word. Benn with his referendum of 1975 and Tebbit with his strike ballots of 1984 had both revealed to moderates that they had much to gain from wider political participation, and this was the direction in which Labour leaders from Kinnock to Blair gradually moved. So with help from new developments in information technology it seems likely that in party structure the participatory rather than the centralizing aspect of the SDP's legacy will ultimately prevail. It would be a development very much in line with British party traditions since the 1860s.

*

Constituency localism, with its down-to-earth and forcibly expressed priorities and taste for the two-party battle, pervades the intermediate structures of both major parties at every level. When the secretary of the Labour Party branch in 'Ashton' offered to read out to the meeting in 1953 a letter about problems in British Guiana, ' "Don't bother", one of the women exclaimed; "We've enough trouble in Ashton".'[68] The simple-majority electoral system does not select the MP through generating a consensus behind him. Indeed, the one area after the 1860s where the MP formally represented the entire constituency was southern Ireland, whose Home Rulers were in retrospect preparing themselves to leave Westminster altogether. But the MP once elected is bound to act in some sense for his entire constituency, not only in his day-to-day activities, but sometimes also when voting in parliament. The simple-majority electoral system, reinforced by the voluntary rather than state funding of parties, renders the relationship between MP and constituent direct, and makes it difficult for party officialdom to distance itself from or manipulate the voter. If anything, the MP has become more exposed to constituency problems during the twentieth century. Constituents are better educated and more self-confident, faster transport and communications make it easier for them to exert pressure, parliamentary seats (at least since the 1960s) have become less secure, and since the rise of the career politician MPs have become keener to hold on to them. Extended public welfare has given constituents more reason to make contact, and during the 1960s MPs holding 'surgeries' for constituents rose from 60 per cent to 90 per cent. Whereas in 1959 the typical MP received between twelve and twenty letters a week, by 1986 he was receiving between twenty and fifty a day.[69]

Politicians did not see the constituency as a mere mathematical unit of opinion: it was a community, whose opinions needed to be weighed up carefully. As late as the 1960s the Boundary Commission 'considered it reasonable to assume that each existing constituency normally represents a community with its own distinct character, problems and traditions'.[70] At a time when opinion was fragmented into localities, the constituency was an important sounding-board, and governments found the MP a useful guide to significant opinion. Indeed, opinion long impinged on government in a fragmented way, through its impact on individual MPs rather than directly or collectively. Twentieth-century commentators often view the nineteenth-century patronage system censoriously, yet ministers needed the MP's guidance on how government appointments would go down in the localities. 'Don't ever lose touch with your constituency,' Baldwin told new MPs in 1924, 'don't ever mistake the voice of the clubman and the voice of the Pressman in London for the voice of the country.'[71]

A constituency often moulded the entire outlook and career of an MP: Grimsby's impact on Crosland, for example, or Sedgefield's on Blair. It was the unemployment of Stockton and Middlesbrough or Jarrow that inspired the distinctive contributions made by Harold Macmillan and Ellen Wilkinson to inter-war parliamentary debates, just as it was in Plymouth that Lady Astor tested out several of her ideas on national welfare policy. The parliamentary preoccupations of Powell and Benn would have been very different if they had not been MPs for Wolverhampton and Bristol, respectively. The MP who fails to gear his party behind constituency interest may well put his constituency first in the division lobby. Powell illustrates the point when he explains why he insisted on publicizing the race question in his Birmingham speech of April 1968. 'Here is a decent, ordinary fellow Englishman, who in broad daylight in my own town says to me, his member of Parliament, that this country will not be worth living in for his children. I simply do not have the right to shrug my shoulders and think about something else.'[72] In both Toulouse and Bristol, well-placed constituency MPs helped in difficult times to shield the vast expenditure on Concorde from cuts.[73]

Constituency representation is so central to the British political system that regional structures within the parties have never acquired much influence. The role of Ulster Unionists in the system has, it is true, been distinctive; but as we saw in Chapter 2, the parties have cut across national loyalties in Scotland and Wales, and in England regional loyalties have been too weak for the parties ever to exploit them. Regionalism may have had some appeal for the Liberals, but for a unionist party its attractions have never been strong. As for the Labour Party, it had a threefold reason for resisting regionalism: the Party was dominated by increasingly central-ized trade unions; it was committed to central planning and nationaliza-tion; and its outlook on social class consciousness, while never showing a Marxian freedom in imputing 'false' consciousness, made it wary of pan-class regional policy priorities. So the role of party structures intermediate between Westminster and the constituencies has not been to dilute gov-ernment's responsiveness to constituents, but to enforce it. Take the role of the party conference, for example. At first it had been sufficient for prominent supporters to mingle with their MPs in the London clubs. But the last great burst of club-building took place in London and provincial cities in the 1860s and 1870s, and thereafter numbers became so large that the party conference did the job better. Disraeli took the initiative in 1867, and set up the National Union of Conservative and Constitutional Associations (NUCCA)—not as a policy-forming agency, but as an aid to the leadership. It turned out to be the ancestor of the modern Conservat-ive Party conference. Through a characteristic local initiative, the Liberals in their turn set up the National Liberal Federation (NLF) in 1877 to co-ordinate the demands of progressive cause groups, using Americanized caucus methods and a participatory local branch structure. Conservatives in the early 1880s responded through the initiatives taken by the up-and-coming young backbencher Lord Randolph Churchill. He worked through the National Union to increase local participation in the Party's manage-ment. Simultaneous effort to extend the Party's appeal and propaganda was made through the Primrose League, founded in 1883. This pseudo-masonic, semi-recreational organization used regalia, ceremonial, and snob-bery to marshal mass male and female volunteer support behind the Party in local branches, or 'habitations'. Children were admitted as Primrose 'buds' from 1889, and by October 1891 there were just over a million mem-bers. 'Vulgar?' said Lady Salisbury, 'of course, it is vulgar! But that is why we have got on so well.'[74]

The NUCCA and the NLF may have originated from different direc-tions, but in both cases the effect was similar: to reward constituency activists with a cross between policy forum and annual jamboree. The Liberal leader W. V. Harcourt grumbled in 1888 that NLF council meet-ings were 'a bore and a mistake'. He hated their carnival atmosphere, especially as he was always cast as an 'ornamental figure' making 'short ornamental speeches'.[75] But he attended none the less. The somewhat pained and weary note struck by Harcourt was certainly echoed on the Conservative side. 'Every habitation thinks it necessary at every crisis to assure us of its unabated confidence,' grumbled Lord Salisbury in 1886; 'and I have to assure them that I have received the assurance with sincere gratification. Touching at first . . . but very tiresome when you come to your hundredth letter.'[76] The new party structures had little direct effect on policy, and on the Conservative side were not normally intended to do so, but constituency activists had now to be humoured. The role of party conferences a century later was not so very different, with Michael Heseltine playing Harcourt to the Conservative conference. Activists needed reassurance that the government, amidst the compromises inevitable in office, was still on course. For Castle in 1975 the Labour Party conference was 'an essential piece of catharsis for our activists frustrated by the limitations on our actions imposed by reality'.[77] Conservative leaders from Heath onwards have thought it worth spending much more time at their conference. In the victory conference of 1979 there was an almost theatrical adulation of the leader, with the organ striking up 'Hello, Maggie' as she entered the conference hall, and there were many comparable performances thereafter. During the 1960s the constituency parties' increasing importance was reflected in mounting interest from political scientists and the media, and in the growth of 'fringe meetings'. There was growing familiarity between party leaders and delegates, though this was disrupted in 1984 by the IRA's attempt to blow up the cabinet at the Party conference. 'The party conferences have been turned into a kind of political bazaar or fairground,' wrote Alan Watkins in 1982: 'see the fat lady, listen to the mad professor, try your strength with the hard Left.'[78]

At this point R. T. McKenzie's classic analysis of party structures, first published in 1955, becomes relevant, for, unlike Conservatives and Liberals, the Labour Party originated as what Duverger called an 'outside party'. Beginning as a cross between mass movement and pressure group, it grew towards Westminster with a power structure that for practical and ideological reasons lent much less influence to the MPs. McKenzie argues, however, that the Labour Party, like other mass organizations, is subject to Michels's 'iron law of oligarchy'. This claims that mass organizations, however radical in their origins, tend to fall into the hands of relatively conservative leaders who soon lose touch with their rank and file. This is because their leaders once in office become complacent, a development facilitated by an apathetic mass membership. In the case of the Labour

Party this distance between leaders and led was widened still further, once Labour had superseded the Liberals and formed a government, by the conventions of the cabinet system. This lent Labour leaders more power than their Party's constitution would have led anyone to expect. The formal position is that the Parliamentary Labour Party (PLP) chooses the shadow cabinet and (together with the mass party organization) helps to decide on a programme. The leader has no personal control over the Party's head office, and his position is especially weak in opposition. Yet the reality is different. MacDonald, McKenzie argues, was well on the way to shaking off conference control by 1914, and shook it off altogether after returning to the leadership in 1922. In 1924 he chose his cabinet ministers without consulting anyone in the Party, and as party leader controlled the Party conference through allying with right-wing trade-union leaders and the PLP, who permeated the Party's National Executive Committee. Attlee consolidated this position after 1945. Far from distancing leaders from voters, this enhancement of their powers aimed at consolidating the relationship. A Labour leader is or may be prime minister, and needs to communicate directly with actual or potential electors unhindered by unrepresentative intermediate bodies. For if forced to choose between activist and voter, the leader who wants an electoral majority must choose the voter, and the governmental party will try to ensure that its intermediate structures are representative enough to prevent that choice from being difficult.

The Conservatives never espoused Labour's ideal of intra-party democracy in so structured a form. So they did not display so glaring and disillusioning a contrast as Labour's between aspiration in opposition and achievement in government. Formally speaking, the Conservative leader, McKenzie pointed out, has complete control over policy, party organization, and appointments to cabinet, and dominates the party conference. Yet in reality he holds office only with the consent of his followers, and there is ample precedent for the Party's withdrawing that consent, most notably at the Carlton Club meeting of 23 October 1922. McKenzie establishes the point through a detailed study of the leadership of Balfour, Austen Chamberlain, and Baldwin. Party leaders who fail to retain contact with party feeling are readily removed: Macmillan in 1963 and (he would now have added) Heath in 1975 and Thatcher in 1990. So whereas Conservative leaders were formally more powerful than they were in practice, the reverse was the case with Labour leaders. The contrast in structure between the parties, while more apparent than real, put Labour at an electoral disadvantage. This was because Labour activists, encouraged by their Party's origins and constitution to hold an inflated view of their own influence, displayed their disappointment to the electors at unfraternal Party conferences. True, Gaitskell's reversal of his conference defeat in 1960 showed how a Labour leader could outmanœuvre one Party conference by working to change the composition of the next. But for McKenzie this was an unnecessary struggle, which could be avoided if the Party admitted the truth: that its leader's main line of responsibility (as an actual or potential prime minister) must lie to the electorate and not to the party activists. Given the mounting importance of centralized media campaigning at general elections, the activists were anyway increasingly marginal to the Party's electoral fortunes.[79] McKenzie wanted the leader to call the activists' bluff.

This trenchant argument, amply backed by empirical detail, aroused much interest at the time, and three of its important features have been vindicated since. On the role of the mass party, the contrast between Labour and Conservative remained substantial at least until the 1990s. McKenzie's advice was not taken. The Labour leader's traditional way of controlling the Party conference—through an alliance with right-wing trade-union leaders wielding their block vote—has more than once since 1963 proved impracticable. At the Party conference of 1970 Wilson tried to hold the line by directly confronting those who believed in conference sovereignty. 'A prime minister is responsible to the House of Commons', he said, 'and acts on the basis of the Cabinet judgement of what is necessary in the public interest in so far as and as long as he commands the confidence of the House of Commons, and he cannot be instructed by any authority from day to day other than Parliament.'[80] Yet something more than assertion was required, and things had to get worse before they could get better. The concessions needed to bring the trade-union leaders back into alliance with the parliamentary party were so substantial between 1970 and 1976 that they helped to undermine the leader's stature and the Party's credibility. For most of the 1980s the contrast between the Conservative and Labour conferences severely handicapped Labour. Indeed, according to Harold Wilson in 1980 the Blackpool conference in September that year was a 'shambles'.[81] The SDP had no need or desire to replicate Labour's structure. As we have seen, it took the argument further than McKenzie had taken it in the 1960s by enfranchising every individual SDP member directly, rather than indirectly through a block vote. The Labour Party in the 1990s belatedly began to move in the same direction. Much has also been done since 1983 to scale down the activists' expectations, but the ambiguity in Labour's power structure persists, and perhaps it was not until Blair's success in getting the commitment to nationalization in the Party's constitution modified in 1995 that the activists' bluff was at last definitively called.

McKenzie's argument on the role of the Labour leader also remains convincing. The broadening number of participants from parliamentary party down to party conference gave some activists the misleading impression that the conference was more likely than the MPs to represent the still wider number of participants who were prepared to vote Labour. In reality, the MPs at the apex of the party pyramid had constituency contacts close enough, and perspectives broad enough, to have better contact with the pyramid's lowest and broadest layer. Kinnock after 1983 appealed repeatedly over the heads of his party activists to the wider public, which his party structures were failing to represent. As he put it in his speech of 1985, repudiating Liverpool's Militant Tendency councillors, 'the voice of the people, not the people in here, the people with real needs is louder than all the boos that can be assembled'.[82] Of Labour's five leaders whose terms have ended since 1963, Smith died before retirement was an option, but the other four have all chosen their own moment for retirement. Undignified as many of Wilson's manœuvres for position within his party may have been, he was not pushed in 1976: he chose to go. Furthermore, Foot's brief period of leadership proved electorally so disastrous that the Party conceded considerable authority to Kinnock between 1983 and 1992 in the hope that he could ensure its continuance as second party in the state. For similar reasons Kinnock's two successors, Smith and Blair, have enhanced the leader's authority still further.

As for the Conservatives, the peculiar combination of strong leaders easily removed has persisted. The Party's move since 1963 to a meritocratic mood and leadership weakened the leader's position. Peel, Disraeli, and Baldwin were all Conservative prime ministers who experienced serious challenges to their authority, yet in no case was the challenge so continuous and even at times contemptuous as that faced by the three Conservative leaders since McKenzie's book was written. Thatcher's fear of 'enemies within', initially justified, flawed her entire style of leadership, and ultimately caused her downfall. Major's energies after his first year as Prime Minister seemed almost entirely absorbed in asserting his competence for his post. If this represents a long-term trend, the Conservatives may now be losing one of their major advantages over parties on the left. So formal structures and procedures are a poor guide to where power lies within political parties. Conservative leaders are as responsive as Labour leaders to their followers. They need to be, because if they diverge from their conference they have no block vote to fall back upon; when conference demanded 300,000 houses per year in 1950 or the accelerated introduction of the poll tax in 1987, the leadership had to acquiesce.[83] Conservative backbenchers acquired a new authority over their leader in 1965 when they acquired the power to select or deselect. They replaced Douglas-Home by Heath in 1965, Heath by Thatcher in 1975, and Thatcher by Major in 1990. Nowhere was the Party's control more strikingly demonstrated than in 1990, when one of the most powerful leaders in its history was removed because thought unlikely to win the next election. Before casting their votes in 1990, backbenchers took some care to consult their constituents.[84] This mutual responsiveness between member and constituency activist is designed to avoid public confrontation, and is no less real for being informal. Likewise, mutual interaction between leaders and conference delegates, as with backbenchers in the House of Commons, takes place continuously and unobtrusively, with the ultimate sanction that disagreement, if not reconciled, will be made public.

To endorse the essentials of McKenzie's argument is to highlight the fact that party machinery above the constituency level in both Labour and Conservative parties has as its function the transmission of constituency opinion to the leadership, the leader being left free to reject conference recommendations if constituency activists seem likely to lose the party the next election. Gaitskell did this over unilateral disarmament in 1960, but Thatcher had no such need because both she and her party activists for most of the 1980s were in closer touch with electoral opinion than Labour's activists in the 1950s or 1980s had been. With the poll tax at the very end of her reign, however, she made the same sort of mistake that Foot had made as Labour leader before 1983.

\*

We are now equipped to turn to the parties at Westminster, and relate the two-party polarization in the constituencies to the two-party conflict between government and opposition. We saw in Chapter 1 that Bagehot was writing mid-way between the second and third of the six near-disruptions of the British two-party system that have occurred since the 1790s, and that it was not then clear that the two-party system had restabilized. By the end of his life, however, he was taking the rightward direction that so many moderate Liberals were beginning to take in a repolarized system. Still worried by Disraelian adventurism, concerned in 1874 that the Conservatives had not yet tempted sufficient ministerial talent from the Liberals, he none the less had high hopes of Lord Salisbury as the safe man of the future. 'In happy states', he wrote in 1874, 'the Conservative party must rule upon the whole a much longer time than their adversaries. In well-framed polities ... great innovation ... can only be occasional.'[85] Yet it was some time before this late-Victorian Conservative haven for the middle classes came to seem really secure. Towards the end of this third phase (1846–86) in the modern history of the British two-party system, the 'swing of the pendulum' was once more in operation—in 1874, 1880, and 1885—and the two-party system seemed to be re-establishing itself. Yet once more it was disrupted at the end of the period: the Irish nationalists won eighty-five seats at the general election of 1885, and this set in train the sequence of events that led Gladstone to declare for home rule. This split his Party, and gave many Whig aristocrats, among others, the excuse they had long wanted for leaving it. Thereby the Conservatives acquired the infusion of ministerial talent that Bagehot thought lacking in 1874.[86] In 1886, however, Britain had for the moment four political groupings: Conservatives, Liberal Unionists, Gladstonian Liberals, and Irish Nationalists. It was not at all clear even to leading politicians after the general election of 1886 what shape the party system would take in the near future.

The fourth phase (1886–1916) once more saw the two-party system gradually restored. Some would say that in backing home rule this had been Gladstone's intention all along. Five linked developments produced this outcome. First, the Liberal leaders regained full control over their Party. Whereas in the early 1880s it looked as though the NLF would enable Joseph Chamberlain to capture it, his secession into Liberal Unionism in 1886 enabled Gladstone to capture the Chamberlain machine outside Birmingham. The NLF's Newcastle programme of 1891 aggregated the demands of Liberals at the grassroots level but did the Party little good, and thereafter the Liberal caucus lost its influence, never fully to regain it. Secondly, Gladstone's actions in 1886 had the effect of disciplining the Irish MPs. Because the Irish Nationalists after 1886 had some hope that the Liberals would get what they wanted, they became in effect a Liberal adjunct, and ceased to disrupt parliament and the party system. Meanwhile Lord Salisbury too was regaining control—of a Conservative Party now renamed Unionist. Hostility to home rule after 1886 was so great that the Conservative appeal could draw heavily upon it, with much less need for the pseudo-progressive policies advocated in the early 1880s by Lord Randolph Churchill. So when Churchill resigned from the Unionist government in 1886 in the hope of increasing his influence over it, Lord Salisbury accepted his resignation and Churchill's career was wrecked.

Conservative leaders henceforth had little trouble from the National Union. The caucus's threat to the leaders of both major parties had gone away.

In the two-party system's fourth phase after 1886, the Liberal Unionists, like the Peelites before them, did not remain a free-standing party group for long: they allied with the Conservatives. This began when Goschen agreed in 1887 to replace Churchill (just resigned) as Chancellor of the Exchequer. In her memorable scrutiny of Jack Worthing (a Liberal Unionist) as a possible son-in-law, Lady Bracknell (a Conservative) in Wilde's *The Importance of being Ernest* (1895) dismissed the divergence as unimportant: 'oh, they count as Tories. They dine with us. Or come in the evening, at any rate.'[87] In the Unionist government of 1895, Chamberlain became Colonial Secretary and Hartington Lord President. Liberal Unionists came to a formal end as a distinct party in 1912, but their distinct existence had really ended nearly twenty years before. In party repolarization's fifth and final dimension, the Liberal and Unionist groups reached out more widely within the community to consolidate their support. The Conservatives moved closer towards the middle class via the tariff reform movement (launched in 1903), with its heavily commercial preoccupations and pressure for middle-class influence in the constituencies. Tariff reform also aimed to attract the working-class vote by consolidating the Party's imperialist image and by funding a welfare programme through taxing the foreigner. Meanwhile, the Liberals were opening out further towards organized labour. Whereas before 1886 two aristocratic parties competed primarily for middle-class support, the two Edwardian middle-class parties competed primarily for working-class support. Between 1900 and 1914 the swing of the pendulum resumed. The Conservative victory in 1900 created the climate within which a pact between the Labour Representation Committee and the Liberal Party could be brought off in 1903. Thence came Liberal victory in 1906 and waning Liberal majorities in the two elections of 1910. Yet once more the period ended with a sudden and unexpected disruption to the newly consolidated two-party system, this time because of the speed and intensity of the First World War's challenges to the Liberal government and its values. These challenges were rendered fatal by the bad feeling that accompanied Lloyd George's supplanting of Asquith as Prime Minister in December 1916.

In the two-party system's fifth phase from 1916 to 1931, left and right competed to eat up the Liberal vote. The liberalizing of the Conservative Party could happen in two ways: either the Conservatives could retain their distinctive policies but ally with anti-socialists in other parties; or they could more overtly trim towards the centre and aim at power on their own. These two strategies were pursued consecutively. Under Bonar Law and Austen Chamberlain from 1918 to 1922, Conservative politicians initially sought to counter the rise of Labour by forming an anti-socialist coalition of Conservatives and centrist Liberals under Lloyd George. But by 1922 Conservative backbenchers' distrust of Lloyd George had increased the attractions of the second strategy, and with help from Baldwin and Bonar Law the coalition strategy was abandoned. As Bonar Law's successor in presiding over the strategy for single-party Conservative government, Baldwin could hope to contain Labour by pursuing coalition of the more traditional kind: that is, through a single-party government whose broad base ran from far right to centre-left under the Conservative label. With vigorous propaganda and loyal backbenchers, he could hope both to attract centrist Liberals and to contain his right-wingers through the familiar operation of the two-party system. This would squeeze out the Liberals from the right in the same way as Labour's leader Ramsay MacDonald hoped to squeeze them out from the left. When Baldwin won the general election of 1924 and formed a government which included the centrist Conservative coalitionist leaders, he seemed on course for success. Meanwhile, Ramsay MacDonald's liberalized Labour Party was tempting the more adventurous Liberals leftwards. This task was much eased in 1920 when the labour movement's Marxists channelled themselves off into the Communist Party ghetto from which they began to emerge only after 1956. It was a recipe for success: Labour's percentage of the votes cast went up from 30 per cent in 1922 to 31 per cent in 1923 to 33 per cent in 1924 to 37 per cent in 1929.

Yet the two-party system's fifth phase once more ended in disruption. The economic crisis in summer 1931 caused Labour temporarily to resume its earlier role as a relatively narrow church. After the general election, with only fifty-two MPs, it was undisciplined by any near prospect of power, and was once more under the trade unions' firm control. At the same time, the crisis split the Liberal Party three ways: the Simonite Liberals joined the National Government and stayed there, becoming in effect Conservatives; the Samuelites joined it but left in September 1932 when the 10 per cent tariff became National Government policy; and the Lloyd Georgian Liberals became a tiny opposition grouping. Once more it was not at all clear how the two-party system was going to be restored, if at all. Yet in the sixth phase (1931–81) restoration began surprisingly quickly, simultaneously through efforts to right and left, helped by the Liberals' rapid demise. The Conservatives digested the National Liberals and National Labour, and the 'National' government gradually became in effect Conservative. The Liberals did not re-emerge as a major force till the 1970s. Labour gradually resumed MacDonald's strategy: that is, it bid for the Liberal Party's former role as the progressive party within a two-party system. That system was already recovering in the general election of 1935, when Labour gained from capitalizing on the National Government's mistakes. The Second World War coalition gave Labour five years' experience of government, together with the credibility which helped to produce its victory at the general election of 1945.

By 1945 both Conservatives and Labour were united, experienced, and strong enough to preside over the two-party scene until the late 1960s. Between 1945 and 1951 the Conservatives bid energetically for the centre ground. The Labour government made this easier by allowing itself to appear more extreme than it really was, but Conservatives were energetic in refurbishing their image, Macmillan going so far as to favour a change of name to 'New Democratic Party'.[88] Winston Churchill made a real effort to draw the Liberals into his own Party, and soon after the defeat in 1945 offered them a clear run in sixty seats if they would agree to an electoral pact. He failed to get their consent, and failed again in 1951 when Clement Davies, the Liberal leader, turned down his offer of a cabinet post after consulting his Party. But Lloyd George's younger son, Gwilym, a former Liberal, was more pliable, and joined Churchill's cabinet in 1951 as Minister of Food, moving on to became his Home Secretary three years later. All this occupied any territory centre parties might otherwise have taken up, and in 1955, for the first time at a general election, both parties contested every seat in the country. At no time during the Conservative governments of 1951–64 did Labour lose its hope of power, for the margin of votes between the parties was narrow even when at its widest in 1959. Labour's class base was steadily broadening almost despite itself; by 1966 nearly two-thirds of Wilson's cabinet were university men.

Once more the period ended with a threat, less sudden than its predecessors, to the two-party system. This time it came simultaneously from several directions: from growing nationalist opinion in Scotland and Wales, beginning in the late 1950s; from Ulster Unionists breaking away from the Conservative Party during the 1970s; and from electors' mounting disillusionment at the Labour leadership's apparent deference to the extreme left. The last of these fuelled both the Liberal revival from the 1950s and, in 1981, the emergence of the Social Democratic Party. In the 1970s, as in the 1920s, the simple-majority electoral system, which had earlier produced reasonably fair results in a two-horse race, began producing unpredictable results in what had become a three-horse race. Pressure built up for electoral reform, which became a major plank in the platform of the Liberal Party and later of the SDP. These two parties reached their apogee at the general elections of 1983 and 1987.

Yet when the centre was unwise enough to split between SDP and Liberal Democrats in 1988, this challenge to the two-party system encountered a severe set-back. It remains difficult, however, to see how the Welsh and Scottish nationalists can be reabsorbed into the two-party system, and European precedents for electoral reform and federal structures move ever closer. Liberal Democrats' gains in local politics, especially in the south of England, together with electors' tactical voting, may produce the first disruption of the British two-party system since the 1780s that proves lasting. On the other hand, there are some signs that we are well into the start of a seventh phase in British party history, whereby two-party polarization resumes through the parties of right and left competing to eat up the centre ground. For Blair's Labour Party has become liberal enough in outlook to shift the Liberal Democrats from their stance of total neutrality between Conservative and Labour. Once the Liberals move towards alliance with Labour there is a danger that they (as the smallest party) will both be absorbed into their larger partner and that they will split in the process. Furthermore, it remains difficult to see how the electoral reform which could launch us into a multi-party system can now come about. The Conservatives oppose it, and if they do not constitute the largest party at the next election their successors in that position will have no interest in introducing it. At the start of the seventh phase in the history of Britain's two-party system, as at the end of the six earlier phases, the lines of party-political evolution remain very unclear.

Why has the two-party system been so resilient? Or to put the question in another way, why have electoral systems that favour multi-party situations never found much favour in Britain? Partly because the two-party system is so compatible with the practice, procedure, traditions, and culture of the House of Commons, with all its ramifications. All this was well known to the cabinet ministers prominent in the first five of the six disruptions of the two-party system so far discussed. The Peelites after 1846, Joseph Chamberlain after 1886, Henderson after 1917, and MacDonald after 1931 were not politicians likely to relish permanent residence in the political wilderness. Knowing well enough how the simple-majority electoral system hinders third parties, they rapidly made it their business to align with one 'side' or the other, both within parliament and within the constituencies. The adversarial shape of the House of Commons encouraged them to do so, for there are no cross-benches. As Winston Churchill pointed out when discussing rebuilding the House, 'we shape our buildings and afterwards our buildings shape us'. The House's oblong rather than semicircular shape was, he said, 'a very potent factor in our political life'.[89] This is one reason why the terms 'left' and 'right' did not catch on in Britain as party designations till the 1920s, for they originated in a legislature whose parties occupied fixed locations according to their opinion. Even by the 1960s only a fifth of a sample from the general public when questioned thought of the parties in right–left terms.[90] In an adversarial seating-plan, by contrast, there is no fixed location for particular opinions, and schismatic groups need to make an early decision on where to sit—a decision which may have important consequences. The Peelites after the split of 1846 first sat on the opposition benches with the radicals and Irish, then found themselves joined in 1847 by the protectionists. The Liberal Unionists after 1886 sat with the Gladstonian Liberals on the opposition benches, but after 1892 the Conservatives joined them there. The Labour MPs in 1906 sat on the opposition benches, but after January 1910 joined the government side, and the 1920s witnessed much jockeying for position between Liberals and Labour on the opposition benches. All Westminster's pressures on the secessionists lay towards either rejoining the group they had just left or burning their boats and joining what had hitherto been the other side.

Yet the shape of a legislature could hardly achieve so much on its own. It is because the two-party system accords well with the decentralized and participatory dimensions of British society, discussed in the first section of this chapter, that it has proved so tenacious. For the secessionists from the two dominant parties at any one time were edged from below towards collaborating with one party or the other. Constituency organizations were if anything more alert than the politicians to the logic of the simple-majority system. 'In London society the idea of a middle party can be understood,' wrote Bagehot in 1874, 'but in the country, in the constituencies which are the ultimate source of power, it would be an unintelligible nondescript.'[91] Constituency parties are campaigning structures recruited from enthusiasts which spring to life when confronting local opponents at general elections. They are hardly likely to sympathize with their MP if he threatens to join what they have long regarded as the other side. Nor would there be much future for a dissident MP who tried to mobilize an alternative constituency structure staffed by moderates who had not hitherto been noted for campaigning zeal.[92] When a Labour or Conservative MP responds to constituency party pressure, he usually moves left or right, respectively, not towards the centre. Where a government tries to use constituency pressure to discipline a recalcitrant MP towards centrist policies, it is likely to fail, as the history of the Conservative 'Euro-sceptic' rebellion in 1994–5 shows.

A brief glance at the last four disruptions to the two-party system will briefly show how each unexpectedly originated at the top but was rendered ephemeral by pressures from below. If Salisbury had acted as Gladstone hoped and had (by imitating Wellington's strategy of 1829) implemented with Liberal support the home rule policy acceptable to the Irish, the Liberal split need never have occurred. Or Gladstone could have prevented it by moving towards home rule more slowly and by trying harder to conciliate the cabinet colleague who became one of its most effective opponents: Joseph Chamberlain. In the outcome, the Liberal Unionists found their position anomalous at Westminster and (in Chamberlain's words) 'without efficient organization, isolated, and uneasy' in their constituencies, loathed by old friends and distrusted by new.[93] R. W. Dale recalled the 'immense difference to my private life' that deserting the Liberals over home rule had made. In Birmingham, he said, 'there are two clubs, and I belong to neither. I have friends on both sides, but the discussions that we had at the old Arts Club before the quarrel I look back upon with lasting regret.'[94] The Liberal Unionist remedy was, in effect, rapidly to join the Conservatives.

The disruption of 1916–18 once more began at the top, though its outcome was more dramatic, in that the result was for one party of the left to supplant the other. The split within Asquith's cabinet was perpetuated thereafter by a vendetta that was cultivated at the highest political levels, and by a sequence of tactical mistakes. If the Liberals had rapidly buried their differences, they could have been the stronger partners in the coalition with the Conservatives. And if Lloyd George had called a general election rather sooner in his premiership—early in 1917, for example— more Lloyd Georgian Liberal candidates and fewer Conservatives would have been returned. Or if Lloyd George had backed that decidedly Liberal cause proportional representation—which was seriously discussed in the debates of 1917 on the Franchise Bill—the Liberal Party might have survived as a third party between the wars in rather the same way as it did in Belgium; the Liberals' failure in this respect has been seen as 'the Party's most disastrous decision this century'.[95] In the outcome, the Liberals after 1918 experienced the third party's penalty in the simple-majority system, and their attempts to resume their pre-war alliance with Labour were fended off by a Labour leadership which now saw a chance of getting power on its own. Liberal constituency organizations could do little to rectify the situation, whereas the labour movement in the country was eager to exploit the opportunity thus presented.

The Labour split of 1931 originated at the highest level in response to the emergency action needed to stave off an economic crisis. As with the Conservative split of 1846 and the Liberal splits of 1886 and 1916, cabinet ministers seceding from the government party were not eager to set up on their own. MacDonald himself made a double contribution in 1931 towards restoring the two-party system: first, by actions which made it easy for the Labour Party to blame him, rather than itself, for being unable to agree on the cuts needed to stave off the crisis. And secondly by strengthening, through his accession to the National Government, centrist tendencies within Baldwin's Conservative Party. So Labour, although severely depleted at Westminster, never lost its position as leading party on the left, and was actually strengthened by the events of 1931 in its traditional trade-union connection. From there its road to recovery was clear.

The decision to form the SDP in 1981, an event which came near to transforming the map of British party politics, was taken by four former cabinet ministers (William Rodgers, Roy Jenkins, David Owen, and Shirley Williams) who again were not eager to form a distinct centre party. Their aim was rather, in alliance with the Liberals, to do in reverse what Labour had done to the Liberals sixty years before: to supplant the old party of the left with a new. Labour's split in 1981 was never inevitable, and would not have occurred if Labour had elected Healey as its leader in November 1980, whereas in the outcome Foot defeated him by 139 votes to 129. The secessionists remained free-floating in the party system for rather longer than the Liberal Unionists after 1886 or the National Liberal and National Labour groupings after 1931, largely because no inter-party coalition emerged to absorb them. But they encountered the same contempt from old colleagues and constituency structures. There could be no future for the so-called 'gang of four' in the Labour Party—even in a Labour Party which after 1983 gradually and unobtrusively adopted almost all their policies. Nor did the Conservatives need to offer the secessionists any bait. In effect, all four of the 'gang' were pushed into the political sidelines.

So at all four climacterics, disruption to the two-party system did not carry down to the constituency level. From the schism of 1981, as from its predecessors of 1886, 1916–18, and 1931, it was the Conservative Party which gained. Why so? Partly because social and educational background and party tradition cause the Party's governing passion to burn more fiercely than in parties further left. Deference to social rank may have declined, but deference to leadership comes naturally to a party with strong public-school and military connections. Furthermore, Conservatives at the Party's higher levels have long experienced that overlapping of the political and the social that occurred within the Labour Party only lower down and at the earlier stages of its history. The Conservative Party 'is in many ways a kind of total party', said Shirley Williams. 'It doesn't *just* have Members of Parliament; it brings them within a circle—a social circle as well as a political circle,' whose members are reluctant to leave for fear that they and their families will be denied social functions and connections which they value.[96]

Usually more businesslike than other parties in handling internal disputes, the Conservatives have been readier to absorb the ideas and talents of refugees from other parties' more prolonged disputes. Labour's unity suffers from a pursuit of orthodoxy in party policy that has made it since 1918 a somewhat narrower church than its Liberal predecessor. By comparison with the situation before 1914, the British left has been weakened not only by the split between Liberals and Labour, but also by Labour's latent split between moderates/revisionists and extremists/Marxists. The second of these splits was widened by the way the left treated the moderates at the Wembley party conferences of 31 May 1980 and 24 January 1981. Both conferences helped to drive the social democrats into secession. But the SDP carried off some of Labour's schismatic tendency in its hand-luggage. In 1987–9 the earlier splits on the left were compounded by two more in rapid succession: first between Liberals and SDP, and then within the SDP itself. The Conservative contrast is striking. Although Thatcher's policies divided the Party, no major Conservative seceded to the SDP. For all his loathing of 'Thatcherism', Heath does not seem even to have considered leaving his Party after 1975. Some Conservatives feared in the mid-1970s that in a crisis he would split the Party by joining a coalition with Callaghan, but no such crisis occurred.[97] And although in November 1981 he said he would be prepared after the next election to serve in a coalition government with the SDP and the Liberals if this seemed in the country's interest,[98] he never joined them. Nor was Jim Prior, perhaps Thatcher's leading 'wet' critic in her first cabinet, ever tempted to join the SDP: 'one is a Conservative because of certain instincts and beliefs about society, about life and about change', he recalled.[99] Instead of splitting off, both Heath and Prior concentrated on defending their own view of Conservative traditions from within.

A folk-memory of past disruptions, now fading and even half-conscious for many Conservatives, also helps to explain the contrast. For Conservative leaders have not forgotten the great electoral damage their Party incurred from the splits of 1829–32, 1846, and 1903–10. Urging the Conservative Party conference to heal its wounds over the Maastricht treaty in 1992, Douglas Hurd as Foreign Secretary pointed out that 'our party broke itself over the Corn Laws and effectively shut itself out of power for 10 years . . . Let us decide to give that madness a miss.'[100] Furthermore, Conservatives know from long experience that the two-party simple-majority system has served them well. They have skilfully exploited its incentives to hold together and make a broad appeal within the community. Thatcher in her final election press conference of 1979, like her predecessors in the 1920s, dismissed the idea that socialism could best be contained through electoral reform. This was 'the easy way of fighting Socialism', whereas 'the only way to fight state Socialism . . . is to fight it head on and beat it head on'.[101]

Given the attacks on the two-party system so fashionable in the early 1990s, it is worth emphasizing in conclusion the role that conviction plays in buttressing a two-party system which, after nearly two centuries in operation, is deeply rooted within Britain's political culture. The arguments against it are at first sight formidable,[102] and after the 1960s were heard as regularly as in the 1920s. Several appear in S. E. Finer's influential collection *Adversary Politics and Electoral Reform* (1975), and gained credibility when parliamentary debates were broadcast after 1978. For the two-party system seems to foment what David Steel called 'Yah-Boo politics',[103] crudely obscuring the subtle gradations and complex options that are the reality of politics. No government performs convincingly because an alternative cast is continuously subverting it from the wings—on Irish and imperial policy from the 1880s to the 1960s, for example, or on incomes policies in the 1970s. Nerving himself for the Conservative sell-out on Ireland which occurred three years later, Austen Chamberlain told Lord Hugh Cecil in April 1918: 'it is clear that we cannot count on 20 or even ten years of a consistent anti-Home Rule policy by the British electorate'.[104] Such a system, said Lord Scarman in 1992, 'neither reflects the complex plurality which is British society today, nor encourages the full expression within Parliament of the views of the many minorities within it'.[105] In his Dimbleby lecture, Jenkins in 1979 saw the confrontation between Labour and Conservative, each with its own social-class image, as divisive. 'If, on the House of Commons floor, it was always the fault of the other side, how could politicians preach convincingly against the prevalence of such a view on the shop floor?'[106] The system also wastes political talent. It condemns half Westminster to languish in opposition, and shuts out those who combine elements from the extremes—social imperialists, for example. It seems undemocratic in so far as it renders much discussion private which ought arguably to be public. Each party in a two-party system embraces a wide range of opinion whose disagreements in a multi-party system would be aired publicly, whereas when confined within a single party they are aired only in cabinets or private party meetings. Worse, the two-party system rests on a simple-majority single-ballot electoral system which ensures that parliamentary representation fails to reflect the exact balance of opinion within the community.

These are powerful objections, and electoral reformers have 'tended always to be better informed and more logically coherent in their arguments'[107] than their opponents. Yet these arguments are overdone. Confrontation occurs at Westminster only on set-piece occasions and in selected policy areas. Collaboration is the day-to-day reality, especially on the all-party committees where MPs spend so much of their time. Besides, even confrontational language may have as its aim the decidedly moderate objective of channelling discontent towards parliament. In attacking the other party, the apparently inflammatory MP is often addressing not so much the other side as dissidents on his own side: backbenchers or party activists outside Westminster angrier than himself. And the private confrontations that continuously occur within the party ensure the continuous mutual influence of extremes and centre, ideologue and pragmatist, to the benefit of both. MPs do of course sometimes come to blows. T. P. O'Connor provoked trouble by repeatedly calling out to Joseph Chamberlain 'Judas, Judas', George Wigg knocked Leslie Thomas down in the members' cloakroom during the Suez crisis, and Jeremy Thorpe was jostled by furious Labour MPs when the Liberals rescued the Heath government on the EEC vote of 17 February 1972. But the violence which occurs inside parliament is a triviality by comparison with the violence that parliament's integrating function helps to prevent.[108] Through this and other routes, parliament's confrontational structure helps to frustrate extremists and shields centrists from taking up seriously exposed positions. The extremes are ultimately at the mercy of the centre, because without the centre they will neither win elections nor govern successfully.

To complain that the polarity between government and opposition is crude is to inflate the importance of content by comparison with tone and situation. For it is through confrontation that what Bagehot described as parliament's informing function[109] is best performed. And in policy areas where choices are clear and where parliament needs to carry out Bagehot's teaching and expressive functions, the electors have everything to gain from criticism articulated by those who are either experienced in government or have a good chance of becoming so. By contrast, the small parties of multi-party systems find it difficult on their own to engage in long-term policy planning, for if unpredictable coalitions mould government policy it is difficult to look very far ahead. Recalling the Liberal–Labour pact which kept the Labour government in power after 1977, Healey was reminded of France under the Fourth Republic, with different coalitions hastily assembled according to the subject in hand: 'no one who lived through that period can believe that proportional representation would necessarily produce better government than the traditional British voting system'.[110] Governments benefit from being continually exposed to integrated opposition instead of facing only the bifurcated opposition (from far left and far right) that centre coalitions normally encounter. The polarity has the more significance because it is one aspect of the opposition party's continuous appeal to the electorate, which must be consulted within a maximum of five years. Besides, in politics and elsewhere, decisions often narrow down to a clear choice between alternatives. Hugo Young thought the SDP–Liberal alliance at a disadvantage during the general election campaign of 1987 because the British character 'may turn out to be more two-party-minded than anyone has recently thought.' Life 'is a more straightforwardly adversarial business than is consistent with a three-party structure permanently installed at Westminster'.[111]

Parties in multi-party systems are more like pressure groups: sectarian in their appeal and difficult to unite behind a co-ordinated governmental programme whose priorities are well considered and decided in advance. 'The whole tendency of proportional representation', said Herbert Morrison in 1924, 'is the elevation of the minority and the subjection of the majority to the special opinion of cranks and freaks of various kinds.'[112] It seemed a natural outcrop of Liberal individualism and hostility to the state, politically and intellectually fragmenting in its effects; progressive collectivists should reject it, together with much other Liberal baggage. A party of government was likely to have rather different priorities, and to welcome a political system which diffused a governmental outlook across a very wide spectrum of opinion. The peak of a House of Commons career is, after all, promotion to the cabinet, and in British politics the incentives are strong to answer Orwell's question: 'in such and such circumstances, what would you *do*?'[113] Some may welcome the variety of goods that are on offer in the electoral reformer's political hypermarket, but others will regard it as a finicking, even sectarian, temperament that seeks only the party that precisely reflects its own desires. For most mortals the position taken up by Bertrand Russell in 1930, when justifying his support for the Labour Party, will suffice: 'I do not like them, but an Englishman has to have a Party just as he has to have trousers, and of the three Parties I find them the least painful . . . I do not think that in joining a Party one necessarily abrogates the use of one's reason. I know that my trousers might be better than they are; nevertheless they seem to me better than none.'[114]

While the two-party system does not enlist the ablest politicians continuously in government, the definition of 'government' should not perhaps be too pedantic, given that in the British political system government and opposition continuously interact. Besides, politicians benefit from the periods of rest, reflection, and consultation which periods of opposition bestow. Such periods are Britain's peaceful and non-violent alternative to the permanent purge. In a recurring cyclical pattern, party leaders drift away from their party activists when in power and return to them when in opposition. In a society where centrist opinion is strong, a party on entering opposition moves closer to the extreme, but moves back towards the centre in the hope of winning the next election. So the gulf between the government and opposition parties opens out shortly after a party has lost power, and narrows as governmental experience gradually moderates the views of the government party, and as the need to win the next election moderates the views of the opposition. As Bagehot pointed out, the British political system 'makes party government permanent and possible in the sole way in which it can be so, by making it mild', through encouraging moderate views in both the leaders and the rank and file of the major political parties.[115] What was clear to Bagehot over a century ago remains true today: 'though a middle party is impossible, a middle government—a government which represents the extreme of neither party, but the common element between the two parties—is inevitable . . . Any extreme government would be plainly contrary to the wishes of the nation.'[116]

So the two-party system, unlike a multi-party system involving centre coalitions, marshals virtually the entire political spectrum behind the parliamentary process and governmental priorities. It ensures that fullness of dialogue between intellectuals and men of government, between dogmatists and pragmatists, which the stability of any political system requires. Such dialogue introduces the extremists to and involves them in the complex processes of formulating policy just as it brings the pragmatists into contact with idealism and the need for change. The crudeness of political polarity within the community is thereby muted. The electorate, too, is enlisted behind the parliamentary process. For in a two-party system the government's complexion is usually determined by electors choosing between two governmental party programmes presented openly at the general election, rather than by politicians choosing between several semi-governmental programmes discussed in private between elections. This scales down the importance of the claim that the two-party system secretes significant political debate within cabinet and party meeting. In reality, the debate should be more about the location than about the incidence of secrecy, given that the negotiations to set up a sequence of multi-party coalitions must also be secret. A two-party system that directly enlists the electorate in choosing governmental policy diffuses political discussion relatively widely, and draws more closely together the opinions expressed by the electorate and the policies the government subsequently pursues. 'Above all, maintain the line of demarcation between parties,' said Disraeli (taking up a position in 1846 which profoundly influenced his successors as leaders of the Conservative Party). 'For it is only by maintaining the independence of party that you can maintain the integrity of public men, and the power and influence of Parliament itself.'[117]

The two-party system does of course deny British government the strength required to implement some types of policy, though few of the system's critics would have favoured the strong government required to uphold coercive British control in southern Ireland and the empire, for example. The system also entails some discontinuity of policy. David Owen at the SDP conference in October 1981 went so far as to claim that the removal of this discontinuity was 'absolutely central to the revival of this country's fortunes'.[118] But that discontinuity is often the (admittedly in-efficient) route towards consensus, and the obvious inconvenience of too many reversals of policy in itself curbs their incidence. Bipartisan policy (in overseas or Irish policy, for example) or compromise between government and opposition (on the 'mixed economy', for example) are the outcome. Compromise is in the interest of both government and opposition parties, because a purely negative reversal of preceding governments' policies will not attract the electors. Besides, alternation between the parties in govern-ment is never inevitable, and occurred at only six of the fourteen general elections between 1945 and 1992 inclusive. And are there really significant policies neglected because of the high threshold the simple-majority elec-toral system erects against third parties? Competition between the parties of government and opposition is usually fierce enough to ensure that any ideas of value are quickly picked up. As for the rest, there is much to be said for Ramsay MacDonald's view, expressed to the conference of the

Labour Party (then itself a third party) in 1914: 'opinions should not be coddled in their infancy; they should have to surmount reasonable obstacles'. Every opinion seeking parliamentary recognition 'should be asked to prove its staying power'.[119]

The argument for electoral reform that has carried most conviction since the 1970s has been the simple-majority system's distortion of opinion within the community in the process of procuring a secure governmental majority. Regionally dispersed parties such as the Liberals and SDP understandably object to this. But in fostering three-party politics under an electoral system that is roughly representative only when there are only two main contenders for power, the new or third parties have themselves created the problem that their reforms claim to solve. Reformers under the two-party system do not need to take on the extra burden of seeking to change the system; they can employ their energies more profitably by permeating one or both of the two main contenders for power. In the early 1980s the obvious candidate for that was the Labour Party. 'They ought to have stayed in and done the infighting and made the extreme left split off,' said Thatcher of Labour dissidents who seceded into the SDP 'They have not. They took the easy way; they split off.'[120] The history of British Conservatism since the 1860s shows how important to a party's electoral success is the capacity to remain united and open out towards centrist opinion. The two-party system penalizes only the sectarian; it rewards those who continuously seek to broaden their appeal. It stabilizes government by rewarding intra-party coalition and rendering inter-party coalition rare and ephemeral. For the choice is not between coalition or no coalition: it is between the intra-party coalition of the British type and the inter-party coalition more frequently found elsewhere. Indeed, the term 'coalition' was originally applied only to the former.[121] The intra-party coalition has the double advantage that it is tried and tested over a long period, and springs from long-term conviction rather than short-term parliamentary convenience.

One last point. Advocates of electoral reform rarely spell out its implications for parliament. After very generalized populist grumbling about confrontation, they merely hint at the need for cross-benches.[122] Proportional representation's earliest and most forceful opponent was well aware of the parliamentary implications. Bagehot knew that British general elections perform a double purpose. 'The judgement of the Parliament ought always to be coincident with the opinion of the nation', he wrote, 'but there is no objection to its being more decided . . . The House of Commons should think as the nation thinks; but it should think so rather more strongly, and with somewhat less of wavering.'[123] General elections are, it is true, tests of opinion, but they are also moments for selecting a stable government in a parliament which among Bagehot's five functions must combine the 'expressive' with the 'elective'. It is partly, one suspects, because politicians and even the general public in practice recognize the advantages of this combination that the two-party system has survived for so long.

# 8

## *Assessing Opinion*

POLITICIANS are not alone in needing to assess public opinion, nor did they pioneer modern techniques for doing so. The pioneers were social investigators grappling with poverty; businessmen trying to predict their markets; media people seeking readers, listeners, and viewers; and pressure groups seeking reinforcement. Indeed, politicians were somewhat behindhand, and for long after the 1860s often wanted the public excluded from moulding policy. During the controversy about the Eastern question in 1876, Disraeli wanted the government to ride out the crisis until the public became bored with the agitators, and urged Lord Derby, his Foreign Secretary, 'not to act, as if you were under the control of popular opinion. If so, you may do what they like, but they won't respect you for doing it.'[1] Lord Salisbury's distaste for public involvement in foreign policy was discussed in Chapter 2, and Sir Edward Grey's secretiveness after 1905 explains much of the left's enthusiasm after 1914 for 'open diplomacy'. Three aspects of the political system shielded the politician from the full blast of opinion: an electoral system that only gradually sought to be representative; a party system whose policy programmes warded off single-issue pressure; and a parliamentary system which protected the MP from being coerced by constituents. Parliament, said Crossman in 1968, was 'the buffer which enables our leadership to avoid saying yes or no to the electorate in the hope that, given time, the situation can be eased away'.[2]

When politicians did need to discover public opinion, whether to follow or reject it, they had their own special source of information: parliamentary elections, which were steadily refined to cope with urbanization and industrialization. Franchise reforms enlarged the electorate in 1832, 1867, 1884, 1918, 1928, and 1969. So did rising affluence, which (without need for further legislation) automatically boosted the numbers qualifying for the votes that until 1918 accompanied ownership of property. Together with the ballot in 1872 and several measures to curb corruption, these changes afforced the politician when confronting pressure groups that claimed to be representative. Yet if the votes cast were anonymous, while at the same time opinions were not as yet interpreted by opinion polls or behavioural political scientists, complexity was compounded. New ways of influencing electors were essential, for in a society gradually coming to see itself as democratic, the voter must ultimately prevail.

As late-Victorian opinion congealed into a single national political community, parliament became an arena where parties returned from combat in one election only to launch a national dialogue that continuously fed into the next. The stakes were high: 'democracy has arrived at a gallop in England', wrote Baldwin privately in 1928, 'and I feel all the time that it is a race for life: can we educate them before the crash comes?'[3] Uncertainty about the electors was manifest in discussions about foreign policy in the early 1930s, when a government with a huge majority nervously eyed pacifists resourceful at manipulating and measuring public opinion. Humiliatingly, in 1935–6, it had to reverse its policy on the Hoare–Laval pact soon after winning an election. Comparable reversals of policy occurred in 1920 during the Black and Tan strategy in Ireland, in 1934 on unemployment benefits, and in 1937 on proposals for a national defence contribution— though not in 1926 on the General Strike.[4] The politician's best safeguard was to refine his own ways of testing opinion through parliament and the parties, and cautiously respond in the face of the new opinion-sounding techniques. The continuing struggle to improve parliament as a guide to opinion will be discussed further in Chapter 9. The focus here will be on improvements to political parties and elections as guides to opinion, especially at general elections. Four challenges emerged to politicians' authority as judges of opinion: from pressure groups, the referendum, the media, and opinion polls. Each will now be discussed in turn.

*

Chapter 6 discussed pressure groups' difficulties with the politicians. Here we discuss politicians' difficulties with pressure groups, whose competing claims often confused the public opinion they set out to clarify. They tended to over-represent the organized at the expense of the unorganized, as Stanley discovered when grappling with slavery in 1833, Bruce when confronting the drink question in 1871, Disraeli's government when regulating vivisection in 1876. Any mid-Victorian politician seeking improved Sunday recreation found himself beset by zealots eager either to open or to close museums and pubs.[5] Gladstone eloquently described the politician's plight in 1860. Seeking a more continental and relaxed attitude to pub licensing, he confronted an alliance of temperance reformers and established drink interests, and found himself 'much in the position of Hercules, as we are encountered by two figures of Virtue and Vice. But instead of Virtue soliciting us to go one way, and Vice pressing us to go another, we have both Virtue and Vice leagued against us . . . I appeal from them to . . . the common sense of the House of Commons and of the country at large.'[6]

Until the franchise was broad enough to capture majority opinion directly, and until party programmes established policy priorities, pressure groups could plausibly claim superior knowledge of opinion. Not until the parties' nation-wide and co-ordinated branch structure matched that of the pressure group did the politician at last touch firm ground. Parliament would have paid far less attention to the Anti-Corn Law League, said John Morley, if there had been universal suffrage in the 1840s.[7] By 1885 even a Conservative leader, Lord Salisbury, was deploying the franchise to counterbalance 'demonstrations, or processions, or meetings, or addresses on railway platforms', pointing out that 'there is no way of ascertaining who are on one side and who are on the other, except by the elementary process of counting them'.[8] We saw in Chapter 6 how late-Victorian party programmes eventually helped to discipline the cause-group world. A politician might then sometimes think it worth risking defiance of a pressure group—as witness the origins of licensing reform in 1902 or votes for women in 1918. When the party system was in abeyance—during wartime, for example, or during multi-party coalitions—the old difficulties with pressure groups returned. Because the peacetime coalitions of 1918 and 1931 had not been returned on a clear party manifesto, their policies lacked clear popular endorsement. So instead of feeling stronger in relation to public opinion, such coalitions were sometimes more timid than single-party governments with smaller majorities. Governments of any complexion needed to run to stay in the same place, given the continuous refinement of techniques for mobilizing and assessing opinion. Edwardian suffragist processions, banners, exhibitions, and public meetings carried the display of sympathetic opinion to its apogee, and greatly embarrassed Asquith's government. Beveridge's skill at manipulating public opinion through more modern methods helped him to outwit the coalition government's ample resources during the Second World War.[9] By the 1960s the abortion law reformers were deploying congenial statistics garnered from their own systematic polls.[10]

Governments counter-attacked by refining their own machinery for gathering and moulding opinion. Only gradually during the nineteenth century did government supersede the cause group's fact-gathering role by building up its own machinery for collecting facts through the census and the departmental committee. This new machinery was the more necessary because the cause groups' facts were often unreliable. Many of their facts aimed to influence opinion, and even (in the absence of opinion polls) opinion about opinion. The late-Victorian politician could never be sure that the cause group's analysis of opinion was reliable. Campaigners for or against temperance reform or votes for women publicized referenda or canvassing results which suited their cause, and were prone (as in the peace ballot of 1935) to ask tendentious questions. Here too the cause group's importance for collecting information diminished over time. The vote (now universal among adults) and the opinion poll gradually became twentieth-century politicians' guide to public opinion, and political scientists and sociologists (rather than pressure groups) became the experts at interpreting it. Lloyd George as Prime Minister presided over an elaborate network of advisers on public opinion,[11] and the Attlee government employed the latest techniques under Morrison's enthusiastic management. 'Public relations work at its best is really part of the process of public accountability,' he wrote.[12] Wilson's second government developed the 'green paper', a tentative statement of policy options in which the Home Office was a pioneer, as a way to test the water without plunging fully in.[13] And as we saw in Chapter 6, government policy could often cause pressure groups to prosper, or even brought them into existence. For example, consent for corporatist economic policies needed to be mobilized not only at elections but between them. As the TUC General Secretary Len Murray pointed out in 1980, 'putting a cross on a ballot paper once every five years is no substitute for democracy'.[14] Incomes policies before 1979 required governments to launch massive exercises in public education—so much so, that their patronage was becoming increasingly important in the advertising trade.

Politicians were sometimes pushed into countering sectional opinion with their own opinion-gathering machinery: the threat or even the reality of a general election. The trade-union movement posed a special problem here, and Heath's decision to call a general election in February 1974 reflected the phrase then current at Westminster: 'the miners have had their ballot and we must have ours'.[15] Heath's attempt failed, and until 1979 an alternative approach to handling the trade-union movement— consultation, co-operation and co-option—was attempted with initial success but ultimate failure. When after 1979 the Thatcher governments aimed to turn opinion away from corporatism, they needed cunning and luck if they were to prevail over entrenched interests. On privatization they succeeded, but in the long-drawn-out battle with the trade-union movement, each side warily executed move and counter-move until the miners' strike was defeated in 1985.[16] Thatcherism questioned whether trade unions accurately represented even their own members, let alone others. Here, as elsewhere, it appealed over the heads of intermediate groups direct to individuals, as Michael Edwardes had earlier done when prevailing over the unions within British Leyland.[17] Success in this delicate enterprise required the government to keep its own opinion-gathering machinery in trim. The price of failure had been thoroughly advertised on three earlier occasions: in 1969 and 1971, when attempts at legislation by the Wilson and Heath governments respectively had failed, and in 1974 when the electorate had not backed Heath's attempt to outmanoeuvre the National Union of Mineworkers.

Thatcher's caution, a shift in intellectual climate, and her Party's eagerness to learn from its mistakes at first brought considerable success. But she undermined her own achievement. Her desire for firm direction of policy paid handsome dividends in many areas but led her to undermine the cabinet as sounding-board for a wide span of party attitudes. Her intimidating style, backed up by her counter-productively loyal press secretary Bernard Ingham, weakened the representation of contrary views at the same time as she had discarded the royal commission as a guide to, and influence upon, opinion. So her third government slipped on a sequence of so-called 'banana skins',[18] and on one of them—the poll tax fiasco—she fell.

\*

The referendum, a second rival to the politician in his opinion-sounding role, became prominent in the Edwardian period, and here too the politicians tamed the new device. Given the mounting strength of party machines, the referendum (as Dicey pointed out in 1894) had 'the great merit of being the only check on party management which is in perfect harmony with democratic sentiment'.[19] Politicians used it to defuse the sort of issue where a national majority could not risk riding roughshod over strongly held local opinion: from 1881 on opening pubs in Wales on Sunday; in November 1972 for discovering opinion in Northern Ireland on the border question; and in 1978–9 to settle the devolution issue in Wales and Scotland. On questions of national policy, politicians have learned to tame the referendum by recommending it only where it will help over-come failures in the party system: in areas where there is no clear party alignment, where the parties are divided, or where (because the parties are united) there is no effective choice at general elections. So the tariff reformers showed some enthusiasm for it when battling within the Con-servative Party after 1903, but less enthusiasm for it once they had prevailed. The referendum also came into play on the women's suffrage issue, where the anti-suffragists rightly suspected that it would usefully embarrass their opponents.[20]

The opponents of referenda, however, have always argued that it rep-resents a transfer of political power from knowledge to ignorance. Some-what surprisingly, this argument was espoused even by the Labour Party and in Harold Laski's inter-war writings on British political institutions, despite the incentive referenda could have provided for massive adult-education campaigns. 'Personally, I am opposed to the Referendum in everything,' wrote Ramsay MacDonald in 1912; 'it is nothing but a fraudu-lent way of destroying the responsibilities of Representatives'.[21] Labour's position reflects the Party's overall rejection of the Liberal taste for con-stitutional tinkering. Furthermore, Labour between the wars felt an increas-ingly Fabian respect for the MP's political expertise, and came to see the socialist and democratic advantages of parliamentary sovereignty; if carefully husbanded, it could enable a socialist government to implement quickly the package the electors had endorsed. A referendum, said MacDonald, would 'break up the wholeness of a programme' and hamper 'the organic development, the all-round advance of the social will'.[22]

Only expediency led Labour to revive the referendum in the 1970s, though a genuinely democratic impulse probably inspired its originator Tony Benn. In 1968 he was already predicting 'electronic referenda' within a generation, to help extend popular participation in government.[23] After 1970 Wilson sought a formula which would in the short term hold together a party bitterly divided on whether Britain should join the EEC. At first unpopular within the shadow cabinet, the referendum suddenly became feasible for Labour in March 1972 when President Pompidou announced a referendum in France on whether the EEC should be enlarged.[24] Nor were Conservatives wholly opposed to the referendum idea: during the run-up to the general election of 1970, Iain Macleod wanted to pre-empt any move by Wilson towards holding a referendum on the EEC by taking the initiative on the matter,[25] but he was overruled. The idea became the weapon of those who opposed Britain's membership of the EEC but was turned neatly against them by the EEC's defenders. *The Times* directed a leader against the referendum, Wilson showed no initial enthusiasm for it, and in 1972 Jenkins was edged further towards resignation by distaste for it. The conventional arguments against it were deployed: it was the weapon of pseudo-democratic dictators and atavistic causes, it threatened the cohesion of government policy, its questions could not be framed clearly, it would undermine parliamentary sovereignty, and so on.[26] As late as September 1974 Jenkins remained 'profoundly un-happy' at the idea.[27] Wilson eventually launched the referendum, together with temporary suspension of cabinet responsibility, remarkably casually; he 'announced a fundamental change in our constitutional convention' in cabinet, wrote Barbara Castle, 'as casually as if he had been offering us a cup of tea'.[28]

The referendum's opponents argued that it would set a 'dangerous pre-cedent'. Ironically these included Thatcher, for whom 'a major constitu-tional change ... should only be made if, after full deliberation, it was seriously thought to be a lasting improvement on present practice'.[29] This was entirely to neglect the partisan origins of constitutional reform in Britain, and within two years she was herself hinting that Conservative governments might need to deploy the referendum if embroiled with the trade unions.[30] The idea kept cropping up among her off-the-cuff remarks thereafter,[31] but was never acted upon. In the outcome, the referendum, when observed overseas and when held in Britain, has been an instrument used by politicians for their own purposes, not a restraint upon them. 'Virtually every new democratic and constitutional device this century has been given a party twist by the government in power,' wrote the *Times* political correspondent, discussing the referendum in 1977: 'What could be an advance in democratic method has been turned into an advantage for the government and its party managers.'[32] This is not to say that the referendum is always undesirable. If the issue is important it compels politicians, at the least, to make sure that the voters are fully informed. That was certainly desirable in the 1970s and may prove desirable again in the 1990s.

\*

A third, continuously evolving, threat came from what we now call the media: first from newspapers, then from radio and television. Newspapers deeply influenced nineteenth-century electors. The trade-union leader Joseph Arch formed his political creed from reading long press reports of

Gladstone's and Bright's speeches, and Lloyd George walked fourteen miles to Portmadoc in 1880 to get a London paper which fully reported one of Gladstone's Midlothian speeches.[33] Newspapers were often read communally in such places as public houses, but mounting affluence gradually brought newspapers to every home. The politicians aimed to control this medium through establishing and funding newspapers and providing them with information. Nineteenth-century party machines were deeply involved with the press at the local level. Some newspapermen, however, had more grandiose notions. W. T. Stead, in a remarkable article of 1886, showed an almost breathless enthusiasm for creating a nation-wide network of between 600 and 1,000 informants on opinion within their localities, presided over by the editor 'filled with his central fire, saturated with his ideas'. A newspaper acting thus 'would . . . be a great secular or civic church and democratic university' which if wisely directed 'would come to be the very soul of our national unity'.[34] Stead's dreams were not realized at the time, though something similar occurred after the 1950s, when newspapers boosted their circulation by sponsoring opinion polls.

Politicians were none the less experiencing unprecedented public scrutiny. In 1868 Chief Justice Cockburn welcomed the prevailing freedom of comment on the conduct and motives of public figures as something new. Comments were 'now made every day, which half a century ago would have been the subject of actions'.[35] By the 1880s the intrusion on politicians' privacy was becoming tiresome. 'I am pestered with incessant telegrams which there is no defence against, but either suicide or Parnell's method of self-concealment,' Gladstone complained in December 1885. A few months later W. H. Smith told his wife how pressmen had pursued him while entering Salisbury's home by the garden entrance during his cabinet-making: 'it is really quite intolerable. These vermin are omnipresent and it is hopeless to attempt to escape observation.'[36] The press was not just inquisitive: it tried to influence policy, especially on defence issues—exposing defective equipment during the Crimean War, inadequate naval expenditure in 1884, and insufficient munitions in 1915.[37] Aroused humanitarian feeling could also mobilize the press behind very different causes: against the 'white slave traffic' in 1885, or in that major sortie of public opinion in 1920 when Hugh Martin's *Daily News* reports helped to destroy the Black and Tan strategy in Ireland.[38] Without opinion polls, press influence on opinion seemed formidable, and Lloyd George assiduously tried to harness it behind his coalition of 1918–22.

The politicians gradually learned to scale down press pretensions, culminating in Baldwin's famous analogy between press barons and harlots in

March 1931. But in neutralizing its dangers, manipulation was at least as effective as confrontation. In 1894 Joseph Chamberlain urged Balfour not to carry his disregard of the press too far. 'After all,' he wrote, 'there is no other way of finding out the trend of public opinion, and the knowledge which is always necessary to a politician. It is very well to know what is right,—but it is also well to know what is possible.'[39] Chamberlain, Lord Randolph Churchill, and (somewhat less obtrusively) Gladstone himself knew the value of press contacts as guides to opinion. Later politicians who were distant from the press—Asquith, McKenna, Heath, and the offspring of the third Marquis of Salisbury, for example—suffered through neglecting this important asset. The opinion poll and universal suffrage have combined to open up the political system to opinion and have scaled down the rival pretensions of the press. By 1959 observers were noting how opinion polls had encroached on press reporters' traditional role of recording public opinion. By 1966 journalists' traditional methods had come to seem positively antique: 'in the old days a journalist savoured the constituencies like a wine-taster, making his forecast on an impression of flavour and bouquet'.[40] Politicians' worries about the press have been further scaled down by the advent of new and rival means of communication: radio and television.

Radio first reached a mass audience in the 1930s. BBC radio was at first timid about reporting elections, so its political impact was smaller and slower than television's. In 1950, for instance, the BBC thought it necessary to pass over in silence headline news of Churchill's proposal for atom talks, and as late as 1955 there were no election discussion programmes at all.[41] It now seems extraordinary that until that year the BBC implemented the so-called fourteen-day rule, whereby matters to be discussed in parliament were banned from radio and television discussion during the preceding fortnight. The rule was suspended experimentally for six months after the Suez crisis and suspended indefinitely in July 1957.[42] Restraints on election broadcasting seemed to David Butler, writing about the general election of 1955, 'absurd', and were soon abandoned.[43] It was ITV that broke down these BBC inhibitions with its programmes on the Rochdale by-election in March 1958.

Radio impinged on the general election campaign, however, much earlier. Snowden's election broadcasts of 1931 made a big impact, and candidates at the general election of 1935 already felt the need to comment locally on national broadcasts.[44] In 1945 the political broadcasts, 'more lucid and intellectually able than that delivered from the local platform', were heard by nearly half the adult population.[45] In safe seats this centralized appeal downgraded the local campaign. By 1959 the election study could claim that 'the most brilliant of agents with the most perfect army of party workers could not change the representation in perhaps 550 of the 630 seats'.[46] Television gradually advanced over radio, though its initial effect was to improve the quantity and quality of radio's political reporting. The moment of transition lies between the general elections of 1955 and 1959: 57 per cent of the electors heard at least one of the sound broadcasts in 1955, 27 per cent in 1959; 33 per cent heard at least one of the television broadcasts in 1955, 61 per cent in 1959.[47] During the 1950s television pushed radio out of the electoral limelight, or at least into a specialized role, for in the next two decades radio made something of a come-back through phone-in programmes which enabled listeners to participate. In February 1974, for example, the BBC's *Election Call* programme at 9 a.m. received up to 9,000 calls and won a million listeners.[48] By 1979 the growth of local radio also produced a modest reverse trend towards the locality, and the parties made a great effort to exploit it.[49]

As early as 1923 Baldwin was making shrewd use of two newsreels to project the image of the calm and confident statesman.[50] During the general election of 1931 the Party deployed twenty-two cinema vans at 543 meetings, staking out territory Labour had yet to occupy.[51] In 1951 the parties first used television for election broadcasts, though these reached less than a tenth of the electorate.[52] The number of viewers for election programmes expanded continuously from the early 1950s, with mounting expertise in producing them. By 1959 between 35 and 40 million people were watching regular weekly political discussion programmes on radio and television.[53] At the general election of 1955, 33 per cent of the electorate said they watched at least one televised party election broadcast, 61 per cent in 1959, 85 per cent in 1966.[54] By the election of February 1974, television broadcasts had become so central to the campaign that Labour installed facilities at its headquarters for recording and playing back all its broadcasts.[55] By 1987, 75 per cent of those sampled had seen a party election broadcast on television, but only 15 per cent had heard one on radio.[56]

Politicians and media people compete as communicators, each wary of the other—hence the long delay before parliament admitted microphones and cameras.[57] During the election of 1970 both parties rejected live audience programmes, and Wilson ruled out 'confrontation' programmes early in the campaign. In 1979 Thatcher refused Callaghan's challenge to a televised debate, saying that issues and policies decide elections: 'we are not electing a president, we are choosing a Government'.[58] Yet she recognized the media's importance well enough, and struggled to improve her technique. Some commentators at this election thought that it was the politicians who were exploiting the media rather than the other way round; for instance, staged 'media events' showed Thatcher for some reason holding a new-born calf at Eye in Suffolk.[59] Labour eventually realized that television could compensate for its unfavourable press coverage. In 1959, when the media first made a really striking impact, the 'Labour Television and Radio Operations Room', run by a small committee chaired by Benn, outclassed the Conservative broadcasts through most of the campaign. Morgan Phillips's daily press conference was brilliantly organized and became for the first time the central feature of the election day.[60] By February 1974, according to Donoughue, 'the 9 o'clock news on BBC television and the 10 o'clock news on ITV became crucial instruments in our campaign', for 'in Britain television has become an essential instrument for any non-Conservative party attempting to influence the election debate'.[61] But media influence over voters should not be exaggerated. In February 1974 a campaign that was amateur from the media point of view did not prevent the Liberals from winning 6 million votes, or 19.3 per cent of the total cast.

The media were steadily centralizing the election campaign. In the early 1950s 'there was extraordinarily little intercommunication or discussion of strategy or tactics'[62] between the leaders of any one party at general elections, but this soon began to change. By 1959 the party leaders were timing their speeches to meet the television networks' technical requirements, delivering them earlier than usual so that they would get into the late-evening newsreels. By 1979 the parties were timing their morning press conferences to feed the midday news bulletins. They were also staging afternoon walkabouts of their leaders for the benefit of local and national evening news broadcasts, and timing major speeches to catch the news bulletins at 9 and 10 p.m. By 1979 television had introduced a paradoxical disjunction into the election campaign: whereas most voters got their information from television, the candidates were far too busy on most evenings to watch television at all.[63] In 1987 'never before had the parties tailored their efforts so single-mindedly to capturing the cameras' attention',[64] though this jockeying for position between politicians and media seemed by 1992 to have drained politicians' utterances of spontaneity.[65] Media technology was beginning to come together. By 1987 electoral registers were available on computer tape and were used in a few areas to prepare canvass cards. When linked with canvass data they could be used to print polling-day knock-up sheets, and when linked to a good printer they could be used to send out direct-mail letters, often targeted at individuals. A fortnight before the general election in 1992 more than a million voters in sixty-seven marginal seats received the first direct mail letter from a prime minister in British history.[66] This programming of the electors was not always smooth. No less than three different agencies vied for Thatcher's attention at the height of the 1987 campaign, each linked to different cabinet ministers, bringing Conservative election plans close to shipwreck.

*

Closely entangled with the media was a fourth potential threat to the politician's opinion-gathering role: the opinion poll. As late as 1945, political opinion was measured so crudely that Labour's victory surprised even the so-called experts. 'Public opinion, as a matter of study, remains a mystery,' wrote the authors of the first Nuffield election book; 'and in seeking to understand it one must be content with approximations to truth and imperfect deductions from infinitely complex evidence'.[67] However much the pollsters assisted the politician by demoting the pressure group as guide to opinion, they at first seemed pushy and unsubtle intruders into his special sphere of expertise.

For the politician, opinions are never of equal value, least of all in the aristocratic England Bagehot knew. 'There is a certain tact in the management of even great affairs which can only be acquired by feeling the pulse of society,' said Disraeli in 1878, regretting Monty Corry's absence as guide in sounding out opinion in 'society'.[68] Discussing the court of Queen Anne, Bagehot pointed out that 'to be able to manage men, to know with whom to be silent, to know with whom to say how much, to be able to drop casual observations, to have a sense of that which others mean, though they do not say . . . in a word, to understand, to feel, to be unable to help feeling, the *by-play* of life, is the principal necessity for a success in courts'.[69] Such quick insights are if anything still more integral to managing a democratic society, whose advent should not in any case be antedated. After three reform acts Sidney Webb could still point out, in 1886, that 'nothing in England is done without the consent of a small intellectual yet practical class in London not 2000 in number'. Justifying 'wire-pulling' to herself in 1929, his wife pointed out that 'the great mass of citizens are uninterested in some or other—many of them in all . . . current political issues. Wire-pulling is only the way in which those who *are* interested and have a certain knowledge of particular questions bring their experience and will into the common pool.'[70]

Assessing relevant opinion is inevitably impressionistic, and the pollster can supply only one among several ingredients for a political decision. Wilson, we are told, 'had a very simple view of the electorate. It was subject to tendencies and moods, which were more important in determining its voting disposition than were specific governmental or organisational actions.'[71] During the Falklands crisis in 1982 Powell felt a shift in national opinion in his bones, and despised the pollsters' skill: 'a change has come about in Britain. I do not need opinion polls, with their question-begging questions, to tell me that. I have the evidence of my own senses, as I go about the country and as I mingle with fellow members.'[72] Some even saw the pollster as threatening the politician's freedom of manœuvre. Adversary politics in Britain frees the politician to neglect short-term opinion about his policy, while requiring him to be judged by the electorate on its longer-term effects. If the pollster caused him merely to execute the citizen's evanescent whim, the politician would lose personal consistency and even dignity. It became a commonplace for party leaders, confronted with unfavourable polls, to say that the only important poll is taken at the next general election.

Furthermore, the pollster can measure only voting intention; he cannot say whether it will result in action, let alone how action will translate into parliamentary seats. What with this, the narrow margin between the parties, a more volatile electorate, late shifts in electoral opinion, and the margin to be allowed for polling error, prediction was hazardous. In four of the five elections between 1950 and 1964 the gap between the major parties was smaller than the average error of the four major polls in 1966,[73] and partly for this reason prediction of the electoral outcome was not growing more accurate. None the less, the polls did correctly predict the outcome of six of the seven general elections between 1945 and 1966, and their prestige mounted during the 1960s. By 1970 the polls dominated election-reporting in the final week,[74] but much to the surprise of Wilson, who had been relying on them, they got the result wrong. An entire page of *The Times* on 23rd June was given up to delighted assaults on the polls. The pollsters met soon afterwards to establish a code of conduct, and recouped themselves somewhat during the general elections of 1974 and the EEC referendum of 1975. Polls shaped the election agenda for both parties and for the media at the general election of 1987, whose analysts say that 'there has never been an election where the strategy of all parties was more directly linked to the evidence of surveys about the preferences of the voters'.[75] Yet the polls were soon once more confounded by a party leader who doggedly discounted their accuracy. Major's triumph in 1992, like

Heath's in 1970, was enhanced by being won in the teeth of the pollsters' predictions.

Quite apart from whether the polls were accurate on what they purported to measure, politicians justifiably questioned whether the polls could ever analyse opinion in the sophisticated way that they so often require—providing guidance on such imponderables as the intensity, stability, and relevance of opinion in several areas of policy at once. The pollsters often measure only inchoate opinion, whereas the politician must judge how opinion would evolve if better informed.[76] Questionnaires reveal that the public often want incompatible things, thereby leaving intact the market for the politicians' traditional skills of weighing up competing pressures. Kenneth Clarke, beset in 1989 as Health Secretary by a long-running ambulance workers' strike, robustly dismissed the opinion-poll evidence of support for a generous settlement. 'Ambulance workers are very popular with all of us . . .', he told an interviewer, 'But . . . the depth of public knowledge about what they earn, what they are being offered and what they want is nil, absolutely nil. You cannot settle pay negotiations in a health service of a million people by going out and holding opinion polls.'[77]

Politicians are often concerned less with present than with future opinion. They must often react quickly to unexpected events and guess at likely trends in unpolled opinion. 'He is a poor democratic leader, of any political party, in any country, who needs public opinion polls to tell him what is likely to be the popular reaction to particular policies,' said Wilson in March 1971. To decide one's policy merely according to the polls, he pointed out, 'would involve violent lurchings of policy, for violent swings in public opinion on particular issues can be brought about by a sudden, perhaps shocking, turn in events or be induced by a well-managed publicity campaign'.[78] When taxed with public hostility to EEC entry, as revealed by the polls, Jenkins in July 1971 noted that four years earlier public opinion was overwhelmingly in favour of entry, and could change again (as, indeed, it did). Besides, he continued, citing appeasement and Suez, 'public opinion is not always right' and it is 'by no means the duty of those who seek to lead always to follow public opinion'.[79] Wilson's handling of opinion on the EEC in the 1970s was in some ways a political masterpiece, though it entailed considerable loss in personal dignity. With him on this issue, as with Thatcher's ministers on privatization, it was necessary to risk moving ahead of public opinion and hope that it would eventually catch up (as, once more, it did).[80] Even when events are expected, the timing and effect of their interaction remain difficult to predict. In such situations the politician's impressionistic hunch or flair, however fallible, remains crucial.

A master of this art was Gladstone, who justifiably laid claim to 'an insight into the facts of particular eras, and their relation one to another, which generates in the mind a conviction that the materials exist for forming a public opinion'.[81] Donoughue ascribes similar qualities to Wilson and Callaghan, who 'had an uncanny sense . . . of when was the right time to act on a policy and when it was more sensible to let matters lie'.[82] To politicians thus placed, statistics on existing public opinion were less valuable than long experience of how opinion evolves and how it can be moulded, together with guidance from shrewd, informed, or significant contacts within the community. 'I believe I know what the people would tolerate and what they would not,' Baldwin told Edward VIII, at their second discussion about his relations with Mrs Simpson in 1936; 'even my enemies would grant me that'. Baldwin's biographer once told him he thought he was 'the only man on Friday who knew what the House of Commons would be thinking on Monday', to which Baldwin replied: 'I have always believed in the week-end. But how they [sc. MPs] do it I don't know. I suppose they talk to the stationmaster.'[83] Baldwin's gift 'was to sense, among countless currents, the relative importance of diverse views, relating them to traditional attitudes and established orthodoxies, and judging with almost intuitive timing the moment when certain things needed to be done'.[84] Here the traditional links between the MP and his constituents were important, as we saw in Chapter 7. Also valuable were the party networks of constituency and area agents. Before the government committed itself publicly on an issue, useful information on sympathetic opinion could be gathered privately. Conservative Central Office did this with some energy before introducing the Trades Disputes Bill in 1927.[85]

All this helps explain politicians' curt response to early mentions of opinion polls. The Gallup poll was invented in the USA and correctly predicted Roosevelt's victory in 1936, in the first major attempt to apply systematic sampling to national politics. It came to Britain in 1938, but in May 1939 when Eleanor Rathbone referred in parliament to poll evidence showing support for an alliance between Britain, France, and the USSR as 'this important and scientific test', R. A. Butler replied: 'I am always interested in any scientific test. When I have applied it in my constituency I have always been returned.' When told by Rathbone in November 1941 that 84 per cent of the public favoured equal compensation for war injury, Walter Womersley airily replied 'I do not take any notice at all of Gallups'.[86] None the less, by the 1950s polls were increasingly prominent in newspapers, and polling agencies were proliferating. In 1959 four of the nine national daily papers published poll results at least weekly, each choosing a different day. By revealing a narrowing gap between the parties they made the campaign more exciting.[87] Psephologists and pollsters were re-introducing a sporting dimension into the election by developing at the national level the idea of a neck-and-neck fight to the finish, though the election of 1966 fell rather flat when the polls put Labour securely ahead. In 1979 there were more nation-wide polls than at any previous general election: twenty-eight nation-wide polls and seven panel surveys. All the mass-circulation papers except the *Mirror* published their own polls.[88] There is a circular relationship here: the papers boost the polls' impact, and the polls boost the papers' circulation.

Opinion polls do not mirror voting behaviour: they can distort it directly and indirectly because they provide the elector with some of the data on which he reaches his decision. In seven successive elections between 1964 and 1983 the party that was ahead in the final surveys fared worse in the outcome than had been predicted,[89] perhaps because the polls had encouraged complacency among the winning party's supporters. Many electors decide how to vote during the campaign itself—6 per cent in 1951, 8 per cent in 1955, 12 per cent in 1959, a third in October 1974, and a quarter in 1979.[90] An informed elector will be tempted to cast tactical votes. In February 1974 the polls, by revealing Liberal strength, may have caused Labour voters to cast tactical Liberal votes in seats where Labour was weak. There were open moves to promote tactical voting at the general election of 1987, though with little effect. Yet the polls' influence on the voter must be kept in proportion. Despite all the efforts of twentieth-century political parties, none has caused electoral turn-out to rise higher than in the first general election of 1910 (87 per cent). Since then the highest turn-out has been 84 per cent in 1950, and neither opinion polls nor televised campaigning have subsequently prevented turn-out from falling. Furthermore, the EEC referendum of 1975 without any organized campaigning produced a turn-out of almost general election proportions.

The polls' indirect influence on voters was most powerfully exercised through private party polls, the most important among the polls' aids to politicians. Whereas the press used opinion polls to predict electoral conduct, the political parties increasingly used them to discover how success-fully their campaigns were influencing opinion. This was safer ground for the polls to occupy, for as Richard Rose pointed out in 1974, margins of error made it always likely that prediction of election results would fail; polls would be more useful if they returned to their original function of assessing opinion.[91] They could provide up-to-date information about likely public attitudes to slogans and possible policies, together with protection against undue partisan optimism. Here too the new methods had at first to compete with more traditional ways of assessing opinion. In 1970 Patrick Cosgrave, on first meeting Oliver Poole (a powerful figure in the Conservative machine during the 1950s), was told to ignore the heap of poll reports on his desk. 'I will tell you, young man, how to predict general-election results. Once the prime minister of the day calls an election, go into a pub. Sit there for an hour or so and listen to what people are saying. Then saunter down a high street, still listening. Finally, count the number of posters in people's windows noting their affiliations. Once you put all this information together you know who is going to win.'[92]

Without always abandoning these older approaches, politicians gradually incorporated opinion polls into their armoury, and denials of their importance became less credible as time elapsed. 'I do not look at opinion polls,' said Thatcher, responding amid 'prolonged Labour cheers' to a claim that Gallup polls indicated her unpopularity in February 1986. 'I do not explain them either. The polls I am interested in are those done on election day, and we have not done too badly at them,' a remark that received 'Conservative cheers'.[93] On the contrary, behind the scenes by 1979 both parties were privately using opinion polls to discover how to influence the electoral outcome.[94] The pace was set throughout by the Conservatives. Labour commissioned a private poll in 1956, and Conservatives sponsored a local survey in 1958 after the Rochdale by-election. In 1959 Conservative advertising agents based their election tactics on research into the party's image, and after the death of Bevan (a strong critic of the polls) Labour was free to follow. From 1962 it made regular use of Mark Abrams.[95] It made unprecedented use of survey research in its major advertising campaign launched in May 1963, outstripping the Conservatives in adventurousness with the new techniques. In 1965 polls were important enough to the Conservatives for Humphrey Taylor, in consultation with the Party's adviser on tactics, to think it worth setting up the Opinion Research Centre, with the Conservatives as his first major client.[96] In February 1974 Labour sponsored daily 'tracking polls' on the salience of the issues for the first time, as well as polls of voting intention.[97]

Events in that year show, however, that even psephologists are fallible (David Butler on 10 February 1974 was privately predicting 'a Tory landslide'[98]), and that private polls might mislead a party. By encouraging Heath in his national unity theme at the general election in October,[99] they contributed to a defeat which sharpened Conservative divisions and gave Thatcher her chance to oust Heath in the following year. Yet this did not cause Bevan's prejudices against the polls to surface among the

Conservatives. Their business connections and thirst for power made it natural for them to seek out existing opinion and then set about catering for it. They did not need the Labour MP Austin Mitchell to tell them that there was 'little point in confusing bad merchandising with high principle'; they knew well enough that the polls could give their party 'a chart of the territory through which the party has to trek', and thereby equip it more effectively to win elections.[100] Labour, by contrast, suffered severely in 1983 through having done no private opinion-polling since summer 1979. Not till well into the campaign did Labour's leaders realize that the electors doubted the Party's claim that it could reduce unemployment to 1 million in five years.[101]

The Social Democratic Party made no such mistake. Launched in 1981, it was often criticized by its enemies for being itself a media creation, tricking itself out in whatever garments the pollsters judged acceptable. Polls can profoundly influence a party's morale, and more. By 1983 the SDP's allegations about likely developments in the polls came near to being self-fulfilling. On 4 June 23 per cent of Conservative voters and 38 per cent of Labour's said that they would be more likely to switch to the SDP–Liberal Alliance if it seemed to have a chance. Alliance leaders then selectively leaked their private poll results to the press and timed their speeches accordingly. After a statistically insignificant improvement in their poll-rating, the Alliance argued that opinion was shifting towards them from Labour, aiming thereby to produce a bandwagon effect. If the shift of opinion had happened earlier it would have affected voting behaviour substantially. The Labour Party under Kinnock after 1983 was quick to learn from all this, and his advisers were alert to the importance of such things as images and impressions. 'I don't let polls dictate my attitude,' said Kinnock in September 1985, dismissing Benn's depreciation of the polls, 'but there is no one on the NEC who doesn't know in their stomachs that what the polls tell us now is true. It's borne out by continual comments of solid Labour supporters.'[102] During the general election of 1987, though, private polling probably counted for less than in the past because the abundance of public polls made it less necessary.[103]

The polls' advent fostered important changes in 'political science', which had originally focused on the comparative study of political institutions, political theory and history, and legal and constitutional questions. After the 1940s it became increasingly quantitative and behavioural, much preoccupied with how voters think and vote. In the 1960s the first nationwide study with panel surveys before and after general elections was organized, leading to the first of three behavioural studies based on poll evidence: Butler and Stokes's *Political Change in Britain* (1969). Political scientists of this new type were not shy of the media. David Butler was the key influence. In his first contribution to an election study—that on the general election of 1945—he complained that journalists' psephological comment was too vague.[104] His subsequent books record substantial improvement, and the political parties have learned much from him. Butler and R. T. McKenzie became well-known television commentators in election programmes of the 1950s, and university experts in 'politics' from the 1970s were active in writing on electoral matters in the press: Hugh Berrington, Ivor Crewe, Dennis Kavanagh, Anthony King, Peter Pulzer.

Psephologists have been especially influential on party attitudes towards marginal seats. In 1951 London Conservatives put special effort into switching their constituency workers from safe to marginal seats. By 1959 Conservatives were concentrating their workers on the marginal seats, and by 1964 both parties were sometimes devoting only nominal attention to the safe seats.[105] In 1966 the Conservatives focused their efforts on over seventy 'critical seats',[106] and in 1970 they devoted far more effort than Labour to ensuring that party workers in safe constituencies concentrated their efforts on the nearest marginal constituency.[107] In February 1974 Heath concentrated his walkabouts in marginal seats,[108] and by 1979 Conservative decisions on where to advertise in the press were influenced by poll evidence on the background and interests of switchable voters.[109] When Thatcher seemed to wave rather indiscriminately to bystanders from her campaign coach in 1983, David Wolfson from her Downing Street staff advised: 'only wave in marginals, Prime Minister'.[110]

*

It will now be clear that politicians, at first feeling threatened in their role as assessors of opinion, gradually refined their own (largely electoral and party) machinery for testing opinion, and appropriated for their own purposes whatever their rivals could usefully offer. A combination of deliberate reform and half-conscious response to social, economic, and technological change has been continuously at work. The outcome has been a complete transformation in the conduct of general elections since Bagehot's day. Given the dwindling importance of local influences, they have become more like referenda, with campaigning simultaneously centred on London and decentralized into each individual home. The rest of this chapter will be concerned with this broad development. The process was well under way by 1884, when single-member constituencies began replacing multi-member. The casualties in terms of political area were the intermediate social units: neighbourhood, community, street, pub, and chapel. In party terms, the casualty was the Liberal Party, in so far as it cherished localism and relied on the religion of locality: nonconformity. The trend also damaged the Labour Party in its original form, for its socialism had always owed much to the working-class community's need to share scarce resources. 'When . . . a working class family buys a motor car', said Gaitskell in July 1959, '. . . it may produce a feeling of a more individual and independent status. Its loyalty ceases to be the simple group loyalty. It begins to function as an independent unit.'[111] The Conservative Party, on the other hand, growing less directly out of the local community, and happy with the concept of the national family, could hardly lose from the simultaneous nationalization and domestication of British electoral politics.

The decline of community politics brought one benefit, however, to all parties. Perhaps the most striking contrast between early-Victorian and present-day general elections is the decline of violence and intimidation. Here, more than elsewhere, change was deliberate. The sequence of nineteenth-century humanitarian crusades discussed in Chapter 6 had already begun to erode the localism of British elections while Bagehot was writing. Owing much to evangelical and utilitarian distaste for traditional and aristocratic manners, and reinforced by concern about the impact of such manners on urban life, these campaigns mobilized 'respectability' within middle and working classes to get things changed. The humanitarians' efforts combined a direct attack on violence and drunkenness with an indirect attack through their attempt to convert elections into debates on questions of national policy rather than squabbles between local personalities or traditional loyalties. 'One of the great objects of their agitation', Samuel Pope told prohibitionists in 1872, '—one of the great lessons they had to teach to political parties in this country was that no party could live long now which associated itself with roughs, and which did not appeal solely to the intelligence of the constituency.'[112]

In 1872 one of these humanitarian campaigns secured the ballot. It 'made the casting of a vote seem more of a deliberate political act and less of a social occasion',[113] and so denied elections much of their excitement. Its impact was slow because many people, especially in country areas, long doubted its secrecy, but it gradually cut away the reasons for bribery and violence. Employers and customers could no longer coerce voters, whose short-term interest was less directly involved in the election result, and the main actors in the electoral drama were increasingly remote from the

community's daily life. At the general election of 1964 the only violence
that occurred was (perhaps predictably) in West Belfast, where republicans
illegally displayed a flag and initiated three days of riot.[114] There were
outbreaks of violence at Sussex and Essex universities during the general
election of 1970 and an arson attack on the Conservative campaign headquarters in Hackney North and Stoke Newington in 1987,[115] but the controversy between government and miners at the general election of February
1974 shows how parties were by then competing for the credit of reducing
violence by seeking to outmanœuvre the potentially violent: terrorists, racists,
and advocates of indiscriminate 'direct action'.

The Victorian campaign for the ballot was linked to a more generalized
attack on electoral corruption. It produced legislation such as the Corrupt
Practices Act (1883), which at last curbed candidates' election expenditure.
Bribery's decline also owed something to better living-standards, for bribes
wither when poverty is no longer desperate, and electoral violence holds
fewer attractions when there are homes to defend and alternative recreations available within them. The fall in average constituency expenditure
per candidate since 1900 has been marked. In 1979 it was in real terms only
a quarter of what it had been in 1945.[116] It is expenditure on central campaigning that has increased since Victorian times. This is higher than the
figures show because subsidized by free broadcasting facilities worth nearly
£7 million to the three major political parties during the period of election
campaigning between summer 1978 and election day in 1979. This was
about the same sum as the parties themselves raised for campaigning.[117]
Lying behind these developments was the mounting articulation of party
structure, which (as shown in Chapter 6) owed much to humanitarians'
promotion of movements concerned with national policy.[118]

Transport changes moulded organizational change. Improved forms of
communication—railways, the popular press, and (from the early twentieth century) motor transport—initiated a circular process. The substruc-
ture necessary for a national political community was brought into existence.
Parties could now mount national campaigns and promote national programmes, contesting all seats and encouraging the party leader forward as
the national campaign's leader. Early-Victorian electoral propaganda took
the form of local fly-bills containing scurrilous references to local personalities,[119] but early twentieth-century election posters, however crudely over-
simplified, concerned issues of national policy and were co-ordinated by
the parties. The general election of 1880 has been described as 'the first
modern election' because a national campaign transcended localized con-
tests, and five-sixths of the constituencies were contested.[120] Better roads

enabled national leaders to campaign more extensively around the country, candidates (especially in rural constituencies) could be seen by more voters, and more voters could be got to the poll. In 1906 between a quarter and a half the nation's motor-cars (then totalling 36,000) were mobilized for election purposes.[121] In the long term all this helped to centre the election campaign on London, though it was still possible at the general election of February 1974 for the Liberal campaign to be directed rather successfully by Jeremy Thorpe from Barnstaple, and at the general election of 1979 David Steel's itinerant 'battle-bus' won much coverage.[122]

The political parties soon exploited the new means of transport. Cars remained a subject of party controversy as long as access to them could be thought to influence votes. The Labour Party limited the ratio of party cars to electors in 1948, a limit that the Conservatives removed ten years later, but at the general election of 1959 neither party thought the change had made much difference. This was not because the party differential had been entirely removed; 33 per cent of Conservative voters were driven to the poll, but only 8 per cent of Labour voters.[123] The secret ballot ensured that, with free lifts as with bribes, the benefactor could never be sure that his investment would produce a return. In 1959 whereas 1 per cent of Labour voters and 1 per cent of Conservative voters admitted to accepting a lift to the poll in the car of another party, as many as 11 per cent of Liberals confessed to this sin.[124] Postal voting was another transport-related source of party controversy in the 1950s. It became available for the first time in 1950, when 470,000 postal votes were cast, most of them for Conservatives. These were enough to get Conservatives returned in at least ten constituencies, and substantially reduced Labour's majority.[125] But for the postal vote in 1964, Labour's majority would have been much larger than four, and its entire parliamentary strategy after forming a government might then have been different.[126] By October 1974 the number of postal votes cast had almost doubled by comparison with 1950.[127] By 1985 transport change had gone so far as to lead the Conservatives to enfranchise 500,000 of the 3 million British citizens living or working overseas, and by 1986 their 'Conservatives Abroad' structure, on an American Republican model, identified 110,000 British citizens living overseas.[128] The media enhanced the tendencies towards simultaneous electoral centralization and decentralization. The national press increasingly dominated electoral comment, with reporting centralized not just on London, but on a small and rather introverted group there. Politicians and media men huddled together in what was by the 1960s almost a private world of their own, and in 1979 Thatcher flew about in a 100-seater plane which was almost entirely funded by the journalists who bought seats in it to accompany her.[129]

Conservatives in the 1950s were quick to learn from American advertising techniques. In the run-up to the general election of 1959, they mounted a nine-month campaign based on the slogan 'Life's better with the Conservatives. Don't let Labour ruin it'. During the campaign itself they launched a major advertising campaign in the press, directed at 'target voters', as a substitute for the pamphlet literature once so prominent in elections. There was a repeat performance in the late 1970s, with the claim that 'Labour isn't working'. At the general election of 1979 advertising expenditure absorbed 64 per cent of the Conservative Party's spending on the central campaign, 40 per cent of Labour's.[130] Rationalistic in tendency, somewhat puritan in mood, and distant from the business world, Labour did not feel comfortable with the new commercial ways of securing publicity and collecting information. Ian Mikardo was applauded at the Party conference in 1970 for attacking 'smart alec advertising agents', Callaghan in the election campaign of 1979 insisted that 'I will not be packaged like cornflakes', and at a Tribune rally in Blackpool in 1988 Ron Todd (General Secretary of the TGWU) angrily attacked the Party's modernizers with their Filofaxes, sharp suits, and clipboards.[131] Labour's campaign was sometimes even counter-productive. In 1983 Conservative headquarters bought 3,000 copies of Labour's manifesto on the night of publication, and Thatcher denounced it as 'the most extreme manifesto that has ever yet been put before the British electorate'. A full-page advertisement in *The Times* on 26th May was headlined 'Like your manifesto comrade', and listed eleven points common to both Labour and Communist manifestos. Not till 1987 did Peter Mandelson enable Labour to seize the media initiative with his sophisticated Red Rose campaign.

With the centralized campaign came the decline of the public meeting. By the 1880s better transport enabled national party figures to address huge audiences at election meetings, though already their aim was as much to influence the national media (then the newspapers) as to address the people who happened to be present at the meeting itself. The microphone enlarged the potential audience for meetings, and Conservatives used cinema vans from 1925 not only to put out propaganda but also to gather a crowd which could then be addressed.[132] Yet the future lay less with the public meeting than with the domestic circle. Already by 1935 the decline of the public meeting was being noted, and a commentator saw Baldwin on radio as speaking 'with his feet on our fenders'.[133] During the 1950s home-based television accelerated this decline, and Tony Benn, seeking new modes of access at Bristol South–East by-election in April 1961, laid claim to 'brilliant success' with his canvassing of people waiting 'icy cold and . . . bored' at bus stops. Television's influence was at first not entirely one-way, however. It was noted in 1959, for instance, that television actually boosted attendance at local meetings addressed by the political leaders whom it had made into nationally recognized figures.[134] Television in the 1970s also created a new type of meeting—the 'walk-about', or meeting that moves. These by February 1974 had become more common than the more traditional type of public meeting,[135] but by 1987 only 5 per cent of the sample had attended an election meeting of any type.[136]

There is still a recreational dimension to elections, but it is a family and national rather than local affair. Going to vote is now a sober and sedate business, rather like going to church. Voters enter the booth silently and alone to cast their secret votes. They then disperse into small domesticated groups of spectators to relish the excitement of cumulated results being cast on a single day over the country as a whole. As in mass spectator sport, a domesticated and passive viewer is entertained by professionals, and the worlds of politics and entertainment compete. In 1964 Wilson persuaded the BBC to postpone its popular serial *Steptoe and Son*, to ensure fair turn-out, and in timing the election in 1970 he was well aware of the likely competition from sporting and recreational events.[137] In the outcome, some 20 million people stayed up for the results, but a fifth of a sample polled said they were more interested in the World Cup than in the election.[138] An opinion poll of 1,000 people aged 16 and above in 1983 showed that only a tenth of the sample thought politics very important in their daily lives; in the lives of a fifth, politics were not at all important.[139] In the 1980s the parties reacted by harnessing sympathetic pop-singers and sporting heroes. Superstar comedians and sportsmen paraded on the platform at Wembley conference centre on 5 June 1983 for the Conservative youth rally, and on 1 April 1992 the Labour Party's pre-election rally at Sheffield 'was a son et lumière within an election rally alongside a pop concert inside a sports hall'.[140] Kinnock behaved too much like a pop star, however, to make him more credible as prime ministerial candidate.[141] Benn was shocked at the emptiness of that year's election campaign: 'I've never seen anything like it. The whole thing's been turned into an entertainment,' and 'the Chartists and the Suffragettes would be horrified'.[142]

It is sometimes claimed that improved communications have made British election campaigns more 'presidential'. If there has been such a trend, it began too early for electronic innovation to be the cause. Peel's Tamworth Manifesto of 1834 first introduced the idea of a party leader issuing a general policy statement for his party, and by the 1840s this had become accepted procedure. Peel was as dominant at the general election of 1841 as Palmerston in 1857.[143] Bagehot reports the comment of a bad speaker when asked how he got on as a candidate at the general election of 1868: ' "Oh", he answered, "when I do not know what to say, I say 'Gladstone', and then they are sure to cheer, and I have time to think".'[144] By 1886 Gladstone's general election campaign had allegedly become 'plebiscitary' in nature. Electoral 'presidentialism' emerges from the interaction between the personality of the prime minister, the nature of the issues, the state of the relevant technology, and the peculiarities of the political situation. The high points of electoral 'presidentialism' by no means cluster in the most recent decades of the twentieth century. They include Lloyd George in 1918, Churchill in 1945, and Wilson in 1966, as well as Thatcher in 1983. Nor are the low points of electoral 'presidentialism' concentrated early in the century. They include Attlee in 1950–1, Home in 1964, and the rather diminished Wilson of February 1974. Personality has always been far more important than technology in explaining a politician's prominence at elections. It could enable a mere cabinet minister to dominate the election in 1900 (Joseph Chamberlain) and January 1910 (Churchill and Lloyd George). In 1983 Thatcher's prominence stemmed not just from her own campaigning skill but from the defects of Foot, her Labour adversary, defects so great that in its party television broadcasts his Party decided to display him to the electors only in the company of colleagues.[145] But we must now turn to the legislature, where opinion, once assessed, is articulated.

# 9

# *Articulating Opinion*

'POLITICIANS rarely alter people's opinions,' Powell once explained. 'Politicians articulate, crystallise, dramatise if you like, render intelligible and therefore render capable of being turned into action . . . something which is present already in people's minds.'[1] It is through parliament that British public opinion is articulated. How successfully since the 1860s has it carried out Bagehot's five 'functions'? When discussing parliament's 'elective' function (that is, its influence over selecting the executive) in Chapter 1 we saw how Bagehot was wrong to think of governments in the 1860s as elected by the House of Commons. The monarch initiated the process of choosing the executive by finding a politician who could command a majority there, and the monarch's backing made it easier for him to get parliamentary support. Nor were governments entirely dependent on parliament when chosen. They inherited many powers from the royal prerogative, and have continued to exercise them ever since, including the right not to answer MPs' questions.[2] The gradual decline in monarchy's formal powers (longer delayed, as we saw in Chapter 1, than Bagehot had supposed) in itself enhanced parliament's 'elective' function. The monarch still initiates the process of forming a government, but what has made this role so much less important since the 1860s has been the growth in the cohesion and discipline of two dominant political parties. Where there are more than two parties, however, and where their mutual relations are fluid—as between 1846 and 1859 or between 1916 and 1931—the monarch still retains considerable discretion in selecting the person who is to organize the government, and such fluid situations could arise again.

Chapters 7 and 8 showed how an expanding electorate forced nineteenth-century parties to mould opinion from two directions: through building up a branch structure in the country, and through mobilizing opinion at the national level under party leaders who could accumulate a national electoral following. This in turn ensured that parliament's 'legislative function' was enhanced only at the price of greatly increased power for the party machines, which required parliament to be much more responsive to the electoral opinion they helped to mould. Flowing from this was a decline in the contribution made by the MP's personal following to parliament's elective function; he must now seek influence primarily through his party. MPs owed their seats increasingly to the party machine and to its leader, who had increasing claims on their parliamentary votes. Mounting government intervention worked in the same direction, especially as politicians' growing professionalism and declining social status made them ever keener to get government posts. Hope of a political career sent more and more people into parliament, and the best career on offer in the House of Commons is through winning government office. So party discipline tightened, especially during the home rule crisis of 1886. Thereafter, both political parties digested their dissident extremists in the course of crusading either for or against Gladstone's bold reform proposals. The percentage of parliamentary divisions in which more than nine-tenths of a party's members voted on the same side rose from 6 per cent in 1860 to 35 per cent in 1871 to 47 per cent in 1881 to 76 per cent in 1894.[3] The pattern of two-party discipline thenceforth persisted across all the temporary set-backs involved in the Labour Party's supersession of the Liberals and also across the four twentieth-century periods of coalition government. At the same time, the concept of an official and loyal opposition to the government grew apace, and by 1927 Balfour could say that the British party system 'pre-supposes a people so fundamentally at one that they can safely afford to bicker; and so sure of their own moderation that they are not dangerously disturbed by the never-ending din of political conflict'.[4] From 1937 an annual salary was paid to the individual who held the post entitled 'Leader of the Opposition'.

So the party with a Commons majority in effect acquired Bagehot's 'legislative function'. If it remained united there was little to hinder it from deploying what remained of the royal prerogative within a unitary system of government. The opposition could do little in the short term except bring moral pressure to bear, but its long-term influence was considerable because the House of Commons became the arena for a continuous election campaign, with speeches aimed at outside opinion. We now know that it is not so much the few weeks of the election campaign that determine an election's outcome, but 'the long campaign' over several preceding months or even years. Kinnock acknowledged as much when, shortly after losing the election in 1987, he said that 'the next general election campaign begins now'.[5] Institutional opposition to the government, from monarchy and House of Lords, gradually dwindled but did not entirely disappear. Legislative curbs on House of Lords powers in 1911 and 1948 did not prevent it from defeating the Heath government twenty-five times and the Thatcher governments over 150 times,[6] partly because the advent of life peers after 1958 increased crossbenchers' influence there. In preserving free school transport in 1980 the Lords' amendments were not overruled, but even where (as with abolition of the GLC in 1984 and persistence with a flat-rate Community Charge in 1988) the government did eventually prevail, the strenuous efforts required to get its way entailed a considerable moral set-back.

Neither Mill nor Bagehot would have welcomed the way these changes in parliament's 'elective' function fostered populism and undermined MPs' discretion. True, Bagehot's claims about monarchy's diminished influence, however inaccurate as description, turned out to be accurate as prediction. But parliament's gain was fleeting. Party discipline, the new source of government's stability, ensured that power over the choice of government rapidly gravitated to an electorate moulded by party machines. These had always aroused Bagehot's suspicion, nor were they likely to enhance the MP's discretion which both writers favoured. As for Mill's safeguard, proportional representation, that has never come about.

*

In Bagehot's second function, the 'expressive', there have also been major changes since the 1860s. Parliament can represent the whole range of relevant political opinion only if its prestige can attract recruits of high quality and from a broad social range. Helpful here were parliament's impressive new buildings begun in 1840—buildings rich in aristocratic symbolism and reference to British traditions. Both houses of parliament in the nineteenth century had the major attraction of being select clubs, closely linked with and resembling the more social types of club nearby in Pall Mall and St James's Street. 'A man gains far more social standing . . . by going into Parliament than he can gain in any other way,' wrote Bagehot, who himself made more than one attempt to get there.[7] Working-class clubs, vestries, and debating societies or local 'parliaments' mimicked House of Commons procedure. By 1883 there were over a hundred houses of commons distributed throughout the country, later co-ordinated through the National Association of Local Parliaments.[8] The scale of popular interest in parliament at the time emerges from the political pottery that sold so widely in its day. By steadily broadening out its membership the House of Commons suffered in social standing but equipped itself better to perform its 'expressive' function. Whereas 24 per cent of MPs in 1832 had hereditary titles, only 16 per cent had them in 1900 and only 5 per cent in 1950.[9] In 1832 land accounted for 66 per cent of the interests represented in parliament but for only 44 per cent by 1865.[10] The aristocracy's intellectual supremacy was waning too. Parliamentary reform in 1832 took away most of the safe seats whence they had earlier launched clever young men from other social classes to defend their cause.[11] At the same time an alignment between intellect and the anti-aristocratic left had already become established among Victorian radicals, and was carried forward into the twentieth-century anti-capitalist left by way of the Fabian Society, the *New Statesman*, and Marxian ginger-groups loosely linked with the Labour Party.

Middle-class influence at Westminster was steadily mounting, though more slowly than the wider franchise might lead one to expect. To get the independence an MP required, the new recruit to parliament needed first to make money. Even an aristocratic younger son like Winston Churchill had first to amass £10,000 by lecturing and writing in the 1890s before he felt able to stand for parliament.[12] As soon as self-funded, the aspiring MP had to find a seat, and in both political parties aristocrats had great influence over the selection of candidates. None the less the middle classes were making sufficient progress by the late 1860s for complaints to be made that the House of Commons was becoming more plutocratic. There was also a marked increase in the number of late-Victorian MPs drawn from the professions. The middle-class advance was bolder even than this, for it began to mould the composition of the late-Victorian House of Lords as well. There were 385 peers in 1837, 400 in 1865, but 544 by 1909 because the number of viscounts and barons was growing so fast.[13] Peerages for a brewer like Arthur Guinness in 1880 or an armaments manufacturer like William Armstrong in 1887 were largely symbolic, but with the advent of life peerages in 1958 the middle classes were drawn into the House's innermost workings. The life peers' proportion of the total rose from 3 per cent in 1960 to 15 per cent in 1970 to 28 per cent in 1980 to 34 per cent in 1993.[14] In 1950 the hereditary element accounted for 96 per cent of the House's membership, but for only 64 per cent in 1993,[15] and its proportion of the House's active membership was smaller still.

The House of Lords' non-elected status, its less partisan mood, and its relatively unpressured atmosphere made it in some respects more representative than the lower house. It was well equipped to ventilate the important problems arising from old age, and the hereditary principle introduced an ordinariness into its composition which the lower house could not rival. In the reform debate of 1968, Viscount Monckton dismissed one speaker's suggestion that the House's composition be settled by lottery as redundant: 'I would almost humbly suggest that we have that in the Peers' bedrooms already.'[16] Add to this the fact that, at least from the time of Lord Shaftesbury, the House felt it held a special brief for working-class interests until they acquired votes and a party of their own.[17] After 1906, for instance, the House—though eager for combat with the Commons on other matters—was careful not to throw out measures relating to social reform and trade-union interests.[18] In the Lords, as in the Commons, there were many lawyers, teachers, and journalists, but a tenth of those in the House of Lords in 1981 had experience in the civil and diplomatic service and 5 per cent were full-time trade unionists.[19] Women accounted for 6.5 per cent of the upper house in 1994, 9.2 per cent of the lower house, but until 1992 the upper house surpassed the lower in its proportion of women members, and in 1975 it acquired a member of West Indian origin when the lower house had none.[20]

Middle-class advance meant greater religious diversity. Catholic emancipation in 1829 enabled Catholics to sit, and their number at first increased roughly in parallel with the number of MPs for southern Irish seats. The Test and Corporation Acts of 1828 expanded dissenting representation. The Quaker presence rose from one during the first ten years of Queen Victoria's reign to between five and ten in the 1860s and 1870s, and between ten and fifteen between 1880 and 1895.[21] The general election of 1906 launched the nonconformists into their apogee; they contributed 180 of the 430 Liberal and Labour MPs, together with seven or eight Unionist MPs.[22] Unbelief can perhaps be viewed as the extreme of dissidence, and by the 1880s there were probably about fifty covertly unbelieving MPs.[23] But only the atheist Charles Bradlaugh pursued religious pluralism to its ultimate. On gaining entry in 1880 he insisted on affirming rather than taking a religious oath of allegiance. This shut him out, but he was thrice re-elected (in 1881, 1882, and 1884), was allowed to take his seat in 1886, and remained there till he died in 1891. The House of Lords broadened out rather more slowly in this respect. Secularization and the gradual integration of nonconformists into British society ensured that the Lords crisis of 1909–11 was the last occasion on which a nonconformist cry against the second chamber could plausibly be mounted. Already by 1869 Gladstone was asking John Bright to suggest a nonconformist manufacturer for a peerage.[24] In the same year Granville told the Queen that ennobling a Rothschild might ease the Jews away from the democratic camp.[25] When the Chief Rabbi, Immanuel Jakobovits, became a life peer in 1988, there were suggestions that a Roman Catholic bishop should go there too.[26] Non-Anglican Protestant groups, however, lacked structures which could produce the officials elected for life who could complement the Church of England's twenty-six bishops and archbishops. They have sat in the House of Lords throughout the twentieth century.

No religious group has attained full social integration until its MPs are distributed fairly evenly between the political parties. Nonconformist MPs were overwhelmingly on the left as late as 1935,[27] but the national government's splitting of the left in 1931 accelerated a rightward shift that was already in progress. The Jews, too, began by clustering only on the Liberal side. The home rule crisis sent some of them towards the Conservatives via Liberal Unionism, but even as recently as the 1950s they contributed between twenty-five and thirty Labour MPs but only two Conservatives. By 1983 they were for the first time contributing more Conservative MPs than Labour,[28] and in recruiting her cabinets Thatcher found Jewish candidates suggesting themselves simply because she 'wanted a Cabinet of clever, energetic people'.[29] The southern Irish connection caused nineteenth-century Catholic MPs too to cluster on the left, but independence in 1922 caused such Irish influence as remained in parliament to benefit the Conservative side. As for mainland Catholics, their mounting social diversity ensures that the left is no longer their inevitable destination. Still more religious diversity came from overseas. Nothing came of the occasional nineteenth-century suggestion that the colonies should send representatives to parliament, though there were discussions as late as 1955 about Malta's being represented in parliament.[30] Representation of formerly colonial peoples did in fact arrive, but by a quite unexpected route when, in 1987, the first Asian MP since 1929 was elected and when parliament welcomed its first Afro-Caribbean MPs. By 1992 there were six non-white MPs, one of them Conservative.

Perhaps the most striking impact on the House of Commons was made not by a class but by a region: by the Irish MPs discussed in Chapter 3. They left a legacy behind. By their social isolation and irreverence, and also (during the 1880s) by recruiting MPs from a lower social grade than was customary in other parties, they influenced the early representatives of the next social group that parliament set out to assimilate: the working men. They could at first get into parliament only if subsidized by working-class organizations, especially trade unions. This was how the first two working-class MPs (both Lib-Labs) got to parliament in 1874: Alexander

Macdonald and Thomas Burt. Even an advocate of working men in parliament such as J. S. Mill did not want MPs funded from taxation for fear
of encouraging 'adventurers of a low class' to stand,[31] and the early Labour
Party MPs were still getting to parliament through institutional self-
funding. But from 1911, when payment of MPs was introduced, the parliamentary road became easier. The earliest working-class MPs, Keir Hardie
and Joseph Arch, for example, were very self-conscious about dress, and
displayed a rather prickly preoccupation with personal integrity. Even in
the 1920s the Clydesider Labour MPs were refusing to accept hospitality
from non-Labour politicians. But Ramsay MacDonald was to Labour
MPs what Gladstone had been to the Irish members: the subtle but
determined foe of sectionalism. Bidding energetically in the 1920s for
ex-Liberal votes, he needed to present Labour MPs in the most respectable light. From his Party's point of view, he pushed ahead too fast,
culminating in his secession of 1931. Yet his departure had the effect of
placing the Labour Party once more firmly within trade-union control,
and this helped to ensure that working men (Bevin, Morrison, Bevan)
were in key positions when Labour at last won power on its own in 1945.

Working men made less impact on parliament than their backers had
hoped. This was not just because they were Lib-Labs rather than socialists. Newcomers influence the ethos of any institution only slowly because
self-confidence and know-how come only gradually. Still more was this
true of an assembly so adept at permeating the outlook of its new recruits.
Virginia Woolf's delicate antennae rapidly picked up such pressures when
visiting the House in 1931. 'It has somehow a code of its own,' she wrote.
'People who disregard this code will be unmercifully chastened . . . nothing
could be easier than to say the wrong thing, either with the wrong levity
or the wrong seriousness.'[32] Alexander Macdonald was subjected to such
pressures almost at once. Rising to an employer's supposed slur upon the
early-morning drinking habits of working men, he 'ventured to think that
he knew as much about the habits of the working men in the country as
the hon. Member'. There were immediate sounds of disapproval, and
W. E. Forster rose to say that 'no hon. Member has a right to say he speaks
on behalf of so large a body as the working classes'.[33]

Nor did working-class MPs grow markedly in number. In society as a
whole, a meritocratic educational system increasingly channelled working-
class talent into middle-class occupations, and the proportion in manual
and craft trades was in long-term decline. Besides, political life is most
readily combined with professional occupations which can be dropped and
picked up again, or pursued continuously but part-time. The proportion of

successful Labour candidates educated at universities rose almost continuously from 15 per cent in 1922 to 61 per cent in 1992.[34] Labour Party
candidates included many teachers in school and university, yet another
way in which the Party inherited the Liberal role, mobilizing progressive
intellectuals and the power of reason against privilege and obscurantism.
But Mill's intellectualism had always fitted awkwardly with the representative principle, and given the twentieth-century spread of class consciousness and populist anti-intellectualism, Labour intellectuals had to be more
deferential than Liberal. There was none the less a danger that parliament's intellectuals would hinder it from being 'expressive' of attitudes
widespread among the less educated electors. The MP's duty, said Enoch
Powell in the year of his 'rivers of blood' speech, is 'not to refrain from
saying what a great number of his constituents wish and think, even though
he agrees with them, just because it runs contrary to fashionable opinion
or to the consensus of the elite', otherwise 'a dangerous estrangement . . .
between electorate, Parliament and Government' might result.[35]

   In view of all this, it is the resilience of the privileged classes that is
striking about parliament's recent history. The British aristocracy was better
integrated than its rivals. It could afford to travel, its education was shared
in the public schools and at Oxford and Cambridge, and the London
season's marriage-market helped to draw its families into a network. Young
aristocrats were trained for political life from a very early age. Their classical education gave them a sense of history, a training in rhetoric, and a
smattering of the classical tags which would identify them as members of
the political élite. They acquired a head start over possible political rivals
by getting into parliament through a family seat relatively early. Their
executive roles within family, neighbourhood, and the armed services
equipped them amply for ministerial decision-making. So by the time
middle-class rivals had accumulated enough to acquire their first seat, the
young aristocrats had become ministers.[36] Aristocrats often arrived in the
House of Commons as younger sons who needed to make their own way,
as the political prominence of the Churchill, Russell, and Stanley families
indicates—so the nineteenth-century House of Commons was on average
younger than it is now. In 1841, 56 per cent of MPs were under 45, and 36
per cent had entered parliament before the age of 30.[37] Once there, the
aristocrats were drawn together by their social functions and their shared
schools, regiments, and clubs. In 1900–10 well over four-fifths of all MPs
(and 95 per cent of all Conservative MPs) belonged to one or more London club. As late as 1974, 66 per cent of Conservative MPs were members
of clubs, but only 8 per cent of Labour MPs.[38] So parliament's rising

middle-class membership did not rapidly change its overall mood, which gave the middle classes ample time to learn from aristocratic governmental experience.

In the 1860s the middle classes were only beginning to acquire the education then thought necessary for politics. Much was made in 1869 of John Bright's blunder when he made his one attempt at classical quotation in parliament;[39] the middle-class provincial was unwise to compete on aristocratic territory. Nor was it much help to have the backing of a vigorous pressure group, promoting such causes as free trade, disestablishment, or financial reform. For the House of Commons, then as now, enjoyed cutting down to size new MPs who had made a reputation elsewhere. Besides, a popular figure accustomed to addressing sympathetic public meetings found it unpleasant as an MP to face (as a matter of routine) a hostile—or, perhaps worse, an indifferent—audience. The House valued character (of which it was a shrewd judge) at least as much as rhetoric or intellect. One recalls the parliamentary success of honest but relatively inarticulate men like Hartington, Althorp, or W. H. Smith, and the parliamentary failure of famous extra-parliamentary names like W. J. Fox, William Cobbett, and Feargus O'Connor, or (for a later example) Ken Livingstone. Even middle-class spokesmen such as Cobden and Bright, who took the trouble to assimilate House of Commons ways, tended to consign themselves—through refusals to take office or resignations from it—to the margins of politics. The first really professional and self-consciously middle-class politician was Joseph Chamberlain, who did not enter the cabinet until 1880. Still, middle-class concerns were gaining ground. The new industrial society demanded more and more legislation of a practical and domestic kind, and aristocratic MPs needed middle-class votes within an expanded electorate. A more factual and statistical approach to parliamentary speaking gained ground, pioneered by Huskisson, Peel, and Gladstone. Perorations became diminishingly high-flown, and subject-matter increasingly economic in nature, and less preoccupied with the constitutional and foreign policy issues that aristocrats relished. Working-class irreverence made its contribution. Classical quotations were in decline by 1874, and ridicule by working-class MPs such as Will Crooks or Jack Jones accelerated the process. Jones (builder's labourer and Labour MP for West Ham's Silvertown division) would greet a speaker's classical tag with the remark 'that's the winner of the two-thirty'.[40]

In opening out to women after 1918, parliament at first moved quickly; there were eight women MPs by 1923. Thereafter progress slowed, until a plateau of about twenty was reached from the 1950s to the 1970s. Only recently has the rise in the number of women MPs resumed, with 19 in 1979, 23 in 1983, 41 in 1987, and 60 in 1992.[41] Yet with women as with working men, the newcomers' initial impact was muted, thus belying both feminist hopes and anti-feminist fears. Anti-suffragists often argued that women MPs would transform parliament's atmosphere,[42] but they were wrong. So few women could hardly have brought off such a transformation even if they had desired it. The polarized party structure made it difficult for them to work together, and nothing came of Christabel Pankhurst's idea of promoting a 'Women's Party'. The fierceness of inter-war conflicts over social class and foreign policy made even the staunchest of feminists—Eleanor Rathbone, for example—subordinate feminism to what then seemed more pressing concerns. Besides, women MPs once elected tended to occupy a limited 'women's sphere' of policy: education, welfare, peace, and 'women's questions'. The early women MPs usually made themselves into 'honorary men', repudiating aggressive variants of feminism, and carefully apprenticing themselves to the parliamentary career. Not till the 1960s did women MPs emerge from their self-imposed policy ghetto. And not till 1979 did a woman MP (Thatcher) move into the centre of political power, thereby concerning herself with the full range of public policy, and even then there were many surreptitious male misgivings about a woman occupying such a post. Most important restraint of all was the fact that the early women MPs were as keen as earlier newcomers to embrace parliament's ways. As the careers of Lady Astor and Eleanor Rathbone amply display, they often ended their careers as proud of it as any male.[43]

\*

For Bagehot's third, 'teaching', function, debates were of central importance. A legislature whose members either make up the government or are continuously at risk of becoming the government is well qualified for this function. MPs with no fixed term are continuously at risk of having to face the electors. The Heath government was returned in 1970 with an overall majority of thirty, for example, but after a mere twenty months its fate depended on the split-second decisions of a handful of individual MPs at the end of the second-reading debate on the Bill endorsing EEC membership on 17 February 1972; it scraped through by only 309 votes to 301.[44] Bagehot made much of the contrast in this respect between parliament and Congress. 'We here listen to parliamentary debates, and have a daily, critical, eager opinion on parliamentary issues, because those issues are decisive. A division and a debate may change our rulers . . . The whole conduct of the government is publicly examined by those who *wish* to destroy it in the presence of those who can destroy it.' He went on to point out that 'if, as in America, there was no decision to make, no issue to settle, no government to discard or retain, public opinion here as there would be apathetic and indeterminate, and the debates of the House of Commons be as long, as dull, and as unheeded as those of the House of Representatives'.[45] Parliament's oft-criticized confrontations should be seen in this context. An adversarial debate, within what is in effect the arena for a continuous election campaign, will be livelier than in assemblies where the stakes are lower, and lively debates inside the legislature will encourage lively debates outside it.[46]

The teaching function requires the MP to retain some discretion in relation to his constituents. Not only must he respond to changing circumstances between elections; as a person better informed on an issue than the man in the street, he must sometimes risk holding out against the populist but ill-judged stance. 'This is exactly the sort of situation in which this House should exercise its qualities of independent judgement and not merely those of reflecting opinion,' said Jenkins, opposing restoration of hanging for terrorists in 1974.[47] Parliament also teaches by less direct routes—most notably through educating its own members, whose new knowledge radiates outwards. By such routes even the home rulers kept southern Ireland within the union for thirty years, and the incorporation of mainland dissenters, women, and Roman Catholics proved permanent. 'The British Parliament, and indeed every free legislature, is a wonderfully educating institution,' wrote Samuel Smith, who entered parliament in 1883. 'No man can sit there for years and follow the debates without being a much wiser man, unless he is an absolute fool. No man can long sit there and be an extreme dogmatist, or can fail to perceive that political truth is many sided, and cannot be put into short verbal formulae.'[48]

MPs were increasingly keen to speak. In the session of 1833, 395 of them gave 5,765 speeches; in the session of 1883, 458 gave 21,160 speeches. For Lloyd George in 1911 this was an argument for paying MPs. By 1970 each MP was averaging about five speeches a year.[49] MPs also became more active in the division lobbies, whose votes were published from 1836 onwards. The number of divisions attracting fewer than 100 MPs was more than a third in 1836, nil seventy years later. Since the 1940s more than three-quarters of the divisions have attracted 300 MPs or more, as compared with less than a tenth in the early-Victorian period.[50] MPs also asked a mounting number of parliamentary questions each year: about 200 in 1850 but 4–5,000 in the 1890s.[51] By 1900 more questions were being asked in one day than in the entire session of 1830,[52] and the total per session has quadrupled since then.[53] 'Starred' questions, requiring an oral reply, have gained increasing publicity, especially when it is the prime minister who must answer. The idea of grouping questions for the prime minister originated with Gladstone in 1881, and their salience increased in 1961 when they were taken at a fixed time, for fifteen minutes twice a week. Skill at parrying questions became one source of Wilson's hold on the House of Commons, and the preparation needed for the occasion increased further in the mid-1970s when 'open' (that is, unpredictable) questions were introduced. The media search for drama enhanced the occasion still further after broadcasting of parliament began in 1978.

From all this, parliament's teaching function probably gained less than its other functions. This was because question-time became less concerned with answering backbenchers' factual questions, more a 'form of theatre'[54] which dramatized divergence on policy and style between government and opposition parties. Because the questions are often parried, question-time is often depreciated, yet it should be viewed in overall context, and not just as a device for gathering information. Furthermore, in preparing for it the prime minister often discovers defects in the implementing of policy,[55] and it is useful not so much for exposing abuses as because it 'puts every minister and civil servant on guard to avoid any impropriety and so improves the whole standard of administration of the government'.[56] Question-time wards off delusions of grandeur. From Macmillan, who often vomited on the day before making important speeches in the House, it evoked 'the same painful anticipation . . . as men feel before a race or a battle' even at the end of his seven-year premiership, and so he made a practice of lunching alone on Tuesdays and Thursdays. Struggling outwardly to appear calm, Callaghan on his own account 'was always paddling like hell under the surface.'[57] Question-time provides, says Nigel Lawson, 'a continuous public examination of the character and competence of the Prime Minister of the day; and I have never known a Prime Minister who did not take it very seriously indeed'.[58] An experience intimidating for prime ministers was still more so for their cabinet colleagues.[59]

Parliament was increasingly opening itself up to public opinion. From 1771 the press were allowed to report its debates, and since then parliament has adjusted (with a longer or shorter interval) in the face of all improvements in communications. The first volume of Cobbett's *Parliamentary Debates* appeared in 1804, and since then parliamentary debates have been reported continuously and with mounting accuracy. More and more House of Commons speeches were directed less at those present in the House than at the wider public outside it. This was especially so with the set-piece annual debates on reforming causes launched by nineteenth-century pressure groups: on corn law repeal, temperance reform, or votes for women. The press acted as intermediary, and reports of parliamentary debates in *The Times* in the 1830s, then a much smaller paper, were far fuller than they are today. Yet it is significant that in 1886 W. T. Stead felt that parliament had 'attained its utmost development' and that there was 'need of a new representative method, not to supersede but to supplement that which exists', more flexible and in closer contact with the people.[60] Parliamentary debates occupy a diminishing proportion of twentieth-century newspapers; debates' percentage of total editorial space fell from 7.3 in 1900 to 3.6 in 1972 in seventeen national dailies.[61] Politics must now jostle for attention with many other interests. But the point should not be overdone: more journalists attend parliament now than in parliament's supposed great nineteenth-century days, and after the House of Commons was bombed in the Second World War it was thought worth doubling the size of the press gallery.[62] Sales of daily *Hansards* by the 1960s were much higher than between the wars, and if sales of weekly and daily *Hansards* are combined, the average annual sale was much higher in the quinquennium 1983–7 (6,321) than in 1956–60 (4,378), though much lower than in 1946–50 (14,895).[63]

As for parliamentary papers, some were being printed for sale or circulation beyond the House from 1780 onwards. Their number vastly increased with the nineteenth-century growth in royal commission and select committee inquiries. During the twentieth century these types of inquiry, though still substantial, gave ground to the departmental inquiry from within the governmental machine, and during Thatcher's reign the royal commission vanished almost entirely. In responding to new developments in the media, too, the House of Commons has been less enterprising in the twentieth century than in the nineteenth. For many years the House prevented radio and television from broadcasting its proceedings, thereby risking a media take-over of its teaching and informing functions. At last in 1978 it nerved itself to admit radio. Then in 1988, prompted by competition from the House of Lords (which in 1985 anticipated it by approving continuance of experimental broadcasts), it allowed itself to be televised, though only under tight restrictions. Experiments began in November 1989, and became permanent in 1990.

Two twentieth-century developments have hampered parliament's teaching role. In wartime, executive power inevitably encroaches on legislative, party conflict is muted, and publicity of government actions suffers. *Hansard* had never been entirely accurate as a record of what was said (for example, the first parliamentary mention of Mrs Simpson during the abdication crisis was never published[64]), but during the Second World War censorship was formalized and carried much further. Quite apart from MPs' self-censorship, there were sixty-five secret-session debates, thirty-seven of them dealing with strategy and security, twenty-eight with air-raid precautions. A second hindrance to the teaching role has been the impact of party discipline on MPs' freedom of speech in open debate. Parliament only slowly became as central to the values of the Labour Party as to those of its Liberal predecessor. We saw in Chapter 7 how Labour, as an 'outside party', only gradually moved towards the other two parties in being Westminster-centred. Furthermore, although parliamentarism has long been central to trade-union values, there is recurrent argument within the labour movement about how far trade unions should be orientated towards the shop floor through workers' control, or orientated towards parliament through intra-party democracy. For Marxist socialists parliament was in theory a mere side-show.

Britain since the Second World War has seen at least three threats to the MP's freedom to diverge from constituents. The first of these, the prominence of the referendum in the 1970s, which in effect transfers important decisions away from MPs to the electors, was discussed in Chapters 3 and 8. The second threat came from the changes in the procedure for selecting party leaders discussed in Chapter 7. No such threat materialized in the Conservative Party, but very different were developments further left. It was understandable that party activists should be given more influence over the choice of the Liberal leader in its reforms of 1976, for the Party's few MPs were by then only the tip of its iceberg. More questionable were the reforms in the Labour Party, at whose special conference at Wembley in January 1981 the constituency parties gained equal weight with Labour MPs in choosing the Labour leader; each contributed 30 per cent of the vote, with the trade unions contributing 40 per cent. This decision reflected a third threat to the MP's discretion: the growing claims of Labour Party activists and trade unions to downgrade the parliamentary party's influence within the movement. In one of twentieth-century Britain's most famous speeches, Gaitskell's defence of Labour MPs as 'men of conscience and honour . . . honest men, loyal men, steadfast men, experienced men, with a lifetime of service to the Labour

Movement'[65] echoed down the decades to rebuke those whose zeal for intra-party democracy subordinated the wider democracy to the narrower. Labour's mandatory reselection mechanism introduced in 1981 made matters worse, and exacerbated the split within the Party in that year. 'MPs are chosen by their constituents to exercise their conscience and judgment,' said three of the SDP's four founders in their open letter to the Labour Party on 1 August 1980. Otherwise they 'cannot be representative of their constituencies in the true sense. They cease to be accountable to the people who elected them and become instead the rubber stamps for a party caucus.'[66]

The House of Lords has been far less exposed to such pressures, given its non-elected recruitment, its less partisan mood, and the presence of experts in its midst. So it became a natural forum for foreign-policy debate during the late nineteenth century, and all foreign secretaries between 1868 and 1905 were drawn from it. For the same reasons, and because party discipline was less fierce, the House became a natural forum for debating issues which party interest excluded from House of Commons discussion: tariff reform after 1903, for example.[67] Not that eloquence has ever been the House's forte. 'Nobody expects a duke to be a great orator . . . his position scarcely requires it,' wrote G. H. Francis, in a *mot* that Bagehot could well have coined.[68] The second chamber's 'teaching' impact came from its expertise and from its relative freedom of expression. Already in 1934 these reasons led Ivor Jennings to see its debates as sometimes superior to those of the Commons.[69] Such a view rang especially true in the 1960s on electorally embarrassing questions such as homosexual law reform, and rings true still on educational and rural questions.[70] The radio broadcasting of debates after 1978 immediately advertised the less confrontational mood of the House of Lords, whose standing in relation to the Commons rose correspondingly.[71] It rose further in 1985 when it allowed its debates to be televised, though the lower house's more frequent opportunities for drama enabled it to regain some of the lost ground when it followed suit three years later. None the less, given the mounting importance of party since Bagehot's day in the lower chamber, the House of Lords has assumed more of Bagehot's teaching function, and in that he would have taken some pleasure. Not so J. S. Mill, who would also have deplored the way the twentieth-century labour movement shook the intellectuals from their nineteenth-century Liberal pedestals.

*

Contrasting Congress with the British parliament, A. L. Lowell noted that 'the very essence of the English system' lay in removing private and local bills from the floor of the House, thereby 'to rivet the attention of Parliament upon public matters'.[72] None the less, Bagehot included the 'informing' (that is, the grievance-presenting) function in his list of parliament's five functions, if only because the electoral system catered so amply for constituency concerns. But parliament's informing function has been subsequently threatened from several directions. Whereas a nineteenth-century MP often went to parliament because his career had already been made, the twentieth-century MP often went there in the hope of making it. There were many more careers to be made at Westminster in the twentieth century: as an MP receiving a salary from the taxpayer after 1911, but more importantly (for the really successful) receiving a ministerial salary as well. Whereas only 6 per cent of MPs held government posts in 1900, 12 per cent did so by 1930, 16 per cent by 1960, 18 per cent by 1980, though there was a modest decline thereafter to 16 per cent in 1992.[73] Such posts did not usually go to MPs careless of party discipline.

All this, together with the mounting importance of party structures, eroded an MP's freedom to dissent from the executive. Fewer MPs now have the secure private income that lends autonomy from the executive and gives access to independent sources of information.[74] The political impact of Churchill or even Macmillan in the 1930s illustrates what has been lost. There was an accompanying shift in the concept of what constituted 'professionalism' in the MP. Hitherto MPs had usually seen themselves as professionals primarily in representing opinion, whereas more and more now sought to be professionals in the sense of full-time politicians. Parliament has steadily extended the length of its sessions within the day and the year. Only during the eighteenth century had it become normal to begin the parliamentary session before Christmas.[75] Between 1865 and 1874 parliament was in session for an average of 111 days, rising to 127 in 1895–1904, 149 in 1925–34, 151 in 1955–64 and 170 in 1974–84.[76] Since the 1940s autumn sessions have been normal. In their concept of parliament under socialism the Webbs in 1920 wanted the MP to be a professional displaying 'no less continuous a devotion to duty, the mastery of no less technique . . . than the vocation of the professional expert or that of the civil servant'.[77] The difficulty with such views is that they so often encourage mistaken views of what professionalism in the MP really is. Its essence is communication, which means that there is much to be said for an MP's not spending all his time at Westminster, otherwise parliament's 'expressive' and 'informing' functions will suffer. Valuable expertise is as easily acquired in non-political avocations as in spending yet more hours in parliamentary committees. True, part-time work is not equally accessible to all members of every party, but legislatures need at least some members whose situation resembles that of their constituents, and who themselves experience the defects of any laws they enact. This is, as John Locke pointed out, 'a new and near tie upon them, to take care, that they make them for the publick good'.[78]

The growth of party discipline does not, however, prevent continuous two-way traffic between back and front benches, particularly when the government's majority is small. With the new specialized select committees at their disposal since 1979, and with ready access to increasingly irreverent media, the backbencher remains well able to exercise his 're-monstrating' function.[79] Through communication with the whips, through party policy committees, and through the plenary meetings held by a party's MPs there are many channels of communication. A government's success in getting its programmes through does not so much reflect draconian disciplinary powers as the fact that the continuous process of mutual persuasion has once more triumphed. Furthermore, some counter-vailing changes since the 1860s have reinforced the backbencher. The House of Commons staff has gradually become more professional. From the mid-nineteenth century the much-respected Erskine May (from 1871 Clerk of the House of Commons) was codifying House of Commons rules. The Clerk became a notable figure in his own right, playing permanent secretary to the Speaker as minister, and presiding over an office that was professionalizing itself into something that now resembles a government department. His department had 167 employees in 1992 and co-operates with five others (Serjeant-at-Arms, Library, Finance and Administration, Official Report, and Refreshment) on matters affecting the House as a whole, and with the Speaker's Office; between them, these bodies were employing 1,272 people by 1992.[80] In 1943 MPs could not use the typewriter 'except under the most archaic conditions', nor could they use the telephone ('an outcast, crowded into odd corners') in conjunction with a desk.[81] All this has now changed, and since the 1960s MPs' offices have gradually been colonizing space within the Palace of Westminster and also to the north of Bridge Street. All MPs now have their own desks, and 435 had a room of their own by November 1993—a facility which will shortly be enjoyed by all.[82] Secretaries now relieve MPs of the more routine aspects of their work. In 1969 a secretarial allowance of £500 a year was introduced for MPs, who were also allowed to make free telephone calls within the United Kingdom. The so-called 'office cost allowance' now accounts for

£40,380 of the combined total of £72,067 that each MP receives.[83] MPs can now cope more easily with constituency paperwork, and no longer have to dictate letters in House of Commons corridors. But parliament's expressive, teaching, and (in some respects) even informing functions will suffer if these changes convert MPs into administrators who see less of their constituents and spend less of their Westminster time in floor debates.

Parliament's informing function has also gained from the broader franchise and the admission (already discussed) of wider categories of MP. Between the franchise extensions of 1832 and 1969 the electorate gradually grew to incorporate almost the entire adult population. Since the number of adults, and still more of voters, rose during the twentieth century, while the number of MPs fell, each MP represented a steadily rising number of people and voters within his constituency. Constituents' pressure has become more continuous. We saw in Chapter 6 how pressure groups concerned with national issues of policy were extending their influence: scrutinizing division-lists, demanding pledges, mounting deputations, organizing processions and petitions, stirring things up at elections. Furthermore, elections have become more frequent. The average life of British parliaments between 1868 and 1885 was five years seven months, but this fell to three years seven months in the period from 1885 to 1915. The Parliament Act of 1911 reduced the maximum term of the House of Commons from seven years to five, and only an exceptional wartime situation justified parliament's allowing ten years to elapse between the general elections of 1935 and 1945. Parliament's average life fell still further between 1918 and 1979—to three years five months. By 1868 the electors rather than the MPs were effectively deciding which party should make up the government. Disraeli, defeated in the general election of that year, acknowledged the fact by giving way to Gladstone before meeting parliament.

\*

The last of Bagehot's five functions is the 'legislative', and if this is defined as efficiency in getting bills enacted, parliament has certainly improved its performance since the 1860s. The decentralizing hopes of both Bagehot and Mill were disappointed, and the scale and complexity of central government's activity escalated. Whereas in 1900 public Acts filled less than 200 pages, by 1974 they filled nearly 2,000, not to mention the mounting tendency to entrust civil servants with implementation.[84] On the days when it considered bills, parliament got through five pages per day in

1906–13 and rose steadily thereafter to sixteen pages per day in the session of 1945–6.[85] All this has required tighter party discipline, reduced the MP's freedom to speak freely in debates, and assigned government a rising proportion of parliamentary time. Debates on petitions ceased from 1842, debates on the first reading of bills ceased from 1849, and gradually the notion gained ground that the government was responsible for organizing parliament's time. Obstruction was possible in principle, and was occasionally practised, well before Irish obstruction in the 1880s. Only Irish irreverence for the House, however, could carry it to the pitch where free debate had to be curbed. In 1932–8, 45 per cent of the session was appropriated by the government, 29 per cent by the opposition, and only 14 per cent by private members.[86] Mill's Commission of Legislation, 'not exceeding in number the members of a Cabinet',[87] was never established, but this was partly because the cabinet itself, in conjunction with civil servants, filled the need.

Legislation has been increasingly entrusted to subordinate bodies. Already by 1848 Lord Normanby thought the time would come when 'the doctrine as to division of labour must be applied to legislation, as it has [been] to everything else'.[88] Two broad types of all-party parliamentary committee emerged during the nineteenth century to cope with the pressure of business. In 1882 parliamentary scrutiny of some impending legislation was devolved to two standing committees—large and constantly shifting groups of MPs who could take some of the strain off the floor of the House in dealing with less controversial measures. As time elapsed, more and more bills were processed in this way, and the standing committees became less specialist in nature.[89] The select committee, by contrast, was a well-established Victorian device for illuminating a policy area. Rather more specialist than the standing committee in tone and composition, its most famous embodiment was the Public Accounts Committee (appointed in 1861), reinforced in 1912 by the Estimates Committee. Competition from Whitehall departmental committees reduced the select committee's role in gathering information, but it persisted as a device for retrospectively scrutinizing government's actions, and its scope was gradually and pragmatically extended during the twentieth century to wider areas of policy.[90] In their make-up these 'miniature parliaments'[91] reflected the party composition of the entire House, their chairmen had powers to discipline discussion, their deliberations were recorded in mini-Hansards, and their conclusions were summarized in published reports.

Select committees moved to the forefront in the 1960s. Congress's powerful committees were the model, MPs were thought to need more technical expertise, and a committee-based career structure might then open out for the MP denied a ministerial career. In 1966 the government appointed select committees on agriculture and science/technology, open to the public, with the power to question civil servants, and promised to introduce two more each year until the whole span of policy was covered. Yet the committees soon found that a legislature which itself supplies the executive possesses few ultimate sanctions against it. Not only did the government choose the chairman and majority membership of each committee; the government could disband it or change its terms of reference if its inquiries became too intrusive, and could limit the publicity its reports received.[92] Besides, as Michael Stewart pointed out in cabinet, a socialist had special reason to oppose the erection of obstacles to a government's carrying out its programme;[93] an interventionist government needed to be able to 'drive a stream of tendency through affairs', as Laski put it.[94] Socialist planning needed to operate inside as well as outside parliament, as Morrison had shown in 1945–50.

Yet here the Labour Party's pluralist tendencies came into play. Michael Foot, a consistent critic of specialist committees, feared that they would deter individual back-benchers and the opposition party from criticizing government. Closeted as small groups in committee rooms, consulting closely with administrators and experts, select committees were in danger of becoming non-party in outlook. 'I only find facts confuse my arguments,' he once told John Mackintosh, playing down the importance of expertise in the MP.[95] Absurd at first sight, Foot's off-the-cuff comment reflects the fact that parliament's professionalism comes, not from the individual MP's technical expertise, nor from a parliamentary committee's collective expertise, but from an entire political party drawing its expertise and impetus from its own resources in the country at large. Parliament's criticism of government must be pointed and passionate enough to rouse opinion in the country, and so cannot be very nuanced or fact-laden. So only one specialist committee was appointed in 1967, and in that year Benn had to overcome stiff opposition from the Ministry of Technology before entering the history books as the first minister ever to appear before a select committee.[96] The Foreign Office and Ministry of Agriculture and Fisheries were most unhelpful to the select committee on agriculture, which was disbanded in 1968. The idea of parliamentary specialization was soon repudiated by Crossman himself.[97] Some years later he confessed that his scheme for specialist committees was unworkable: 'there's always this difficulty. If a man is too much of a nuisance on a committee, your damned Chief Whip can either remove him or promote him . . . the backbencher's

life . . . really is just waiting for a job.'[98] When, in 1978, the select committee on nationalized industries embarrassed Callaghan's government with
powerful criticisms of the British Steel Corporation, even the committee's
Labour chairman came into line and voted against acceptance of his own
report.[99]

The experiments of the 1960s should be seen, not as a failure of parliament to adapt, but as a failed attempt to divert it from its proper purpose
in a political system where powers are concentrated rather than separated.
Besides, Congress's committees can acquire their power only in a society
whose traditions are non-interventionist and decentralized, with political
parties relatively unprogrammatic in nature. Democracy required British
governments, elected on a clear policy programme, ultimately to be able to
force their legislation through. Even the interests of opposition required
this, for, as Foot pointed out, 'the cosier the committee, the more likely
it will be that we shall have bipartisan politics. Every Minister worth
his salt knows how to diddle a committee of that nature.'[100] The British
MP's main priorities must be floor debates and constituency work. But
the history of the twelve specialist committees which began work in 1980
shows clearly enough that modest improvements in parliamentary scrutiny
are feasible if expectations of parliament as monitor of the executive are
less high-flown, and if change does not proceed on false American analogies. The idea of dovetailing select-committee responsibilities with those
of government departments was not at all new. The Haldane report had
recommended it in 1918, and Ivor Jennings and Harold Laski had both
supported the idea in 1934.[101] The limits to the power of these committees
were advertised in 1986 during the Westland affair and in 1989 during the
salmonella-in-eggs crisis.[102] Yet in each case the individual or government
involved in blocking inquiry lost face when forced into such tactics. Furthermore, on numerous occasions committee proceedings when broadcast
turned out to provide major opportunities for dramatic confrontation. By
1992 the number of committees had risen to sixteen.

The two types of committee so far discussed were complemented by a
network of single-party committees which grew up rather less formally.
These take two forms: committees of the entire parliamentary party, assembling to question their leaders on general questions of policy; and party
committees which draw together the party's parliamentary expertise on a
particular subject. The first type of single-party committee ensures that
party discipline grows out of two-way communication between front and
back bench. MPs will toe the party line only if they have been informally
consulted when policy is framed. Such committees can be intimidating.

What he called 'a fairly disagreeable meeting' of the 1922 Committee helped to push Lord Carrington into resigning as Foreign Secretary in 1982, and on 4 December 1984 Sir Keith Joseph received 'one of the angriest grillings given to a minister for many years'.[103] It was what *The Times* described as 'one of the biggest backbench revolts, and one of the most fundamental breakdowns in political communication between government and support- ers, for many years' and produced 'the humiliation and embarrassment' of a rapid climb-down.[104] As for the single-party subject committee, the Conservatives seem to have pioneered it with the Unionist Agricultural Committee, established before 1914. There were seventeen such Conser- vative committees by 1970, and by 1977 twenty-three subject and seven regional committees. By then Labour had a comparable number,[105] though the all-party specialist committee's advance after 1979 caused party subject committees to lose impetus.[106] Yet committees should not be defined too formally, if only because parliament is riddled with informal groupings. 'Put a dozen Conservative MPs on a desert island', wrote Julian Critchley in 1986, 'and within a week they would have set up two dining clubs, the membership of one unknown to the other.'[107]

Parliament has found yet more ways of getting legislation processed more efficiently. One expedient is simply to devolve work to other legis- latures. Bagehot pointed out that since the Reform Act of 1832, 'the House of Lords has become a revising and suspending House'.[108] He welcomed the change in principle, partly because he knew that the lower house legislated so inefficiently. He also favoured life peers because he thought the predominantly landed composition of the second chamber made it biased and prone simply to delay change. The Lords' revising function was not performed very efficiently until well into the twentieth century.[109] By the 1940s, however, a prominent Labour minister like Morrison was as keen as anyone for bills to be revised and even initiated in the Lords,[110] and the advent of life peers after 1958 made the House still more useful for the purpose. Since the 1950s the House has revised its committee system on Commons lines in order to accelerate the process.[111] Changes of this kind rendered somewhat anachronistic Benn's call in 1980, reminiscent of Millite Liberalism, for the next Labour government to abolish the House of Lords by creating within its first month 'a thousand peers and then abolishing the peerage'.[112] Two types of devolution proposed since the 1860s parliament did not adopt. Chapter 3 discussed the failure of the first of these: devolution to subordinate regional assemblies. Still less successful were proposals after the First World War to devolve social and economic matters into a 'social parliament'. The idea was most fully developed by the Webbs in their *Socialist Constitution* (1920), but was also advocated by Winston Churchill in his Romanes lecture of 1930. It is astonishing that so impractical a proposal, prising apart inseparable areas of policy, could ever have won such distinguished support.

An over-pressed House of Commons could also draw upon civil-service resources. Unlike Prussia, Britain reformed its parliament first and its civil service second, so that from the 1830s politicians were in firm control of government. Mid-Victorian governments got civil servants to draft legislation and later even to implement it in detail. By the 1880s legislation on complicated matters was already taking the form of a framework which civil servants could apply in detail through statutory instruments. Lord Hewart might, in his book *The New Despotism* (1929), detect incipient tyranny here, but his outlook was partisan and misleading, though it called into existence a parliamentary committee on statutory instruments in 1944. Equally inflated were many of the fears expressed by enthusiasts for parliamentary reform in the 1960s. The accumulating staff and information at the disposal of modern British governments did not necessarily threaten a parliament whose members themselves fill the government posts. Nor was the bureaucratization of parliament itself—spawning secretaries, sophisticated research staff, and specialist committees—necessarily the right course for a parliament whose greatest strength has always been its 'expressive' capacity to articulate opinions widely held within the community.

The reformers were on firmer ground in the 1960s when they worried about parliament's failure to keep up with the information revolution. Right up to the 1940s the House of Commons library was more like a gentleman's country-house literary library than a research aid for the serious legislator. In 1914 Snowden envied the New Zealand parliament its library, 'stocked with all the recent books on sociology, economics, monetary problems and politics'.[113] In 1934 Ivor Jennings, too, found the House of Commons library 'grossly defective in most branches of learning with which Parliament is concerned', with MPs driven to use the library of the London School of Economics instead.[114] This began to change fast after the Second World War, with research and statistical services established in 1946, and continuous improvements thereafter. The library became a separate department of the House in 1967, and the MP and his assistants are now serviced by a library staff of more than 200; these include lawyers, economists, scientists, and linguists. They preside over a collection of 160,000 volumes and offer 'a research and briefing service on the full range of topics which may arise in the course of Members' parliamentary duties'.[115]

Crick wanted more than this: 'the deliberate creation of a "counter-bureaucracy" to Whitehall'.[116] Yet one bureaucracy is not necessarily the best monitor of another, and for parliament to cast envious eyes at the Library of Congress was inappropriate. A parliament whose front bench has access to the civil service's full resources is better employed in strengthening its access to the opinion that is spontaneously generating within the community. Parliament in the nineteenth century achieved this through its backbenchers' wide local contacts and ample resources. Sir Charles Dilke, his scissors snipping away in the House of Commons library, made himself a mine of information on labour questions in his later career, and even between the wars Winston Churchill's overseas contacts equipped him to monitor government foreign policy. Few backbenchers now have the financial resources of a Heseltine,[117] and although Frank Field continues to demonstrate what one backbencher's open-minded and dedicated industriousness can still achieve, it is through broadening the channels of information from the political party machines and pressure groups—not through imitating Congress—that parliament today can capitalize on the information revolution.

Discussion of parliament's legislative function should perhaps conclude by noting that parliament's accumulating legislative burdens result from choice. In 1922 and 1979 a rather different approach to conserving parliament's time was tried: reducing the overall ambitions of the state. This unwound the whole dynamic, reducing the pressures on parliamentary time, as well as the need for parliamentary specialization and for proliferating committees. Such a strategy was integrally linked to Thatcher's profound traditionalism on constitutional matters, though her campaign to reduce the role of the state was so energetic that it had the paradoxical short-term effect of keeping parliament very busy.

\*

'It is impossible to overrate the importance of the English Parliament . . . ,' wrote Bagehot in 1860, 'the most efficient instrument for expressing the practical opinion of cultivated men which the world has ever seen.'[118] How has parliament's reputation changed since Bagehot's day? Complaints about parliament's decline are perennial. To take only one example: James Bryce included a chapter on the decline of legislatures in his *Modern Democracies* (1921), and admitted that the House of Commons 'seems to hold a slightly lower place in the esteem of the people' than in the 1830s. He claimed that over the intervening years 'its intellectual quality has not risen', its proceedings were less fully reported, obstruction impoverished the quality of its debates and legislation, and party discipline had eroded its members' independence. Somehow a legislature more democratic in its composition and more exposed to press comment had, he thought, lost status. Given the growth of extra-parliamentary political meetings and pressure groups and the mounting complexity of public affairs, parliament inevitably also became less dominant over public discussion.[119] Yet Bryce's tone remained moderately optimistic: earlier high hopes had been disappointed, but no clear alternative approach to representation was in view. His analysis illustrates the complexity of the question under discussion, for it shows how there is no single (let alone statistical) measure of parliament's overall impact; that its impact is many-layered; and that subjective factors (quality of legislation and debate, for example) will affect the assessment. Nor is there any clear linear tendency in parliament's overall status. All that can be offered here are considerations that would be relevant in reaching an assessment, together with emphasis on how difficult that assessment is.

One must first ask: with what is parliament's reputation being compared? If with the prestige of legislatures elsewhere, parliament's standing has inevitably fluctuated with the world influence of the British people, and with Britain's changing status within the Commonwealth. Bagehot thought the mid-Victorian Australian legislature a mere 'degraded imitation'; British institutions were not then envisaged as being for export to such places,[120] and imperialists later thought similar aspirations by Indian nationalists misplaced.[121] But as self-government began to spread through the empire, the 'Westminster model' was widely imitated, and pride was increasingly taken in that fact. For Mackenzie King in 1926, the British constitution represented 'the highest achievement of British genius at its best', and was 'the magnet which counteracts all tendencies to separation from Britain'.[122] Self-government eventually led to independence, yet the Westminster model continued to influence even the nationalist movements once so bitterly critical of British rule. 'We choose this system of parliamentary democracy deliberately,' said Nehru in the Indian legislature in 1957; it was, he said, in tune with Indian traditions, but 'we choose it also—let us give credit where credit is due—because we approved of its functioning in other countries, more especially the United Kingdom'.[123] Still, the Westminster model often failed when transplanted, and after the 1940s the relative decline of the British economy eroded parliament's prestige. Parliament—like the civil service or the ancient universities—became scapegoat for national problems whose causes really lay elsewhere. The obvious comparison lay with Congress, which from the 1940s gained ground over parliament for two reasons: America was rapidly outpacing Britain in world status generally, and its legislature was advancing in relation to the American executive. Much of the impulse to parliamentary reform in Britain during the 1960s was transatlantic.

If we try to assess parliament's changing status by comparison with other British institutions, the trends are not all downhill. Parliament has gained over the monarchy, for instance. Queen Victoria supposed that the legislature was advancing at the expense of the executive,[124] but in reality executive power was shifting from monarch to cabinet, and it is from parliament that the cabinet's members are drawn. The cabinet increasingly depended, however, on the civil service and political parties to get the rising quantity of legislation initiated, drafted, enacted, and even enforced. So parliament's autonomy from outside pressures was eroded, and by the 1970s it became clear that parliament's status suffered when politicians made promises which they could not deliver. Matters were made worse after 1974 when the operation of the simple-majority electoral system was distorted by the growth of a third party. Liberals and later the SDP could then plausibly complain of unfair discrimination, and mounted populist complaints against what was seen as a crude polarity between government and opposition. Thatcher viewed the increasing influence of the labour movement's extra-parliamentary elements with growing alarm, and parliament's primacy was integral to her programme after 1979. Her remedy was to reduce expectations of what the politician could deliver, to reject consensus coalitionism, and to repolarize the party system. Polarization failed to occur because the opposition fragmented, but she did much to restore and advertise the politician's primacy over civil service and powerful pressure groups.[125] No longer did parliament need to watch the trade unions anxiously to see whether its legislation would be obeyed, nor did Howe or Lawson think it necessary to bargain with them about the content of their budgets. It is not yet clear whether events since 1979 have permanently revived either the two-party system or the salience of parliament. The complete exposure of Communist failure in the Soviet Union and Eastern Europe cannot fail to validate parliamentary institutions in general, but in the late 1980s the critics of the traditional oppositional style within the House of Commons—feminists, Liberal Democrats, and electoral reformers of all kinds—were if anything gaining ground, and acquired some credibility from Britain's growing interaction with EEC countries that operated political systems very different from those of the English-speaking nations.

Parliament is bifurcated into a lower and upper house whose standing does not necessarily move in parallel. The advance of democracy inevitably threatened an upper chamber whose status stemmed from rank and birth, so that after 1832 the House of Lords slipped in prestige by comparison with the Commons. Yet the radicals of the 1830s would have been surprised to see the second chamber still in vigorous existence 150 years later. Its survival stems from imperfections in the lower house as a guide to opinion. Elected on average every four years, moulded in its composition by party, it can easily lose touch with public opinion, especially when overpressed with business. Furthermore, as Bagehot pointed out, even the lower house is not one house but several, with moods that shift from day to day. The corrective value of a scrutiny from the upper house became increasingly apparent during the twentieth century. After 1958 the House of Lords reinforced itself further with its increasingly meritocratic composition, and from the 1970s by making itself relatively accessible to the media, and attractively so. Yet a boost for the Lords does not necessarily signify a set-back for standing of the Commons, for much of the Lords' 'new professionalism' since the mid-1970s reflects the fact that House of Commons attitudes and practices have made converts higher up.[126]

Confining the discussion to the status of the lower house, one might expect to find guidance from comparing the MP's salary with the national average for wages and salaries during the year in question. On this criterion, there is no striking evidence of decline. Although the MP's salary has never subsequently reached seven times the national average, as occurred in 1911, it has remained at about twice the national average, and has more than retained its purchasing power; indeed, its present real purchasing power has been surpassed since 1911 only in 1964.[127] If the criterion is whether the functions of the lower house are effectively carried out, one cannot assume that these move in parallel either. House of Commons influence is often equated with the power of the backbencher, and thus with its informing and expressive roles. Yet the backbencher's overall influence waxes and wanes with circumstances, and depends heavily on his party. There are far fewer grumbles about parliament from Labour and Conservative backbenchers than from inter-war Liberals like Ramsay Muir or post-war Liberals like Ashdown, whose Party has less influence over parliamentary debate, let alone over legislation.[128] Other factors shaping backbench influence are the size of the government's majority, the number of political parties, and the relations between them. The mid-Victorian period is sometimes seen as the golden age of the backbencher, whereas at times when the two-party system is in clear operation backbenchers grumble that they are lobby fodder.

Yet anyone tempted to underestimate the backbencher in the 1960s and 1970s need only glance at the way a small minority prevented successive governments from making concessions to Argentina on the Falkland Islands. Furthermore, since the 1960s backbenchers have made important gains. Through the free vote they helped settle controversial moral issues such as abortion and penal law reform in the 1960s and Sunday opening and the age of consent in the 1990s. As Conservatives they selected Heath, Thatcher, and Major as leaders of their Party. As members of a divided Labour Party they were crucial in determining the outcome of the debate over entry to the EEC. And when government's majority was small—as in 1964–6, 1974–9, and since 1992—their influence with the cabinet was enhanced. In the ten years between 1982 and 1992, no less than five Conservative ministers resigned after losing the confidence of backbenchers in their Party; Thatcher was among their number.[129] Perhaps backbenchers' greatest collective triumph was in 1968, when they defeated the two front benches on House of Lords reform. The power of a single twenty-minute speech from the back benches was memorably demonstrated on 18 November 1990, when it destroyed one of the twentieth century's most powerful prime ministers.

There are wheels even within these wheels, for a decline in backbenchers' contribution towards parliament's elective function has been accompanied by an increase in their contribution towards its informing function (through representing constituents more efficiently); indeed, this 'is becoming the predominant part of their parliamentary work'.[130] Furthermore, any increase in the backbencher's influence may threaten parliament's legislative role. At times when the two-party system cannot deliver stable majorities, parliament seems vacillating and inefficient, and loses status: between 1846 and 1859, at some points in the 1920s and 1970s, and in the early 1990s. Until the Peelites had decided whether their home lay to right or to left, much confusion was caused. And in the course of replacing the Liberals, the Labour Party introduced the instability that results from trying to operate a three-party system with an electoral and parliamentary system designed for two. In such situations there is a strong temptation for third parties to grumble about parliament and its workings, rather than to concentrate on winning the electoral support or making the party alliances that will enhance their influence within it. Committees and collaboration have, as we have seen, enabled both houses greatly to enhance their legislating function if judged in terms of quantity of legislation passed. The broadened recruitment of both houses has equipped them better for the expressive function, though the consequent loss of social standing has made it difficult for parliament to attract the highest talent. To that extent, the elective function has suffered. Parliament was also slow to exploit the new media to promote its teaching and informing functions, though it now shows some signs of catching up.

Another guide to parliament's influence is the impact made by its critics. Criticism of the upper house tended to focus on its composition and fluctuated with the influence of party. As for the lower house, the lamentations are continuous but have only spasmodic impact, and often reflect less a desire to repudiate parliamentary institutions than to participate in them. Complaints are often little more than refined variants of customary British grumbles about mothers-in-law and the weather, or they make parliament the scapegoat for some more personal discontent. They involve humorously or resignedly emphasizing defects in an institution which there is no real intention to replace. Yet some critics must receive more attention because they are very much in earnest. They were active, for instance, during the years of political and economic difficulty from the 1820s to the 1840s, years when the notion of the anti-parliament or rival legislature (modelled on the convention from which the USA had emerged in the 1780s) gained much currency. Those who promoted such structures were usually radicals keen to make parliament more representative, but in the historian Thomas Carlyle during the 1840s parliament found a critic who rejected democracy. Indeed, parliament's critics have always included authoritarians and revolutionaries impatient with their fellow human beings, people who want their own way, and quickly. The last of the anti-parliaments were the Chartist conventions of 1839, 1842, and 1848. Thereafter, franchise extension extended parliament's hold on opinion, and from the early 1840s until about 1900 parliament's prestige rose concomitantly with the growth in Britain's economic power and world status. Conventions or assemblies subsequently claiming the status of parliament were engaged in mimicry rather than criticism, and (like the so-called Muslim Parliament launched in Kensington in 1992[131]) were really little more than pretentiously labelled pressure-group conventions.

After the 1840s the House of Commons's critics were rather eccentric: men who (like Fitzjames Stephen or Milner) wanted to wield political power within the system but lacked popular support; or anarchists and socialists who challenged the system. In the utopia outlined by William Morris in *News from Nowhere*, the Parliament House was converted into a dung-market.[132] For critics of this type, party conflict and parliamentary delay seemed to obstruct much-needed firm government and rapid action. But imperialism of an authoritarian variety never captured the

British Conservative Party, parliament was at the heart of the nineteenth-century Liberal Party's values, and the twentieth-century Labour Party's enthusiasm for social justice never diverted it from the parliamentary road. From 1900 to 1939, however, a challenge came from the fashion for 'direct action' to right and left. The successful inter-war entrenchment of the Labour Party saw off threats from the left, but for some on the right the inter-war depression made anti-parliamentarism seem chic. British Fascists in the 1930s, for instance, were impatient with the parliamentary chatter that 'unfits man physically, mentally, and spiritually for any serious executive task'.[133] But the allied victory during the Second World War once more caused a rise in Britain's world status to rub off on its institutions, and the tide turned. Under the Attlee government, furthermore, parliament showed itself well able to meet the rising demand for legislation. A ripe pride in the institution pervades Herbert Morrison's *Government and Parliament* and the memoirs of Harold Wilson. The two-party dominance from 1945 till the early 1970s ensured that the electoral system seemed fair, and the polarity between government and opposition seemed to combine stable government with effective criticism in ways that foreigners (notably the French and the Italians) might envy.

Much of this parliamentary self-confidence collapsed amid disillusion with the Wilson governments during the 1960s. The British political system seemed less capable than other European political systems of delivering economic growth, and anti-parliamentary fashions helped to make Britain in the 1970s seem 'ungovernable'. Since Thatcher's political demise, the complaints have returned, compounded in their impact by economic depression since 1990 and by small parliamentary majorities since 1992. Heath told parliament in May 1995 that when he entered parliament in 1950 'we recognized every Member of Parliament . . . as a person of integrity. We have now reached a stage at which every man and woman in the House is an object of suspicion.'[134] The complaints are, however, largely democratic in flavour, and parliament's less democratic critics should be pressed to suggest practicable remedies for its alleged defects. For since Bagehot's day parliament has shown considerable resilience in the face of major social, political, and economic change. Its procedures peacefully evolved through periods of great prosperity and major depression, in periods of imperial growth and imperial decline. The complaints made by some of its critics (Carlyle, Mosley, Belloc, and Chesterton, for example) sprang from concern about their own failures or lack of influence, or from their impatience with the common run of their fellow human beings whose characteristics parliament is there to represent. Laski rightly pointed out that 'the alternative to the "talking-shop" is the concentration camp'.[135] Indeed, it is sometimes worth recalling J. S. Mill's curt rejoinder to those who complain that parliament talks too much: 'I know not how a representative assembly can more usefully employ itself than in talk, when the subject of talk is the great public interests of the country.'[136]

# 10

## *Power and Decision*

BRITAIN has a strong executive. Some of its powers still reflect its origins in an untrammelled medieval monarchy. It operates within a political system whose powers are concentrated, not separated; within a unitary rather than federal system; and through a 'winner takes all' electoral system operated by a two-party majoritarian parliamentary structure. Nor is it constrained by any written constitution. The cabinet, central instrument of the executive, has no official existence and is free to adapt and evolve unobtrusively. In its modern form the cabinet originated between 1868 and 1914. In these years, says Mackintosh, it 'operated in a delightfully simple manner'.[1] It was still meeting weekly during the parliamentary session, with a vacation in the autumn. Although by 1914 public welfare was beginning to involve government more fully in domestic policy, political issues were less complex in themselves and less intertwined. The pattern of aristocratic life kept cabinet ministers in continuous social contact, and 'there was no sharp line dividing what happened at cabinet meetings from a continuous but less formal process of discussion and intrigue from which policy also emerged'.[2]

Still, pressures on cabinet ministers' time were mounting. Political parties seeking to mobilize the expanded electorate had to develop a national structure, and party leaders aiming to control that structure needed to become nationally more visible. People were beginning to expect more from government, and politicians needed to spend more time cultivating popular support. The press was extending public interest in imperial questions, and Britain was gradually moving towards overseas alliances. Imperial and foreign policy were becoming entangled at a time when there were rivals in the field for colonies. Already by 1846 Peel had complained to Gladstone that 'the mass of public business increased so fast that he could not tell what it was to end in'. By 1884 Gladstone was receiving at least

20,000 letters a year.[3] The political system was becoming more difficult to manage. Up to 1886 the aristocracy had been influential enough in cabinet and parliament to fend off conflicts between Lords and Commons, but the expanded electorate and aristocratic secession from Gladstone's Liberal Party over home rule made such conflicts more likely. Conservatives needed to pay more overt attention to public opinion. In 1885 Lord Salisbury warned Lord Randolph Churchill, then at the India Office, against the double burden involved in public speaking and executive decision-making. 'The strain of doing the two things together is enormous: and if you once go a step too far—if you once break the spring—you may take years to get over it.'[4] Liberals were increasingly beset by a House of Lords with a built-in Conservative majority, which might oblige their governments to seek backing from the electorate earlier than they might otherwise have chosen.

Only one change moderated this increasing complexity of government: although the monarchy remained more actively involved in politics than Bagehot had thought, it now caused less trouble to the cabinet because monarchs could not risk clashing directly with the electorate. This gain for the prime minister was not undiluted because early-Victorian prime ministers had sometimes been able to rely on the Queen to help them deal with recalcitrant colleagues. As late as 1877 Disraeli was prepared to explain to the Queen the seven opinions held within the cabinet on the Eastern question.[5] With the aid of the Queen and Salisbury, the Prime Minister (in an extraordinary situation) managed in that year to outmanoeuvre his Foreign Secretary (Derby), who favoured a policy Disraeli thought too sympathetic to Russia. But by 1885 Gladstone was resisting the Queen's requests for information on disagreements within the cabinet as unconstitutional. His successful resistance reflects the growth of party loyalties during this period.

The growing pressure of cabinet business enhanced formality, with greater reliance on cabinet subcommittees and on civil servants to draft legislation. By the end of the nineteenth century, printed memoranda were circulating within the cabinet. Formality also advanced within the opposition party. As early as the 1830s the opposition was summoning 'cabinets', 'quasi-cabinets', and 'anti-cabinets', and the modern notion of a 'shadow cabinet' certainly existed by 1876, though the actual term was not used until 1907.[6] Before the 1870s oppositions focused on detaching individual MPs from the party of government between elections and on getting government bills significantly amended. Tighter mid-Victorian party discipline made this more difficult, however, and the opposition had to concentrate instead on fighting a continuous election campaign in the hope of defeating the government party at the next general election. As the party struggle intensified in the 1880s, shadow cabinets met more regularly. Their membership remained fluid, and was the source of some dispute, but the leader's role in determining it gradually became clear during the twentieth century.

Pressure of business forced the cabinet to take control of more House of Commons time, both through restrictions on freedom of debate that culminated in Balfour's rules of 1902, and through disciplining backbenchers more tightly. This was all the easier because the MP increasingly owed his seat to his party machine and party leader. The parliamentary division-lists reflect the changed situation, especially after 1886, when home rule raised the temperature of politics. The party's situation in parliament and country led it to elevate the party leader above his cabinet colleagues. He was now required to inspire and co-ordinate the party machine in the country, and to co-ordinate MPs' support for a larger and more complex legislative package. At the same time MPs' personal followings became less important both as a qualification for getting into parliament and for acquiring influence once there. Backbenchers now owed more to the party machine, which was increasingly influential in getting them selected and elected. Likewise with cabinet ministers. The growth of party in the country made them individually less important within cabinet, to whose support they could no longer bring their own semi-autonomous parliamentary 'followings'. Furthermore, politicians were now less likely to have private incomes. Like other middle-class groupings at the time, they were also becoming more career-minded. Politics was becoming an increasingly complex and specialized art, and at its highest levels was attracting recruits from outside the aristocracy. The careerist politician was more eager to get into the cabinet, and the prime minister was in a position to make or break him. Bagehot in 1867 wrongly assigned the cabinet to the 'efficient' sector of the constitution: like the monarchy it was at once dignified and efficient. People wanted to get into it partly for status reasons.

From 1856 the cabinet usually met in the prime minister's house (10 Downing Street), and from the 1870s it became clear that he alone could summon the cabinet. Gladstone in the 1880s doubted whether he had the right as prime minister to dismiss a cabinet colleague, but any such doubts were abandoned after the First World War. So also were any doubts about whether a prime minister needed to consult leading colleagues on whom to put into the cabinet. Balfour formed his cabinet in 1902 without prior consultation, as have all subsequent prime ministers. And in 1905 Balfour for the first time took the decision to dissolve parliament entirely on his own, without consulting cabinet colleagues—a practice which became normal after the First World War. So the prime minister had now risen well above merely being first among equals within the cabinet.

The First World War carried further the trends developed between 1868 and 1914. In some respects the cabinet's task grew simpler. The monarchy after 1914 no longer threatened the prime minister's authority within the cabinet, and after the death of George V it also lost its arbitrating role. The House of Lords was curbed by the Parliament Act of 1911, and serious conflicts with the House of Commons were minimized by the fact that the Conservative Party was usually in power between the wars. But in other respects the cabinet's task grew infinitely more complex. So much so that in 1916 the need for rapid and secret executive action caused what had earlier been a committee of cabinet, the Committee for Imperial Defence, in effect itself to become the cabinet. And at the same time the Committee's secretariat under Sir Maurice Hankey in effect became the war cabinet's secretariat. This dramatic change occurred when Lloyd George became prime minister in 1916, after which Asquith's cabinet of twenty-two was replaced by a war cabinet of only six. Contrast the situation in the Boer War, the Second World War, and in smaller wars such as the Korean and Falklands wars, where the war was run by a committee of cabinet.

Lloyd George's war cabinet met daily, and only one of its members (Bonar Law) was responsible for running a government department. Departmental ministers attended the war cabinet only when needed, though they gathered collectively on Mondays for a war briefing. Non-war business was delegated to cabinet committees. There was a huge increase in cabinet business: before 1914 about 200 memoranda were circulated in the cabinet each year; by 1918 this had risen to its peak of 3,400, but between the wars it did not usually exceed 500.[7] The sole record of cabinet decisions had hitherto been the prime minister's letter to the monarch. Hence occasional controversy over what decisions had been reached. There was no secretariat, and Asquith thought it would be unconstitutional to have any secretary present. Administrative tidiness might have weakened his hold; after a long and inconclusive discussion, his practice was to weigh in and get his way. But this could not last; the professionalization of politics, together with the growing pressure of business, made a secretariat essential, and everything changed in 1916. In its first year the cabinet secretariat consisted of Hankey and ten assistant secretaries, together with more than 40 clerical staff. It prepared minutes which were circulated to those ministers not in the war cabinet, and generally organized the cabinet's paperwork and helped the prime minister. By 1922 the cabinet secretariat had a total staff of 114. In addition, Lloyd George created the (quite distinct) prime minister's small secretariat under Professor W. G. S. Adams, which worked in parallel with Hankey's cabinet secretariat, and which by 1922 had a staff of twenty.[8] The role of this 'garden suburb' (as it was called) was not, as its enemies supposed, conspiratorial or presidential; its purpose was simply to help co-ordinate government policy in a situation of wartime bureaucratic complexity and to protect Lloyd George's position as a Liberal within a largely Conservative wartime coalition. All this contrasts markedly with the staff of four which had catered for pre-war prime ministers.

We saw in Chapter 2 how the First World War saw the move towards imperial unification impinging even on the war cabinet, and how the 'imperial war cabinet' came to nothing. Australia in the Second World War wanted a representative in the British war cabinet, but Churchill resisted the idea because no such representative could be responsible to parliament in the way that British members were, and because he did not want the war cabinet unduly enlarged. An Australian representative was allowed to attend on matters concerning Australia, but no further 'imperial' modifications to the cabinet took place.

The wartime enhancement of the prime minister's power did not cease in 1918, if only because Lloyd George's peacetime coalition of 1918–22 set out with such ambitious plans for reconstruction. The normal cabinet size of twenty was restored in October 1919, but Lloyd George's control of the government machine was increased by the integration of the civil service in 1919. Sir Warren Fisher was made directly responsible for the civil service to the prime minister, who thereby gained more influence over appointments. At this point John Mackintosh, the cabinet's leading historian, introduces his image of the cone. He portrays the prime minister as presiding over widening circles of advisers, of which the cabinet is only one, though still the most important.[9] The Re-election of Ministers Act (1919) removed the need for a by-election when an MP accepted office, so that prime ministers could henceforth reshuffle ministers without risking electoral embarrassment. They did not miss the opportunity.[10] It was perhaps symbolic of the prime minister's new authority that Lloyd George in September 1921 felt able to summon the cabinet to meet at Inverness Town Hall, though not without evoking resentment. Wilson cited this precedent when he summoned a full cabinet meeting at the Labour Party conference in Brighton in 1966.[11] The arrest to the growth in the prime minister's authority when Lloyd George was defeated in 1922 proved only temporary. Increased inter-war demands on government and tighter party discipline soon caused the trend to resume. As we saw in Chapter 9, an increased role for government meant that more and more MPs held government posts, which weakened parliament's capacity to criticize the executive.

In 1920 all cabinet committees except the Committee of Imperial Defence and the Home Affairs Committee were disbanded, and because cabinet ministers still often met one another socially, much business that would now require a committee could be settled informally. None the less, cabinet committees proliferated even in peacetime after 1918. Over 700 cabinet committees and subcommittees existed between 1923 and the Second World War, holding over 6,000 meetings.[12] In any one year between the wars there were twenty cabinet committees of some sort, *ad hoc* or standing. Problems of a new type forced the creation of the Industrial Unrest Committee in 1918, for instance; in the same year a Home Affairs Committee was established, and a Finance Committee in 1919.[13]

The formalization of the cabinet also survived Lloyd George's decline. By 1923 the cabinet secretariat had been reduced to eleven, but the secretary to the cabinet has continued since then to attend cabinet proceedings. Only on rare occasions has he been asked to leave: in 1923 when ministers were in sharp dispute about protection, for example, or twice during the Attlee government when party matters were being discussed.[14] His crucial role as framer of the minutes was captured in an anonymous limerick: 'racking his brains to record and report what he thinks that they think they ought to have thought'.[15] Inter-war civil servants participated in more and more cabinet subcommittees, and between 1928 and 1938 Cabinet Office staff numbers (stationary for most of the 1920s) rose from forty-six to 158.[16] The culmination of civil servants' involvement in cabinet perhaps took place in 1973–4, when Edward Heath mingled civil servants with politicians to sort out such problems as Stage III of his incomes policy.[17] Heath developed a particularly close personal relationship with the head of the home civil service Sir William Armstrong, who recalled that Heath sometimes 'asked me to say something which was not normal for a civil servant and when at press conferences he had me on the platform with him, then it began to edge into a different kind of relationship'.[18]

The Second World War required Churchill to carry government intervention to new heights, though he did not approach the matter in quite Lloyd George's way. He reduced the size of the cabinet to between seven and eleven, most with departmental duties. He personally directed the war effort, first as chairman of the cabinet's Defence Committee and of the

Chiefs of Staff Committee. There was no war cabinet as such. The war was directed through the Defence Committee, which merged with Churchill's personal entourage, and he was more and more left to run the war on his own. Weekly briefings of all ministers on the war situation were given every Monday. Anderson, and later Attlee, chaired the Lord President's Committee, which looked after most domestic matters. It was a kind of subcabinet, acting for the cabinet as a whole over a wide field, with much delegation to subcommittees on particular matters such as food and manpower. As Prime Minister from 1945 to 1951 Attlee did not disband the elaborate committee structure set up in 1941, but presided in peacetime over Mackintosh's conelike structure. He appointed a Home Affairs Committee to consider all proposed legislation, a Future Legislation Committee for domestic affairs, and more committees for economic policy, production, and agriculture. Each of these had its own subcommittees. Attlee himself presided over the Defence, Economic Policy, Commonwealth Affairs, and Nuclear Defence committees. Cabinet committees were now beginning to encroach on the power of the full cabinet. The history of the Education Act in 1944 shows that by then, when there was no dispute in a cabinet committee, an important piece of legislation did not need to come before the full cabinet at all. Furthermore much business was being done, as always, in direct conversations outside cabinet between the prime minister and his cabinet colleagues.

Churchill between 1951 and 1953 tried out a new way of reconciling executive control with the efficient handling of mounting business: L. S. Amery's scheme for cabinet 'overlords', or co-ordinating figures whose presence in a rather smaller cabinet would provide firmer direction, each presiding over several ministers who were outside the cabinet. This scheme had many drawbacks: it antagonized the House of Commons because all three 'overlords' were peers; it disappointed the ministers who had been left out of the cabinet; and parliament could not decide where to pin responsibility for a department's actions. So the experiment was discontinued in 1953. Similar ways of co-ordinating business had occurred within earlier governments, but because they had been informal, they did not encounter constitutional objections.[19] By the mid-1950s the cabinet had become only the most important among the several circles of committees under the prime minister: cabinet, committees of cabinet, and subcommittees including junior ministers and civil servants. Because cabinet reshuffles were more frequent, cabinet ministers found it more difficult to develop the expertise demanded by increasingly complex business. Subsequent governments responded by gradually increasing the staff available to the prime minister and to the cabinet as a whole—though never on the scale promoted by Lloyd George between 1916 and 1918.

Shadow cabinet ministers, Labour and Conservative, in the 1950s and 1960s tended increasingly to specialize. Surprised by the casual arrangements then prevailing, Crossman in 1955 argued that 'to be an alternative Government, Labour must look and behave like an alternative Government'. His views impressed Gaitskell, whose mind was working along the same lines, and Attlee for the first time allocated shadow-cabinet responsibilities across the entire policy spectrum.[20] Crossman was somewhat taken aback when such firm action was taken along the lines he had sketched out. 'I never dreamt that they would envisage setting themselves up so pretentiously as a full-scale Shadow Government,' he grumbled in his diary, 'looking very much like the Labour Government in its worst, last phase in 1950.'[21] Argument persisted, particularly in the Labour Party, about how far the shadow cabinet was bound by conventions of 'collective responsibility'. Heath denied that there was any such thing inside the Conservative shadow cabinet, and in 1968 did not require Sir Edward Boyle to resign after abstaining on a resolution about race issues where the Party had decided to oppose the government.[22] When Heath after February 1974 refused to discuss monetary policy in the shadow cabinet,[23] Sir Keith Joseph was free to mount his own separate campaign to discuss it— the Centre for Policy Studies—thus launching what became 'Thatcherism' on its remarkable journey. In 1981, however, Benn claimed freedom to oppose the shadow cabinet when it diverged from party policy, and was soundly rebuked by Foot as party leader. The doctrine of collective responsibility, Foot declared, 'is not some old constitutional theory. It is much more concerned with common sense, good faith and comradeship among those who must act together in Parliament.' Labour would have no hope of winning the next election 'unless members of the Shadow Cabinet and the Party demonstrate fraternity'.[24] Close observers thought the Labour Party hindered itself through choosing most shadow cabinet members by election. Instead, they argued, the Labour leader should choose for himself what he saw as the most powerful team for rousing the country and defeating the Conservatives, as he was free to do when in office and appointing his cabinet.[25]

When Wilson became Prime Minister in 1964 he increased the prime minister's personal staff by setting up a personal political office under Marcia Williams. Cabinet meetings were becoming more frequent. Whereas before 1914 the cabinet met about forty times a year, between the wars this had risen to about sixty, and after 1964 to about ninety.[26] And although the size of the cabinet did not change appreciably (it has remained at about twenty throughout the twentieth century[27]), the pressure of business was dealt with partly by extending the authority enjoyed by the cabinet's committees. Ever since 1919 it has been agreed that no question could be brought before the cabinet until the cabinet secretariat had submitted it to all the departments concerned. Furthermore, the cabinet's committees gradually became 'each . . . a microcosm of the Cabinet',[28] and in 1967 Wilson told the cabinet that matters could be brought up from committees to full cabinet only with the agreement of their chairmen. The prime minister's power of appointing committee chairmen further reinforced his patronage. Wilson's 'European Strategy Committee', which wore down the opponents of EEC membership in spring 1974, illustrates the great strategic influence a cabinet committee could wield. Composed of three marketeers and three anti-marketeers, with Wilson and Callaghan holding the ring, it scaled down issues of principle to practical demands. With the aid of the civil servants it overwhelmed the anti-market case with a wealth of information, so that British membership could continue without obviously breaching Labour's manifesto commitments.[29]

By the 1970s the Secretary to the Cabinet, though serving the cabinet as a whole, was also acting as a sort of permanent head of the prime ministerial department, relieving the pressure on the prime minister himself. The massive increase in civil-service numbers by the 1960s led to serious problems of control. Whereas in 1900 about sixty ministers controlled 50,000 civil servants, eighty years later about 100 ministers were expected to control about 700,000.[30] In 1970 Heath introduced the Central Policy Review Staff with the aim of producing 'creative tension' (a phrase popular at the time) in the formation of policy. He hoped that by forcing policy options up to cabinet level for decision, the CPRS would prevent crucial policy choices from being pre-empted by decisions taken lower down. The cabinet would then emancipate itself from civil-service orthodoxy. The CPRS was also designed to enable the cabinet occasionally to distance itself from the day-to-day business of government and periodically review the directions it was taking. Headed by Lord Rothschild, it had acquired fifteen members by 1973. Yet even under Heath, the CPRS degenerated into a sort of all-purpose standing royal commission, entrusted with advising on particular problems as they became urgent. After 1974 it lost its overall strategic function, and in the late 1970s gradually lost impetus and direction, surviving only precariously in 1979. At the same time the idea of having partisan political advisers at 10 Downing Street was gaining ground. The Social Policy Unit was established by Wilson in 1974 under Bernard Donoughue, and drew together the (politically committed) special advisers who accompanied ministers into their separate departments, together with six senior civil servants. Smaller than the CPRS, and designed for shorter-term purposes, it co-ordinated the government's social policy, and was responsible directly to the prime minister. It is the ancestor of the policy unit that remained at No. 10 Downing Street thereafter.

By the time Mackintosh was writing his third edition (published in 1977), the situation seemed ominous: government seemed diminishingly in control of events because increasingly dependent on reluctant collaboration from extra-parliamentary bodies. Mackintosh thought that governments, in trying to get control over the situation, were dangerously increasing the prime minister's power. They were also sacrificing both the cabinet's collective responsibility and the minister's individual responsibility for his department's actions. Yet Mackintosh's argument assumed that prime-ministerial power would continue to be driven forward by mounting government intervention. We now know that events took a most unexpected direction in 1979, the year after Mackintosh died. If government attempted to do less, its 'overload' (another fashionable phrase of the time) would diminish. The bold enterprise involved in sending the whole process into reverse itself enhanced the pressures on the cabinet at first, but these were eased by a further change: by Thatcher's increasing tendency to do business through meeting cabinet ministers individually rather than bring everything to relatively formal committees, let alone to full cabinet. Even so important a manifesto commitment as abolishing the GLC emerged in 1983 from informal consultation between Thatcher and colleagues outside the cabinet, and was pushed into the manifesto only a few days after the cabinet's manifesto meeting had been held.[31]

Thatcher was reinforced by a small staff of political advisers at No. 10, covering a wide area of policy. They were direct successors of Donoughue's Social Policy Unit, but their role was more strategic, and was not confined to any particular area of policy. In 1983 Thatcher abolished the CPRS, whose power had been waning for some time, and whose role had always been to advise the cabinet as a whole rather than the prime minister. Some of its functions were transferred to the Downing Street policy unit, which advised the prime minister on immediate issues, and had nine members by October 1985. It included people with business experience, and was quite ready to look beyond Whitehall for some of its ideas, drawing some of these from the think-tanks that were so prominent in developing the philosophy of Thatcherism.

In this situation cabinets could become less frequent, and by 1987 between forty and forty-five were being held in any one year, about half as many as under Attlee and Churchill. Found drinking coffee in his room one cabinet morning, Peter Walker was asked why he was not in cabinet, and allegedly replied: 'oh, we don't have them any more'.[32] The same de-escalation affected cabinet committees. In the six years up to 1986 Thatcher accumulated less than 165, whereas Attlee had accumulated 461 in six and a quarter years and Churchill 246 in three and a half.[33] Here, as so often elsewhere, her affinity with Churchill was more tenuous than she publicly liked to imply. Cabinet committees none the less remained important in the 1980s, and seem to have taken five forms: standing (that is, perman-ent); *ad hoc* (single-issue); ministerial (with civil servants present but not participating); official (entirely composed of civil servants); and mixed (containing ministers and civil servants, both participating).[34] Some of the official cabinet committees under Thatcher were very important. Her 'dry' economic policy, like Wilson's non-devaluationist strategy after 1964, was pushed through after 1979 by appointing sympathetic ministers in that area; but she also ensured that policy was formed in the cabinet's 'E' committee on future economic policy.[35] The so-called 'wets', unco-ordinated and uninformed, were continually at a disadvantage. Jim Prior, a leading 'wet', learned of budget plans for almost doubling VAT to a single rate of 15 per cent in 1979 only from the Director-General of the CBI, and the government's overall economic strategy was not discussed in full cabinet till July 1980.[36] Another important committee, MISC 57, chaired by Robert Wade-Gery, planned the government's victory over the miners after 1981. Both the Falklands and Gulf wars were run by cabinet committees with five members. Both included the Prime Minister, Foreign Secretary, and Defence Secretary. In the Falklands case these were afforced by two trusted party figures: Parkinson (party chairman) and Whitelaw (Home Secret-ary). In the Gulf War, under Major, the other two were Lamont (Chan-cellor of the Exchequer) and Wakeham (Energy Secretary). In both cases, experts—including ministers, civil servants, and members of the armed services—were on call.

Thatcher as Prime Minister acquired more influence over cabinet than any of her predecessors since Churchill. By her public actions and remarks she often denied her ministers the loyalty they deserved, and more than once announced important shifts in policy without full cabinet consulta-tion. 'Never underestimate the effectiveness of simply just announcing something,' she told Kenneth Baker.[37] Yet despite her strength of person-ality and hold over her Party, her management of the cabinet reflected a continuous sense of insecurity: a fear that even the closest of colleagues might conspire to supplant her. Her memoirs record a remarkable sense of vulnerability at the heart of government policy-making. She felt able to inform herself about the plans of Nigel Lawson, her secretive Chancellor of the Exchequer, for example, only through contacts with Treasury civil servants who 'furtively filled me in—with the strictest instructions not to divulge what I knew'. She even claims to have remained unaware for eight months that Lawson was shadowing the Deutschmark, thereby pursuing 'a policy without my knowledge or consent'.[38] The so-called 'Westland affair' of 1986 suggests that her vulnerability in cabinet between 1979 and 1981 led her permanently to underestimate her strength, for only a timid prime minister could have allowed a dispute on policy between colleagues on such a matter to remain public for so long. Something similar happened in her dispute with Lawson in 1988–9. The price for her in 1986 of keeping off the cabinet's agenda a subject which a minister (Heseltine) wanted discussed was high indeed, in both the short and long term. 'I may not be prime minister by six o'clock tonight,' she told one associate before leaving 10 Downing Street to defend herself on the issue in the House of Commons on 27 January 1986.[39]

Westland exposed a degree of distrust and manœuvre at the highest levels that had not hitherto been revealed. Whereas previous prime ministers had used discussion within cabinet to pre-empt public disagreement, Thatcher almost reversed the process, provoking public argument by off-the-cuff remarks in order to get her way in cabinet. When Heseltine thought he could not get his views properly aired in full cabinet, his resignation had as its long-term consequence the ousting of Thatcher herself. Several factors contributed to her political demise in 1990: increasing concern at her strident views and conduct on the EEC; disquiet at the crudities of the poll tax; concern that, with a general election impending, her somewhat frenetic public image was a waning electoral asset; and worries about the state of the economy. But one further factor, lying beneath them all and perhaps ultimately more important than any, was concern about the way she was running the cabinet. For her precautions against conspiracy were in the long term counter-productive.

Sceptical backbenchers during her second leadership contest included several former colleagues who had watched her methods from the inside and disliked them, or even thought them dangerous. 'The strains of office in any modern government are . . . considerable,' wrote David Howell, 'but they only become overwhelming when the enemy is not just in front but also behind, when those who should be reinforcing are undermining, and those who should be calming the waters are stirring them up.' Thatcher's press secretary, Bernard Ingham, aroused special resentment. By rather conspicuously failing to defend cabinet ministers in difficulties, he seemed eventually to become part of Thatcher's machinery for prising them out. 'A Minister with the Lobby poisoned against him . . .', wrote Howell, 'is really caught in a vortex. The more he tries to get on with the job the more he is rubbished for "not being up to it". The more he counters or objects to the stories, the more he is marked as a drowning man.'[40] Heseltine and Howe would no doubt have endorsed Lawson's view that the prime minister had a perfect right to dismiss a minister, but that 'what is unacceptable conduct . . . is to recoil from sacking a Minister, and systematically to undermine him instead'.[41] The undermining came not only from Ingham but from Thatcher herself, who was prone to subvert careful work done by her ministers with what Howe described in his resignation speech as publicly subversive 'background noise', supplemented by 'casual comment or impulsive answer'.[42]

Thatcher announced before winning office that in cabinet she 'couldn't waste time having any internal arguments', and in cabinet discussion she led from the chair.[43] Yet paradoxically this, too, weakened her position because the cabinet ceased to be an effective sounding-board which could reflect the diverse opinion within the Party and the country. Its role as monitor of the prime minister was also increasingly at risk. Given that the Party welcomed Thatcher's electoral success and legislative achievements, the few cabinet dissidents could find very little ground outside the cabinet on which to stand. Yet Thatcher's downfall in 1990 owed much to the persistence in the mind of one cabinet colleague (Howe) of an important and rather traditionalist notion: that cabinet government, like the EEC, 'is all about trying to persuade one another from within . . . Plain speaking certainly—but matched always by mutual respect and restraint in pursuit of a common cause.'[44] Ultimately the government was endangered by the mood of distrust evoked by Thatcher's unsavoury combination of covert subversion and outright rudeness to cabinet colleagues. Genuine cabinet government was quietly restored by John Major, and it will be some years into the 1990s before we know whether the Thatcher years will act as a salutary warning to any potential imitators of her style, or will be seen as a good reason for getting the entire political system reformed. It will also be some time before we know whether 1979 will eventually come to resemble 1922, and constitute only a temporary halt to a long-term interventionist trend, with all the consequences for cabinet structure thereby entailed.

A few major themes are worth drawing out of what has so far been said.

The first will be obvious: the cabinet's continuous and unobtrusive adaptability in the face of escalating government business, together with the implications of this for the prime minister and for the network of cabinet committees. This flexibility stems from the fact that, as A. B. Keith pointed out, 'it is essentially by the growth of conventions that the Cabinet system exists': by rules which have no stronger force than that of custom whose authority accumulates over time.[45] There are two other themes, of which the first is the mounting problem of publicity that has subverted cabinet secrecy. Within the cabinet there was little love of secrecy for its own sake, but much awareness of the practical gains to be made from pooling full and frank views on policy, together with much commonsensical concern to ensure that discussions about the country's welfare should not be unduly distorted by participants' vanity, by intimidation, or by other selfish and short-term personal motives. Cabinet secrecy also reflected a desire to uphold collective cabinet and individual ministerial responsibility to parliament for the policies undertaken, and to preserve a direct relationship between a government's policy and its commitments to the electorate. Several episodes before 1914 illustrate how confidentially cabinet proceedings were then regarded. Anyone who attempted to take notes in cabinet was firmly discouraged. In the Aberdeen cabinet Lord Granville once refused to continue a statement until Sir William Molesworth ceased his note-taking, and 'Hansardizing' was firmly discouraged by Lord Salisbury.[46] Asquith took a similar line, though simultaneously and secretly providing Venetia Stanley with remarkably frank accounts of what went on in cabinet. In the 1970s both Wilson and Callaghan took exception to colleagues' note-taking during cabinet discussions, especially by Benn.[47] Until the 1960s it would have been inconceivable for anyone to publish a diary of what was said in cabinet.

Cabinet confidentiality was vigorously enforced until the 1960s. In 1934 George Lansbury's son was prosecuted under the Official Secrets Act for quoting papers circulated to the cabinet in 1930–1 in his biography of his father; in 1943–4 Norman Brook as Secretary to the Cabinet plundered the Lansbury papers for secret cabinet material; Anthony Nutting submitted a proof of his book on the Suez crisis to Burke Trend as Cabinet Secretary, and had to suppress some details, though nothing like as many as were requested; and when John Mackintosh had written his book on the cabinet, the Cabinet Office asked him (in vain) to show them the entire text before publication.[48] Until very recently even the existence, let alone the membership, of cabinet committees was kept secret, on the ground that otherwise it would be unclear which minister was responsible to parliament for which department. When David Butler asked him in an Oxford seminar of 1966 why he could not even admit that cabinet committees existed, Crossman thought it a fair question. Benn was amused in 1978 to discover that at least one member of the Labour cabinet did not know what cabinet committees there were: 'open government is needed for *Ministers* to know what is going on', he wrote, 'let alone anybody else'.[49]

Cabinet secrecy could not survive intact in an increasingly democratic and participatory society. More direct means were required to keep cabinet and public opinion in line. Among the four leading devices developed, the unattributable leak is the first, and has a long history. Joseph Chamberlain's attempts to open up late-Victorian public discussion on policy were discussed in Chapter 8, and by 1938 Laski could claim that 'there are few Cabinet meetings in which the modern Press is not a semi-participant'.[50] Media contacts with cabinet ministers have continued to extend up to the present day. Harold Wilson's attempts to stem leaks stumbled upon his colleagues' recognition that he was at least as prone to leak as they were. During the Thatcher cabinets, a competitive leaking to the press was part of the weaponry deployed by 'wets' and 'dries' in their battle for control over policy, and by the early 1990s the art of competitive leaking was being practised even within the royal family. 'These days', wrote Norman Fowler in 1991, 'no self-respecting up-and-coming minister or shadow minister would be without a lunch diary crammed full of political correspondents.'[51] A more formal version of the unofficial leak is a second device: the public agreement to differ, which was seen in operation on women's suffrage between 1905 and 1914, on protection in 1931–2, and on membership of the EEC in 1974–5.

Reinforcing these two devices were two more that were concerned with publications. In 1958 the fifty-year rule governing the release of government documents was introduced, relaxed to thirty years by the Public Records Act (1967). This automatically made most cabinet documents available thirty years back from the present. A fourth device was less deliberate, with Crossman as pioneer. Not only did he write diaries when a cabinet minister from 1964 to 1970, but he insisted on publishing them. In 1975 a legal action retrospectively justified him in doing so, and this enabled Castle and Benn to follow suit. The fashion for revelation has continued during the 1980s, with numerous autobiographies of Conservative ministers, some of them illuminating. Labour ministers' revelations in their diaries about the scale of the disputes at the heart of the Labour governments in 1960s and 1970s were demoralizing and damaging for the Party in the aftermath, especially when not paralleled by Conservative

revelations in equal detail. We cannot as yet say how deeply this change
has hindered free discussion within cabinet. Jenkins felt that in practical
executive decision-making, far more urgent considerations were likely to
affect cabinet discussion than concern about what posterity might think of
any one person's contribution. Castle felt rather ashamed in retrospect at
her 'priggishness' in having opposed Crossman in his desire to publish,
given the democratic advantages of wider understanding—especially as
cabinet discussion seemed little affected by the change.[52]

A third long-term theme underlying this discussion is the change in
the prime minister's role. In 1963 Crossman consigned the cabinet to the
'dignified' dimension of the British constitution because he thought he
detected the growth of 'prime ministerial' government. He made much
of Mackintosh's remark that the prime minister 'can keep any item off
the agenda indefinitely'. He enlarged on how Neville Chamberlain had
bypassed the Foreign Office during the appeasement period; on Attlee's
alleged failure to bring nuclear weapons tests to full cabinet discussion
in the government of 1945; and on the planning of the Suez venture by
a cabinet subgroup after Nasser nationalized the canal in 1956. Prime-
ministerial power was enhanced, he thought, by the power to appoint
chairmen of cabinet committees. The complexity of modern departmental
business worked in the same direction by hindering a departmental minister from acquiring any overall grasp of policy. Crossman and others in
the 1960s tended to emphasize the influence over opinion (and therefore
over election results) that prime ministers then enjoyed through their prominence in the media, through access to opinion polls, and through their
hold on economic management. Crossman claimed that cabinet government 'finally disappeared under the Churchill war régime' because Attlee's
peacetime management of the cabinet involved 'no return to normalcy'.
Prime-ministerial government was therefore the outcome.[53] After nearly
six years in the cabinet, Crossman felt no need to alter his view.[54] In the
1970s similar ideas influenced notions, peddled on right (by Hailsham) and
left (by Benn), that an 'elective dictatorship' existed.[55] The history of the
poll tax highlights yet another prime-ministerial weapon: the power to
determine the type of meeting in which decisions are taken. For the decisive
meeting on that issue occurred at Chequers on 31 March 1985, and took
the form of an informal presentation, with some cabinet ministers present;
its format in itself helped to produce the outcome.[56]

Crossman's views were not endorsed, however, by a second former
Oxford don who (unlike Crossman) had seen the Attlee cabinet from the
inside: Patrick Gordon Walker. Mackintosh was a maverick Labour MP

who never reached the cabinet, and his interpretation reflected his anti-establishment radicalism. His view of power was somewhat conspiratorial, and his narrative of mounting prime-ministerial power was too linear in conception. Still more was this so with Crossman's popularization of Mackintosh's views. In truth, the prime minister's power depends more on fluctuations in personality and situation, and on changes in the interaction between the two, than on any long-term or institutional trend. Even prime-ministerial dominance of general elections can be found well before the advent of the mass media and other modern devices for moulding public opinion: in 1857, 1868, 1874, and 1880. The prime minister's power within the cabinet began to rise early in the nineteenth century and in 1916–18 reached a height never subsequently equalled. And under Neville Chamberlain in 1937–9 and Churchill in 1940–5 it reached levels not seen again until the extraordinary Thatcher regimes of the 1980s. Conversely, even after the advent of psephology, economic planning, and the mass media, there were prime ministers far weaker than Peel or Gladstone: Ramsay MacDonald in his declining years, for example, Neville Chamberlain after the occupation of Prague, and Harold Wilson after the pound was devalued in 1967. We also now know that the prime minister's gender can introduce yet another variable. 'A few tears occasionally, the odd tantrum, then a bit of coquetry were all permissible,' Prior recalls.[57] Once asked what she did when a minister displeased her, Thatcher replied 'I withdraw my love.'[58]

'I believe the British constitution always invents the power to counteract too much power,' said R. A. Butler.[59] If for any reason a prime minister does gain unusual influence, a reaction is likely to set in. Thatcher's premiership illustrates how a Conservative prime minister now has a built-in and cumulative counteractive mechanism even while in power. For the reshuffles that are inevitable during a prolonged premiership cause discarded and resentful cabinet ministers to gather on the back benches, all with votes to cast in a leadership challenge. Prime-ministerial pretensions are not cumulative; after Lloyd George came Bonar Law, after Thatcher came Major. Bonar Law set the new tone by referring a delegation from the unemployed in 1922 to the Ministry of Labour; and Baldwin in 1927 refused to answer a question on the subject in place of the minister responsible.[60] In the history of twentieth-century British prime ministers there is a continuous interaction of style and policy, and a recurrent oscillation in either or both as one holder of the office succeeds another. Neville Chamberlain's authoritarian style of the late 1930s was followed by Churchill's careful deference to parliament during the Second World War, a situation very different from what had happened during the First. Heath in 1970 reacted against Wilsonian interventionism, Callaghan's bluff and commonsensical directness was welcomed after Wilson's taste for intrigue, Thatcher in 1979 repudiated the interventionism of Callaghan, and in 1990 Major's conciliatory tone made a refreshing change from Thatcher's abrasiveness.

Crossman's view of how the cabinet works was implausible—surprisingly so for a politician as experienced as he was by 1963, and still more surprisingly so for the ex-cabinet minister of 1972. In retrospect it is astonishing that during Wilson's prime, when an insecure prime minister put so much into reshuffling his cabinet ministers and playing one off against another, the theory of 'prime-ministerial power' should have been so widely accepted. First Brown, then Callaghan, then Jenkins were narrowly scrutinized by Wilson as potential rivals for his own position. Only exhaustion or wilful blindness can explain how in 1970 Crossman could have retained his views of 1963. He had himself played a prominent part in frustrating the Wilson/Castle scheme for trade-union reform in 1969, an episode which vividly illustrates the need for a prime minister who wishes to launch major innovations in policy to do so only after consulting the cabinet. Crossman vividly describes the denouement: Wilson was reduced to 'really shouting I won't, I can't, you can't do this to me'. Consuming three double brandies in the course of the discussion, he became 'a little man, for the first time dragged down on our level. It was painful because in a sense he was sabotaged and utterly nonplussed.'[61]

The greater complexity of government may confine a minister's perspective to his departmental grindstone, leaving overall strategy to the prime minister. But for many modern cabinet ministers this was not so: Callaghan on trade-union reform in 1969, Benn and Crosland in the Labour governments of 1974–9, Lawson and Howe on EEC strategy under Thatcher. Besides, the expertise that flows from a departmental brief may give cabinet ministers a professionalism unavailable to the prime minister. True, this increased complexity creates the cabinet committee with its chairman (not necessarily the prime minister) and power to decide. But the need for such delegation itself removes important decisions from the prime minister's eye, and distributes power and experience more widely within the cabinet. As for the prime minister's salience with the media, this too can work both ways, as Wilson's premiership shows. If things are going well, the media will enhance the prime minister's position; if things are going badly, the media will worsen it, and other cabinet ministers (Jenkins, for instance, in 1968–70) will steal the limelight. The media are media. It is also far less clear in the 1990s than it seemed in the 1950s that the prime minister can use opinion polls and economic management to manipulate the electorate. Not only are his powers limited by the state of the economy, by no means always manipulable since the 1950s, but prime ministers lost three of the four general elections held in the 1970s (1970, February 1974, and 1979) despite enjoying all the help that opinion polls can provide.

Any full understanding of how the cabinet works needs to emphasize the cabinet's beleaguered situation when operating in an adversarial parliamentary structure. The problems of government bear down upon cabinet ministers, who daily confront an opposition in parliament that is eager to expose incompetence. At the same time the government party in parliament (and still more in the constituencies) is on the watch for sell-outs and compromises of principle. Unless prime minister and cabinet ministers trust one another, the cause is lost. Far from narrowly scrutinizing the prime minister for increases in his power, busy departmental ministers welcome the efforts (often visibly strenuous) of a prime minister who will 'manage' the cabinet for them. If anything, the mounting pressure of business enhances the cabinet's integrating role as the one institution which draws together all the divergent strands of policy and influences upon policy. It is, says Lord Wakeham, 'the cement which binds the Government together',[62] and no prime minister can afford to downgrade it.

Cabinet ministers also welcome a prime minister who will protect them from indiscretion by acting as curator of secrets. When Crossman found Attlee (whom he loathed) confining decisions on the nuclear deterrent to a cabinet committee, he saw himself as 'whisking aside' the 'drapery' from myths about how the British constitution works; yet Gordon Walker rightly pointed out that ministers 'do not wish to be burdened with secrets that they need not know'.[63] And although the decision was taken by the defence subcommittee of cabinet, the minutes were circulated to all cabinet ministers, and the decision was notified to parliament in answer to a question on 12 May 1948.[64] Under Churchill in 1954, the decision to manufacture a British hydrogen bomb was deliberately taken in full cabinet on 25 July. A prime minister who inspires distrust among cabinet colleagues weakens the unity and morale of the team. The policy must be got through, the next general election must be won, otherwise the entire team (and perhaps, in their view, the country) suffers. On the other hand a prime minister who humiliates cabinet colleagues, as Macmillan seemed to do with his mass sackings of 1962, risks piling up trouble on the back benches by arousing sympathy for the victim. Thatcher in the 1980s, by sacking cabinet ministers often in humiliating circumstances, steadily built up resentment. Nor could her forcefulness destroy her Party's instinct for power. Conservatives will tolerate much from a prime minister who can win elections—but if not, not. Cabinet colleagues are always potential rivals for the premiership, and in exceptional circumstances (1916, 1940, 1990) one colleague can oust another.

In this situation, no prime minister could keep off the agenda for long an item that significant members of the cabinet wanted discussed. Nor could he appoint to cabinet committees chairmen unacceptable to the majority. The appearance of manipulation in this area during the Westland affair of 1986 seriously damaged Thatcher. Besides, a determined minister can always threaten to resign (as Kenneth Baker did on curricular reform in 1987, claiming that the Prime Minister had slanted the minutes).[65] In dealing with Thatcher, he pointed out, 'it was no good being a wimp: if people stood their ground . . . then she respected them for it'.[66] As for the 'partial cabinet' of which Crossman makes so much, this is less likely to reflect any conspiracy against colleagues than the need to get agreed decisions implemented more efficiently, secretly, and quickly. This can certainly be said of the way Asquith and Grey ran foreign policy before the First World War, of 'the six' who ran the National Government, or of Eden planning the Suez venture in 1956. The 'partial cabinet' results more from the need to speed up business and preserve confidentiality—for example, on foreign policy, especially before 1914, and on finance—than from any prime-ministerial desire to 'divide and rule'. For Nicholas Ridley, Thatcher's taste for settling matters through informal discussion with the relevant ministers 'seemed eminently sensible . . . For the most part, Cabinet ministers were so busy that they were only too thankful that other people's complex problems were sorted out without their having to be involved.'[67] But cabinet government is flexible enough to accommodate differing prime-ministerial tastes, and since 1990 the standing committee has once more gained ground over the partial cabinet.[68]

To a surprising extent, people see what they are looking for. On all counts, Gordon Walker's view of the cabinet is preferable to Crossman's. A brilliant tutor at New College, Oxford, in the 1930s—more brilliant, by all accounts, than Gordon Walker at Christ Church—Crossman liked putting forward stimulating ideas in a situation where there was little need for responsibility or balance. Though he later pursued a long career in politics, he never lost the habit of provoking and stimulating in a profession where such habits are perilous. Wilson, reviewing Crossman's diaries, pointed out that 'Dick Crossman never understood cabinet government, either as a philosophical student lecturing and writing about it, or as a minister'.[69]

# 11

# *Administration and Execution*

TWENTIETH-CENTURY Britain, like all industrial societies, has seen a massive growth in the service sector, especially in administrative employment. As a percentage of the occupied population in Great Britain, managers rose from 3 per cent in 1911 to 14 per cent in 1981; clerical and related employees from 5 per cent to 15 per cent.[1] This growth reflects the mounting complexity of manufacturing and retailing processes and the continuous improvement in communications, all accelerated by two world wars. To cope with it there arrived new secretarial methods and office technology which transformed the nature and recruitment of administrative work. The typewriter crossed the Atlantic to Britain in 1874, the telephone was in general office use by the early 1880s, shorthand made rapid progress during the same decade, and clerical occupations rapidly began recruiting women. Since then, the service sector has progressed through a sequence of world-wide technological upheavals: from electric typewriter to word-processor, from cash register to computerized accounting, from photocopier to optical scanner, from dictaphone to fax machine. Add to all this the complexities that arise from interventionist policy within a democratizing society that is subject to mounting international pressures.

British civil-service numbers grew from a low base. Unitary states like the United Kingdom need fewer civil servants per head of population than federal states. Furthermore, British industrialization took place within a free-market framework. Non-interventionist unitary states like mid-Victorian Britain need fewer civil servants per head of population than interventionist unitary states such as twentieth-century Britain. Still, civil-service numbers rose fast during the nineteenth century. By 1914 they had reached 282,000, excluding industrial staff, and by 1938 this total had risen to 376,000. War accelerated growth in civil-service numbers, but whereas after the First World War these fell markedly, numbers after the Second fell only slightly, given the increased responsibilities the Attlee government assumed. Numbers of non-industrial civil servants had risen by 1950 to 575,000 and by 1960 to 637,000.[2] Total government employment is of course much larger because it includes Post Office and local-authority employees and industrial civil servants in governmental and related public bodies such as nationalized industries. By 1956, 4 per cent of the total employed population were employed in central government, 6 per cent in local authority work, and 12 per cent in other public bodies—that is, a fifth of the whole.[3]

The long-term pattern of government growth persisted well into the 1970s, and took a marked downward turn only after 1979 as a result of deliberate government policy. Between 1981 and 1986 total civil-service numbers fell from 690,000 to 594,000, with cuts in almost all departments. By 1994 numbers had fallen to 533,000,[4] but there had been no concomitant decline in the number of ministerial posts since 1979—a discrepancy which attracted some ironic comment from senior civil servants. Proportionate cuts at that level would have reduced the number of ministers from eighty-one in Thatcher's first government to sixty-two, a change with major implications for cabinet–backbench relations; their number had in fact risen to eighty-seven.[5] Nor have the politicians incurred the civil service's cuts in accommodation. On the contrary, at Whitehall's Westminster end the politicians with their new accommodation seem to be advancing into the space the civil servants have vacated.

Moving from size to shape, relative changes in departmental size reflect changes in the overall functions of government and in attitudes to them. Chapter 2 showed that Britain's declining international status was slow to produce proportionate cuts in the overseas and defence aspects of administration. The twentieth-century growth in administration involving domestic welfare has fluctuated according to the party in power. Discontinuities in the distribution of power between government departments have reflected shifting administrative fashion rather than the party composition of governments. The vogue from the late 1950s to the early 1970s, both inside and outside government, for amalgamation and size reflected a belief that the super-department would concentrate responsibility and promote economies of scale. So in three broad policy-areas government departments have amalgamated—in the first two (foreign policy and defence) because government's role has contracted, in the third (welfare) because it has grown.

The merging of the diplomatic service and the Foreign Office began in 1943. Independence for India made it sensible to merge the India Office with the Dominions Office into the renamed Commonwealth Relations Office in 1947. In the 1960s the Foreign Office's commercial sections integrated with the diplomatic service, the Foreign Office merged with the Commonwealth Relations Office, and the Colonial Office faded away. Yet Britain's imperial decline by no means reduced international contacts. Better communications extended contact, and decolonization within European empires greatly increased the number of independent states with which relations had to be maintained. The numbers involved in defence simultaneously fell. Co-ordination between the services was slow in coming. There was much inter-service rivalry early in the twentieth century, and much squabbling between the armed services before the Air Force acquired its separate place in Whitehall during the 1920s. None the less, co-ordination produced a single Ministry of Defence from 1946, and from 1964 a single Secretary of State for Defence, presiding over the defence ministers.

In the welfare area, amalgamation resulted from growth, not from decline. Nineteenth-century central government was almost entirely preoccupied with war, diplomacy, and taxation, whereas in the twentieth century it was increasingly involved in providing welfare, driven on as we saw in Chapter 2 by competition for votes between the parties, and by spontaneous bureaucratic expansion. The political impulse was, however, discontinuous. Numbers in civil-service welfare departments grew under governments of the left (in 1905–14, 1945–51, 1964–70, and 1974–9) and contracted under governments of the right (after 1922, 1951, and 1979). Noting a decline in civil-service numbers of 50,000, the Conservative manifesto in 1955 associated socialism with ration book and food subsidy, adding that 'we are sure that it is the customer, and not "the gentleman in Whitehall", who knows best'.[6] The Wilson governments in 1964–70 created a super-department, the Department of Health and Social Security, whose minister became a Secretary of State with a seat in cabinet. Further co-ordination in welfare occurred through the creation of the Social Policy Committee, chaired by Bernard (now Lord) Donoughue, to assist the Labour governments of 1974–9.[7] But the amalgamated DHSS of 1968 turned out to be too large, and in 1988 Health was once more separated from Social Security, each with its own cabinet minister. If one looks at the overall distribution of non-industrial civil servants as at January 1971, the biggest department remained Defence (which had fallen to 24 per cent of the total), but Health and Social Security now accounted for 15 per cent, Inland Revenue for 15 per cent, and Environment for 8 per cent. If industrial civil servants are included, Defence and the Environment increase still further in importance, with 37 per cent and 11 per cent, respectively. With subsequent privatization and defence cuts, the relative size of Defence declined still further. The Foreign and Colonial Office was, by comparison, tiny, contributing only 3 per cent of the non-industrial civil servants.[8]

In civil-service relationships as a whole, the overriding tendency, at least until the late 1980s, was one of increasing co-ordination.[9] The advantages of interchange between departments became clear when Lloyd George's national insurance scheme of 1911 was organized by a team of talented young civil servants drawn from several departments, one of whom was Warren Fisher. A leap forward in co-ordination occurred in 1919 when the post entitled 'Head of the Civil Service' was created for the Permanent Secretary to the Treasury. Fisher got the job at the remarkably early age of 39 and stayed in it till 1939. The need to re-establish Treasury control, relaxed during the First World War, lay behind these measures, but it was Treasury control of a mild and collaborative kind. After 1919 Fisher helped to integrate the civil service by moving civil servants frequently between departments. He was a great believer in what was later pejoratively called the 'generalist'. Administration was for him an art that needed to be learned on the job. He promoted integration in other ways too—by setting up co-ordinated civil-service sports facilities, holding periodic meetings between heads of government departments, and improving the Treasury's relations with other government departments. Since Fisher's day only ten people have been Head of the Civil Service, including Sir Robin Butler, the present head. Throughout the period the Treasury has retained its overall control. During the Wilson governments of 1964–70 the Department of Economic Affairs was set up to promote 'creative tension' with it, and the Civil Service Department was set up in 1968 to take over its role in managing the civil service. But the Treasury soon recovered its economic role, and regained its overall control of the civil service in 1981. Conservative on constitutional matters, Thatcher had little time for the fashions of the 1960s.

The scale of civil-service co-ordination has sometimes been exaggerated by those such as Crossman and Benn who see civil servants as conspiratorially colluding in pursuit of power. In reality 'the departments disagree with one another . . . very much', Healey recalled in 1981, countering recent remarks by Benn; 'and some departments notoriously fight through the ages with one another: Defence both with the Treasury and with the Foreign Office to take an obvious example'.[10] Politicians sometimes promote their own purposes by playing off civil servants against one another. This most notoriously occurred in the 'creative tension' mentioned above, but also when Heath and Armstrong covertly prepared an interventionist Industry Act (1972) which they knew would be unpopular with the relevant departments (the Treasury and the Department of Trade and Industry).[11] The diplomatic service long remained aloof from the rest of the civil service. Its aristocratic flavour led it to postpone meritocratic recruitment for longest. The Foreign Office's reception on the Queen's birthday was a major social event in late-Victorian London—in Lady Gwendolen Cecil's words, 'a vast gathering of all who were distinguished in the official, political, and social worlds of London'.[12] Until 1919 the Foreign Secretary was not limited in his patronage of appointments by anything stronger than a 'qualifying test', and no candidate could take even that unless recommended to him 'by men of standing and position'.[13] Until after the First World War, candidates needed a private income of at least £400 a year. This separatism within a small but élite department persists, despite the fact that overseas contacts have become so common in Whitehall as to erode the Foreign Office's distinctive role. This process began with the armed services, which had overseas attachés before the First World War, and moved on to trade and other dimensions of government. Extended trade, improved transport, and the growth of international structures have all required government employees to exploit the improved communications that are now feasible.

There have been significant changes since the 1850s in the civil-service hierarchy. Civil servants have long been classified as 'industrial' and 'non-industrial'. This classification takes into account a combination of three factors: type of employment, type of trade-union organization, and negotiating procedure. 'Industrial civil servants are manual workers, skilled, semi-skilled, and unskilled, employed in dockyards, ordnance factories, research and other establishments.'[14] They are particularly numerous in the armed-services departments and Post Office. The female proportion of the non-industrial category in 1955 was, at 47 per cent, predictably much higher than the proportion of the industrial (11 per cent).[15] The percentage of non-industrial by comparison with industrial has risen—reflecting the three-fold process of privatization, declining defence commitments, and the broadening concerns of government. Non-industrial civil servants' percentage of the total rose from 36 in 1914 to 65 in 1938 to 71 in 1971 to 81 in 1984 to 91 in 1993.[16] Whereas in 1950 there had been 396,900 industrial civil servants, by 1993 there were only 51,000.[17] So within the civil service, as in society as a whole, the twentieth-century trend is away from heavy-industry occupations towards white-collar employment. Taking the situation in 1955, the non-industrial civil servants were distributed in numbers proportioned roughly inversely to a department's political importance. The Post Office (with 247,901) had by far the most, followed by the three armed-services departments (99,023) and the Inland Revenue (51,953), whereas the Foreign Office (with only 5,714) and the Treasury (with 1,263) came well down the list.[18]

The hierarchy among civil servants within the non-industrial category has changed significantly since the 1860s. By the 1870s a three-tier system was crystallizing out: the ancestors of the present (small, policy-orientated, and managerial) administrative grade at the top of the service; of the present executive grade (larger, with some executive responsibility); and of the present clerical grade (concerned with routine paperwork). These three grades broadly corresponded to the three-tiered late-Victorian class structure. The top grade was recruited largely from public-school, university-educated entrants; the middle grade from grammar-school leavers at age 17; and the bottom grade from other secondary-school leavers at about the same age. In April 1939 only 0.5 per cent were in the administrative grade, 5 per cent in the executive grade and 29 per cent in the clerical grade, the rest being in lower and specialist categories.[19] H. E. Dale memorably describes these grades arriving for work shortly before the Second World War: the lower-middle-class clerical officers (male and female) before 10 a.m.; the higher clerical and executive officers, assistant principals, and principals (with a higher proportion of men) soon after 10; and the potentates (all men) between 10.15 and 10.45.[20] This pyramid persists, except that in the late 1980s large sections of its lower (non-policy) levels were sent out of London, leaving policy to the higher sections who remained there. This accelerated a long-term pattern of civil-service geographical dispersal. Whitehall was and remains the area where the higher civil servants, concerned more with policy than with execution, cluster—close to the London clubs, which many of them join. As a distinctively governmental area, nineteenth-century Whitehall had grown up only slowly, and did not shine by comparison with its equivalents in Berlin or Paris. Many of Britain's government departments were first housed in what had once been aristocratic town houses, but grew out of them during the nineteenth century and moved into purpose-built administrative offices. The Home, Foreign, Colonial, and India Offices were built in the 1850s and 1860s, and the spaces between the buildings gradually filled up. One of the last was the big Edwardian block of offices facing Parliament Square, built to house several government departments.

The civil service has dispersed geographically partly for political reasons, as we saw in Chapter 3,[21] but more important has been the dispersal that results from organic growth—from localities to centre and from centre to localities. During the early twentieth century the two lines of development came together to form a system. Transport changes, population growth, and regional discrepancies in wealth forced inter-war local government to embrace regional planning and national funding. Organic growth from the centre caused individual departments to spread out tentacles into other parts of London after 1939. By the 1950s Whitehall departments were acquiring their own provincial outposts and even regional networks of outposts. Central government now required far more at the local level than the post offices and taxation departments which had once sufficed. The Board of Trade, in administering labour exchanges and unemployment insurance, was probably the first department to employ a large local staff to administer welfare policy. Bureaucratic growth at regional level was nourished during the First World War by the Ministries of Food, National Service, and Munitions. In 1918 three government ministries (National Service, Munitions, and Labour) collaborated to divide Great Britain into nine grouped localities for their joint administrative purposes.[22] So closely were local and central administrations moving together by 1920 that Beveridge sought to substitute the phrase 'public service' for 'civil service'.[23] Job creation and cost-cutting later caused whole sections of national government to move out from London. An early example was to locate the central office of the new Ministry of National Insurance during the Second World War at Newcastle. Considerations of national defence inspired similar moves. Also during the Second World War the regional commissioners' staff tended increasingly to be used as outposts for central-government ministries which sought to keep in touch with local authorities, though these staffs were disbanded at the end of the war.[24] By the mid-1950s, however, most government departments had a regional structure or provincial offices, and by 1956, 65 per cent of non-industrial civil servants were located outside London.[25]

All this relocated administration; it did not relocate power. Indeed, several trends have centralized control over policy during the twentieth century: nationalization and the advent of public welfare (at the expense of the poor law), to name only two. It was the lower grades of civil servant who were expected to be regionally mobile, whereas power-seekers stayed in London, where the (policy-orientated) administrative class was mainly located. And not only in London, but in the right part of London. Successive secretaries of state for social security, for example, found Elephant and Castle far too distant from Westminster. It was, wrote Crossman in 1969, 'desperately remote and inconvenient' and 'psychologically . . . miles away' from Whitehall; 'no set of departmental ministers were more often on their feet than us', wrote Norman Fowler, recalling his time there in the 1980s, 'yet no set were further away'.[26] Among the gains to be made from the latest bout of administrative decentralization, launched in 1988 by the *Next Steps* report, is that policy-makers can move closer to Westminster. The work hitherto done in the big London ministries can be decanted elsewhere, and expensive London buildings sold off. The aim lying behind *Next Steps* is to get the civil service better managed by hiving off many of its functions into separate agencies. A certain decentralization of power to middle management is involved in this, but also the concentration of policy-making in Whitehall. By April 1993, 249,000 out of 554,000 civil servants were working in ninety-four agencies.[27]

On civil-service recruitment, the main trend has been meritocratic. Throughout the twentieth century, recruitment at the top levels has been meritocratic. This for decades entailed channelling industrious and impecunious middle-class 'scholarship boys' from the grammar schools through the non-scientific courses at Oxford and Cambridge (especially Greats and modern history)—a tradition persisting into the 1950s. At least until the 1940s there was much interaction between Oxford and Cambridge syllabuses and civil-service entrance requirements; between 1900 and 1986, 45 per cent of permanent secretaries came from Oxford, 23 per cent from Cambridge.[28] Meritocratic pressures within the civil service mounted after 1945 and reached a peak in the 1960s and 1970s. The country-house method of admission was modelled on the selection process for army officers. It was introduced after the Second World War, which had disrupted many people's formal education, and after 1948 it continued in parallel with the written examination. Like many established British institutions in the 1960s, the civil service was compared unfavourably with its European equivalents; a considerable impact was made by the high quality of the civil servants from the EEC countries (especially France) with whom British politicians were then negotiating. This influence combined with the meritocratic mood of the time to produce the Fulton committee's recommendation of 1968 for merging the clerical, administrative, and executive grades so as to produce a single career-ladder. The aim was especially to improve the opportunities for government employees with technical expertise. 'The word "class", and the structure it represents', said the committee, 'produce feelings of inferiority as well as of restricted opportunities.'[29] Direct entry to the higher regions of the civil service from the universities persisted, but given the universities' increasingly meritocratic recruitment this meant a further enhancement for meritocratic trends. The continued prominence of Oxford and Cambridge in civil-service recruitment now reflected, not privilege or favouritism, but their own broadened recruitment.

A second important recruitment theme is gender. Women clerical workers first arrived in state employment at the lower levels, when the telegraph system was transferred to the Post Office in 1870. Women employees in Great Britain working in central and local government at all levels rose steadily thereafter: 17,000 in 1891; 29,000 in 1901; 50,000 in 1911; 81,000 in 1921.[30] The First World War produced a massive temporary substitution of women for men within the civil service, so that women were contributing 56 per cent of its total non-industrial employees by November 1918.[31] Their competence at the higher levels was now manifest, and the aftermath of women's enfranchisement in 1918 rendered their elevation permanent. Still, progress was slow. By 1939 there were only forty-three women in the administrative grade (3 per cent of the grade's total),[32] partly because of a requirement that women should resign on marriage. The separation of spheres operated here as in parliament: women civil servants tended to cluster in the social services departments, made slower progress in the defence area, and were actually excluded till the Second World War from the 'male sphere' of the diplomatic service.[33] The marriage bar was temporarily suspended in the Second World War, but was not removed till 1946. In the Second World War, as in the First, the female proportion of non-industrial civil servants advanced fast—from a quarter of the total in April 1939 to nearly half by October 1944.[34] The first woman ambassador, Dame Barbara Salt, was appointed to Israel in 1963, but illness prevented her from taking up the post. Women also continued to cluster at the civil-service pyramid's lower levels, accounting in 1955 for 98 per cent of the typing class, 36 per cent of the clerical, 16 per cent of the executive and only 6 per cent of the administrative.[35]

Civil-service recruitment also broadened to take in those at lower social levels. Already by the 1880s the Liberal government was appointing working men as inspectors of mines.[36] The Asquith government's legislation on labour exchanges and national insurance created numerous managerial posts. These were used to co-opt many trade unionists into the state machine, complementing their earlier co-option into the parliamentary structure.[37] The First and Second World Wars drew trade unions further in, and the Attlee government's nationalization channelled many leading trade unionists into top administrative posts. Thereafter trade unionists' integration with government varied in intensity with the party in power, but under governments of both parties in the 1960s and 1970s it reached new heights. Only with the repudiation of national plans, incomes policies, and 'fine tuning' in economic management after 1979 did the need for such collaboration decline.

Women and trade unionists were not the only outsiders recruited into the civil service during the two world wars. The desperate search for expertise in a situation of total war powerfully boosted meritocratic pressures. This advanced the middle classes during the First World War. In running the Ministry of Munitions in 1915 Lloyd George secured the unpaid services of many businessmen, and their success caused him to carry them further into government when he became Prime Minister a year later. Many were self-made radical provincial nonconformists. 'Theirs was a long-delayed revolt of the provinces against London's political and cultural dominance,' wrote A. J. P. Taylor, 'a revolt on behalf of the factories and workshops where the war was being won.'[38] Lord Rhondda at the Ministry of Food was one of the most successful, but the many others included Alfred Mond, the chemicals manufacturer, and Sir Albert Stanley, manager of the London Underground. The Second World War saw a middle-class incursion of a rather different kind. Right up to the 1970s there was a close kinship between the worlds of Oxford, Cambridge, and the higher regions of the civil service. In wartime, academics (especially economists and scientists) naturally gravitated to Whitehall from Oxford and Cambridge in large numbers. By March 1940 movement from Oxford had been so great that centralized arrangements had to be made within the University to control it.[39] Lord Franks was a distinguished example of an academic who chose to stay on after the war had ended. There was a further incursion in 1964, when 'a positive flight into Whitehall' caused Oxford's economics subfaculty to be rapidly almost denuded of teaching talent.[40] These incursions, together with the growth in government intervention, kept up the prestige of a civil service which in other ways was becoming less attractive. Hours were becoming longer, and job security—once a distinctive feature of public employment—was becoming much more common elsewhere.

Resistance to central government within Britain continues to mould civil-service attitudes, which are often misunderstood. The civil-service mood is, on the whole, secretive. This stems, rather paradoxically, from government's responsiveness to the general public. It reflects the civil servant's strong feeling that it is the politicians, as representatives of the public, who should take responsibility for executive acts. If civil servants are publicly identified with particular policies, they are hindered in serving the politicians of whichever party happens to be in power, and the idea of the career civil servant (which has many advantages) is put at risk.

Secrecy was enhanced for a second reason: national security. The Official Secrets Act (1889) was reinforced in 1911 and 1920, and only recently, with the ending of the cold war, has the dynamic behind such legislation begun slowly to unwind. The higher civil servant aims professionally to be unobtrusive. He is expected to merge with the community, not to separate off into a caste with inappropriately specialized training. 'The really important point about the social life of high permanent officials', wrote Dale in 1941, 'is that they do not form a society of their own. I should say that outside official hours they rather prefer to mix with people of other professions.'[41]

Since the Second World War civil servants have done much to reduce such barriers as remain between themselves and the public. The report of the inquiry into the Crichel Down affair (published in 1954) revealed the dangers of civil-service arrogance towards private citizens, and made a major impact.[42] In 1967 the Parliamentary Commissioner for Administration (or 'Ombudsman') was appointed to chase up cases of alleged civil-service misconduct that were referred to him by MPs. Sir Ernest Gowers's *Plain Words* (1948) was written at the instigation of the then head of the civil service, Sir Edward Bridges, to initiate new civil servants in writing plain English. Stilted officialese has been curbed—phrases such as 'Sir, I am directed by the Minister . . . to refer to your letter of . . . He instructs me to say that . . .'.[43] And in the 1980s Thatcher's blue pencil assaulted jargon and obfuscation at the highest levels; she was unafraid to exclaim 'That is gobbledygook' on civil servants' drafts.[44] Furthermore, since the 1960s some opening out of government has occurred—for example, through the mounting accessibility of secret documents and the writing of diaries discussed in Chapter 10.[45]

The mood of the higher civil servant, who helps to mould policy, is sceptical. This again reflects the nature of the British political system, which discourages civil-service initiative and commitment to particular policies. The initiatives are expected to come from elsewhere, and the civil servant is trained primarily as an intermediary who must do the politicians' bidding. British civil servants, with their longer-term perspective, understandably acquire a certain scepticism about what politicians can achieve. Added to this is the pragmatism that springs from continuous administrative responsibility, which renders British civil servants wary of dramatic innovations in policy. Moderation and prudence are bred into the higher civil servant from the start—though as Dale wryly pointed out, 'it is possible to be enthusiastic for moderation and prudence'.[46] Such an outlook represented, not cynicism, but 'stoical realism'. The civil servant's situation in Britain oddly combines security with vulnerability: the security of a lifetime's career with the vulnerability of depending on others for ideas, energy, and initiative. In 1941 Dale thought that if the higher civil servants were polled, half would say they voted for Liberal candidates, and 'the general temper of mind and character is Left Centre'.[47] In 1976 Lord Armstrong, head of the home civil service from 1968 to 1974, said that most senior civil servants were Butskellites: 'after all those years you tend to be within a narrow line either side of the centre. Most of them would like a government with Heath as prime minister and Jenkins as chancellor.'[48]

A higher civil servant whose prime role is that of intermediary needs political more than technical skills. As Sir Douglas Wass pointed out in 1987, 'finesse and diplomacy are an essential ingredient in public service'.[49] Judgement, common sense, wisdom, grasp of the political process, experience of how the government machine works—these are the (highly professional) qualities essential in the British civil servant at the higher level. For the very special skill that is involved in administration, it is desirable to train the young civil servant by switching him frequently between jobs. From the Second World War onwards, however, partly under the influence of respected foreign models, pressure for formalized and specialist in-house training of the civil servant mounted. The Assheton committee's report in 1944 led to a Training and Education Division being set up at the Treasury, and a central school for civil servants in 1945. The pressure for training moderated in the 1950s but resumed in the early 1960s, and in 1963 the Centre for Administrative Studies was established in London to provide in-house courses in relevant disciplines such as economics and statistics. This pursuit of technical expertise in the 1960s owed much to European civil-service models and was taken up by the Fulton committee. Such a view took insufficient account of the British civil servant's essentially political situation, and neglected his need for generalist skills, which it also undervalued. Partly for this reason, the committee's proposal of 'preference for relevance' in civil-service recruiting was rejected, though a Civil Service College was established in 1970. Experts are of course needed for specific purposes within the British civil service, as in any large organization, but the wider role that they could usefully perform was exaggerated in the 1960s. To take only one example: the continuous increase in the number of economists in the Government Economic Service—from twenty-one in 1964 to 317 in 1975—was not so obviously beneficial as to be thought worth continuing into the 1980s.[50] Healey struck a note of disillusion in his budget speech of 1978. Economics, he said, 'is a useful tool of policy but still far from being an exact science—if it is a science at all'.[51]

What changes have taken place since the 1850s in the influence of the civil service? One must distinguish between the influence of the civil service in British society as a whole, a structural question; and the influence of the permanent secretary on the government minister, partly a matter of personal chemistry. Any attempt to assess the distribution of power in the first of these two relationships at once stumbles against the fact that the civil service is not monolithic. The power of civil servants in any one ministry will not necessarily move in parallel with civil servants in other ministries. Take education, for example. Even in the 1970s the powers of central government were very small. In the Tameside dispute of 1976 the House of Lords upheld the view that the Conservative-run local council could resist the directions of a Labour government and refuse to adopt the comprehensive system for its secondary schools.[52] In 1977 Max Wilkinson's *Lessons from Europe*, the booklet which so deeply influenced Keith Joseph's policy at the Department of Education and Science after 1981, stressed the circularity of the problem involved in getting more public participation in educational decision-making. By European standards, he said, the Department was extraordinarily weak, and 'hardly ever interferes in the running of school courses'.[53] A similar contrast with Europe is provided by the Department of the Environment, whose ignorance of local-government finance is a major theme in the poll tax fiasco.[54]

It seems in general fair to say, though, that shifts in civil-service power reflect shifts in its relative access to information, personnel, and expertise. British administration has never been tightly integrated at the centre. Central-government power in Britain is fragmented between civil service, parliament, judiciary, and (diminishingly) monarchy—with much influence left to local government, pressure groups, and voluntary bodies. The British have never entertained that clear concept of the state, set apart from the community, which is present in many European countries. In modern times there has been no British equivalent of the French prefect—no local agent of the central government with extensive executive powers. In the General Strike or the Second World War there was never any question of appointing civil servants as regional commissioners. Indeed, the radicalism of Mosley's Fascist package in the 1930s emerges from his proposal to appoint Fascist MPs with executive functions to supersede the committee-based flavour of British local administration.

All this reflects the fact that in Britain most initiatives on policy are expected to come from outside government, which has the effect of reinforcing the political against the administrative arm. The British civil servant's timetable and priorities are moulded by the parliamentary timetable. 'The main object to which all others yield', Sir Charles Trevelyan complained in 1848, when discussing the civil service, 'is to get well through the session and then after some necessary relaxation, to consider how to get through the next.'[55] The situation has not appreciably changed since. Dale in 1941 described how a civil servant, when confronted by the green file that denoted a parliamentary question, got to work on it at once, looking anxiously for the date when an answer was needed.[56] Drawing on his experience in the 1970s, Gerald Kaufman claimed that 'cabinet minutes are studied in Government Departments with the reverence generally reserved for sacred texts, and can be triumphantly produced conclusively to settle any arguments'.[57] So however much the civil servant's influence gains from growing professionalism, numbers, and co-ordination, his overall influence will increase only to the extent that the politicians encourage it.

The free-market non-interventionist state of the Victorians could supply little information on important subjects because information flows primarily from intervention. Profound ignorance lay at the heart of some major government bills in their early stages. The Whigs floundered more than once in 1832 for lack of crucial information when preparing their Reform Bill.[58] Lord Welby many years later recalled the haste with which Gladstone's first Home Rule Bill had been introduced in 1886;[59] the departments did not possess the necessary data, yet a government which came to power only in February introduced its bill in April. In a free-trade economy, information on untaxed trades was seriously lacking. 'In the course of our inquiry', complained the royal commission on the depression of trade and industry in 1886, 'we have frequently experienced the want of accurate statistics with regard to the details of our home trade'.[60] We saw in Chapter 6 how this required the Tariff Reform League to appoint its own inquiry in 1904. The poor law commission in 1909 complained that 'we are still without any reliable data of the average earnings in many trades, especially those of an unskilled or casual nature'.[61] On educational matters, central government remained surprisingly ignorant well into the interventionist period because the local authorities retained so much power.[62] In this policy area, what Morrison had once called 'a campaign for statistical floodlighting'[63] became one of Thatcher's several raids on the left's techniques after 1979.

Still, central government's role in economic and welfare matters advanced markedly during the twentieth century. During the First World War the politicians wanted the state to mobilize the economy for war-making purposes quickly, but the interventionist impetus waned in the 1920s. This was because the war emergency had disappeared, because Conservatives were reacting against Lloyd George's methods and policies, and because they felt bound to respond to attacks on the advance of delegated legislation—most notably from Lord Hewart's forceful *The New Despotism* (1929). The inter-war split between Liberals and Labour prevented the growing influence of Fabian interventionism within the labour movement from moulding government policy. Despite rising unemployment in 1930, the minority Labour government had no Ministry of Economic Affairs to pursue Sweden's actively interventionist policy, for example. The Treasury did not then feel the need even to co-ordinate government information on the economy, let alone to plan the economy as a whole.

Intervention did, however, take a significant step forward in 1932 when protection was resumed, with its ancillary plans for industrial rationalization. It advanced further still in 1941, when for the first time the budget moved forward from accounting balance sheet towards planning-document for the economy as a whole. Social research—initially collected outside the civil service by free-lance social investigators, by royal commissions, and by parliamentary committees—was over a long period gradually being built into the government machine. Even at the height of Victorian localism, inspectors had been encouraged to send reports to London. That arch-enthusiast for local self-government J. S. Mill thought central government should set up a national bank for statistical information: 'power may be localized', he wrote, 'but knowledge, to be most useful, must be centralized'.[64] Thereafter, the collection of information prepared the empirical basis for the advance of the state. Departmental inquiries laid the basis for the Beveridge report of 1942, and the Attlee government's enthusiasm for planning had important implications for civil-service manpower. After a short hiatus in the 1950s the interventionist pressure resumed in the early 1960s, reaching its denouement with the failed National Plan in 1965. Interventionism persisted as a fashion till 1979, urged on by enthusiasm for French 'planification' and Italian corporatism, and with incomes policies as its most ambitious manifestation. All this thrust many higher civil servants into unaccustomed public prominence.

But asking more from civil servants does not necessarily empower them to deliver. Interventionist policies tended to generate an equal and opposite reaction. The growth in civil-service influence led to countervailing pressures for closer scrutiny of its activities. Anti-socialist hostility to Whitehall interventionism was vociferous under the Attlee government, and by the late 1960s Conservative backbench grumbles of this kind were building up once more. As we have already seen, civil servants were themselves sometimes embarrassed at their new prominence.[65] Civil-service activism became even more vulnerable in the 1970s when Britain's relative economic decline persisted despite all the interventionist and institutional reforms of the 1960s. The civil service was one of several British political institutions seriously strained by the incomes policies of the 1970s. At the end of his career, Lord Armstrong was in despair at the country's plight, and retired after a nervous breakdown.[66] In June 1974 one journalist referred to the 'utter gloom . . . to be encountered in Whitehall these days', with fears of uncontrollable inflation and political disintegration in the offing once the so-called 'social contract' between the Labour government and the trade unions had broken down. 'When Sir Douglas Allen, head of the Treasury, imagines walking to work one morning to find the tanks drawn up on Horseguards Parade nobody is quite sure that he is joking. Nobody knows what to do, few any longer pretend to know what to do.'[67]

When Thatcher succeeded Heath in 1975, Conservative backbench critics of interventionism at last found a voice. When after 1979 the Thatcher governments scaled down the role of the civil service and undermined its morale, much talent was drained off into other areas of British life. This was, indeed, Thatcher's intention, for her governments were acting in accordance with J. S. Mill's *Liberty*, where a high concentration of ability in central government is seen as undermining a society's capacity for self-help. 'The absorption of all the principal ability of the country into the governing body', he wrote, 'is fatal, sooner or later, to the mental activity and progressiveness of the body itself.'[68] In so far as the Thatcher revolution needed information at all, it was as likely to come from right-wing 'think-tanks' or outside sympathizers as from civil servants. The royal commission went virtually into abeyance during the 1980s and decisions on policy tended to emerge from the quick and decisive departmental inquiry. Sir Derek Rayner, a director of Marks and Spencer, acted as Thatcher's adviser on improving efficiency in government from 1979 to 1983, and from that stemmed a major reduction in civil-service numbers and a massive administrative devolution among those who remained. Thatcherism strikingly demonstrated the primacy of the politician within the British political system.

How can this salience of the politician be reconciled with complaints from the extremes on right and left that civil servants obstruct reforms that they do not like? Such a question switches attention from the influence of the civil service on British society at large to the relationship between minister and permanent secretary within the government department.

Crossman, for example, deprecated the growth of cabinet committees when writing his introduction to Bagehot's *English Constitution* in 1963. His fears were reinforced by a few months' experience of ministerial office: 'the really big thing I completely failed to notice', he wrote, 'was the network of civil-service committees running in parallel with cabinet committees. 'This means that very often the whole job is pre-cooked,' and 'this is the way in which Whitehall ensures that the Cabinet system is relatively harmless'.[69] Yet Crossman's view was distorted. It simultaneously underestimated the need for co-ordination in a huge governmental machine and exaggerated the civil servants' yearning or capacity to outmanoeuvre the politicians. If the cabinet co-ordinates higher up, the civil servants must co-ordinate lower down. Besides, a civil servant wants his departmental minister to succeed in his efforts to influence policy in cabinet and parliament; in that battle, he and his minister are on the same side. Armstrong told parliament in 1972 that ministers were fully entitled to get their civil servants to participate 'in what I might call various stratagems: arranging to talk out a motion ... arranging the order of clauses in a Bill to fit with anticipated action in Parliament', and the like.[70] In truth, criticisms of the civil service by outsiders often unintentionally reflect inexperience in government, together with a somewhat conspiratorial view of how things happen. Such criticisms are also sometimes a device for shuffling off the blame from where it should rest: with the failings of individual politician and party, whether on right or left. If civil servants resist ministers, this is likely to reflect their responsibility for implementation. If only to ensure success for a policy they dislike, they must ensure that decisions take account of practical difficulties. Castle was intrigued, as Minister of Transport, with how civil servants, 'even when they have done their utmost to persuade one to accept a different policy, identify themselves with the success of the measure once it has been introduced'.[71]

Conversely, if governments follow civil-service advice, this is as likely to indicate that ministers have agreed with their civil servants as that they have been coerced. As Warren Fisher pointed out, civil servants are keen for their minister to do well, but 'if the Minister ... has neither the courage nor the brains to evolve a policy of his own, they will do their best to find him one; for after all it is better that a department should be run by its civil servants than that it should not be run at all'.[72] John Burns was undoubtedly a failure as President of the Local Government Board from 1905 to 1914, as was J. H. Thomas when minister responsible for employment in the Labour government of 1929—but their failure stemmed from conceit and lack of ideas, so that civil servants had to fill the vacuum. No civil servant, whatever his social standing, could have overruled personalities as strong as those of Snowden (Chancellor of the Exchequer in 1924 and 1929–31) or Bevin (Foreign Secretary from 1945 to 1950). Macmillan's success in getting his annual 300,000 houses stemmed not only from his shrewd choice of subordinates and skill at getting colleagues to co-operate. It reflected his close partnership with a civil servant who appears in Crossman's diaries as a sort of malign presence: Evelyn Sharp, in Macmillan's words 'the ablest woman I have ever known'.[73]

Benn's experience in the 1970s led him to paint a very different picture of the politician's relations with civil servants.[74] Yet his complaints were brusquely dismissed by Healey, his cabinet colleague: 'a minister who complains that his civil servants are too powerful is either a weak minister or an incompetent one'.[75] Benn was undermined by lack of commitment to his policies both from his Party and from the prime minister. 'The point of the manifesto is not to persuade the voter', said Crossman, with characteristic exaggeration, but 'to give yourself an anchor when the civil service tries to go back on your word.' A politician seeking to promote a policy without manifesto commitment 'is lost',[76] whereas if forearmed by the manifesto he would find that the civil servants 'will do it for you with knobs on'.[77] Labour voters after 1974 were never whole-heartedly behind Benn's policies, and both Wilson and Callaghan as prime ministers knew it. The prime minister, as judge of public opinion on a continuing basis, must estimate whether even adhering to the manifesto is justified, and whether it will be endorsed by the electorate at the next election if circumstances have significantly changed since it was drafted.[78] Wilson and Callaghan as prime ministers suspected that Benn's ambitious interventionism lacked sufficient support from cabinet colleagues, from the Party, and still more from the electorate. When confronted by Benn, the civil servants (who knew where power lay within the government, and were in any event bound to consult the Treasury about any expenditure that Benn's policies might involve) displayed the political skills which their profession requires.

The influence of individual civil servants with their ministers—the 'Yes Minister' syndrome—is a relationship moulded by interactions of personality. Behind the long-term trends will be marked contrasts between one department and another. When he became Secretary of State for Education, for example, Kenneth Baker noticed that civil servants were far more powerful at the Department of Education and Science than they had been at his two earlier departments: environment and trade. 'Of all Whitehall Departments, the DES was among those with the strongest in-house ideology. There was a clear 1960s ethos and a very clear agenda which permeated virtually all the civil servants.'[79] None the less, some overall changes have slanted the relationship towards the civil servant more than was once the case. If pay is an index of status, permanent secretaries have overtaken cabinet ministers by quite a large margin since the Second World War.[80] By 1984 forty-one civil servants were paid more than the prime minister, 157 more than leading cabinet ministers.[81] On the other hand, the relative social status of the civil servant has been declining during the twentieth century. In the nineteenth century, before the distinction opened up between the professions of politician and civil servant, the higher civil servant might well surpass the politician in social status. But twentieth-century meritocratic recruitment of the civil service made it likely that, while the higher civil servant was perhaps more industrious or even more intelligent than the politician, he would be inferior in social status as long as the politician's links with the social élite persisted.[82] The Labour Party's advance threatened those links, and the broadening out of political recruitment since the 1950s has carried that process still further, so that by the 1980s politicians and civil servants were drawn largely from the same social levels.

It should by now be clear that since Bagehot's day British government's central administrative machinery has proved adaptable—in war and peace, under governments Conservative and Labour, under strategies corporatist or free-market. The machinery of local government, too, has adapted to remarkable changes, though much less satisfactorily. One theme consistently runs through these changes: the retreat of protocol and ceremonial before utilitarian and businesslike procedures. As recently as 1908 Lowell pointed out that one incentive for a Unionist to vote with his party was his fear that otherwise he would not be invited to Foreign Office functions: 'the weakness of the Liberals for nearly a score of years after the split over Home Rule was due in no small part to the fact that they had very little social influence at their command'.[83] At the local level the symbols of tradition and authority were often paraded through the streets on Victorian municipal occasions, with trade and friendly societies displaying their banners in procession, and with the Chartists as willing as any to participate.[84] Somehow Gladstonian cheese-paring in nineteenth-century Whitehall and in nineteenth-century town halls did not preclude high ceilings, splendid stairways, and impressive façades.

No longer so: hardboard partitions cut through the grand architecture of Whitehall's high-ceilinged rooms, and filing-cabinets clutter its splendid corridors. The worlds of high society and government administration have drawn apart, and even the Foreign Office has lost something of its social cachet. Likewise in local government, the tall and ornamented nineteenth-century town-hall towers and imposing pediments have retreated in the face of a more pinched and utilitarian twentieth-century approach to administration. The decline in ceremonial began with the Victorians themselves, for the flummery of local ceremonial, the grand meals, and the ample cellars of the municipal corporations were fixed narrowly in the sights of the early-Victorian municipal reformers, their zeal often reinforced by a dissenting and puritan moralism. 'It is pitiful to see a Mayor of Manchester imitating the obsolete sensuality of the Cockney [sc. City of London] Corporation,' Cobden grumbled in 1849.[85] The arrival of Chartist and radical working men as councillors brought to local government a passion for economy,[86] and much of this carried forward into the London County Council, whose plain dress contrasted markedly with the paraphernalia of the City corporation when addresses were presented to Edward VII on his accession in 1901.[87] The Labour Party between the wars inherited this tradition, and mayoral regalia were still being spurned and mayoral chauffeurs returned to the municipal car pool under the regime of Ken Livingstone shortly before the Greater London Council was abolished in 1986.

There was of course another side to this story. The shelves of second-hand bookshops groan with the many ceremonial centenary histories of local-government authorities, replete with photographs of local worthies and showy bindings. To some extent, utility merely transferred the location and style of ceremonial. If the Labour Party came into being partly in order to incorporate working people fully into the political system, a certain amount of municipal splendour under a Labour council arguably acknowledged the Party's achievement. Twentieth-century mayors retained something of their traditional ceremonial role, and it was through observing the children's disappointment at a Christmas party when Mayor of Hackney that Morrison—as concerned as any for economy in local government—came to regret the early Labour mayors' rejection of their regalia.[88] Benn was astonished in 1976 at the Ruritanian splendour accompanying the enthronement of the new Bishop of Bristol, complete with coachmen in cocked hats and knee-breeches: 'it is astonishing that seventy years after the Labour Party was founded this sort of thing should still be going on' other than at a folk festival.[89] From the late-Victorian period onwards it was royal occasions that often provided the excuse for such municipal ceremonial as survived,[90] and ceremonial and formality have become more and more the speciality of the one remaining major British political institution to be discussed: the monarchy.

# 12

# *Symbolism and Ceremony*

A SURVEY of 416 informants in Glasgow in 1968 showed that the general
public then knew far more about the monarchy than about leading politicians: 73 per cent of respondents could name at least three children in the
royal family, whereas only 56 per cent could name at least three party
leaders. So visible an institution must be in some sense important. Is its
importance in any sense political? If the political system is defined narrowly, as a system concerned with the formal distribution of institutional
power, the monarchy has been declining at least since the early nineteenth
century. Yet the study of formal institutions exaggerates decline—it is the
study of the informal that highlights growth. G. M. Young said of the
British monarchy that 'as its power pursued its inevitable downward curve,
its influence rose in equipoise'.[1] This Chapter will show that here, as so
often with British political institutions, new functions have emerged spontaneously since Bagehot's day, and old functions have acquired new twists,
without any need for formal institutional change.

To take first the sphere the monarchy had occupied from earliest times,
relations between Britain and foreign powers, we saw in Chapter 1 how
Bagehot's inevitable ignorance of what went on behind the scenes led him
to underestimate the Queen's importance. But her death, by removing the
British monarch from the heart of Europe's dynastic network, immediately
freed politicians to extend their powers. Despite the mythology, Edward
VII lacked the energy, connections, and experience required for significant
foreign-policy initiatives of his own,[2] and George V, even in his personal
relations with other monarchs, had to defer to the politicians. His impulse
to help Manuel, the dethroned King of Portugal, received no backing from
the Foreign Secretary.[3] The war undermined the monarchy still further by
destroying so many of the royal families whose correspondence had reinforced Queen Victoria against her ministers. Since 1850 the monarchies

of only seven European states have remained in continuous existence—in the Benelux countries, Sweden, Norway, Denmark, and the United Kingdom—and the monarchies of fourteen European states have fallen. So there are fewer candidates for any British dynastic alliance. At the same time, apart from Japan, the growing powers after 1918—the United States, the USSR, and Germany—have been self-consciously republican. Besides, the fact that the First World War occurred at all undermined the idea that the dynastic marriage promoted peace. 'It is not *every* day that one marries the eldest daughter of a Queen of England,' Queen Victoria had said, when the idea was mooted that her daughter Vicky should marry the future Emperor Frederick III in 1857.[4] The marriage contributed to Anglo-German misunderstanding, and the First World War was fought between nations led largely by Queen Victoria's grandchildren. So the British inter-war monarchy retreated into splendid isolation. It renamed itself the House of Windsor in 1917, the Battenbergs changed their name to Mountbatten, and between the wars George V's domesticated tastes accorded with necessity. He paid only two state visits abroad—to Belgium in 1922 and to Italy in 1923—and resisted pressure for more on the ground that state visits now lacked political importance. From 1918 until his death he spent only eight weeks overseas, five of them on a cruise convalescing from an illness. During her twenty-eight years as a widow, Queen Mary never left the British Isles.[5]

The Prince of Wales, later Edward VIII, was much readier to travel than his father, but his reputation as an international ambassador stemmed largely from his tours of what was rapidly becoming the Commonwealth. Furthermore, by 1936 his links with Nazi organizations, his carelessness with official papers, and the fact that Mrs Simpson was seen as a security risk caused Foreign Office papers for the first time in history to be screened before being sent to the King,[6] who continued to be seen as a security risk even in the later stages of the Second World War.[7] In the dangerous context of the late 1930s there was no necessary conflict between support for closer relations with Nazi Germany and the monarchy's duty to safeguard the national interest. But given that events seemed subsequently to vindicate the Churchillian anti-appeasement strategy, the Duke of Windsor's German contacts and George VI's support in the Munich crisis for Neville Chamberlain (during which he appeared with the King on the balcony of Buckingham Palace) did nothing to enhance monarchy's influence in foreign policy. When George VI corresponded with European monarchs, the initiative was seldom his, and ministers were always kept fully informed. The Second World War further undermined the dynastic alliance as a peace-preserving agency. An expanding sphere of influence for George VI was as trouble-shooter amidst the entanglements the war produced among European royal families.[8]

Since 1945 earlier trends have continued. In thirteen European states monarchy has come to an end, and in eight it has never existed.[9] Although there has been a striking revival of monarchy in Spain, and some talk of further revivals in Eastern Europe, its world-wide decline has almost destroyed the political power that British monarchs accumulated through their international dynastic connections. By 1986 less than a tenth of the world's population lived within monarchical political systems.[10] Although in 1990 a sixth of the Queen's 570 official engagements were undertaken while on official tours abroad,[11] such visits rarely entail much diplomatic activity by the Queen herself. So during the twentieth century the diplomatic constituent of royal power has greatly declined. On the other hand, by discrediting more charismatic styles of personal leadership, the Nazi defeat did something to validate the concept of constitutional monarchy. Like other British institutions at that time, the monarchy gained from Britain's being on the winning side. Furthermore, even with international relations the monarchy has gained new roles to replace the old—notably the promotion of international trade. Already by 1925 the South American visits of the Prince of Wales had the revival of British trade in view,[12] and by the 1960s this new role was well established. In autumn 1967, for instance, the Ogilvies linked an eleven-day tour of the USA to a series of British Weeks in department stores, and during one month of 1969 Princess Margaret went to Tokyo, and Princess Alexandra to Vienna, both with the aim of crowning a British Week.[13]

This was by no means the first of the monarchy's growing international roles, for at the end of Bagehot's life a new bond was developing with empire. Disraeli told the Queen in 1858 that her name should 'be impressed upon' the Indians' 'native life', and had earlier told parliament that 'you can only act upon the opinion of Eastern nations through their imagination'.[14] The Royal Titles Bill (1876) sought to consolidate the British connection through cultivating a feudal relationship between British monarchs and the Indian princes. 'In India the monarchy must seem to be as little constitutional as possible . . .', wrote Lord Salisbury later; 'it is of great importance to obtrude upon the native Indian mind the personality of the Sovereign and her family'.[15] None of this had been foreseen by Bagehot, who as a good Liberal was unlikely to welcome feudal revivals. His *English Constitution* was written at a time when republicanism seemed on the rise and shortly before 'imperialism' gathered strength. 'The English people', he wrote, in an attack on the Bill, 'is not one on which it is safe to try innovating experiments in matters of mere sentiment.'[16] The Queen, by contrast, was keen on the Bill, and resented such attacks. Her enthusiasm for empire was strong enough to influence her day-to-day routine: her plan for an Indian native bodyguard was rejected by the cabinet in 1883, but in 1887 she was taking lessons in Hindustani so as to improve communication with her Indian servants.[17] In letters to her ministers, she invariably saw defence of the imperial frontier as part of a world crusade to uphold civilization and trade. A later critic might see the monarchy in the age of imperialism as 'a fig leaf to cover the shocking reality of exploitation',[18] but for the Queen it protected the weak against the strong: the Africans against the Boers and the slave-traders, the Indians against the Russians.

Her successors identified even more firmly with empire. The first member of the royal family to tour India was the Duke of Edinburgh in 1869, but the Prince of Wales made a six-month visit in 1875–6, and in May 1886 he was closely involved with organizing the colonial and Indian exhibition in South Kensington.[19] Joseph Chamberlain's initiative encouraged the future George V and Queen Mary on their empire tour in 1901, and on ascending the throne George V told Chamberlain that 'it has always been my dream to identify myself with the great idea of Empire'.[20] The future Edward VIII, in his turn, made his name with a sequence of empire tours in the 1920s. When depressed about the Congress Party's hostility during his visit to India in 1921, he was reassured by his father that the Indian princes were now much more loyal than they had been in the 1850s.[21] George VI's ministers denied him his wish to be crowned, like his father, at a durbar in Delhi, and in 1942 he was 'amazed' to learn from Churchill that India would have to be given up to the Indians after the war.[22] Thereafter, the princes were pushed somewhat unceremoniously into accepting independence for India, whose linkage between monarchy, imperialism, and ceremonial was destroyed in 1949 when allowed to remain in the Commonwealth as a republic. 'When one thinks of the attitude of the Princes in both World Wars, and that of Congress in 1942', Monckton told Churchill in May 1946, 'one wonders if we must always be driven to let down our friends and appease our enemies'.[23]

Thereafter the imperial connection seems in retrospect to have been, from the monarchy's point of view, a waning asset. Yet it began to seem so only after the 1960s. The tour in 1939 of Canada and the USA ('that tour made us', said the present Queen Mother[24]) and the tour of South Africa in 1947 were high points in George VI's reign, and at the beginning of the new reign there was much talk of a 'new Elizabethan age'. Elizabeth II's close knowledge of the Commonwealth, buttressed by her personal rapport with many of its leaders, proved a diplomatic asset on more than one occasion—most notably in 1979, when her influence with Kenneth Kaunda at the Commonwealth conference in Zambia helped to get a Rhodesian settlement.[25] Heath as Prime Minister, however, had already been vigorously defending British national self-interest against Commonwealth pressures, and by the mid-1980s Powell was not alone in thinking that the prominence of the Commonwealth, and of immigrants from the Commonwealth, among the Queen's priorities was beginning to distance her dangerously from her British subjects.[26] In 1987 Powell ridiculed the idea that a British monarch can also be head of independent countries such as Fiji, where the Queen's attempts to brand a coup as illegal came to naught.[27] Conflicts of responsibility are likely to arise in powers so extended, but will diminish to the extent that the fifteen Commonwealth countries for whom the Queen is still head of state decide to replace her. The Duke of Edinburgh told Benn in February 1968 that in twenty-five years the Queen would no longer be nominal head of state in countries such as Canada: 'they don't want us and they will have to be a republic or something'.[28] If that happens, the monarchy will be freed yet again to assume new roles in place of the old. But as long as the Commonwealth survives, the Queen seems the only head for it who is likely to win general acceptance,[29] and old roles will merge with new to the extent that the royal family helps to integrate former Commonwealth immigrants into the United Kingdom. Thereby it will carry into new areas Edward VII's integrating role, as when he helped to get Jews fully accepted into British life. Already the Prince of Wales has made the cause of East London Bengali immigrants his own.[30]

Running in parallel with the monarchy's new imperial role was a further novelty: its ceremonial function. This was not welcomed by Queen Victoria. She disliked ceremony, regretted its cost, and feared assassination. Bagehot showed more insight. Urging her out of retirement in 1871, he claimed that by her long seclusion she had 'done almost as much injury to the popularity of the monarchy . . . as the most unworthy of her predecessors did by his profligacy and frivolity'. He pointed out three years later that 'to be invisible is to be forgotten', and that 'to be . . . an effective symbol, you must be vividly and often seen'.[31] As the monarchy's formal powers wane, its ceremonial role seems to wax. There was a false dawn in ceremonial with George IV, whose coronation in 1821 cost more in real terms than George V's and far more when related to gross national product than any subsequent coronation. William IV, unenthusiastic about ceremony, cut down coronation expenditure, and when walking down St James's after his accession was kissed by a prostitute.[32] Court ceremonial remained rather casual in Queen Victoria's early years, though as long as ceremonial was confined within an aristocratic élite this did not matter greatly. The more publicly the monarchy displayed itself, however, the greater the need for sophisticated planning and staging. Prince Albert recognized the importance of ceremonial, and supervised arrangements for his eldest daughter's wedding to the Crown Prince of Prussia in 1858. Edward VII continued where his father left off. His famed punctilio in dress was more than a mere quirk; he knew that with monarchy, appearances matter. His own wedding in 1863 set the pattern for many late-Victorian ceremonial occasions. The year 1866 saw the first of Queen Victoria's seven openings of parliament in person after Albert's death, but the real turning-point occurred in 1872. The alleged 'invention' of tradition in that year, when a thanksgiving service was held for the Prince of Wales's recovery from serious illness, has been somewhat overdone. True, the cabinet discussed the arrangements extensively, and the whole subject took up much of Gladstone's time. But in planning the service, Gladstone was able to compile a list of precedents before bringing the subject before the Queen.[33] He sought a solemnity in the occasion that would bring out its religious dimension. In the late-Victorian monarchy's emphasis on ceremonial there was a high-church ingredient: an adjustment of religious forms to suit secular purposes.

MEDIA
    Ceremonial and preoccupation with changes in the media went hand in hand. The thanksgiving of 1872 was the first ceremonial royal occasion where seats were deliberately assigned to representative groups such as nonconformists and working men, and in 1937 four working people received invitations to the coronation.[34] In 1874 the press facilities for reporting the Duke of Edinburgh's wedding were fuller than those granted in 1863. In the Abbey for the jubilee service in 1887 were ninety places for the press.[35] The Prince of Wales was a keen photographer, and was already making himself accessible to press photographers in the 1880s.[36] The jubilee boosted photography in rather the same way as the coronation of 1953 boosted television. 'Perhaps at no previous period have so many outdoor subjects been portrayed by photography in a single week,' wrote the *British Journal of Photography* on 1 July; '. . . in every provincial town, village, and hamlet there have been rejoicings, mementoes of which have been portrayed by photography . . . cameras of all sizes and shapes . . . were brought into requisition.' Royal ceremonial soon associated itself with philanthropy, civic functions, and the distribution of honours. The diamond jubilee of

1897 firmly wedded empire to royal ceremonial, whose apogee occurred under Edward VII. Given growing national wealth, the cost seemed affordable. Despite the coronation's rising real cost in the twentieth century, it remained a tiny and static proportion of gross national product—0.0001 per cent in each twentieth-century coronation year,[37] and by 1969 the British monarchy was cheaper in relation to population than in any other European monarchy.[38] George V readily carried on where his father left off, except that his less cosmopolitan outlook rendered imperial and domestic occasions more prominent.

Its ceremonial role required monarchy to respond flexibly to all changes in the media. As we saw in Chapter 5, modern media have deprived monarchs, like all much-photographed people, of their privacy. George V greatly disliked the press, but recognized its importance in 1918 when a full-time salaried press secretary was first appointed. The post has persisted ever since, except for a gap between 1931 and 1944. George V's voice was first heard on radio in 1924 when he opened the British Empire exhibition at Wembley. Reith first invited him to deliver a Christmas or New Year radio broadcast in 1923, but the King did not succumb till 1932. Even in the timing of his death, arranged by the doctors to suit the needs of the respectable morning papers, George V involuntarily acknowledged the enhanced importance of the media.[39] Invited by the Prince of Wales soon after the First World War to comment on how he was faring in the role, Sir Frederick Ponsonby replied: 'if I may say so, Sir, I think there is risk in your making yourself too accessible . . . The Monarchy must always retain an element of mystery.' The advice was not acted upon, and in some ways Edward responded too readily to media demands. When photographed as King walking to an appointment in the rain beneath an umbrella, instead of taking the Daimler, some shock was caused.[40] Yet he missed the full significance of the change, for it was not the least among his blindnesses that he thought he could combine the monarch's public role with a private life that would remain informal, unconventional, and unobserved. George VI, given his speech defect, was ill-equipped for the monarch's new-found media role, but he struggled to overcome it, just as his daughter has struggled to overcome her distaste for being televised. Television was excluded from the Abbey for the coronation in 1937, though cameras were placed on the processional route and the King helped to ensure that opposition to radio broadcasts of the coronation was defeated.[41] Again in 1953 it was the monarch who helped the new media forward. The Queen prevailed over the politicians and ensured that television cameras were inside the Abbey.[42] The coronation's television audience included

7,800,000 people viewing at home, 10,400,000 viewing with friends, and 1,500,000 viewing in public places.[43]

Under Elizabeth II the monarchy has responded more alertly than the politicians to changes in the media, though it did not welcome initiatives from its staff in that direction: the family ostracized the Queen's nanny Marion Crawford ('Crawfie') for publishing *The Little Princesses* in 1950.[44] The Queen gave her first televised Christmas broadcast in 1957, and with the appointment of Sir William Heseltine as press secretary in 1968 monarchy's exploitation of the new media accelerated. The hour-long television film 'The Royal Palaces of Britain', first shown in 1966, let the cameras into the royal palaces for the first time. It prepared the way for a television film on the royal family in 1969 which marked a major breakthrough in publicity.[45] In the same year, much trouble was also taken to launch the Prince of Wales. 'The monarchy is back in business,' wrote the *Observer* in July, 'and much more professional, devoted, potent, and slick than we had ever supposed it could be.'[46] Helped by her work for the Save the Children Fund, Princess Anne did much to carry these developments further. In 1973 she and Mark Phillips gave a ninety-minute interview to the press before their wedding,[47] and in 1985 she became the royal family's first senior member to participate in a radio phone-in.[48] The announcement of the Prince of Wales's engagement in February 1981 was important enough to prompt speculation in the companies likely to benefit from souvenirs and tourism.[49] Public interest in the wedding was so great during the televised wedding-service that national electricity demand acted (in the words of Mr Glyn England of the Central Electricity Generating Board) as a 'barometer of national emotions'. It declined at all the peak moments of ceremonial, while people were quietly watching their televisions; it shot up at other times, when people seized the chance of putting on the kettle or of going to the loo, all of which set off the pumps at the pumping-stations.[50] The interaction of media and ceremonial was symbolized by the fact that the streets were deserted except where the action was taking place; people were either watching events indoors on their televisions or monitoring them on their portable radios and televisions while waiting in the crowd on the processional route.[51] In 1986 the first of two television programmes showing the Prince and Princess of Wales at home drew 13,550,000 viewers, and claimed sixth place in the 'top ten' for that week on all television channels.[52]

The monarchy's ceremonial role has the advantage of diverting from the politicians some of the prestige that often accompanies power. The televised broadcast on the royal family in 1969 claimed that 'the great strength of the monarchy does not lie in the power it gives to the sovereign but in the power it denies to anybody else'.[53] This became increasingly necessary after Bagehot's time because the articulation of party structure and the centralization of state power made politicians' delusions of grandeur more likely. The inter-war fashion for Fascist styles of leadership came to nothing in Britain; yet during the Second World War, despite his respect for the formalities, even Winston Churchill sometimes threw King George VI into the shade.[54] Delusions of grandeur reached new heights in the 1980s, and may well have fuelled the allegedly bad relations between Queen and Prime Minister.

The ceremonial role required training and self-discipline in the monarch, and substantial organizational backing. Edward VIII did himself and his family a disservice in his memoirs when he reported one of the few pieces of advice he ever received about how to be a king: 'only two rules really count', an old courtier told him. 'Never miss an opportunity to relieve yourself; never miss a chance to sit down and rest your feet.'[55] There is far more to the ceremonial role than this: physical courage, for instance. The more visible yet special the head of state becomes, the more valuable he is as a target for those who seek the spectacular and symbolic protest, whether on behalf of themselves or in the hope of advancing some wider cause. Queen Victoria was shot at six times during her reign, and was once knocked momentarily unconscious with a cane,[56] a fact which goes some way towards explaining her distaste for public ceremonial. The massacre of the Serbian court in 1903 and the attempted assassination at the wedding of Queen Ena of Spain in 1906 helped to cultivate in British monarchs the sort of guild loyalty to their order that profoundly influenced Edward VII and caused George VI to ensure the dignified reburial of the three Stuart Pretenders buried in Rome.[57] Police efforts foiled Fenian efforts to produce explosions in parliament and at Westminster Abbey during the jubilee of 1887,[58] but Chapter 3 showed how the IRA in recent years has greatly limited the scope for royal ceremonial in Northern Ireland, and even elsewhere. The security risk led the government to advise Princess Margaret to call off her visit to Washington in July 1981, and elaborate precautions were taken during that month to limit the terrorist risk during the royal wedding, with pillar-boxes *en route* blocked, sewers underneath the route inspected, and 400 detectives mingling with the sightseers.[59]

The danger from individuals with a personal grievance is even more difficult to ward off, because so unpredictable. Jerome Bannigan's loaded gun designed for Edward VIII in 1936, the attempt to kidnap Princess

Anne in March 1973, and what at first looked like an assassination attempt on the Prince of Wales in Australia in January 1994 all illustrate the need for physical courage in modern monarchs. Danger for them 'is a permanent possibility', as Princess Anne pointed out; 'we just have to live with it'.[60] The danger is made still less predictable by the vanity of individuals for whom any type of publicity is better than none. Marcus Sarjeant, the 17-year-old who fired six blank shots at the Queen at the Trooping of the Colour in 1981 allegedly vowed to become 'the most famous teenager in the world'.[61] Yet none of this prevented the Queen in 1990 from being present at 125 official visits, opening ceremonies, and other appearances, or from attending fifty-nine receptions, lunches, dinners, and banquets. Even the Queen Mother (then aged 90) managed sixty-three and thirty-eight, respectively.[62] Furthermore, the increasing importance of the media has diminished the terrorist threat to the extent that when monarchs communicate with the public mainly through radio and film, access to them can be much more closely monitored than in public functions indiscriminately attended.

Potentially more threatening to monarchy than terrorism was the decline in formality after the 1950s. Refusal to stand for the national anthem was fashionable in some inter-war intellectual circles, to the disgust of Ramsay MacDonald and George Orwell,[63] but in the 1960s a less principled, more casual, and more generalized rejection of the ritual caused it to be phased out in cinemas and theatres.[64] The royal family responded constructively to the situation, and itself became less formal. The present Queen Mother had done much to overcome the problems posed by her husband's shyness by cultivating just the right mix of friendliness and dignity in her public appearances. Her example was influential. Royal ceremonial requires a delicate balance to be struck between visibility and distance: between seeming at once ordinary, yet also elevated. The balance shifts from one generation to another, and by the 1970s a further move towards informality seemed required. In 1970 the first royal 'walk-abouts' took place, in New Zealand in March and in Coventry in June.[65]

The monarchy's ceremonial role was a unifying influence at home as well as in the Commonwealth, for the non-party head of state rose above a political system designed to advertise party conflict. The eighteenth-century monarchy attained political neutrality of a sort when fathers identified with one political faction and sons with another. A faint late-Victorian residue of this can be seen when the Prince of Wales kept on good terms with Dilke and Gladstone, of whom his mother did not approve, and in the friction between Buckingham Palace and the office of the present

Prince of Wales. The late-Victorian Conservative Party's patriotic self-image might well have endangered the monarchy's precariously established neutrality between the parties. However, Conservatives had nothing to gain from being identified with too obviously partisan a symbol, and they refrained from exploiting the identification with monarchy too crudely. While publicly presenting a neutral face, all twentieth-century British monarchs have been moderate Liberals or moderate Conservatives in private. Removal from direct participation in politics early in the nineteenth century enabled monarchs to cultivate political neutrality in a new guise: to arbitrate overtly between the parties in situations of conflict. Queen Victoria mediated in 1884 between Salisbury and the more moderate Conservatives in the hope of settling the franchise question without conflict between Lords and Commons. George V made mediation central to the monarch's role—notably in the Buckingham Palace conferences on home rule in 1914–15 and in the formation in 1931 of the National Government, a coalition less partisan in its origin than it later became in practice, let alone in legend.

This overt neutrality added weight to monarchs' intuitive insights into public opinion—insights which owed nothing to elections, and concerned topics absent from party programmes. Queen Victoria's rapport with public opinion has already been discussed.[66] Her letters reveal a woman whose interests—Jack the Ripper, cruelty to animals, the strange marriage of Baroness Burdett-Coutts—reflected those of her subjects. On social questions such as providing counter-attractions to the pub on Sundays or moving the housing question up the political agenda, she displayed a common sense not always present within her governments. Likewise, George V's biographer refers to the King's belief that there was 'some almost mystical association between the Sovereign and the common people', and to his feelings which often 'reflected immediately and precisely the thoughts and feelings of the ordinary British citizen'. They were feelings held by a man who, in his beloved York Cottage, wanted above all things to live as far as possible without pretension.[67] 'There is nothing to differentiate the cottage from any of the villas at Surbiton,' wrote Harold Nicolson: 'it is almost incredible that the heir to so vast a heritage lived in this horrible little house.'[68]

Twentieth-century monarchs' insights into public opinion may owe something to the rural and sporting connections that distance monarchy from its more cerebral critics. The solitudes of Balmoral and the pheasant shoots of Sandringham nourish a sense of proportion and a range of connections that are elusive in Westminster and Whitehall. It was on a sporting issue that the royal family had one of its most bruising encounters with Thatcher, who in 1980 espoused the dubious cause of boycotting the Moscow Olympics as a protest against the Soviet invasion of Afghanistan. Sport could draw together people from all social classes, and Queen Victoria was doing rather more than suit her taste when displaying herself annually to her people at Ascot. The substantial volumes *King Edward VII as a Sportsman* (1911) and *King George V as a Sportsman: An Informal Study of the First Country Gentleman in Europe* (1935), besides revealing what now seems a royal indifference to the slaughter of animals, illuminate the simple, squire-like tastes and relationships of both monarchs. Harold Wilson, plucked by his weekly audiences from the almost continual political storms of the mid-1960s, seems to have found the Queen's robust common sense refreshing.[69] And once the Duke of Edinburgh in the 1950s had broadened out what the monarch's associates could acceptably say in public, the way was cleared for a Prince of Wales who could champion the ordinary man against the experts in matters such as agriculture, architecture, film-making, medicine, and theology.

The integrating role, once assumed, commits the monarchy to continual adaptation in the face of social change. For as soon as one source of division is muted, another manifests itself. A social divide that is always present, however, which the monarchy is peculiarly equipped to moderate, is the gulf between the generations. A royal, rather than presidential, family symbolizes continuity across the generations—a symbolism all the more necessary when continuity is sought amidst dramatic shifts in the country's international standing and social structure, and across governments of changing political composition. The hereditary principle—in monarchies of any type, as contrasted with dictatorships—has the merit of enhancing continuity by at least narrowing the options when it comes to choosing a head of state. By comparison with a presidential system, a constitutional monarchy is less inevitably or completely dominated by an ageing public figure. A family, which continuously rejuvenates itself, has the potential for a wider appeal within age-groups. 'By preserving the method of nature in the conduct of the state', wrote Burke, 'in what we improve we are never wholly new; in what we retain we are never wholly obsolete.'[70] In an opinion poll of 1978, 77 per cent of the age-group between 16 and 24 supported the idea of a monarch as head of state, and only 16 per cent preferred a presidency.[71] So Bagehot's comment remains true: 'a *family* on the throne is an interesting idea . . . it brings down the pride of sovereignty to the level of petty life'. As Burke had earlier pointed out, 'binding up the constitution of our country with our dearest domestic ties' involves 'adopting our fundamental laws into the bosom of our family affections'.[72]

There are of course difficulties about this aspect of monarchy. The indeterminate role of Prince of Wales has never been easy to carry off, and clearly puzzles Prince Charles. Here, too, constitutional monarchy needs to strike a delicate balance. The gulf between reigning monarch and Prince of Wales in the eighteenth century was often too wide to reinforce political stability. Conversely, the virtual absence of any such gulf between Edward VII and a successor who waged a 'private war with the twentieth century'[73] brought the opposite risk: that the monarchy would become dull and out of touch. The gulf between Queen Victoria and the future Edward VII, however, was sufficiently wide and narrow for each successfully to complement the other. In the 1920s the same could perhaps be said of the future Edward VIII's relationship with his father, for there were always severe limits to the scale of his youthful rebellion. 'In truth, all that I ever had in mind was to throw open the windows a little,' he writes; his aim was simply 'to be a successful King, though a King in a modern way'.[74] Besides, if the monarchy's younger generation can be rebellious, it can also help to harness the potentially rebellious. As late as 1935 the Prince was still performing the role that comes naturally to Princes of Wales: taking a special interest in organizations and charities catering for youth. It was a theme the present Prince of Wales took up in his second speech in the House of Lords.[75] But the work of the Silver Trust Fund was disrupted by the abdication crisis. 'After I am dead the boy will ruin himself within twelve months,' is George V's alleged comment on the Prince's fortieth birthday.[76] This strained relationship had helped to protect the monarchy from the conservatism of the father, but had not ultimately brought maturity, balance, and judgement to the son.

There is also a price to be paid for a family on the throne—a family which, under the present Queen, has been growing. Already by December 1987, 73 per cent of those surveyed thought junior members of the royal family should pursue a career or combine a career (in the armed services, or in the civil service, for example) with ceremonial tasks.[77] The financial problem is being solved, and much would be lost if the idea of family-based ceremonial leadership were jettisoned. Not only does such a system relieve the pressure on the head of state. Monarchy also has the advantage of operating on a timetable that is contrapuntal to the political timetable: far more predictable, and longer-term in perspective. Monarchs are not obliged to retire at 60 or 65, and have not done so. 'I think continuity is very important,' said the Queen in 1992; 'it is a job for life.'[78] The royal timetable reflects the longer-lasting non-political human relationships with which all can identify. Monarchs carefully record in their diaries the anniversaries which are central to their function. Surveying George V's diary, his biographer says that he 'was enthralled less by events than by their anniversaries, which he noted again and again'.[79] In the words of the Duke of Edinburgh, 'our life is very much bounded by things that happen annually, more than by things that happen daily':[80] birth, marriage, parenthood, anniversaries, and death, each likely to evoke some sort of formal occasion. With nations as with families, such recurring functions stabilize and unify. Indeed, most British people would probably find a chronicle of modern British history centring on royal festivities more congenial and familiar than any election-based timetable, if only because often commemorated by special issues of stamps and coins. It would centre upon jubilees (1887, 1897, 1935, 1977), coronations (1838, 1901, 1911, 1937, 1953) and weddings (the Princess Royal in 1858, the Prince of Wales in 1863, the Duke of York in 1893, the Princess Royal in 1922, the Duke of York in 1923, the Duke of Kent in 1934, Princess Elizabeth in 1948, Princess Margaret in 1960, Princess Anne in 1973, and the Prince of Wales in 1981). It would be complemented by silver weddings (of George VI in 1948, of Elizabeth II in 1972) and by numerous birthdays, funerals, and state openings of parliament. The mere recital of the list illustrates the twentieth-century extension of public ceremonial beyond the immediate royal family to consorts (Queen Alexandra's state funeral in 1925, Queen Mary's lying-in-state in 1953) and relatives.[81]

The monarchy's role in drawing together the regions was discussed in Chapter 3. In the case of Wales and Scotland the role was eased by the religious outlook of British monarchs, who played down regionally divisive subgroups within protestantism. Religious leaders, especially clergymen, were influential in the media of their day, and had to be cultivated. From Queen Victoria onwards, British monarchs displayed a middle-of-the-road, undoctrinaire, unsectarian, and commonsensical variant of protestantism that broadened out further during the twentieth century. Edward VII extended monarchy's connections by relaxing sectarian attitudes towards nonconformists and Jews, and in 1918 George V and Queen Mary made a point of attending the free-church service of thanksgiving for victory, thereby pleasing John Clifford, the Baptist leader. Since the monarchy is intimately linked with the established church, much less could be achieved in Ireland. But Edward VII tried to liberalize attitudes towards Roman Catholics by protesting against the anti-Catholicism inherent in the coronation oath. George V began his reign by getting the oath rendered less offensive to Roman Catholics, and Edward VIII wanted to dispense with his declaration of Protestant faith when opening parliament in 1936, though he decided not to press the matter.[82] George VI deeply respected the loyalty shown by Cardinal Hinsley during the Second World War, and would have liked to send a representative to his funeral in 1943.[83] Elizabeth II carried these trends further in 1982 when she received the Pope at Buckingham Palace, and Prince Charles seems likely to carry the trend further'.[84]

Bagehot generalized from Queen Victoria's conduct to develop an emphasis upon the moral dimensions of the monarch's religious role, portraying the monarch as moral exemplar to the nation. This was to put the cart before the horse and mistake the contingent for the permanent. The monarchy cannot afford to diverge too markedly from opinions held in society at large. Its status depends, as with the Supreme Court in the United States, on preserving a delicate but unobtrusive affinity with public opinion, which usually entails lagging somewhat behind it. The Queen's 'Victorian values', nourished by the Prince Consort, largely reflected an astute perception that the future lay with the middle classes, permeated as they then were by evangelical and domesticated values. When *The Times* claimed in 1972 that 'the Queen, the Duke and their children have set a standard of family life and family happiness that everyone must respect and many envy',[85] it was reporting a situation that could scarcely last. The broken marriages of the Queen's sister and of her three married children may be regrettable, but they cannot be seen as yet another threat to a major British institution, for the monarchy's representative role ultimately takes priority over any role as moral exemplar. Besides, the change is less one of substance than of appearances and attitudes. Marriages of convenience or 'arranged' marriages, as distinct from marriages founded on romantic love, were once commonplace in upper-class circles because marriage was an instrument for promoting international alliances or consolidating landed estates. The conventions governing the arranged marriage were not entirely cynical or without justification. Those who marry only for love can fall out of it, and the marriages of those who do not marry for love are likely to survive only if a separation of spheres frees the partners from being continuously thrown into one another's company, and if sexual liaisons outside marriage are widely condoned. This is the context within which to view Edward VII's notorious amours, the fact that George V as a young man kept a mistress at Southsea and shared another with his brother at St John's Wood,[86] not to mention the future Edward VIII's calculated loss of virginity to a French prostitute, Paulette, in 1916.[87]

It was a sign, however, of Queen Victoria's middle-class allegiance that she embraced the middle-class concept of romantic love—a concept difficult to reconcile with institutions orientated round inheriting property and social status. Cupid's darts do not necessarily alight upon those equipped for their role by personal qualities or by prolonged grooming. The abdication crisis of 1936 exposed the conflict between old and new attitudes at two levels. First, a monarch who could not carry his heavy burden of responsibility without the help of the unsuitable woman he loved would have to choose the one or the other. As Wallis Simpson told her aunt, when trying to persuade him not to insist on abdicating to marry her, 'it's a tragedy that he can't bring himself to marry without loving'.[88] Second, the crisis stretched beyond endurance the press discretion which had hitherto concealed the King's sequence of earlier sexual liaisons. Baldwin during the crisis told the King that the British people had responded to falling moral standards since the war by requiring a higher standard of their monarch than they applied to themselves.[89] If that was so in 1936, the requirement did not prove lasting. We can now see that the examples in personal life set by George V and George VI were unusual in the long history of the British monarchy. What has happened since 1972 is simply that the monarchy in this sphere, as in others, has moved into line with social trends, and the press has ceased to collude in pretending otherwise, leaving Princess Margaret as an unfortunate victim of the transition. What was new from the 1980s onwards was not the adultery, but the combination of adultery with publicity.

The British people tend to regard sexuality as morality's prime component, but British monarchs set an example in many other areas, especially at times of national crisis. The monarchy's military role goes back to its remote origins, and even Queen Victoria saw herself as inheriting a special role in this area. But by then the monarch's symbolic role took priority, and during the First World War neither George V nor the Prince of Wales were allowed to go too near the Front, though the King used all his influence to defend the service leaders against political interference. The entire royal family could, however, set an example to the nation in other ways. Just as the King set the pace for national self-denial through taking what was called 'the King's Pledge' against drink in 1915, so the Queen's example drew women into channelling their customary charitable role towards the war effort. Example-setting within the United Kingdom was if anything accentuated during the twentieth century by the monarchy's closer identification with the nation state. In 1940 George VI refused to leave London, and practised revolver-shooting in the grounds of Buckingham

Palace, where he intended to die fighting.[90] 'It makes me feel I can look the East End in the face,' said the Queen Mother, after Buckingham Palace was bombed in 1940,[91] and the King visited Coventry directly after its serious bombing raids. A faint echo of the monarchy's wartime role can be found in the attention paid to Prince Andrew's role in the Falklands War, and in the doubts expressed during the Gulf War of 1991 about whether the royal family was playing its full part. Example-setting is required in peacetime crises too. In 1931, for instance, the civil list was reduced by £50,000 for as long as the economic crisis lasted. But the monarchy's example-setting is not confined to crises, as the Princess of Wales's prominence in fashion magazines shows. In clothing, speech, and conduct, the monarchy is expected in day-to-day matters to indicate 'how things should be done'.

As the preoccupations of political parties moved from religion to social class, the monarchy's reconciling role could extend into class relations. This might be thought particularly difficult, for if pre-Marxian alignments persisted, monarchy's interests would hardly be separable from those of the aristocracy, whose hereditary principle it shared to the full. On the other hand if Marxian alignments prevailed, monarchy could hardly forsake Queen Victoria's bourgeois alignment. In the outcome, the complexities and fluidity of British class relations freed the monarchy from the embarrassment of having to make any clear choice. Neither Marxian nor pre-Marxian class polarity has been dominant since Bagehot's day. Not only has class dialogue been tripartite rather than Marxian, involving aristocracy as well as bourgeoisie: the monarchy has not even been clearly identified with the aristocratic participant in the debate. But is aristocracy an outwork that requires defending if monarchy's citadel is to be preserved? Benn's attack on the House of Lords led Norman St John-Stevas to articulate this notion at the Conservative Party conference in 1980: 'with the Lords gone, how long would the Crown itself remain free from pressure to go the same way?'[92] George VI himself shared the notion in his more depressed moments. 'Everything is going nowadays,' he told Vita Sackville-West in 1948, raising his hands in despair when she said Knole had gone to the National Trust. 'Before long, I shall also have to go.'[93] Yet neither he nor his successor had to go, partly because the socialist revolution was at that moment losing momentum, but mainly because the fates of monarchy and aristocracy are not integrally linked. The twentieth century has seen the first left standing amidst the ruins of the second.

Monarchy was being distanced from aristocracy long before Bagehot published his *English Constitution*. Evangelical religion and a Whiggish

alertness to revolutionary danger led Queen Victoria to reject an aristocratic extravagance and frivolity, and prepared her family to grow up 'fit
for *whatever station* they may be placed in—*high or low*'. As she told her
eldest daughter in 1868, 'I do feel so strongly that we are before God all
alike, and that in the twinkling of an eye, the highest may find themselves
at the feet of the poorest and lowest.'[94] Prince Albert's death gave her an
excuse for allowing the court virtually to go out of existence, thereby
distancing her still further from the aristocracy. Although the Prince of
Wales later wielded immense power in 'society',[95] he took care to dilute it
with Jewish and Bohemian newcomers. George V retreated even from this
role: Queen Mary had no small talk, and he preferred shooting and stamps.
'Society's' somewhat patronizing dismissal of the court as dull was transferred in full measure to the household of George VI after the sparkling
but brief interlude provided by Edward VIII.[96] 'Society in England is a
national institution,' wrote Lowell in 1908. 'It is not a collection of separate
groups in different places, but a single body with ramifications all over the
country, and a central meeting ground in London during the season.'[97]
At no stage since the Second World War has this been so. 'Society' as
an integrated political influence has slowly died away, together with the
political hostess who could once make or break a political career. Lord
Altrincham might complain in 1957 that the Queen moved among people
who were 'almost without exception people of the "tweedy" sort',[98] but the
tweeds were adapted for country and sporting pursuits, not for any power-
wielding role in the metropolis, and his wish that presentation parties
should be abolished was granted in the following year. The gulf between
monarchy and aristocracy was widened further by the independent-minded,
plain-speaking, and even combative personalities central to the history of
twentieth-century monarchy—the Duke of Windsor, Earl Mountbatten,
and Prince Philip—men who would never integrate smoothly with any
cosy establishment.

Its combination of distance from and familiarity with aristocracy equipped
the monarchy for the first of its class-integrating roles: stabilizing relations
between aristocracy and middle class. Early- and mid-Victorian radicalism
as articulated by Cobden, Bright, and Joseph Chamberlain was strongly
anti-aristocratic in mood, but threats to the middle class from below, together with the removal of dissenting and other middle-class grievances,
prepared the ground for a courtship. With help from the honours system,
a marriage was effected: by 1897 Queen Victoria had instituted or enlarged
fourteen orders.[99] In the late-Victorian move against home rule and towards
imperialism, middle class and aristocracy could join together behind the

consolidated Unionist grouping that the Queen had unobtrusively done more than most to bring about.

By this time the monarchy had already embarked upon a second class-integrating task: helping to integrate organized labour. Once more, Britain's broadly tripartite class structure was helpful. The nineteenth-century landowner was not normally entangled directly in the materialist contest between employer and employee, and sometimes (most notably in the case of Lord Shaftesbury) made a name for urban social concern. The Tory-radical alliance was an evanescent but recurring alignment in nineteenth-century politics, and the House of Lords was always careful before clashing with the lower house on matters of social reform. Paternalist instincts were traits which monarchy shared with landed aristocracy, but which distanced it from manufacturing and commercial employers in some areas of policy. Furthermore, inheritance is not an exclusively aristocratic concern; preoccupation with it pervades society from top to bottom. Inheritance is not concerned solely with the transfer of property, and property can be owned at the lowest levels of society.

None the less, George V was apprehensive. Fearful for the security of his throne it was he, and not the politicians, who in 1917 prevented asylum being given to the Tsar and his family in their distress[100]—a step that he thought would inflame disloyal opinion. A two-pronged approach was required: direct influence over working-class opinion and good relations with its representatives. To promote the first of these, the royal family committed itself publicly to industrial conciliation. Tours of mining areas and the potteries in 1912–13 were complemented by a tour of munitions factories in 1917 that aimed to moderate industrial discontent in the north of England.[101] George V did what he could to moderate extremes of repression during the General Strike, protesting against the *British Gazette*'s mood, for example, and urging the government not to provoke the strikers. As Duke of York, George VI was active in the Industrial Welfare Society. The first 'Duke of York's Camp', organizing collaboration between industrial employees and public schoolboys, was held in 1921, and the Duke attended all but one of the eighteen camps that took place. A recent echo of this approach can perhaps be seen in the Prince of Wales's visit to a trade-union annual conference in 1979. Such activities help to explain how the monarchy came to occupy, in Hoggart's words, 'a quite special position, belonging neither to Them nor to Us—at society's heart, yet somehow outside the social class order'. For Alan Fox's East London working-class parents between the wars, the royal family did not seem linked in a hierarchy that included the politicians and employers.

These they were quite prepared to criticize, but the royal family 'occupied a separate fairy-tale world of infinitely higher quality than our own mundane, rub-along existence'.[102]

Under Elizabeth II, monarchy's social-class contacts and appeal have widened still further. Clive Wigram, George V's assistant secretary, was already pushing for wider access to Buckingham Palace functions in 1919, on the analogy of the White House reception.[103] Under a broadened basis of invitation, Buckingham Palace garden parties by 1983 were attended by 35,000 people each year.[104] From 1956 a sequence of small and informal lunch-parties enabled the Queen to meet leading figures from many walks of life—about 1,200 of them by 1983.[105] In 1919 Lady Patricia Ramsay pioneered the idea that members of the royal family could marry a commoner, a development carried further with Princess Anne's marriage in 1973. Prince Charles was the first heir to the British throne educated with other children away from home instead of by private tutors. The criteria for honours also steadily broadened. Despite Conservative prominence in government since 1964, few hereditary honours have been awarded, and none at all by Labour governments. The automatic award of honours to holders of particular posts has been drastically curtailed, and 30,000 silver-jubilee medals were distributed as a personal award from the Queen in 1977.[106]

Establishing good relations with labour leaders was a task the royal family had begun even before the creation of the Labour Party. The future Edward VII did his best to put the Lib-Lab leader Henry Broadhurst at ease when entertaining him at Sandringham, and as King he cultivated good relations with John Burns, the Liberal cabinet minister from 1905 to 1914. George V was much helped in this task by his sporting interests and by a set of personal values akin to Queen Victoria's, for he impressed on his children the idea that they were neither different from nor better than other people, and tried to imbue them with a strong sense of duty.[107] He did much to ease Labour smoothly into power in its two minority governments of 1924 and 1929, and established a particularly good personal relationship with J. H. Thomas. Endorsement by monarchy was, in a sense, the culmination of the Labour Party's purpose: to integrate working-class structures fully into the political system and simultaneously to broaden access to political careers for labour's leaders. 'You have found me an ordinary man, haven't you?' was George V's parting remark to Ramsay MacDonald, when requesting a dissolution in October 1924.[108] Although George V's vigorous promotion of the National Government in 1931 had disastrous short-term consequences for the Labour Party, this was not at all the King's intention. Indeed, to enlist the personal and patriotic loyalties of Ramsay MacDonald in a crisis constituted the ultimate acknowledgement of the Labour Party's historic integrating role. The King saw an all-party resolution of the economic crisis as very much in the interests of all social classes. Relations between later monarchs and Labour prime ministers seem to have been at least as good. 'The King is dead; he was always very nice to me,' was Attlee's laconic but heartfelt comment in 1952 when announcing George VI's death to a Labour Party meeting; it was noticed how deeply moved he seemed to be by the event.[109] Nor were the 1960s disturbed by any of the rumours about friction between monarch and prime minister that rumbled through the 1980s. Indeed, there seems to have been something more than a formality about Wilson's favourable comments on his relations with the Queen.[110]

The impact made by the monarchy's class-reconciling role should not be exaggerated. In none of these areas of potential division in British society has its healing role been crucial, and it can help to unify only if it works with the grain of opinion and of social and political change. Nobody did more than Gladstone to incorporate the middle class into the nineteenth-century political structure. If anyone's example during the First World War transformed national morale, it was Lloyd George's. And if any individual ensured that the General Strike ended peacefully and later fended off Fascism, it was Baldwin. Still, in improving class relations, as in other areas of national reconciliation, the British monarchy since Bagehot's time has shown itself continuously resourceful. 'The special position of the royal family cannot survive without gradations of class,' Jeremy Paxman has claimed.[111] This is questionable, but the issue is hardly worth pursuing since it is difficult to imagine in the near future any society without social gradations of some kind. Besides, monarchy seems secure enough in several European countries less class-conscious than our own.

The monarchy's twentieth-century achievements have taken place against a background of scepticism from progressive-minded people, among whom Bagehot himself should perhaps be included. Of all the groups it has cultivated, the British monarchy has made least effort with the intellectual world. Princes of Wales have attended university, but Britain has seen no equivalent of the Scandinavian scholar-monarch. George V dismissed clever men as 'eyebrows', and according to his son 'had always been suspicious of college dons and professors', regarding them 'as unpractical, unworldly people whose lives and ways were alien to his own'.[112] Queen Mary's search for self-education and artistic expertise in so philistine a family was indeed an uphill struggle, and not without pathos.[113] In 1926 when told that the Prince of Wales was to address the British Association's annual meeting, the King remarked that he had refused a similar invitation; no member of the family since Prince Albert, he said, had felt up to it, 'and he was an intellectual'.[114] The royal family's anti-intellectual tradition and indifference to the arts persisted under George VI, and have not yet entirely disappeared. In its anti-intellectualism the British royal family once again reflects national traits, but the intellectuals have certainly sought their revenge. For it is intellectuals drawn predominantly from the middle class who have tended to move from scepticism about monarchy to full-blown republicanism. 'Amongst the educated classes', wrote the positivist Frederic Harrison in 1872, 'there is a quiet pooh-poohing of monarchy as a living institution.'[115] Commenting on Elizabeth II's fiftieth birthday, *The Times* noted that 'she has had to face one of the most difficult periods for monarchy in human history, a period in which almost all the trends of intellectual fashion were running against the principle of monarchy itself.'[116] The fire in Windsor Castle in 1992, the Queen's 'annus horribilis', seemed to symbolize the threat to monarchy that mounting expense and marital difficulties were beginning to evoke from its critics.[117]

Objections to monarchy boil down to three linked arguments: that it is irrational, that its connections and values foster ideas of social hierarchy, and that it is expensive for what it does. The first objection stems from the eighteenth-century enlightenment, when progressive people thought that the advance of reason would chase away monarchy together with other mystical, medieval, and warlike institutions and attitudes. Tom Paine's *Rights of Man* (1791–2) claimed that because it is impossible to plan the inheritance of ability, monarchy is irrational as a form of government. Indeed, he thought monarchy hardly a form of government at all, because it changes with the personality of every individual who so unpredictably ascends the throne. 'Every succession is a revolution, and every regency a counter-revolution,' whereas government 'ought to be a thing always in full maturity . . . superior to all the accidents to which individual man is subject'.[118] For the Chartist William Lovett, monarchy fostered the ultimate irrationality: war, which 'has ever been the sport and hobby of kings, and conquest and dominion their greatest delight'.[119] Although radicals grew less sharply critical of tradition during the Victorian period, their enthusiasm for open government, education, and a free press reflected their marked distaste for inherited privilege, whether in aristocracy or monarchy.

This branch of the republican argument has some force. Gladstone thought that 'the strength and vitality of the monarchy is solely dependent on the individual on whom the crown rests'.[120] So much in monarchy depends on the accidents of personality, health, and fertility; so much that is important cannot be planned and predicted. The history of the British royal family is riddled with unexpected developments and dangers narrowly averted. Between 1837 and 1840, when the Princess Royal was born, only Queen Victoria stood between the throne and the deeply unpopular Duke of Cumberland. Her health and fertility proved robust enough, but from the constitutional point of view the Duke of Clarence's death in 1892 could only be welcomed, as removing from the direct line of succession a man who seems to have lacked both character and ability. The failure of the Prince of Wales to marry, and even the possibility that he was sterile,[121] led Queen Mary in 1920 to 'mention' to the future George VI the idea of getting married.[122] Uncertainties reached a climax in the abdication crisis, when the thought of directly appealing to the people from his balcony in Buckingham Palace did at least cross the mind of Edward VIII,[123] and when otherwise inexplicable delays in the negotiations suggest doubts at the highest level about whether the future George VI was capable of succeeding his brother.[124] Even what seems the most predictable of successions turns out on closer inspection to be uncertain. Elizabeth II remained only heir presumptive throughout her father's reign, for a brother might at any time have supplanted her. George VI's death, too, was premature. 'In a way I didn't have an apprenticeship,' she recalled fifty years later: '. . . it was all very sudden . . . taking on and making the best job you can.'[125]

The republican's second claim, that monarchy fosters notions of social hierarchy, also has some plausibility. 'Royalty, though politically powerless, or nearly so, is socially very strong and very mischievous,' said its positivist critic E. S. Beesly in 1863.[126] Such complaints became less current after the 1870s, if only because the middle classes were by then turning to monarchy and aristocracy for protection against threats from below. But they still persisted among Labour leaders of the 1960s. We have seen how the complexities of the British class system subsequently blurred its links with class exploitation, but complaints at its links with a distorted distribution of wealth are readily roused. There might not be many takers for Paine's claim that monarchy is 'the popery of government; a thing kept up to amuse the ignorant, and quiet them into taxes',[127] but complaints about the contrast between royal salaries and the plight of old-age pensioners are still often heard. In 1971 William Hamilton claimed in parliament that it was 'obscene' to award £95,000 a year to the Queen Mother when his constituents were asking him why pensions could not be increased to prevent pensioners 'dying from cold and starvation this winter'.[128] Crossman's diaries reflect a surprised and somewhat irritated discovery that the monarchy could remain so popular; as he pointed out in 1971, if we were 'rational' men, we 'would all like an elected president'.[129] Labour leaders' diaries portray consciences repeatedly under strain. Benn 'left the Palace boiling with indignation' after being sworn in as privy councillor in October 1964.[130] 'This is what I have been dreading' was his response to being invited to a sherry party there in November, and he sent his apologies.[131] 'The Privy Council is the best example of pure mumbo-jumbo you can find,' wrote Crossman in 1966.[132] The ceremony of kissing hands as a privy councillor, wrote Benn in the same year, was 'a little ceremony which we all knew was ridiculous',[133] and in the following year Crossman 'really was dreading' having to hire morning dress for the state opening of parliament.[134]

Another aspect of the social-hierarchical critique of monarchy was concerned less with capitalist exploitation than with the aristocratic privilege that seemed to discourage modernization. This seems to have been the intention behind the famous, though somewhat imprecise, complaint by the playwright John Osborne: that the British monarchy is 'the gold filling in a mouthful of decay'.[135] In the hunt during the 1980s for scapegoats to explain Britain's relative economic decline, monarchy and aristocracy were criticized for fostering backward-looking attitudes. It was noted that monarchs rendered themselves artificially antique by clinging for ceremonial purposes to forms of road transport that others had long since abandoned. It was claimed that monarchy's increasingly elaborate and antique rituals, enhanced by Richard Dimbleby, 'provided a comfortable palliative to the loss of world-power status'.[136] The monarchy, argues Stephen Haseler, 'perpetuates a culture of backwardness in a nation desperately needing to modernise itself', a nation whose difficulties are cultural rather than economic in origin.[137] This branch of the republican argument also carries some conviction. The royal palaces have indeed been prominent in the growth of the nostalgic 'heritage industry', and in its royal wedding number under the headline 'Day of Romance in a Grey World', *The Times* in 1981 thought that 'in a troubled nation smarting from a crown of social and political thorns, it was a day of unbridled romance, colour, and celebration'.[138] The monarchy, with its imperial and military connections and its ceremonial functions, can hardly be said to have discouraged Britain's retention, ultimately unsuccessfully, of expensive overseas commitments and grandiose pretensions.

The third branch of the republican case centres on the discrepancy between the monarchy's cost and its diminished function, and it too has plausibility. We have seen how the decline of monarchies elsewhere and the collapse of Britain's world influence reduced the monarchy's importance in foreign policy and empire, and how the growth of disciplined and articulated parties at home eroded monarchy's domestic role. Edward VIII was forcibly reminded in 1936 of how weak is a modern constitutional monarch who obeys the rules and refrains from appealing directly for public support—an aspect of the crisis for which his autobiography sought some credit. Baldwin, he recalled, 'controlled all the levers of power', and as soon as the King accepted the cabinet's decision not to allow him to broadcast directly to his people, his cause was lost.[139] 'How lonely is a Monarch', he wrote, 'in a struggle with a shrewd Prime Minister backed by all the apparatus of the modern State!'[140] By presenting the electorate with two disciplined parties, each of whose leaders enjoyed a high public profile, the two-party system has subsequently restricted the monarch's constitutional role still further. Macmillan became Prime Minister in 1957 not as a result of Elizabeth II's free choice but because she felt bound to follow the wishes of the Conservative Party. And thereafter, election by MPs replaced the Party's choice of its leader through informal consultation, thus excluding the monarchy altogether. Yet despite this diminished role, the royal family, with expensive recreations and large private houses that bear no relation to its public responsibilities, enjoys what is by modern standards an extravagant life-style, however conscientious individual monarchs may be.

So the republican case remains in theory strong. Yet despite the spread of education and the diffusion of political information, the three branches of the case do not carry much weight with the general public, however many grumbles there may be about individual members of the royal family. The *New Statesman*'s 'anti-jubilee number' of 3 June 1977 was a lighthearted and self-mocking issue, more akin to *Private Eye* than to a strongly felt and serious political manifesto, though the *Times*'s political correspondent Ronald Butt thought he found 'pathetic and spluttering malevolence' in it.[141] Does this lack of republican impact stem from the poor calibre of republican spokesmen? Republicanism has never captured a major political party, and leading republicans have been politically insubstantial. The leading republican of the 1960s, William Hamilton, was a marginal figure whom Crossman (himself no zealot for monarchy) described as 'a curiously egotistical, wayward character, unreliable, publicity-seeking, bloody-minded'.[142] Republicanism tends to wither on the careerist vine when it comes to politicians of republican inclinations but real ability:

Joseph Chamberlain, Dilke, and Benn, for example. Before assuming office in 1880, Dilke was required to write Granville a rather ingratiating little letter, designed for the Queen's eye, making it clear that he repudiated republicanism in the British context.[143] In 1963 Benn declined an invitation to write an article against the monarchy because 'I am vulnerable at the moment and I don't want to be impatient and take on more of the battle than I can manage.'[144] And in the 1980s there was tactical shrewdness in his desire to focus republicans on the monarchy's powers rather than on its personalities,[145] for as soon as Labour criticizes the monarchy in the mildest manner, the Queen's popularity causes Conservatives to leap eagerly into the fray, if only out of self-interest, as Jack Straw found in 1994.[146]

Yet to ascribe republican failure simply to the low calibre of republican spokesmen is to put the cart before the horse. If republicanism had any hope of widespread support, political parties would readily cater for it, and republican careers could then be made. Why does the cause fail to attract abler politicians? Because the three branches of the republican case are not ultimately convincing. The first, 'irrational', argument simultaneously exaggerates the reason behind the process that would produce an elected head of state and the prominence of unreason in a constitutional monarchy. Such a structure seems in practice to strike a nice balance. The unpredictability of its talent is far less damaging than it would be in authoritarian regimes of any type. And the oppressiveness of its continuity is mild by comparison with the alternatives: rule by committee, for example—in the Catholic Church or in Communist regimes.[147] Furthermore, many of heredity's accidents can be corrected by the sustained training for the role, and experience in conducting it, that monarchy's relatively predictable succession makes possible. Whereas the average tenure (sometimes discontinuous) for seventeen twentieth-century prime ministers was five years as at December 1990, the average tenure (continuous) for the five monarchs up to that point was seventeen. If Elizabeth II were to die tomorrow, the average length of reign since 1837 would be twenty-six years.[148]

In 1872 Disraeli pointed out that 'information and experience . . . whether they are possessed by a Sovereign or by the humblest of his subjects, are irresistible in life'.[149] Long life cannot of course guarantee continuously accumulated experience in a single individual, given that old age brings disability. Queen Victoria towards the end of her life was so blind that documents had to be read to her by Princess Beatrice, and her officials feared that her constitutional powers were at risk.[150] But there is a further safeguard: the efficient palace bureaucracy that has grown up to reinforce a sequence of conscientious and industrious monarchs. Prince Albert himself acted as the Queen's private secretary until his death, and thereafter the Queen and her private secretary made themselves into what was in effect 'one of the great Departments of State'.[151] The post of private secretary to the monarch requires great tact. Not only is he 'the sovereign's eyes and ears'; he 'is responsible for interpreting the sovereign to the government and the government to the sovereign'.[152] With the Labour government's advent in 1924, the scope of this machinery was enlarged still further. Labour could not supply enough people to fill the great court posts, and these henceforth became non-political and permanent holders of office, to be joined from the 1960s by media experts. Cautious and conservative the palace officials might be, but Edward VIII took a serious risk in so distancing himself from them in 1936.[153] Harold Wilson soon found after 1964 that for audiences with the Queen he needed to be well briefed.[154]

These safeguards, reinforced by cultural influences and a measure of good luck, have lent considerable professionalism to monarchs since 1837. Queen Victoria combined a strong sense of duty with a grasp of public opinion that sometimes surpassed that of her political leaders. 'The phrase, "my people", with its dependent variations, which appeared so frequently in her public utterances', writes Lady Gwendolen Cecil, 'was, in her eyes, no conventional locution. It represented a real relation of whose responsibility she never ceased to be conscious.'[155] Such attitudes carried on down the line. The Duke of Windsor recalled how his father placed a quotation from an American Quaker on his desk, to remind him not to miss opportunities for acts of kindness. His mother placed 'duty, in the stoic Victorian sense, before everything else in life. From her invincible virtue and correctness she looked out as from a fortress upon the rest of humanity, with all its tremulous uncertainties and distractions.'[156] One newspaper in 1992 thought it 'impossible to think of an occasion when Elizabeth II has made a serious mistake', and 'impossible to think of a time when she has displayed greed or vanity or neglected her duties'.[157] And should the necessary qualities be lacking in any individual monarch, the abdication's outcome illustrates how an individual's defects can be transcended by loyalty to the institution, for the popularity of Edward VIII was readily transferred to his very diffident and relatively introverted successor.

The republican's second, social-hierarchical, argument also seems overdone, if only because some sort of social gradation seems inevitable, and because many other aspects of Britain's social hierarchy seem more oppressive and less justified. Perhaps this is why monarchy's links with exploitation seem unperceived by most of the alleged victims. The early socialists were relatively unconcerned about monarchy. This was partly because the Labour Party's nonconformist background distanced it from the militantly rationalistic mood of nineteenth-century radicalism. The Labour Party drew much of its support from a working class whose traditionalism and patriotism rendered it more monarchist in outlook than the Party's middle-class supporters.[158] Many a late-Victorian family had its matriarch who performed the Queen's role within her humbler circle. For H. G. Wells's mother, Queen Victoria acted as 'compensatory personality, her imaginative consolation for all the restrictions and hardships that her sex, her diminutive size, her motherhood and all the endless difficulties of life, imposed upon her'.[159] Furthermore, the socialist pioneers were preoccupied with economic relationships throughout society, and this sidelined what seemed a rather antique anti-monarchical set of priorities. Their attack on the maldistribution of wealth was by no means specific to wealth that was inherited. 'In theory I am a Republican,' said Snowden in 1907, 'but I attach so little importance to this as a practical question at present that I would not lift my little finger to interfere with the Monarchy.'[160] The jubilee of 1977 was by no means merely an upper- or middle-class function; a *Times* correspondent (echoing reports of what had happened at the coronation of 1937) pointed out that on 6 June 'a sound working rule ... in London was: "the wealthier the street, the less likely it is to have a party" '.[161] Callaghan as Labour Prime Minister during the jubilee celebrations was determined to accept the Queen's invitation to the naval review at Spithead. 'My father had taken me aboard the *Victoria and Albert* when I was a toddler, but I do not suppose it ever crossed his mind that one day his son would be invited to return as the Prime Minister of the United Kingdom.'[162] In this as in so much else, he spoke for Labour's mass following.

Grumbles about the monarchy in the diaries of Labour's cabinet ministers of the 1960s reveal much about the gulf between the more rationalistic among Labour's middle-class leaders and its working-class following. Crossman, after discussing 'the most idiotic flummery' of a privy council meeting in 1965, had the honesty to admit that 'my attitude is partly a piece of conscious arrogance—I want to prove to myself that I don't like these things, although I sometimes find myself mildly enjoying them'.[163] In 1969 he confessed that the cabinet's working-class members were less inhibited; they were happy to participate in 'all the flummery' of the Prince of Wales's investiture, whereas he, Castle, Jenkins, and Crosland kept away.[164] When she attended such functions, Castle always felt the need to justify doing so, either in terms of her husband's needs and tastes or through preening herself that she felt no intellectual snobbery about such matters. 'I love sweeping up the grand staircase at Buckingham Palace', she wrote in 1969, 'between the lines of immobile flunkeys, grinning at the thought that they are probably secret members of the Labour Party, grumbling under their breaths about their working conditions.'[165]

Although a substantial number of Labour MPs voted against a royal pay-rise in 1971 and 1975, Benn when powerful in his Party never thought it worth pushing his attack on the hereditary principle to the ultimate. An opinion poll in 1978 showed that 97 per cent of the sample thought the Queen did a good job, and even in 1994 only a fifth of the population when sampled said they were republicans.[166] One remaining escape-route for the republican is to explain the British monarchy's continuing polarity in terms of deception. Yet this analysis was implausible even in the 1860s, for the 'deception' took effect at higher levels in society than Bagehot allowed—so much so, that it is perhaps better to speak of the monarchy's perceived utility at the time.[167] Political explanation cast in terms of false consciousness always verges on the patronizing, and is certainly unhelpful here. Extended education, information gained from the media, and long experience of voting make it unnecessary for government now to be rendered 'intelligible' in Bagehot's sense and by Bagehot's means. Laski might claim in 1938 that 'the Monarchy, to put it bluntly, has been sold to the democracy as the symbol of itself',[168] but what is striking is the eagerness of the purchaser.

The attempt to link monarchy with anti-modernizing forces also lacks force. Not only does it ignore the speed with which 'modernization' has in fact occurred in many areas of twentieth-century British life. It also manufactures too close a correlation between monarchy's antique aspects and the nation's decline. In 1821, when Britain was the world's pioneer in industrialism, medievalism pervaded George IV's coronation, with the King's Champion in full armour riding a white charger borrowed from Astley's circus and capering beneath a specially erected Gothic triumphal arch.[169] In 1937, well before national decline had moulded national attitudes, Mass Observation pointed out that coronations tend to call forth 'obsolete or unusual language'.[170] In reality, the heritage industry stems not from national decline but from the mass leisure and affluence that are nourished by national prosperity. A nostalgic preoccupation with the past attracts hordes of tourists in all modern industrial societies, in republics as much as in monarchies, and seems to tap needs that run deeper than sentimentality or self-indulgence. Furthermore, whereas hostility to modernization comes from many areas of British society, the British monarchy's energies have by no means been directed solely at nostalgia. Ventures such as the Duke of Edinburgh's award scheme, his work for conservation, his daughter's work for the Save the Children Fund, and the Queen's awards to industry can hardly be seen as backward-looking. Indeed, Wilson took a wry pleasure in the fact that the idea for awards to industry came in 1965 from a politician who then saw himself as an arch-modernizer: Tony Benn, who himself bracketed trade unions, the civil service, and the Conservative Party with the monarchy in his list of conservative influences in Britain at the time.[171]

The republican's third argument, which stresses the monarchy's cost in relation to its loss of formal role, can be turned against its proponents, for the advantages of a republic over a monarchy have always been difficult to detect once monarchs ceased to be absolute. As Crossman pointed out in 1971, 'because we are not rational but emotional creatures it is good for us to have something we can look up to, to admire and respect, and it is safer to have it impotent'.[172] Nor does this third branch of the republican case allow for the way informal roles rush in to fill the void left by the retreat of the formal, thereby making 'a family on the throne' seem worth the price. Republicans do not feel much responsibility for indicating who will effectively fill some of the roles monarchy performs, for by no means all of them are redundant. The demand for non-partisan public figures who can lend dignity to formal occasions, for example, is enhanced, rather than diminished, by aristocracy's decline. As for the cost of monarchy, that can be (and is being) adjusted without any necessary threat to the institution.

There is a negative tone about the republican argument that ultimately fails to appeal. A republic is 'a lesser evil rather than a preferred alternative', and republican zeal is not normally the reason why monarchies are toppled.[173] 'It is unlikely that his book will make many converts,' wrote John Grigg (himself no idolater of monarchy) of William Hamilton's book *My Queen and I*: 'Mr Hamilton has virtually nothing to say about the positive advantages of a republic; his argument is essentially destructive.'[174] Because the critics lack influence, closely reasoned defence has no more been required for monarchy than for the simple-majority electoral system. 'The serious arguments for monarchy all resolve themselves into this,' said Frederic Harrison, '—that it is there.'[175] This is not to say that no formal defence of monarchy can be mounted, or that there is no substance behind the monarchist's inarticulate loyalties. Monarchy survives largely because since Bagehot's day it has brought tangible practical benefits. These include the stabilizing emphasis on continuity that it can offer a nation whose international status is in marked decline, and whose social structure is in the process of continuous and bewildering change. Perhaps this function assists objectives of which even Benn would approve. Authoritarian responses to Britain's diminished world status are perhaps best warded off if the nation is symbolized by a non-political figure, and if national decline is not too brutally advertised. 'From the chaos of the world around them', it has been said of George V's popularity, 'the nation turned with increasing devotion to the one stable institution in their midst.'[176] The British monarchy seems to win either way: profiting from the nineteenth century's enhancement of British national power, yet also from its twentieth-century decline.

In this chapter we have seen how in Queen Victoria's early years the monarchy helped to integrate the newly self-conscious middle class into the established order, and both adopted and advanced its moralistic values. From the 1870s to the First World War it performed the roles that empire seemed to require. From then until the 1950s it adapted again to cater for the ceremonial traditionalism that provided the nation with reassurance and continuity in a world that was becoming less congenial. After the Second World War the monarchy changed again, this time accommodating itself (despite the personal inclinations of individual monarchs) to the modest instalment of socialism and egalitarianism that the Attlee government entailed. Egalitarianism British-style might require the abolition of the debutante, but never equality in Scandinavian measure. In recent writing about the British monarchy there has been a tendency towards 'unmasking': towards demonstrating in a knowingly sarcastic tone how the monarchy has assumed new guises over the years. The implication is that the author, at least, has not been taken in by its pretensions to continuity or by the alleged antiquity of its traditions. It is strange that anybody should be surprised by such discontinuities and disguises, or see them as doing anything other than illuminate the monarchy's flexibility as an institution. Even in Bagehot's day the mysticism and magic were seen by intelligent observers as instrumental and not as the reality. It is one of the British political system's many paradoxes that this ancient institution, with the hereditary principle at its heart, should have shown itself since the 1860s to be at least as flexible an instrument as any so far discussed.

# 13

# *The British Political System*
# *in the 1990s*

THIS book began by showing how the British political system worked when Bagehot wrote his *English Constitution*. It then explained the formidable challenges to that system presented by the growth of empire and social welfare, and showed how the United Kingdom survived as a political entity, though eventually without southern Ireland. In Chapters 4 to 12 it went on to survey how the system evolved in each of its dimensions. These chapters showed how gradually, pragmatically, unobtrusively, and to a large extent effectively British political institutions adapted in the face of formidable challenges. Adaptation has been a response more to social and technological change than to any pressure from the politicians. Few of the adaptations were planned, and planned adaptations owed more to party interest than to any pursuit of improvement for its own sake. Peaceful evolution of this kind can occur more readily in a flexible structure that is not tied down by formal bodies with statutory functions or by written documents around whose interpretation lawyers foregather. These piecemeal changes interacted to produce the political system we now know, and whose essential features do not require elaboration here. The piecemeal process of adaptation continues. British pressure groups and political parties, ever pursuing public support, harness the latest methods of communication, only to find that these have important structural and tactical implications. Reform of constituency boundaries is a continuous procedure and reform of local-government boundaries has in recent years been if anything too frequent. Parliament is experimenting with a modified timetable, and is still elaborating a committee system that is only fifteen years old. Government in the 1990s is abandoning secrecy in striking ways, and is decentralizing control within its civil service to a remarkable extent. Even the monarchy has initiated significant changes in its funding arrangements.

Yet it was symptomatic of the nation's loss of self-confidence by the 1990s that the system was more frequently condemned for failing to change its outward forms than it was praised for its unobtrusive flexibility. The overall balance of public comment seemed to attach little value to the political continuity and stability which the system had helped to secure over so long and changeful a period. This flexible system, once widely admired at home and abroad, has lost prestige since the 1950s and has become controversial even between the political parties. Proposals for constitutional reform raise large theoretical and practical questions of cost, complexity, and implementation. With these this chapter does not grapple. Its aims are more limited: to complement Chapter 1 by outlining some of the constitutional issues now under discussion. The aim is not to criticize them, but to emphasize their range and diversity, and to re-emphasize a theme that has run through earlier chapters: the uncertainty about the immediate future with which politicians must continuously grapple. It will not be clear for some time in what direction the British political system is evolving in the 1990s, and only then will the direction it has taken come to seem inevitable. For it is as true now as it was when Bagehot wrote the preface to the second edition of his *English Constitution* that a 'living' constitution is portrayed at any one moment only with difficulty: 'a contemporary writer who tries to paint what is before him is puzzled and perplexed; what he sees is changing daily'.[1]

Given the strength of pressure for constitutional reform by the late 1980s, some Conservatives thought it necessary to mobilize resistance. John Patten was early in the field. 'We . . . reject the grand theoretical design,' he declared in 1991. 'Instead, we concentrate on improving the present and on tackling proven abuses.'[2] Two years later he stressed that 'we British have a knack of not trying to fix that which is not broken'.[3] He light-heartedly dismissed the reformers, while claiming for his Party an alert recognition of the need for piecemeal improvement: franchise extension from 1867 onwards, for example, life peerages in 1958, a reformed committee system in 1979. Conservative pamphlets and lectures from Kenneth Minogue, Philip Norton, and Nevil Johnson reinforced the position. Minogue in a swashbuckling performance treated the new-found enthusiasm for reform as a sort of illness: 'constitutional mania', which involved a strange enthusiasm for the political institutions of the foreigner. He also dwelt upon contradictions not only within the reforming case (simultaneously rendering government more democratic and then clipping its wings with bills of rights, for example[4]), but also between reforming organizations. More cautiously and therefore more impressively, Philip Norton contested reformers' claims to have won the debate, for, he wrote, 'there has been no sustained debate'.[5] The constitution's defenders had hardly yet entered the field, but their case was no less powerful for that. He pointed out that not only did organizations like Charter 88 have nothing to say on important questions—on Northern Ireland, for instance, or on the implications of their reforms for the operation of parliament. They also failed to think through how their specific reforms would interact, and so had no vision of how the new written constitution would operate.[6] Above all, the reformers failed to grasp the interaction between a constitution and the 'values and attitudes that are embedded in the minds and instincts of the governors and the governed'. British governments are constrained by checks and balances, says Norton, but these are not all cramped in their operation by formal documents, and 'are not confined to bodies that enjoy political muscle'.[7] Most Conservatives, however, have confined themselves to resistance in specific areas, as we shall see from following through reforming proposals in each of the ten dimensions of the political system to which Chapters 3 to 12 were assigned.

*

In their rather direct strategy for holding the United Kingdom together, the Conservatives since 1979 have been anything but reformers. As we saw in Chapter 3, Thatcher terminated the Party's dalliance with devolution. Conservative objections to it have partly been practical. In July 1991, for instance, John Patten claimed that Labour's plans for regional assemblies would convert the United Kingdom into the most over-governed, over-taxed, and over-administered of nations.[8] He also questioned whether regional assemblies would attract much support if their costs were fully spelt out. Local government, he pointed out, 'is strongest when it is closest to the people it serves', and 'if we really want to devolve powers then we should remove, not add to, existing layers of bureaucracy'.[9] But the main thrust of Conservative resistance is emotional and traditionalist, founded on recognizing the benefits for the United Kingdom as a whole of economic and cultural inter-fertilization and enhanced international influence. It rests on a semi-articulated supra-nationalism that transcends the smaller nationalisms of ethnic and cultural loyalty. John Major's vigorous defence of the union—'nearly 300 years of success together'[10]—seems to have been a turning-point in the general election of 1992. He admitted that 'no nation can be held irrevocably in a union against its will' and that 'we can do it. We can break up the United Kingdom.'[11] But for him the choice was 'between the Conservative Party, which would stand up for Britain, and the Labour and Liberal parties, which could break up Britain if they follow the policies they are discussing'. At his last big rally before the election he reserved his strongest language for this 'sleeping issue'. Urging his fellow countrymen to 'wake up now, before it is too late', he claimed that 'the United Kingdom is in danger', and on his first visit to Scotland after the election he claimed that devolution is 'a half-way step across a chasm'.[12] Major's strategy at the end of 1995 still seemed directed primarily at undermining the case for Labour's devolution plans: that is, by giving Scottish local authorities more autonomy and by increasing the powers of the Scottish and Welsh grand committees.[13]

For Major, devolution would not improve relations between England, Scotland, and Wales, but worsen them, setting 'Scot against Scot, Scot against Briton in other parts of the United Kingdom'.[14] Yet the wavering stance of his Party before 1979 shows that this is far from being the only possible Conservative strategy for dealing with nationalism, whose cross-class local loyalties can readily be seen as 'wholly natural and fully conservative'. For Ian Gilmour in 1976 'there is nothing unconservative in the diffusion of power . . . it is very much Conservative doctrine that the diversity within the state is to be encouraged and that centralization should be diminished'.[15] It was indeed strange that a party drawing so deeply on a sense of nationality south of the border should discourage any such sense north of it.[16] So, although there are as yet few signs of it at the highest level, Conservative devolutionism may well re-emerge. This would have the double advantage of enabling Scottish Conservatives to poach on nationalist preserves, and of opening up a subtler way to preserve the union. For to combine concession (thereby breaking up nationalist opinion) with co-option into the horizon-lowering, practical business of government was a tactic that in franchise reform was long applied in Britain with success by the Whigs. The Fabians later applied it successfully in the labour movement through encouraging participation in local government. Whigs and Conservatives applied it to the empire in the form of devolution. There is of course a gamble involved. If devolution were to exacerbate Anglo-Welsh and Anglo-Scottish relations, it would be impossible to go back, and some sort of federal or even fragmented future for the United Kingdom would be inevitable. For not even the keenest enthusiast for the union with Scotland and Wales believes that it can be preserved in any way other than through consent.

Liberals have been more consistently enthusiastic for devolution because the Liberal wariness of governmental power combines with a genuine belief in local self-government and a party interest in pleasing the localities where it is strong. For Labour, devolution is more problematic. A local government that is subordinate to central government and acts as vehicle for its good intentions is of course well rooted in Labour's Fabian traditions. Less congenial to Labour are structures that are more or less federal, involving regional assemblies. While devolution of this kind may realize Labour's egalitarian ideal at the political level, it obstructs it at other levels by hindering central planning and economic equality. On the other hand, a commitment to regional assemblies might consolidate Labour's hold on Scotland and Wales and undermine nationalist rivals. Not surprisingly, during the 1980s a Party seriously threatened in its non-English heartland showed much interest in the early non-statist variants of socialism which had eventually succumbed before the statist variant of the 1940s, and gave a renewed attention to the socialist values of 'fraternity' and 'community'.[17] But even if Labour decides it is worth sacrificing the considerable amount of legislative time that devolution would require, especially in its first year of office, there will be little enthusiasm from constituency activists for an objective so tangential to the Party's main purposes and traditions.

Unlike Wales and Scotland, Northern Ireland once enjoyed local self-government within the United Kingdom. But when it failed to gain consensus support within a deeply divided community, the mainland government felt obliged to terminate it. Northern Ireland's political violence also singles it out. When British troops went to Northern Ireland in 1969, Wilson predicted that 'they're going to be there for seven years at least'. The Catholics first welcomed them as protectors, but Crossman presciently feared that once Catholics and Protestants grew accustomed to the troops' presence 'they will hate us more than they hate each other', and wondered whether the United Nations could be usefully involved.[18] By September 1994 'the troubles' had produced about 3,168 killed in Northern Ireland and 237 elsewhere, together with many thousands more injured, some maimed for life, not to mention the imprisonments and all the loss of liberty and dignity involved in fear and intimidation. The economic cost to Ireland north and south in lost tourism and trade was enormous, and was compounded by the security costs and compensation that taxpayers had to fund.[19] Television pictures of misery in the former Yugoslavia in the early 1990s conjured up fears that something even worse might be in the offing. Implicitly drawing the parallel in December 1992, when discussing demands that British troops should withdraw from Northern Ireland, Sir Patrick Mayhew pointed out as Secretary of State for Northern Ireland that 'properly understood, "Brits out" means the ethnic cleansing of a million human beings'.[20]

Until the unexpected IRA ceasefire of 1994 the only 'political solution' that seemed possible was the stalemate involved in direct rule, which at least gave something to both sides: to the Protestants, security from Dublin's rule; to the Catholics, security from Protestant rule. It was far from being an ideal outcome, if only because for diplomatic reasons it could be acquiesced in only as a matter of fact and not openly embraced with enthusiasm. But, short of a determination on both sides of the border to make counter-terrorism as effective as in some European countries, direct rule seemed the least bad of the options available. In 1972 direct rule did at least help to reduce levels of violence; it subsequently helped to stave off violence of much worse kinds. The Anglo-Irish agreement of 1985 and the Anglo-Irish declaration of 1993 did not embody any retreat from commitment to the union by Thatcher or Major, both of whom are personally firm unionists. Their purpose was simply to make it clear that peace in Ireland could come only through consent, and to harness the Irish Republic behind resistance to any coercive approach. The secret communications between the IRA and British government during 1993, unexpectedly publicized in November, show that the British government was saying in private what it had long been saying in public. Its policy (confirmed by the Anglo-Irish declaration in the following month) required firm, if unannounced, evidence of an end to terrorism as the pre-condition for talks; and talks without pre-condition as to the outcome, provided that a settlement emerged through consensus rather than coercion.[21]

But what of the declaration's assertion in 1993 that the British government 'have no selfish strategic or economic interest in Northern Ireland'? That 'it is for the people of the island of Ireland alone, by agreement between the two parts respectively, to exercise their right of self-determination on the basis of consent, freely and concurrently given, North and South, to bring about a united Ireland, if that is their wish'? And that 'the role of the British Government will be to encourage, facilitate and enable the achievement of . . . agreement . . . through a process of dialogue and co-operation based on full respect for the rights and identities of both traditions in Ireland'? For some, this is the British government showing a culpable even-handedness: abdicating responsibility, and retreating from the union in the face of violent intimidation. It has even prompted the suggestion that the Scots and Welsh would have got further if they too had espoused violence.[22] Such suspicions and suggestions are surely melodramatic. The agreement had the admirable result of enabling the IRA to back down from its self-created impasse without making any concession of substance. Respect for 'both traditions' in Northern Ireland can hardly give the republicans all that they seek; still less would any such concession be endorsed by the necessary referendum in Northern, and possibly even in southern, Ireland. It is simply a statement of fact (which needs no spelling out in Wales and Scotland) that no democratic society can or would wish to impose a political regime on people who clearly repudiate it. By removing the terrorist obstacle to progress, the cease-fire removed the Ulster Unionists' excuse for being narrowly defensive and unconstructive. So the opportunity for peace lay precariously open.

Yet the IRA decision to de-escalate violence in 1994 could prove as ephemeral as its earlier cease-fires of 1939 and the late 1950s. There could, at the least, be a republican split, with terrorism resuming from a fraction—though that would, together with the cease-fire itself, constitute a gain. But what is certain is that neither republican nor Ulster Unionist can win all that they desire, for their positions are incompatible and each has in practice a veto on the other. 'As with all the other colonial situations we have been in,' said Ken Livingstone in November 1987, 'eventually Britain will go.'[23] His 'political solution', which could be dismissed as naïve if it had not dangerously encouraged so many false hopes, can only be set beside Powell's entirely unrealistic 'solution' put forward thirteen years earlier: Northern Ireland's full integration with the mainland. 'The political remedy', he said, 'is to remove the ambiguity of the past and make it clear by deeds ... that the Union is beyond the reach of violence, however brutal, however persistent.'[24] In the long term, both positions seem likely to be transcended. The nationalist dream of a complete break between a united Ireland and the mainland runs not only against the integrating tendency of the European Union, but also against the still more powerful integrating and world-wide tendency of modern communications, even though there is as yet no Irish equivalent of the Channel tunnel. Despite all the mythology, southern Ireland's independence did little to erode Anglo-Irish interdependence. By the mid-1960s half the Republic's homes had television sets, and more than a third of those could receive mainland as well as Irish programmes.[25] Statistics for travel movements, telephone calls, and freight traffic show that contacts with the mainland in 1974–5 were as great (population allowed for) from the Republic as from Northern Ireland.[26] Given the impact of such powerful integrating influences on the individual, it is difficult to see how in the longer term, and in the absence of revived terrorism, the old hatreds can be perpetuated indefinitely by the politicians.

\*

In local government the Conservatives have shown some interest in constitutional reform, though mainly only as a by-product of trying to solve problems elsewhere. The Thatcher governments' reforms (discussed in

Chapter 4) cut local-government employment from 2,480,000 in 1979 to 2,100,000 in 1994, overwhelmingly through shedding male manual labour.[27] But Thatcher's reforms were left incomplete, even truncated, and their long-term effect is as yet unclear. Yet if anything, Conservative enthusiasm for local-government reform for its own sake increased after Thatcher's departure. The Conservatives do favour devolution, but in a form more practical and down-to-earth than any Liberal or nationalist favoured. It involved operating at much lower levels and creating smaller units—privatized concerns, opted-out schools, trust hospitals—in which more power could be wielded by customers, parents, and employees, each simultaneously enhancing efficiency and choice. The constraints of national wage agreements, incomes policies, and domination by local authorities and public-sector trade unions were cast aside. Predicting 'another colossal row with the educational establishment' when power was shifted from local authorities to parents, Major in his Party conference speech of 1992 thought it 'a row worth having. A row where we will have the vast majority of parents . . . squarely on our side'.[28]

For John Stewart, these changes involved a partial reversion to the unelected local structures that had prevailed before 1888. 'A new magistracy is being created', he warned, 'in the sense that a non-elected elite are assuming responsibility for a large part of local governance.'[29] In countering such claims, William Waldegrave thought the key point 'not whether those who run our public services are elected, but whether they are producer-responsive or consumer-responsive. Services are not necessarily made to respond to the public simply by giving citizens a democratic voice . . . in their make-up.'[30] Major viewed central government as the agency for ensuring responsiveness by state structures to the consumer, whose choice was reinforced with more information on educational and welfare facilities and rights. This seemed to procure an accountability far more practical and effective than any generalized, and in practice unreal, ministerial responsibility to parliament. 'Which is more genuinely accountable to the public,' Thatcher had asked in 1983, '—a private firm which has to satisfy its customers or the nationalized monopolies where it sometimes seems that the customers have to satisfy the demands of the producers?'[31] Nonetheless, some critics remained concerned about the alleged 'democratic deficit' at the local level, and worried about the imperfections of the so-called 'market' established in areas of public responsibility.

There were hesitant experiments, too, under Major in reforming the administration of local authorities. 'Too many councillors spend too much time achieving too little,' said Heseltine in March 1991. Reduced or better-paid committee work for councillors and enhanced opportunities for achievement in local government seemed the way to attract talent for city government on a Victorian scale.[32] Such policies tied in naturally with the idea of 'the enabling council', which should not itself carry out many services, but should get them contracted out. Nothing came of Heseltine's scheme for elected mayors (an idea which Peter Walker had also favoured in the 1970s),[33] but in 1993 the government tentatively floated the idea of extending cabinet-style government to local government authorities through small groups of relatively well-paid 'cabinet' councillors selected by the leaders of the largest party. With stronger executive direction from the elected authority, fewer permanent officials would be needed.[34] The most substantial change in local government under the Major governments, however, seems likely to be reform of local-government boundaries. The reform is not at all as ambitious as the government would originally have liked. Like the poll tax, the idea of orientating local government round single-tier authorities, attracted Conservative governments because it offered some hope of improving the voters' understanding of how their money was being spent, and was implemented in Scotland and Wales in full. But a much more variegated picture emerged in England as a result of discovering how indifferent the public were to any ambitious reform. Working in the same direction were electoral considerations, changes of minister, in-fighting between the bodies representing the different types of local authority, together with pressure from Sir John Banham (chairman of the Local Government Commission), and from interested parties among professional organizations.

In local government, more than in any other area of British government in the early 1990s, there remains a strong sense of unfinished business, even of long-term institutional failure. London's County Hall, that grand monument to municipal vitality now absurdly consigned to the role of hotel which never opens, confronts Conservative governments as a standing reproach. Before 1914 local government's vitality was nourished by long-standing national and local traditions and loyalties, buttressed by widespread participation in religious institutions, and by a relatively lively commitment through party politics to the public life as distinct from the private. Long-distance communication, then relatively expensive and slow, focused ambitions and ideals more firmly on the localities. All these influences have waned in the twentieth century, at the same time as central-government intervention and funding have spread. Yet promising suggestions for reviving participation in local government tend unobtrusively to fail. For example, Labour councillors at Coventry in August 1981 launched a referendum to discover whether ratepayers would vote for higher rates to preserve the services threatened by cuts in the government grant. They were heavily defeated, and Heseltine spoke of using such referenda to help curb excessive rate rises, yet in December a scheme to that effect was withdrawn.[35] Somehow local-government reform comes low among the priorities of governments whether Labour or Conservative, and the poll tax fiasco is hardly likely to change matters.

*

Rights and liberties in the early 1990s seemed beset by contradictory tendencies. On the one hand, the judges' standing seemed to rise in parallel with the politicians' decline, especially when Lord Chief Justice Taylor set out to communicate more directly with the public on succeeding Lord Lane in 1992.[36] On the other hand, the sequence of recent serious miscarriages of justice (most notably the so-called 'Cardiff three', the 'Maguire seven', the 'Birmingham six', the 'Guildford four') prompted much pressure for reforms in the legal system.[37] Uncertainty also stemmed from change in science and technology. Information technology has already evoked legislation on data protection, and new methods and attitudes in the mass media have led governments to contemplate legislation in defence of privacy.[38] Doctors' newly won capacity to prolong life soon after birth and shortly before death raises very difficult libertarian and humanitarian issues, most notably and tragically with the Hillsborough casualty Anthony Bland in 1993. He was kept artificially alive for more than three years, yet with no hope of recovery, and *Airedale NHS Trust* v. *Bland* made it possible for his life-support system to be switched off. Also important are libertarian issues arising from the patient's relationship with the doctor. As Secretary of State responsible for hospitals, Crossman brooded over their power structure in 1968: 'the patient is completely unrepresented and the public completely excluded. It is all controlled by the doctors and the men who work with them, the Chairmen of the boards of governors, professional men, remote, detached, confident and absolutely undemocratic.'[39] Much has been done since the 1960s to change this situation.

Issues far more traditional in the area of rights and liberties continued to thrust themselves forward at the political level. For Thatcher and Major, 'negative' liberty took priority over 'positive'. They were encouraged in this by revelations about liberty's absence in the Soviet Union—for all its written constitutions, and for all its attachment to liberty of the 'positive' variety. They sought to strengthen the individual against the state by separating political from economic power. The 'Citizen's Charter' idea acknowledged that government will continue to provide many services, but sought to set up equivalents of the profit incentive which encouraged the commercial provider to care for his customers: refunds to passengers when trains failed to arrive on time, penalties to hospitals when waiting-lists were too long, and so on.[40] By July 1991 the Cabinet Office had machinery in place, headed by Sir James Blyth (chief executive of Boots PLC) to enforce the Charter. Thereafter charters spread into many areas of British life, culminating in the updated parent's charter, which outlined the parent's educational rights and duties and was sent to every home in 1994. In all this Major was usefully repackaging and drawing out the implications of Thatcherism. Neither he nor Thatcher have had any truck with bills of rights. Here populist Conservatives could tap into widespread suspicion of the legal profession. As Waldegrave put it, noting that slavery was both promoted and abolished within the same American constitution, 'smart lawyers can do almost anything with written constitutions'.[41] In some areas, however, Major's libertarian concerns have moved into new territory, not just in his significant moves towards open government, but also in championing civil liberties overseas. Thatcher had long been championing freedom against totalitarianism in general terms, and in August 1990 moved forward to specific proposals for safeguarding liberty on an international basis, suggesting that basic rights be entrenched through a European magna carta.[42] In September the following year Major publicly championed civil rights during his visit to China, and in October urged the Commonwealth to assume a new identity as standard-bearer for 'a responsive democratic culture'.[43] Four years later he demonstrated that this was more than mere talk when he joined with the rest of the Commonwealth in suspending Nigeria, under its undemocratic government, from continued membership.

A bill of rights, complemented by devolution and electoral reform, became almost an orthodoxy from the late 1980s among Liberal and Labour critics of Conservatism who, after three consecutive Conservative electoral victories, were seeking some new way of putting Conservatives on the defensive. Such critics found their ablest champion in Lord Scarman. Arguing in 1992 for a bill of rights, he pointed out that the British political system had once possessed a mechanism of checks and balances, given that the constitutional settlement of 1688–9 had distributed power between crown, Lords, and Commons. But with increasingly democratic elections, organized by the rival parties of government and opposition, the mechanism had, he thought, been 'capsized', leaving the requirement for periodic general elections as the sole remaining check on the Commons.[44] Eager to capture the ground occupied by the Liberal Democrats, whose libertarian pedigree reached far back into their Whig ancestry, Labour under Kinnock began to abandon the statist variant of socialism that had been the Party's dominant trend for fifty years. From the late 1980s onwards Labour also aimed to capitalize upon the enthusiasm for constitutional reform that Thatcher's centralism had evoked. Reinforcement came from the Party's new-found Europeanism. The Party could advertise its sincerity in that area by showing enthusiasm for political institutions that were more prevalent in Europe than among Britain's traditional American and Commonwealth allies. An untrammelled authority for an interventionist government within a unitary state had suited socialist planners eager to redistribute wealth more equitably between the regions. A Labour opposition less statist in aspiration could afford to think differently.

By June 1991 Roy Hattersley, who had hitherto firmly opposed bills of rights, could claim to find such ideas 'increasingly attractive',[45] though he still thought such a bill would cause the judges unduly to encroach on parliamentary sovereignty. At the general election in 1992, Labour committed itself to specific bills defending particular rights, complemented by a charter of rights. In 1993 John Smith went further, and became the first Labour leader to back a bill of rights, claiming that he wanted to see 'a fundamental shift in the balance of power between the people and the state'. Labour's bill would incorporate the European Convention on Human Rights into British law, and the Act would be monitored by an independent Human Rights Commission. Lord Plant argued in 1978 that the most important function of a bill of rights 'would be the benefit derived from it as a course of public education in the values of a democratic society.[46] But there was a risk that any such bill would mislead the general public on where the safeguards for democracy in Britain really lay. Smith was determined to maintain parliamentary sovereignty, and defended his proposal for a ministry of justice by arguing that 'the task of judges is to interpret the law, not make it'. He claimed that 'democracy demands that fundamental rights protecting citizens' freedoms should be decided by parliament and not by the judges', who are not elected.[47]

Religion, which to many seemed the greatest threat to liberty in Bagehot's day, has long retreated from the centre of the libertarian stage. Even in the 1930s the fear of competition from commercial radio prevented Reith from getting very far with a BBC Sabbath,[48] and what we now call multiculturalism has proceeded so far as to render disestablishment of the Church of England a mere tidying-up operation, congenial even to many Anglicans. Yet with multiculturalism come religious minorities of unaccustomed fervour, some of which revive very old libertarian issues. Against the puppet caricature of Jesus in the television programme *Spitting Image*, it was Muslim rather than Christian protest that proved effective,[49] and it was offence given by his writings to Muslim beliefs that placed Salman Rushdie's life at risk. On the other hand, the rights of these religious minorities seemed, to Lord Scarman in 1978, one further justification for a bill of rights, which would give the judges guide-lines on the new problems thus presented. Common law, he pointed out in 1978, has 'never succeeded in tackling the problem of the alien . . . the woman and . . . religious minorities'.[50]

*

British voluntarism in the 1990s was as vibrant as ever, as the political salience of constitutional reform itself illustrates. Gay liberation publicized the continued vitality of the older techniques of pressure, for the procession now advertises the number of homosexuals as usefully as it advertised the number of teetotalers in the 1830s. 'It may be a celebration', said one participant in Gay Pride's demonstration of 1995, 'but the simple act of being here is a political statement'.[51] Furthermore, the new electronic media, often seen as threats to 'civil society', in reality furnish it with new opportunities. We saw in Chapter 6 how central to the pressure group's role are collecting and diffusing ideas. By the early 1990s, computer-based networks seemed likely to transcend the long-standing conflict between the public and the private life, for new links between home-based people and public causes seemed likely at last to realize Mill's dream that electoral opinion groups could be mobilized on a nation-wide basis. Domesticity now had the potential for reinforcing rather than eroding community action and the cause group.

Perhaps the most vivid testimony to voluntarist vitality in the 1980s, however, appears in Ruth Finnegan's book *The Hidden Musicians* (1989). This remarkable analysis of music-making in Milton Keynes shows each citizen selecting a personal combination of 'pathways' through the community. The musical pathway leads to the numerous rehearsals, festivals, concerts and competitions that are mounted in local schools, clubs, homes, churches and pubs. Self-organized and often self-sacrificing, the music-makers cultivate in their brass bands, their choirs and their pop groups entrepreneurial skills that are driven by values often distant from the commercial. Individuality and creativity are nurtured at least as vigorously in the rock group's gig as in the classical concert. And the new technology, far from threatening this susurration of self-help, offers new aids and supports. Cassette records enable the novice to sharpen technique, computers enable secretaries to drum up support from an ever-widening circle, microphones and amplifiers boost the profits of local music shops, and sophisticated recording equipment ensures that freelance studios preserve the best of the amateur performances for posterity. Despite their overtly cultural preoccupations, the music-makers of Milton Keynes fuel the political process in three important ways. First, they create and manage structures that are complementary or even antithetical to the better-known and more formal hierarchies, thereby training themselves in the give-and-take that lies at the heart of politics. Secondly, in their grouping, overlapping and re-grouping, they set up a rich complex of committees, publications and networks that draw together the social classes, the age-groups and the sexes. And thirdly, in edging reticent people on to the public stage, they introduce amateur to professional, local enthusiast to national maestro, thereby diffusing self-confidence more widely. Such talent—reinforced from similar self-created structures in sport, charity, hobbies, trade unions, commercial ventures, and the professions—then becomes available to those who need it for wider local and national public and political purposes. From such ingredients over the centuries has the United Kingdom's 'civil society' been composed.

At the national level, Chapter 8 showed how willing the political parties were during the 1980s to apply new techniques towards raising funds, mobilizing support and gathering new ideas. But for Lord Scarman in 1992, a bill of rights was needed 'if defenceless and grossly under-represented groups are to have their human rights and their freedoms safeguarded'.[52] He was running behind the times, for he underestimated parliament's capacity for upholding liberty through acting as arena for an opposition party which is adept at articulating sentiments widely held in the country at large. Thatcher's departure had by then loosened up the relationship between pressure group and political party. The changed parliamentary mood after 1990 and the changed party situation at Westminster after 1992 compelled Major to exercise the politician's co-ordinating and reconciling skills more overtly than Thatcher had thought necessary. So the private or public inquiry, launched from outside government—into education, local government, the electoral system, criminal law, and the welfare structure, for example—made something of a come-back after 1990. And it was seen as significant during Major's first month in office that the government abandoned the position Thatcher had taken up only a month before, and agreed to pay a further £42,000,000 to haemophiliacs infected with the AIDS virus through contaminated health-service products.[53] Major's position on liberties abroad responded to the concerns of Amnesty International in the same way as his retreat from government secrecy appeased the Campaign for Freedom of Information.

As Prime Minister, Major was conciliatory by temperament but also by circumstance. After a divisive succession, it was not easy to hold his Party together in the run-up to a general election, and after that election his tactics inevitably reflected his small majority and Labour's new vitality. The 1990s witnessed splits within and among the right-wing think-tanks in attitudes to Europe and to Major himself, for his strategy and temperament revealed him as less uniformly Thatcherite than his backers had supposed. He could not afford to show his predecessor's contempt for organized opinion, nor could he rely so exclusively on the pressure groups, think-tanks, and partisan inquiries that had fuelled Thatcherism. The poll-tax fiasco had driven home at least two lessons: that bright new ideas from right-wing think-tanks needed to be viewed cautiously, and that 'market testing' should apply as much to legislation as to the functions of government. A recurring theme in the history of the poll-tax during the 1980s is the failure adequately to consider its likely impact on opinion, the failure to operate pilot schemes and exploit opinion-poll techniques.[54] Yet the political agenda in domestic policy was still being driven from the right, and on the trade unions Major beat no retreat from Thatcher; it was from the TUC's new General Secretary, John Monks, that the policy shift emerged. His structural reforms and public statements early in 1994 highlighted a contraction in the range of policy that trade unions now sought to influence. This made it possible in the same year for David Hunt, the Employment Secretary, to become the first Conservative cabinet minister to address the TUC for decades. Overtures to Sir Ian McKellen as spokesman for homosexual rights apparently produced no advance on the earlier reform of civil-service vetting rules in homosexuals' favour.[55] And under Major as under Thatcher, relations with the professions—teachers, doctors, civil servants, scientists, lawyers, the armed services—were strained by a radical government's continued assaults on traditional practices.

Whereas the Conservatives after 1990 became somewhat more receptive to organized opinion, Labour increasingly distanced itself from what had until recently been the most powerful pressure group of all: the trade-union movement. In January 1984 Hattersley pointed out that trade unions 'are going to be a diminishing force in British political and industrial life'; the Labour Party could not in future rely so heavily upon them. At the Party conference in 1993 John Smith's scaling down of their direct influence precariously prevailed, and the Party set about reforming conference voting procedure; both trends have since been carried further. At the same time, the Party was opening itself up to pressures that it had neglected for too long: regional, feminist, and libertarian. A new-found enthusiasm for pluralism pervaded the reports of the Party's working party on electoral reform. 'We begin to see a new and exciting role for the voluntary sector', Tony Blair told a Jewish charity in 1994; '—not an optional extra but a vital part of our economy, helping to achieve many of our key social objectives'. The defence of regional interests and individual rights was now grist to the mill of 'New Labour', a Party which was opening up links with think-tanks as fast as Majorite Conservative pragmatism was phasing them out. The two new think-tanks that appeared on the right in 1995—'Politeia', the think-tank seeking non-statist solutions for social problems which was set up with Major's approval, and the 'Conservative 2000 Foundation' created by his rival for the leadership John Redwood—were as yet unknown quantities, but seemed modest both in terms of their resources and their radicalism.[56]

\*

In their relationship to opinion, the government and opposition parties in a two-party system jointly perform the role of established church: they have the potential for disciplining and harnessing the irrational, the self-centred, the violent, and the impulsive. The decline of church and party is likely to prompt the rise of black magic and anarchy, respectively. Political parties are the engines of opinion, the instruments of participation, the mechanism for securing consensus and co-ordination. Fortunately for democracy in Britain, the two-party system showed every sign of life in the early 1990s. By ousting its leader in 1990, well before the election was due, the Conservative Party brought off a remarkable act of self-renewal, thereby freeing itself to capitalize on the widespread national feeling that it was time for a change. Major and Kinnock in their respective parties resumed the party leader's traditional role of broadening support by opening out towards the centre, thereby fending off political polarization. Major's relations with Kinnock were far less frosty than Thatcher's, and early in 1991 there was a notable improvement in the exchange of courtesies between government and opposition parties.[57] The House of Commons 'need not necessarily be a perpetual cockpit of confrontation', Major declared on 6 December 1990 at prime minister's question-time, a ritual confrontation whose reform he favoured. In the same month he made a point of crossing the floor to shake hands with Eric Heffer, the left-wing Labour MP, then terminally ill with cancer. In March 1991 Major invited Callaghan to Chequers for the first time since he had ceased to be Prime Minister in 1979.[58] Major's relatively centrist tone prompted restiveness on the right of his Party, and by 1995 he was facetiously telling Chancellor Kohl that 'I am a coalition government on my own.'[59] None of this involved any retreat in domestic policy from what Thatcher had achieved. The Conservative Party remained the party of home ownership, privatization, expanded opportunity, smaller government, and market forces within such government structures as survived—all at the expense of corporatist structures and public-sector trade unions. Major's meritocratic journey on the 'long road from Coldharbour Lane to Downing Street' lent him a special advantage in overcoming social-class barriers to opportunity, and Conservative racist criticisms of a black candidate in Cheltenham gave him the opportunity to emphasize that barriers of race, too, were 'not sentiments which have any place in our party'.[60]

When David Owen finally wound up the SDP in 1990, it seemed only a matter of time before he brought four-party politics to an end by joining one of the two parties he had so vigorously attacked since forsaking Labour in 1981. Indeed, he seems to have made tentative overtures to both. Conservative leaders bid publicly for his support in 1987–8.[61] Not surprisingly, they failed, because after 1987 the Conservatives encountered the difficulty they had so often experienced since the 1950s: voters disillusioned with a Conservative government flee at least temporarily to the Liberals. The Liberal Democrats recruited still more deserters after 1992 when the Conservatives experienced serious set-backs in economic policy and began squabbling about Europe. Discussing this in-fighting, Jenkins discerned a 'concentration of mutual venom, extraordinary by the standards of past disputes within parties', and branded the Conservative ministers as 'a group of political pygmies'.[62] None the less, during the general election campaign in 1992 Owen advised voters to support the Conservatives. Furthermore, the Conservatives attracted many SDP subordinates, most notably Owen's adviser Robert Skidelsky and the Social Market Foundation, a think-tank whose director, David Finkelstein, also became a Conservative. Still more valuably for the Conservatives, the opposition parties were slow to draw together, and Conservatives could in the short term only gain from the friction generated by Labour's attempts at self-reform under Kinnock, Smith, and Blair. Nor was the Party's modernization much of an asset if it could be presented as more opportunistic than idealistic.

By 1992 Labour's programme closely resembled what the SDP had put before the electorate nine years earlier, and in electing Blair as Party leader, Labour in 1994 made what Jenkins described as 'the most exciting Labour

choice since the election of Hugh Gaitskell'.[63] The SDP since its foundation had been steadily scaling down its ambitions: at first aiming to replace
the Labour Party, then from 1983 seeking to remain a major player in the
political game by collaborating with the Liberals, then from 1987 quietly
claiming credit for compelling Labour towards self-reform. It is an uncon-
vincing claim, if only because the fight for social democracy within the
Labour Party has been unceasing. The SDP leaders had long played a
distinguished part in that fight, and the effect of their secession in 1981 was
simultaneously to benefit Thatcher and to complicate greatly the task of
the social democrats they left behind. As the SDP's trade-union sympa-
thizer Frank Chapple had pointed out in February 1981, 'if a Labour split
is inevitable, then it should be the undemocratic Left and infiltrators who
should be forced to quit'.[64] Fortunately for Labour's long-term prospects,
Blair in 1994–5 did not dismiss in sectarian fashion SDP–Liberal overtures,[65] but encouraged his Party to revert to being the broad church of
MacDonald and Attlee. Labour, he emphasized, 'has got to be a party that
is capable of building a new coalition of support in the country that reaches
out beyond its traditional boundaries of support to be a vehicle for the
national renewal that I want to see'.[66] Furthermore, in moving towards the
centre he was less hampered than Kinnock had been by a left-wing past,
and was bolder by temperament and instinct than Smith. So Labour's
revisionism at last seemed to spring from conviction. This was important
not only for the Party's national image, but for rank-and-file morale. As
Foot had once pointed out, with a sidelong glance at Wilson, 'no left-wing
party can be sustained by the appeal to the business of manipulation'.[67]

If Labour was once more to be a party of conviction, however, substantial reforms of image and structure were required from a leader who would
have to take risks and show courage. Here again Labour, in Blair, seemed
to have found its man. The Archer committee, which knew that 'too much
of our time is consumed in talking to one another, instead of talking to
those who are not yet converted', recommended in 1993 that 'to alter the
name would be a dramatic symbol that the Party had disowned its history'.[68] In view of manual labour's long-term decline in the British economy,
there was much to be said for this, but perhaps it was wise not to tempt
providence. 'New Labour', however, a label widely used by 1995, was a
half-way house that got the worst of both worlds, as though the Party was
some sort of improved washing-powder. On the other hand, it was undoubtedly important in 1995 to replace Clause 4 of the Party's constitution.
Everybody knew that a Labour government would not act upon it, and the
Party's growing reputation for honesty had to be nurtured at a time when

a Conservative government seemed to be moving in the other direction. Abolition loosened up the Party's discussion on economic policy and accelerated the move away from mere formulae and symbols. It made the Labour Party once more a haven for the Gaitskellites who had been long wandering.

In some ways still more important were the structural reforms concerned with policy-making. After its defeat in 1992 the Party at last set about democratizing its structure, and its conference in that year set up the National Policy Forum. Meeting privately in winter and spring each year, and including among its representatives people from local government, trade unions, and women's groups, it meshed in with the Party conference but ensured that policy was formulated in a more considered, consensual, and participatory way than had been possible in the crowded agenda of an assembly closely scrutinized by the media. The Party also played its part in reviving the public inquiry, which Thatcher had almost killed off. It launched detailed and published investigations of its own, drawing on others besides its own supporters, into important policy issues: the working party on electoral systems (final report, 1993), the commission on social justice (final report, 1994), and the commission on wealth creation (appointed, 1995). The last two of these were conducted in association with the Institute for Public Policy Research, one of the new think-tanks that were now fertilizing policy on the left in rather the same way that the Centre for Policy Studies had once fertilized policy on the right. These inquiries generated a fruitful interaction between the academic and the practical, and did much to educate the general public as well as the Party. In 1995 the Party still had much further to travel: the trade unions' hold could not be broken without a rapid build-up of membership in the constituency parties, only timid moves were made to remove the Party's self-crippling restraints on its leader's free choice of his shadow cabinet,[69] and 'one member one vote' needed to be made more of a practical reality. But the Party seemed at last to be on its way, and the two-party system was coming back to life.

*

Debate in the early 1990s about how best to assess public opinion fleetingly grappled once more with the merits of the referendum. During the debates on the Maastricht treaty it was a weapon of anti-marketeers on right and left, somewhat paradoxically egged on by European precedents. With all-party consensus on the issue, asked Thatcher, 'how . . . will the people make their views known on whether or not they want their powers taken away?' Economic and political union seemed to be occurring without consulting the British people.[70] In vain: other countries (France and Denmark) might have their referenda, but Major pointed out that in Britain it was parliament which scrutinized international treaties, and brought far more stringency to the task than any referendum, so the campaign came to naught.[71] But inevitably, with a smaller government majority, Major's cabinet sounded a less decisive note and a somewhat more watchful eye was kept on opinion polls. The main debate on assessing opinion, however, centred on the merits of the simple-majority electoral system.

Here Major closely followed Thatcher. Opposition to proportional representation since 1979 partly reflects Conservative self-interest, for Conservatives have benefited from the simple-majority system, given that their enemies have been divided. Thatcher realized in the mid-1970s that electoral reform, then favoured by some leading Conservatives, risked generating a multi-party system which would end her Party's chance of holding office on its own. She also thought interests best represented through the free market rather than through a fragmented party structure, for as Friedman pointed out, the market 'is a system of effectively proportional representation',[72] and ensures representation of far more groups than any amount of electoral reform. Furthermore, Conservatives suspect that the simple-majority system's virtues are appreciated by more people than could be guessed at from the balance of comment that appears in recent books, academic journals, and newspapers—or would be appreciated if substantial reform were at all imminent. So the campaign for electoral reform has recently flourished only on the left, and it was from the *New Statesman*'s offices that the campaign gained renewed impetus with the formation of Charter 88 in 1988.[73] The Labour Campaign for Electoral Reform carried the pressure inside the Labour Party, arguing in 1991 that this was '*the* issue on which Labour can appeal to a new constituency of voters, the great middle ground of middle England, the very voters Labour needs to win the next election'.[74]

Yet electoral reform faced powerful obstacles even on the left. Some Labour politicians thought their programme required a strong executive, some had harboured a deep distrust of coalitions since 1931, some felt the left's perennial desire to preserve the true faith unsullied. There would be 'no pacts. No alliances. No deals before the election', Hattersley told the Party conference in 1990, dismissing notions of a Lib-Lab electoral pact. The Party 'did not survive the betrayal of 1981 to go into cosy huddles with the men and women who helped to keep Margaret Thatcher in power'.[75]

The critics of a well-entrenched political institution usually need to be more articulate than its defenders, and in the late 1980s it was the electoral reformers who made the running in public discussion. Hattersley increasingly found himself fighting a rearguard action when deploying the well-rehearsed arguments for the simple-majority system: the undemocratic implications of post-election coalitions held in 'smoke-filled rooms', the benefits of the constituency MP, the excessive power small parties enjoy in multi-party coalitions, and so on.[76] Labour's appointment of a working party on electoral reform, chaired by Raymond Plant, combined education of the Party with education of the general public on an important constitutional issue. The inquiry encouraged academic and political opinion to interact; indeed, its interim report of 1991 was perhaps too heavily academic to attract many readers even among politicians. The debate took place not just inside the Labour Party, but inside its working party, where the two sides fair-mindedly and informatively exchanged argument and counter-argument. The reformers made much of the damage done to the existing electoral system, and to the country as a whole, by the increasing regional divide between the Labour and Conservative parties, and it was the belief that electoral reform would help to cure this that converted its chairman.[77] Yet the working party's members who defended first-past-the-post thought this 'defeatist'. They argued that 'Labour is a nationally-based party', and that if some areas failed to elect Labour MPs 'then it is to our policies, our organisation and our presentation that we should turn for an examination, rather than to an alteration of the electoral system'.[78]

The best argument against the simple-majority electoral system, much discussed within the working party, is that it perpetuates the over-representation of white men in parliament because it divides the country into constituencies each of which is contested by only one candidate from each party. The parties play safe, and so do not seek out candidates from women and the ethnic minorities. Electoral reform's Labour supporters thought it 'the quickest, most effective way to achieve a gender balance' in the House of Commons, and thus to transform 'one of the last bastions of male privilege' with its 'macho style of politics'.[79] Yet there are counter-arguments. The simple-majority system's conservatism can offer no more than temporary resistance to any change that is widely demanded; the political parties cannot resist broader recruitment of candidates if the electors really want it. So here too the supporters of the simple-majority system within the Plant working party preferred to attain that broadening 'by a process of encouragement and by changing attitudes'.[80] The change is already in progress. During the 1980s the proportion of women candidates for parliament took a leap forward. At the same time, women were advancing into new types of career and gaining new educational opportunities. Within those two great generators of political talent Oxford and Cambridge, they had emerged from their single-sex college ghetto. They were also breaking out of the less visible but far more important ghetto of the mind that stems from centuries of separated gender roles within the family. Some feel that these changes are too slow, and that progress would be faster if parliament's hours of sitting were reformed. But the fact remains that women were elected in a record number (sixty) to parliament at the general election of 1992. And Thatcher's career, which owed so little to feminist inspiration, acclimatized people to the idea of women succeeding at the very highest levels in politics. It also did much to destroy that important—though since the Edwardian period, covert—constituent of anti-feminist attitudes: doubt about the stability of women's political judgement. A 'role model' was set up for all to see.

Labour's working party merely postponed the moment of decision, and Kinnock found it increasingly difficult to remain securely on the fence. His difficulty lay not only in convincing himself that electoral reform was intrinsically desirable, but in presenting his convictions as stemming from anything more than short-term electoral calculation. If proportional representation must come, he said, 'it must be for the right reasons'.[81] For all the working party's technical expertise on electoral systems, neither side within it grappled firmly with the tactical situation the Labour Party faced when blocked off from much of the centre ground by Liberal Democrats who retained substantial electoral credibility. So three-party politics survived. The overt pursuit of the centre was a strategy that Conservative leaders had abandoned in 1975, and the Thatcher–Joseph strategy had been to shun compromise and thereby initiate a right-wing ratchet effect in the entire political system. This policy, which Tebbit called 'pumping up Paddy Ashdown', had the effect of leaving the centre ground free for overtly centrist parties, and so of enabling the Conservatives to profit all the more from a split opposition, even after 1992.[82]

None the less, some Conservatives thought it necessary in the late 1980s to formulate a defence of the simple-majority system that had not hitherto been required. In May 1987 the Conservative MP Robert Jackson dismissed the idea that British economic failure since 1945 could be blamed on the system's exaggeration of fluctuations in government policy. It was, he claimed, the all-party corporatist continuity in economic policy up to 1979 that had done the damage. Proportional representation would merely entrench interest groups, and make it still less likely that governments would take the national view.[83] A more comprehensive case was put forward by Nevil Johnson, who had changed his view on the matter since the mid-1970s, in his resourceful booklet for the Centre for Policy Studies: *The Political Consequences of PR* (1992). The defenders of the simple-majority system, seeing beyond the superficialities of its failure exactly to replicate public opinion in the make-up of the House of Commons, recognized that it maximizes the span of opinion that is forced to concern itself with what should be done in government, thereby broadening the range of opinion that is drawn towards Westminster. A system which had grown up piecemeal also had the virtue of being operated by politicians with long experience of its workings. With the notable exception of Anglo-Irish relations, it had been made to work compatibly with political continuity and relative social harmony over a very long period—a period during which Britain had experienced the rise and decline of empire and of industrial supremacy.

So at the general election of 1992, whereas Kinnock said he would admit other political parties to his Party's inquiry into electoral reform, Major firmly opposed opportunist compromises on the subject with any other party, and roundly condemned the uncertainties involved in 'backstairs deals' and cobbled coalitions.[84] Ashdown in September recalled Major's last-minute appeal against hung parliaments as 'a seminal moment' in promoting the fourth consecutive Conservative victory. Claiming to have been 'shocked by the shift in opinion' on the subject, he argued that electoral reform could be sold only to an electorate better prepared for the politics of pluralism.[85] At any point after 1979 overt Lib-Lab coalition or merger, as distinct from a mere electoral pact (whose outcome would be precarious[86]), could have reaped for Liberal Democrats and Labour all the anti-Tory benefits of the simple-majority system without any need to divert energy into struggling to abolish it. But any such option foundered on the difficulties presented by institutional and individual self-interest, traditionalism, and lack of imagination. Restoration of that winning combination on the left which had thrown the Conservatives on to the defensive between 1905 and 1914 now seems likely to come from quite another direction: from a broadened Labour Party with the imagination to heal the wound on reforming opinion that its own quite unexpected secession from the Liberals had inflicted after 1916.

For it is now difficult to see how electoral reform can be obtained except by a party which has gained power through the first-past-the-post system, or which (like Labour in February 1974) has a good chance of doing so. Having gained power in that way, it would then hardly seem sensible for a minority Labour government to use up its early months in office by kicking away its electoral ladder. Besides, the electors do not need to wait for the politicians: they have it in their power to end Conservative rule for themselves, regardless of any artificially preserved Liberal–Labour division. For the present electoral system does not prevent them from voting tactically. Indeed their readiness to do so halved the Conservative majority at the general election of 1992.[87] So the Conservatives are kept in power not by the electoral system, but by anti-Conservatives' relative failure to work it to their advantage, and by its consequent distortion of representation when three parties try to operate a representative and parliamentary system designed in effect for two. When a car performs erratically on the road, it may be the driver that is to blame.

It performs no service to the simple-majority system, however, to defend it indiscriminately:[88] to dismiss proportional representation for elections to the European parliament as 'the thin end of the wedge' for electoral reform at home, as did Castle in 1979.[89] During the late 1970s, when the electoral system for devolved assemblies was being planned, many thought proportional representation well suited to those areas of the United Kingdom that were simultaneously cut across by cultural as well as class issues— areas that therefore seemed likely to divide into more than two major political parties. It was incorporated into the Scottish devolution Bill by House of Lords amendments, and although the lower house threw these out, their supporters constituted the largest House of Commons vote for proportional representation on a free vote up to that date.[90] The simple-majority system also seems unsuited to electing representatives whose purpose is not to form a government; or to electing those who, if they do constitute a government, do not operate within an adversarial legislature. Elections to local-government authorities and to the European parliament (within whose large constituencies the simple-majority system unduly distorts opinion) spring at once to mind. When the electoral system for EEC elections was under discussion in 1977, Edward Heath, no radical on constitutional matters at home, was forceful in rejecting the simple-majority system as suited to such large constituencies; besides, the EEC elections were for an assembly which (unlike the Westminster parliament) had as its sole function the representation of opinion. The Conservative Party, he said, had nothing to lose by going for a regional list system.[91] The merits of proportional representation, in certain circumstances, are well advertised by the average turn-out in the four EEC elections (1979, 1984, 1989, and 1994). This was 34 per cent in Great Britain, where the simple-majority system applied, but 54 per cent in Northern Ireland, where the single transferable vote applied. The Liberals were understandably angry when, after winning an eighth of the vote in the Euro-election of June 1979, they gained none of the eighty-one seats. In the following month ten Liberals seized the opportunity presented by empty seats in the European parliament during a mealtime to get themselves photographed occupying what they saw as their rightful places.[92]

*

As vehicle for articulating opinion, parliament gained substantially from Thatcherism, which firmly asserted Westminster's primacy over other areas of the political system: over party activists, pressure groups, local authorities, and the civil service. At the same time, Thatcher warded off the subordinate legislatures which nationalist, Liberal, and Labour parties hoped to create. Referenda, which on three major occasions in the 1970s transferred to electors decisions customarily made by politicians, faded into the background in the 1980s. So a well-informed observer could still write in 1990 that 'the Commons, its lobbies and corridors, its bars and terraces, its dining room and smoking room, its gossip and ambience, *are* the political world in Britain'.[93] Never in its long history has parliament more strikingly demonstrated its capacity for political theatre than during the confidence debate on 22 November 1990, the day when Thatcher resigned.

Change in parliament after 1979 took the form of gradually working out the implications of reforms introduced from the 1950s to the 1970s. Parliament has, in other words, followed its customarily pragmatic and gradualist course. The new committees established in 1979 explored and developed their powers. They have undoubtedly enhanced parliament's expertise, its links with pressure groups, and its capacity to monitor the executive. But they were the dog that failed to bark during the gestation of the poll tax, and the necessary limits on their powers as against the executive were advertised in 1995 when the government's abolition of the Department of Employment entailed abolition of its associated parliamentary committee.[94] And as we saw in Chapter 11 there has been no cut in the number of ministerial posts to accord with civil-service cuts: governments find such posts too valuable as a way of influencing ambitious backbenchers. The advance of radio and television into parliament has still further enhanced the importance of prime minister's question-time. So much so, that the gains from its enhancement of political theatre must now be weighed against the cost of the substantial preliminary briefings for government ministers that are needed. Yet the media incursion has changed debating styles less than opponents feared, while at the same time enhancing public understanding of how parliament works. Office accommodation for MPs has been extended and library facilities have improved. A major parliamentary as well as educational opportunity was lost in the 1980s when a short-sighted government failed to see the newly vacant County Hall as a prize site for the London School of Economics, which in turn could have made powerful academic resources available to parliament. Nor is it yet clear what will be the long-term effect (as from 30 November 1993) of supplanting a spring budget that is concerned only with plans for government income by an integrated discussion earlier in the year of both income and expenditure.

Although Benn still wishes to abolish the House of Lords, its new professionalism and vigour caused attacks upon it to fall out of fashion after the early 1980s. This was partly because the Thatcher dynamic was forcing more and more legislation through the lower house (2581 pages of it in 1989, surpassing the Attlee government's previous all-time high). Quality inevitably suffered; the second chamber's revising function was all the more needed, and had been further elaborated from the mid-1970s.[95] Furthermore, life peers drawn from a wide spectrum of British life demonstrated the value of an assembly which can draw directly on expertise, and debate matters in a less partisan way than in the lower house. Some House of Lords committees (most notably those on European Communities legislation and on science and technology) gained considerable weight. No major political party manifesto now recommends abolishing the House. The reformers' aim is simply to make it more effective by democratizing its composition and removing some of its anomalies, though that runs into the familiar difficulty that such changes might have the effect of undermining the authority of the lower house.

Parliament's most radical reform in the 1990s has been its adoption of the Nolan Committee's recommendation that MPs should make their outside earnings public, cease initiating parliamentary proceedings in the interests of clients who pay them, and allow their conduct to be monitored by an outside commissioner. This change, achieved in November 1995 against substantial but ill-argued Conservative opposition, strikingly illustrates judges' growing prominence as instruments of an aroused public opinion. The impact of the change is as yet unclear, but two dangers will need to be warded off. Firstly, the paradoxical possibility that in this instance open government will, by distancing MPs from pressure groups, produce the insulation from outside opinion against which the Prime Minister rightly warned: the danger of 'a monastic Commons, a chamber of high minds, a conventicle of saints'.[96] Secondly, the reform may well lower the calibre of candidates for parliament, with consequences for policy on the pay and even the number of MPs. Nolan's reform is, however, by no means as radical in its implications for parliament as the bills of rights and the reformed electoral system that hold the centre of the constitutional reformers' stage. In their implications for the operation of parliament, these proposals have so far been very inadequately explained, still less have they been justified. It needs at least to be argued that multipartism will improve parliament as forum of public discussion, yet nowhere do reformers highlight any worked-out version of their case. Nor is it always clear that they appreciate what parliament's present role is. It is not intended to be a photograph of public opinion at a particular moment: the House of Commons is 'a representation in local terms, place by place of the nation . . . for the purpose of saying yea or nay. It is not an attempt to find out the exact shadings of opinion across the whole spectrum. It is a means of arriving at valid, sustainable decisions.'[97]

*

In the area of power and decision, the most important development of the early 1990s was the revelation of how little Thatcher's long reign had changed the nature of the cabinet. In this special area of institutional flexibility, relationships fluctuate not as a result of constitutional reform but with the personality and situation of prime minister and party. The new mood was set from the start: 'well, who would have believed it?' Major is said to have remarked, when embarking on his first cabinet meeting. Thatcher's way of doing business, through *ad hoc* informal meetings with small groups of ministers, now gave way to the more traditional formal cabinet committees with fixed membership.[98] Cabinet discussions became more collaborative, and with Gus O'Donnell supplanting Bernard Ingham as prime minister's press secretary, Conservative cabinet ministers no longer feared being surreptitiously undermined by prime-ministerial press briefings. Press rumours of splits within the cabinet were nourished less by the reality of any such splits than by the fact that the cabinet's new chairman once more treated it as a sounding-board for free-ranging discussion. This reversion did not rescue the government from slipping on a sequence of 'banana skins', but there were none to compare with the poll tax or even Westland. One small but significant and no doubt permanent change has, however, come about: publicity for the workings of the cabinet's committee system. On 15 May 1992 the full list of cabinet subcommittees was published in *Hansard*. In his budget speech of November 1993, Kenneth Clarke's praise for 'my colleagues on the Cabinet known as the EDX Committee' took the new openness about cabinet procedures so much for granted that nobody seems to have noticed it.[99]

As for Major himself, the early 1990s certainly vindicated R. T. McKenzie's emphasis on Conservative leaders' vulnerability within their own Party, though in 1995 Major skilfully turned the Party's electoral procedures against his enemies by putting himself up for election and daring them to elect an alternative. His personality and situation combined to produce a leader more collegial and conciliatory than his predecessor. The only 'presidential' feature from Thatcher's reign that he continued was the habit of staging press conferences in the street outside No. 10 Downing Street. Before the general election of 1992 he was inhibited as Prime Minister by the speed of his rise from obscurity, and by having to live in the shadow of a formidable predecessor who had divided his Party and who remained hyperactive. As Alan Watkins coarsely put it in November 1991: 'the old bat is still up there in the rafters'.[100] After an unexpected election victory boosted his standing in 1992, Major had to cope with the small and dwindling size of his Commons majority, unsure about how far he could rely on the votes of Ulster Unionist MPs, and beset by controversy among colleagues about Britain's role in Europe whose intensity would have sorely tested any leader. Here, as often elsewhere, Major found himself landed with problems that earlier prime ministers had evaded. For the European Union's long-term political purpose, hitherto rarely advertised even by British 'Europeans', could now no longer be disguised. Many likened Major's European difficulty to the protection issue that had bedevilled Balfour's premiership between 1902 and 1905. Together with the Irish issue it required from Major an acrobatic skill that his music-hall ancestors would have relished.

All this meant that the thrust of the government's achievements had to be administrative and executive rather than legislative, with civil-service reform and improved Anglo-Irish relations as the centre-pieces. Major's dismissed Chancellor of the Exchequer Norman Lamont missed the mark when he complained in his resignation speech that 'there is too much short-termism, too much reacting to events, not enough shaping of events' and that 'far too many important decisions are made for 36 hours' publicity'.[101] So did Lawson, with his unsolicited reminder that 'to govern is to choose'.[102] For in the difficult parliamentary situation Major faced after 1992, charismatic leadership and a cavalier approach to public opinion were no more possible than they had been for MacDonald when Prime Minister of minority governments in the 1920s or for Wilson with his wafer-thin parliamentary majorities of 1964–6 and 1974. Major was forced, in his own words, 'to tack a little here, manœuvre a little there',[103] because 'a strong government needs political skills . . . when leading a democratic society and, in particular, handling a lively House of Commons with a small majority'.[104] Major turned out to be the great survivor among twentieth-century prime ministers, once more illustrating the contingent and non-cumulative nature of prime-ministerial power. His premiership also revealed the continuing importance for a prime minister of patience, tenacity, resilience, good manners, and a basic decency—qualities that, despite all the ridicule, eventually won for him a certain grudging respect.

\*

In the administration and execution of policy, Thatcher presided over the most ambitious reform of the century—a reform that throws the Fulton report thoroughly into the shade. Major's small parliamentary majority after 1992 might seriously hamper legislation, but it did not prevent this revolution from continuing. After 1990 there occurred a modest reshuffling of ministries more reminiscent of the 1960s and 1970s than of the 1980s: the Department of Energy's responsibilities went to the Departments of Environment and Trade; a new Heritage department was set up; the Department of Employment was abolished and its responsibilities reassigned; and a non-governmental minister was appointed to promote the Citizen's Charter. The last of these, however, testifies to the way the Major governments confronted a problem Thatcher had not tackled so resolutely: the need to find ways of applying market disciplines to activities that government could not hive off. The Charter brought to the public sphere all that concern with enfranchising the consumer which had inspired the privatization programme whose 'lineal descendant' it was.[105]

In 1994 Major explained the five ways in which his government was breaking down the boundaries between the private and public sectors: through privatizing where possible and regulating where impossible; through the private-finance initiative to draw in private funds for public purposes; through competition and choice within the public sector; through devolving decision-making within the public services; and through diffusing more information about public services. Under the 'Next Steps' programme, instituted in 1988, 70 per cent of the civil service had been organized into agencies by October 1993, and in 1995 a stir was created when the chief executive of an agency, with no Whitehall experience, was recruited as Permanent Secretary at the Department of Employment over the heads of internal candidates.[106] Also persisting is Thatcher's policy of hiving off and contracting out functions from local-government authorities. This has most obviously occurred in education and health, but it has continued elsewhere.

The call for even faster progress in slimming down central-government staffing was made in 1993 by a pioneer of 'Next Steps', Sir Peter Kemp, whose *Beyond Next Steps* argues that a civil service that provides such diverse services should not be monolithic, and should always ask itself whether it needs to provide any particular service at all. 'There is in reality no such thing as a monolithic civil service, which can be designed and run in the sort of tidy way some people would like. What we have instead is a vast variety of activities that must be carried out using different skills and different management methods.'[107] He argues that the agencies should now be cut loose from their parent departments and that their chief executives should be made directly responsible to parliament through select committees. He regrets that the civil service's central staffing in Whitehall has not been cut down so as to reflect its loss of functions to the agencies. 'It is amazing that a government dedicated to market testing and contracting out has failed largely to apply these disciplines to its own centre.'[108] Still, the Major governments' changes in the civil service have been radical, and under the reforms Waldegrave announced in July 1994, a further cut of 50,000 in overall civil-service numbers was planned over four years.[109] And in so far as the reforms then announced included enhancing management discretion over departmental costs and recruitment, additional and built-in piecemeal reductions, not centrally planned, seem likely thereafter. Additionally, in October the Treasury set the pace for further cuts at the centre by announcing that its senior posts would be cut by a third.[110]

These reforms have not been universally welcomed. The notion of a 'democratic deficit', already briefly discussed in the context of recent reforms in local government, has also been marshalled against reforms in central government. Agency status moves large areas of the civil service not only geographically away from the seat of government in many cases, but also formally away from the minister in so far as it devolves autonomy to managers, or even eventually privatizes the function concerned. Critics also question whether business attitudes are appropriate for governmental decision-taking which must subordinate efficiency to fairness. There are worries, too, about the impact of continuous criticism and cuts on the morale and corporate sense of civil servants.[111] Waldegrave's consumer-orientated reply to such fears has already been discussed in the local-government context, and the critics' fears do seem exaggerated. Accountability in many areas of British life—commercial, professional, technical—is not the less real or the less democratic for operating outside parliamentary or local-authority structures, and it is not obvious that large areas of public admin-istration need to be treated so very differently, nor do many enthusiasts for direct political accountability appear to favour re-politicizing the manage-ment of private concerns. As for those areas which must be monitored more directly by parliament, those in pursuit of political accountability sometimes speak as though the ministerial resignation solves every prob-lem and should be much more frequent. But recurrent resignations con-stitute a very clumsy instrument, a recipe for discontinuity and even an incentive to the abdication of responsibility. Nobody suggests that resig-nation should be such a frequent resort elsewhere in British life. It seems better, with activities inevitably conducted by the state, to institute correc-tives that are continuous, detailed and automatic in their operation. Market or near-market operations seem a good way to secure this. After all, as Vernon Bogdanor has pointed out, 'what is needed is not a resignation but a *remedy*'.[112]

The Next Steps reforms have in their essentials won all-party agree-ment, and are promoted with some enthusiasm by the head of the civil service, Sir Robin Butler. Nor do the critics give sufficient attention to the defects of the system Next Steps set out to replace: to the vagueness of the ministerial control that prevailed in a civil service that before 1979 was so large and varied in its functions; to the difficulty of assessing state services when there were so few comparative statistics on their performance; and to the lack of financial and other incentive on managers and rank and file to restrain the costs of activities over which they had so little direct con-trol. Corporate morale and incentives hardly gained by the civil service's sheer size and centralization before Next Steps, nor by the trade unions' strategic disruption of essential services in the pursuit of standardized pay levels unrelated to performance or local costs. Such a system was also difficult to justify to the taxpayer, let alone in terms of equity.

The Major governments' democratic credentials are evident enough from changes in attitudes to secrecy. Doubts about the ambitions and impartial-ity of the secret services in the 1970s helped to launch a movement for more open government that bore much fruit in the early 1990s. The National Coordinating Committee against Censorship, founded in 1974, aimed to yoke free speech and censorship issues with attacks on the Official Secrets Act,[113] but its successors in the 1980s had a bleak time, given Thatcher's traditionalism in this area. Less secret procedures in other countries, how-ever, most notably in the United States, produced international anomalies on access to documents, and made the British government's line increasingly difficult to hold. Waldegrave in 1993 announced substantial concessions, monitored by the Parliamentary Commissioner.[114] The culture of British politics took a surprising turn when the Director-General of MI5 posed for official photographs on 16 July and issued a booklet on the security service. Still more surprising was the press conference given by the head of MI6 (without photographs) in November, together with the announcement that social-security expenditure would for the first time feature among spending commitments announced in the budget.[115] When reinforced from April 1994 by publication of the minutes of the monthly meetings between the Chancellor of the Exchequer and the Governor of the Bank of England,[116] and in June by a televised lecture from the Director-General of MI5 on her department's role,[117] such concessions were substantial enough to deny the open-government lobby much of its impetus, which was no doubt partly the intention. Something similar happened with the panel of independent forecasters set up late in 1992 to open up policy formation by advising the Treasury; their disagreements were so extensive and so public that by August 1994 their existence had almost been forgotten.[118] The Central Statistical Office, an executive agency, made considerable efforts under Bill McLennan to make government statistics (some of whose collection was contracted out) more widely available, not to mention the wealth of statistics on education and public health that Conservative policy generated.[119] Like Gladstone's last Liberal government of 1892–4, the Major government from 1992 made a virtue of its parliamentary weakness by directing much of its energy into making significant administrative reforms.

\*

On the role of monarchy, Thatcher's successor is at least as adventurous. Major resolutely defended monarchy in December 1992 as 'an essential part of our landscape in this country', and relations between Prime Minister and monarch rapidly became warm,[120] but he is pursuing a Peelite policy of reforming in order to preserve, a Gladstonian policy of removing the indefensible so as to safeguard the rest. Conservatives know that Bagehot's mysticism and reverence are no longer sufficient to safeguard monarchy or any other British political institution. Stability and continuity of government can now be promoted only through wider understanding. Without explaining how his stance on monarchy or his recommendation of a baronetcy for Denis Thatcher could be reconciled with his desire 'to get rid of old, class-based distinctions',[121] Major at last made a start in 1993 on removing class distinctions from within the honours system. A Conservative prime minister could hardly secure the 'logical Labour alternative to the honours list' that Benn had sought in May 1963,[122] but he did at least achieve the more modest reform in this area which Castle had sought unavailingly from Wilson in 1966.[123] Seventy of the 970 honours announced in December 1993 came as a result of nominations by the public; 130 more were also thus nominated, but had already been under consideration.[124] Also under Major's premiership the monarchy's financial basis was at last clarified. *The Times* thought the Queen's decision in 1993 to pay tax on her private wealth 'a peculiarly British form of constitutional change—gradual, voluntary, uncoded by law'.[125] Focusing the civil list on the needs of the Queen, the Duke of Edinburgh, and the Queen Mother may simultaneously render her children's shortcomings less objectionable and strengthen her control over them.[126] At the same time the Queen's decision in 1994 to renounce her right to free private travel in RAF planes and to give up the royal yacht *Britannia*[127] may help to defuse resentment about the royal family's life-style. And if the rebuilding of Windsor Castle is funded by the proceeds of wider access to royal premises, this involves carrying forward the welcome policy initiated when the rebuilt chapel at Buckingham Palace was opened to the public as an art gallery in 1962, two desirable objectives thereby being attained for the price of one.

One aspect of Conservative policy after 1979, increasingly endorsed by Labour in the 1990s, has the effect of enhancing a long-standing role that the nineteenth-century monarchy built up for itself: the promotion through voluntary action of welfare and charitable activity. Like so many of the monarchy's new roles, this had accumulated pragmatically and gradually in response to the mood of the time.[128] It had the effect not only of drawing together the social classes, but of placing the monarchy at their head. In the first half of the twentieth century, however, state intervention became increasingly the vogue, so the monarchy's 'welfare' role became less central to its prestige—a role that Edward VIII when Prince of Wales was much less keen than his predecessors to develop. Under George VI the role seemed about to disappear. Yet state action had never entirely ousted voluntary action, and during the 1950s the Duke of Edinburgh vigorously identified himself with environmental and youth causes. When voluntarism once more came into fashion after 1979 the monarchy was well placed to profit by the change, for its central role in the state was buttressed by prolonged voluntarist experience.[129] However repugnant the Prince of Wales in the 1980s might privately find Thatcher's values, he resourcefully built on new wings to the monarchy's voluntarist edifice, and in 1993–4 his mother was giving away more than £200,000 a year.[130]

Liberal and Labour party comment on the monarchy has been sparse. The overall thrust of their reforming impulse—in the early 1990s, as in the late 1950s—consists in attacking mysticism and class privilege and pursuing the educational and economic benefits of 'modernization'. Indeed, some stalwarts from the 1950s persist in old age with the causes of their youth. Yet Labour's modernization rarely incorporates an attack on the hereditary principle that goes beyond reforming the House of Lords. True, Benn's *Common Sense* substitutes an elected president for the monarch, but it is significant that when Labour was at the crest of its leftward wave in 1980, with Benn at the height of his influence within his Party, he did not carry his attack on the hereditary principle as far as the monarchy. Likewise with the Institute for Public Policy Research's draft constitution published in 1991. Its concern is only to remove the monarch's prerogative powers, and in listing the monarch's duties it draws upon the Spanish constitution.[131] If the agenda of public discussion and of party programmes offers any guidance, the British monarchy in the 1990s is at least as secure as it was in Bagehot's day. And if the views of the Prince of Wales offer any guidance, the monarchy itself seems likely to be more radical than the Labour Party on some matters. The Prince claimed in his televised documentary of June 1994 that his proper role as monarch in a multicultural nation was to be 'Defender of faith, not the faith'. Despite the subsequent fuss among Anglicans,[132] the British constitution's flexibility will no doubt ensure that common sense prevails in this area as so often earlier elsewhere.

\*

This book does not aim to predict which, if any, of the reforms in the British political system discussed in this chapter are likely to win through. If precedent is any guide, the British political system will not be suddenly transformed, but will adapt in a piecemeal and undoctrinaire way to confront new problems. Powerful elements of both Conservative and Labour parties have no desire for electoral reform, the SDP came to naught, the Liberal Democrats can wield no direct power without either merging with Labour or securing electoral reform, and it is not at all clear how electoral reform can be extracted from a government whose majority or even minority power comes through the existing electoral system. Entrenched interests in the legal profession are powerful, and constitutional reform is hardly a cause that enthuses the masses. Nor do Major's governments fuel movements for constitutional reform, as Thatcher's did, by carrying to an extreme the existing system's potential for strong government. Vulnerable elements of the system—monarchy, parliament, and the political parties, and perhaps even the judiciary—continue to pre-empt drastic change by responding with timely concession.

Yet precedents need not be constraints; we may at last have arrived at the sort of conjuncture, absent hitherto, where Britain can embark in peacetime on the sort of grand institutional revolution that elsewhere tends to occur only in war or revolution—on constitutional reforms deliberately promoted from motives that transcend party interest. Changes in local government and civil service since 1979 show how quickly and substantially the British political system can change if the political will is there. Nor do we lack non-political impulses to change. Chapters 8 and 9 have shown how changes in the media have done as much since the 1950s as the railways did throughout the nineteenth century to transform the conduct of elections and the role of parliament, nor have we even begun to appreciate information technology's potential for change in the political structure. Already by 1993 experiments were being conducted with automated counting of votes at elections;[133] the ease and cheapness of computerized voting could transform parliament and the electoral process, and make referenda much easier and cheaper to organize.[134] Membership of the European Union, accompanied by the slow draining away of Commonwealth influences, brings new constitutional and legal attitudes to bear, and has important implications for the politics of the regions. Britain's relative economic decline has not been reversed, and changes in the political system that are offered as remedies are likely to win followers.

There are ample defects in the working of British institutions to fuel the fire: modern technology's threats to individual liberty and privacy, disquieting faults in the police force and prison service, apathy in local government, crude polarities in national government, under-representation of women and ethnic minorities in parliament, and above all the serious under-representation of centre parties at Westminster since the 1960s. We may be evolving towards a multi-party system reinforced by some form of proportional representation. We may involve lawyers more fully in the political process. We may move towards a Scandinavian style of monarchy, or to no monarchy at all. But no remedy through constitutional reform will be effective unless its enactment allows for its likely effects within the British political context. This will require a full understanding of the historical background, if only to ensure that the virtues (whether intended or accidental) of the relevant British institutions are not sacrificed lightly. The historian's insights by no means discourage political change. On the contrary, they highlight the political system's flexibility by providing case-studies of the range of options that were available in the past, and by illustrating how unpredictably some were accepted, some rejected. In grappling with uncertainty, whether we are reformers or not, we can only gain from starting out with a thorough understanding of how Britain's political institutions came to be what they now are.

# 14

# *International Perspectives*

THE widespread present-day dissatisfaction with the British political system is part of a world-wide restiveness with political structures. British political culture does not evolve in isolation from what happens in other countries. Mr Podsnap was no guide to attitudes even in nineteenth-century Britain, let alone later. For although nineteenth-century travel was less frequent and methods of communication much poorer, British political institutions and attitudes were deeply influenced by sympathy with or distaste for political systems elsewhere. 'The English people do not easily change their rooted notions,' wrote Bagehot, 'but they have many unrooted notions. Any great European event is sure for a moment to excite a sort of twinge of conversion to something or other.' Or as the future Lord Salisbury put it in 1871, 'our agitations, like our dramas, are generally translated from the French'.[1] Observation (from a distance) of politics in Europe led the Victorians to congratulate themselves on combining liberty with stability. Indeed, until the 1950s one could almost argue that the entire apologia for British political institutions was cast in terms of a double distaste: for the authoritarian and often Catholic political traditions of Europe, and for the political instability that had resulted from French and Italian attempts to escape from them. During the nineteenth century the bench-marks were usually France and Prussia, whose continuously or fitfully authoritarian regimes provided Bagehot with so many of his improving texts. British complacency was nourished by European Anglophilia. Josef Redlich, introducing his fine study *Local Government in England* in 1903, wanted a book written which would explain 'the most curious phenomenon in the modern political history of Europe'. For him this was 'the . . . always prevailing influence of the English political institutions in the evolution and revolution of modern political thought, as well as of constitutional law and practice on the Continent during the eighteenth and nineteenth centuries'.[2]

Overseas influences on Britain did not come only from Europe. The United States moulded nineteenth-century Liberal and radical attitudes to their Party's ideas and organization; hence the close interest that Britain took in the American civil war. In the early nineteenth century the United States had been the radical's utopia. 'The American constitutions were to liberty, what a grammar is to language,' wrote Tom Paine. 'They define its parts of speech, and practically construct them into syntax.'[3] With its continually extending frontier, America seemed the archetypal land of freedom and opportunity. But as the Liberal Party's notion of liberty evolved from negative to positive, the British left's American enthusiasms waned. As exemplar of capitalism, the United States had even less attraction for a twentieth-century Labour Party whose priorities were class-conscious and socialist. None the less, Labour inherited much of the Liberal Party's zest for freedom, and so American libertarianism retained a certain appeal. The aggressive methods of American pressure groups in monitoring commercial activity were an important influence on the British left from the 1960s, and the exposure of President Nixon by American investigative journalism in the early 1970s prompted British imitation. 'The Watergate story is a cautionary tale for all politicians,' wrote Peter Jenkins in 1986, 'the moral of which is that it pays to come clean and come clean quickly.'[4]

The nineteenth-century Conservative Party's distaste for egalitarian and secular ideas distanced it from the United States, but the Party's twentieth-century individualist and meritocratic tendency gradually changed this, and by the 1950s the Republicans' election-winning methods were continuously influencing the Party's tactics.[5] Thirty years later the influence extended to government policy, given the affinity between Thatcher and Reagan and the Party's search for an alternative to corporatism. The remedy for unemployment, said Nigel Lawson in 1984, was to repatriate to Britain the enterprise which Britain had earlier exported to the United States.[6]

Influence can come as much through antagonism as through affinity. As the self-consciously patriotic party, the Conservatives were unlikely to find political exemplars overseas, and few were enthusiasts for the European Fascist counter-attack on Communism between the wars. Whereas Tsarist Russia had been a bugbear of the left till 1917, during the twentieth century the USSR became the bugbear of the right, uniting Conservatives in distaste far more effectively than it united the left in enthusiasm. Russian Communism seriously divided the British left. 'Nothing has contributed so much to the corruption of the original idea of socialism', wrote Orwell in 1947, 'as the belief that Russia is a socialist country and that every act of its rulers must be excused, if not imitated.' In his last speech to a

Labour Party conference Bevan claimed that the USSR's commitment to planning would eventually enable it to outpace the West.[7] Even during the 1960s, after the USSR's influence on the British left had waned, Marxism—with a new, non-Soviet, pedigree—for some time retained a following, and Marxist utopias were discovered in places as far afield as Yugoslavia, Cuba, and China. But by the end of the decade the apolitical influence of oriental religions was gaining ground with the young. Between March and October 1970 the British embassy in Kabul was issuing an average of two one-way tickets back to London every week to British pilgrims who wanted to go home but lacked the means.[8]

Much more influential than Europe as an overseas influence on British Conservatism was what was once called the British empire, an influence with considerable popular appeal, though viewed somewhat sceptically by the Party's leaders. On Conservatism its influence was authoritarian, especially in its Indian dimension. Liberals like Cobden, Bright, and J. A. Hobson thought it corrupted domestic politics. For Hobson in 1902, the south and south-west of England was 'richly sprinkled' with retired imperial soldiers and administrators, 'men openly contemptuous of democracy, devoted to material luxury, social display, and the shallower arts of intellectual life', and working their way into British politics.[9] However much imperialism might benefit 'certain lower races', he argued in 1909, 'such gain may be purchased dearly by the damage done to democracy at home'.[10] Authoritarianism and paternalism were kindred sentiments, however, and Conservative ideas on welfare at home did not necessarily suffer. As for the Labour Party, the empire of white settlement was a source of democratic and egalitarian ideas. Labour found the democratic tone and welfare measures of Australia and New Zealand at least as congenial as New Zealand's free-market experiments now seem to the British right.[11] The Scandinavian democracies too, especially Sweden, nourished British social-democratic ideas and were still a potent influence on Labour's egalitarian and open-government policies in the 1960s. Sweden, for instance, contributed the idea of the ombudsman.

Many of these overseas influences on right and left nourished complacency about British political institutions, which till the 1950s were scarcely questioned as suitable constituents of the nation's export drive. Britain's industrial and imperial achievement, founded on a long period of political continuity, seemed to validate such complacency. But during the 1950s all this began to change. Together with the mounting imports of foreign manufactured goods came foreign political attitudes and institutions. The first major political import was the French model of indicative planning.

Contacts with the French civil service during negotiations for entering the EEC made it a model for British civil-service reforms. Labour's National Enterprise Board, established in 1975, owed much to Italian precedent, and in the late 1980s Labour and the Liberals showed increasing interest in the constitutional arrangements of West European nations. This was partly because the British left sympathized with the continuing corporatism prevailing within the EEC at a time when in Britain it had gone out of fashion. And if Japan's political system in the 1980s did not directly influence Thatcherism, the political impact made by its manufacturing methods and labour relations was profound.

These overseas influences have never since the 1860s led to any wholesale British appropriation of a political system developed elsewhere. Where specific practices and structures have been lifted from other political systems, they have been adapted for British purposes and grafted on to British institutions. Care was taken, for instance, to subordinate Sweden's ombudsman to parliament in 1967, and experience soon disabused anyone with Americanized expectations of parliament's new select committees appointed in the mid-1960s. No serious attempt was made to import French civil-service structures into Britain after the Fulton report; such appearances of borrowing as did take place did not long outlast the 1970s. And however much the British monarchy has opened itself up to public view, it has not embraced the Scandinavian model. This insularity may well not persist. So rapidly is overseas travel extending, so rapidly are industrial societies becoming intermeshed, and so completely has British confidence in British institutions declined that in some ways Herbert Morrison has more in common with Walter Bagehot than with us. In 1954 Morrison could still write of French institutions with the combination of amused and somewhat patronizing puzzlement, laced occasionally with apprehension, that Bagehot had displayed a century before. No such thing happens now. If this change signifies diminished British arrogance, it is indeed welcome. But if it brings the danger that home-grown institutions will be jettisoned out of hand, and if it leads to foreign-grown institutions being imported regardless of context and tradition, it can only be damaging. Institutional changes hastily imported will have unexpected and by no means always desirable results.

*

The most important source of overseas influence on British political institutions after 1973 was not a single country but a group of countries: what is now the European Union. Its impact on the political system needs to be distinguished from the separate impact made by aspects of its constituent countries—the Dutch monarchy, French planification, Italian corporatism, and so on. Its impact on the political system should also be distinguished from its effect on specific areas of policy. Sir Keith Joseph might launch himself as Secretary of State for Education and Science in 1981 by circulating the booklet *Lessons from Europe*, but his concerns in doing so were educational rather than European.[12] Bundesbank precedents might prompt Chancellors of the Exchequer from 1992 to render Treasury relations with the Bank of England less secretive, but their motives were less European than economic. To focus attention on the EEC's collective impact is to highlight significant ways in which the British political system operates. Of these, the first is the flexibility on policy of the two leading parties when it comes to dealing with a major issue—a flexibility that springs from the vigour of their competition. On the European issue the Liberals alone among the parties showed consistency, nourished by their distance from power after 1945. By contrast, Labour and Conservative have been almost shameless in pursuing electoral advantage through syncopations of policy over six broad phases between 1945 and the present. The phases can be labelled Conservative Europeanism (1945–51), British isolationism (1951–61), revived Conservative Europeanism (1961–7), all-party Europeanism (1967–70), revived Conservative Europeanism (1970–5), and revived all-party Europeanism (1975 to the present).

During the first phase (1945–51) Winston Churchill showed far more sympathy than Labour with Europe's aspirations to unity, but for him this did not entail any choice between Europe and the open seas. His Party's manifesto in 1950 favoured 'ever closer association with Western Europe and the United States', while placing 'in the forefront of British statesmanship . . . the vital task of extending the unity, strength and progress of the British Empire and Commonwealth'.[13] On taking office in 1951, Churchill disappointed some Conservative 'Europeans' by opting clearly for the open seas, thereby launching the second (isolationist) phase (1951–61). Macmillan's European sympathies before 1951 did not lead him as Foreign Secretary in 1955 to perceive opportunities for Britain in the Messina conference which led to the foundation of the EEC. Indeed, 'embrace destructively' was the Foreign Office phrase for British policy on such discussions, and the invitation to join them was spurned.[14] Pressure for a change of policy owed much to the fact that the EEC in its early years proved an unexpected success. Furthermore, the Suez venture revealed that Britain needed new friends, given friction with the United States and disunity in the Commonwealth. The Commonwealth was now becoming so flexible a structure that membership of the EEC seemed no longer incompatible with it, and some hoped that the relative prosperity of 'the Six' in the late 1950s would rub off on Britain if she joined. Still, no prominent Conservative publicly advocated EEC membership before 1960 and the initiative for a change in policy came from the top, first with committees of civil servants and then from Macmillan himself. EEC membership would, he hoped, offer his government a new image for modernity, a new sphere for British influence, a new way to poach on Liberal preserves, a new mechanism for pushing Labour on to the defensive, and thus a much-needed route to electoral victory. Yet given his Party's imperial past, the widespread British hostility to Germany in the 1950s, and the lack of 'European' pressure from below, Macmillan's remains in retrospect a bold move.

With the first application for entry in 1961, launching the third phase (revived Conservative Europeanism, 1961–7) Britain had at last reached the situation where the government was in favour, and Macmillan handled things so skilfully at home that in the crucial division of 2 August 1961 there were only thirty abstentions and one hostile vote from his own Party. The opposition had yet to be convinced, for Gaitskell came out against British membership at his Party conference in 1962, influenced partly by personal distaste for Macmillan and his partisan motives. Diverging on this from many of his revisionist disciples, who divided three to one in favour in the early 1960s,[15] Gaitskell was at one with many of the traditionalists in his Party who had earlier opposed his attempt to jettison its constitution's fourth clause. As Dora Gaitskell put it, after he had concluded his speech, 'all the wrong people are cheering'.[16] Macmillan's bid failed with de Gaulle partly because of the conflict between the downbeat campaign Macmillan had to conduct at home and the need to convince the French that Britain was psychologically 'ready' for the change. Besides, de Gaulle knew that Macmillan had not abandoned his pursuit of the 'special relationship' on defence and other matters with the United States. In Heath, however, the Conservatives found a leader who was not inclined to postpone choices, whose instincts on foreign policy were far more radical, and who was ready to use his influence within his Party energetically to push Euro-sceptics into a minority. So Wilson's application for entry in 1967 launched a fourth phase (1967–70), during which for the first time Europeanism captured both government and opposition. The Conservatives took the unusual step of imposing a three-line whip in favour of Wilson's decision to apply.

In the complicated European dance being performed by the parties,

Labour loyalties were not yet predictable. Whereas the leaders in both parties now favoured membership, their rank and file contained dissidents, and Labour's dissidents were determined after 1970 to exploit the European issue as a way of repudiating Wilson governments that had deeply disappointed them on other issues. So in the fifth phase (1970–4), Europeanism reverted to being a single-party alignment. Wilson had long ago pointed out that the EEC's pedigree was Cobdenite Liberal rather than socialist,[17] and this perception made it easier for his Party to go along with the little Englandism of its working-class following in the guise of pursuing 'socialism in one country'. This was not at all acceptable to Jenkins, for whom internationalism was 'quite fundamental to socialism', and John Mackintosh reminded the Party's special conference on the EEC in 1975 that the Party's song was 'The Red Flag', not 'Land of Hope and Glory'.[18] Westminster's holes and corners now witnessed significant but secret cross-party deals. Labour's Europeans refused to prevent Heath from getting Britain into the EEC, and their secret discussions with the government eased the Bill through parliament with the aid of the free vote which William Rodgers had privately requested.[19] Conversely, several discussions between Wilson and Powell in a parliamentary lavatory edged Powell into declaring for Labour, then decidedly Euro-sceptic, at the general election of February 1974.[20]

Once in power, Labour set about restoring the situation of 1967: all-party agreement on EEC membership. It negotiated amended terms of accession, subject to the referendum which (as we saw in Chapter 8) crept up on the Party after 1969 as a device for holding its Europeans and Euro-sceptics together. The speech of the West German Chancellor Helmut Schmidt at Labour's special conference on the EEC in November 1974, insisting that 'your comrades on the Continent want you to stay', was warmly received,[21] but only the electors could overcome Labour's Euro-sceptics. The New Left historian E. P. Thompson thought the referendum's endorsement of EEC entry would 'put the bourgeoisie 20 years ahead at one throw', by enabling the European employers to mobilize far ahead of their employees.[22] However that may be, the two-to-one referendum victory for the Europeans certainly threw Labour's Euro-sceptic left on the defensive. Party activists, who prided themselves on being more closely in touch with opinion than the leaders they criticized, received a severe shock. A demoted Benn was still nursing his wounds when looking back over the year on 31 December: it was 'a far bigger defeat for the Left—and for me in particular—than I had realised'.[23] Throughout this phase, Wilson's main objective had not been to get Britain securely into the EEC, but to hold his Party together. 'For many years I have been accused of putting party interests or the requirements of party unity before all else,' he told a dinner of Labour mayors in December 1974. 'I do not think party unity is necessarily an unworthy aim, particularly for the leader of the party.'[24]

The stage was set for the sixth and final phase (1975 to the present): all-party Europeanism. Although both Labour and Conservative governments saw themselves as European throughout this phase, both parties were divided. Labour at first remained sufficiently Euro-sceptic for defence of Britain's continued EEC membership to fuel the SDP's secession in 1981. As early as January 1971 Benn in conversation with Jenkins had sketched out the possibility that the EEC issue might split Labour and create a broad European centre party flanked by left- and right-wing Euro-sceptic groupings.[25] By December 1976 Jenkins, battered by his experience in a Labour Party that still seemed moving left and against Europe, expressed his weariness of Westminster's gladiatorial politics[26] and soon retreated to Brussels. He later came to see the Europeans' all-party referendum campaign of 1975 as the beginning of the end for the two-party divide; in enabling him to work with sympathizers from other parties, it had brought him 'a considerable liberation of the spirit'.[27] By summer 1980 Labour's Europeans were on the defensive, and three members of the future 'gang of four' (Williams, Owen, and Rodgers) issued a statement deploring the revived threat to leave the EEC.[28] In October the Party conference in 1980 ignored David Owen's plea and voted overwhelmingly to take Britain out of the EEC without a referendum. Not surprisingly, the SDP listed securing 'international co-operation' among its twelve tasks in March 1981, with Britain playing a full role in EEC and NATO.[29]

As long as the EEC saw itself as a community of nation states that provided an enlarged free market for British goods, Thatcher had no difficulty with membership. 'My own vision of Europe can be summed up in two words,' she said in November 1990. 'It should be *free*, politically and economically. And it should be *open*.'[30] She was able to straddle the incipient divide in her Party after 1979 by her forthright campaign to improve the financial basis of Britain's membership—to 'get our money back'. Two developments in the 1980s made this position difficult to sustain. The contrast between a free-market Britain and an interventionist EEC progressively widened as the Thatcher revolution took shape, while the EEC moved steadily forward from free-trade area to economic and then political union. By the mid-1980s the dance between the two parties was taking another turn, with Labour becoming more sympathetic to the EEC than the Conservatives. Given that socialism was now on the defensive at home, the EEC began to seem for Labour a last redoubt for the old values[31] and at the same time—with the accession of Greece (1981), Spain, and Portugal (1986)—a mechanism for consolidating democracy within countries hitherto authoritarian in tendency. In December 1989 Labour went further, and for European reasons abandoned its support for the closed shop. The EEC's proposed social charter endorsed the right to take a job without being required to join a trade union, and only by changing its stance could Labour plausibly attack the government for failing to endorse the charter. By this time Thatcher was losing a sequence of important ministers—Heseltine, Lawson, and (most damagingly of all) Howe—who for one reason or another disliked the anti-European direction she now seemed to be taking. With serious trouble from Euro-sceptics in the Party conference of 1992, and with a Euro-sceptic 'party within a party' separating out in 1994–5, it was now Major's Conservative Party that was inclining away from Europe.

What does this sixfold sequence reveal about the working of the two-party system? Firstly, because the parties compete continuously for electoral advantage through seeking new sources of support within the community, full ventilation for Euro-sceptic and Europhile opinion has been assured, even at the expense of party consistency on policy. So although Labour attacked Macmillan's first bid for membership, it was itself making the second bid within five years. At that point, Conservative Euro-sceptics were suppressed by the strength of Heath's European convictions and by the brevity of the interval between application and de Gaulle's veto. But when Heath took Britain into Europe after 1970, Labour almost immediately abandoned its earlier European commitment, to protests from some of the more honest former Labour ministers who had supported it, and preserved a Euro-sceptic tone until the referendum of 1975. Thereafter, the two parties have successively taken up the Euro-sceptic role. Secondly, Britain's EEC story reveals the continuing importance of divisions within as well as between parties in the process of scouring the community for opinion likely to be electorally helpful: Powell versus Heath, Benn versus Wilson and Callaghan, Thatcher versus Howe, Tebbit versus Major. Thirdly, although European union is difficult to fit into the traditions of both Conservative and Labour parties, it did not in itself prompt the emergence of a centre party, still less the electoral system favouring centrist government that some Europeans would have liked. The two-party system has been tenacious enough to survive continuous comparison with the proportional representation and centre-government coalition systems in the European Union. Fourthly, there is the two-party system's capacity to present to the world, even more on this issue than on some others, a national image of indecision, inconsistency, and even bad faith. This has done nothing to boost Britain's reputation within the EEC, though such wavering and hesitation probably reflects quite accurately the state of British opinion on the issue since the 1950s.

This raises the rather different question of how public opinion on the European issue has impinged on the political system since 1945. Pressure groups directly concerned with the matter have been relatively unimportant. Interest and cause groups concerned with specific areas of policy, gravitating as they instinctively do to the centres of power, have of course been active at the European level. The TUC did not long maintain its initial boycott of EEC institutions,[32] and after 1973 agricultural and environmentalist groups often bypassed the House of Commons and operated in Brussels,[33] where there was often more money and support to be had than at Westminster. Feminist and humanitarian causes have also benefited considerably since 1973 from support within the EEC. Yet Britain's three applications to join the EEC did not result from pressure-group activity. And in so far as pressure groups were later formed to promote membership, they drew heavily on élite connections. Their opponents, by contrast, responded to less expert but popular sentiments relatively distant, geographically and psychologically, from the centres of power. 'Yes' campaigners in 1975 did not need to exert themselves much because backed by a majority of the cabinet, and almost unanimously by the press and the larger interest groups, apart from the trade unions.[34] They were able to spend eleven times as much as the 'noes', more than any political party had hitherto spent centrally on any general election.[35] Tied as they were so closely to the establishment, they aimed to avoid provoking the anti-establishment vote, so diffused and dispersed their efforts and spread out into the community. Confronted by this relatively united, affluent, expert, and in media terms sophisticated movement, the 'noes', by contrast, sought to concentrate their campaign.[36] Unlike opponents who were disparate by design, the 'noes' were rendered disparate by fate. One of their leading supporters (Benn) even refused to appear on the same platform as another (Powell). The Euro-sceptics' relative weakness persists. For if the British cannot bring themselves to express enthusiasm for European union, they express no enthusiasm for its opponents either. Backing from both Benn and Thatcher for a referendum on the Maastricht treaty in January 1993 could not draw more than a few hundred to a meeting in Trafalgar Square, at which Benn refrained from applauding the supportive statement from Thatcher when it was read out.[37]

If pressure groups were relatively unimportant, how was public opinion carried along with the idea that Britain should not only enter the EEC but accept, however reluctantly, the steady extension of its aspirations? The general public have seldom been overtly enlisted in the process. General elections have never centred upon the European issue, and there has been only one referendum. One reason for lack of public involvement is simply that at each of Britain's three applications for entry—in 1961–3, 1967, and 1970–5—the prime minister's overriding concern was to avoid splitting his party. Macmillan's move towards the EEC advanced in stages: first, should negotiation begin? With that agreed, what should be the terms of accession? With the terms discovered, could they be improved? With improvements won, the negotiation was presented as a hard-earned success which it would be foolish to reject, and so Macmillan's Conservative MPs remained as united as Wilson's cabinet ministers during the second try in 1967. No single moment of choice was presented to the public, and no attempt was made directly to rouse it, if only because this might simultaneously divide the government and weaken its bargaining hand in Europe. As we have seen, such a low-key campaign had the unintended effect of convincing de Gaulle that the British people were not ready for the change: hence his first veto, in 1963. Something similar happened with Wilson's second attempt at entry in 1967. By avoiding questions of principle and concentrating on the practical details of what terms might be offered, Wilson, too, managed to avoid any clear moment of decision, and so (much to his pride) was able to keep his cabinet united while the application was prepared and considered.[38] Powell complained in 1971 that Heath was doing just the same, and that once the details had been settled surprise would be expressed when anyone objected to the principle.[39]

But did not the 1975 referendum at least involve the public in reaching a decision? Some say not, because Wilson's handling of the entire issue since 1970 had loaded the decision in favour of entry in several ways. Before taking office he had focused Labour's objections to entry on the terms the Heath government had obtained. On taking office, discussion centred entirely on the terms, and when these had been settled they carried the government's endorsement. What with this and the fact that Britain was by then already in the EEC, 'safety first' dictated the referendum's outcome. There was also plausibility in the complaint Benn made in cabinet: that during the referendum campaign 'the real case for entry has never been spelled out, which is that there should be a fully federal Europe in which we become a province', and that 'it hasn't been spelled out because the people would never accept it'.[40] From Macmillan onwards, the EEC's supporters had chosen to emphasize the economic benefits of membership, and to keep its political implications in the background. Heath and Jenkins did not conceal their belief in ultimate political union, but that was presented as a distant prospect which could be scrutinized when it came more closely into view, decision not having been pre-empted by the economic union then under discussion. The EEC 'was never intended solely as a charter for economic liberty', Heath rightly pointed out in 1989. 'The aim was, and is . . . ever closer political union. The means for bringing this about were, and are, economic.'[41] Yet this was not at all the tone the Europeans struck during the referendum campaign. Even economic and monetary union was, Wilson told the cabinet in December 1974, 'as dead as mutton': a mere form of words, a pious aspiration that need not be taken seriously.[42] At the key meeting of the cabinet in March, Castle said she opposed membership because 'we were asking the British people to remain in an organization in whose principles we said we did not believe', and Benn claimed that 'we are at the moment on a federal escalator, moving as we talk, going towards a federal objective we do not wish to reach'.[43]

In this, Labour's anti-marketeers of 1975 anticipated the Conservative Euro-sceptics of the early 1990s. Once Britain had become a full member, the EEC's influence was neither immediate nor dramatic. The scale of its aspirations and impact was not at once perceived, or was perceived only with a blind eye; people assumed, or wanted to assume, that for the time being they could carry on as though nothing much had happened. But by the early 1990s economic integration had gone so far that political integration seemed the EEC's natural destination, and to oppose it seemed likely to damage the British economy seriously. 'The history of our dealings with the European Commission', Thatcher told parliament in 1991, 'seems to consist of our conceding powers, of reassurances being given about their limits, of those limits being breached, and of the European Community then coming back with a new set of demands for more power for the Commission.'[44] Hence the Euro-sceptics' enthusiasm once more for a referendum. The outcome of any such referendum is uncertain, and the circumstances demanding it are as yet unclear, but it would have the major merit of forcing British Europeans to mobilize, and to educate and involve the public in deciding the matter.

For it will now be clear that public opinion has not been prominent as a direct player in Britain's European party-game. Opinion polls in the 1960s were much boosted by the need to discover public attitudes to the EEC,[45] but the polls merely provided the politicians with their raw material. The

Europeans have never needed to mount sustained campaigns because at every stage in the European advance it is governments that have taken the initiative: Macmillan (prompted by civil servants and the need for an up-to-date image and an election-winning issue) in 1961; Wilson (seeking a distraction from serious set-backs on Rhodesia and the economy) in 1967; Heath (responding to personal conviction and prior party commitment) in 1970–3; Wilson again (having negotiated revised terms) in 1974–5; Callaghan (amidst strong opposition within his Party but with Conservative support) moving forward to direct elections for the European parliament in 1977; Thatcher (somewhat apprehensively, after getting safeguards) acquiescing in the Single European Act in 1985 and then reluctantly entering the Exchange Rate Mechanism in 1990; Major withdrawing from it in 1992 (only because market pressures made continued membership impossible) and in 1992–3 (again after getting concessions) narrowly getting the Maastricht treaty through parliament without seeking endorsement from the referenda that were thought necessary in Denmark and France.

If the British Europeans had needed to rouse public opinion, they would not have found it easy. Among the EEC's six founding members, enthusiasm and idealism have never been lacking. Defence against Soviet and resurgent German ambitions and pursuit of prosperity through economies of scale have been present among the arguments for union from the start, but so has a yearning to avoid any recurrence of the jealousies and hatreds within Europe that produced two disastrously destructive world wars. As a precedent for political union flowing from economic union, the *Zollverein* which united nineteenth-century Germany has been helpful, though it is the United States rather than Bismarck's German empire that acts as political exemplar. Because Britain's fortunate geographical situation in 1940 enabled her to 'stand alone' against Hitler, and because the scale of her destruction and humiliation in the Second World War never even approached those of 'the Six', the British people have felt neither their yearning for European unity, nor their unalloyed pleasure at the demise of the old frontiers. And while federalism is an approach to government which Britain was happy to export to her colonies, it is alien to her own unitary structure. All this helps to explain British fatalism and indifference towards EEC and European Union.

When Heath returned to Downing Street after parliament had endorsed British entry to the EEC, he played Bach's first prelude and fugue for the well-tempered clavier on his clavichord to a few close friends. But combined controversy and apathy about British entry, the musical and cultural 'fanfare for Europe', organized to celebrate British entry into the

EEC, seemed somewhat incongruous, even élitist, and fell rather flat.[46] The metrication associated with the move towards the EEC in the 1970s evoked continuous grumbles, so much so that politicians were afraid to push it fully home. They allowed themselves to be diverted in 1970 by a sentimental campaign to preserve the sixpence,[47] and successive governments showed a 'pusillanimous attitude' on metrication, 'each in turn giving way to the temptation of simplistic populist appeal'.[48] The vote for continued British membership in 1975 was of course overwhelming, but it was hardly enthusiastic. The Labour Party for at least a decade thereafter remained only grudgingly acquiescent, and the Conservatives in 1975 acquired as leader someone who drew from the Second World War lessons quite different from Heath's. As Prime Minister, Thatcher showed no enthusiasm for EEC ideals, consistent impatience with EEC politicians and their style, and uncompromising hostility to European political union. Here Euro-sceptic politicians were probably more in tune with public opinion than Heath and Jenkins, both sidelined in British politics after 1975. Overwhelming votes were cast in Labour Party conferences against direct elections to the European parliament in 1976, a divided cabinet was slow to legislate for it in 1977, and heavily dependent on Conservative support to get it through. The parties were relatively inactive at Euro-elections, and turn-out was scarcely more than half that for any other European country and lower than in local-government elections. As we have seen, this was largely because, uniquely in the EEC, Britain had adopted a voting system ill suited to the purpose, but that in itself indicated how distant Britain still was from Europe. In the circumstances, *The Times*'s claim in December 1977 that Britain was 'now slowly acquiring the habit of thinking in European terms, taking the European dimension of policies into account, comparing its experiences and institutions with those of fellow Europeans' looked like wishful thinking.[49]

The Euro-sceptic position rests on significant misunderstanding. The role and power of the European Commission is widely misinterpreted in Britain, whose attachment to the concept of the nation state is stronger than in most of the European Union. A more interactive concept of nationality is more appropriate in the situation that now prevails in communications and technology; and if this is so, a new understanding of what is meant by 'sovereignty' needs to be promoted. Whereas the Commission is a modest administrative structure responsible for implementing decisions reached by national governments through the Council of Ministers, it came to be seen by Thatcher in the late 1980s as a malign and scheming body with interventionist designs. British Euro-sceptics came to see 'federalism', an

entirely respectable concept concerned with the fragmenting of government power and frequently applied by the British in ex-colonial contexts,[50]
as a sort of bogy when promoted from Brussels. In 1991 the President of
the Commission, Jacques Delors, thought it necessary to point out that it
is 'a word you should speak out loud. It's not a pornographic word.'[51]

This was one among many insights Howe compressed into his brief but
memorable resignation speech in November 1990, together with a plea for
a more subtle approach to the whole concept of sovereignty. The European enterprise, he said, should not be seen as 'some kind of zero sum
game';[52] interaction between EEC states involved mutual persuasion within
a continuing set of relationships, and sovereignty could not be equated
with virginity: 'now you had it, now you did not'.[53] Sovereignty within the
EEC was pooled; any one nation lost some control over its own affairs but
at the same time gained some control over the affairs of partner nations.
The EEC was, said Heseltine, 'a *political* market place—a process of
wheeling and dealing—as well as an economic market'.[54] British Europeans from the 1960s onwards knew that given the prevailing economic
interdependence, Britain faced a choice only between different types of
subordination: between on the one hand operating independently on the
international economic stage but with her fate decided in private discussions among EEC powers, or on the other hand trading in some sovereignty for the right to join in those discussions. Drawing on his recent
experience as Chancellor of the Exchequer, Jenkins in 1971 'did not wish
to see a continuation of the position in which the Six decide . . . matters
which are crucial to this country and all that we can do is to have a little
chat with the Americans'.[55]

As long as the EEC's aspirations remained purely economic, they could
be accepted by Labour and endorsed by Thatcher even with enthusiasm.
But in the changed situation of the 1990s, it is arguable that the British
Europeans need to become more active. The European Union's drawbacks
are daily advertised, whereas the problems withdrawal would pose are conveniently distant, and it is on a diet of indignation rather than of contentment that cause groups march furthest. Withdrawal from the European
Union would now be really damaging to the economy, not just for inward
investment, but also for the City, which aims to make itself Europe's
financial centre.[56] The stock exchange FT-SE index immediately rose ten
points when the news of Thatcher's resignation in 1990 flashed on the
screen, and rose another 24.5 points within minutes.[57] Politicians in the
British political system cannot ultimately act autonomously from articulated opinion, and in their continued European commitment they will

need firm evidence of backing from the public—perhaps even in the second referendum which even Douglas Hurd, when Foreign Secretary, did not rule out.[58]

So methods of handling public opinion that have sufficed since 1973 seem unlikely to suffice for much longer. Government initiatives on Europe have hitherto freed British Europhiles from any need to keep their muscles in trim, but muscle may well soon be required if they are to make their aspirations clear and organize vigorously in their defence. For the Euro-sceptics in their manifesto of 1994 and Blair in his statement to businessmen in Brussels in 1995 are correct: 'European integration cannot happen by stealth, by closet agreement among governments. It must be with the people's consent,' and 'for any European policy to work it must enjoy the consent of the people'.[59] Manipulation by politicians and parties may have secured Britain's formal enlistment in European union, whether economic or political, but only public involvement and even enthusiasm for it can render this new alignment beneficial or even democratic for Britain. To generate such enthusiasm, rather more energy will be required from British Europeans than has been needed in the past. Geoffrey Howe records 'with some sadness' in his memoirs how the courage of some 'Europeans' in Thatcher's last cabinet 'often faltered' in the face of Europhobia from the chair. Jenkins in 1972 complained of populists who appealed only to people's 'superficial reactions, to the prejudices of the moment, to their worst rather than their better instincts',[60] and felt no enthusiasm for a Euro-referendum which then seemed merely a populist instrument. His insistence on the MP's autonomy reflected, among other things, a certain fastidiousness about campaigning to change opinions he disliked. Yet for the continued vitality of the European venture in Britain, a campaigning mood combining reason and emotion more akin to that of William Wilberforce, Richard Cobden, and Josephine Butler may eventually be required.

It remains to consider how British involvement with Europe since 1973 has affected the separate parts of its political system.[61] Europe's impact on pressure groups has already been discussed, together with its substantial impact on the agenda of political parties. In other respects, the EEC changed the parties less than might be supposed. Both Labour and Conservative parties were slow to affiliate with their equivalents in the European parliament,[62] if only because their traditions were not easily assimilated. The German social democrats had long offered Labour a model of how it might adjust to new class relationships, but the model had never been whole-heartedly or overtly embraced. As for the Conservatives, European conservative parties were more coalitionist, less secular, and less distant from parties of the left. European electoral systems helped to strengthen the Liberal and SDP pressure for electoral reform, and exerted some influence on the Labour Party but little influence on the Conservatives after Heath had ceased to be leader. On ways of influencing the electorate, we saw in Chapter 8 how the United States remained the major influence, especially on the Conservative Party. The Labour Party, too, was profoundly affected by the campaigns which made Kennedy and Clinton presidents. The only powerful European influences on party policy, at least until the late 1980s, came from individual countries rather than from the EEC as a whole: during the Conservative and Labour parties' corporatist phase, from the interventionist structures of France, Germany, and Italy. After 1979 British economic policy was, if anything, for export, though as we have seen, the EEC countries' interventionism provided Labour with some solace.

Of the other major institutions, the most deeply affected was parliament. Because the parties were divided, it was not easy to get Britain into the EEC in the 1970s or into the European Union in the 1990s. Backbenchers had to be courted, and there was much less talk of MPs having become mere lobby fodder. Parliament on key occasions became the focus of everyone's attention. On the other hand, MPs had good reason to be suspicious of the EEC. Parliament's longevity and paramountcy, as Powell pointed out in 1971, bound it more closely than other European national parliaments into the national self-image.[63] The House of Commons took pride in its long record of challenging the executive, and British MPs, when they first arrived in the European parliament, thought themselves specially qualified to make suggestions for its improvement.[64] By closeting the elected heads of state in the European Council two or three times a year, the EEC seemed to accentuate the danger from the executive, if only because the Council often gave prime ministers the excuse to escape their troubles at home and perform on an international stage. Some thought it ominous that Heath chose to announce the success of the EEC negotiations, not in parliament, but at Lancaster House on 12 July 1971 in an international press conference that was presidential in style.[65] Powell and Foot were the two backbenchers who had successfully resisted House of Lords reform in 1969 on the ground that it would unduly promote executive power. It was no coincidence that in 1972 they collaborated again in resisting membership of the EEC.[66] Labour's backbench suspicions were accentuated by what Foot called the 'kind of lawyer's conjuring trick'[67] whereby the government hoped to rush the Bill through the House of Commons by making it unexpectedly brief. Furthermore, the roles of civil servant and politician were less clearly delimited in many European countries than in Britain. The effect of membership, said Benn in 1978, 'has been to produce a radical transfer of power from the British parliament to the British Government, from the British Government to Europe, and from Ministers to officials'.[68]

Europe also threatened parliament's authority from quite another direction, because the Euro-sceptics were inconsistent in their parliamentarism. They espoused the referendum in the hope that it would go against the EEC. But the referendum infringed the MP's autonomy from the voter, who on the issue in question was being required to assume the politician's function of reaching a decision. 'After all,' grumbled an opponent of the referendum, 'one doesn't keep a dog and bark oneself.'[69] The infringement was minimized by requiring the referendum count to be taken nationally rather than by county (as many Euro-sceptics favoured) or by constituency (as Benn favoured). A national count would avoid divisively identifying particular regions as hostile, and would minimize threats to good relations between MP and constituency.[70] The government argued that the referendum could not erode parliamentary sovereignty because parliament could not be bound by it,[71] but when Heath attacked Wilson for his 'major constitutional innovation', Wilson felt bound to explain that this was 'a very special situation, which I do not think anybody will take as a precedent'.[72] Thatcher too objected that the precedent would be held to justify the referendum's wider application—somewhat ironically, given the fact that she espoused just such an extension on several later occasions. In 1992 she was advocating a referendum on the Maastricht treaty at a time when Major was insisting that the House of Commons offered scrutiny 'line by line, clause by clause . . . a more effective scrutiny than referenda'.[73]

There were several other ways in which the EEC issue threatened parliament. As with delegated legislation earlier, the sheer volume of information requiring scrutiny brought the danger of parliamentary overload, and led to the appointment of the select committee on European secondary legislation in 1974. There were also accentuated threats from rival assemblies. The European parliament itself set up MEPs as potential rivals, and the Westminster parliament even in the late 1980s was still treating them 'almost like pariahs.'[74] The European parliament for the time being provided a training-ground for aspiring MPs (Ann Clwyd, Robert Jackson), or a rest-home for retiring ones (Castle), but they could occasionally cause trouble. When thirty-two Labour MEPs challenged Blair's plans for the Labour Party constitution's Clause 4 in 1995, for instance, he was quick to brand their conduct as 'infantile'. And when, later in the year, Major was struggling to hold his Party together on Europe, the chairman of the Conservative MEPs argued that 'parliamentary control lost at national level should be regained at European level', and specified several ways in which the powers of the European Parliament should be extended.[75] The EEC also increased potential rivalry from subordinate assemblies elsewhere in the United Kingdom. One strand in the Euro-sceptic case was always the fear that those parts of the United Kingdom closest to Europe would gain at the expense of those (often Labour heartland) areas furthest away, and this regional imbalance of fear was reflected in votes on European issues. Even more threatening to Labour's traditionalists, though, was what might happen if European union, in transcending the nation state, released the subordinate peoples the nation state had subjugated for a new European role. In a nationalist upsurge that transcended both class and party, and bypassed Paris, Madrid, and London,—the Corsicans, Bretons, Basques, Scots, and Welsh might eventually go their own way. The European Union's macro-federalism might in other words produce micro-federalism within the United Kingdom—the term 'federalism' being used, of course, in its proper sense of fragmented sovereignty.

The fear that the EEC would have the effect of enhancing the powers of the British executive was not fully borne out. For much of the period the EEC was too controversial for the monarchy to be too closely identified with it, and Euro-sceptic MPs were on the watch for any lapses from the monarchy's complete neutrality. A state visit to France in 1972, the first since 1957, set the seal on the new Anglo-French accord, but Hamilton and Shore were quick to raise objections to the monarchy being used in this way, and Euro-sceptics did the same again when the Queen addressed the European Commission in 1980 and the European parliament in 1992.[76] By providing the occasion for the loss of key cabinet ministers, the EEC connection also undermined one of twentieth-century Britain's most powerful prime ministers, and European factors do much to explain why she ultimately lost power. The Foreign Office had at first opposed British involvement with the EEC, but by the 1970s found in this new alignment a new role for itself. The mere fact that the EEC involved Britain in closer international linkages in itself lent value to the Foreign Office's special skills, and both Council of Ministers and European Council provided valuable locations for informal diplomacy on non-European matters—on Anglo-Irish relations, for example. The Foreign Office found its new role the more valuable because, as we saw in Chapter 11, improved communications were strengthening the foreign connections of many government departments, thereby denying the Foreign Office its earlier distinctive role. All this helps to explain Thatcher's strained relations with her foreign secretaries. It was a former diplomat worried by Thatcher's distaste for the EEC who first issued a challenge to her as Conservative leader: Sir Anthony Meyer in 1989. And Heseltine, her leading challenger in the following year, had first publicly fallen out with her on a European question.[77] There was one further 'European' limitation on executive power in Britain: through the mounting concern with civil liberties. The European convention on human rights grew out of the Second World War and antedated the EEC, but Britain's European connection after 1973 increased the visibility of the European Court of Human Rights at Strasbourg, and in the 1970s its influence restrained repressive army techniques in Northern Ireland and curbed caning in schools. And despite its rejection of the railwaymen's case for the closed shop in 1981, the Court was one of the influences enhancing preoccupation with civil liberties in the 1980s at a time when the dominant Party was highly unsympathetic.

*

In discussing the international context for Britain's political institutions, something must be said about the attitudes projected by Britain's political leaders. 'The leading statesmen in a free country . . .', wrote Bagehot, 'settle the conversation of mankind. It is they who . . . determine what shall be said and what shall be written for long after.'[78] With some exceptions—Palmerston, Disraeli, and Joseph Chamberlain, for instance—nineteenth-century statesmen were privately and even publicly keen to play down Britain's aspirations to a world role. Their Christian and classical culture rendered the decline of empires a familiar concept. At the same time, their concern about the national debt, their pursuit of cheap government, and their faith in free trade made them wary of overseas adventures. Twentieth-century political leaders have been slow to wean the British people away from inflated notions of their world role. They have settled our conversation largely by pretending either that national decline has not occurred, or that it can be reversed. They have lingered too long over the precariously won successes of the Second World War, they have encouraged revivals of 'the Dunkirk spirit', and have even propagated the notion of a 'new Elizabethan age'. They have misled the voters into expecting far more from politicians than they can possibly deliver. In the 1970s their belief in planning fostered inflated expectations in domestic policy as well, with the result that British political institutions were overstretched and there was talk of the country becoming 'ungovernable'; the 1980s did at least remove that danger, but there still persists a yearning, as the phrase goes, to 'punch above our weight' on the world's stage. Hence an undignified clinging to a seat on the United Nations' Security Council which makes Britain look ridiculous and insults more influential nations.

At least since the late 1950s it has been with the politicians, not with the Foreign Office, that the blame has rested, for those who move professionally in international circles can retain few illusions about British power. Powell's 'nest of vipers, that nursery of traitors'[79] has been made into a scapegoat by politicians for diplomatic set-backs that stem from the politicians' failure to inject realism into public discussion. 'One of the few points on which the Foreign Office and I agreed', Thatcher recalls, 'was the need for British embassies to be architecturally imposing and provided with fine pictures and furniture.'[80] She seems genuinely to have believed that Britain's long-lost military and diplomatic status could and should be recovered. Less robust politicians, however, have kept up the illusions as much from timidity as from conviction. The very concept of the 'Commonwealth' was used to conceal from the public the speed of Britain's imperial decline. Foreigners might detect hypocrisy in the attempt to present the loss of 400 million citizens as a gain, wrote Harold Nicolson, discussing Britain's stage-managed retreat from India in August 1947, but 'it is not that. We do not desire to deceive others; we wish only to comfort ourselves.'[81] Many British Europeans saw themselves as calling a new European empire into existence to compensate for loss of the old. British parliamentary institutions and practices, already exported far beyond Europe, would at last come to rest in Brussels and Strasbourg. All this was accompanied by dismissive asides about Scandinavian-style monarchies and by depreciating references to prosperous and rather attractive small nations such as Switzerland as unsuitable destinations for Britain. There is nothing inherently discreditable to a nation in smallness, nor, in a world of increasing international integration, is smallness the drawback it once was.

British statesmen since 1914 have privately known well enough that Britain could not in practice match her public pretensions. Such recognition was integral to the highly practical and down-to-earth strategy of the 1930s that is so often ignorantly scorned as 'appeasement'. British involvement on the winning side during the Second World War delayed the nation's recognition of the truths that appeasement acknowledged. How can politicians' public acquiescence in national self-deception be explained? 'Giving up what one has is always a bad thing,' Queen Victoria told the

Marquis of Salisbury, reluctantly consenting to cede Heligoland to Germany in 1890.[82] Desire to minimize the disruptions and even humiliations involved in national decline is understandable, and was perhaps even necessary for a time, yet one cannot but feel that there has been a long-term failure of leadership here. Britain's reduced world standing offered an unrivalled opportunity for a British statesman to transcend petty detail and short-term party interest and enlist public opinion behind a new and less showy but more constructive destiny for the country. Guiding public opinion towards the constructive exploitation of necessity is integral to statesmanship. In Joseph Chamberlain from 1903 the British people discovered a man of vision who sought simultaneously to reassess Britain's overall situation and to educate the public on the new directions British society should take. There was ample room at the time, and still more now, for questioning the direction Chamberlain favoured. But at least he showed a courage and breadth of vision about Britain's international role that has been lacking in the politics of decline since 1945.

The failure of statesmanship may owe something to the types of explanation which Cobden would have found congenial: to such things as the vanity of statesmen who preen themselves on the world role their country's power enables them to pursue, to the continuing influence of outdated school textbooks and imperial festivals,[83] and to the interest felt by the armed services and by diplomats in preserving their careers and perquisites. In 1969 the Duncan committee on overseas representation recommended that the diplomatic service should aim at only selective coverage of the world, and at more interaction between the service and industry, but it was not energetically acted upon. Still less acceptable to the diplomats was the CPRS report of 1977 which wanted diplomatic expenditure scaled down. Sir Geoffrey Howe when Foreign Secretary tried to secure 'a medium-term framework' within which Britain's scarce resources for defence, diplomacy and overseas aid (material and cultural) could be most effectively deployed. Yet he made no progress: 'it always seemed impossible to open up to objective analysis the thought processes of the Ministry of Defence'.[84] Still, Cobden's types of explanation never quite carry conviction. After the successive economic set-backs since 1945, politicians must take some responsibility. It would have been difficult for party leaders on the right to achieve any such redirection. The Europeanism of Macmillan and Heath came close to it, but in the first case was accompanied by too much tactical manoeuvring and national self-assertion to be effective for the purpose under discussion. In the second case, the proponent was too controversial in personality and domestic policy to retain widespread support within his own

Party, let alone elsewhere. Besides, in both instances the case for Britain's joining the EEC was presented in terms of new worlds for Britain to conquer, rather than as a way out of insularity, and this understandably aroused de Gaulle's suspicion. As for Churchill and Eden in the 1950s and Thatcher in the 1980s, let alone Portillo in the 1990s, their signposts all pointed the wrong way. Even in 1993 there seemed positive daring in the confession by Douglas Hurd as Foreign Secretary, when opposing American demands for British troops in Bosnia, that 'obviously we cannot be everywhere and we cannot do everything'.[85]

The failure of the left energetically to promote readjustment in the face of international decline is more surprising. A Cobdenite Liberal party could readily have made a virtue of this necessity. It would also have seized the internationalist opportunity presented by European union with enthusiasm, instead of hesitantly and after a long delay. How can the delay be explained? It is not as though the opportunity was not perceived. In 1945 Attlee privately questioned the value of Britain's defence commitments in the Middle East and east of Suez, yet he failed to influence Bevin.[86] Benn in 1963 wanted Britain to deal with her 'central African colonial encumbrances', deal with Aden and Oman, and then adopt a Scandinavian line at the United Nations in support of underdeveloped countries.[87] Crossman in June 1966 thought the government's commitment to involvement east of Suez 'all a fantastic illusion', and six months later claimed that clinging to the parity with the aim of keeping Britain great had been 'the basic reason for all our economic troubles and our difficulties at home'. He thought most electors would 'be perfectly content to accept the end of our imperial pretensions and to cut-back the mumbo-jumbo and humbug' for a realistic foreign policy. By June 1967 he privately despised the House of Commons for its wishful thinking on how, in the event of Israeli victory, Britain could now shape the future of the Middle East.[88] And yet as a cabinet minister he did nothing to draw the British public towards his view. In April he thought that it might have been possible a year earlier to abandon the sterling area and withdraw from east of Suez, but the moment had passed.[89] Jenkins and his supporters, imbued with Liberal values, readily grasped the vision that lay behind the EEC. Yet after a courageous battle for the European ideal inside the Labour Party during the 1970s, they were forced, as events turned out in the 1980s, to become Liberals also in name.

The explanation for Labour's failure involves far more than just Wilson's taste for discovering Britain's frontier on the Himalayas. It lies partly in the nature of the Party: heavily dependent on areas of heavy industry, its constituencies had much to lose by the cessation of British defence commitments. More heavily dependent on working-class support than its Liberal predecessor had been, Labour had fewer and weaker middle-class progressives to draw upon. But there are other reasons less specific to Labour: for example, the fact that although (as pointed out in Chapter 2) empire impinged surprisingly late on the British governmental machine, its influence persisted there for a surprisingly long time. British politicians in the 1940s and 1950s were slow to appreciate how quickly African nationalists would learn from Irish and Indian. They were also encouraged by the United States to co-operate in holding back the advance of world communism. This role came as naturally to the Labour Party as to any other, for its advance to the status of party of government occurred during the 1920s in the course of fending off Communist infiltration. Well into the 1980s the Communist threat seemed as menacing as ever. The Americans wanted Britain's anti-Communist influence maintained in Asia and Africa,[90] and as reciprocal favours supplied nuclear secrets and defended Britain's ailing pound. In this they were supported by anti-Communist national leaders such as Lee Kuan Yew, who felt they had some claim on the British government for continued support.[91] None the less, a weakened economy soon forced Wilson's second government to abandon Britain's role east of Suez. 'The real trouble is that we have never done things in time,' wrote Crossman in December 1968. 'Every decision has visibly been extracted from us.'[92]

It was difficult to disentangle Britain from her former connections. Imperial myths remain so tenacious partly because they reflect a cultural and demographic reality. Britain's colonial moment was both preceded and followed by long periods of less formal linkage. Stressing the importance of Commonwealth links in December 1974, Wilson pointed out that 'I have forty-three close relatives in Australia, descendants of my four grandparents, more than four times as many as I have in Britain.' His Commonwealth enthusiasm had been nourished by accompanying his mother in 1926 in a visit to his sick grandfather in Australia, and had been carried further in the 1950s by his involvement with War on Want and by writing his book *The War on World Poverty* (1953). Such influences help to explain why rejuvenation of the Commonwealth remained central to a Labour general election campaign as recently as 1964.[93] Commitments of a cultural as well as military kind long outlasted the colonial connection, and gave rise to special expectations of Britain in many parts of the world. Reminding MPs and peers in May 1993 of Britain's long involvement in South Africa, Nelson Mandela claimed that the mingling of Britons and

South Africans 'demands of you that you should assist us, and therefore yourselves as well, to rediscover for ourselves as a people the practice of democracy'.[94]

The British political system in some ways made it difficult for politicians to prepare Britain for its diminished world role. Bagehot long ago acknowledged that in foreign policy the two-party system failed to produce that public education for which he so valued it in other spheres. 'In a case affecting the nation's honour . . .', he pointed out, 'no party dares to take the side which is, or is said to be, opposed to that honour,' so that 'as a nation never hears anything against its own side, it naturally comes to believe that side to be unassailable and incontrovertible'.[95] Such influences were of course powerful on the right, but they also influenced Labour, for the Party's problem was always to yoke a down-to-earth working-class vote with a high-minded middle-class one. To take a recent example: because of fear of what Castle privately called the 'absolute howl of anger in Parliament'[96] that a deal on the Falklands with Argentina would provoke, the politicians directing foreign policy did not feel able publicly to sell the Foreign Office's proposal for a deal on the matter. Hence the misunderstandings which caused Argentina to invade in 1982.[97] The Falklands victory, together with Thatcher's highly unusual conjuncture of personal relationships with the American and Soviet heads of state, postponed the recognition of reality for still longer. 'Really', Castle had added, 'the problem of winding up the last outposts of empire is almost ludicrously difficult.'[98]

Yet one can adopt a rather different perspective on this story. Instead of regret at Britain's reduced international economic and strategic importance, or yearning to recover it, perhaps the dominant emotion should be one of surprise that so small a nation could once have wielded such power in the world. And given the economic and perhaps even moral costs of such influence, British pride in past glories should perhaps now give way to pride in the way it retreated from them: in that 'managed decline' which in the Foreign Office evoked such scorn from Thatcher. By world standards, Britain's exercise in extrication from impossible responsibilities was skilfully brought off, and with remarkably little disruption of British political structures. This success perhaps even provides some excuse for the politicians' failure to scotch national self-deception, for they were shielding the British public from the full shock of the British decline. The politicians' long delay before endorsing British membership of the EEC, for example, made it easier for both Commonwealth and United Kingdom to adjust psychologically and practically to the new and necessary alignment. National withdrawal and retreat were continuously presented as mere evolution, or even billed as presenting new opportunities. Perhaps it is unreasonable to want the successful self-extrication, the social stability, and the political continuity that twentieth-century British politicians have achieved without the accompanying national self-deception. But it takes no party-political or personal courage for a political leader to inflate the self-image of his audience, considerable courage for him to scale it down. Britain's transition from her one-time role is now almost complete. A party leader bold enough to say so, and imaginative enough to highlight the benefits of that transition, might settle the conversation of the British people in new and more fruitful directions.

# 15

## *Cultural Prerequisites*

THIS book has been concerned with a political system whose unusual features are perhaps too much taken for granted. We have seen how central government from the 1860s till the First World War grew substantially at the expense of local government, reached a plateau between the wars, then advanced further until 1979, then fell back rapidly, so that civil-service numbers declined by a third within a decade. All this occurred piecemeal, with remarkably little public discussion, let alone with any formal consideration of the administration's role within the political system. We have seen how an adversarial party system which grew up informally, with parties unknown to the law, proved remarkably tenacious. It rested upon an electoral system transformed by changes in transport and the media, yet it retained the simple-majority procedures thought acceptable before railways were invented. We have seen a parliament which can respond to wartime emergencies by prolonging its life and concealing its debates, yet which in peacetime can subject its governments to continuous criticism from an opposition whose structure grew up unexpectedly and became formalized only over a very long period. And at the apex of the system we have observed in action a cabinet which has no formal existence and which changes its structure, as required, according to the personality and circumstances of party and prime minister; and a monarchy which adapts its functions according to needs imperial or domestic, peaceful or warlike, aristocratic or democratic. In several contexts earlier chapters have stressed the advantages of such flexibility: the directness of the relationship it makes possible between government policy and shifts in opinion, the relative speed and cheapness of its procedures for implementing policy, the stream of continual but relatively responsible criticism that is made possible, and the government's relative freedom to focus on objectives rather than on mechanisms.

Yet therein also lie the system's drawbacks, for with flexibility comes the danger of abuse. 'Procedure is all the Constitution the poor Briton has', said Pickthorn in 1960, 'now that any Government which can command 51 per cent of the House [of Commons] can at any moment do anything they like, with retrospective or prospective intention'. Bagehot's political system assumed for its successful working a quite specific social situation, now long gone. It assumed that 'common sense' and integrity would be widespread at the highest political levels, and that those qualities would be widely respected lower down. Nineteenth-century Liberals knew that these qualities need to be nurtured, and with that in view they treated the world as a classroom, presided over by high-minded intellectuals. Given good laws, broad political participation, and the free exchange of ideas within and between states, the citizen's understanding would steadily advance. We are now less optimistic about the citizen's capacity and appetite for political instruction, less rationalistic about how that instruction is best conveyed. None the less, the Hansard Society's working party on political education in 1978 was entirely right to emphasize that the subject is not to be confused with slots in a school timetable labelled 'civics', 'politics', or 'British constitution'.[1] As adults we all absorb political understanding more effectively and continuously in informal and practical contexts long after we have fitfully absorbed it as schoolchildren. This informal political education grows out of British political culture, and its qualities are all the more important for the fact that, as Chapters 3–6 showed, so many initiatives in the British political system are expected to come from outside government. Yet these qualities would remain important even for a society which introduced a written constitution, for only in an environment compatible with its purposes could it ever take effect.

So this book will not conclude with an agenda of desirable reforms; that is already abundantly available elsewhere. Instead it will focus on cultural prerequisites for the continued successful working of the system. Many of these could be considered, but the emphasis here will be on four (each worthy of a book in itself) that affect attitudes to the political process, for it is from this quarter that threats to the long-standing British tradition of incremental institutional change are most likely to come. The discussion will concern political ideas, and will successively consider their generation, their communication, their interaction with participation, and their interpretation.

*

The British political system works well only if those who operate it can reach broad agreement on its agenda and methods. As Gladstone pointed out, the British constitution 'presumes, more boldly than any other, the sense and good faith of those who work it'. It assumes 'that the depositaries of power will all respect one another; will evince a consciousness that they are working in a common interest for a common end; that they will be possessed, together with not less than an average intelligence, of not less than an average sense of equity and of the public interest and rights'. Otherwise, 'the British Constitution will be in danger'.[2] For most of the period since the 1860s this posed no serious difficulty. The subject-matter of politics was by our standards relatively uncomplicated. The landed aristocracy who operated the system were trained from birth in how to operate political institutions, and they readily recruited experts and professional administrators to help them. Their political influence long outlasted their formal political control; even within a democratized electorate the management of politics remained in the hands of very few until surprisingly recently, especially where economic and diplomatic questions were involved. Furthermore, through their close links with the public schools, Oxford, and Cambridge, the landed aristocracy readily imbued the rising middle class with their political values and understanding during the nineteenth century. In the process, Jews, Roman Catholics, and nonconformists were with some difficulty harnessed to the working of the system.

The spread of democratic ideals, reinforced by the requirements of planning and social stability, made it necessary to incorporate new groups into the political system even more quickly during the twentieth century, at precisely the time when the supply of political talent became less predictable. The attempt to assimilate the Irish into the political system after 1914 signally failed, and the absorption of Protestant Ireland after 1922 turned out to be precarious. The harnessing of organized labour to the system was a lengthy process, still causing major difficulty in the 1970s, though valiant efforts had been made to bequeath to the Labour Party elements of the old aristocratic political inheritance.[3] After 1918 women were drawn into the parliamentary process relatively smoothly, though the continued separation of spheres ensured that Westminster remained largely in the hands of men. By the 1960s this compromise with feminism seemed no longer satisfactory, but attempts to move beyond it were accompanied by the new challenges. New waves of immigrants needed to be drawn towards the political system, together with a group which had not hitherto been allowed to develop in Britain: a potentially disaffected group within the intelligentsia. These challenges have by no means yet been surmounted.

When access to a political system broadens out so quickly, those who operate it will not necessarily have been trained for their role by tradition, background, and education. Political ideas are no longer generated within a 'political class' that meets frequently at clubs, country houses, and social functions regardless of political party, as occurred in Bagehot's day. Nor can political ideas now be ventilated in the well-informed and mature national forum that the great Victorian periodicals and reviews provided. The links between the political and intellectual élite are weakening, and high seriousness is now dispersed to the learned journals. The national press embraces with growing enthusiasm the largely visual and recreational priorities of the mass media. Correspondence columns of a much-diminished *Times* and fragmented debates on *Any Questions* or *Panorama* provide no substitute for the sustained argument that was conducted within mid-Victorian periodicals like the *Fortnightly Review*, and from which Bagehot's *English Constitution* emerged. The demotion of politics within the national press since Bagehot's day has been striking. While nobody would now want a return to the 1830s, when more than a quarter of *The Times* carried verbatim reports of parliamentary debates, it does seem regrettable that the national press no longer fosters the national conversation that once took place on matters of political importance. The scope and seriousness of political discussion conducted within, say, the Edwardian *Manchester Guardian* would indeed be welcome in at least one of our national newspapers. The hopes that were placed in the *Independent* in its early days have been disappointed, and alone among modern newspapers the *Financial Times* approaches the level of public discussion that was once taken for granted in leading national papers. Yet its scope is inevitably specialized, and in other papers political comment grows increasingly superficial. So rapid has been the decline, fuelled by the advent since the 1960s of increasingly frothy supplements, that columnists like Alan Watkins, who themselves pioneered a lighter approach to political comment in their day, now seem positively serious. Direct reporting of parliamentary debates dwindles, and parliamentary speeches on topics of major importance (Heath's, for example, on terrorism on 8 June 1993) are hardly noticed.[4]

These developments are the more serious because the agenda of politics has simultaneously become more complex and the electoral mood less predictable. Many of the issues central to British politics since the 1930s have been highly technical in nature. The nineteenth century had already encountered this problem in the medical and scientific area, and by the 1930s the difficulty increasingly lay in the field of economics. Keynes, says his biographer, 'never ceased to believe that the well-being of society depended on the strong, clear thinking of the few'. He told R. F. Kahn in 1940 that the problem of exchange control, central to the nation's prosperity, yet never prominent in a general election, was 'frightfully technical . . . I should think there are hardly more than half a dozen people in the country whose opinion is worth having.'[5] Governments in the 1960s and 1970s had to open out more widely than this, if only because incomes policies and the restraint of inflation required them to reach into the daily lives of every individual, and so to promote expensive schemes of public education. Yet as Heath complained in the mid-1960s, 'abstract conceptions are extremely difficult to put across to a mass electorate. If one speaks of preserving market forces or the need to diversify the centres of power in society one is understood by only a small minority of the electorate.'[6]

The political parties offered one of the earliest substitutes for the inherited experience that was husbanded within the old aristocratic system, but their inevitably partisan and short-term perspectives inhibited sustained thought. One reason why the Labour Party failed to expose the potential hostility to the poll tax was that the money voted to it in its capacity as opposition party was spent on boosting the parliamentary effectiveness of individual shadow cabinet ministers, not on collectively investigating the likely effects of the tax.[7] Furthermore, the parties depend too heavily on private funding for continuous research and constructive discussion to be at all easy. Private funding does, however, have the virtue of forcing parties to reach out for support into the community at large,[8] and of increasing the incentive for politicians to retain contact with the voter. This is more than can be said for much of what happens in the social studies departments of universities, which might otherwise have been expected to take over from country house and London club in the generation of policy. The careers of Beveridge, Tawney, and Titmuss amply reveal the potential. But academic specialization proceeds so fast that the worlds of academic study and political practice are diverging. University teachers in the social sciences, reverential towards the natural sciences, pursue quantification and abstraction, and will perhaps frown on the fact that this book has required neither tables nor diagrams. The academic study of politics, economics, and sociology moves steadily beyond comprehension by the practising politician, let alone by the layman.

Hence the need that has increasingly been felt since the 1950s for a bridge-building that will ward off mindless pragmatism and unworldly abstraction and draw together theory and practice. It is a divide that since the decline of aristocratic government has been wider in Britain than in the United States, but governments since the 1960s have recognized that the problem exists, and have sought a solution in such ventures as the Civil Service College, the Central Policy Review Staff, the Social Policy Unit, and the Policy Unit at 10 Downing Street that developed under Thatcher, not to mention proposals for ministerial cabinets or a British Brookings Institution. These ventures achieved less than their creators had hoped. More successful have been initiatives from outside government. By 1962 Anthony Sampson was noting the growth of 'new institutes', which provided 'a kind of shadow civil service': the Royal Institute of International Affairs (founded in 1920), for example, which revived in the 1960s to supplement the Foreign Office. Similar bodies related to government departments were the National Institute for Economic and Social Research (supplementing the Treasury), the Institute for Strategic Studies (supplementing the Ministry of Defence), the Institute of Education (supplementing the Ministry of Education), and the Institute for Overseas Development (supplementing the Department of Technical Co-operation). 'While Oxford and Cambridge have remained proudly aloof from most contemporary studies', wrote Sampson, 'the institutes are beginning to provide an academic circumference to Whitehall.'[9] In the natural sciences and in subjects that were of interest to the professions, the field was also well cultivated by interest and pressure groups.

In social and economic policy, where such groups were less in evidence, the 1970s saw a crucially important contribution emerging from the 'think-tanks' that assisted at the birth of 'Thatcherism'. Bagehot rightly pointed out in 1862 that public opinion on any issue is more fluid at any one time than appears on the surface. Many people derive their opinions from what they think others think. 'In secret, each has his doubts, which he suppresses, because he fancies that others who have thought more about the matter have no such misgivings; but if a shrewd examiner were to scrutinise each man's mind, they would find much tacit, latent, accumulated doubt in each.' The think-tanks' role was to release such doubts and mobilize them. Thereby public opinion could be prepared for ideas the politicians had earlier dismissed as unthinkable. 'What we can do', said Madsen Pirie of the Adam Smith Institute in December 1987, 'is to introduce ideas into the public arena and make it acceptable to talk about them.'[10] To the busy politician such bodies offered the great boon of access to the ideas and expertise of the intellectually leisured. In their pursuit of practical aims, they fertilized public discussion by breaking down the barriers and obscurities of academic specialism. Their brain-power complemented and even counteracted the muscle-power of the pressure group.[11] At the Centre for Policy Studies, an energetic merging of disciplines, a tapping of networks, and an effecting of introductions excited all who participated. And at the Institute of Economic Affairs 'Arthur Seldon managed to everyone's surprise to persuade economists to write English prose.'[12] The impetus from such groups on the right ran out during the 1980s. The failure of the poll tax revealed the limits to what thinking alone can achieve in politics, and advertised the crucial importance of political judgement. Since then the Thatcher Foundation, which could have made itself very useful in Britain in the early 1990s, seems to have achieved little, and Major's reduced parliamentary majority after 1992 made bold and imaginative Conservative plans for the future less feasible.

Yet such methods are not ineluctably conservative, and are capable of wide extension. From the late 1980s there was widespread imitation on the left, reinforced by the charitable foundations whose role Thatcherism had enhanced: the Rowntree Trust and the Leverhulme, Nuffield, and Wellcome Foundations. The careers of John Gray, David Marquand, Raymond Plant, and David Willetts—to name only four of those whose minds are playing on the boundary of academic and political life—suggest that the Thatcher episode will have as one of its unplanned consequences a revival of that interaction between the active and the contemplative life which a healthy democratic society requires. If that is so, there is some hope that politics may recapture some of the talent that in recent years has been flowing so freely into the entertainment media.

\*

'The ignorance ... is in many classes profound,' wrote Bagehot of popular attitudes to the working of the British political system. 'If any one will investigate what his servants say ... probably he will begin to be awake to a difficulty which our common habits conceal from us.'[13] He was complacent amidst such ignorance, and under universal suffrage his nonchalance is no longer feasible; in a democracy, the communication of policy becomes of central importance. Yet instead of political literacy extending in parallel with the franchise, there is some evidence of a reverse tendency. 'The popular constituency for serious discussion of politics in Edwardian Britain', it has been claimed, 'was probably larger in proportion to population than at any time before or since.'[14] Between the wars the need for improved communication in politics seemed urgent enough to generate the vigorous and progressive though perhaps somewhat earnest Association for Education in Citizenship, launched in 1934.

The Association was a rationalistic analogue of Moral Rearmament, born out of the totalitarian threat. Alarmed at the way propaganda could mould opinion, it wanted British democracy to match its Fascist rivals in educational self-defence. Its aim was 'to advance the study of and training in citizenship, by which is meant training in the moral qualities necessary for the citizens of a democracy; the encouragement of clear thinking in everyday affairs; and the acquisition of that knowledge of the modern world usually given by means of courses in history, geography, economics, citizenship and public affairs'.[15] Key figures in its promotion were Ernest Simon and Eva Hubback,[16] and it owed much to support from the sort of feminist, adult educationist, and Liberal intellectual who had been left politically high and dry by Labour's supersession of the Liberal Party. Too rationalistic to welcome the emotions and loyalties of the Labour Party, such people pined for the progressive intellectualism of the governmental Liberal Party that had now been lost for good. The Association operated inside the educational establishment on a non-party basis, and concentrated on making informal approaches to influential individuals and on organizing conferences of the cultivated. Based on 'red-brick' universities, it advanced its cause through discussion groups, bibliographical guides, handbooks, and aids for those who were teaching sixth-formers economics and politics. Its membership at its height in 1938–9 was only 1,650.[17] During the Second World War its branch structure collapsed, and later its chief donor Ernest Simon (by then Lord Simon of Wythenshawe) acquired other interests and ceased to subscribe. With the widening of school curricula after the war, and with democracy's triumph over Fascism, there seemed less need for the Association, and in 1957 it was wound up.

The Association's concerns, however, were shared by many who knew nothing of it, both before and after its short life. 'The urgency of effective civic education speaks for itself,' wrote Laski in 1938. Failure to interest more people in public affairs was 'one of the great failures of imagination in British democracy'. This meant that 'most of the population grows to maturity with little conception of even the purposes, let alone the methods, of modern administration'.[18] Margaret Cole, impressed in 1942 by the morale-boosting impact of education on both the Nazi and the Soviet war effort, thought it 'one of the more staggering facts, and a comment upon our civilization's survival-value' that elementary politics was nowhere taught in British schools.[19] Now that both Fascist and Communist threats to democracy have crumbled, the Association's fears seem somewhat dated, and in any event the classroom and the moral-reform movement as weapons against totalitarianism seem inadequate—even sinister, the closer they came to mimicking the enemy.

Yet the threat to democracy is ever taking new forms, and the Association's concerns seem in the 1990s as relevant as ever. In 1962 the majority of a sample interviewed for the *Sunday Times* could not name any political figure in either Labour or Conservative parties other than the leader, and in the following year a Gallup poll showed that several million electors thought Britain already belonged to the EEC.[20] When the Hansard Society surveyed 4,027 15-year-olds in state secondary schools for their political awareness in summer 1975, only a quarter chose the correct figure (635) for the number of MPs out of a choice of six figures, well dispersed, between sixty-five and 820.[21] The survey was also concerned with the use the teenagers made of their political information, and this showed that their understanding did not go very far. More than a quarter thought that the Conservative Party wanted more nationalization, for example, and only 42 per cent contested the suggestion that the IRA was a Protestant organization set up to prevent Irish union. For Bernard Crick, 'the extent of political awareness among this group is truly appalling ... only a little more appalling than that of the mass of the ordinary population'.[22] Given the decline of a leisured class, the decay of civic consciousness, the increasing tendency of women to take paid work, and the growth of recreational diversity, there are now more distractions from political understanding and participation than seems healthy in a democratic society.

The mass media have done something to meet the need. Television has taken British politicians off the precariously high pedestals they occupied until the 1950s. Only this can explain the scale of the impact made on Macmillan's public image, for example, by an irreverent entertainer like Peter Cook in the early 1960s. The media have helped to break down some of the unnecessary secrecy which until very recently surrounded British governmental decision-making. They have also greatly extended public comprehension of political issues, personalities, and information. New developments in technology make it likely that information about government will soon become much more widely and cheaply available, and that the opportunities for citizens conveniently to impinge on government will greatly extend. If this occurs, the media will be receiving as much as they give out. The beginnings of this tendency are already evident in the growth of concern about audience response and in the recent spread of phone-in and feedback programmes. So the media have helped to diffuse some of the raw materials necessary for political understanding, and promise to diffuse more. Yet knowledge of political facts is not sufficient for understanding the political process—the 'art of politics'—any more than to assemble the ingredients is to make the cake. Have the media helped to advance understanding of the political process itself? Here their contribution is more equivocal, and has been criticized not only by outsiders but also by distinguished media personalities such as Robin Day and John Birt.

We now have an almost continuous generation of news-as-entertainment, enhanced and glamorized by noisy musical and/or dramatic visual introductions. There is mounting visibility for the personalities and methods involved in news-gathering, together with frequent references to 'news desks', and even televised representations of them that seem drawn from science fiction. It will soon be forgotten how recent was the decision to dramatize the news in this way, for the change creeps up on us gradually and unannounced. News, if it does not exist, is manufactured. This is a world very distant from the early days of radio. 'When there was not sufficient news judged worthy of being broadcast', writes the BBC's historian, 'no attempt was made to fill the gap, and the announcer simply said "there is no news tonight".'[23] So complete has been our retreat from this outlook that it now seems laughable. When the distinguished pioneer news-broadcaster Alvar Lidell dared to say, in 1979, that 'news has a right to be boring and dull on occasion' and that '*synthetic* excitement'[24] is above all to be avoided, some of the responses were incredulous.

From the point of view of communicating to the general public a sense of what politics is about, this new climate has its drawbacks. The yearning for visual and aural impact is at risk of ousting balance and proportion.[25] There is a somewhat breathless media pressure towards preoccupation only with the immediate and the up-to-date, even with attempts to predict the future. Contrast with this the essence of the political and diplomatic process—cautious, prolonged, and often (if it is to be really effective) secret. As Birt puts it, broadcasters 'need to ensure that we address long-term as well as short-term issues'.[26] *The Times* in a thoughtful leader of 1993 pointed out that 'journalists who work to tight daily deadlines are tempted to seize upon events, rather than processes. If something happens suddenly, it is more likely to be covered than if it happens gradually.'[27] This is not calculated to bring out the full complexity of the situations with which politicians and diplomats have to deal. It may even foster a pressure for publicity and for instant solutions that actually hinder reconciliation of disputes. In a speech of 1993 that was only cursorily reported, and which received somewhat dismissive comment, Douglas Hurd as Foreign Secretary expressed concern about the difficulties that resulted from the widening news coverage of international relations since the 1950s. He stressed that secrecy is inevitable if diplomatic negotiations are ever to succeed, and emphasized that 'the camera is an actor', both in making a choice about what to record, and in its impact on events once that decision is taken. He pointed up the contrasts between two professions: the reporters who (in Bosnia at least) were 'founder members of the "something must be done" school'; and the decision-makers who must take responsibility for their actions.[28] A mere endorsement of ill-considered compassion would in the statesman be culpable, and would probably create more suffering than it removed.

Then there is the impact made by reporting of this type on the pace and mood of politics. The problem is epitomized by the *Sun*'s headline on 11 January 1979: 'CRISIS—WHAT CRISIS?' The paper was summarizing Callaghan's response at London Airport to journalists' allegations of 'mounting chaos' in the country on his return from the Guadeloupe summit.[29] News-reporting speeds up the pace and intensity of life, and there is a perpetual search for the stimulation that crises and emergencies will provide. 'News bulletins are too much a kaleidoscope of visual happenings rather than explanation of issues,' Robin Day claimed in 1980. He thought 'those in charge of television' should 'restrain themselves from using its power solely to project the visual aspects of world affairs, because the most important things are not always visual'.[30] When Martyn Lewis raised the 'bad news' issue, fellow broadcasters and journalists were dismissive. He thought it 'high time' that 'we who work in television news with its remorseless emphasis on disaster, conflict and failure, started treating the complaint of too much bad news seriously'.[31] It was not deliberately biased reporting that worried him, but unconscious bias in the selection of news items. He complained of 'a relentless drip-feed into the viewer's mind that we live in a society where achievement takes a back seat to conflict, disaster and failure', and that therefore 'we consign viewers to growing up in a relentless culture of negativity—of naturally expecting things to go wrong'.[32] He rightly emphasized that news programmes in their contents reflect a deliberate act of choice on the part of people who are not required to identify themselves publicly or explain the principles that govern their selection.

Instead of subsequent discussion throwing light on the selection process, let alone justifying it, Lewis's concerns were dismissed as naïve or self-promoting. Comment was largely confined, not to considering his arguments at their face value, but (somewhat impertinently) to providing biographical portraits of a colleague who could so strangely choose to step out of professional line. Dismissing misinterpretation of his views, Lewis pointed out that 'I am simply asking for TV news editors ... to bring to news bulletins as a whole, over the year, the same balance we all strive for in each individual video report.' He went on to say that 'where there is disaster, there are people trying to recover from it. Where there is suffering, there are people trying to help. Where there is conflict, there are people trying to end it.'[33] The search for bad news risks not only distorting the climate within which politicians operate. It risks devaluing the very business of politics. There is the danger that the media will transfer the glamour that was once the politician's to others far less deserving: that the 'macho' values of gangster films will move from the world of recreation to the world of news-reporting, and that viewers will fail to distinguish fact from fiction. The problem has been confronted only in the context of terrorism based in Northern Ireland, but the danger is more pervasive. News reporters need to know that terrorists arrange their actions so as to create maximum media effect, and that they exploit people whose aims and methods diverge markedly from their own.

The devaluing of politics is even more direct than this. Broadcasters, said Birt, relish the disputatious and thereby discourage reflection, so that 'the media resounds [*sic*] with acrimony, allegations of incompetence, demands for resignation'.[34] No chairman of the BBC could now brave press hostility, as Lord Simon of Wythenshawe did in 1950, by banning a repeat performance of a comedy whose plot turned on politicians' cynical venality: Val Gielgud's 'Party Manners'.[35] The media have done much to produce a salutary decline of 'deference' in modern British society, and it is certainly important that politicians should be prevented from manipulating the means of communication in self-interested ways. Yet there is now a danger that the deference once accorded to elected politicians will be transferred to their unelected critics. If cynicism is what replaces deference, the last state may be worse than the first. The pedigree of this change in media attitudes goes back to the irreverent strategy of Aidan Crawley at ITN in the 1950s, as implemented by Robin Day,[36] and thence to the satirical television programmes of the early 1960s. The line continues through *Private Eye*, the journalism of Alan Watkins and Frank Johnson,[37] and through numerous plays and films of the 1970s and 1980s. Wilson's style of political leadership after 1964, confirmed by the diaries of his cabinet colleagues, lent credibility to a cynical outlook on politics, and was reinforced by the Poulson and Stonehouse affairs.

It is of course the beginning of political maturity to avoid utopian expectations of other human beings. Indeed, the British two-party adversarial system is designed precisely to avoid that, and to subject government to a continuous barrage of criticism. But there is a distinction between scepticism and cynicism: between a critical approach to the actions of a government and rejection of the entire political process for some unstated alternative. The parties in Britain are, after all, far more than groupings of 'ins' and 'outs': in contrast to some party systems, their battle is fought over policies and programmes. With their knowing yet over-simplified attribution of motives, their elaborate detection of 'subtexts', commentators run the risk of causing public figures to live down to their reputation, or else to vacate public life altogether. Healthy criticism can become a negative carping, effecting from a quite unexpected direction what was attempted between the wars by extremists of right and left: the devaluing of politics as an activity. Fortunately politicians have not been entirely bereft of sympathizers within the media. By 1970 Paul Johnson was deploring 'the spectacle of TV professionals—not notorious for the gravity or sincerity of their opinions—attempting to corner politicians into admitting that they are liars, manipulators or even scoundrels. In my experience', he went on, 'the great majority of our politicians are honest, with genuine convictions, trying to serve their country to the best of their ability.'[38]

From the mid-1960s onwards, politicians were becoming increasingly and justifiably wary of how television was affecting their profession—one reason for the long delay before they voted for parliament to be televised. Tony Benn, discussing with media people over lunch what should replace the programme *That was the Week that Was* in September 1964, sensed that the mood was anti-political—not in a radical extremist sense, but 'in a scornful and contemptuous way'.[39] Callaghan as Prime Minister at formal media gatherings twice deplored 'the trendy cynicism that has crept into our national life . . . more often destructive than creative'.[40] Hurd in 1993 referred to the imbalance that had grown up in British life since the 1950s between the doers and the sceptics: to the 'marked shift of talent and effort away from achievement into criticism',[41] and in the following year Portillo spoke of the 'new British disease' of national self-depreciation that had grown up since the 1960s among 'the chattering classes'.[42] For the Prince of Wales in 1994 there was 'a persistent current that flows along undermining the integrity and motives of individuals, organisations and institutions', and in the same year John Major attacked the prevalent 'knocking, carping and sneering' in British politics. 'I know politicians of all parties', he said, and 'they are not the cynical, power-hungry, self-servers that fiction so often portrays'.[43]

The media should not be made scapegoat for a cynical tendency that has much broader causes. They reflect tendencies which are widespread in society; nor are politicians exempt from responsibility. Those who, with Thatcher, favour 'conviction politics' would perhaps say that Macmillan's ingenuity in holding his party together was bought at too high a price. And there were many in the Labour Party during the 1960s who felt that Wilson's parliamentarism degenerated into something close to opportunism. Already in March 1972 Jenkins was hinting at the problem: 'unless we can demonstrate that we, at least, do not see politics as a mere game of "ins" and "outs", an arcane affair of House of Commons tricks and manœuvres, public disillusionment with the present Government will spill over into a more general disillusionment with the parliamentary system itself. Cynicism about politics and politicians is already widespread. It is the deadliest single enemy of any party which wishes to change society through the ballot box.'[44] Jenkins went on to channel much idealism into the Social Democratic Party, whose failure no doubt added to the ranks of the disillusioned. None the less, both the survival of John Major amidst his sea of troubles and the wave of enthusiasm for the leadership of Tony Blair suggest that there are still political gains to be made by decent men articulating decent values.

Political life has many attractions. MPs' salaries are well above the national average, their secretarial facilities are generous, their role is varied and potentially fulfilling, with what is in some sense the nation's highest (though not highest-paid) post as the ultimate prize. There is also the excitement of being at the heart of events. 'I have tried all forms of excitement', said Lord Randolph Churchill once in conversation, 'from tip-cat to tiger-shooting; all degrees of gambling, from beggar-my-neighbour to Monte Carlo; but have found no gambling like politics, and no excitement like a big division'.[45] There is no shortage of applicants for adoption as parliamentary candidates, and to judge from the imbalance of MPs drawn from women and ethnic minorities, large areas of national talent remain untapped for parliamentary purposes. But parliament no longer offers its members the social standing it could still offer between the wars, the pay is low by business and even higher civil-service standards, and lower than many at Westminster might get if they worked elsewhere. MPs' formidable hours and work-pressures hardly make for good health, the insecurity of the career (and still more of success in it) is endemic and worsening the more volatile the voters become, the threat to family life is considerable, and press scrutiny becomes ever more intrusive. While the voters in their own lives share fully in relaxed standards of personal conduct, they now require a puritanism from public figures that is as stringent as at any time in our history. Coming on top of all this, the unobtrusive and even unintentional devaluing of politics as an activity by the media, supplemented by direct attacks on the politicians, is likely to accentuate a draining of talent from political life which has now gone far enough.

Censorship cannot now be the remedy. The only remedy lies in creating a discriminating public and encouraging self-criticism within the media. This requires decision-makers of all kinds, especially diplomats and politicians, to ensure (often at the risk of their careers, given the power of the media) that their critics are not in full possession of the field, and not only to explain and justify their specific decisions but also to propagate wider understanding of what their professions involve. It also perhaps requires practitioners in the media to respond somewhat less self-righteously to lay criticism, and to avoid instinctively interpreting criticism of their actions as an attempt to infringe free speech or stifle artistic creativity. 'We quite properly demand the right to attack, criticise and analyse every other sector of society,' writes Lewis, 'and yet some of us are surprisingly sensitive when someone . . . asks us to turn that same probing spotlight on ourselves.'[46] Decisions taken within the media, like decisions taken by politicians and diplomats, have a widely ramifying and often subtle impact on society as a whole. The affinity between freedom of reporting and the health of democracy cannot merely be assumed. Those responsible for deciding which subjects to report and how should be ready to identify themselves and explain and justify their priorities. For as Birt points out, 'there is no higher democratic legitimacy than Parliament's . . . we should . . . remember that individual MPs and parties have stood before the public and have been elected by them, which we have not'.[47]

*

In 1978 two well-informed enthusiasts for political education in schools rightly pointed out that political literacy concerns action as well as knowledge: 'there are still some who appear to want "good citizenship" without the trouble of having citizens'.[48] If political education involves training for action as well as possession of facts and ideas, local self-government, the third theme of this chapter, is important. Here the case for substantial institutional change seems strong. For the problem which the poll tax clumsily addressed has not gone away: communities lack the incentive closely to monitor what local authorities do on their behalf. Already by 1926 Ernest Simon was depressed at Manchester's distance from the Athenian ideal. In a book on the city council dedicated to 'my fellow citizens', he regretted the fact that a 'cynical attitude towards municipal service is unfortunately common amongst all classes'.[49] At the start of his book *The Devolution of Power* in 1968, John Mackintosh asked 'why should the words "local government" induce a sense of boredom in even the most politically interested citizens?'[50] Nothing highlights the lowered twentieth-century expectation of local government better than a glance at what now seem the absurdly inflated late-Victorian hopes of parish councils. Turn-out at local elections, well below that at national elections,[51] shows no sign of improvement, and a marked fall in electoral registration in the late 1980s showed that for many people the vote was less important to them than the chance of avoiding the poll tax. Thatcher yearned to revive the civic pride and local participation that once set limits to the power of central government and did so much to beautify British cities. Yet her one practical proposal for effecting that revival came to naught, and the incidental effect of her policies elsewhere was to erode the prestige of local government. The remedy is often seen in terms of merely restoring to local government the powers that Thatcher eroded, whereas something more substantial seems required. For Thatcher's impatience with local authorities reflected her concern at their distorted representation of public opinion, a problem which stemmed, in its turn, from an apathy among local-government electors that was manifest well before 1979. So it is not mere restoration of local-government powers that is required, but their re-establishment on a basis that will advance the health of local democracy.

In no year between 1945 and 1987 was the turn-out in English local-government elections higher than the 51 per cent attained in 1947—except in the freak year 1979, when district council elections coincided with a general election. The average for the eight years from 1980 to 1987 was 42 per cent.[52] In 1967 between a fifth and a half of those surveyed could not name any service provided by their local authority, and only 7 per cent had ever been to a council meeting.[53] In the following year Crossman felt nostalgic for his dreams as a young WEA lecturer of a broadened political participation: 'what we now have is mass-indifference and mass-alienation—a greater gap between government and people than . . . in the time of Disraeli and Gladstone'.[54] This disappointment has not of course been confined to government at the local level. In 1936, when the Germans reoccupied the Rhineland, George Orwell went into a pub in Barnsley to hear the 9 o'clock news. 'I . . . remarked at random, "The German army has crossed the Rhine". With a vague air of remembering something, someone murmured "Parley-voo". No more response than that . . . So also at every moment of crisis from 1931 onwards.'[55] Still, apathy in local politics is in some ways more worrying than at the national level because it is at the local level that most people have their best chance of political participation, and it is through local democracy that many of the recruits for national democracy begin their careers and sharpen their wits. If local democracy is unhealthy, the outlook for national government is not healthy either. Yet a survey in 1981 showed that 57 per cent of informants could not name any councillor for their area, and 56 per cent could not name their own local authority.[56]

It would be absurd to expect a high proportion of citizens to prefer sitting in committees to cultivating their gardens, associating with their families, or drinking in the pub. Political activism will always be a minority taste. Nor should local government become, as it has sometimes been with its Liberal advocates, a substitute for considered reflection on national policy, a populist accommodation with parochialism, a blurring of the distinction between pressure group and party. There was truth in Alan Clark's complaint of 1990: 'their trick is to *degrade* the whole standard of political debate. The nation, wide policy issues, the sweep of history— forget it . . . the Liberal technique is to force people to lower their sights, teeny little provincial problems about bus timetables, and street lighting and the grant for a new community hall.'[57] None the less, present-day levels of apathy in local government would have shocked the Victorians, and do not suggest that British local government is in a healthy state. How, then, can it be revived? Britain may well have something to learn here from other countries. Some have argued that a more professional, less participatory style of local government on the German model is desirable, and perhaps this would be preferable to what we have at present. Yet such a response would not have satisfied John Stuart Mill, for whom 'a democratic constitution, not supported by democratic institutions in detail, but confined to the central government, not only is not political freedom, but often creates a spirit precisely the reverse, carrying down to the lowest grade in society the desire and ambition of political domination'. Voluntarist vitality in other areas of British life—in pressure groups, think-tanks, and charities, for instance—shows that the participatory impulse has not vanished, but has simply been transferred away from local government. How could it be encouraged to return? All three major parties have an interest in finding the answer, and have long-standing traditions that will help them to do so.

The problem does not lie simply at the level of the voter; there is a need to foster the ideal of public service in local institutions, for some modern equivalent needs to be found for the social responsibility, almost automatic in nature, that in earlier periods went with aristocratic status, professional and commercial self-interest, and working-class self-defence. There may be something in the idea of reviving the concept of 'citizenship', whose unifying impulse made it preferable to Marxism as an influence on many pioneers of the Labour Party.[58] The concept was also integral to Edwardian 'new Liberalism' and the early Labour Party, and is implicit in many Conservative attitudes. But its early twentieth-century vitality owed much to a residual religious commitment, and to the localism which preceded the advent of public welfare, let alone motorways and the mass media. It is difficult to see how a less diverse and more secular and relatively hedonistic society could revive a concept so heavily dependent on voluntarism of a highly idealistic kind. Devolution in Scotland and Wales might call out public-spiritedness at the regional level, though no equivalent seems yet forthcoming within England. It is also a matter for nice calculation whether such a change will enhance the collaboration between peoples more than it inhibits it.

More practical and earthbound remedies at the level of local government include such things as simplifying boundaries, better arrangements for councillors' job release and better compensation for their lost earnings, local referenda, and voting by post in local elections. There is a case for proportional representation at the local level, where the virtues of the simple-majority system are far less clear than in national government. For Sir Ian Gilmour this was one of Thatcher's lost opportunities. He thought that, under proportional representation, none of the 'loony left' councils that led her to conduct such an assault on local-government powers would ever have been elected.[59] There is much to be said for paying welfare benefits through local authorities that acquire some discretion over entitlement.[60] But ultimately there can be no better way to revive local government than by simplifying perception of where authority lies through promoting the idea of the single-tier authority, a reform from which the government now seems largely to have retreated; and by increasing the proportion of local-authority expenditure that has to be raised locally. Ratepayers' interest in local elections would soon revive if local authorities gained more control over their budgets, and if their rising expenditure became immediately visible in rising rates. The poll tax may have been clumsily introduced and unfair in its details, but its collapse did more than damage Thatcher's career: it threatened to divert local government from the promising overall direction towards which she was guiding it.

*

Our fourth and final theme is the interpretation of politics, a theme briefly raised in the introduction. This, too, is an area where the worlds of politics and the intellect seem to be drifting apart. It is highly paradoxical that at precisely the time when more people are receiving formal instruction in politics than ever before, the quality of debate about politics in the national press has so greatly declined. There are some areas, of course, in which reporting has improved; the Nuffield election studies and the growth of opinion polls have transformed the analysis of election results, for instance. But even there the emphasis has switched unduly towards prediction and statistics. Attention has shifted away from the influences which weigh so heavily with politicians: away from their less measurable but none the less crucially important professional skills and from the inherited constraints they experience. The twentieth century has seen a major growth in writing and research on the political process, but historians, particularly those writing since 1945, have played only a small part in it. This is a surprising development if politics 'is concerned with the creative conciliation of differing interests, whether . . . primarily material or moral',[61] especially as the continuity of British political evolution has ensured that British historical writing offers a treasure trove of well-documented case-studies in such activity.

History has retreated from the serious discussion of politics because the students of 'politics' have turned away from the past and the students of the past have turned away from politics. Many political scientists, defining themselves into a new discipline, thought that this required them to define themselves out of the discipline from which their subject was emerging. Hence the decline of that fruitful interaction between the study of politics past and present that could still be found in the work of Dicey and Laski, let alone earlier. For one political scientist studying British political parties in the 1950s, the lack of any history of the Conservative Party since Peel was 'an appalling gap', and he 'found that before I could attempt to explain the institutional arrangements of either party I have had to try to repair some of the gaps left by the historians'.[62] How many political scientists would complain in such terms now? Such historical interests became scarce among students of 'politics' trained in the 1960s, influenced as they were by American behavioural and sociological models or by a Marxism for which politics was a mere side-show.

Conversely, the historians, by neglecting the study of recent politics, have paradoxically encouraged in current political debate a certain parochialism in time. Historians' wariness of 'contemporary history' reflects their desire to avoid the bias that so readily intrudes when interpreting recent events. They feel professionally less vulnerable if their subject-matter is safely distanced in the past and if it rests upon the documents, secret at the time, that reveal the real impulse behind events. The Thatcher crusade for 'Victorian values' might have been expected to lead historians both to see the Victorians from a new angle and to offer some special insights into Thatcherism. Yet the latter was consigned to the political scientists, economists, and journalists. Some of these responded with panache, and the literature is rich; Hugo Young's biography of Thatcher, for instance, compares well with any political biography that historians have written in the past century, despite being written in circumstances much more difficult than historians usually experience. The historians lost the opportunity for bringing their own distinctive perspectives to bear. This development is self-reinforcing because the political scientist's ahistorical approach deters the historian still further.

The situation was made worse by the decline of what was called 'constitutional' history. In university history courses from the 1950s onwards constitutional history succumbed before subjects less governmental in their concern, and historians grew increasingly interested in history of the social, economic, and intellectual varieties. They rightly felt that they should be concerned with the entire society, and should not limit themselves to underpinning the study and practice of government. They were also often impatient with the legalism of 'constitutional history', with its tendency to ignore the importance of social and even political context. If only for the purposes of understanding government, it seemed important to study the history of the governed. This was particularly so with the growing study of 'labour history', given that the Labour Party (unlike the Liberal and Conservative parties) grew towards Westminster from outside. Working in the same historiographical direction was Marxism, a major influence on historical writing even in Britain since 1945, let alone elsewhere. Its unconcern with problems of government, its devaluing of the politician's profession, its subordination of political influences on social change all played their part.

Yet the collapse of supposedly Marxist regimes in the USSR and in eastern Europe during the 1980s prepares the ground for a modest historiographical revolution nearer home: for history's return to a more central place in the study of politics. Events or non-events east of the iron curtain forcibly remind us both how important are political institutions and how profoundly they are moulded by events deeply rooted in the past, often in the remote past. A new emphasis has been given to the tenacity of the collective historical memory, whereby problems allegedly new turn out to be old problems in disguise. A mere glance at recent British political history illustrates this. The Conservatives remain profoundly influenced by the appeasement crisis of 1938 and the Suez crisis in 1956 and even by the split over free trade in 1846. Likewise, Labour's outlook is still moulded by the mythology of the General Strike and the crisis of 1931. The understanding of the present requires fertilization from that speciality of the historian: the study of change. A major difficulty involved in writing this book has been the need to draw a chronological sequence out of the many static analyses that political scientists have compiled.

Fortunately, historians have never entirely forsaken the study of politics. Political biography has if anything absorbed too much talent, and there have been valuable studies of major political structures and issues such as the growth of party organization, pressure-group activity, appeasement, and empire. Historians have never entirely lost interest in what politicians do and how they think. Nor have all students of 'politics' taken a sectarian view of their subject. Indeed, many of the best historical studies of British political institutions have been written by people who did not see themselves primarily as historians at all, or for whom the gulf between history and politics did not seem sensible: by S. H. Beer, Vernon Bogdanor, David Butler, D. N. Chester, R. T. McKenzie, John Mackintosh, Kenneth Wheare, and Philip Williams, for example. This book owes much to them, and if it helps to increase their number, it will have served its purpose. With a new infusion from history, other advantages would accrue. If any intellectual activity should aim to be accessible to the informed public, it is the study of 'politics'. More than many disciplines, history has sought to retain contact with the informed public, and has been less seduced than the social sciences by the natural-science model. Historians have not shown an undue preoccupation with what can be measured, or with an esoteric vocabulary and its attendant cluster of flow-charts. Not that the history which interacts with the study of 'politics' will be unchanging. Given British membership of the European Union, for instance, action will no doubt be taken on the recommendation of a *Times* leading article in 1971: that students 'should be taught a European history, related to the history of the whole world, rather than the narrowly British history which is still too common . . . schools will . . . have to educate for a European future'.[63]

A historical approach to the study of political institutions seems particularly important for understanding the political culture that is central to this book. In a society which lacks any written constitution, political institutions depend heavily for their successful working on the attitudes of those who run them. These institutions can be studied only through investigating, with access to sources once private, how the political system operated over a long time-span: that is, historically. The historian at his best will be alert to the subtleties of how the past differs from the present. He will have a rich understanding of context, of the inherited practices and attitudes that mould the working of political institutions. Baldwin once pointed out that whereas the historian could say what constitutional practice was at any given period, it would be difficult to be so specific about the present because the constitution is 'a living organism': 'at almost any given moment ... there may be one practice called "Constitutional" which is falling into desuetude and there may be another practice which is creeping into use but is not yet called Constitutional'.[64] If an instrument so flexible as the British constitution—unwritten and with only a subordinate role for the judiciary—is to be compatible with democratic and libertarian values, those who operate it must be imbued with those values and skilled at promoting them, and those who monitor governments must understand how they work. The inheritance of these qualities is not automatic. Hence this book.

# Notes

Place of publication is London unless otherwise stated. Items are cited in full only at their first citation.

## Introduction (pp. 1–11)

1. David Marquand, 'The Devolution Debacle', *Listener*, 8 Mar. 1979, 335–6.
2. W. Hutton, *The State We're In* (1995), p. xii (preface).
3. D. E. Butler and A. King, *The British General Election of 1964* (1965), 33.
4. Institute for Public Policy Research, *The Constitution of the United Kingdom* (1991), 1.
5. A. Benn and A. Hood, *Common Sense: A New Constitution for Britain*, ed. R. Winstone (1993).
6. See John Grigg's powerful criticisms in *Times Literary Supplement*, 29 July 1994, 22 of Anthony Barnett (ed.), *The Power and the Throne: The Monarchy Debate* (1994).
7. *Independent*, 9 Oct. 1991, 21.
8. M. Thatcher, *The Downing Street Years* (1993), 282.
9. Benn and Hood, *Common Sense*, 120. T. Benn, *Diaries 1980–1990*, ed. R. Winstone (1992), 564 (9 May 1989).
10. Anthony Barnett, in Barnett (ed.), *Power and the Throne*, 12.
11. M. Beloff, 'Beware the Prattling Reformers', *Independent*, 9 Oct. 1991, 21; cf. Nevil Johnson's letter in *The Times*, 30 Apr. 1992, 13.
12. W. Bagehot, Introduction to the 2nd (1872) edn. of 'English Constitution', in *Works*, v (1974), 165. S. Low, *The Governance of England* (first pub. 1904; rev. edn. 1914), 6, 12.
13. A. Adonis, *Parliament Today* (Manchester, 1990), 169.
14. Low, *Governance of England*, 2.
15. J. Paxman, *Friends in High Places: Who Runs Britain?* (first pub. 1990, paperback edn. Harmondsworth, 1991), 8.
16. H. J. Laski, *Parliamentary Government in England: A Commentary* (1938), 388.
17. H. Nicolson, *Diaries and Letters 1945–1962*, ed. N. Nicolson (1968), 161.
18. Benn and Hood, *Common Sense*, 119.
19. Cf. F. Mount, *The British Constitution Now: Recovery or Decline?* (1992), 93.
20. J. Cannon, 'The Survival of the British Monarchy', *Transactions of the Royal Historical Society* (1976), 143.

21. P. King (ed.), *The Study of Politics: A Collection of Inaugural Lectures* (1977), 13.

22. A. King (ed.), *The British Prime Minister: A Reader* (1969), pp. vii–viii.

23. N. Stammers, *Civil Liberties in Britain during the Second World War: A Political Study* (1983), 1.

24. R. I. Morgan, 'The Introduction of Civil Legal Aid in England and Wales 1914–1949', *Twentieth Century British History* (1994), 39.

25. In the introduction to S. A. Walkland (ed.), *The House of Commons in the Twentieth Century: Essays by Members of the Study of Parliament Group* (Oxford, 1979), 1, Walkland complained of 'the general lack, until recently, of Parliamentary scholarship this century', which left 'large tracts of twentieth-century procedural development . . . uncharted'. Compare Laski in King (ed.), *The Study of Politics*, 11–12.

26. J. P. Morgan, *The House of Lords and the Labour Government 1964–1970* (Oxford, 1975), 247, cf. p. vii (foreword).

27. A. Adonis, *Making Aristocracy Work: The Peerage and the Political System in Britain 1884–1914* (Oxford, 1993), 7.

28. For a cluster of examples, see N. Lawson, *The View from Number 11: Memoirs of a Tory Radical* (1992), 1015–16.

29. D. Butler, A. Adonis and T. Travers, *Failure in British Government: The Politics of the Poll Tax* (Oxford, 1994), 12.

30. W. Bagehot, 'The Character of Sir Robert Peel', in *Collected Works*, ed. N. St J.-Stevas, iii (1968), 255. Churchill, speech (6 June 1885) on 'Political Life and Thought in England' to the Cambridge University Carlton Club, in his *Speeches . . . 1880–1888*, ed. L. J. Jennings (1889), i. 255–7.

31. H. Young, *The Crossman Affair* (1976), 20.

32. T. Benn, *Out of the Wilderness: Diaries 1963–1967* (1987), 379 (26 Jan. 1966).

33. Quotation from 'Lord Althorp and the Reform Act of 1832' (1876), in Bagehot's *Works*, iii (1968), 201. See also xv (1986), 67.

34. V. Bogdanor, in D. Kavanagh and A. Seldon (eds.), *The Thatcher Effect* (Oxford, 1989), 142.

35. K. D. Ewing and C. A. Gearty, *Freedom under Thatcher: Civil Liberties in Modern Britain* (Oxford, 1990), 7.

36. D. E. Butler and R. Rose, *The British General Election of 1959* (1960), 9.

## Chapter 1: Bagehot's System (pp. 13–53)

1. W. Bagehot, 'The Advantages and Disadvantages of Becoming a Member of Parliament' (1874), in Bagehot, *Works*, vi (1974), 57.

2. Lady G. Cecil, *Life of Robert Marquis of Salisbury*, i (1921), 78. See also K. Rose, *The Later Cecils* (1975), 29.

3. Mrs Russell Barrington, *Life of Walter Bagehot* (1914), 5.

4. Letter (Feb. 1846) to his mother, in *Works*, xii (1986), 210. See also his 'Mr Disraeli' (1859), in *Works*, iii. 487.

5. Quoted in N. St J.-Stevas, *Walter Bagehot: A Study of his Life and Thought together with a Selection from his Political Writings* (1959), 46.

6. Bagehot, 'Parliamentary Reform' (1857), in *Works*, vi. 188.

7. Bagehot, 'The Late Mr Mill' (1873), in *Works*, iii. 555.

8. Bagehot, 'Principles of Political Economy' (1848), in *Works*, xi (1978), 194.

9. Bagehot, 'English Constitution', in *Works*, v. 311.

10. Bagehot, 'Principles of Political Economy' (1848), in *Works*, xi. 193.

11. J. S. Mill, *Principles of Political Economy*, ed. W. J. Ashley (1917), 758.

12. Bagehot, *Works*, vi. 390.

13. Ibid. xiv (1986), 316 (18 Aug. 1860); cf. Benn, *Against the Tide: Diaries 1973–76* (first pub. 1989, paperback edn. 1990), 619, 641.

14. e.g. in his 'The Reform Bill', *Quarterly Review* (Apr. 1866), repr. in P. Smith (ed.), *Lord Salisbury on Politics* (Cambridge, 1972), 210–13.

15. Bagehot, 'The Residence of the Queen' (1870), in *Works*, v. 421.

16. A. J. P. Taylor, *English History 1914–1945* (1965), 1.

17. C. B. Fawcett, *Provinces of England: A Study of Some Geographical Aspects of Devolution* (first pub. 1919, rev. W. G. East and S. W. Wooldridge, 1960), 151.

18. Ibid. 28.

19. B. Keith-Lucas and P. G. Richards, *History of Local Government in the Twentieth Century* (1978), 161–2.

20. J. Redlich, *Local Government in England*, ed. F. W. Hirst (1903), ii. 257.

21. Speech at Edinburgh, 25 Nov. 1882—see Lady G. Cecil, *Life of Robert Marquis of Salisbury*, iii (1931), 67.

22. Speech at Newport, 7 Oct. 1885, quoted in Cecil, *Salisbury*, iii. 265.

23. For a good discussion of lords-lieutenant, see Paxman, *Friends in High Places*, 62–6.

24. T. H. S. Escott, *England: Its People, Polity and Pursuits* (1885), 9.

25. R. Cobden, *Speeches on Questions of Public Policy*, ed. J. Bright and J. E. T. Rogers (1870), i. 363 (speech at Manchester, 15 Jan. 1846).

26. Mill, *Principles of Political Economy*, 947.

27. For good accounts of this religious impulse, see E. P. Hennock, *Fit and Proper Persons: Ideal and Reality in Nineteenth-Century Urban Government* (1973), 140–53; H. Meller, *Leisure and the Changing City 1870–1914* (1976), 87–90.

28. *The Charter*, 13 Oct. 1839, 593.

29. *Ernest Jones, Chartist: Selections from the Writings and Speeches . . .*, ed. J. Saville (1952), 184.

30. E. P. Hennock, 'Finance and Politics in Urban Local Government in England 1835–1900', *Historical Journal* (1963), 216–17.

31. W. C. Lubenow, *The Politics of Government Growth: Early Victorian Attitudes towards State Intervention 1833–1848* (1971), 190 n. 10 says the phrase has been credited to Joshua Toulmin Smith and to C. B. Adderley.

32. Redlich, *Local Government in England*, i. 231.

33. For Joseph Hume's pioneering efforts here, see ibid. 164, 167–9.

34. Ibid. 193. See also ii. 164–7.

35. Ibid. i. 193–4.

36. Mill, 'Representative Government', in *Works*, xix (1977), 539–40.

37. There is a good table in C. H. Wilson (ed.), *Essays on Local Government* (Oxford, 1948), 127.

38. K. B. Smellie, *A History of Local Government* (4th edn. n.d.), 64. See also Redlich, *Local Government*, i. 156–61.

39. Quoted in A. Offer, *Property and Politics 1870–1914: Landownership, Law, Ideology and Urban Development in England* (Cambridge, 1981), 216.

40. For more detail on this, see Hennock, 'Finance and Politics', 224.

41. For good discussions of this, see Smellie, *History of Local Government*, 110–22; W. I. Jennings, in H. J. Laski, W. I. Jennings, and W. A. Robson, *A Century of Municipal Progress: The Last Hundred Years* (1935), 432.

42. Redich, *Local Government in England*, ii. 7–9.

43. Bagehot, 'English Constitution', in *Works*, v. 393, 336.

44. Mill, *Principles of Political Economy*, 949–50.

45. J. Butler, *Memoir of John Grey of Dilston*, rev. edn. (1874), 48; cf. B. Webb on Herbert Spencer in her *My Apprenticeship* (first pub. 1926, 2nd edn. n.d.), 22.

46. Mill, 'Autobiography', in *Works*, i (1981), 45.

47. *Oxford Chronicle*, 25 May 1850, 3. I owe this reference to Raphael Samuel of Ruskin College, Oxford.

48. Bagehot, 'France or England' (1863), in *Works*, iv (1968), 94.

49. Mill, 'On Liberty', in *Works*, xviii (1977), 224.

50. Quoted in A. Buchan, *The Spare Chancellor: The Life of Walter Bagehot* (1959), 205.

51. Mill, 'On Liberty', in *Works*, xviii. 261.

52. Mill, *Principles of Political Economy*, 957. See also C. F. Brockington, *A short History of Public Health* (1966), 149.

53. Mill, 'Representative Government', in *Works*, xix. 397.

54. Bagehot, 'Physics and Politics', in *Works*, vii (1974), 55.

55. Mill, 'Representative Government', in *Works*, xix. 404.

56. K. Willis, 'The Introduction and Critical Reception of Marxist Thought in Britain 1850–1900', *Historical Journal* (1977), 450.

57. J. Tulloch, *Movements of Religious Thought in Britain during the Nineteenth Century* (first pub. 1885, repr. Leicester, 1971), 229 n. 1.

58. *Oxford English Dictionary*, Supplement Se–Z (1986), 1188.

59. Taylor, *English History 1914–1945*, 174–5.

60. Bagehot, 'English Constitution', in *Works*, v. 308.

61. Mill, 'Representative Government', in *Works*, xix. 461.
62. Ibid. 381.
63. Quoted in W. L. Burn, *The Age of Equipoise: A Study of the Mid-Victorian Generation* (first pub. 1964, Norton paperback edn. New York, 1965), 58.
64. G. Eliot, *Felix Holt* (first pub. 1866, vol. v in Blackwood edn. of her *Novels*, n.d.), 2.
65. *H.C.Deb.* 14 Feb. 1845, c.485, cf. cc.491, 494.
66. Mill, 'Representative Government', in *Works*, xix. 406.
67. Ibid. 382, 381.
68. G. Orwell, 'Writers and Leviathan' (1948), in *Collected Essays, Journalism and Letters*, iv (first pub. 1968, paperback edn. Harmondsworth, 1970), 469.
69. Speech at Abingdon, *Oxford Chronicle*, 25 May 1850, 3. I owe this reference to Raphael Samuel of Ruskin College, Oxford.
70. Bagehot, 'Lord Palmerston at Bradford' (1864), in *Works*, iii. 281.
71. Bagehot, 'Lombard Street', in *Works*, ix (1978), 53; J. A. Hobson, 'The General Election: A Sociological Interpretation', *Sociological Review* (Apr. 1910), 112–13.
72. Mill, 'On Liberty', in *Works*, xviii. 268.
73. Bagehot, 'English Constitution', in *Works*, v. 276.
74. J. T. Mills, *John Bright and the Quakers* (1935), ii. 161, cf. 297.
75. *H.C.Deb.* 17 Feb. 1843, c.838.
76. Bagehot, 'Trades Unions and Reform' (1859), in *Works*, viii (1974), 16.
77. Bagehot, 'Parliamentary Reform' (1859), in *Works*, vi. 209.
78. For more on this point, see my 'A Genealogy of Reform in Modern Britain', in C. Bolt and S. Drescher (eds.), *Anti-slavery, Religion, and Reform: Essays in Memory of Roger Anstey* (Folkestone, 1980), 119–48.
79. Quoted in *Financial Times*, 12 July 1986, 7. See also D. C. Moore, 'Social Structure, Political Structure, and Public Opinion in Mid-Victorian England', in R. Robson (ed.), *Ideas and Institutions of Victorian Britain* (1967), 23, 38. P. Joyce, *Work, Society and Politics: The Culture of the Factory in Later Victorian England* (Brighton, 1980), 205.
80. For a good discussion, see P. F. Clarke, *Lancashire and the New Liberalism* (Cambridge, 1971), 21.
81. On this, see Joyce, *Work, Society and Politics*, 279, 295.
82. See the useful table analysing constituencies in F. W. S. Craig (ed.), *British Electoral Facts 1832–1987* (Dartmouth, 1989), 161–2.
83. For valuable election timetables, see ibid. 151–2.
84. Calculated from table 1 in W. O. Aydelotte, 'Opportunities for Quantitative Research in Modern British Political History' (unpublished paper for AHA conference on quantitative data, Ann Arbor, Mich., 1967).
85. D. Close, 'The Formation of a Two-Party Alignment in the House of Commons between 1832 and 1841', *English Historical Review* (1969), 258.
86. M. Ostrogorski, *Democracy and the Organization of Political Parties*, tr. F. Clarke (1902), i. 466.

87. See e.g. Clarke, *Lancashire and the New Liberalism*, 15. S. Pankhurst, *The Suffragette Movement: An Intimate Account of Persons and Ideals* (1931), 135.

88. See C. C. O'Leary in S. E. Finer (ed.), *Adversary Politics and Electoral Reform* (n.p., 1975), 179, 181–3.

89. Lord Rosebery, *Lord Randolph Churchill* (1906), 111.

90. T. O. Lloyd, *The General Election of 1880* (1968), 76.

91. H. J. Hanham, *Elections and Party Management: Politics in the Time of Disraeli and Gladstone* (1959), 20.

92. *H.C.Deb.* 30 Aug. 1848, cc.709–10.

93. Speech at the Oxford Union, *Oxford Mail*, 9 May 1958, 3.

94. Buchan, *Spare Chancellor*, 135.

95. P. D. G. Thomas, *The House of Commons in the Eighteenth Century* (Oxford, 1971), 210.

96. Disraeli to Lord Derby, 3 Apr. 1859, quoted in W. F. Monypenny and G. E. Buckle, *The Life of Benjamin Disraeli: Earl of Beaconsfield* (first pub. 1910–20, rev. edn. 1929), i. 1612.

97. Bagehot, 'Mr Gladstone and the People', in *Works*, iii. 461.

98. Bagehot, 'Parliamentary Reform' (1859), in *Works*, vi. 235.

99. Quoted in A. Aspinall, 'English Party Organisation in the Early Nineteenth Century', *English Historical Review* (1926), 406.

100. Quoted from N. Gash, *Mr Secretary Peel: The Life of Sir Robert Peel to 1830* (1961), 4. See also Gash's *Sir Robert Peel: The Life of Sir Robert Peel after 1830* (1972), 433–4, 436.

101. Bagehot, 'The Character of Sir Robert Peel' (1856), in *Works*, iii. 260.

102. Bagehot, 'The Practical Difficulties of Secret Voting' (1859), in *Works*, vi. 310–13; J. S. Mill, 'Of the Mode of Voting', in 'Representative Government' (1861), in *Works*, xix, ch. 10.

103. Mill, 'Representative Government', in *Works*, xix. 378; 'De Tocqueville on Democracy in America' (1840), in *Works*, xviii. 165; 'On Liberty', in *Works*, xviii. 269.

104. Quoted in G. Martin, *The Durham Report and British Policy: A Critical Essay* (Cambridge, 1972), 21.

105. [Lord John Russell], *The Causes of the French Revolution* (1832), 85.

106. Bagehot, 'English Constitution', *Works*, v. 218, cf. J. P. Mackintosh, *The British Cabinet*, 3rd. edn. (1977), 102, but see also 224–8.

107. As W. R. Greg argued in 'The Newspaper Press', *Edinburgh Review* (Oct. 1855), 479.

108. Bagehot, 'English Constitution', in *Works*, v. 304.

109. Bagehot, 'Lord Althorp and the Reform Act of 1832' (1876), in *Works*, iii. 229.

110. W. I. Jennings, *Parliament* (first pub. 1939, 2nd edn. Cambridge, 1957), 2–3.

111. G. M. Young, *Portrait of an age: Victorian England*, ed. G. Kitson Clark (1977), 151.

112. In 1861 Bagehot assigned to parliament four duties, as follows: 'to pass laws; to express public opinion on the critical events of the time, and especially on the foreign events; to choose, maintain, and check an efficient ministry; to vote and to regulate the national expenditure'. See his 'The Present Session of Parliament', *Works*, vi. 116. In the 'English Constitution', *Works*, v. 292 Bagehot brusquely dismissed the last of these because the House 'has long ceased to be the checking, sparing, economical body it once was'.

113. J. R. Seeley, *Introduction to Political Science* (1896), 223.

114. On this, see L. S. Amery, *Thoughts on the Constitution*, 2nd edn. (1964), 15.

115. Bagehot, 'English Constitution', in *Works*, v. 213.

116. See e.g. his 'Mr Gladstone and the People' (4 Nov. 1871), in *Works*, iii. 461–4.

117. Bagehot, 'English Constitution', in *Works*, v. 289–90.

118. Mill, 'Representative Government', in *Works*, xix. 433.

119. Letter to G. L. Browne, 23 Oct. 1849, in Monypenny and Buckle, *Disraeli*, i. 1038.

120. *H.C.Deb.* 28 Oct. 1943, c.404–5.

121. Bagehot, 'English constitution', in *Works*, v. 290, 314, 216.

122. Ibid. 314.

123. Mill, 'Representative Government', in *Works*, xix. 432.

124. *H.C.Deb.* 13 Apr. 1866, cc.1259–60. 'Representative Government', in *Works*, xix. 405. See also J. M. Robson, *The Improvement of Mankind: The Social and Political Thought of John Stuart Mill* (Toronto, 1968), 259. For Bagehot's view, see 'English Constitution', in *Works*, v. 315.

125. Bagehot, Introduction to the 2nd (1872) edn. of 'English Constitution', in *Works*, v. 174.

126. Ibid. 177.

127. Mill, 'Representative Government', in *Works*, xix. 515.

128. Bagehot 'A Suggestion for the Future Government of France' (1874), in *Works*, viii. 239, 241.

129. Bagehot, Introduction to the 2nd (1872) edn. of 'English Constitution', in *Works*, v. 181.

130. Bagehot, 'English Constitution', in *Works*, v. 295.

131. B. L. Kinzer, 'J. S. Mill and the Problem of Party', *Journal of British Studies* (Fall, 1981), 106–8 points out that Mill was hostile only to the type of non-ideological party conflict prevalent in the 1860s. But this is to neglect the continuous yearning in Mill for reconciling opposites and for bringing more technical expertise to bear on the political process. See 'On Liberty', in *Works*, xviii. 254; 'Representative Government', in *Works*, xix. 463.

132. Bagehot, 'Considerations on Representative Government' (1861), in *Works*, vi. 344.

133. Bagehot, 'English Constitution', in *Works*, v. 296.

134. Mill, 'Representative Government', in *Works*, xix. 514.

135. Ibid. 439.
136. Bagehot, 'The Late Mr Mill' (1873), in *Works*, iii (1968), 556–7.
137. See e.g. the footnote in 'Representative Government', in *Works*, xix. 452.
138. Mill, 'On Liberty', in *Works*, xviii. 250. Fitzjames Stephen thought few public issues were settled by free discussion most were settled by physical force or by the half-way house involved in taking a vote: *Liberty, Equality, Fraternity*, ed. R. J. White (Cambridge, 1967), 70.
139. Bagehot, 'English Constitution', in *Works*, v. 212.
140. Ibid. 213.
141. G. H. L. Le May, *The Victorian Constitution: Conventions, Usages and Contingencies* (1979), 97.
142. It will be obvious to any reader of John Mackintosh's *The British Cabinet* (first pub. 1962, 3rd edn. 1977) how much this discussion owes to that fine book.
143. Low, *Governance of England*, 156.
144. Bagehot, 'English Constitution', in *Works*, v. 332.
145. Ibid. 327.
146. K. Marx, *Capital* (ed. F. Engels Moscow, 1954), i. 9 (preface to first German edn.).
147. H. Parris, 'The Origins of the Permanent Civil Service 1780–1830', *Public Administration* (1968), 157; E. Hughes, 'Civil Service Reform 1853–5', *Public Administration* (1954), 17. See also the helpful discussion in H. Parris, *Constitutional Bureaucracy: The Development of British Central Administration since the Eighteenth Century* (1969), 22.
148. Bagehot, 'English Constitution', in *Works*, v. 341.
149. H. J. Hanham (ed.), *The Nineteenth-Century Constitution 1815–1914: Documents and Commentary* (Cambridge, 1969), 341.
150. Bagehot, 'Competitive Tests for the Public Service' (1862), in *Works*, vi. 73.
151. Bagehot, 'Lord Althorp and the Reform Act of 1832' (1876), in *Works*, iii. 228.
152. Bagehot, 'The House of Peers' (1871), in *Works*, vi. 37. See also Parris, *Constitutional Bureaucracy*, 145.
153. J. W. Wheeler-Bennett, *King George VI: His Life and Reign* (1958), 132.
154. Bagehot, 'English Constitution', in *Works*, v. 208.
155. Ibid. 240.
156. Ibid. 369, 226.
157. Ibid. 379.
158. Ibid. 378–9.
159. Ibid. 229.
160. Ibid. 243.
161. e.g. ibid. 208, and 'The Ultimate Evil of French Politics' (1873), in *Works*, viii. 220.
162. Letter to editor, *Spectator*, 21 Apr. 1866, 440.
163. As C. H. Sisson points out in his *The Case of Walter Bagehot* (1972), 129.

164. Bagehot, 'Sir Charles Dilke on the Civil List' (1874), in *Works*, v. 416.

165. Queen Victoria, *Letters: Third Series*, ed. G. E. Buckle, i (1930), 48 (writing in her journal on 6 Feb. 1886).

166. *Your Dear Letter: Private Correspondence of Queen Victoria and the Crown Princess of Prussia 1865–1871*, ed. R. Fulford (1971), 235.

167. Queen Victoria, *Letters: Third Series*, i. 48 (journal, 6 Feb. 1886).

168. Amery, *Thoughts on the Constitution*, 27, cf. 21–2.

169. V. Bogdanor, '1931 Revisited: The Constitutional Aspects', *Twentieth Century British History*, 2/1 (1991), 24–5.

170. Quoted in J. Wilson, *CB: A Life of Sir Henry Campbell-Bannerman* (1973), 165.

171. J. Pope-Hennessy, *Queen Mary, 1867–1953* (1959), 343.

172. Speech in House of Lords, 25 Jan. 1901, quoted in Cecil, *Salisbury*, iii. 186.

173. Mackintosh, *British Cabinet*, 7.

174. R. H. S. Crossman, *Inside View: Three Lectures on Prime Ministerial Government* (1972), 39.

## Chapter 2: Empire and Welfare (pp. 55–83)

1. Bagehot, 'English Constitution', in *Works*, v. 165.

2. Ibid. 335–6.

3. A. Briggs, *The Age of Improvement 1783–1867* (1959), 359.

4. Ibid. 360.

5. R. Blake, *Disraeli* (1966), 668; R. B. Pugh, 'The Colonial Office 1801–1925', in J. H. Rose, A. P. Newton, E. A. Benians, and H. H. Dodwell (eds.), *Cambridge History of the British Empire*, iii: *The Empire–Commonwealth 1870–1919* (Cambridge, 1959), 748.

6. The colonial administrator Alfred Lyall in 1859, quoted in Sir Henry M. Durand, *Life of the Right Hon. Sir Alfred Comyn Lyall* (1913), 92.

7. Queen Victoria, *Letters: Second Series*, ed. G. E. Buckle, iii (1928), 491 (28 Mar. 1884). See also Rosebery to Sir Henry Ponsonby, 24 Apr. 1885, ibid. 641, cf. 629, 632. For a good discussion of frontier problems generally, see J. S. Galbraith, 'The "Turbulent Frontier" as a Factor in British Expansion', *Comparative Studies in Society and History*, 2 (1959–60).

8. Queen Victoria, *Letters: Third Series*, 195, cf. Lord Wolseley to Queen Victoria, 22 Mar. 1885, quoted in her *Letters: Second Series*, iii. 632.

9. Lord Randolph Churchill to the Tsar in 1888, quoted in W. S. Churchill, *Lord Randolph Churchill* (first pub. 1906, 1 vol. edn. 1907), 720.

10. Quoted R. R. James, *Lord Randolph Churchill* (1959), 162.

11. G. Orwell, *Works*, i. 270, writing in 1936.

12. C. A. Bodelsen, *Studies in Mid-Victorian Imperialism* (first pub. 1924, New York edn. 1968), 48–9.

13. A. B. Keith (ed.), *Selected Speeches and Documents on British Colonial Policy 1783–1917* (1918) (henceforth cited as *Colonial Documents*), i. 140.

14. N. Mansergh, *The Commonwealth Experience* (1969), 24, 187.

15. Lord Salisbury to Lord Lytton, 9 Mar. 1877, quoted in Lady G. Cecil, *Life of Robert Marquis of Salisbury*, ii (1921), 130.

16. R. B. Pugh, in *Cambridge History of the British Empire*, iii. 716.

17. To Howick, 6 Feb. 1833, quoted by R. C. Snelling and T. J. Barron, 'The Colonial Office', in G. Sutherland (ed.), *Studies in the Growth of Nineteenth-Century Government* (1972), 142.

18. C. Buller, 'Responsible Government for Colonies', repr. in E. M. Wrong (ed.), *Charles Buller and Responsible Government* (Oxford, 1926), 151.

19. Buller quoted from Wrong (ed.), *Buller*, 143. For statistics, see C. C. Eldridge, *England's Mission: The Imperial Idea in the Age of Gladstone and Disraeli 1868–1880* (1973), 32–3. For complaints about parliament, see J. Clive, *Macaulay: The Shaping of the Historian* (New York, 1973), 309.

20. Colquhoun, MP for Newcastle-under-Lyme, quoted in S. Walpole, *The Life of Lord John Russell*, 2 vols. (1889), i. 339, cf. Buller, 'Responsible Government for Colonies', in Wrong (ed.) *Buller*, 142–3.

21. See e.g. Queen Victoria, *Letters: Third Series*, i. 48, 211.

22. See H. Temperley's excellent article 'Secret Diplomacy from Canning to Grey', *Cambridge Historical Journal* (1938), 1, 12; and V. Cromwell, 'The Private Member of the House of Commons and Foreign Policy in the Nineteenth Century', in *Liber Memorialis Sir Maurice Powicke: Studies Presented to the International Commission for the History of Representative and Parliamentary Institutions*, xxvii (Paris, 1965), 216.

23. Monypenny and Buckle, *Disraeli*, ii. 938–9.

24. Quoted in Adonis, *Making Aristocracy Work*, 72.

25. Cecil, *Salisbury*, iv (1932), 162.

26. D. C. M. Platt, *Finance, Trade, and Politics in British Foreign Policy 1815–1914* (Oxford, 1968), 371, cf. 373–5.

27. Ibid. 108–11.

28. T. Paine, *Rights of Man* (first pub. 1791–2, ed. H. Collins, Harmondsworth, 1971), 230.

29. Cobden, *Speeches*, ii. 228 (House of Commons speech, 28 June 1850). See also J. A. Hobson, *Richard Cobden: The International Man* (1919), 34.

30. Bagehot, 'English Constitution', in *Works*, v. 281.

31. Salisbury to Lansdowne, 30 Aug. 1899, quoted in Lord Newton, *Lord Lansdowne: A Biography* (1929), 157.

32. Temperley, 'Secret Diplomacy', 32.

33. Quoted in Hanham (ed.), *Nineteenth-Century Constitution*, 100. See also Wilson, *CB*, 530–1.

34. H. W. V. Temperley, *Life of Canning* (1905), 102; W. R. Brock, *Lord Liverpool and Liberal Toryism* (Cambridge, 1941), 114.

35. Quoted in J. L. Garvin, *Life of Joseph Chamberlain*, iii (1934), 282. See also ii (1933), 191.
36. Eldridge, *England's Mission*, 116.
37. L. Stephen, *The Life of Henry Fawcett*, 3rd edn. (1886), 343–4, 352. For Bright, see J. L. Sturgis, *John Bright and the Empire* (1969).
38. A. H. Nethercot, *The First Five Lives of Annie Besant* (1961), i. 363.
39. On this, see M. Cumpston, 'Some Early Indian Nationalists and their Allies in the British Parliament 1851–1906', *English Historical Review* (1961), 281–6.
40. Marquess of Zetland, *Lord Cromer: Being the Authorized Life of Evelyn Baring First Earl of Cromer* (1932), 150–1.
41. Newton, *Lansdowne*, 61.
42. Quoted in Adonis, *Making Aristocracy Work*, 79.
43. J. E. Wrench, *Alfred, Lord Milner: The Man of no Illusions, 1854–1925* (1958), 259, cf. 233; Amery, *Chamberlain*, iv (1951), 100; A. M. Gollin, *Proconsul in Politics: A Study of Lord Milner in Opposition and in Power* (1964), 314. For Lloyd, C. F. Adam, *Life of Lord Lloyd* (1948), 48, 124–5, 180–3.
44. M. Swartz, *The Union of Democratic Control in British Politics during the First World War* (Oxford, 1971), 89.
45. Ibid. 221.
46. See e.g. P. M. Williams, *Hugh Gaitskell: A Political Biography* (1979), 479–80, 483.
47. *H.C.Deb.* 4 Nov. 1943, c.887.
48. D. Goldsworthy, *Colonial Issues in British Politics 1945–1961: From 'Colonial Development' to 'Wind of Change'* (Oxford, 1971), 249–50.
49. J. Ehrman, *Cabinet Government and War: 1890–1940* (Cambridge, 1958), 9–13. I. M. Cumpston (ed.), *The Growth of the British Commonwealth 1880–1932* (1973), 77.
50. Quoted in Keith (ed.), *Colonial Documents*, ii. 212–13.
51. J. Amery, *The Life of Joseph Chamberlain*, iv (1951), 384–5.
52. Sir Joseph Ward, quoted in Keith (ed.), *Colonial Documents*, ii. 248–9.
53. Amery, *Joseph Chamberlain*, vi. 528.
54. On de Redcliffe, see Hon. A. D. Elliot, *The Life of George Joachim Goschen, First Viscount Goschen, 1831–1907*, 2 vols. (1911), i. 197.
55. For the Foreign Office, see K. Rose, *Superior Person: A Portrait of Curzon and his Circle in Late Victorian England* (1969), 297; cf. W. Hinde, *George Canning* (1973), 426. For the Colonial Office, see Sir Norman Chester, *The English Administrative System 1780–1870* (Oxford, 1981), 283; cf. Barron and Snelling, in Sutherland (ed.), *Nineteenth-Century Government*, 141.
56. R. B. Pugh, in *Cambridge History of the British Empire*, iii. 748.
57. Ibid. 747, 764.
58. On this, see Steiner and Cromwell, in Sutherland (ed.), *Nineteenth-Century Government*, 170. Mackintosh, *British Cabinet*, 267–8.
59. See K. O. Morgan, *Labour in Power 1945–1951* (Oxford, 1984), 201 for the

'excitement and . . . economic initiative' within the Colonial Office prevailing at that time.

60. D. and G. Butler, *British Political Facts 1900–1994*, 7th edn. (1994), 291. These figures are of course not necessarily internally consistent, but their general upward tendency cannot be denied. Compare the figures in F. M. G. Willson, *The Organization of British Central Government 1914–1964: A Survey by a Study Group of the Royal Institute of Public Administration* (first pub. 1957, 2nd edn. D. N. Chester, 1968), 194, 380.

61. Willson, *Central Government*, 238.

62. e.g. in Cumpston (ed.), *Commonwealth*, 17–18, 20.

63. R. MacG. Dawson (ed.), *The Development of Dominion Status 1900–1936* (1937), 4, 52–63. See also Gollin, *Proconsul in Politics*, 395–8, 596.

64. I. M. Drummond, *British Economic Policy and the Empire 1919–1939* (1972), 18. See also Amery, *Joseph Chamberlain*, vi (1969), 1028–30.

65. F. W. S. Craig (ed.), *British General Election Manifestos 1918–1966* (Chichester, 1970), 88.

66. The phrase is Sir Michael Hicks-Beach's (Colonial Secretary), quoted in Keith (ed.), *Colonial Documents*, ii. 143.

67. Quoted in J. A. Cross, 'The Beginning and End of the Commonwealth Office', *Public Administration* (1969), 116. See also the Marquess of Ripon's comment of 1895, quoted in Keith, *Colonial Documents*, ii. 156 ff.

68. Cumpston (ed.), *Commonwealth*, 35. See also 26, 28, 34.

69. Quoted in A. B. Keith (ed.), *Speeches and Documents on the British Dominions 1918–1931* (n.d.) (henceforth cited as *Dominions Documents*), 55–6. See also 84, 209.

70. Dawson, *Dominion Status*, 87, 99, 101–2.

71. R. B. Pugh, in *Cambridge History of the British Empire*, iii. 762.

72. J. A. Cross, 'Whitehall and the Commonwealth: The Development of British Departmental Organization for Commonwealth Affairs', *Journal of Commonwealth Political Studies*, ii (1963–4), 189–90.

73. Cross, 'Beginning and End of the Commonwealth Office', 119. See also J. Garner, *The Commonwealth Office 1925–68* (1978), 146–7, 422, 424.

74. R. B. Pugh, in *Cambridge History of the British Empire*, iii. 735.

75. An idea which attracted Lulu Harcourt as Colonial Secretary in 1911. See Cross, 'Whitehall and the Commonwealth', 196.

76. H. Morrison, *Government and Parliament: A Survey from the Inside* (first pub. 1954, 3rd edn. 1965), 77.

77. H. Macmillan, *The Middle Way: A Study of the Problem of Economic and Social Progress in a Free and Democratic Society* (first pub. 1938, 1966 edn.), 367.

78. Sir William Beveridge, *Social Insurance and Allied Services: Report . . . Presented to Parliament . . . November 1942* (Cmd. 6404) (henceforth *Beveridge Report*), 6.

79. B. Webb, *Our Partnership*, ed. B. Drake and M. I. Cole (1948), 331 (9 Feb. 1906).

80. Quoted in K. Sinclair, *A History of New Zealand* (first pub. 1959, paperback edn. Harmondsworth, 1960), 183.

81. *H.C.Deb.* 9 July 1908, c.152, in debate on the third reading of the Old-Age Pensions Bill.

82. For municipal enterprise, see B. Donoughue and G. W. Jones, *Herbert Morrison: Portrait of a Politician* (1973), 83. For nationalization, see G. N. Ostergaard, 'Labour and the Development of the Public Corporation', *Manchester School* (1954), 203–4. For compulsory arbitration, see H. Pelling, *Popular Politics and Society in Late Victorian Britain*, 2nd edn. (1979), 73. For family allowances, see *H.C.Deb.* 8 Mar. 1945, cc.2296 (Adamson), 2298 (Butcher). For sweated labour, see R. Churchill, *Winston S. Churchill*, ii: *Young Statesman 1901–1914* (1967), 298; S. and B. Webb, *The Webbs' Australian Diary 1898*, ed. A. G. Austin (Melbourne, 1965), 78, 86.

83. W. H. Beveridge, *Power and Influence* (1953), 309; *Beveridge Report*, 8–9.

84. *H.C.Deb.* 8 Mar. 1945, c.2284. Australian and New Zealand precedents were often cited as precedents for paying family allowances directly to the mother, *H.C.Deb.* 8 Mar. 1945, c.2280 (Rathbone), cf. c.2319 (Summerskill); *H.C.Deb.* 3 Nov. 1944, c.1171 (Rathbone); *H.C.Deb.* 10 May 1945, cc. 2062 (Griffiths), 2064 (Summerskill).

85. R. A. Lewis, *Edwin Chadwick and the Public Health Movement 1832–1954* (1952), 331–2.

86. Beveridge, *Power and Influence*, 56, 58, cf. 80–1. Lloyd George, *H.C.Deb.* 4 May 1911, c.615. See also W. J. Braithwaite, *Lloyd George's Ambulance Wagon: Being the Memoirs of William J. Braithwaite 1911–1912*, ed. Sir Henry N. Bunbury (1957), 71, 82–3.

87. Churchill, *Winston S. Churchill*, ii: *Young Statesman*, 308.

88. Beveridge, *Power and Influence*, 80.

89. *Beveridge Report*, 5.

90. For a full treatment of this, see my 'State Intervention and Moral Reform in Nineteenth-Century England', in P. Hollis (ed.), *Pressure from without in Early Victorian England* (1974), 289–322.

91. M. Arnold, 'Culture and Anarchy', in *Complete Prose Works*, v, ed. R. H. Super (Ann Arbor, Mich., 1965), 215, cf. 94, 95, 112, 219. Compare William Morris, 'The Socialist Ideal, 1: Art', *New Review* (Jan. 1891), 5.

92. T. Carlyle, 'Past and Present', in *Works*, Ashburton edn., 17 vols. (1886–93), ii. 126, cf. 178.

93. See H. E. Dale, *The Higher Civil Service of Great Britain* (1941), 72. G. B. Grundy, *Fifty-Five Years at Oxford: An Unconventional Autobiography* (1945), 139–40.

94. This paragraph owes much to Henry Pelling's essay 'The Working Class and the Origins of the Welfare State', in his *Popular Politics*, 1–18.

95. For a fuller discussion of this theme, see the chapter 'Traditions of Respectability in British Labour History', in my *Peaceable Kingdom: Stability and Change in Modern Britain* (Oxford, 1982), 157–216.

96. B. C. Roberts, 'Industrial Relations', in M. Ginsberg (ed.), *Law and Opinion in England in the Twentieth Century* (1959), 366.

97. Jim Radford, discussing the Committee of 100 in *Observer*, colour suppl., 26 Aug. 1973, 16.

98. *H.C.Deb.* 21 Nov. 1929, c.752; cf. *H.C.Deb.* 16 Dec. 1929, c.1140.

99. As reported by Balfour to Lord Salisbury, 22 Mar. 1886 in B. E. C. Dugdale, *Arthur James Balfour, First Earl of Balfour*, i (1939), 78.

100. B. de Jouvenel, *Problems of Socialist England* (1949), 158.

101. See my *Drink and the Victorians: The Temperance Question in England 1815–1872*, 2nd edn. (Keele, 1994), ch. 9.

102. R. H. S. Crossman, *The Role of the Volunteer in the Modern Social Service*, Sidney Ball Memorial Lecture 1973 (Oxford, n.d.), 20.

103. Quoted in Webb, *My Apprenticeship*, 218.

104. de Jouvenel, *Problems of Socialist England*, 44.

105. J. Harris, *William Beveridge: A Biography* (Oxford, 1977), 448, 459.

106. C. Cross, *Philip Snowden* (1966), 66; E. Halévy, 'Socialism and the Problem of Democratic Parliamentarism' (1934), in *The Era of Tyrannies*, tr. R. K. Webb (New York, 1965), 258.

107. *Beveridge Report*, 17.

108. A. H. Halsey (ed.), *British Social Trends since 1900: A Guide to the Changing Social Structure of Britain* (1988), 501.

109. R. Rose, 'Class and Party Divisions: Britain as a Test Case', *Sociology* (1968), 156.

110. P. Smith, *Disraelian Conservatism and Social Reform* (1967), 244–9, 256.

111. Garvin, *Chamberlain*, ii (1933), 427; P. Marsh, *The Discipline of Popular Government: Lord Salisbury's Domestic Statecraft 1881–1902* (Hassocks, 1978), 170–1.

112. J. Roach, 'Liberalism and the Victorian Intelligentsia', *Cambridge Historical Journal* (1957), 75; cf. Baldwin in 1931, quoted in C. S. Emden, *The People and the Constitution: Being a History of the Development of the People's Influence in British Government* (first pub. 1933, 2nd edn. 1956), 252.

113. Bagehot, introduction to the 2nd (1872) edn. of 'English Constitution', in *Works*, v. 173.

114. Adonis, *Making Aristocracy Work*, 78.

115. Lord Askwith, *Lord James of Hereford* (1930), 247.

116. B. Webb, 12 Feb. 1906, in *Our Partnership*, 332.

117. S. Reynolds and B. and T. Woolley, *Seems So! A Working-Class View of Politics* (1911), 166.

118. P. Townsend, *Poverty in the United Kingdom: A Survey of Household Resources and Standards of Living* (Harmondsworth, 1979), 155.

119. M. E. Bulkley, *The Feeding of School Children* (1914), 109.

120. E. F. Rathbone, *The Disinherited Family: A Plea for the Endowment of the Family* (1924), 287–8.

121. In B. Shaw *et al.*, *Fabian Essays* (first pub. 1889, Jubilee edn. 1948), 33, cf. 57.

122. H. L. Wilensky, *The Welfare State and Equality: Structural and Ideological Roots of Public Expenditures* (Berkeley, 1975), 19.

123. Henry Aaron, cited ibid. 10.

124. R. Lambert, *Sir John Simon 1816–1904 and English Social Administration* (1963), 457. This paragraph owes much to O. MacDonagh, 'The Nineteenth-Century Revolution in Government: A Reappraisal', *Historical Journal* (1958).

125. K. Marx and F. Engels, *Selected Works*, 2 vols. (Moscow, 1962), i. 383.

126. D. H. Blelloch, 'A Historical Survey of Factory Inspection in Great Britain', *International Labour Review* (Nov. 1938).

127. S. Webb, in *Fabian Essays*, 47–8.

128. Young, *Portrait of an Age*, 54.

129. A. T. Peacock and J. Wiseman, *The Growth of Public Expenditure in the United Kingdom* (first pub. 1961, 2nd edn. 1967), 101–2, 200.

130. Ramsay MacDonald, *The New Unemployed Bill of the Labour Party* (1907), 6; cf. R. Owen, *A New View of Society* (first pub. 1813, Everyman edn. 1927), 83.

131. Royal Commission on Population, *Report* (Cmd. 7695, 1949), 113.

132. Julia Parker, in A. H. Halsey (ed.), *Trends in British Society since 1900: A Guide to the Changing Social Structure of Britain* (1972), 375.

## Chapter 3: Fragmentation and Union (pp. 85–113)

1. J. C. Banks, *Federal Britain?* (1971), 30.

2. K. Robbins, 'Core and Periphery in Modern British History', *Proceedings of the British Academy*, 70 (1984), 276.

3. Bagehot, 'The Meaning and the Value of the Limits of the Principle of Nationalities' (1864), in *Works*, viii. 152.

4. Wilson, *CB*, 129.

5. J. Prior, *A Balance of Power* (1986), 197.

6. *H.C.Deb.* 17 May 1866, c.1089.

7. 21 June 1846, quoted in Sir Robert Peel, *Memoirs* (1856), part III, 302.

8. Cecil, *Salisbury*, iii. 302–3.

9. F. Engels, *The Condition of the Working Class in England*, tr. and ed. W. O. Henderson and W. H. Chaloner (Oxford, 1958), 105.

10. Scotland strikingly surpassed England in university places per head of population 1830–1950. See T. C. Smout, in F. M. L. Thompson (ed.), *The Cambridge Social History of Britain 1750–1950*, i: *Regions and Communities* (Cambridge, 1990), 278.

11. Smout, ibid. 212.

12. See B. Crick, 'Sovereignty, Centralism and Devolution', in R. Holme and M. Elliott (eds.), *1688–1988: Time for a New Constitution* (1988), 65.

13. Queen Victoria, *Letters: Second Series*, iii. 162.

14. Young, *Portrait of an Age*, 89.

15. Bagehot, 'The Irish Viceroyalty' (1876), in *Works*, viii. 134.

16. Lloyd George to his wife, 2 Sept. 1920, in *Lloyd George Family Letters 1885–1936*, ed. K. O. Morgan (Cardiff, 1973), 192.

17. F. Hardie, *The Political Influence of the British Monarchy 1868–1952* (1970), 163.

18. S. Bradford, *George VI* (1989), 527.

19. e.g. from Dr Garret Fitzgerald, *Guardian*, 11 Aug. 1979, 1.

20. For de Valera's offer of 1958, see *Daily Telegraph*, 3 Jan. 1992, 2. See also the leader in *Guardian*, 29 Aug. 1979, 12, taking up a suggestion from a reader, Alan Hart.

21. *The Times*, 11 Aug. 1977, 2; cf. security arrangements for the preceding and preparatory visit of Princess Anne, *The Times*, 24 Mar. 1977, 2.

22. David Thomas, 'Workers Unmoved', *Financial Times*, 12 July 1986, 7.

23. e.g. when George VI's proposed visit to Northern Ireland was under consideration in Feb. 1951: see P. Howarth, *George VI: A New Biography* (1987), 250. Biographers of British monarchs since 1922 show remarkably little interest in the monarchy's impact, or lack of it, in Northern Ireland. Edward VIII's biographers say nothing about his ungracious demeanour, as Prince of Wales, during his visit to Belfast in November 1932. It is discussed frankly in St J. Ervine, *Craigavon: Ulsterman* (1949), 525–6.

24. For Princess Anne's visit on 23 Mar. 1977, during which 'troops and policemen flooded the castle and the village of Hillsborough', see *The Times*, 24 Mar. 1977, 2. It was a 'trial run' for the Queen's jubilee visit which followed, see *The Times*, 11 Aug. 1977, 2.

25. Sir Reginald Coupland, *Welsh and Scottish Nationalism: A Study* (1954), 273.

26. H. A. Bruce MSS (in family possession): Queen Victoria to Bruce, 1 Nov. 1869.

27. *The Times*, 28 May 1977, 1.

28. *Lloyd George Family Letters*, 53.

29. Joint Committee of Parliament on Indian Constitutional Reform, quoted in St J.-Stevas, *Bagehot*, 117.

30. *The Political Correspondence of Mr Gladstone and Lord Granville 1876–1886*, ed. A. Ramm (Oxford, 1962), i. 92. See also J. Vincent, 'Gladstone and Ireland', *Proceedings of the British Academy* (1977), 219.

31. P. Guedalla (ed.), *The Queen and Mr Gladstone*, ii: *1880–1898* (1933), 177; *Gladstone–Granville Correspondence*, ii. 11.

32. Speech at Aberdeen quoted in Vincent, 'Gladstone and Ireland', 234; C. C. O'Brien, *Parnell and his Party 1880–90* (Oxford, 1957), 162.

33. *H.C.Deb.* 8 Apr. 1886, c.1039.

34. Queen Victoria, *Letters: Second Series*, iii. 294. See also J. L. Hammond, *Gladstone and the Irish Nation* (1938), 312–13.

35. For a good discussion of this, see O'Brien, *Parnell and his Party*, 59–61, 72, 77–8.

36. A. G. Gardiner, *The Life of Sir William Harcourt* (1923), i. 553.

37. K. R. M. Short, *The Dynamite War: Irish-American Bombers in Victorian Britain* (Dublin, 1979), 50, 55, 91, 104–5, 160, 162, 176, 184, 200, 205, 207, 208, 229, 232–3, 259. For Gladstone's disgust at such tactics, see e.g. Queen Victoria, *Letters: Second Series*, iii. 453. For the ending of the bombing campaign, see Short, *Dynamite War*, 225, 229.

38. Chamberlain to Gladstone, 17 Apr. 1882, in his *A Political Memoir 1880–92*, ed. C. H. D. Howard (1953), 35. See also Garvin, *Joseph Chamberlain*, i. 344, 352. For Parnell condoning violence in 1877, see F. S. L. Lyons, 'The Political Ideas of Parnell', *Historical Journal*, 16/4 (1973), 759.

39. To Labouchere, 3 Jan. 1886, quoted in A. L. Thorold, *The Life of Henry Labouchere* (1913), 278.

40. Quoted from Churchill, *Lord Randolph Churchill*, 474–9; cf. Gladstone's response in Queen Victoria, *Letters: Third Series*, i. 170.

41. H. Pelling, *The Social Geography of British Elections 1885–1910* (1967), 377. Statistics from J. G. Kellas, *Modern Scotland: The Nation since 1870* (1968), 240.

42. H. C. G. Matthew, introduction to W. E. Gladstone, *Diaries*, x and xi (Oxford, 1990), p. cxlvi.

43. J. A. Spender and C. Asquith, *Life of Herbert Henry Asquith, Lord Oxford and Asquith* (1932), ii. 216–17. See also R. Jenkins, *Asquith* (1964), 275. For an excellent account of Bonar Law, see J. Smith, 'Bluff, Bluster and Brinkmanship: Andrew Bonar Law and the Third Home Rule Bill', *Historical Journal* (Mar. 1993), 161–78.

44. For a particularly good discussion of this, see H. Berrington, 'Partisanship and Dissidence in the Nineteenth-Century House of Commons', *Parliamentary Affairs*, xxi (1967–8), 338–74.

45. See the valuable discussion in V. Bogdanor, *Devolution* (Oxford, 1979), 19, 24.

46. Bagehot, 'Mr Gladstone on Home Rule for Ireland' (1871), in *Works*, iii. 459.

47. W. E. Gladstone in 1897, published in his *Autobiographica*, ed. J. Brooke and M. Sorensen (1971), 112.

48. Bagehot, 'The Ultimate End of Fenianism' (1867), in *Works*, viii. 90.

49. Quoted in D. G. Boyce, *Englishmen and Irish Troubles: British Public Opinion and the Making of Irish Policy 1918–1922* (1972), 37.

50. Speech at Aberdeen, quoted in Vincent, 'Gladstone and Ireland', 236.

51. e.g. Hubert Bland, in *Fabian Essays*, 197.

52. Quoted in J. Morley, *The Life of William Ewart Gladstone* (first pub. 1903, 2 vol. edn. 1905), i. 893.

53. To Parnell, 30 Aug. 1889, quoted in Hammond, *Gladstone and the Irish Nation*, 645.

54. Quoted in H. J. Hanham, *Scottish Nationalism* (1969), 91–2.

55. K. O. Morgan, *Wales in British Politics: 1868–1922* (Cardiff, 1963), 112–13; *Rebirth of a Nation: Wales 1880–1980* (Oxford, 1982), 32.

56. J. G. Kellas, 'The Liberal Party in Scotland 1876–1895', *Scottish Histor-ical Review* (Apr. 1965), 15. By operating vigorously within the NLF the Welsh were more successful than the Scots in pushing their claims on the Party.

57. Bogdanor, *Devolution*, 91.

58. J. T. Ward, *Sir James Graham* (1967), 220; Walpole, *Lord John Russell*, ii. 443 n. 1.

59. Quoted in B. Holland, *The Life of Spencer Compton, Eighth Duke of Devon-shire* (1911), ii. 265. See also Hammond, *Gladstone and the Irish Nation*, 405–6.

60. For some of its backers, see R. F. V. Heuston, *Lives of the Lord Chancellors 1885–1940* (Oxford, 1964), 143 (for Lord Loreburn); Hanham, *Scottish Nation-alism*, 97 (for Winston Churchill); S. Gwynn and G. M. Tuckwell, *The Life of the Rt. Hon. Sir Charles W. Dilke Bart. MP* (1917), ii. 148 (for Dilke).

61. Fawcett, *Provinces of England*, 19 (preface to 1919 edn.).

62. P. Jalland, 'United Kingdom Devolution 1910–14: Political Panacea or Tac-tical Diversion?', *English Historical Review* (Oct. 1979), 760, 770, 784–5. Bogdanor, *Devolution*, 37–8. Robbins, 'Core and Periphery', 293–4.

63. *H.C.Deb.* 17 Oct. 1944, cc.2312–13.

64. Quoted in E. Wertheimer, *Portrait of the Labour Party* (1929), 57.

65. See the useful table in D. E. Butler, *British General Elections since 1945* (Oxford, 1989), 72.

66. Coupland, *Nationalism*, 374; Morgan, *Rebirth of a Nation*, 207.

67. See the useful table in A. H. Birch, *Political Integration and Disintegration in the British Isles* (1977), 43.

68. Craig (ed.), *Manifestos*, 270.

69. T. C. Smout, in *Cambridge Social History of Britain*, i. 242.

70. *The Times*, 29 Oct. 1969, 2.

71. *The Times*, 20 May 1968, 3.

72. Heath, *H.C.Deb.* 16 Dec. 1976, c.1776; Thatcher, *H.C.Deb.* 13 Dec. 1976, cc.997–1005. There were serious divisions within the Party on the issue, see *The Times*, 9 Dec. 1976, 1.

73. Heath speech to the Employment Institute, *Guardian*, 5 Mar. 1986, 9. Prior, quoted in 'Pro-consul of the New Wales', *Observer*, 12 Feb. 1989, 13. Robert Harris, 'Springing out of Exile', *Sunday Times*, 16 Apr. 1989, sect. B, 3 (Walker).

74. Lawson, *The Times*, 24 Nov. 1987, 2. Rifkind, *Independent*, 23 Dec. 1987, 4; *Guardian*, 4 Apr. 1988, 2.

75. *Daily Telegraph*, 14 May 1988, 2.

76. For views within the cabinet, see R. H. S. Crossman, *The Diaries of a Cabinet Minister*, ed. J. Morgan, iii (1977), 69 (19 May 1968); B. Castle, *The Castle Diaries 1974–1976* (1980), 283 (17 Jan. 1975).

77. Castle, *Diaries 1974–1976*, 173 (15 Sept. 1974).

78. H. Wilson, *Final Term: The Labour Government 1974–1976* (1979), 46; cf. 212.

79. *H.C.Deb.* 9 May 1978, c.1108 (Abse); *H.C.Deb.* 15 Nov. 1977, c.475 (Kinnock), and cf. W. Hamilton at the Labour Party's Scottish conference, quoted in *The Times*, 27 Mar. 1976, 2.

80. *H.L.Deb.* 4 Apr. 1978, c.55.

81. Leader in *The Times*, 18 Sept. 1980, 15; cf. 1 for Whitelaw's reaction.

82. D. E. Butler and M. Pinto-Duschinsky, *The British General Election of 1970* (1971), 456, cf. 462.

83. Edward Taylor, *H.C.Deb.* 14 Dec. 1976, c.1250; cf. Norman Buchan, *H.C.Deb.* 22 Feb. 1977, c.1295 and Jeremy Thorpe's response to Thatcher's retreat from Heath's position on Scottish devolution, *Guardian*, 16 May 1977, 2.

84. On this, see F. S. L. Lyons *Ireland since the Famine* (1971), 718, 721, 723.

85. *H.C.Deb.* 4 June 1974, c.1167. For Ulster protestantism, see Halsey (ed.), *Trends in British Society*, 409, 414, 416.

86. Birch, *Political Integration and Disintegration*, 43. Bogdanor, *Devolution*, 65.

87. J. Campbell, *Edward Heath: A Biography* (1993), 429.

88. *Guardian*, 22 May 1974, 6.

89. Craig, *British Electoral Facts*, 69–71; D. E. Butler and D. Kavanagh, *The British General Election of 1992* (1992), 286.

90. For a more detailed discussion, see Finer (ed.), *Adversary Politics*, 175–82.

91. *Guardian*, 14 Nov. 1983, 1. *Daily Telegraph*, 19 June 1989, 2.

92. Tim Pat Coogan, in 'The Last Colony' (Channel 4 television programme, 4 July 1994).

93. As Michael Foot and Peter Shore were well aware at a private dinner reported in Benn, *Diaries 1973–1976*, 495.

94. É. de Valera, *Daily Telegraph*, 3 Jan. 1992, 2; Fitzgerald, *Guardian*, 11 Aug. 1979, 1.

95. A suggestion put forward by a reader, Alan Hart, and supported by a leader in *Guardian*, 29 Aug. 1979, 12.

96. Census figures discussed in *The Times*, 29 Aug. 1983, 1; opinion discussed in *Guardian*, 16 Oct. 1979, 3. According to Department of Health and Social Security, *Northern Ireland Census 1981: Religion Report* (Belfast, 1984), 1 there were in 1981 28% Catholics, 23% Presbyterians, 19% Church of Ireland, 4% Methodist, 8% other denominations, and 19% not stated (which due to Catholic boycotting may include many Catholics).

97. Crossman, *Diaries*, iii. 620 (17 Aug. 1969).

98. M. R. D. Foot, 'IRA and the origins of SOE', in M. R. D. Foot (ed.), *War and Society: Historical Essays in Honour and Memory of J. R. Western 1928–1971* (1971), 67–9.

99. *The Times*, 13 Oct. 1984, 3.

100. C. Pankhurst, *Unshackled: The Story of how we Won the Vote* (1959), 153. For parallels with suffragette militancy, see 'The Act of Militancy: Violence and the Suffragettes 1904–1914', in my *Peaceable Kingdom*, 26–81.

101. E. Burke, *Reflections on the Revolution in France* (1790, ed. C. C. O'Brien, Harmondsworth, 1969), 156.

102. Benn, *Diaries 1973–1976*, 457 (6 Nov. 1975).

103. *Daily Telegraph*, 27 Sept. 1979, 1.

104. Kevin McNamara, *Daily Telegraph*, 4 Nov. 1989, 1. Compare the argument in C. C. O'Brien, 'The Spiral into Civil War', *Observer*, 26 Aug. 1979, 34.

105. Speech on 12 Oct. 1979, as reported on BBC television later that day.

106. See the useful analysis in *The Times*, 15 Nov. 1985, 5. See also *Guardian*, 15 Nov. 1985, 15; 16 Nov. 1985, 17.

107. See e.g. the MORI poll cited in *The Economist*, 26 Mar. 1988, 28.

108. See the figures in C. Cook and B. Keith, *British Historical Facts 1830–1900* (1975), 103; Butler, *British Political Facts 1900–1994*, 222–3.

109. On this point, see West Sussex Record Office, Chichester: Cobden papers No. 33: Cobden to George Combe, 21 Mar. 1854.

110. A. D. Macintyre, *The Liberator: Daniel O'Connell and the Irish Party 1830–1847* (1965), 15.

111. Ibid. 43.

112. To Sir Herbert Taylor, 9 Jan. 1836, quoted in J. Prest, *Lord John Russell* (1972), 112.

113. Macintyre, *Liberator*, 273 (1843). Peel to Wellington, 21 June 1846, quoted in his *Memoirs*, part III, 290–1.

114. Hammond, *Gladstone and the Irish Nation*, 95, 220–1. A. B. Cooke and J. Vincent, *The Governing Passion: Cabinet Government and Party Politics in Britain 1885–1886* (Brighton, 1974), 53, 316–18.

115. O'Brien, *Parnell and his Party*, 34, cf. 14, 33, 155.

116. H. A. L. Fisher, *James Bryce (Viscount Bryce of Dechmont, OM)* (1927), i. 206.

117. See e.g. Marchioness of Londonderry, *Henry Chaplin: A Memoir* (1926), 183; Lord E. FitzMaurice, *The Life of Granville George Leveson Gower, Second Earl Granville KG 1815–1891*, 3rd edn. (1905), ii. 468–9, 473–4.

118. Chamberlain, *Political Memoir*, 186; Garvin, *Joseph Chamberlain*, i. 352.

119. Spender and Asquith, *Asquith*, ii. 170.

120. C. Tsuzuki, *H. M. Hyndman and British socialism* (1961), 70; T. Jones, *Lloyd George* (1951), 15.

121. H. H. Asquith, *Letters to Venetia Stanley*, ed. M. and E. Brock (Oxford, 1982), 469.

122. M. Lloyd-George, *H.C.Deb.* 17 Oct. 1944, c.2237; *The Times*, 16 Feb. 1982, 5.

123. Alan Watkins, 'Westminster's Orange Lodge', *New Statesman*, 26 Mar. 1971, 411.

124. Crossman, *Diaries*, iii. 451 (22 Apr. 1969), cf. 871 (24 Mar. 1970). Prior, *Balance of Power*, 180.

125. Robert Chichester-Clark, Ulster Unionist MP for Londonderry, *H.C.Deb.* 3 July 1970, c.249.

126. There is a good organizational chart in P. Hennessy, *Whitehall* (first pub. 1989, rev. paperback edn. 1990), 471.

127. Coupland, *Nationalism*, 404.
128. Kellas, *Modern Scotland*, 174–7.
129. Morgan, *Rebirth of a Nation*, 130, 379, 388.
130. Bogdanor, *Devolution*, 131–5.

## Chapter 4: County and Borough (pp. 115–131)

1. T. Byrne, *Local Government in Britain: Everyone's Guide to how it all Works* (first pub. 1981, 5th edn. 1990), 17.
2. Escott, *England*, 45; cf. Sir Norman Chester, *Administrative System*, 347.
3. R. C. K. Ensor, *England 1870–1914* (1936), 214.
4. For a good discussion, see K. Young (ed.), *New Directions for County Government* (Oxford, 1989), 16–17.
5. A. W. W. Dale, *The Life of R. W. Dale of Birmingham*, 2nd edn. (1899), 412.
6. B. Webb, *My Apprenticeship*, 110.
7. Garvin, *Joseph Chamberlain*, i. 384–5.
8. J. F. C. Harrison, 'Chartism in Leeds', in A. Briggs (ed.), *Chartist Studies* (1959), 92. J. F. Harris, 'The Transition to High Politics 1880–1914', in M. Bentley and J. Stevenson (eds.), *High and Low Politics in Modern Britain: Ten Studies* (Oxford, 1983), 69.
9. M. E. Rose, *The Relief of Poverty 1834–1914* (1972), 54–5.
10. Redlich, *Local Government in England*, ii. 251.
11. Ibid. i. 352; Laski, in Laski *et al.* (eds.), *A Century of Municipal Progress*, 97.
12. Redlich, *Local Government in England*, i. 350.
13. Ibid. ii. 34, 31; see also 20–3 and i. 325.
14. In Laski *et al.* (eds.), *A Century of Municipal Progress*, 106.
15. E. D. Simon, *A City Council from Within* (1926), 136.
16. Ibid. 188.
17. Ibid. 190; see also 165.
18. Ibid. 135; cf. 190 and Redlich, *Local Government in England*, i. 261, 263.
19. Calculated from Butler, *British Political Facts 1900–1994*, 438. See also Hennock, 'Finance and Politics', 224.
20. Table in Wilson (ed.), *Essays on Local Government*, 127.
21. Ibid. 74.
22. See Lloyd George's excellent exposition of the problem in *H.C.Deb.* 4 May 1914, c.67.
23. J. Burnett, *A Social History of Housing* (1978), 237–8.
24. See the useful table listing joint boards in Wilson (ed.), *Essays on Local Government*, 212.
25. Fawcett, *Provinces of England*, 30.
26. H. G. Wells, *Mankind in the Making*, 2nd edn. (1903), 281. His paper on administrative areas is printed as an appendix to Wells's volume.

27. This paragraph owes much to A. Sancton, 'British Socialist Theories of the Division of Power by Area', *Political Studies* (1976), 158–70.

28. C. Ponting, *Breach of Promise: Labour in Power 1964–1970* (first pub. 1989, Penguin edn. 1990), 115.

29. By Byrne, *Local Government in Britain*, 17–19.

30. See the valuable discussion in R. Millward and R. Ward, 'From Private to Public Ownership of Gas Undertakings in England and Wales 1851–1947: Chronology, Incidence and Causes', *Business History* (July 1993), esp. 17–19.

31. Laski *et al.* (eds.), *A Century of Municipal Progress*, 309, 322, 324, 326.

32. See e.g. *Fabian Essays*, 142–3, 174–5; A. M. McBriar, *Fabian Socialism and English Politics 1884–1918* (Cambridge, 1962), 108; W. Wolfe, *Radicalism to Socialism: Men and Ideas in the Formation of Fabian Socialist Doctrines 1881–1889* (New Haven, 1975), 249.

33. As Susan Lawrence pointed out in Labour Party, *Report of 27th Annual Conference* (1927), 227.

34. There is a good discussion of this by J. H. Warren in Lord Campion *et al.*, *British Government since 1918* (1950), 200, 204–5.

35. Wilson (ed.), *Essays on Local Government*, 104–5.

36. For R. Jackman's excellent discussion of these points, see M. Loughlin, M. D. Gelfand, and K. Young (eds.), *Half a Century of Municipal Decline 1935–1985* (1985), 150–3, 157.

37. W. J. M. Mackenzie and J. W. Grove, *Central Administration in Britain* (1957), 403.

38. Keith-Lucas and Richards, *History of Local Government in the Twentieth Century*, 119–20.

39. G. W. Jones, *Borough Politics: A Study of the Wolverhampton Town Council 1888–1964* (1969), 164.

40. K. Young, in A. Seldon and S. Ball (eds.), *Conservative Century: The Conservative Party since 1900* (Oxford, 1994), 417 n. 47.

41. B. Keith-Lucas, epilogue to J. Redlich and F. W. Hirst, *The History of Local Government in England: Being a Reissue of Book 1 of 'Local Government in England'* (first pub. 1958, 2nd edn. 1970), 236.

42. Keith-Lucas and Richards, *History of Local Government in the Twentieth Century*, 117–18.

43. H. Finer, *English Local Government* (first pub. 1933, 3rd edn. 1946), 233, 242; cf. Laski, in Laski *et al.* (eds.), *A Century of Municipal Progress*, 99–100.

44. Byrne, *Local Government in Britain*, 169–70.

45. Hennock, *Fit and Proper Persons*, 335.

46. Simon, *City Council*, 139, 143; Laski, in Laski *et al.* (eds.), *A Century of Municipal Progress*, 102–3.

47. L. Hill, in Laski *et al.* (eds.), *A Century of Municipal Progress*, 120.

48. See J. P. R. M[aud], 'Experiment in the Social Sciences', *Oxford Magazine*, 29 Oct. 1936, 89; D. N. Chester, *Economics, Politics and Social Studies in Oxford 1900–1985* (1986), 132–4.

49. For a useful discussion of this by J. D. Stewart, see Loughlin *et al.* (eds.), *Half a Century of Municipal Decline*, 100.

50. P. G. Richards, *The Local Government System* (1983), 141.

51. Quoted in M. Harrison and A. Norton, *Local Government Administration in England and Wales* (1967, pub. as vol. 5 of the papers of the Ministry of Housing and Local Government's Committee on the Management of Local Government), 38. See also Hennock, *Fit and Proper Persons*, 337.

52. In Laski *et al.* (eds.), *A Century of Municipal Progress*, 106.

53. See Bruce Wood's useful tables in Halsey (ed.), *Trends in British Society since 1900* (1972), 282 and in its revised edition: *British Social Trends since 1900* (1988), 325.

54. Royal Commission on Local Government in England, *Report*, Cmnd. 4040 (1969), 27.

55. Maud Commission, *Report*, 31.

56. Simon, *City council*, 167, cf. 144. See also Keith-Lucas and Richards, *History of Local Government*, 180–2, 195, 219.

57. Butler *et al.*, *Failure in British Government*, 220–1, 276–7.

58. Maud Commission, *Report*, 28–9.

59. See Des Wilson's 'Neighbourhood Muscle', *Observer Colour Supplement*, 26 Aug. 1973, 16–23. Compare David Wood's attack on community politics in 'Parish Pump Comes to Westminster', *The Times*, 11 Dec. 1972, 15.

60. For a good survey, see 'How the Tories Muffed Reform', *The Economist*, 16 Mar. 1985, 38–40.

61. Byrne, *Local Government in Britain*, 21, 235.

62. For figures, see Maud Commission, *Report*, 130.

63. Byrne, *Local Government in Britain*, 185.

64. N. Ridley, *The Local Right: Enabling not Providing*, Centre for Policy Studies, study no. 91 (1988), 26.

65. For a useful discussion, see *Financial Times*, 11 Mar. 1991, survey number, 'Contracted Business Services', p. ii. See also H. Butcher, R. Leach, and M. Mullard, *Local Government and Thatcherism* (1990), 68.

66. Ridley, *Local Right*, 27.

67. P. Beresford, *'Good Council Guide': Wandsworth 1978–1987*, Centre for Policy Studies, study no. 84 (1987), 5.

68. *Financial Times*, 26 May 1992, 6 has a valuable discussion. See also 16 for leading article.

69. See the valuable table and graph in G. C. Baugh, 'Government Grants in Aid of the Rates in England and Wales 1889–1990', *Historical Research* (1992), 234–7.

70. See e.g. Heseltine's response to visiting the Meadow Well estate, Tyneside, *Financial Times*, 14 Nov. 1991, 7.

71. *The Times*, 13 Oct. 1990, 9. For the pioneers of the shift in educational opinion, see *Independent*, 23 July 1987, 11; *Financial Times*, 19 Nov. 1988, 6.

72. K. Baker, *Turbulent Years: My Life in Politics* (1993), 211.

73. Ibid. 244–5.
74. Ibid. 234.
75. Keith-Lucas and Richards, *History of Local Government in the Twentieth Century*, 98. For obituaries of Poulson and T. Dan Smith, see, respectively, *The Times*, 4 Feb. 1993, 19; 28 July 1993, 17.
76. M. Thatcher, *Speeches to the Conservative Party Conference 1975–1988* (1989), 128 (speech on 9 Oct. 1987).
77. *Guardian*, 17 May 1986, 30; cf. *Daily Telegraph*, 1 Oct. 1979, 21 (Birkenhead demolition).
78. A. Beaumont-Dark, *H.C.Deb.* 11 Dec. 1985, c.957.
79. For a good discussion, see S. Dalby, 'Heseltine's Vision of Land Regeneration Takes Shape', *Financial Times*, 30 Oct. 1990, suppl., 'Urban Development in the Thatcher Era', p. vi; 'Hammered, One Way or Another', *The Economist*, 2 Dec. 1989, 33–4.
80. J. Willman, 'Charm and a Challenge', *Financial Times*, 18 Sept. 1992, sect. IV (Urban Development), 1.
81. Thatcher, *Downing Street Years*, 661.
82. Ridley, *The Local Right*, 15; cf. Baker, *Turbulent Years*, 121.
83. Thatcher, *Downing Street Years*, 645, 653, 648.
84. S. and B. Webb, *A Constitution for the Socialist Commonwealth of Great Britain* (first pub. 1920, Cambridge, 1975), 186.
85. *Independent*, 24 Nov. 1987, 2.

## Chapter 5: Rights and Liberties (pp. 133–156)

1. Mill, 'Representative Government', in *Works*, xix. 547.
2. Bagehot, 'Physics and Politics' (1872), in *Works*, vii. 54.
3. I. Berlin, 'Two Concepts of Liberty' (1958), in *Four Essays on Liberty* (1969), 122.
4. D. Coleman and J. Salt, *The British Population: Patterns, Trends, and Processes* (Oxford, 1992), 150.
5. C. Booth, *Life and Labour of the People in London, 3rd ser: Religious Influences*, vii (1902), 429.
6. P. Willmott and M. Young, *Family and Class in a London Suburb* (1960), 130.
7. H. Ellis, *Sexual Inversion*, Studies in the Psychology of Sex (first pub. 1897, 2nd edn. Philadelphia, 1908), 28, cf. 30.
8. Quoted in M. Young and P. Willmott, *Family and Kinship in East London* (first pub. 1957, rev. Penguin edn. 1962), 92.
9. *People's Paper*, 28 Aug. 1852, 1.
10. *A King's Story: The Memoirs of HRH the Duke of Windsor, KG* (1951, Reprint Society edn. 1953), 42.

11. A. Horne, *Macmillan 1894–1956*, i (1988), 341–2. A. Lambert, 'The Prime Minister, his Wife and her Lover', *Independent*, 23 Feb. 1994, 21.

12. *Guardian*, 30 June 1994, 3.

13. *Sinister Street* (first pub. 1913, Penguin edn. Harmondsworth, 1983), 35–6.

14. G. Raverat, *Period Piece: A Cambridge Childhood* (first pub. 1952, 1960 edn.), 102; cf. P. Thompson, *The Edwardians: The Remaking of British Society* (1975), 314.

15. B. Bond, 'Recruiting the Victorian Army 1870–92', *Victorian Studies* (June 1962), 334.

16. J. R. Dinwiddy, 'The Early Nineteenth-Century Campaign against Flogging in the Army', *English Historical Review* (1982), 308, 319–20.

17. See G. H. L. Le May, *British Government 1914–1963: Select Documents* (first pub. 1955, 1964 edn.), 19–20.

18. Ibid. 306. J. B. Christoph, 'Political Rights and Administrative Impartiality in the British Civil Service', *American Political Science Review* (1957), 84.

19. J. Bryce, preface to his *Modern Democracies* (1921), vol. i, p. xii.

20. S. and B. Webb, *Soviet Communism: A New Civilization?* (1935), 1030 n. 1.

21. Sir Edward W. Hamilton, *The Diary . . . 1880–1885*, ed. D. W. R. Bahlman (Oxford, 1972), ii. 562–3 (20 Feb. 1884, Freeman). V. Woolf, *Letters*, vi, ed. N. Nicolson (1980), 250 n. 2 (Davies).

22. C. Darwin, *On the Origin of Species* (first pub. 1859, Penguin edn. Harmondsworth, 1968), 453.

23. Stephen, *Henry Fawcett*, 101. See also his reproach to Lyell in F. Darwin (ed.), *The Life and Letters of Charles Darwin* (1887), iii. 11.

24. Professor Jeffrey Gray, *The Times*, 6 Sept. 1986, 18.

25. G. Orwell, *Works*, iii (1968), 27; iv (1968), 452, 464.

26. V. Woolf, *Diary*, v, ed. A. O. Bell and A. McNeillie (1984), 229.

27. Cunningham quoted in A. Kadish, *The Oxford Economists in the Late Nineteenth Century* (Oxford, 1982), 242; Hough, *New Statesman*, 5 Apr. 1947, 237. Compare Alan Walters, *Independent*, 26 Oct. 1989, 16.

28. Orwell, 'The Freedom of the Press' (unused preface to *Animal Farm*), quoted in B. Crick, *George Orwell: A Life* (1980), 319. See also *The Times*, 4 Dec. 1974, 17 (letter from Joseph); *Guardian*, 5 Apr. 1974, 7.

29. *Independent*, 9 Dec. 1993, 2.

30. Bogdanor, *Devolution*, 50–1.

31. Bagehot, 'English Constitution', *Works*, v. 393.

32. *H.C.Deb.* 26 Nov. 1970, c.296.

33. *H.C.Deb.* 26 Nov. 1970, c.295.

34. H. T. Buckle, *Introduction to the History of Civilization in England* (first pub. 1857–61, rev. edn. J. M. Robertson, 1904), 651.

35. J. S. Mill, 'Autobiography', in *Works*, i. 73; see also 47.

36. Mill, 'Representative Government', *Works*, xix. 479.

37. In 1851, quoted in C. Woodham-Smith, *Florence Nightingale 1820–1910* (1950), 93.

38. A. V. Dicey, *Letters to a Friend on Votes for Women* (1909), 31; 'Woman Suffrage', *Quarterly Review* (Jan. 1909), 285.

39. Mill, *Principles of Political Economy*, 958.

40. For more on the Liberal basis of the campaign, see my *Separate Spheres: The Opposition to Women's Suffrage in Britain* (1978), 39–40.

41. I have elaborated this argument in my 'Women's Suffrage at Westminster 1866–1928', in M. Bentley and J. Stevenson (eds.), *High and Low Politics in Modern Britain: Ten Studies* (Oxford, 1983), 99–102.

42. J. Bentham, *Introduction to the Principles of Morals and Legislation* (first pub. 1789, 1823 edn. repr. as Hafner paperback, New York, 1961), 310–11.

43. K. Rose, *King George V* (1983), 242.

44. Bagehot, 'Newspapers as Property' (1863), in *Works*, vii. 294.

45. Bryce, preface to his *Modern Democracies*, vol. i, p. xi.

46. See my *Drink and the Victorians*, 192–5.

47. T. H. Green, 'Liberal Legislation and Freedom of Contract', in *Works*, ed. R. L. Nettleship, 3rd edn. (1891), iii. 371.

48. E. Burke, 'First Letter on a Regicide Peace' (1796), in *Writings and Speeches*, ix, ed. R. B. McDowell (Oxford, 1991), 242.

49. G. Grosvenor, 'Statistics of the Abatement in Crime in England and Wales during the Twenty Years ended 1887–88', *Journal of the Royal Statistical Society* (Sept. 1890), 386 (table 6).

50. Quotations from H. Spencer, *The Man versus the State* (first pub. 1884, Thinker's Library edn. 1940), 130, 21.

51. Tsuzuki, *Hyndman*, 79. See also H. Pelling, *The Origins of the Labour Party 1880–1900* (1954), 100, 190, 201.

52. Engels, *Condition of the Working Class*, 89, cf. 92–3, 124.

53. Quoted in C. F. Brand, *The British Labour Party: A Short History* (Stanford, Calif., 1965), 82.

54. B. Russell, *Autobiography*, iii: *1944–67* (first pub. 1969, paperback edn. 1971), 222.

55. A thorough and scholarly study is needed of the Society of Labour Lawyers and of the interaction between the Labour Party and the judiciary.

56. See the interesting letter from J. Melville Williams, QC in *The Times*, 4 June 1977, 15.

57. To the annual conference of the Union of Post Office Workers, *Guardian* 16 May 1977, 1. When Conservatives attacked him, Callaghan, Powell, and Professor K. W. Wedderburn defended his view: see *H.C.Deb.* 17 May 1977, c.235 and *The Times*, 21 May 1977, 15.

58. K. W. Wedderburn, letter to *The Times*, 21 May 1977, 15.

59. See e.g. Eric Heffer in *H.C.Deb.* 18 Dec. 1972, c.971; *The Times*, 24 Jan. 1973, 2; *Observer*, 18 Feb. 1973, 10; and Hugh Scanlon, *The Times*, 7 Sept. 1972, 4. For a useful discussion, see Pelling, 'Trade Unions, Workers and the Law', in his *Popular Politics and Society*, 62–81.

60. See Benn's comments in *Sunday Times*, 23 July 1972, 2.
61. On this, see *Listener*, 16 May 1985, 12. *Observer*, 5 May 1985, 3.
62. S. and B. Webb, *Constitution for the Socialist Commonwealth of Great Britain*, 270.
63. For these episodes, see *The Times*, 28 July 1972, 17; 27 Feb. 1974, 10–11; 14 Jan. 1977, 1–2, 6; 15 Jan. 1977, 15; 17 Jan. 1977, 1; 27 Jan. 1982, 1; 29 Jan. 1982, 6; 23 Sept. 1982, 2.
64. See his letter in *The Times*, 10 Feb. 1982, 11.
65. See the law report in *The Times*, 6 Nov. 1986, 34. For Thatcher's views on Labour's boycott of Murdoch journalists, see *The Times*, 31 Jan. 1986, 1.
66. See Remington's comments in H. G. Wells, *The New Machiavelli* (first pub. 1911, Penguin edn. Harmondsworth, 1985), 245.
67. E. Halévy, 'Socialism and the Problem of Democratic Parliamentarism' (1934), in *The Era of Tyrannies*, 258.
68. In 1890, quoted in P. Thompson, *The Work of William Morris* (1967), 242.
69. *Financial Times*, 20 May 1987, 12.
70. Mill, 'On Liberty', in *Works*, 18 (1977), 261.
71. C. A. R. Crosland, *The Future of Socialism* (1956), 522.
72. B. Crick, *The Reform of Parliament* (1964), 181–2.
73. *H.L.Deb.* 18 June 1969, c.1040; compare Larry Gostin's reasons for resigning as General Secretary, *Financial Times*, 3 May 1985, 8.
74. *Guardian*, 10 Nov. 1972, 14; cf. her important Derbyshire speech, *Guardian*, 22 Jan. 1977, 6.
75. G. Orwell, *Works*, ii (1968), 78. See also iii (1968), 27–8.
76. *H.C.Deb.* 7 Feb. 1978, cc.1355–6 (Lawson); *Daily Telegraph*, 14 Dec. 1978, 10 (Prior).
77. T. Benn, *Conflicts of Interest: Diaries 1977–1980*, ed. R. Winstone (1990), 412 (7 Dec. 1978).
78. Burke, *Reflections*, 151.
79. M. J. Oakeshott, *Rationalism in Politics* (first pub. 1962, paperback edn. 1967), 43.
80. Bodleian Library, Oxford: MS Bryce 4, fo. 247: Bryce to Dicey, 22 July 1920.
81. Quoted in M. Cockerell, *Live from Number 10: The Inside Story of Prime Ministers and Television* (first pub. 1988, paperback edn. 1989), 345.
82. Quoted in Thatcher, *Downing Street Years*, 753.
83. Interview with Trevor Grove, in *Sunday Telegraph*, 15 Apr. 1990, review section, p. iii.
84. Liberal Industrial Inquiry, *Britain's Industrial Future* (first pub. 1928, new edn. 1977), 261.
85. Interview with Brian Connell, *The Times*, 9 May 1977, 8.
86. *The Times*, 28 Feb. 1981, 1 (Georgetown University speech). The link between freedom and economic prosperity was regularly made in her speeches, e.g. *The Times*, 11 Oct. 1975, 4; *Sunday Telegraph*, 13 May 1979, 4.

87. *Guardian*, 6 Apr. 1973, 24.

88. *H.C.Deb.* 1 Mar. 1976, c.951.

89. *The Times*, 3 Jan. 1984, 3.

90. F. A. von Hayek, preface (1976) to *The Road to Serfdom* (first pub. 1944, paperback edn. 1976), p. vii; cf. Crosland, *Future of Socialism*, 500.

91. Hayek, *Road to Serfdom*, 136.

92. Ibid. 16.

93. Milton Friedman, *Capitalism and Freedom* (first pub. 1962, paperback edn. Chicago, 1969), 201.

94. Hayek, *Road to Serfdom*, 108.

95. K. Joseph, *Stranded on the Middle Ground? Reflections on Circumstances and Policies* (1976), 63–4.

96. Quoted in S. Letwin, *The Anatomy of Thatcherism* (Fontana paperback edn. 1992), 74.

97. M. and R. Friedman, *Free to Choose: A Personal Statement* (first pub. 1979, paperback edn. Harmondsworth, 1980), 89–90.

98. *H.C.Deb.* 23 July 1970, c.769.

99. Friedman, *Free to Choose*, 289–90.

100. Friedman, *Capitalism and Freedom*, 108, cf. 110.

101. The unofficial view prevailing in some local parties was less liberal. See the controversy in Cheltenham about a black Conservative candidate John Taylor, *Independent*, 5 Dec. 1990, 3.

102. See John Torode, 'Self-Help is Better than State Help', *Guardian*, 11 Feb. 1986, 23, discussing Chief Rabbi Immanuel Jakobovitz's *From Doom to Hope: A Jewish View on 'Faith in the City'* . . . (Office of the Chief Rabbi, 1986).

103. *The Times*, 17 Nov. 1977, 1.

104. C. Parkinson, *Right at the Centre: An Autobiography* (1992), 231.

105. Hayek, *Road to Serfdom*, 109.

106. Ibid. 42.

107. Speech at Worsley, *Observer*, 12 Mar. 1972, 2.

108. *The Times*, 12 Oct. 1984, 1.

109. Thatcher, *Downing Street Years*, 425.

110. O. Mosley, *My Life* (first pub. 1968, Nelson paperback edn. 1970), 290, cf. 293, 295, 298, 301.

111. John Tyndall, letter in *The Times*, 23 Aug. 1977, 11.

112. H. Ellis, *The Task of Social Hygiene* (first pub. 1912, 2nd edn. 1927), 394.

113. H. Ellis, *The Nineteenth Century: A Dialogue in Utopia* (1900), 80.

114. Orwell, *Works*, iii. 27.

115. P. Whiteley, P. Seyd, and J. Richardson, *True Blues: The Politics of Conservative Party Membership* (Oxford, 1994), 20–1, 53.

116. Bodleian Library, Oxford: Conservative Party archive NUA 6/2/7: Final Report of the Committee on Party Organisation (dated 27 Apr. 1949), 6.

117. Quoted in K. Harris, *Attlee* (1982), 131.

118. Castle, *Diaries 1974–1976*, 233 (22 Nov. 1974).
119. Jennings, *Parliament*, 61–2.
120. Morgan, *House of Lords and the Labour Government*, 6–7, cf. 8, 222.
121. J. Patten, *Political Culture: Conservatism and Rolling Constitutional Change*, 1991 Swinton Lecture (Conservative Political Centre, 1991), 9.
122. Cockburn, in W. C. Costin and J. S. Watson, *The Law and Working and Working of the Constitution: Documents 1660–1914*, ii (first pub. 1952, 2nd edn. 1964), 292 (*Wason v. Walter*). Simon writing in *The Times*, 27 Apr. 1950, quoted in G. Wilson, *Cases and Materials on Constitutional and Administrative Law* (first pub. 1966, 2nd edn. Cambridge, 1976), 21.
123. R. Muir, *How Britain is Governed: A Critical Analysis of Modern Developments in the British System of Government* (1930), 153.
124. Ibid. 144.
125. Scarman, 'Why Britain Needs a Written Constitution', 4.
126. Wilson, *Cases and Materials*, 454.
127. *H.C.Deb.* 14 Dec. 1921, c.27.

## Chapter 6: Interests and Pressures (pp. 157–179)

1. Quoted in R. Terrill, *R. H. Tawney and his Times: Socialism as Fellowship* (1974), 180.
2. N. C. Hunt, 'Pressure Groups in the USA', *Occidente*, 12/2 (Mar.–Apr. 1956), 114.
3. Mackenzie and Grove, *Central Administration*, 430.
4. *The Times*, 18 May 1978, 4. For the Women's National Commission, see *The Times*, 22 July 1969, 3.
5. P. Hollis, preface to Hollis (ed.), *Pressure from Without*, p. vii.
6. J. Turner (ed.), *Businessmen and Politics: Studies of Business Activity in British Politics 1900–1945* (1984), 4–5.
7. R. Cobden, in *The League*, 2 Dec. 1843, 146.
8. S. and B. Webb, *Constitution for the Socialist Commonwealth*, 187.
9. Quoted in R. A. Butler, *The Art of the Possible: The Memoirs of Lord Butler* (1971), 51.
10. Cobden, *Speeches on Questions of Public Policy*, i. 133 (speech in London, 8 Feb. 1844).
11. W. A. S. Hewins, *The Apologia of an Imperialist: Forty Years of Empire Policy* (1929) vol. i, chs. 3 and 4.
12. *The Times*, 18 Dec. 1968, 14; 18 Apr. 1973, 2.
13. *Public Petitions in the House of Commons*, House of Commons factsheet no. 32 (Feb. 1993 ed.), 3.
14. Benn, *Diaries 1980–90*, 582 (15 Dec. 1989).

15. See also 'The Act of Militancy: Violence and the Suffragettes 1904–1914', in my *Peaceable Kingdom*, 26–81.

16. See my *Separate Spheres*, 177–99.

17. For a portrait, see *Guardian*, 27 Sept. 1976, 7.

18. P. Norton, *Does Parliament Matter?* (1993), 63–4.

19. Viscount Cecil, *A Great Experiment* (1941), 191–2.

20. Compare David Hunt, Secretary of State for Employment, in *Financial Times*, 23 Aug. 1993, 6 with Thatcher at Glasgow in *The Times*, 10 Jan. 1978, 1.

21. For a good discussion of this, see Chester, *Administrative System*, 117–18.

22. R. H. S. Crossman, *Backbench Diaries*, ed. J. Morgan (1981), 944 (15 May 1961); *Diaries of a Cabinet Minister*, ii (1976), 701 (11 Mar. 1968).

23. For the slow dawning of such recognition in one pressure group, see my 'Women's Suffrage at Westminster', in Bentley and Stevenson (eds.), *High and Low Politics in Modern Britain*, 80–122.

24. For a good discussion of this, see W. Rüdig, 'Wilting Greenery', *Times Higher Education Supplement*, 17 Sept. 1993, 17.

25. K. O. Morgan, *Consensus and Disunity: The Lloyd George Coalition Government 1918–1922* (Oxford, 1979), 168.

26. For an extended argument to this effect, see my 'Women's Suffrage at Westminster', 80–122.

27. D. S. Birn, *The League of Nations Union 1918–1945* (Oxford, 1981), 49; cf. R. B. McCallum, *Public Opinion and the Last Peace* (1944), 146 and the situation of the family allowance movement as discussed in M. D. Stocks, *Eleanor Rathbone: A Biography* (1949), 145.

28. B. Donoughue, *Prime Minister: The Conduct of Policy under Harold Wilson and James Callaghan* (1987), 110. See Baker, *Turbulent Years*, 254 for a very similar comment.

29. R. McKibbin, *The Ideologies of Class: Social Relations in Britain 1880–1950* (Oxford, 1990, paperback edn. 1991), 279.

30. See e.g. the Liberals' manifesto in *The Times*, 18 Sept. 1974, 4.

31. Thorpe, in Liberal Party advertisement, *The Times*, 19 Feb. 1974, 3; Heath, speech at Manchester Free Trade Hall, *Guardian*, 21 Feb. 1974, 6.

32. *Financial Times*, 19 Jan. 1984, 10.

33. Burke, *Reflections*, 119.

34. Quoted in Adonis, *Making Aristocracy Work*, 13.

35. L. S. Amery, *My Political Life*, i (1953), 459.

36. *H.C.Deb.* 20 July 1954, c.1217.

37. Lord Robert Cecil, 'The Theories of Parliamentary Reform', in *Oxford Essays, Contributed by Members of the University 1858* (1858), 56.

38. Quoted in Adonis, *Making Aristocracy Work*, 13.

39. J. Morley, *The Life of Richard Cobden* (first pub. 1879, 11th edn. 1903), 152. B. Disraeli, *Lord George Bentinck: A Political Biography*, 5th edn. (1852), 309.

40. Monypenny and Buckle, *Disraeli*, i. 1043, 1047.

41. M. J. D. Roberts, 'Pressure-Group Politics and the Church of England: The Church Defence Institution 1859–1896', *Journal of Ecclesiastical History* (Oct. 1984).

42. As D. A. Hamer points out in his preface to *The Politics of Electoral Pressure: A Study in the History of Victorian Reform Agitations* (Hassocks, 1977), p. x.

43. Amery, *Joseph Chamberlain*, vi. 773–4.

44. Jo Richardson, *H.C.Deb.* 15 Dec. 1982, c.334.

45. See my *Separate Spheres*, 113–14, 239.

46. Quoted in Vincent and Cooke, *Governing Passion*, 370.

47. Quoted by A. Taylor in Seldon and Ball (eds.), *Conservative Century*, 509.

48. For fuller treatment of this, see my 'Mrs Thatcher and the Intellectuals', *Twentieth Century British history*, 5/2 (1994), 213–20.

49. *Times Higher Education Supplement*, 27 Apr. 1994, 2.

50. H. J. Hanham, 'Liberal Organizations for Working Men 1860–1914', *Bulletin of the Society for the Study of Labour History*, 7 (Autumn, 1963), 5–7.

51. G. M. Young, 'Mr Gladstone', in W. D. Handcock (ed.), *Victorian Essays* (1962), 107.

52. Gladstone, *Autobiographica*, 136.

53. *H.C.Deb.* 14 June 1881, c.559.

54. Speech at Birmingham on 5 Jan. 1885, in J. L. Garvin, *The Life of Joseph Chamberlain*, i (1932), 548.

55. Snowden, *Autobiography*, ii. 650, 652.

56. See pp. 197–200.

57. *Guardian*, 13 Nov. 1980, 15.

58. Wells, *New Machiavelli*, 245–6.

59. Nicolson, *Diaries and Letters 1945–1962*, 171, diary entry for 10 June 1949, commenting on the Attlee government's attitude to the National Trust. Nicolson had stood as a Labour candidate in a by-election of the previous year.

60. *Oxford English Dictionary, Supplement Se–Z* (1986), 1188 (first citation, 1957).

61. *The Times*, 26 Jan. 1971, 12; 17 Nov. 1980, 3. See also Benn, *Diaries 1977–1980*, 508 (23 May 1979), 595 (16 May 1980).

62. Webb, *Constitution for the Socialist Commonwealth of Great Britain*, 145. Cousins quoted in L. Panitch, *Social Democracy and Industrial Militancy: The Labour Party, the Trade Unions and Incomes Policy 1945–1974* (Cambridge, 1976), 272.

63. *Guardian*, 8 July 1975, 5 (at Scarborough).

64. *Financial Times*, 7 Jan. 1986, 10.

65. Bagehot, 'The Advantages and Disadvantages of Becoming a Member of Parliament' (1874), in *Works*, vi. 57.

66. *Guardian*, 12 Apr. 1976, 10.

67. Baker, *Turbulent Years*, 172, 167.

68. J. Loughlin, *Gladstone, Home Rule and the Ulster Question 1882–1893* (Atlantic Heights, NJ, 1987), 53.

69. On this, see A. E. Dingle, *The Campaign for Prohibition in Victorian England: The United Kingdom Alliance 1872–1895* (1980), 141–4, 150, 162, 172. See also my *Drink and the Victorians*, 356–60.
70. Letter in *The Times*, 24 June 1969, 9.
71. *Observer*, 23 Dec. 1990, 18. In 1993 the matter was resolved by parliament selecting from a range of options.
72. A. A. Rogow, *The Labour Government and British Industry 1945–1951* (Oxford, 1955), 124.

## Chapter 7: Co-ordinating Opinion (pp. 181–217)

1. Bagehot, 'History of the Unreformed Parliament, and its Lessons' (1858), in *Works*, vi. 273.
2. W. O. Aydelotte, 'The House of Commons in the 1840s', 254; M. Rush, in Walkland (ed.), *House of Commons in the Twentieth Century*, 87–8, 121 (his categories 'direct' and 'area' provide the comparison).
3. Craig (ed.), *British Electoral Facts 1832–1987*, 161–2.
4. S. Smith, *My Life-Work* (popular edn. 1903), 174.
5. See e.g. Muir, *How Britain is Governed*, 158. M. Linton, *Labour's Road to Electoral Reform: What's Wrong with First-Past-the-Post?*, ed. M. Georghiou (Labour Campaign for Electoral Reform, [1993]), 26.
6. *H.L.Deb.* 8 June 1885, c.1361: Earl of Kimberley, speaking in committee stage of the Parliamentary Elections (Redistribution) Bill.
7. J. Ramsden, *The Age of Balfour and Baldwin 1902–1940* (1978), 259–60.
8. R. Heath, MP, President of Stoke-on-Trent Constitutional Club, quoted in R. T. McKenzie, *British Political Parties* (first pub. 1955, 2nd edn. 1963), 161.
9. For more on this, see Clarke, *Lancashire and the New Liberalism*, 6.
10. C. Cook, 'Liberals, Labour and Local Elections', in G. Peele and C. Cook (eds.), *The Politics of Reappraisal 1918–1939* (1975), 171, 177–87.
11. M. Pinto-Duschinsky, *British Political Finance 1830–1980* (Washington, 1981), 77–9.
12. For a good discussion, see R. McKibbin, *The Evolution of the Labour Party 1910–1924* (Oxford, 1974), 162. See also Pinto-Duschinsky, *British Political Finance*, 77–8, 159.
13. D. H. Close, 'The Collapse of Resistance to Democracy: Conservatives, Adult Suffrage, and Second Chamber Reform 1911–1928', *Historical Journal* (1977), 907–8.
14. Pinto-Duschinsky, *British Political Finance*, 27, 52–3, 126.
15. Ramsden, *Age of Balfour and Baldwin*, 248.
16. For the campaign, see B. Pimlott, *Labour and the Left in the 1930s* (Cambridge, 1977), 116–18, 123–4, 128–9, 131, 136–9. For the proposed conferences, see M. Harrison, *Trade Unions and the Labour Party since 1945* (1960), 253.

17. Seldon and Ball (eds.), *Conservative Century*, 291.

18. J. D. Hoffman, *The Conservative Party in Opposition 1945–1951* (1964), 118; see also 55–6, 59–60.

19. Pinto-Duschinsky, *British Political Finance*, 283.

20. Butler and Pinto-Duschinsky, *British General Election of 1970*, 291; cf. Butler and King, *British General Election of 1964*, 215; Butler and Rose, *British General Election of 1959*, 120.

21. D. E. Butler and D. Kavanagh, *The British General Election of October 1974* (1975), 244–5.

22. D. E. Butler and D. Kavanagh, *The British General Election of 1979* (1980), 308.

23. 'Interim report of the [Wilson] sub-committee on party organization' (hereafter cited as 'Wilson Report'), in *Report of the 54th Annual Conference of the Labour Party, Margate 1955* (n.d.), 66.

24. Ibid.

25. Ibid. 65. See also McKenzie, *British Political Parties*, 543.

26. Wilson Report, 66, 71.

27. Crossman, *The Diaries of a Cabinet Minister*, i (1975), 254 (18 June 1965).

28. Ibid. 159 (14 Feb. 1965); cf. McKenzie, *British Political Parties*, 546.

29. Benn, *Diaries 1973–1976*, 635 (2 Nov. 1976).

30. Pinto-Duschinsky, *British Political Finance*, 151; cf. 126.

31. McKenzie, *British Political Parties*, 546.

32. S. H. Beer, 'Labour—an Ageing Party', *Observer*, 7 Oct. 1973, 12; cf. L. Minkin, *The Labour Party Conference: A Study in the Politics of Intra-party Democracy* (1978), 131.

33. *Guardian*, 8 July 1975, 5.

34. For figures, see Pinto-Duschinsky, *British Political Finance*, 314–15.

35. *The Times*, 27 Aug. 1976, 4.

36. e.g. David Wood, ibid. 1.

37. As argued with abundant supporting evidence in Pinto-Duschinsky, *British Political Finance*, 292–6.

38. *Daily Telegraph*, 21 Apr. 1979, 1.

39. *Castle Diaries 1974–1976*, 565 (16 Nov. 1975).

40. Benn, *Diaries 1977–1980*, 656 (14 Dec. 1979).

41. Interview in *The Times*, 8 June 1981, 3.

42. Benn, *Diaries 1980–1990*, 507 (21 May 1887).

43. Figures in Butler, *British Political Facts 1900–1994*, 213–19.

44. *The Times*, 14 Sept. 1967, 8; 11 Dec. 1972, 15; 30 June 1973, 5 (Crosland).

45. Open letter of S. Williams, W. Rodgers, and D. Owen to the Labour Party, 1 Aug. 1980, *Guardian*, 1 Aug. 1980, 11.

46. *The Times*, 12 June 1981, 2.

47. *Financial Times*, 9 Jan. 1984, 1.

48. Ibid., 2 Oct. 1984, 8.

49. D. E. Butler and D. Kavanagh, *The British General Election of February 1974*

(1974), 220. Butler and Kavanagh, *British General Election of October 1974*, 224, 228. *The Economist*, 9 Feb. 1974, 21.

50. Butler and Pinto-Duschinsky, *British General Election of 1970*, 98–101.

51. Whiteley *et al.*, *True Blues*, 226.

52. As pointed out by T. Lloyd, 'Uncontested Seats in British General Elections 1852–1910', *Historical Journal* (1965), 265.

53. R. B. McCallum and A. Readman, *The British General Election of 1945* (1947), 155.

54. D. E. Butler and U. Kitzinger, *The 1975 Referendum* (London, 1976), 273; see also 282.

55. McKenzie, *British Political Parties*, 648; cf. Peter Jenkins, in *Guardian*, 22 Oct. 1980, 15.

56. Parkinson, *Right at the Centre*, 186.

57. Clive Cookson, *The Times*, 25 May 1983, 4.

58. P. Riddell, 'Trying to Box Clever', *Financial Times*, 27 Jan. 1987, 21. See also J. Haber, 'A Vote of Confidence', *Guardian*, 8 May 1986, 13.

59. D. E. Butler and D. Kavanagh, *The British General Election of 1987* (1988), 213. *Financial Times*, 23 May 1987, 6.

60. N. Tebbit, *Upwardly Mobile* (1988), 247.

61. Benn, *Diaries 1980–1990*, 526 (3 Nov. 1987).

62. Butler and Kavanagh, *British General Election of 1992*, 238.

63. Butler and Pinto-Duschinsky, *British General Election of 1970*, 293.

64. Hansard Commission on Electoral Reform, *Report, June 1976* ([1976]), paras. 47–8.

65. Whiteley *et al.*, *True Blues*, 21.

66. Parkinson, *Right at the Centre*, 187.

67. *Financial Times*, 28 Mar 1983, 8.

68. N. Dennis, F. Henriques, and C. Slaughter, *Coal is our Life: An Analysis of a Yorkshire Mining Community* (1956), 165–6.

69. Norton, *Does Parliament Matter?*, 148–50.

70. Wilson (ed.), *Cases and Materials*, 118, cf. 112, 113.

71. S. Baldwin, speech at the Albert Hall, 4 Dec. 1924, in his *On England, and Other Addresses* (1926), 73.

72. *The Times*, 22 Apr. 1968, 2.

73. On this, see D. Healey, *The Time of my Life* (first pub. 1989, paperback edn. 1990), 408–9. Benn, *Diaries 1973–1976*, 123–5 (19–21 Mar. 1974); 162 (24 May 1974).

74. J. H. Robb, *The Primrose League 1883–1906* (New York, 1942), 87.

75. M. Barker, *Gladstone and Radicalism: The Reconstruction of Liberal Policy in Britain 1885–1894* (Hassocks, 1975), 160.

76. Hatfield House MSS, Third Marquis of Salisbury/D48, fo. 277: Salisbury to Lady John Manners, 26 Apr. 1886 (typescript copy); cf. Cecil, *Salisbury*, iii. 108.

77. *Castle Diaries 1974–1976*, 510 (29 Sept. 1975).

78. *Observer*, 17 Oct. 1982, 7.

79. For more on this, see pp. 192, 227–8.

80. Quoted in Pimlott, *Harold Wilson*, 580; cf. A. Morgan, *Harold Wilson* (1992), 422.

81. Interviewed on BBC *Panorama*, *The Times*, 17 Nov. 1980, 1.

82. *Guardian*, 2 Oct. 1985, 6.

83. Butler *et al.*, *Failure in British Government*, 249.

84. See e.g. Julian Critchley, 'The Battle Smoke did not Cloud our Judgement', *Independent*, 21 Nov. 1990, 19.

85. Bagehot, 'The Chances for a Long Conservative Régime in England', in *Works*, vii. 226.

86. Ibid. 233.

87. Wilde, *Works*, ed. G. F. Maine (1948), 332.

88. Horne, *Macmillan*, i. 298.

89. *H.C.Deb.* 28 Oct. 1943, c.403.

90. D. E. Butler and D. Stokes, *Political Change in Britain: Forces Shaping Electoral Choice* (1969), 206. See also D. Thomson, *England in the Twentieth Century 1914–1963* (1965), 116.

91. W. Bagehot, 'Not a Middle Party but a Middle Government' (1874), in *Works*, vii. 198.

92. I have discussed the centrist's plight more fully in 'The Centrist Theme in Modern British Politics', in my *Peaceable Kingdom*, 309–77.

93. Chamberlain, *Political Memoir*, 276.

94. Dale, *R. W. Dale*, 634.

95. V. Bogdanor, *The People and the Party System: The Referendum and Electoral Reform in British Politics* (Cambridge, 1981), 134. In 1925 Lloyd George regretted his failure as prime minister to seize this opportunity: *The Political Diaries of C. P. Scott 1911–1928*, ed. T. Wilson (1970), 485.

96. In a Radio 3 programme 'The Gang that Fell Apart', 11 Sept. 1991.

97. See Ronald Butt, *The Times*, 7 Oct. 1976, 18.

98. Ibid., 28 Nov. 1981, 1.

99. Prior, *Balance of Power*, 263.

100. *Daily Telegraph*, 7 Oct. 1992, 1.

101. Ibid., 3 May 1979, 8; cf. Bogdanor, *People and the Party System*, 133.

102. For examples of such complaints, see John Morley, 'Old Parties and New Policy', *Fortnightly Review* (Sept. 1868), 325 and Barbara Wootton, *Testament for Social Science: An Essay in the Application of Scientific Method to Human Problems* (1950), 58.

103. Speech at Louth, *Guardian*, 18 Apr. 1979, 4.

104. Quoted in Boyce, *Englishmen and Irish Troubles*, 36; see also 37 for his letter to Hoare; cf. Newton, *Lansdowne*, 73.

105. Lord Scarman, 'Why Britain Needs a Written Constitution', 4th Sovereignty Lecture, Charter 88 Trust, 20 July 1992, 7.

106. *The Times*, 23 Nov. 1979, 5.
107. D. E. Butler, *The Electoral System in Britain 1918–1951* (Oxford, 1953), 41.
108. For the 'Judas' episode, see Guedalla (ed.), *The Queen and Mr Gladstone*, ii. 472–3. For Wigg, see T. Benn, *Years of Hope: Diaries, Letters and Papers 1940–1962*, ed. R. Winstone (1994), 205; cf. 200 and S. Ball, 'Parliament and Politics in Britain 1900–1951', *Parliamentary History* (1991), 275. For Thorpe, see Campbell, *Edward Heath*, 439.
109. See above, pp. 41–2.
110. Healey, *Time of my Life*, 458.
111. 'An Alliance Hung up on a Hung Parliament', *Guardian*, 5 Jun. 1987, 19. A. L. Lowell comments on the British tendency to discuss political questions in terms of rival teams in his *The Government of England* (first pub. 1908, 1921 edn.), i. 447. Low, *Governance of England*, 128 speaks of rival 'armies' or 'sides'.
112. *H.C.Deb.* 2 May 1924, c.2020. In 1917 Lloyd George held similar views—see *The Political Diaries of C. P. Scott*, 274—but not later.
113. G. Orwell, 'Rudyard Kipling' (1942), *Works*, ii (1968), 228.
114. B. Russell, *Autobiography*, ii (first pub. 1968, Bantam paperback edn. 1969), 280.
115. Bagehot, 'English Constitution', in *Works*, v. 297.
116. Bagehot, 'Not a Middle Party but a Middle Government' (1874), *Works*, vii. 198–9.
117. *H.C.Deb.* 22 Jan. 1846, c.123; cf. Disraeli, *Bentinck*, 310.
118. *The Times*, 9 Oct. 1981, 6. See also Liberal Party manifesto in *Financial Times*, 11 Apr. 1979, 13. For similar claims by Pardoe and Thorpe, see *The Times*, 24 Feb. 1977, 7.
119. Quoted in Linton, *Labour's Road to Electoral reform*, 6.
120. Interview in *Financial Times*, 14 Nov. 1985, 28.
121. G. R. Searle, *Country before Party: Coalition and the Idea of 'National Government' in Modern Britain 1885–1987* (1995), 25.
122. As did David Owen at the SDP conference on 8 Oct. 1981, *The Times*, 9 Oct. 1981, 6.
123. Bagehot, 'Parliamentary Reform' (1859), in *Works*, vi. 215.

## Chapter 8: Assessing Opinion (pp. 219–243)

1. Disraeli to Derby, 4 Sept. 1876, quoted in Monypenny and Buckle, *Disraeli*, ii. 925; see also 933–4, 944.
2. Crossman, *Cabinet Diaries*, iii. 30 (27 Apr. 1968).
3. Quoted by P. Addison, *The Road to 1945: British Politics and the Second World War* (1975), 28.

4. Jennings, *Parliament*, 8. See also V. R. Markham, *Return Passage: The Autobiography of Violet R. Markham, CH* (1953), 199.

5. See my *Peaceable Kingdom*, 138–50, 429–30; *Drink and the Victorians*, 2nd edn., 245–9, 252–3, 256, 273.

6. *H.C.Deb.* 7 May 1860, cc.828–9.

7. Morley, *Richard Cobden*, 407.

8. Speech at Glasgow on 1 Oct. 1885, quoted in H. Jephson, *The Platform: Its Rise and Progress* (1892), ii. 544.

9. Harris, *William Beveridge*, 421, 435, 438.

10. K. Hindell and M. Simms, 'How the Abortion Lobby Worked', in R. Kimber and J. J. Richardson (eds.), *Pressure Groups in Britain: A Reader* (1974), 156, 159.

11. K. Middlemas, *Politics in industrial Society: The Experience of the British System since 1911* (1979), 129–31, 349–52.

12. Morrison, *Government and Parliament*, 278. See also Donoughue and Jones, *Herbert Morrison*, 358–9.

13. H. Wilson, *The Labour Government 1964–70: A Personal Record* (1971), 380. See also *H.C.Deb.* 13 May 1969, cc.1218–20; *New Society*, 24 Aug. 1967, 253.

14. *Financial Times*, 29 May 1980, 12. See also S. H. Beer, in E. Frank (ed.), *Lawmakers in a Changing World* (Englewood Cliffs, NJ, 1966), 45–6.

15. *The Times*, 8 Feb. 1974, 2.

16. See e.g. Philip Bassett's 'British Rail Letting off more Steam in Public', *Financial Times*, 22 Jan. 1982, 10.

17. *Daily Telegraph*, 2 Nov. 1979, 1.

18. See the interesting discussion in H. Young, 'Hole in the Corner Decisions that can only Lead to Blunders', *Guardian*, 10 Dec. 1984, 14.

19. House of Lords Record Office, Strachey MSS S/5/5/1: Dicey to St L. Strachey, 24 Jan. 1894. I owe this reference to Vernon Bogdanor. See also his *The People and the Party System*, 12–15.

20. On this, see my *Separate Spheres*, 158–60.

21. Cumbria County Record Office, Catherine Marshall MSS, box 8, file 'CEM January 1912': MacDonald to Mrs Fawcett, 29 Jan. 1912.

22. Quoted in J. Meadowcroft and M. W. Taylor, 'Liberalism and the Referendum in British Political Thought 1890–1914', *Twentieth Century British History*, 1/1 (1990), 51.

23. Speech at Llandudno, *Guardian*, 27 May 1968, 2. His ideas evoked an unperceptive and jaundiced response in Crossman, *Cabinet Diaries*, iii. 80 (27 May 1968).

24. For the origins of the referendum, see Bogdanor, *People and Party System*, 39–41. *The Times*, 28 Apr. 1975, 13.

25. T. Benn, *Office without Power: Diaries 1968–1972* (1988), 414 (16 Mar. 1972). Prior, *Balance of Power*, 85.

26. See *The Times* leader on 1 Aug. 1970, 13 in response to Douglas Jay's advocacy. For Jenkins, see *The Times*, 11 Apr. 1972, 4.

27. Castle, *Diaries 1974–1976*, 182 (16 Sept. 1974).

28. Ibid. 287 (21 Jan. 1975); cf. N. Johnson, *In Search of the Constitution: Reflections on State and Society in Britain* (Oxford, 1977), 147: the referendum 'evoked practically no constitutional discussion of a significant kind: the conceptual context was simply not present to permit this'.

29. *H.C.Deb.* 11 Mar. 1975, c.316.

30. Thatcher, *Speeches to the Conservative Party Conference*, 34–5 (14 Oct. 1977). *Guardian*, 19 Sept. 1977, 1.

31. e.g. *Sunday Telegraph*, 18 Nov. 1990, 19; *Observer*, 24 Nov. 1991, 3; *H.C.Deb.* 21 Nov. 1991, cc.464–5.

32. D. Wood, 'The Great Referendum Gimmick', *The Times*, 7 Feb. 1977, 15.

33. For Lloyd George, see Lloyd, *General Election of 1880*, 96. For Arch, see J. Arch, *The Story of his Life*, ed. Countess of Warwick (1898), 49.

34. W. T. Stead, 'The Future of Journalism', *Contemporary Review*, Nov. 1886, 677–8.

35. Costin and Watson, *Law and Working of the Constitution*, ii. 292.

36. Quotations from Holland, *Devonshire*, ii. 99; Viscount Chilston, *W. H. Smith* (1965), 212.

37. Emden, *The People and the Constitution*, 100.

38. On the last of these, see Boyce, *Englishmen and Irish Troubles*, 58, 63, 71, 193–5 and Orwell, *Works*, iii. 24.

39. Quoted in Dugdale, *Balfour*, 158.

40. C. Seymour-Ure, in Butler and King, *The British General Election of 1966*, 152. See also Butler and Rose, *British General Election of 1959*, 109.

41. H. G. Nicholas, *The British General Election of 1950* (1951), 127. Butler and Rose, *British General Election of 1959*, 75.

42. Cockerell, *Live from Number 10*, 58; see also 8–9 and A. Briggs, *The BBC: The First Fifty Years* (Oxford, 1985), 292–3.

43. D. E. Butler, *The British General Election of 1955* (1955), 64.

44. T. Stannage, *Baldwin Thwarts the Opposition: The British General Election of 1935* (1980), 178.

45. McCallum and Readman, *British General Election of 1945*, 154–5.

46. Butler and Rose, *British General Election of 1959*, 119.

47. Ibid. 93.

48. Butler and Kavanagh, *British General Election of February 1974*, 157.

49. Butler and Kavanagh, *British General Election of 1979*, 218.

50. Ramsden, *Age of Balfour and Baldwin*, 235.

51. A. Thorpe, *The British General Election of 1931* (Oxford, 1991), 188.

52. D. E. Butler, *The British General Election of 1951* (1952), 75.

53. Butler and Rose, *British General Election of 1959*, 96.

54. Ibid. 93. Butler and King, *British General Election of 1966*, 144.

55. Butler and Kavanagh, *British General Election of February 1974*, 123.

56. Butler and Kavanagh, *British General Election of 1987*, 215.

57. See above, p. 257.

58. *Daily Telegraph*, 4 Apr. 1979, 1. A. Raphael and G. Wansell, 'The Selling of Maggie', *Observer*, 22 Apr. 1979, 9, 10 claim that Thatcher had wanted to take up Callaghan's challenge but was dissuaded by her advisers.

59. Butler and Kavanagh, *General Election of 1979*, 206.

60. Butler and King, *British General Election of 1964*, 153 n. 1.

61. Donoughue, *Prime Minister*, 41.

62. Butler, *British General Elections since 1945*, 82.

63. Butler and Kavanagh, *British General Election of 1979*, 293.

64. M. Harrison, in Butler and Kavanagh, *British General Election of 1987*, 139.

65. Butler and Kavanagh, *British General Election of 1992*, 249.

66. Butler and Kavanagh, *British General Election of 1987*, 214; cf. Butler and Kavanagh, *British General Election of 1992*, 238. S. Hogg and J. Hill, *Too Close to Call. Power and Politics—John Major in No. 10* (1995), 218.

67. McCallum and Readman, *British General Election of 1945*, p. xi.

68. Monypenny and Buckle, *Disraeli*, ii. 1154 quoting his letter to the Queen, 3 Apr. 1878.

69. Bagehot, 'Bolingbroke as a Statesman' (1863), in *Works*, iii. 61.

70. S. Webb to Edward Pease, 24 Oct. 1886, in S. and B. Webb, *Letters*, ed. N. Mackenzie, i (1978), 101. B. Webb, *Diaries 1924–1932* (1956), 224.

71. Butler and Pinto-Duschinsky, *British General Election of 1970*, 47.

72. *The Times*, 14 May 1982, 10.

73. Butler and King, *British General Election of 1966*, 175.

74. Butler and Pinto-Duschinsky, *British General Election of 1970*, 169.

75. Butler and Kavanagh, *British General Election of 1987*, 137.

76. See James Fishkin's attempts to get round this problem through the 'deliberative opinion poll', reported in *Independent*, 22 Sept. 1993, 25.

77. *Financial Times*, 14 Dec. 1989, 9.

78. *Observer*, 14 Mar. 1971, 29.

79. *The Times*, 13 July 1971, 4; cf. his speech at Birmingham on 18 June, *The Times*, 19 June 1971, 1.

80. Lawson, *View from No. 11*, 233; cf. 368, 375–6 for his rather similar reaction to poll evidence on taxation policy and welfare expenditure.

81. Morley, *Gladstone*, i. 875; cf. ii. 745.

82. Donoughue, *Prime Minister*, 13.

83. G. M. Young, *Stanley Baldwin* (1952), 242. For the weekend's continuing importance in Conservative Party politics, see M. Kettle, 'The Weekend to do the Deed', *Guardian*, 24 June 1995, 25, discussing the manœuvring behind John Major's re-election as leader.

84. Duke of Windror, *A King's Story*, 304; J. Barnes and K. Middlemas, *Baldwin: A Biography* (1969), 1079.

85. K. Middlemas, *Politics in Industrial Society: The Experience of the British System since 1911* (1979), 203. See also Butler and King, *British General Election of 1964*, 52.

86. *H.C.Deb.* 10 May 1939, cc.452–3.

87. Butler and Rose, *British General Election of 1959*, 98.

88. R. Rose, in H. R. Penniman (ed.), *Britain at the Polls 1979: A Study of the General Election* (Washington, 1981), 183.

89. Butler, *British General Elections since 1945*, 110.

90. Butler and Rose, *British General Election of 1959*, 1–3. Butler and Kavanagh, *British General Election of 1979*, 320.

91. R. M. Worcester, *British Public Opinion: A Guide to the History and Methodology of Political Opinion Polling* (Oxford, 1991), 47.

92. Obituary, in *Independent*, 29 Jan. 1993, 27. See also Butler and King, *British General Election of 1964*, 49–50.

93. *H.C.Deb.* 13 Feb. 1986, c.1092, cf. *The Times*, 14 Feb. 1986, 4 (for background noise).

94. Penniman (ed.), *Britain at the Polls 1979*, 186–7.

95. Butler and King, *British General Election of 1964*, 206–7.

96. Butler and King, *British General Election of 1966*, 66–7.

97. Butler and Kavanagh, *British General Election of October 1974*, 200–1. *Sunday Times*, 24 Feb. 1974, 18.

98. Benn, *Diaries 1973–1976*, 106.

99. Butler and Kavanagh, *British General Election of October 1974*, 198–9.

100. Worcester, *British Public Opinion*, 72–3.

101. D. E. Butler and D. Kavanagh, *The British General Election of 1983* (1984), 140–1, 143.

102. *Guardian*, 30 Sept. 1985, 30.

103. Butler and Kavanagh, *British General Election of 1987*, 132.

104. McCallum and Readman, *British General Election of 1945*, 290.

105. Butler, *British General Election of 1951*, 142. Butler and Rose, *British General Election of 1959*, 135. Butler and King, *British General Election of 1964*, 216.

106. Butler and Pinto-Duschinsky, *British General Election of 1970*, 101.

107. Ibid. 319.

108. Butler and Kavanagh, *British General Election of February 1974*, 226.

109. Butler and Kavanagh, *British General Election of 1979*, 275–6.

110. Thatcher, *Downing Street Years*, 293.

111. Butler and Rose, *British General Election of 1959*, 13.

112. In Bath, reported in *Alliance News*, 3 Feb. 1872, 98.

113. C. O'Leary, *The Elimination of Corrupt Practices in British Elections 1868–1911* (Oxford, 1962), 86.

114. Butler and King, *British General Election of 1964*, 222 n. 1.

115. For these incidents, see *Guardian*, 3 June 1970, 1 (Sussex); *The Times*, 3 June 1970, 1 (Essex); *Sunday Telegraph*, 14 June 1987, 1.

116. Penniman (ed.), *Britain at the Polls 1979*, 237.

117. Ibid. 233. For a table showing candidates' election expenses by party, see Butler and Kavanagh, *British General Election of 1979*, 315.

118. See above, pp. 36, 161–2.

119. For a good discussion, see J. Vincent, *The Formation of the Liberal Party 1857–1868* (1966), 96–126.

120. M. Pugh, *The Making of Modern British Politics 1867–1939* (first pub. 1982, 2nd edn. Oxford, 1993), 1.

121. A. K. Russell, *Liberal Landslide: The General Election of 1906* (Newton Abbot, 1973), 127.

122. Butler and Kavanagh, *British General Election of February 1974*, 79, 130; *Guardian*, 10 Apr. 1979, 32.

123. Butler and Rose, *British General Election of 1959*, 141.

124. Ibid. 142.

125. Nicholas, *British General Election of 1950*, 6–9.

126. Butler and King, *British General Election of 1964*, 226.

127. *The Times*, 9 Jan. 1978, 2.

128. *The Times*, 18 Aug. 1986, 10. Cf. Craig, *British Electoral Facts 1832–1987*, 99.

129. Penniman (ed.), *Britain at the Polls 1979*, 225.

130. Ibid. 226.

131. *Guardian*, 3 Oct. 1970, 20 (Mikardo); *Financial Times*, 2 May 1979, 22 (Callaghan); *Guardian*, 6 Oct. 1988, 19 (Todd).

132. T. J. Hollins, 'The Conservative Party and Film Propaganda between the Wars', *English Historical Review* (Apr. 1981), 362.

133. Stannage, *Baldwin Thwarts the Opposition*, 179.

134. T. Benn, *Diaries 1940–1962*, 383. Butler and Rose, *British General Election of 1959*, 96.

135. Butler and Kavanagh, *British General Election of February 1974*, 224.

136. Butler and Kavanagh, *British General Election of 1987*, 216.

137. Cockerell, *Live from No. 10*, 107, cf. 129. B. Castle, *The Castle Diaries 1964–1970* (1984), 799 (14 May 1970); Crossman, *Cabinet Diaries*, iii. 846 (8 Mar. 1970).

138. Butler and Pinto-Duschinsky, *British General Election of 1970*, 154 n. 1; 337.

139. *The Times*, 18 May 1983, 2.

140. Jon Hibbs, in *Daily Telegraph*, 2 Apr. 1992, 4. See also *Guardian*, 6 June 1983, 1, 24; *The Times*, 6 June 1983, 1.

141. Butler and Kavanagh, *British General Election of 1992*, 125.

142. *Guardian*, 3 Apr. 1992, 9, cf. *The Times*, 3 Apr. 1992, 12.

143. For Peel, see C. S. Parker (ed.), *Sir Robert Peel from his Private Papers*, ii (1899), 475. For Palmerston, Emden, *People and the Constitution*, 240.

144. Introduction to 2nd (1872) edn. of 'English Constitution', in *Works*, v. 171. There is endorsement for this in Vincent, *Formation of the Liberal Party*, 233.

145. For Chamberlain, see Garvin, *Chamberlain*, iii. 593, 598, 606; for Churchill and Lloyd George, N. Blewett, *The Peers, the Parties and the People: The General Elections of 1910* (1972), 110. For Foot, see Butler and Kavanagh, *British General Election of 1983*, 153, 161.

## Chapter 9: Articulating Opinion (pp. 245–275)

1. *Guardian*, 22 Feb. 1971, 11.
2. See the good discussion in Chester, *Administrative System*, 82, 86–7, 89.
3. A. L. Lowell, 'The Influence of Party upon Legislation in England and America', in *Annual Report of the American Historical Association* (1901) i. 327.
4. Quoted in R. T. McKenzie and A. Silver, *Angels in Marble: Working Class Conservatives in Urban England* (1968), 48 (writing in 1927); cf. his speech at Fulham in 1902 discussed in Low, *Governance of England*, 118.
5. *Sunday Telegraph*, 14 June 1987, 1, addressing the Scottish Miners' Gala.
6. M. Rutherford, 'The Rise of the House of Lords', *Financial Times*, 23 Mar. 1984, 19; P. Norton, *Does Parliament Matter?* (1993), 27.
7. Bagehot, 'The Advantages and Disadvantages of Becoming a Member of Parliament' (1874), in *Works*, vi. 55.
8. H. C. G. Matthew, 'Rhetoric and Politics in Britain 1860–1950', in P. J. Waller (ed.), *Politics and Social Change in Modern Britain: Essays Presented to A. F. Thompson* (Brighton, 1987), 37.
9. G. D. H. Cole, *Studies in Class Structure* (first pub. 1955, 1961 edn.), 135.
10. J. A. Thomas, *The British House of Commons 1832–1901* (Cardiff, 1939), 9.
11. Bagehot, 'Lord Althorp and the Reform Act of 1832' (1876), in *Works*, iii. 226–8.
12. Lady V. Bonham-Carter, *Winston Churchill as I Knew Him* (first pub. 1965, paperback edn. 1967), 77–9.
13. E. Halévy, *The Rule of Democracy 1905–1914* (first pub. 1932, tr. E. I. Watkin, paperback edn. 1961), 309.
14. Butler, *British Political Facts 1900–1994*, 205; J. Mitchell and A. Davies, *Reforming the Lords* (1993), 5.
15. Norton (ed.), *Parliament in the 1980s* (1985), 104; Mitchell and Davies, *Reforming the Lords*, 5.
16. *H.L.Deb.* 19 Nov. 1968, c.822. See also c.703 (Lord Denham).
17. See Disraeli's comments (3 Apr. 1872) at Manchester in *Selected Speeches of the Late Right Honourable the Earl of Beaconsfield*, ed. T. E. Kebbel (1882), ii. 501.
18. Halévy, *Rule of Democracy*, 120; Spender and Asquith, *Herbert Henry Asquith*, i. 233, 239.
19. Norton (ed.), *Parliament in the 1980s*, 105.
20. Norton, *Does Parliament Matter?*, 142. For figures on the House of Lords in 1994 I am most grateful to Mrs Mary Bloor, Clerk of the House of Lords Information Office.
21. E. Isichei, *Victorian Quakers* (1970), 203.
22. Halévy, *Rule of Democracy*, 64 n. 2. The figures in S. Koss, *Nonconformity in Modern British Politics* (1975), 228 differ slightly, but the overall alignment is the same.

23. W. L. Arnstein, *The Bradlaugh Case: A Study in Late-Victorian Opinion and Politics* (1965), 57, 223.

24. Though without success: see J. D. Clayton, 'Mr Gladstone's Leadership of the Parliamentary Liberal Party 1868–1874', D.Phil. thesis, Oxford University, 1960, 244–5.

25. Quoted in J. D. Fair, *British Interparty Conferences: A Study of the Procedure of Conciliation in British Politics 1867–1921* (Oxford, 1980), 284.

26. *Sunday Telegraph*, 3 Jan. 1988, 1.

27. Koss, *Nonconformity*, 236.

28. Butler and Kavanagh, *British General Election of 1987*, 199. See also G. Alderman, 'Converts to the Vision in True Blue', *Times Higher Education Supplement*, 10 July 1987, 15.

29. Thatcher, *Downing Street Years*, 509.

30. Crossman, *Backbench Diaries*, 440, 499.

31. Mill, 'Representative Government', in *Works*, xix. 499.

32. V. Woolf, *The London Scene* (New York, 1975), 39–40; cf. George Orwell's critical comment in his *Works*, iii. 98.

33. *H.C.Deb.* 5 June 1874, cc.1093 (Macdonald), 1099 (Forster).

34. Butler, *British Political Facts 1900–1994*, 175.

35. *Sunday Times*, 8 Sept. 1968, 2.

36. There is a good discussion of this in J. Cornford, 'The Parliamentary Foundations of the Hotel Cecil', in Robson (ed.), *Ideas and Institutions of Victorian Britain*, 279–80, 289, 311.

37. W. O. Aydelotte, 'The House of Commons in the 1840s', *History* (June–Oct. 1954), 253.

38. M. Rush, in Walkland (ed.), *House of Commons in the Twentieth Century*, 118.

39. Earl Curzon of Kedleston, *Modern Parliamentary Eloquence* (1913), 12; cf. A. C. Benson, *The Life of Edward White Benson sometime Archbishop of Canterbury by his Son*, ii (1900), 659.

40. Mosley, *My Life*, 211; cf. F. Bealey and H. Pelling, *Labour and Politics 1900–1906* (1958), 200.

41. See the table in Butler, *British Political Facts 1900–1994*, 243.

42. See my 'Women in a Men's House: The Women MPs 1919–1945', *Historical Journal* (Sept. 1986), 623.

43. On this, see my *Prudent Revolutionaries: Portraits of British Feminists between the Wars* (Oxford, 1987), 94, 120.

44. Campbell, *Edward Heath*, 439.

45. Bagehot, 'The Federal Constitution Responsible for Federal Apathy' (1863), in *Works*, vi. 170.

46. For an interesting discussion on this point, see Nevil Johnson, *The Political consequences of PR: The British Idea of Responsible Government* (Centre for Policy Studies, 1992), 22.

47. *H.C.Deb.* 11 Dec. 1974, c.636. Cf. his speech on capital punishment in *H.C.Deb.* 1 Apr. 1987, c.1146.

48. Smith, *My Life-Work*, 146.
49. Mackintosh, *British Cabinet*, 194 n. 64. Lloyd George, *H.C.Deb.* 10 Aug. 1911, c.1368. *Times*, 21 Oct. 1970, 10 (speeches of 10 *Hansard* lines or more).
50. W. O. Aydelotte, *Quantification in History* (Reading, Mass., 1971), 117.
51. D. N. Chester and N. Bowring, *Questions in Parliament* (Oxford, 1962), 29.
52. Ibid. 16.
53. Calculated from Butler, *British Political Facts 1900–1994*, 176–8: 86,604 questions were asked in the ten sessions from 1901 to 1910 inclusive, 373,398 in the 11 sessions from 1974 to 1984 inclusive.
54. John Major's phrase, *Daily Telegraph*, 15 June 1994, 2.
55. D. Hurd, *An End to Promises: Sketch of a Government 1970–1974* (1979), 33.
56. N. St J.-Stevas, 'The Political Genius of Walter Bagehot', in *Works*, v. 158.
57. H. Macmillan, *Winds of Change 1914–1939* (1966), 41. See also L. A. Siedentop, 'Mr Macmillan and the Edwardian Style', in V. Bogdanor and R. Skidelsky (eds.), *The Age of Affluence 1951–1964* (1970), 40. Callaghan, *Financial Times*, 15 Mar. 1995, 12.
58. Lawson, *The View from No. 11*, 12. For Thatcher's careful preparation for, and nervousness at, question time, see Baker, *Turbulent Years*, 271.
59. For a junior minister with 'butterflies in my stomach' at the prospect, see A. Clark, *Diaries* (1993), 23.
60. Stead, 'The Future of Journalism', 678.
61. C. Seymour-Ure, in Walkland (ed.), *House of Commons in the Twentieth Century*, 564.
62. Ibid. 548.
63. R. Butt, *The Power of Parliament* (1967), 379. Dr C. Pond, of the House of Commons Public Information Office, who has been most helpful in response to my enquiries, referred me to *H.C.Deb.* 26 Oct. 1988, c.239W for figures going back to 1980. Given the high proportion sold to official customers it is difficult to know how far such figures reveal changing levels of interest in parliament. The whole subject deserves further investigation. Sales trends are complicated by important price changes in the 1980s. For figures on prices and overall circulation, see A. Lester, L. Mackie, and M. Renshall, *What Price Hansard?*, Hansard Society King Hall Paper no. 1 (1994), 6, 9, 10, 12–13, 19.
64. P. Ziegler, *King Edward VIII: The Official Biography* (1990, Fontana paperback edn. 1991), 296.
65. Quoted in Williams, *Gaitskell*, 611.
66. *Guardian*, 1 Aug. 1980, 11.
67. Elliot, *Goschen*, ii. 268–9.
68. G. H. Francis, 'Contemporary Orators, no. xi: Corn-Law Speakers, Pro and Con', *Fraser's Magazine* (July 1846), 93.
69. W. I. Jennings, *Parliamentary Reform* (1934), 124.
70. For homosexual law reform, see Eric Clark, 'House of Lords: Abolition or

Reform?', *Observer Magazine*, 31 Mar. 1974, 31 and Lord Brockway in *H.L.Deb.* 19 Nov. 1968, c.772. For education, see M. Beloff, 'British Universities and the Public Purse', *Minerva* (Summer 1967), 520.

71. See e.g. the comments of John Stokes in *H.C.Deb.* 2 Apr 1980, c.446 and the letter of Professor Alan Thompson in *The Times*, 11 Aug. 1980, 11.

72. A. L. Lowell, *The Government of England* (first pub. 1908, 1921 edn.), i. 391.

73. Percentages calculated from Butler, *British Political Facts 1900–1994*, 66; Norton, *Does Parliament Matter?*, 37.

74. For a useful analysis of MPs' interests as at 1976, see Pinto-Duschinsky, *British Political Finance*, 245.

75. P. D. G. Thomas, *The House of Commons in the Eighteenth Century* (Oxford, 1971), 89.

76. S. H. Beer, in S. H. Beer, A. B. Ulam, N. Wahl, *Patterns of Government: The Major Political Systems of Europe* (first pub. 1958, 2nd edn. New York, 1962), 235; Butler, *British Political Facts 1900–1994*, 176–8; cf. M. Rush, in Walkland (ed.), *House of Commons in the Twentieth Century*, 73.

77. S. and B. Webb, *Constitution for a Socialist Commonwealth*, 145 n. 1.

78. J. Locke, *Two Treatises on Government*, ed. P. Laslett (first pub. 1960, Cambridge, 1963), 382.

79. Mount, *The British Constitution Now*, 161.

80. *The House of Commons Service*, House of Commons factsheet no. 55 (Sept. 1992 edn.), 3–6.

81. *H.C.Deb.* 28 Oct. 1943, c.449 (J. C. Wilmot).

82. Norton, *Does Parliament Matter?*, 20; *H.C.Deb.* 4 Nov. 1993, c.418W.

83. *Members' Pay and Allowances*, House of Commons factsheet no. 17 (Dec. 1993 edn.), 4, 6.

84. M. Rush, in Walkland (ed.), *House of Commons in the Twentieth Century*, 73.

85. Campion *et al.*, *British Government since 1918*, 29–30.

86. Ibid. 28.

87. Mill, 'Representative Government', in *Works*, xix. 430.

88. Walpole, *Lord John Russell*, ii. 96.

89. For a useful discussion, see Walkland, in Walkland (ed.), *House of Commons in the Twentieth Century*, 255–9.

90. Ball, 'Parliament and Politics in Britain 1900–1951', 254–5 documents this development in helpful detail.

91. Jennings, *Parliament*, 275.

92. See e.g. the restraints of 1972 on the select committee on science and technology, in Wilson (ed.), *Cases and Materials*, 349–50.

93. Crossman, *Diaries*, ii. 308 (11 Apr. 1967).

94. H. Laski, *A Grammar of Politics* (first pub. 1925, 4th edn. 1941), 346.

95. Quoted (1973) in P. Kellner and Lord Crowther-Hunt, *The Civil Servants: An Inquiry into Britain's Ruling Class* (1980), 255.

96. Benn, *Diaries 1963–1967*, 498 (11 May 1967).

97. J. Mackintosh, 'Dwindling Hopes of Commons Reform', *The Times*, 13 Mar. 1969, 11. See also Mackintosh's complaints reported in *The Times*, 3 Apr. 1970, 4.

98. *Listener*, 14 Mar. 1974, 328.

99. R. Butt, 'The Rise and Fall of the Select Committee', *The Times*, 6 Apr. 1978, 16.

100. Quoted in Butt, *Power of Parliament*, 350, cf. 322.

101. Ministry of Reconstruction, *Report of the Machinery of Government Committee*, Parl. Papers 1918 XII, Cd. 9230, 15; Jennings, *Parliamentary Reform*, 85; Laski, *Grammar of Politics*, 349–50. F. W. Jowett's scheme, endorsed by the ILP conference in 1926, was somewhat different: it envisaged the minister chairing the committee, which would monitor the details of the department's administration. See the criticism of it in Morrison, *Government and Parliament*, 168.

102. For these episodes, see Hugo Young, 'Parliament Joins Westland's Body Count', *Guardian*, 4 Feb. 1986, 21; *Daily Telegraph*, 9 Feb. 1989, 1 (Currie); *Financial Times*, 14 Jan. 1992, 7; 18 Jan. 1992, 7 (Maxwell).

103. *Reflect on Things Past: The Memoirs of Lord Carrington* (1988), 371; cf. Prior, *Balance of Power*, 147. *The Times*, 5 Dec. 1984, 1 (Joseph).

104. *The Times*, 6 Dec. 1984, 1.

105. P. Norton, in Walkland (ed.), *House of Commons in the Twentieth Century*, 36–8. For Labour's committees, see 44–7.

106. P. Norton, in Seldon and Ball (eds.), *Conservative Century*, 128.

107. 'Plotting Tory Policy with Knife and Talk', *Daily Telegraph*, 20 May 1986, 17.

108. Bagehot 'English Constitution', in *Works*, v. 268.

109. Adonis, *Making Aristocracy Work*, 60–9.

110. Morrison, *Government and Parliament*, 207–8.

111. Grantham and Hodgson, in Norton (ed.), *Parliament in the 1980s*, 115.

112. *The Times*, 30 Sept. 1980, 4 (at the Labour Party conference on 29 Sept.).

113. P. Snowden, *An Autobiography*, i (1934), 343.

114. Jennings, *Parliamentary Reform*, 161.

115. House of Commons Library, *Services for Members of Parliament*, leaflet given to Members (1993 edn.).

116. Crick, *Reform of Parliament*, 194, cf. 170.

117. P. Riddell, 'Heseltine Remains Active in the Wilderness', *Financial Times*, 27 May 1987, 48.

118. Bagehot, 'The Non-legislative Functions of Parliament', in *Works*, vi. 43.

119. Bryce, *Modern Democracies*, ii. 370 ff.

120. Bagehot, 'The American Constitution at the Present Crisis' (1861), in *Works*, iv. 310.

121. Mansergh, *Commonwealth Experience*, 249.

122. Keith (ed.), *Dominions Documents*, 159–60.

123. Final speech (28 Mar. 1957) before dissolution of the first parliament of independent republican India, in A. F. Madden (ed.), *Imperial Constitutional Documents 1765–1965: A Supplement* (first pub. 1953, 2nd edn. Oxford, 1966), 100.

124. F. M. Hardie, *The Political Influence of Queen Victoria 1861–1901*, 2nd edn. (1938), 79.

125. See esp. her speech of 8 Oct. 1976 in her *Speeches to the Conservative Party Conference*, 20–1, and her attack on Healey's budget speech in *H.C.Deb.* 6 Apr. 1976, c.285.

126. Adonis, *Parliament Today*, 166.

127. *Members' Pay and Allowances*, House of Commons factsheet no. 17 (Dec. 1993 edn.), 4. Wage/salary data from C. Feinstein, *National Income and Output of the UK 1865–1905* (Cambridge, 1972), tables 21, 57, and 11.10; *National Income and Expenditure* (1983 edn.), tables 1.12 and 4.1; *UK National Accounts* (1993 edn.), tables 4.1, 17.1. RPI from Feinstein, *National Income and Output 1865–1905*, table 140, supplemented by *Economic Trends*. I am most grateful to Andrew Glyn of Corpus Christi College, Oxford for guidance on RPI and national income statistics. National average pay/salary excludes employers' national insurance and pension contributions.

128. R. Muir, *The Political Consequences of the Great War* (1930), 127–8.

129. Norton, *Does Parliament Matter?*, 63.

130. Ibid. 152.

131. On which, see *New Statesman*, 10 Jan. 1992, 14–15.

132. W. Morris, *News from Nowhere*, in *Selected Writings and Designs*, ed. A. Briggs (Harmondsworth, 1962), 283.

133. Quoted (1937) in R. Skidelsky, *Oswald Mosley* (1975), 311.

134. *H.C.Deb.* 18 May 1995, c.506.

135. Laski, *Parliamentary Government in England*, 155.

136. Mill, 'Representative Government', in *Works*, xix. 433.

## Chapter 10: Power and Decision (pp. 277–296)

1. Mackintosh, *British Cabinet*, 4.

2. Vincent and Cooke, *Governing Passion*, p. xi.

3. Hamilton, *Diary*, ii. 750 (6 Dec. 1884); cf. Morley, *Gladstone*, i. 297.

4. Quoted in Churchill, *Lord Randolph Churchill*, 371.

5. Monypenny and Buckle, *Disraeli*, ii. 1066.

6. Mackintosh, *British Cabinet*, 152. McKenzie, *British Political Parties*, 56 n. 2.

7. S. S. Wilson, *The Cabinet Office to 1945* (1975), 39.

8. J. R. Starr, 'The English Cabinet Secretariat', *American Political Science Review* (May 1928), 392, 395, 399.

9. Mackintosh, *British Cabinet*, 388.

10. R. Rose, 'The Making of Cabinet Ministers', in V. Herman and J. E. Alt (eds.), *Cabinet Studies: A Reader* (1975), 22 compares duration of ministers in office 1900–14 (34.4 months per minister) and 1955–70 (26.1 months).

11. P. Gordon Walker, *The Cabinet* (first pub. 1970, rev. paperback edn. 1972), 100. Wilson, *Labour Government 1964–1970*, 290.

12. Statistics from Wilson, *Cabinet Office*, 12; see the interesting diagram in Gordon Walker, *Cabinet*, 174–5.

13. Sir Ivor Jennings, *Cabinet Government* (first pub. 1936, 3rd edn. Cambridge, 1961), 319–20. Gordon Walker, *Cabinet*, 39.

14. Gordon Walker, *Cabinet*, 47, 53.

15. Wilson, *Cabinet Office*, p. ii (epigraph).

16. Ibid. 64, 174 (figures include Committee of Imperial Defence staff).

17. S. Fay and H. Young, in *Sunday Times*, 22 Feb. 1976, 33–4; W. Whitelaw, ibid., 29 Feb. 1976, 34.

18. *The Times*, 27 Mar. 1974, 6.

19. As Attlee pointed out, *H.C.Deb.* 6 May 1952, c.191.

20. R. H. S. Crossman, 'Shadow Cabinet or Caucus?', *New Statesman*, 25 June 1955, 875. See also Crossman's *Backbench Diaries*, 432–3 (28 June 1955) and R. M. Punnett, 'Her Majesty's Shadow Cabinet', in Herman and Alt (eds.), *Cabinet Studies*, 146.

21. Crossman, *Backbench Diaries*, 437 (15 July 1955).

22. *The Times*, 25 Apr. 1968, 1.

23. Author's tape-recorded interview with Lord Joseph of Portsoken, 7 Aug. 1992.

24. *The Times*, 14 Nov. 1981, 2. See also *The Times*, 2 June 1981, 13 (leader); 4 June 1981, 1.

25. A. Marr, 'More Beauty Contest than Shadow Cabinet', *Independent*, 21 Oct. 1993, 21. 'Nonsensical Election', *The Times*, 22 Oct. 1993, 21 (leader).

26. Gordon Walker, *Cabinet*, 36.

27. See the useful table 2.3 in J. E. Alt, 'Continuity, Turnover, and Experience in the British Cabinet 1868–1970', in Herman and Alt (eds.), *Cabinet Studies*, 43.

28. Crossman, *Inside View*, 56.

29. For a good discussion, see *Sunday Times*, 9 June 1974, 17.

30. Kellner and Crowther-Hunt, *The Civil Servants*, 220.

31. K. Young, 'The Party and English Local Government', in Seldon and Ball (eds.), *Conservative Century*, 439.

32. *Observer*, 25 Nov. 1990, 13. See also Peter Hennessy in K. Minogue and M. Biddiss (eds.), *Thatcherism: Personality and Politics* (1987), 60 (10 Aug. 1966).

33. P. Hennessy, *Cabinet* (Oxford, 1986), 99–101.

34. Ibid. 30–1.

35. M. Burch, 'Mrs Thatcher's Approach to Leadership in Government 1979–June 1983', *Parliamentary Affairs* (1983), 411; cf. Castle, *Diaries 1964–1970*, 160–1.

36. H. Young, *One of Us: A Biography of Margaret Thatcher* (1989), 149–50.

37. Baker, *Turbulent Years*, 192; cf. Thatcher, *Downing Street Years*, 578–9.

38. Thatcher, *Downing Street Years*, 672, 703; see also 701.

39. Young, *One of Us*, 454.

40. *Times Literary Supplement*, 7 Jun. 1991, 20.

41. Lawson, *View from No. 11*, 971.

42. *H.C.Deb.* 13 Nov. 1990, cc.464–5. Cf. Howe's review of her memoirs in *Financial Times*, 23 Oct. 1993, sect. 2, VII.

43. Interview with K. Harris, *Observer*, 25 Feb. 1979, 34.

44. Resignation letter in *Financial Times*, 2 Nov. 1990, 8; cf. resignation speech, *H.C.Deb.* 13 Nov. 1990, c.465.

45. A. B. Keith, *The British Cabinet System 1830–1938* (1939), 2.

46. Jennings, *Cabinet Government*, 269. Cecil, *Salisbury*, ii. 223.

47. Crossman, *Cabinet Diaries*, iii. 885 (13 Apr. 1970); Benn, *Diaries 1973–1976*, 207 (26 July 1974), 300 (14 Jan. 1975), 457 (6 Nov. 1975); *Diaries 1977–1980*, 351 (28 Sept. 1978).

48. R. Postgate, *The Life of George Lansbury* (1951), pp. vii, viii. Young, *Crossman Affair*, 110, 128.

49. Crossman, *Cabinet Diaries*, i. 511–12 (4 May 1966). Benn, *Diaries 1977–1980*, 339 (14 Sept. 1978).

50. Laski, *Parliamentary Government in England*, 255.

51. N. Fowler, *Ministers Decide: A Personal Memoir of the Thatcher Years* (1991), 62.

52. Both in Anthony Howard's Radio 3 programme *Chroniclers of Power* on 29 Apr. 1990 on political diaries.

53. R. H. S. Crossman, introduction to Bagehot's *English Constitution* (Fontana edn. 1963), 49.

54. Crossman, *Inside View*, 9–10.

55. For Benn, see *Sunday Telegraph*, 15 July 1979, 4. For Hailsham, see his Richard Dimbleby lecture, in *Listener*, 21 Oct. 1976, 496–500.

56. Butler *et al.*, *Failure in British Government*, 194–5.

57. Prior, *Balance of Power*, 139. For a useful discussion of Thatcher's exploitation of her femininity, see Melanie Phillips, 'That's Why the Lady was a Champ', *Guardian*, 23 Nov. 1990, 19.

58. Adam Raphael, 'Maggie's Enemies within', *Observer*, 25 Nov. 1990, 13; cf. R. Harris, *Good and Faithful Servant: The Unauthorized Biography of Bernard Ingham* (first pub. 1990, paperback edn. 1991).

59. Interview with Norman Hunt, 16 Sept. 1965, repr. in Herman and Alt (eds.), *Cabinet Studies*, 196.

60. Ramsden, *Age of Balfour and Baldwin*, 172. Barnes and Middlemas, *Baldwin*, 463.

61. Crossman, *Cabinet Diaries*, iii. 523–4 (17 June 1969).

62. Wakeham, *Cabinet Government: Lecture, 10 November 1993 at Brunel University, Uxbridge*, 8.

63. Crossman, introduction to Bagehot *English Constitution*, 54; Gordon Walker, *Cabinet*, 114, cf. Benn, *Diaries 1968–1972*, 159 (14 Apr. 1969).

64. R. Blake, *The Office of Prime Minister* (1975), 52; G. Strauss, letter to *The Times*, 26 Mar. 1969, 11.

65. Baker, *Turbulent Years*, 196–7.

66. Ibid. 222.

67. N. Ridley, *'My Style of Government': The Thatcher Years* (1991), 29–30. Lawson, *View from No. 11*, 128–9, however, thinks that Thatcher's 'bilaterals', convenient as they were for many cabinet ministers, degenerated into a 'divide and rule' tactic.

68. Wakeham, *Cabinet Government*, 12.

69. *Listener*, 5 Jan. 1978, 4.

## Chapter 11: Administration and Execution (pp. 297–316)

1. Halsey (ed.), *British Social Trends since 1900*, 164.

2. Butler, *British Political Facts 1900–1994*, 287.

3. Mackenzie and Grove, *Central Administration*, 403.

4. G. Drewry and T. Butcher, *The Civil Service Today* (first pub. Oxford, 1988, 2nd edn. 1991), 59. Latest figure from *Financial Times*, 14 July 1994, 9.

5. *Financial Times*, 13 July 1994, 8.

6. Craig (ed.), *Manifestos 1918–1966*, 166.

7. See above, pp. 285–6.

8. Sir Richard Clarke, *New Trends in Government*, Civil Service College studies no. 1 (1971), 119.

9. There is a remarkable diagram illustrating this in detail in E. N. Gladden, *Civil Services of the United Kingdom 1855–1970* (1967), 10.

10. In Radio 4's programme *No Minister*, 14 June 1981; cf. Healey, *The Time of my Life*, 256.

11. Campbell, *Edward Heath*, 446–8.

12. Cecil, *Salisbury*, ii. 272.

13. R. T. Nightingale, 'The Personnel of the British Foreign Office and Diplomatic Service', *The Realist*, 2/3 (Dec. 1929), 331.

14. Mackenzie and Grove, *Central Administration*, 15.

15. Ibid. 22, 24.

16. Butler, *British Political Facts 1900–1994*, 287.

17. Ibid. 291. Drewry and Butcher, *Civil Service Today*, 199.

18. Mackenzie and Grove, *Central Administration*, 24.

19. Calculated from figures in Gladden, *Civil Services of the United Kingdom*, 4.
20. Dale, *Higher Civil Service*, 21–2.
21. See above, p. 112.
22. Fawcett, *Provinces of England*, 37.
23. Sir William Beveridge, *The Public Service in War and Peace* (1920), 3, cf. 62.
24. Keith-Lucas and Richards, *History of Local Government in the Twentieth Century*, 47.
25. Willson, *British Central Government*, 37.
26. Crossman, *Diaries*, iii. 605 (4 Aug. 1969). Fowler, *Ministers Decide*, 276.
27. Butler, *British Political Facts 1900–1994*, 289–90.
28. K. Theakston and G. K. Fry, 'Britain's Administrative Elite: Permanent Secretaries 1900–1986', *Public Administration* (Summer 1989), 132.
29. *Report of the [Fulton] Committee* (Cmnd. 3638, 1968), 67–8.
30. B. R. Mitchell, *British Historical Statistics* (Cambridge, 1988), 104. The figures include Post Office workers, but not telephonists and telegraphists.
31. Calculated from figures in B. Drake, *Women in Trade Unions*, Labour Research Department trade union series no. 6 (n.d.), app., table III.
32. M. Zimmeck, 'Strategies and Stratagems for the Employment of Women in the British Civil Service 1919–1939', *Historical Journal* (Dec. 1984), 922.
33. Compare my 'Women in a Men's House: The Women MPs 1919–1945', *Historical Journal* (Sept. 1986), 634–42.
34. Royal Commission on Equal Pay 1944–46, *Report*, Cmd. 6937 (1946), 8.
35. Mackenzie and Grove, *Central Administration*, 26.
36. T. Burt, *An Autobiography* (1924), 260.
37. B. C. Roberts, 'Industrial Relations', in Ginsberg (ed.), *Law and Opinion*, 366. Halévy, *Rule of Democracy*, 446–7.
38. Taylor, *English History 1914–1945*, 67.
39. R. G. C. L[evens], 'Oxford and Whitehall', *Oxford Magazine*, 7 Mar. 1940, 247–8.
40. See the complaints of Max Beloff in *Oxford Magazine*, 28 Jan. 1965, 171; 18 Feb. 1965, 226.
41. Dale, *Higher Civil Service*, 108.
42. J. Delafons, 'Working in Whitehall: Changes in Public Administration 1952–1982', *Public Administration* (1982), 256.
43. Ibid. 255.
44. H. Young and A. Sloman, *The Thatcher Phenomenon* (1986), 47.
45. See above, pp. 291–2.
46. Dale, *Higher Civil Service*, 93.
47. Ibid. 107.
48. *The Times*, 15 July 1980, 14.
49. Quoted in Hennessy, *Whitehall*, 150.
50. *The Times*, 24 Nov. 1975, 1. Cf. *Independent on Sunday*, 29 July 1990 (business suppl.), 11 for the marked subsequent decline in numbers.

51. *H.C.Deb.* 11 Apr. 1978, c.1189.

52. Richards, *Local Government System*, 120–1.

53. M. Wilkinson, *Lessons from Europe: A Comparison of British and West European Schooling*, Centre for Policy Studies (1977), 1; cf. B. Miller, 'Citadels of Local Power', *Twentieth Century* (Oct. 1957), 329.

54. Butler *et al.*, *Failure in British Government*, 220–1.

55. To Lord John Russell, 16 Dec. 1848, quoted in J. Hart, 'Sir Charles Trevelyan at the Treasury', *English Historical Review* (Jan. 1960), 106–7.

56. Dale, *Higher Civil Service*, 28; cf. Lord Brooke of Cumnor in *H.L.Deb.* 24 July 1968, c.1053 and Mount, *British Constitution Now*, 161.

57. G. Kaufman, *How to be a Minister* (1980), quoted in Hennessy, *Whitehall*, 65.

58. M. G. Brock, *The Great Reform Act* (1973), 157–9, 215.

59. Loughlin, *Gladstone, Home Rule and the Ulster Question*, 62, 70.

60. *Parl. Papers* 1886 XXIII, C. 4893, p. xxv.

61. *Parl. Papers* 1909 XXXVII, Cd. 4499, 48.

62. Wilkinson, *Lessons from Europe*, 1; cf. Miller, 'Citadels of Local Power', 329.

63. H. Morrison, *The Peaceful Revolution: Speeches* (1949), 15 (speech of 1946).

64. Mill, 'Representative Government', in *Works*, xix. 544.

65. See above, p. 282.

66. Benn, *Diaries 1973–1976*, 422 (22 July 1975). See also Hennessy, *Whitehall*, 240–1.

67. *Guardian*, 21 June 1974, 14.

68. Mill, 'On Liberty', in *Works*, xviii. 308.

69. Crossman, *Cabinet Diaries*, i. 198 (18 Apr. 1965).

70. Quoted in Wilson (ed.), *Cases and Materials*, 80; cf. Mackenzie and Grove, *Central Administration*, 380.

71. Castle, *Diaries 1964–1970*, 372 (13 Feb. 1968), cf. 394 (11 Mar. 1968).

72. K. B. Smellie, *A Hundred Years of English Government* (1937), 427.

73. Quoted in Horne, *Macmillan*, i. 336.

74. Outlined in his Bristol lecture, in *Guardian*, 4 Feb. 1980, 9.

75. Radio 4 programme *No Minister*, 14 June 1981.

76. Lecture of 1972, quoted in K. Theakston, *The Labour Party and Whitehall* (1992), 61. See also M. Rutherford, 'Believing the Manifestos', *Financial Times*, 24 Apr. 1979, 22.

77. R. H. S. Crossman, *Socialism and Planning*, Fabian Tract no. 375 (1967), 12.

78. See the interesting exchanges between Shore and Benn in Benn, *Diaries 1973–1976*, 498 (18 Jan. 1976) and between Healey and Benn in *The Times*, 15 Sept. 1981, 4.

79. Baker, *Turbulent Years*, 168.

80. For ministerial salaries, see Butler, *British Political Facts 1900–1994*, 49. For civil servants' salaries, see A. Sampson, in *Observer*, 28 Feb. 1971, 19.

81. R. Rose, 'The Political Status of Higher Civil Servants in Britain', in E. N. Suleiman (ed.), *Bureaucrats and Policy Making: A Comparative Overview* (New York, 1984), 152.

82. For a good discussion, see Dale, *Higher Civil Service*, 133–4, 193–4.
83. Lowell, *Government of England*, i. 468.
84. For a good discussion of this, see N. Kirk, *The Growth of Working Class Reformism in Mid-Victorian England* (1985), 162–3.
85. Cobden to Ashworth, 13 Dec. 1849, quoted in J. Skinner, 'John Bright and the Representation of Manchester in the House of Commons 1847–57', MA thesis, Cardiff University, 1965, 33.
86. See J. F. C. Harrison, 'Chartism in Leeds', in Briggs (ed.), *Chartist Studies*, 92. Hennock, *Fit and Proper Persons*, 197–8, 330.
87. H. C. White, *Willoughby Hyett Dickinson 1859–1943* (Gloucester, 1956), 35.
88. Donoughue and Jones, *Morrison*, 46, 59.
89. Benn, *Diaries 1973–1976*, 514 (7 Feb. 1976).
90. Joyce, *Work, Society and Politics*, 278.

## Chapter 12: Symbolism and Ceremony (pp. 317–347)

1. G. M. Young, *Portrait of an Age*, 90. For Glasgow, see D. Kavanagh and R. Rose, 'The Monarchy in Contemporary Political Culture' (1976), in D. Kavanagh, *Politics and Personalities* (1990), 288.
2. Newton, *Lansdowne*, 293; Halévy, *Rule of Democracy*, 124, 418; Hardie, *Political Influence of the British Monarchy*, 102.
3. E. Longford, *Elizabeth R: A Biography* (1983), 3.
4. To the Earl of Clarendon, 25 Oct. 1857, in Queen Victoria, *Letters: First Series*, ed. A. C. Benson and Viscount Esher, iii (1908), 253.
5. Pope-Hennessy, *Queen Mary*, 527.
6. Bradford, *George VI*, 211, cf. 216.
7. Ibid. 566–7, 575; R. Lacey, *Majesty: Elizabeth II and the House of Windsor* (first pub. 1977, rev. paperback edn. 1979), 174.
8. Bradford, *George VI*, 427, 561–2.
9. Statistics (updated) from D. Kavanagh, 'The Monarchy in Contemporary Politics' (1976), in his *Politics and Personalities*, 308.
10. J. Cannon, 'The Survival of the British Monarchy', 144.
11. *The Times*, 4 Jan. 1991, 1.
12. Ziegler, *Edward VIII*, 211–12.
13. *Observer*, 26 Oct. 1969, 6.
14. Monypenny and Buckle, *Disraeli*, i. 1566 (Disraeli to the Queen, 24 June 1858); Blake, *Disraeli*, 376 (27 July 1857).
15. Churchill, *Randolph Churchill*, 408.
16. Bagehot, 'The New Title of the Queen' (1876), in *Works*, v (1974), 448.
17. Gwynn and Tuckwell, *Dilke*, i. 522; Queen Victoria, *Letters: Third Series*, i. 344, 447.

18. W. S. Adams, 'The People and the Monarchy', *Modern Quarterly*, 8/3 (Summer 1953), 163.

19. *The Times*, 5 May 1886, 11–12.

20. Amery, *Joseph Chamberlain*, vi. 953; see also iv. 10.

21. Duke of Windsor, *A King's Story*, 164.

22. Wheeler-Bennett, *George VI*, 703.

23. Quoted in Lord Birkenhead, *Walter Monckton: The Life of Viscount Monckton of Brenchley* (1969), 221; cf. 229 and P. Ziegler, *Mountbatten: The Official Biography* (1985), 415.

24. Bradford, *George VI*, 372, cf. 377, 383, 396.

25. Young, *One of Us*, 491; cf. Callaghan's letter quoted in Longford, *Elizabeth R*, 247.

26. Powell at Leicester, *Daily Telegraph*, 21 Jan. 1984, 8; cf. P. Worsthorne, in *Sunday Telegraph*, 20 July 1986, 20 (leader).

27. *The Times*, 2 Oct. 1987, 16; see also *Independent*, 3 Oct. 1987, 12 (leader).

28. Benn, *Diaries 1968–1972*, 38, cf. *The Times*, 20 Oct. 1969, 9 (leader).

29. V. Bogdanor, *The Monarchy and the Constitution* (Oxford, 1995), 273–5 argues powerfully to this effect.

30. See *The Times*, 2 July 1987, 1, 20 for his visit to Bengalis in Brick Lane.

31. Bagehot, 'The Monarchy and the People' (22 July 1871) and 'The Income of the Prince of Wales' (10 Oct. 1874), in *Works*, v. 431, 419.

32. R. Fulford, *Hanover to Windsor* (1960), 27.

33. W. M. Kuhn, 'Ceremony and Politics: The British Monarchy 1871–1872', *Journal of British Studies* (Apr. 1987), 151, 153, 156.

34. Mass-Observation, *May the Twelfth*, ed. H. Jennings and C. Madge (1937), 6.

35. L. Brown, 'The Treatment of the News in Mid-Victorian Newspapers', *Transactions of the Royal Historical Society* (1977), 28, 35. J. L. Lant, *Insubstantial Pageant: Ceremony and Confusion at Queen Victoria's Court* (1979), 85.

36. On this, see *Photographic News*, 4 June 1886, 360; 27 May 1887, 328.

37. Calculated from the figures presented by D. Cannadine in E. Hobsbawm and T. Ranger (eds.), *The Invention of Tradition* (first pub. 1983, paperback edn. Cambridge, 1984), 163.

38. Total annual cost £2,592,000, representing 11d. per head of population. The heads of state in West Germany, Finland, and Eire were cheaper. *Observer*, 16 Nov. 1969, 10.

39. Bradford, *George VI*, 200.

40. Duke of Windsor, *A King's Story*, 132, 261.

41. A. Briggs, *The BBC: The First Fifty Years* (Oxford, 1985), 166.

42. *Financial Times*, 30 Apr. 1986, 19.

43. A. Briggs, *History of Broadcasting in the United Kingdom*, iv: *Sound and Vision* (1979), 467.

44. Bradford, *George VI*, 175.
45. *The Times*, 23 June 1969, 9.
46. Michael Davie, 'How they Packaged the Prince', *Observer*, 6 July 1969, 9.
47. *The Times*, 12 Nov. 1973, 6.
48. Ibid., 4 Sept. 1985, 3.
49. Ibid., 25 Feb. 1981, 2.
50. *Financial Times*, 31 July 1981, 30.
51. *The Times*, 30 July 1981, 4.
52. *Daily Telegraph*, 27 Sept. 1986, 3.
53. *New Statesman*, 27 June 1969, 901.
54. Bradford, *George VI*, 449.
55. Duke of Windsor, *A King's Story*, 128.
56. Longford, *Elizabeth R*, 2–3. For more details, see *The Times*, 21 Mar. 1974, 3.
57. Wheeler-Bennett, *George VI*, 145, 733–4.
58. Short, *Dynamite War*, 232–3.
59. *Guardian*, 30 June 1981, 1; *The Times*, 28 July 1981, 3. See also *The Times*, 30 July 1981, 1, 4 (souvenir number).
60. Quoted in *The Times*, 27 Jan. 1994, 3. See also Ziegler, *Edward VIII*, 264; *The Times*, 21 Mar. 1974, 15 (leading article on the attempted kidnap).
61. *The Times*, 27 Jan. 1994, 3.
62. Ibid., 4 Jan. 1991, 1.
63. D. Marquand, *Ramsay MacDonald* (1977), 246; Orwell, *Works*, i. 592.
64. Ernest Dewhurst, 'When Anthem and Audience are not in Harmony', *Guardian*, 1 Feb. 1969, 5.
65. Longford, *Elizabeth R*, 266.
66. See above, pp. 52, 343.
67. H. Nicolson, *King George V: His Life and Reign* (1952), 86, 83; cf. Bradford, *George VI*, 8, 24.
68. Nicolson, *Diaries 1945–1962*, 175 (4 Oct. 1949).
69. Lacey, *Majesty*, 362. For the Olympics, see *The Times*, 24 Apr. 1980, 1.
70. Burke, *Reflections*, 120.
71. *The Times*, 24 Oct. 1978, 4.
72. Bagehot, 'English Constitution', in *Works*, v. 229; Burke, *Reflections*, 120.
73. The Duke of Windsor's phrase, quoted in Pope-Hennessy, *Queen Mary*, 551; cf. Duke of Windsor, *A King's Story*, 177.
74. Duke of Windsor, *A King's Story*, 260, 258.
75. *H.L.Deb.* 25 June 1975, cc.1418–23; cf. Ziegler, *Edward VIII*, 217.
76. Ziegler, *Edward VIII*, 199.
77. *The Times*, 24 Dec. 1987, 1.
78. *Guardian*, 6 Feb. 1992, 4.
79. Rose, *George V*, 10.

80. *Listener*, 4 Dec. 1969, 791.
81. On this, see D. Cannadine's, 'Splendor out of Court: Royal Spectacle and Pageantry in Modern Britain, *c*.1820–1977', in S. Wilentz (ed.), *Rites of Power: Symbolism, Ritual and Politics since the Middle Ages* (Philadelphia, 1985), 229.
82. Nicolson, *George V*, 162; Wheeler-Bennett, *George VI*, 308; Duke of Windsor, *A King's Story*, 298.
83. Wheeler-Bennett, *George VI*, 743–4.
84. *Daily Telegraph*, 27 June 1994, 3.
85. *The Times*, 20 Nov. 1972, 17 (leading article on the silver wedding).
86. Rose, *George V*, 20.
87. Ziegler, *Edward VIII*, 89–90.
88. M. De-la-Noy, *The Queen behind the Throne* (first pub. 1994, Arrow paperback edn. 1995), 34.
89. H. M. Hyde, *Baldwin: The Unexpected Prime Minister* (1973), 452.
90. Wheeler-Bennett, *George VI*, 463. Taylor, *English History 1914–1945*, 493 n. 1.
91. Wheeler-Bennett, *George VI*, 470; see also 448–9, 466–9.
92. *Guardian*, 8 Oct. 1980, 4. See also Gladstone, quoted in A. Jones, *The Politics of Reform. 1884* (Cambridge, 1972), 144.
93. Nicolson, *Diaries 1945–1962*, 124.
94. Quotations from Queen Victoria to the King of the Belgians, 11 July 1848, in Queen Victoria, *Letters: First Series*, ii. 184. Fulford (ed.), *Your Dear Letter*, 206, cf. 165. See also P. Magnus, *King Edward VII* (first pub. 1964, Penguin edn. 1967), 102, 105, 143.
95. See the excellent anonymous account in *Society in London: By a Foreign Resident* (1885), 26 ff.
96. Bradford, *George VI*, 273. See also 222, 226, 297–8.
97. Lowell, *Government of England*, ii. 509.
98. Lord Altrincham *et al.*, *Is the Monarchy Perfect?* (1958), 9.
99. A. West, 'Some Changes in Social Life during the Queen's Reign', *Nineteenth Century* (Apr. 1897), 641–2.
100. Rose, *George V*, 208–18.
101. W. Kendall, *The Revolutionary Movement in Britain 1900–1921: The Origins of British Communism* (1969), 158.
102. Hoggart, quoted in T. Nairn, *The Enchanted Glass: Britain and its Monarchy* (1988), 22; A. Fox, *A very Late Development: An Autobiography* (Coventry, 1990), 17.
103. Rose, *George V*, 227.
104. Longford, *Elizabeth R*, 209.
105. Ibid. 207–8; Lacey, *Majesty*, 277.
106. *The Times*, 9 June 1977, 1.
107. Duke of Windsor, *A King's Story*, 36.
108. Rose, *George V*, 336.

109. Crossman, *Backbench Diaries*, 70, cf. 71 (6 Feb. 1952).
110. H. Wilson, *Memoirs 1916–64: The Making of a Prime Minister* (1985), 2. See also Pimlott, *Harold Wilson*, 524.
111. Paxman, *Friends in High Places*, 331.
112. Duke of Windsor, *A King's Story*, 83; Bradford, *George VI*, 539. See also Altrincham *et al.*, *Is the Monarchy Perfect?*, 26.
113. See e.g. J. Gore, *King George V: A Personal Memoir* (1941), 128.
114. Duke of Windsor, *A King's Story*, 204.
115. F. Harrison, 'The Monarchy', *Fortnightly Review* (1872), quoted in Hanham (ed.), *Nineteenth-Century Constitution*, 35.
116. *The Times*, 21 Apr. 1976, 17 (leading article).
117. The phrase used in her Guildhall speech; *The Times*, 25 Nov. 1992, 3. For a collection of references to criticism of the monarchy in the early 1990s, see S. Haseler, *The End of the House of Windsor: Birth of a British Republic* (London, 1993), 35–9.
118. Paine, *Rights of Man*, 204, 194.
119. W. Lovett, *The Life and Struggles* (1876), 404, cf. 402; Paine, *Rights of Man*, 183.
120. As reported in *The Diary of Sir Edward Walter Hamilton*, i. 34 (10 Aug. 1880).
121. Bradford, *George VI*, 59.
122. Ibid. 134.
123. Duke of Windsor, *A King's Story*, 335–6.
124. Lacey, *Majesty*, 124–9.
125. *Guardian*, 6 Feb. 1992, 4.
126. *Bee-Hive*, 7 Mar. 1863, 4.
127. Paine, *Rights of Man*, 206.
128. *H.C.Deb.* 14 Dec. 1971, c.348.
129. *H.C.Deb.* 21 Dec. 1971, c.1333.
130. Benn, *Diaries 1963–67*, 169 (21 Oct. 1964).
131. Ibid. 187 (16 Nov. 1964), cf. 191 (20 Nov. 1964).
132. Crossman, *Diaries of a Cabinet Minister*, ii. 44 (20 Sept. 1966), cf. i. 29 (22 Oct. 1964).
133. Benn, *Diaries 1963–1967*, 446 (5 July 1966).
134. Crossman, *Diaries of a Cabinet Minister*, ii. 534.
135. Quoted by D. E. Cooper, in Bogdanor and Skidelsky (eds.), *Age of Affluence*, 260.
136. Cannadine, 'Splendor out of Court', 233; see also 215–16.
137. Haseler, *The End of the House of Windsor*, 3.
138. *The Times*, 30 July 1981, 1.
139. Duke of Windsor, *A King's Story*, 359, cf. 335–6, 347, 356.
140. Ibid. 359.

141. *The Times*, 9 June 1977, 14.
142. Crossman, *Diaries of a Cabinet Minister*, iii. 157 (24 July 1968). For a portrait of Hamilton, see *Observer*, 19 Dec. 1971, 9.
143. R. Jenkins, *Sir Charles Dilke: A Victorian Tragedy* (1958), 161.
144. Benn, *Diaries 1963–1967*, 21 (20 May 1963). See also his *Diaries 1940–1962*, 369 (interview with David Butler).
145. Benn, *Diaries 1980–1990*, 142.
146. 'A Right Royal Furore', *The Economist*, 10 Dec. 1994, 34.
147. As pointed out in Orwell, *Works*, iv. 515.
148. Butler, *British Political Facts 1900–1994*, 52, 419.
149. Disraeli, *Selected Speeches*, ii. 493 (Manchester, 3 Apr. 1872).
150. Pope-Hennessy, *Queen Mary*, 345.
151. Hardie, *Political Influence of the British Monarchy*, 56.
152. Ziegler, *Edward VIII*, 256.
153. Ibid. 255–6; Duke of Windsor, *A King's Story*, 337.
154. Lacey, *Majesty*, 360–1.
155. Cecil, *Salisbury*, iii. 187.
156. Duke of Windsor, *A King's Story*, 307; see also 35.
157. *Daily Telegraph*, 7 Feb. 1992, 18 (leading article).
158. Butler and Stokes, *Political Change in Britain*, 115.
159. Quoted in N. and J. Mackenzie, *The Time Traveller: The Life of H. G. Wells* (1973), 18; cf. Grandmamma Collen, in E. Pethick-Lawrence, *My Part in a Changing World* (1938), 21.
160. Quoted in C. Cross, *Philip Snowden* (1966), 88.
161. *The Times*, 7 June 1977, 3; cf. Mass-Observation, *May 12th*, 42.
162. J. Callaghan, *Time and Chance* (1987), 461.
163. Crossman, *Diaries of a Cabinet Minister*, i. 257 (17 June 1965).
164. Ibid. iii. 543 (1 July 1969).
165. Castle, *Diaries 1964–1970*, 688 (15 July 1969); cf. *Diaries 1974–1976*, 445 (2 July 1975), 467–8 (17 July 1975).
166. *The Times*, 24 Oct. 1978, 4. *The Economist*, 10 Dec. 1994, 34.
167. See the argument in Mount, *The British Constitution Now*, 43.
168. Laski, *Parliamentary Government in England*, 392.
169. R. Fulford, *George IV* (1935), 225, 230.
170. Mass-Observation, *May 12th*, 7.
171. Wilson, *Final Term*, 221; Benn, *Diaries 1963–1967*, 201, cf. 211 (27 Jan. 1965), 232 (10 Mar. 1965).
172. *H.C.Deb.* 21 Dec. 1971, c.1333.
173. Bogdanor, *Monarchy and the Constitution*, 299.
174. *Observer*, 2 Feb. 1975, 29.
175. Harrison, 'The Monarchy', *Fortnightly Review* (1872), quoted in Hanham (ed.), *Nineteenth Century Constitution*, 34.
176. Fulford, *Hanover to Windsor*, 189.

## Chapter 13: The British Political System in the 1990s (pp. 349–384)

1. Bagehot, 'English Constitution', in *Works*, v. 165 (preface to 2nd edn.).
2. J. Patten, *Political Culture, Conservatism and Rolling Constitutional Change*, 1991 Swinton Lecture (Conservative Political Centre, 1991), 21.
3. J. Patten, 'Just Keep Rolling Along', *Spectator*, 30 Jan. 1993, 9. An expanded version is in the European Policy Forum's *Modernising British Government: Approaches to the Constitution and Constitutional Reform* (n.d.), 12–30.
4. K. Minogue, *The Constitutional Mania*, Centre for Policy Studies, policy study no. 134 (1993), 18.
5. P. Norton, *The Constitution: The Conservative Way Forward*, 1992 Swinton Lecture (1992), 5.
6. Ibid. 9.
7. Ibid. 7, cf. 12.
8. *Daily Telegraph*, 31 July 1991, 2.
9. J. Patten, 'Beware a Balkans Effect in Britain', *Guardian*, 21 Jan. 1992, 17.
10. J. Major, speech at Glasgow on 22 Feb. 1992, pub. as *Scotland in the United Kingdom* (1992), 9.
11. Ibid. 10.
12. *Independent*, 7 Apr. 1992, 10; *Daily Telegraph*, 6 Apr. 1992, 1; *Daily Telegraph*, 2 June 1992, 4.
13. *Financial Times*, 1 Dec. 1995, 12.
14. *H.C.Deb.* 12 Jan. 1995, c.276.
15. To OUCA May 1976, quoted in Bogdanor, *Devolution*, 113.
16. See Allan Massie, 'Mr Rifkind, Please do a Brooke', *The Times*, 14 July 1990, 12; cf. *Financial Times*, 9 May 1991, 9 (Philip Stephens).
17. See e.g. A. Wright, 'Decentralisation and the Socialist Tradition', in A. Wright, J. Stewart, and N. Deakin, *Socialism and Decentralisation*, Fabian Tract no. 496 (1984), 1–7.
18. B. Pimlott, *Harold Wilson* (1992), 549. Crossman, *Diaries*, iii. 619–20 (14, 17 Aug. 1969).
19. *Guardian*, 13 Sept. 1994 education suppl., 11. See also *Financial Times*, 16 Nov. 1985, 7.
20. Speech at the University of Ulster, Coleraine, *Independent* 17 Dec. 1992, 2.
21. The correspondence is printed at length in *Daily Telegraph*, 30 Nov. 1993, 12–13.
22. See e.g. the remarkable position taken up in C. Moore's 'Mr Major would not be Dismissive of the Scottish Nationalists if they had the Wit to Commit Atrocities', *Spectator*, 6 May 1995, 8.
23. *Financial Times*, 17 Nov. 1987, 15.

24. Speech at Ulster Hall, Belfast on 18 Apr. 1974, *Guardian*, 19 Apr. 1974, 20. See also *H.C.Deb.* 14 Nov. 1977, cc.88–9, 92.
25. Lyons, *Ireland since the Famine*, 680.
26. Birch, *Political Integration and Disintegration*, 40, 47.
27. *Financial Times*, 13 Dec. 1995, 6.
28. *Daily Telegraph*, 10 Oct. 1992, 11.
29. J. Stewart, 'The Rebuilding of Public Accountability', paper delivered to the conference of the European Policy Forum, 9 Dec. 1992, in its *Accountability to the Public*, 7.
30. W. Waldegrave, *The Reality of Reform and Accountability in Today's Public Service* (Public Finance Foundation 1993), 13 (referring to the views of Madsen Pirie).
31. Speech to Institute of Directors on 23 Feb. 1983, *The Times*, 24 Feb. 1983, 1.
32. *H.C.Deb.* 21 Mar. 1991, c.402.
33. A proposal endorsed by Douglas Hurd: see *Financial Times*, 10 Oct. 1991, 10. For Walker, see Seldon and Ball (eds.), *Conservative Century*, 427.
34. See John Redwood's plans discussed in *Independent on Sunday*, 23 May 1993, 1.
35. *The Times*, 28 Aug. 1981, 1; 25 Sept. 1981, 1; 17 Dec. 1981, 1. *The Economist*, 16 Mar. 1985, 38.
36. See J. Rogaly, 'Why Judges are Jumping', *Financial Times*, 2 Nov. 1993, 22.
37. See *Guardian*, 26 Mar. 1994, 9 and 'Civil Justice in Britain: Trial and Error', *The Economist*, 14 Jan. 1995, 29–31.
38. For the Green Paper on infringement of privacy, see *Financial Times*, 30 July 1993, 8.
39. Crossman, *Cabinet Diaries*, iii. 275 (28 Nov. 1968).
40. The origins of the 'Citizen's Charter' idea are discussed in *The Times*, 23 July 1991, 7.
41. Waldegrave, *Reality of Reform*, 14; cf. Norton, *The Constitution*, 8.
42. At the Aspen Institute, *The Times*, 6 Aug. 1990, 8.
43. Ibid., 16 Oct. 1991, 17 (leader).
44. Lord Scarman, 'Why Britain Needs a Written Constitution', 4th Sovereignty Lecture, Charter 88 Trust, 20 July 1992, 5–6.
45. H. Young, 'Unbound by a Bill of Rights', *Guardian*, 11 June 1991, 18.
46. *H.L.Deb.* 29 Nov. 1978, c.1349.
47. Speech on 1 Mar. 1993 to Charter 88, *Guardian*, 2 Mar. 1993, 8.
48. For useful discussion, see B. G. Cooper, 'The Reith Sunday Controversy 1922–30', *London Quarterly and Holborn Review* (1964), 62, 64, and his thesis 'Religious Broadcasting in Britain 1922–39', (B.Litt. thesis, Oxford University, 1961), 238–9, 244–5, 256.
49. *Sunday Telegraph*, 18 Oct. 1992, 1.
50. *H.L.Deb.* 29 Nov. 1978, 1346 (Bill of Rights select committee report).
51. Jeremy Philpott, *Observer*, 25 June 1995, 6.

52. Scarman 'Why Britain Needs a Written Constitution', 8.

53. *Guardian*, 12 Dec. 1990, 20 (leader).

54. D. Butler, A. Adonis, and T. Travers, *Failure in British Government. The Politics of the Poll Tax* (Oxford, 1994), 57, 126, 217.

55. For Monks, see the leading article 'Divorce may Lead to Happier Unions', *Independent*, 2 Mar. 1994, 17. For McKellen, *Guardian*, 25 Sept. 1991, 22.

56. Blair quoted in F. Prochaska, *Royal Bounty. The Making of a Welfare Monarchy* (New Haven and London, 1995), 272. For *Politeia*, see *Times*, 19 Oct. 1995, 12. For the Conservative 2000 Foundation, see *Guardian*, 17 Aug. 1995, 6; *Independent*, 17 July 1995, 2.

57. *Daily Telegraph*, 9 Feb. 1991, 5.

58. For question-time see *H.C.Deb.* 6 Dec. 1990, c.447. for Callaghan, *The Times*, 18 Mar. 1991, 10.

59. At the G7 summit, *Daily Telegraph*, 17 June 1995, 2.

60. Quotations from *Daily Telegraph*, 12 Oct. 1991, 9; *Guardian*, 5 Dec. 1990, 22. For more on the Cheltenham episode, see *Independent*, 5 Dec. 1990, 3.

61. Hurd at Dulwich, *Guardian*, 23 June 1987, 1. Thatcher interview with Brian Walden, *Sunday Times*, 8 May 1988, sect. c, 2.

62. *Observer*, 13 June 1993, 22.

63. *The Times*, 23 July 1994, 15, cf. Rodgers, ibid., 3 Aug. 1994, 2.

64. *Guardian*, 27 Feb. 1981, 3.

65. As Jack Straw initially proposed, *The Times*, 5 Aug. 1994, 2.

66. *Financial Times*, 11 June 1994, 8.

67. *Guardian*, 1 Apr. 1976, 20.

68. P. Archer (chairman), *A New Constitution for the Labour Party*, Fabian Society special (1993), 1, 4.

69. On 19 July 1995 Blair persuaded the PLP to allow him to appoint the three top whips, *Financial Times*, 20 July 1995, 9.

70. Transcript of television interview, *Observer*, 24 Nov. 1991, 3; cf. her confrontation with Heath, *H.C.Deb.* 21 Nov. 1991, c.465. The Conservative MP Bruce Campbell had taken up the same position as Thatcher on 10 Dec. 1969 when advocating a referendum motion: see Butler and Kitzinger, *1975 Referendum*, 10. For complaints about failure to consult the British people, see H. Young, 'A Mountain Made out of a Muddle', *Guardian*, 5 Nov. 1991, 24; 'Government from Paris', *Guardian*, 8 Sept. 1992, 18; *Independent*, 29 Sept. 1992, 6 (Benn).

71. *Financial Times*, 8 Sept. 1992, 2 (speech to UK presidency conference, London); cf. *H.C.Deb.* 29 June 1992, c.596 (Major).

72. Friedman, *Capitalism and Freedom*, 23.

73. Anthony Barnett's 'Charting a New Course in Democracy', *Sunday Times*, 4 Dec. 1988, sect. B, 4 and Stuart Weir's 'A Child of its Times', *New Statesman*, 3 Dec. 1993, 16 describe how it happened.

74. Labour Campaign for Electoral Reform, *Arguments for Electoral Reform* (1991 edn.).

75. *The Times*, 5 Oct. 1990, 1.

76. For Hattersley's arguments, see *The Times*, 3 Oct. 1987, 4; *Guardian*, 5 Oct. 1990, 6; *Daily Telegraph*, 3 Oct. 1991, 1.

77. Labour Party, *Report of the Working Party on Electoral Systems 1993*, 9. R. Plant, 'Why Changing the System Gets my Vote', *New Statesman*, 17 Sept. 1993, 17.

78. Labour Party, *Report of the Working Party on Electoral Systems 1993*, 26, cf. 11–12.

79. Labour Campaign for Electoral Reform, *Arguments for Electoral Reform*.

80. Labour Party, *Report of the Working party on Electoral Systems 1993*, 26.

81. *The Times*, 17 Sept. 1990, 1.

82. *Independent*, 6 Mar. 1991, 8.

83. R. Jackson, 'Why the Alliance Case is a Fraud', *Sunday Telegraph*, 10 May 1987, 22.

84. *Financial Times*, 3 Apr. 1992, 1. See also *The Times*, 8 Apr. 1992, 7.

85. *The Times*, 14 Sept. 1992, 6.

86. For a shrewd argument to this effect, but favouring only a covert coalition, see I. Crewe, 'Tories could be Trounced without Lib-Lab Pacts', *Independent on Sunday*, 9 May 1993, 2.

87. Butler and Kavanagh, *British General Election of 1992*, 280, 336–7.

88. As did several speakers (though not Edward Heath) in *H.C.Deb.* 13 Dec. 1977 on direct elections to the EEC parliament.

89. *Guardian*, 6 Sept. 1979, 5.

90. *The Times*, 7 July 1978, 1.

91. *H.C.Deb.* 13 Dec. 1977, cc.334–5.

92. *Financial Times*, 19 July 1979, 2.

93. Adonis, *Parliament Today*, 52.

94. For the poll tax, see D. Butler *et al. Failure in British Government*, 227–32, cf. 293. For the employment committee, see *Times*, 4 Nov. 1995, 4.

95. Howe *Conflict of Loyalty*, 622–3. For Benn, see Benn and Hood *Common Sense*, appx. 1, cl. 42.

96. Speech (14 Nov.) at Lord Mayor's banquet, *Guardian*, 15 Nov. 1994, 6.

97. E. Powell in Sir R. Day . . . *But with Respect* (1993), 184 (4 Feb. 1979).

98. For Major, *Independent*, 9 Mar. 1991, 12. See also Lord Wakeham *Cabinet Government*, 12.

99. *H.C.Deb.* 30 Nov. 1993, c.933.

100. Headline to his article in *Observer*, 24 Nov. 1991, 23.

101. *H.C.Deb.* 9 June 1993, c.285.

102. *H.C.Deb.* 25 Mar. 1991, c.637 (a phrase of Mendès-France); cf. *Independent*, 9 Mar 1991, 12.

103. Speech to Scottish Conservatives on 14 May 1993, *The Times*, 15 May 1993, 1.

104. *H.C.Deb.* 9 June 1993, c.298.

105. Hogg and Hill, *Too Close to Call*, 104.

106. Major's speech to European Policy Forum, *Guardian*, 28 July 1994, 2. Statistics from Sir Peter Kemp, *Beyond Next Steps: A Civil Service for the 21st Century* (Social Market Foundation, 1993), 20. For Michael Bichard's appointment, see *Financial Times*, 3 Mar. 1995, 11.

107. Kemp, *Beyond Next Steps*, 17.

108. Ibid. 28.

109. *Financial Times*, 14 July 1994, 1.

110. *The Times*, 20 Oct. 1994, 5.

111. For a useful (though more worried) account of these developments, see 'How to Control Quangos', *The Economist*, 6 Aug. 1994, 19–21.

112. V. Bogdanor, in his article (whose overall position on the issue diverges from mine) 'Tell us where the Buck Stops', *Independent*, 24 Sept. 1994, 24.

113. *The Times*, 26 Mar. 1974, 3.

114. Ibid., 16 July 1993, 7.

115. *Financial Times*, 25 Nov. 1993, 8. For reactions to the first release of information, see 25 Mar. 1994, 11.

116. Ibid., 14 Apr. 1994, 9.

117. On 12 June 1994, reported in *Guardian*, 13 June 1994, 18.

118. P. Norman, 'Wise-Eyed and Legless', *Financial Times*, 15 Aug. 1994, 15.

119. *Financial Times*, 10 Jan. 1995, 16.

120. *The Times*, 22 Dec. 1992, 6; cf. Peter Kellner, 'It will Take many a Bad Year to Bring down the Monarchy', *Sunday Times*, 13 Dec. 1993 (sect. 2), 5.

121. *Financial Times*, 4 Feb. 1993, 9, Carlton Club speech of 3 Feb.

122. Benn, *Diaries 1963–1967*, 16 (12 May 1963).

123. Castle, *Diaries 1964–1970*, 172. For comment on Major's reform, see *Independent*, 23 Dec. 1993, 16; *Financial Times*, 5 Mar. 1993, 15.

124. *Guardian*, 31 Dec. 1993, 1; cf. *Independent*, 31 Dec. 1993, 13 (leading article).

125. *The Times*, 12 Feb. 1993, 17.

126. Ibid. (leader).

127. *Financial Times*, 24 June 1994, 12.

128. Prochaska, *Royal bounty*, 280.

129. Ibid., 274.

130. Ibid., 277.

131. Institute for Public Policy Research, *Constitution of the United Kingdom*, commentary, 27.

132. *Guardian*, 30 June 1994, 3, cf. *Daily Telegraph*, 27 June 1994, 3.

133. *Financial Times*, 5 Oct. 1993, 13.

134. Tony Benn was making such predictions as early as 1968: see his speech at Llandudno, *Guardian*, 27 May 1968, 2.

## Chapter 14: International Perspectives (pp. 385–410)

1. Bagehot, 'English Constitution', in *Works*, v. 327. [Lord Robert Cecil], 'The Commune and the Internationale', *Quarterly Review* (Oct. 1871), 550.
2. Redlich, *Local Government in England*, vol. i, p. xii (preface).
3. Paine, *Rights of Man*, 117.
4. *Sunday Times*, 26 Jan. 1986, 12.
5. W. Fletcher, 'The Persuaders Prepare for the Polls', *Financial Times*, 15 Mar. 1979, 21.
6. *Guardian*, 11 Oct. 1984, 19.
7. Orwell, *Works*, iii. 458. For Bevan, see Pimlott, *Wilson*, 230; cf. 198, 276, Bevan's was also the view of Wilson and Balogh.
8. *Observer*, 15 Aug. 1971, 2.
9. J. A. Hobson, *Imperialism: A Study* (1902, Ann Arbor paperback edn. with intro. by P. Siegelman 1965), 151.
10. J. A. Hobson, *The Crisis of Liberalism: New Issues of Democracy* (first pub. 1909, Harvester reprint, Hassocks, 1974), 259.
11. For a summary of New Zealand's welfare reforms, see *Independent on Sunday*, 30 May 1993, 9.
12. For the sake of conciseness, I use the term 'European' to describe those who were enthusiastic for closer integration with the EEC and later the European Union. But of course 'Europe' even now is much larger than the area covered by the Union, as the 'Eurosceptics' (a term from the 1990s which I use throughout to denote the opponents of the 'Europeans') often emphasize.
13. Craig, *British General Election Manifestos 1918–1966*, 123.
14. Horne, *Macmillan*, i. 363; cf. ii. 35.
15. Haseler, *Gaitskellites*, 228–9.
16. Williams, *Gaitskell*, 736; cf. 739.
17. Morgan, *Harold Wilson*, 204.
18. *Listener*, 19 July 1973, 75. *Sunday Times*, 27 Apr. 1975, 4.
19. Prior, *Balance of Power*, 86. P. Whitehead, *The Writing on the Wall: Britain in the Seventies* (1985), 67.
20. Pimlott, *Wilson*, 611.
21. *The Times*, 2 Dec. 1974, 4.
22. *Sunday Times*, 27 Apr. 1975, 32.
23. Benn, *Diaries 1973–1976*, 485 (31 Dec. 1975).
24. *The Times*, 9 Dec. 1974, 6.
25. Benn, *Diaries 1968–1972*, 324 (13 Jan. 1971).
26. *Listener*, 16 Dec. 1976, 775.
27. R. Jenkins, *A Life at the Centre* (1991), 424.
28. *The Times*, 9 June 1980, 2.

29. Ibid., 27 Mar. 1981, 2.
30. M. Thatcher, 'My Vision of Europe: Open and Free', *Financial Times*, 19 Nov. 1990, 17.
31. As Benn was already detecting in his *Diaries 1980–1990*, 421 (21 Sept. 1985).
32. Jenkins, *The Times*, 7 Sept. 1973, 1. Mackintosh, *Sunday Times*, 27 Apr. 1975, 4.
33. P. Dunleavy, A. Gamble, I. Holliday, and G. Peele (eds.), *Developments in British Politics*, iv (1993), 59–60, 172, 273.
34. Butler and Kitzinger, *1975 Referendum*, 95, 171.
35. Ibid. 95; see also 85–6 and *Guardian*, 8 Oct. 1975, 24.
36. See D. Spanier, 'Man in the Background who Master-Minded the Pro-European Campaign', *The Times*, 7 June 1975, 12 for a useful account of Ernest Wistrich, Director of the European Movement.
37. *The Times*, 18 Jan. 1993, 2.
38. Wilson, *Labour Government 1964–1970*, 387. Ponting, *Breach of Promise*, 209–10, 213.
39. *The Times*, 18 Jan. 1971, 5 (speech at Banbridge, Co. Down).
40. Benn, *Diaries 1973–1976*, 346 (18 Mar. 1975).
41. Speech in Brussels, *Daily Telegraph*, 30 May 1989, 2.
42. Castle, *Diaries 1974–1976*, 249 (12 Dec. 1974).
43. Ibid. 342 (18 Mar. 1975). Benn, *Diaries 1973–1976*, 346 (18 Mar. 1975).
44. *H.C.Deb.* 20 Nov. 1991, c.294 (Thatcher).
45. Butler and King, *British General Election of 1964*, 204–5.
46. Campbell, *Edward Heath*, 405, 556.
47. Crossman, *Cabinet Diaries*, iii. 822 (17 Feb. 1970), 895 (21 Apr. 1970).
48. *H.L.Deb.* 31 Jan. 1980, c.1048 (Lady White, Lord Orr-Ewing's deputy on the Board for four years); cf. *The Times*, 30 Apr. 1975, 21.
49. Leading article, 'Five Years On', *The Times*, 31 Dec. 1977, 13.
50. As Heath twice pointed out, *H.C.Deb.* 26 June 1991, c.1036; *Guardian*, 9 Oct. 1991, 9.
51. *The Times*, 9 Dec. 1991, 1.
52. *H.C.Deb.* 13 Nov. 1990, c.463; cf. 20 Nov. 1991, c.306.
53. *H.C.Deb.* 20 Nov. 1991, c.306.
54. *Financial Times*, 20 Nov. 1990, 21.
55. *H.C.Deb.* 22 July 1971, c.1703.
56. As Howe pointed out in his resignation speech, *H.C.Deb.* 13 Nov. 1990, c.463; cf. Heath, *H.C.Deb.* 21 Nov. 1991, c.459; M. Heseltine, 'Co-operation, not Federation', *Financial Times*, 20 Nov. 1990, 21.
57. *The Times*, 24 Nov. 1990, 37.
58. BBC radio, 25 Nov. 1994, *Daily Telegraph*, 26 Nov. 1994, 1.
59. Quotations respectively from T. Blair, *Financial Times*, 11 Jan. 1995, 1; manifesto of the eight Conservative rebels, *Guardian*, 20 Jan. 1995, 6.
60. Howe, *Conflict of Loyalty*, 632; cf. 685; Jenkins, *The Times*, 4 Oct. 1972, 4.

61. The discussion which follows suffers from the absence of a really good book on this subject. Nobody would be better qualified to write it than Mr Nevil Johnson, of Nuffield College, Oxford, who in correspondence most generously shared some of his ideas with me on the subject. But he must in no way be blamed for what follows.

62. On this, see Castle, *Diaries 1974–1976*, 637 (26 June 1975). N. Ashford, in Layton-Henry (ed.), *Conservative Party Politics*, 119–20.

63. Speech to the Association des Chefs d'Entreprises Libres on 12 Feb., in *The Times*, 13 Feb. 1971, 10.

64. *The Times*, 17 Jan. 1973, 1.

65. *Guardian*, 13 July 1971, 18. See also Cockerell, *Live from No. 10*, 173–6, 190.

66. Powell, in *H.C.Deb.* 13 July 1972, c.1925, noted the lack of paradox involved in this second cross-party collaboration.

67. *The Times*, 27 Jan. 1972, 5.

68. Benn, *Diaries 1977–1980*, 400 (28 Nov. 1978).

69. G. E. Milner, letter in *The Times*, 30 Sept. 1974, 15.

70. Butler and Kitzinger, *1975 Referendum*, 55. Castle, *Diaries 1974–1976*, 305 (6 Feb. 1975).

71. Edward Short, introducing the debate on the referendum White Paper, *H.C.Deb.* 11 Mar. 1975, cc.292–3.

72. Wilson, *H.C.Deb.* 23 Jan. 1975, c.1748; Thatcher, *H.C.Deb.* 11 Mar. 1975, c.316.

73. Speech to U.K. E.E.C. presidency conference in London, *Financial Times*, 8 Sept. 1992, 2.

74. Howe, *Conflict of Loyalty*, 615.

75. *Financial Times*, 12 Jan. 1995, 1; see also *Guardian*, 10 Jan. 1995, 1 (for Labour MEPs). *Financial Times*, 19 June 1995, 1 (for Conservative MEPs).

76. *H.C.Deb.* 25 May 1972, c.1620 (Hamilton). *The Times*, 19 May 1972, 1 (Shore, speech at Enfield on 18 May). *H.C.Deb.* 28 Nov. 1980, c.705 (Shore). *H.C.Deb.* 12 May 1992, c.493.

77. Sir Anthony Meyer, 'Why I am Challenging Thatcher', *The Times* 30 Nov. 1989, 14.

78. Bagehot, 'English Constitution', in *Works*, v. 171 (preface to 2nd edn.).

79. Blaming Foreign Office responsiveness to foreigners for British government mistakes in Northern Ireland, *The Times*, 4 Jan. 1980, 3.

80. Thatcher, *Downing Street Years*, 458.

81. Bradford, *George VI*, 526.

82. Queen Victoria, *Letters: Third Series*, i. 615.

83. On these, see J. MacKenzie, *Propaganda and Empire: The Manipulation of British Public Opinion 1880–1960* (Manchester, 1984), 193. Goldsworthy, *Colonial Issues in British Politics*, 166–9.

84. Howe, *Conflict of Loyalty*, 318. See also Benn, *Diaries 1968–1972*, 12 (12 Jan. 1968), 210 (6 Nov. 1969).

85. Quoted in J. Rogaly, 'At Unease with Itself', *Financial Times*, 29 Jan. 1993, 14.

86. K. O. Morgan, *Labour People: Leaders and Lieutenants, Hardie to Kinnock* (Oxford, 1987), 141.

87. Benn, *Diaries 1963–1967*, 41 (12 July 1963).

88. Crossman, *Cabinet Diaries*, i. 540 (15 June 1966); ii. 182 (1 Jan. 1967), cf. 381–2 (13 June 1967), 592 (26 Nov. 1967).

89. Ibid. ii. 335 (30 Apr. 1967).

90. J. Darwin, *Britain and Decolonisation: The Retreat from Empire in the Post-war World* (1968), 41.

91. Jenkins, *Life at the Centre*, 228.

92. Crossman, *Cabinet Diaries*, iii. 278 (1 Dec. 1968).

93. Quoted from Wilson, *Final Term*, 258. See also Wilson's *Memoirs: The Making of a Prime Minister 1916–1964*, 20, 146 and P. Foot, *The Politics of Harold Wilson* (Harmondsworth, 1968), 238, 247.

94. *Independent*, 6 May 1993, 12.

95. Bagehot, 'No more Guarantees' (1870), in *Works*, viii. 193.

96. Castle, *Diaries 1964–1970*, 520 (24 Sept. 1968), cf. 413 (28 Mar. 1968).

97. Young, *One of Us*, 258–60. See also 'Britain's Foreign Office', *The Economist*, 27 Nov. 1982, 25–9.

98. Castle, *Diaries 1964–1970*, 520 (24 Sept. 1968).

## Chapter 15: Cultural Prerequisites (pp. 411–432)

1. Pickthorn, *H.C.Deb.* 8 Feb. 1960, c.70. B. Crick and A. Porter (eds.), *Political Education and Political Literacy: The Report and Papers of . . . the Working Party of the Hansard Society's 'Programme for Political Education'* (1978), 1 (report).

2. W. E. Gladstone, 'Kin beyond Sea' (1878), repr. in *Gleanings of Past Years*, i. (1879), 245–6. I owe this reference to Professor P. Hennessy of Queen Mary and Westfield College, University of London.

3. For illustrations of this, see my 'Oxford and the Labour Movement', *Twentieth Century British History*, 2/3 (1991), 226–71.

4. These grumbles about the press are not mine alone. See the proposal to remedy them with a new periodical, *Inquiry*, to look at the 'serious public policy issues. As the world becomes more complex, most media have become briefer and more presentation-obsessed' (*Observer*, 19 June 1994, business suppl., 1).

5. Quoted in R. F. Harrod, *The Life of John Maynard Keynes* (first pub. 1951, paperback edn. Harmondsworth, 1972), 585.

6. Ibid. 765; Heath, quoted in J. Ramsden, *The Making of Conservative Party Policy: The Conservative Research Department since 1929* (1980), 241.

7. D. E. Butler *et al. Failure in British Government*, 257.

8. As argued in *Times*, 8 Nov. 1978, 19 (leader).

9. A. Sampson, *The Anatomy of Britain* (1962), 242–4.

10. Quotations from W. Bagehot 'Count your Enemies and Economise your Expenditure' (1862) in his *Works*, viii, 50; *The Times*, 22 Dec. 1987, 13.

11. For more on this, see my 'Mrs Thatcher and the Intellectuals', *Twentieth Century British History*, 5/2 (1994), 213–20.

12. Letwin, *Anatomy of Thatcherism*, 80.

13. Bagehot, 'The Ultimate Evil of French Politics' (1873), in *Works*, viii. 220.

14. J. Harris, *Private Lives, Public Spirit: A Social History of Britain 1870–1914* (1993), 196.

15. *New Statesman*, 14 July 1934, 63.

16. See M. D. Stocks, *Ernest Simon of Manchester* (Manchester, 1963) and my *Prudent Revolutionaries*, ch. 10 ('Catalyst and Facilitator: Eva Hubback'). See also Guy Whitmarsh, 'Society and the School Curriculum: The Association for Education in Citizenship 1934–57', M.Ed. thesis, Birmingham School of Education, 1972. The Association deserves further, and perhaps more sympathetic, scholarly treatment.

17. Whitmarsh, 'Society and the School Curriculum', 105.

18. Laski, *Parliamentary Government in England*, 347–8; cf. R. Bassett, *The Essentials of Parliamentary Democracy* (1935), 170–2.

19. M. Cole, *Education for Democracy: A Report Presented to the Fabian Society* (1942), 35.

20. Butler and Stokes, *Political Change in Britain*, 26.

21. R. Stradling, *The Political Awareness of the School Leaver*, Programme for Political Education, Hansard Society (n.d.), 13.

22. *The Times*, 12 Aug. 1977, 1. See also Stradling, *Political Awareness of the School Leaver*, 19, 22.

23. A. Briggs, *History of Broadcasting in the United Kingdom*, ii: *The Golden Age of Wireless* (1965), 154.

24. *Listener*, 3 May 1979, 620. His remarks responded to comments on his 'Newsweeding', ibid., 5 Apr. 1979, 478. See also the letters ibid., 19 Apr. 1979, 551; 17 May 1979, 685; 24 May 1979, 713.

25. See the vigorous complaints of Peter Jenkins in 'How TV Fails in Politics', *Guardian*, 13 May 1969, 9.

26. J. Birt, 'Why our Interviewers should Stop Sneering and Start to Listen', *The Times*, 4 Feb. 1995, 16.

27. *The Times*, 18 Nov. 1993, 21 (leader).

28. Quotations from D. Hurd, 'The Power of Comment', talk at the Travellers Club, 9 Sept. 1993, typescript, 7, 9.

29. On this episode, see Cockerell, *Live from Number 10*, 243.

30. *The Times*, 5 May 1980, 3.

31. Martyn Lewis, as reported in *Daily Telegraph*, 27 Apr. 1993, 4.

32. M. Lewis, 'The Distorted Mirror of TV News: A Bias against Fairness?', typescript, kindly supplied by the author, 3, 9.

33. M. Lewis, 'Good/Bad/Real News', Royal Society of Arts lecture, 15 Nov. 1993, 2, 9. I am most grateful to Mr Lewis for providing me with this typescript.

34. *The Times*, 4 Feb. 1995, 16.

35. Stocks, *Ernest Simon*, 133.

36. Cockerell, *Live from Number 10*, 43–4.

37. For Edward Heath's hostile view of Johnson's approach to political reporting, see *H.C.Deb.* 20 Nov. 1985, c.289.

38. *New Statesman*, 19 June 1970, 858.

39. Benn, *Diaries 1963–1967*, 138 (8 Sept. 1964).

40. On opening the BBC's new northern HQ in Manchester on 18 June, see *Guardian*, 19 June 1976, 4, cf. his address at the British press awards presentation lunch, *The Times*, 21 Apr. 1977, 3. See also Benn, *Diaries 1968–1972*, 209 (30 Oct. 1969). For politicians' wariness generally, see Butler and King, *British General Election of 1964*, 158; Butler and Pinto-Duschinsky, *British General Election of 1970*, 200.

41. *Daily Telegraph*, 13 Mar. 1993, 4 (speech at Oxford). For a politician's over-reaction against the cynical tendency, however, see Portillo's speech at Southampton in *Guardian*, 5 Feb. 1994, 1.

42. *Independent on Sunday*, 16 Jan. 1994, 2.

43. Prince Charles, speech to editors of regional papers of the Newspaper Society, *The Times*, 5 May 1994, 1. Major, address to the Scottish Conservative Party conference at Inverness, *Independent*, 14 May 1994, 2.

44. Speech at Worsley, *Observer*, 12 Mar. 72, 2.

45. James, *Lord Randolph Churchill*, 255.

46. Lewis, 'Good/Bad/Real News', 3.

47. *The Times*, 4 Feb. 1995, 16.

48. B. Crick and I. Lister, 'Political Literacy', in Crick and Porter (eds.), *Political Education and Political Literacy*, 41, cf. 6.

49. Simon, *A City Council from Within*, 234.

50. Mackintosh, *The Devolution of Power*, 9 (its first sentence).

51. For a useful table on turn-out, see Byrne, *Local Government in Britain*, 367.

52. Craig (ed.), *British Electoral Facts 1832–1987*, 134; cf. G. M. Harris, *Municipal Self-Government in Britain* (1939), 263.

53. Byrne, *Local Government in Britain*, 312.

54. Crossman, *Cabinet Diaries*, ii. 780 (14 Apr. 1968).

55. Orwell, *Works*, ii. 447–8.

56. Byrne, *Local Government in Britain*, 312.

57. Clark, *Diaries*, 284 (3 Mar. 1990).

58. See R. Plant's admirable *Citizenship, Rights and Socialism*, Fabian tract no. 531 (Fabian Society, 1988), esp. 1–2.

59. I. Gilmour, *Dancing with Dogma: Britain under Thatcherism* (1992), 218.
60. A proposal floated by Peter Lilley in *Financial Times*, 17 Jan. 1995, 12.
61. Crick and Porter (eds.), *Political Education and Political Literacy*, 4 (report of the working party).
62. Preface to the first edn. of his *British Political Parties*, repr. in 2nd edn. 1963, p. v. The 'appalling gap' has of course since been filled.
63. *The Times*, 29 Oct. 1971, 15.
64. *H.C.Deb.* 8 Feb. 1932, c.530–1.

# Further Reading

This bibliography does not follow the structure of the book, but takes institutional themes from it and devotes separate sections to each. It lists only items concerned with the history of British political institutions. The many other types of source drawn upon in this book (biographies, diaries, newspapers and historical monographs) are specified in the endnotes. All items were published in London unless otherwise stated. D. E. and G. Butler, *British Political Facts*, 7th edn. (1994) is invaluable for all reference purposes.

## Monarchy

There is a vast literature, but little of historical value, and only a small proportion even of that is concerned with anything other than biography. There has been nothing since 1867 to compare with Bagehot's *English Constitution*. So John Cannon's 'The Survival of the British Monarchy', *Transactions of the Royal Historical Society* (1986) is wide-ranging and invigorating, but hindered by the lack of secondary material on which to draw. Frank Hardie's *The Political Influence of Queen Victoria 1861–1901* (2nd edn. 1938) and *The Political Influence of British Monarchy 1868–1952* (1970) are useful, and owe much to the valuable volumes of Queen Victoria's letters that were published between 1907 and 1932 (1st ser. ed. A. C. Benson and Viscount Esher, 3 vols., 1907; 2nd and 3rd ser. ed. G. E. Buckle, 3 vols., 1926–8, 1930–2). They have been supplemented by *Further Letters of Queen Victoria* (tr. Mrs J. Pudney and Lord Sudley, ed. H. Bolitho, 1938) and by the volumes of the Queen's letters to the Princess Royal (ed. R. Fulford and A. Ramm, 1964– ).

Biographies include P. Magnus, *King Edward the Seventh* (1964) and the two complementary biographies of George V: H. Nicolson's *George V: His Life and Reign* (1952), which covers the public life, and John Gore's more intimate and domestic *King George V: A Personal Memoir* (1941); for its day, Gore's biography was informative and not too reverential, and still has value. These two biographies are supplemented by K. Rose, *King George V* (1983). J. Pope-Hennessy's *Queen Mary 1867–1953* (1959) poignantly shows how a female member of the royal family subordinated her own tastes, abilities, and inclinations entirely to what she saw as being the interests of her husband and her country. An admirably judged and comprehensive study of a subject riddled with historiographical difficulty is Philip Ziegler's *King Edward VIII: The Official Biography* (1985). J. W. Wheeler-Bennett's *George VI: His Life and Reign* (1958) is uninformative by comparison with

S. Bradford's excellent *King George VI* (1989). Well-informed, judicious, and comprehensive on Elizabeth II is Robert Lacey's *Majesty: Elizabeth II and the House of Windsor* (1977, rev. edn. 1979). Also revealing is Philip Ziegler's *Mountbatten: The Official Biography* (1985). Jonathan Dimbleby's *The Prince of Wales: A Biography* (1994) is penetrating, informative, and refreshingly unreverential. Michael De-la-Noy's *The Queen behind the Throne* (1994) takes an important subject (the Queen Mother), but makes all too little of it.

A more interesting (because social anthropological) approach to modern monarchy was pioneered by Mass-Observation's *May 12th* (ed. H. Jennings and C. Madge, 1937). The first historian to take up this approach was J. L. Lant in his *Insubstantial Pageant: Ceremony and Confusion at Queen Victoria's Court* (1979)—a book which has not received due prominence by comparison with D. Cannadine's essay 'The Context, Performance and Meaning of Ritual: The British Monarchy and "The Invention of Tradition" *c.*1820–1977', in E. Hobsbawm and T. Ranger (eds.), *The Invention of Tradition* (1983). Useful correctives to Cannadine are W. M. Kuhn, 'Ceremony and Politics: The British Monarchy 1871–1872', *Journal of British Studies* (Apr. 1987) and W. L. Arnstein, 'Queen Victoria Opens Parliament: The Disinvention of Tradition', *Historical Research*, 63 (1990). Also revealing are sociological studies of opinion; for example, J. G. Blumler, J. R. Brown, A. V. Ewbank, and T. J. Nossiter, 'Attitudes to the Monarchy: Their Structure and Development during a Ceremonial Occasion', *Political Studies* (June 1971) and F. I. Greenstein, H. Valentine, R. N. Stradling, and E. Zureik, 'The Child's Conception of the Queen and the Prime Minister', *British Journal of Political Science* (July 1974). An astringently irreverent view of monarchy can be found in W. S. Adams, 'The People and the Monarchy', *Modern Quarterly*, 8/3 (Summer 1953). Frank Prochaska's *Royal Bounty. The Making of a Welfare Monarchy* (1995), on the monarchy's charitable role from George III to the present, reveals some of the treasures in this area that await the historian with imagination. J. Walker's *The Queen has been Pleased: The British Honours System at Work* (1986) collects useful information on a subject where precise knowledge is all too scarce. With ample historical documentation, Vernon Bogdanor's *The Monarchy and the Constitution* (Oxford, 1995) judiciously analyses the British monarchy's powers today.

## Cabinet and Prime Minister

It will be obvious to the reader how much my discussion of these subjects owes to J. P. Mackintosh's *The British Cabinet* (3rd edn. 1977). It is one of the few really substantial historical studies of any modern British political institution, and a model for the many others that need to be written—though it now badly needs updating in the light of what happened after 1979. The classic statement of the cabinet's role is of course in Bagehot's *English Constitution*, but it was followed by studies that now seem unduly legalistic in their approach: A. B. Keith's *The British Cabinet System 1830–1938* (1939) and Sir Ivor Jennings's *Cabinet Government* (3rd edn. 1961). It was partly in reaction against Keith's approach that Mackintosh's book was embarked upon, for Mackintosh says in the preface to his first edition that he began by trying to produce a third edition of Keith, and then decided that 'an adequate revision would alter the original text to such an extent that the book could scarcely continue to be attributed to Keith'.

There have been valuable smaller-scale studies on limited aspects of the cabinet's history. These include D. N. Chester, 'The Development of the Cabinet 1914–49', in Sir George Campion *et al.*, *British Government since 1918* (1950); J. R. Starr, 'The English Cabinet Secretariat', *American Political Science Review* (May 1928); and J. Turner, *Lloyd George's Secretariat* (1980). Controversy provoked by R. H. S. Crossman's introduction to the Fontana edition of Bagehot's *English Constitution* in 1963 produced some stimulating writing in the academic journals about the position of the prime minister in the cabinet. Among the less known but better-balanced of the contributions is A. H. Brown, 'Prime Ministerial Power', *Public Law* (1968, 2 parts). Out of this controversy emerged Crossman's own somewhat disappointing *Inside View: Three Lectures on Prime Ministerial Government* (1972) and Patrick Gordon Walker's much more useful *The Cabinet* (rev. edn. 1972), which has not been superseded by P. Hennessy's *Cabinet* (Oxford, 1986). There is no full-scale historical study of the prime minister's changing role, though Lord Blake's *The Office of Prime Minister* (1975) provides a brief introduction. S. Hogg and J. Hill's *Too Close to Call. Power and Politics—John Major in No. 10* (1995) penetrates behind the scenes at 10 Downing Street, and captures something of the breathless pace and scope of policy-making under John Major between 1990 and 1992. Anthony King (ed.), *The British Prime Minister*, in both its editions (1969 and 1985), collects valuable material on the prime minister's recent history.

## Parliament

There is unfortunately no equivalent for later periods of P. D. G. Thomas's excellent *The House of Commons in the Eighteenth Century* (Oxford, 1971), though D. N. Chester's 'The British Parliament 1939–66', *Parliamentary Affairs*, 19/4 (Autumn 1966) gives some idea of what is wanted for a rather wider period, and Roland Quinault's 'Westminster and the Victorian Constitution', *Transactions of the Royal Historical Society* (1992) valuably brings together the constitutional and architectural approaches to its historical study. Ivor Jennings's *Parliament* (2nd edn. 1957) is more analytic than historical, though it contains some valuable material. Much more valuable, though inevitably unintegrated and insufficiently historical, is S. A. Walkland (ed.), *The House of Commons in the Twentieth Century: Essays by Members of the Study of Parliament Group* (1979). J. A. Thomas's *The House of*

*Commons 1832–1901: A Study of its Economic and Functional Character* (1939) accumulates a wealth of valuable material on the parliament's composition. Stuart Ball's article 'Parliament and Politics in Britain 1900–1951', *Parliamentary History* (1991), 243–76 operates at just the right level of detail. Although A. Adonis will probably dissent from the overall thrust of this book, his *Parliament Today* (Manchester, 1990) provides a clear, concise, and informative introduction to how parliament works now. P. Norton's *Does Parliament Matter?* (1993) adopts a different perspective, and adds valuable up-to-date detail.

There is no up-to-date history of the House of Lords. P. A. Bromhead's *The House of Lords and Contemporary Politics 1911–1957* (1958) contains useful material, but badly needs updating. A. Adonis's admirable *Making Aristocracy Work: The Peerage and the Political system in Britain 1884–1914* (Oxford, 1993) shows what life there still is in 'constitutional history' for those with energy and imagination. J. P. Morgan's *The House of Lords and the Labour Government 1964–1970* (Oxford, 1975) is a somewhat disappointing book on an important phase in the history of the House. There is much need for a concise and scholarly history of the House since the eighteenth century that draws all this material together and a great deal more.

On party discipline in the House of Commons H. Berrington's article 'Partisanship and Dissidence in the Nineteenth-Century House of Commons', *Parliamentary Affairs*, 21 (1967–8) is valuable. But in writing about parliament I had to rely primarily on a wide range of scattered monographs and primary sources. Interviews could make a major contribution towards understanding changes since 1945 in how parliament works. The need is not for interviews with great men about great events, for information of this kind is already abundant, and such reminiscence is often unreliable. Much more valuable would be the reminiscences of relatively obscure backbenchers or parliamentary officials on how the mood and daily operation of parliament—the sociology and social life of the two houses—have changed. Such interviews would produce much valuable information (lacking in this chapter) on changes in the use of different parts of the building, changed provision of facilities, changed attitudes to the whole business of being an MP or peer.

## Political Parties

There has been more innovative scholarship in this area since 1945 than in most others covered by this book. Excellent introductions can be found in S. H. Beer, *Modern British Politics: A Study of Parties and Pressure Groups* (3rd edn. 1982); S. E. Finer, *The Changing British Party System 1945–1979* (1980); and M. Pugh, *The Making of Modern British Politics 1867–1939* (2nd edn. 1993). Important work has been done on the evolution of party organization. Robert McKenzie's *British Political Parties: The Distribution of Power within the Conservative and Labour Parties*

(2nd edn. 1964) is a classic for drawing together a mass of historical detail into a clear and important argument with relevance for contemporary politics. Also important are N. Gash, *Politics in the Age of Peel: A Study in the Technique of Parliamentary Representation 1830–50* (1953) and H. J. Hanham, *Elections and Party Management: Politics in the Time of Disraeli and Gladstone* (1959). M. Pinto-Duschinsky, *British Political Finance 1830–1980* (1981) presents a wealth of valuable information on a highly technical subject, supplemented by his article on 'Trends in British Party Funding 1983–1987', *Parliamentary Affairs* (Apr. 1989).

It is important not to neglect the interaction between parties, as pointed out in my essay 'The Centrist Theme in Modern British Politics', in my *Peaceable Kingdom: Stability and Change in Modern Britain* (Oxford, 1982), but there are many fine historical studies of individual parties. Outstanding on the Liberal Party are J. Vincent, *The Formation of the Liberal Party 1857–1868* (1966); D. A. Hamer, *Liberal Politics in the Age of Gladstone and Rosebery: A Study in Leadership and Policy* (1972); P. Clarke, *Lancashire and the New Liberalism* (1971). For the Conservatives, see E. J. Feuchtwanger, *Disraeli, Democracy and the Tory Party: Conservative Leadership and Organization after the Second Reform Bill* (1968); P. Smith, *Disraelian Conservatism and Social Reform* (1967); and J. Ramsden's two judicious and thoroughly researched volumes in the Longman history of the Conservative Party: *The Age of Balfour and Baldwin 1902–1940* (1978) and *The Age of Churchill and Eden, 1940–1957* (1995). R. McKibbin's important 'Class and Conventional Wisdom: The Conservative Party and the "Public" in Inter-war Britain', in his *The Ideologies of Class: Social Relations in Britain 1880–1950* (1990) should be read in conjunction with P. Williamson's excellent 'The Doctrinal Politics of Stanley Baldwin', in M. Bentley (ed.), *Public and Private Doctrine: Essays in British History Presented to Maurice Cowling* (Cambridge, 1993). A. Seldon and S. Ball's *Conservative Century: The Conservative Party since 1900* (1994) contains factual material in perhaps excessive abundance, and is variable in the quality of its contents. It does, however, contain an excellent essay by V. Bogdanor on 'The Selection of the Party Leader'. M. Pugh's admirably penetrating and clear *The Tories and the People 1880–1935* (1985) illuminates the Primrose League's integration of the Conservative Party and society. For the Labour Party, see H. Pelling, *The Origins of the Labour Party: A Historical Profile* (1958); R. McKibbin, *The Evolution of the Labour Party 1910–1922* (1974); M. Harrison, *Trade Unions and the Labour Party since 1945* (1960). I. Crewe and A. King's *SDP. The Birth, Life and Death of the Social Democrat Party* (Oxford, 1995) is comprehensive and authoritative. Two books cover the important subject of grassroots support: P. Seyd and P. Whiteley, *Labour's Grass Roots: The Politics of Party Membership* (Oxford, 1992), based on a questionnaire of 1989, and P. Whiteley, P. Seyd, and J. Richardson *True Blues: The Politics of Conservative Party Membership* (Oxford, 1994), based on a questionnaire of 1992. Both contain important data, but their self-conscious preoccupation with social-science techniques limits how much they can learn from their informants and how far they can convey the flavour of their subject to the reader. Better from this point of view is the participant–observer approach adopted in, for example, chapter 4 of A. H. Birch's *Small-Town Politics: A Study of Political Life in Glossop* (1959); but no book comes near to achieving for politics what Ruth Finnegan achieved for popular culture in her *The Hidden Musicians. Music-making in an English Town* (Cambridge, 1989).

Excellent on political ideas are M. Richter, *The Politics of Conscience: T. H. Green and his Age* (1964); W. Wolfe, *From Radicalism to Socialism: Men and Ideas in the Formation of Fabian Socialist Doctrines 1881–1889* (New Haven, 1975); S. Yeo, 'A New Life: The Religion of Socialism in Britain 1883–1896', *History Workshop Journal*, 4 (Autumn 1977); A. M. McBriar, *Fabian Socialism and English Politics 1884–1918* (1962); and S. Macintyre, *A Proletarian Science: Marxism in Britain 1917– 1933* (1980).

## Elections and the Electoral System

By no means every modern British general election has received its published study. The following are at present available: T. Lloyd, *The General Election of 1880* (1968); A. K. Russell, *Liberal Landslide: The General Election of 1906* (Newton Abbot, 1973); N. Blewett, *The Peers, the Parties and the People: The General Elections of 1910* (1972); A. Thorpe, *The British General Election of 1931* (Oxford, 1991); T. Stannage, *Baldwin Thwarts the Opposition: The British General Election of 1935* (1980); R. B. McCallum and A. Readman, *The British General Election of 1945* (1947); H. G. Nicholas, *The British General Election of 1950* (1951). Since then D. E. Butler's remarkable achievement has been to publish studies in the Nuffield series on every subsequent election, usually collaboratively—with R. Rose in 1959, with A. King in 1964 and 1966, with M. Pinto-Duschinsky in 1970, and subsequently with D. Kavanagh. See also two volumes edited by H. R. Penniman for the American Enterprise Institute for Public Policy Research, *Britain at the Polls: The Parliamentary Elections of 1974* (Washington, 1975) and *Britain at the Polls 1979: A Study of the General Election* (Washington, 1981); and I. Crewe and M. Harrop (eds.), *Political Communications: The General Election Campaign of 1983* (Cambridge, 1986). For by-elections, see C. Cook and J. Ramsden (eds.), *By-elections in British Politics* (1973). There is no overall history of British elections, but for those since 1945, see D. E. Butler's convenient *British General Elections since 1945* (Oxford, 1989).

There are several invaluable digests of electoral information edited by F. W. S. Craig—notably his *British Electoral Facts 1832–1987* (Dartmouth, 1989). See also his *British Parliamentary Election Results 1832–1885* (1977), *British Parliamentary Election Results 1885–1918* (1974), *British General Election Manifestos 1900–1974* (1975), *British General Election Manifestos 1959–1987* (Aldershot, 1990), *British Parliamentary Election Results 1918–1949* (rev. edn. 1977), *British Parliamentary Election Results 1950–1970* (Chichester, 1971), and *Minor Parties at British Parliamentary Elections*

*1885–1974* (1975). An important attempt to analyse voting trends over a long time-span is D. E. Butler and D. Stokes, *Political Change in Britain: The Evolution of Electoral Choice* (2nd edn. 1974). An impressive study of electoral geography is H. Pelling, *Social Geography of British Elections 1885–1910* (1967).

On franchise reform, M. Pugh's Historical Association booklet *The Evolution of the British Electoral System 1832–1987* (1988) provides a useful introduction. D. E. Butler pioneered the study of British electoral systems with his *The Electoral System in Britain 1918–1951* (Oxford, 1953). A fine study of attitudes to the electoral system which links a rich collection of historical material with current political problems is V. Bogdanor, *The People and the Party System: The Referendum and Electoral Reform in British Politics* (1981).

## Civil Service

There is a serious lack of synoptic secondary literature on the British civil service, perhaps because the subject lacks drama and because it is difficult to write about. M. Abramovitz and V. F. Eliasberg, *The Growth of Public Employment in Great Britain* (Princeton, 1957) and E. W. Cohen, *The Growth of the British Civil Service 1780–1939* (1941) are now seriously out of date. One would welcome for a later period the sort of comprehensive survey provided in D. N. Chester, *The English Administrative System 1780–1870* (Oxford, 1981). For a first-rate study of the civil service at the end of the 1930s, see H. E. Dale, *The Higher Civil Service of Great Britain* (1941). For a later period, rather unexciting but very informative, are W. J. M. McKenzie and J. W. Grove, *Central Administration in Britain* (1957) and F. M. G. Willson, *The Organization of British Central Government 1914–1964* (2nd edn. 1968). E. N. Gladden, *Civil Services in the United Kingdom 1855–1970* (1967) is again unexciting, but has material of value. The mood of the civil service is admirably evoked in C. H. Sisson, *The Spirit of British Administration and some European Comparisons* (1959). There are numerous volumes on the history of individual departments, notably M. Wright, *Treasury Control of the Civil Service: 1854–1874* (1969); R. Davidson, *Whitehall and the Labour Problem in late-Victorian and Edwardian Britain* (1985) and R. Lowe, *Adjusting to Democracy: The Role of the Ministry of Labour in British Politics 1916–1969* (1986).

## The Welfare State

Maurice Bruce's *The Coming of the Welfare State* (4th edn. 1968) is old-fashioned in its approach but is still useful as a synthesis. An interesting debate grew up in the late 1950s about the dynamic of nineteenth-century government intervention. For a comprehensive and little-known discussion of how this happened in one area, see D. H. Blelloch, 'A Historical Survey of Factory Inspection in Great

Britain', *International Labour Review* (Nov. 1938). See also O. MacDonagh, *Early Victorian Government 1830–1870* (1977); MacDonagh's classic article 'The Nineteenth-Century Revolution in Government: A Reappraisal', *Historical Journal* (1958); J. Veverka, 'The Growth of Government Expenditure in the UK since 1790', *Scottish Journal of Political Economy*, 10 (1963) and A. T. Peacock and J. Wiseman, *The Growth of Public Expenditure in the UK* (2nd edn. 1967). Important aspects of nineteenth-century state intervention are usefully studied in S. E. Finer's *The Life and Times of Sir Edwin Chadwick* (1952) and D. Roberts's *Victorian Origins of the British Welfare State* (1960). M. E. Rose provides a usefully concise summary of one important aspect in his *The Relief of Poverty 1834–1914* (1972).

The Edwardian period was exceptionally creative in this area, and its structures and thought continued to permeate British welfare attitudes for several decades. See J. Harris, *Unemployment and Politics: A Study in English Social Policy 1886–1914* (1972) and *William Beveridge: A Biography* (1977); Asa Briggs's *Social Thought and Social Action: A Study of the Work of Seebohm Rowntree, 1871–1954* (1961). On the impulse to this creativity, Henry Pelling's essay 'The Working Class and the Origins of the Welfare State', in his *Popular Politics and Society in Late Victorian Britain* (2nd edn. 1979) is provocative. Also useful is D. Collins, 'The Introduction of Old Age Pensions in Great Britain', *Historical Journal*, 8 (1965). For the origins of the Attlee government's welfare reforms, see A. Marwick's important article 'Middle Opinion in the Thirties: Planning, Progress and Political "Agreement"', *English Historical Review* (Apr. 1964); Paul Addison's *The Road to 1945: British Politics and the Second World War* (1975); and Harold Macmillan's *The Middle Way: A Study of the Problem of Economic and Social Progress in a Free and Democratic Society* (1966 edn.). G. C. Peden's *British Economic and Social Policy: Lloyd George to Margaret Thatcher* (1985) provides an overview. For developments in public welfare since the 1940s, see Richard Titmuss's *Essays on 'the Welfare State'* (2nd edn. 1963). For a valuable comparative perspective, see H. Wilensky's *The Welfare State and Equality* (1975). Important on one significant area of change is the Finer Report (*Report of the Committee on One Parent Families*, Cmnd. 5629, HMSO, 1974).

## The Impact of Overseas Policy on British Government

Historians have rather neglected this aspect, though much that they have published is relevant to it. On the colonial dimension, R. B. Pugh's essay on the Colonial Office in J. H. Rose, A. P. Newton, E. A. Benians, and H. H. Dodwell (eds.), *The Cambridge History of the British Empire*, iii: *The Empire–Commonwealth 1870–1919* (Cambridge, 1959), 711–68 covers a lot of ground, and can be supplemented by the essay 'The Colonial Office', by R. C. Snelling and T. J. Barron, in G. Sutherland (ed.), *Studies in the Growth of Nineteenth-Century Government*

(1972). Joe Garner's *The Commonwealth Office 1925–68* (1978) is much more interesting than it sounds. The articles by J. A. Cross in *Journal of Commonwealth Political Studies*, 2 (1963–4) and *Public Administration* (1969) are also useful.

N. Mansergh's *The Commonwealth Experience* (1969) surveys the general scene, and is usefully supplemented by D. W. Harkness's *The Restless Dominion: The Irish Free State and the British Commonwealth of Nations 1921–31* (1969). For the more recent period, there are D. Goldsworthy, *Colonial Issues in British Politics 1945–1961: From 'Colonial Development' to 'Wind of Change'* (Oxford, 1971) and J. Darwin's two books: *Britain and Decolonization: The Retreat from Empire in the Post-war World* (1988) and *The End of the British Empire* (1991). For the mood and context of policy-formation, R. Robinson, and J. Gallagher, with A. Denny, *Africa and the Victorians* (1962) is a classic, supplemented by J. A. Gallagher's provocative and somewhat quirky *The Decline, Revival and Fall of the British Empire* (1982). A. B. Keith and I. M. Cumpston made useful collections of documents in, respectively, their *Selected Speeches and Documents on British Colonial Policy 1783–1917* (2 vols. 1918) and *The Growth of the British Commonwealth 1880–1932* (1973).

For the administration of foreign policy, see R. A. Jones, *The Nineteenth-Century Foreign Office: An Administrative History* (1971) and Z. Steiner, *The Foreign Office and Foreign Policy 1898–1914* (1969). H. Temperley's 'Secret Diplomacy from Canning to Grey', *Cambridge Historical Journal* (1938) remains important. D. C. M. Platt's *Finance, Trade, and Politics in British Foreign Policy 1815–1914* (Oxford, 1968) is excellent on the interaction between public opinion and government policy.

## Nationality and Devolution

For historical background, see K. Robbins, *Nineteenth-Century Britain: Integration and Diversity* (Oxford, 1988). On nationalist movements, Sir Reginald Coupland, *Welsh and Scottish Nationalism: A Study* (1954) is wide-ranging and still valuable. J. C. Banks's curiously neglected *Federal Britain?* (1971) is unusual for two qualities rarely found in combination: ample empirical information on important aspects of the subject, and sympathy with the devolutionary point of view. V. Bogdanor, *Devolution* (Oxford, 1979) is a fine example of historical research being brought to bear on a current political problem. For 'home rule all round', see P. Jalland, 'United Kingdom Devolution 1910–14: Political Panacea or Tactical Diversion?', *English Historical Review* (Oct. 1979).

R. F. Foster *Modern Ireland 1600–1972* (1988) provides the best historical introduction. There are many books on 'the Irish question'. J. L. Hammond, *Gladstone and the Irish Nation* (1938) is still valuable, and should be supplemented by C. C. O'Brien, *Parnell and his Party 1880–90* (Oxford, 1957) and by J. Vincent and A. B. Cooke, *The Governing Passion: Cabinet Government and Party Politics in Britain 1885–86* (Brighton, 1974). Also valuable is Vincent's article 'Gladstone and

Ireland', *Proceedings of the British Academy*, 63 (1977). For Northern Ireland, see J. Loughlin, *Gladstone, Home Rule and the Ulster Question 1882–92* (Atlantic Highlands, NJ, 1987); R. J. Lawrence, *The Government of Northern Ireland: Public Finance and Public Services 1921–1964* (Oxford, 1965) and P. Buckland, *The Factory of Grievances: Devolved Government in Northern Ireland 1921–1939* (Dublin, 1979). For Scotland, see H. J. Hanham, *Scottish Nationalism* (1969) and J. N. Wolfe (ed.), *Government and Nationalism in Scotland* (Edinburgh, 1969). For Wales, see K. O. Morgan, *Wales in British Politics 1868–1922* (Cardiff, 1963) and *Rebirth of a Nation: Wales 1880–1980* (Oxford, 1982) and A. Butt Philip, *The Welsh Question: Nationalism in Welsh Politics 1945–1970* (1975).

## Local Government

For a classic study of regionalism in England, see C. B. Fawcett, *Provinces of England: A Study of Some Geographical Aspects of Devolution* (1919). For a short introduction to local government, see B. Keith-Lucas, *English Local Government in the Nineteenth and Twentieth Centuries* (Historical Association pamphlet, 1977). Fuller treatment can be found in the austerely factual but unfootnoted K. B. Smellie, *A History of Local Government* (4th edn. 1968), supplemented by B. Keith-Lucas and P. G. Richards, *A History of Local Government in the Twentieth Century* (1978). Two most informative surveys of the current scene are Tony Byrne's *Local Government in Britain: Everyone's Guide to how it all Works* (1st edn. 1981, 5th edn. Harmondsworth, 1990) and William Hampton's *Local Government and Urban Politics* (1st edn. 1987, 2nd edn. 1991).

For an erudite and admirably informative but older and to modern eyes over-enthusiastic treatment, see J. Redlich, *Local Government in England* (2 vols., first pub. 1903, ed. F. W. Hirst); this major work gains much from viewing the English scene through continental eyes, and combines both breadth of perspective with wealth of detailed information. P. G. Richards provides a clear and informative digest of how the system worked in the early 1980s in his *The Local Government System* (1983). G. C. Baugh provides a valuable long-term historical synoptic survey in his 'Government Grants in Aid of the Rates in England and Wales 1889–1990', *Historical Research* (1992). An admirable study, which concerns far more than local government, is *Failure in British Government: The Politics of the Poll Tax* by D. Butler, A. Adonis, and T. Travers (Oxford, 1994), though its authors will dissent from much that is said in this book.

The classic nineteenth-century statement of the case for local self-government is in chapter 15 of J. S. Mill's *Representative Government* (1861). For trenchant and classic advocacy, see J. Toulmin Smith, *Local Self-government* (1851). For socialist attitudes to local government, see Andrew Sancton's useful 'British Socialist Theories of the Division of Power by Area', *Political Studies* (1976). Valuable discussions of specialist aspects are to be found in J. P. D. Dunbabin's two articles

'The Politics of the Establishment of County Councils', *Historical Journal* (1963) and 'Expectations of the New County Councils and their Realization', *Historical Journal* (1965); J. Prest, *Liberty and Locality: Parliament, Permissive Legislation, and Ratepayers' Democracies in the Nineteenth Century* (Oxford, 1990); V. D. Lipman, *Local Government Areas 1834–1945* (Oxford, 1949); E. P. Hennock, 'Finance and Politics in Urban Local Government in England 1835–1900', *Historical Journal* (1963); C. Cunningham, *Victorian and Edwardian Town Halls* (1981); P. Hollis, *Ladies Elect: Women in English Local Government 1865–1914* (Oxford, 1987); B. Keith-Lucas, *The English Local Government Franchise: A Short History* (Oxford, 1952).

There are many studies of local government in particular areas. K. Young (ed.), *New Directions for County Government* (Oxford, 1989) covers a neglected subject, and has valuable historical and statistical material, though its main concern is with the county councils' present-day responsibilities. For more specific rural studies, see J. M. Lee, *Social Leaders and Public Persons: A Study of County Government in Cheshire since 1888* (Oxford, 1963) and R. J. Olney, *Rural Society and County Government in Nineteenth Century Lincolnshire* (Lincoln, 1979). Of the many studies of nineteenth-century urban history, the following are noteworthy: E. P. Hennock, *Fit and Proper Persons: Ideal and Reality in Nineteenth-Century Urban Government* (1973); D. Fraser, *Urban Politics in Victorian England* (Leicester, 1976); D. Fraser, *Power and Authority in the Victorian City* (Oxford, 1979); P. J. Waller, *Town, City, and Nation: England 1850–1914* (Oxford, 1983). M. Loughlin, M. D. Gelfand, and K. Young (eds.), *Half a Century of Municipal Decline 1935–1985* (1985), particularly good on financial and administrative aspects, complements H. J. Laski, W. I. Jennings, and W. A. Robson (eds.), *A Century of Municipal Progress: The Last Hundred Years* (1935), which breathes an unfamiliar tone of enthusiasm, but still contains material of value. There are numerous histories of individual cities, and many studies of local government within them. See, for example, G. W. Jones, *Borough Politics: A Study of the Wolverhampton Town Council 1888–1964* (1969); R. V. Clements, *Local Notabilities and the City Council: The Role of Bristol's Business and Social Leaders in the City's Government* (1969); J. Davis, *Reforming London: The London Government Problem 1855–1900* (Oxford, 1988). H. E. Meller, *Leisure and the Changing City 1870–1914* (1976) is particularly good on the cultural and recreational background of local government in Bristol.

## Pressure Groups and Voluntary Organizations

No textbook surveys this complex scene comprehensively and historically, though there is useful material in G. Wootton, *Pressure Groups in Britain 1720–1970* (1975). There are many studies of individual pressure groups. Some of those by students of politics have now become historical documents in their own right: for example, J. D. Stewart's *British Pressure Groups: Their Role in Relation to the House of Commons*

(1958), S. E. Finer, *Anonymous Empire: A Study of the Lobby in Great Britain* (1958), H. Eckstein, *Pressure Group Politics: The Case of the British Medical Association* (1960) and J. B. Christoph, *Capital Punishment and British Politics: The British Movement to Abolish the Death Penalty 1945–57* (1962). There are many historical studies of individual cause groups, for which N. McCord's *The Anti-Corn Law League 1838–1846* (1958) and R. T. Shannon, *Gladstone and the Bulgarian Agitation: 1876* (1963) must stand as exemplars. For a study of the interaction between cause and interest group, see my *Drink and the Victorians: The Temperance Question in English Politics* (2nd edn. Keele, 1994). There are many biographies of pressure-group leaders, though they are often misleading on the movements' overall impact. C. S. Emden's *The People and the Constitution* (2nd edn. 1956) is one of the best and most wide-ranging historical studies. Valuable nineteenth-century studies can be found in D. A. Hamer, *The Politics of Electoral Pressure* (1977), J. T. Ward (ed.), *Popular Movements c.1830–1850* (1970) and P. Hollis (ed.), *Pressure from without in Early Victorian England* (1974). I have discussed some of the general issues that arise in my contribution to B. Harrison and N. Deakin, *Voluntary Organizations and Democracy* (Sir George Haynes Lecture, National Council for Voluntary Organizations, 1988). Ruth Finnegan's *The Hidden Musicians. Music-making in an English Town* (Cambridge, 1989), by painting a remarkable portrait of 'civil society' in its cultural aspect, pioneers an approach that could be carried into many other areas of British life.

J. Turner (ed.), *Businessmen and Politics: Studies of Business Activity in British Politics 1900–1945* (1984) pioneers research on the important frontier between politics and economics between the wars. The problems posed by corporatism can be followed up in A. A. Rogow, *The Labour Government and British Industry 1945–51* (1955) and in K. Middlemas, *Politics in Industrial Society: The Experience of the British System since 1911* (1979). For an excellent account of the opinion groups which, in an unusual combination of ideas from the right and methods from the left, helped to destroy corporatism, see Richard Cockett's *Thinking the Unthinkable: Think-Tanks and the Economic Counter-revolution 1931–1983* (1994). For the interaction between voluntarism and the state on welfare issues, see Geoffrey Finlayson's substantial *Citizen, State, and Social Welfare in Britain 1830–1990* (Oxford, 1994).

## Rights and Liberties

Legal historians have not so far made the way plain for non-lawyers who are interested in this area. A. H. Manchester's *A Modern Legal History of England and Wales 1750–1950* (1980) operates in the right territory, but is too technical and rather narrow in approach. For collectivist Liberalism, see M. Richter, *The Politics of Conscience: T. H. Green and his Age* (1964). For the persistence of individualist Liberalism, see K. Willis, 'The Introduction and Critical Reception of Marxist

Thought in Britain 1830–1900', *Historical Journal*, 20/2 (1977). There are numerous studies of the libertarian cause groups that fed into Victorian Liberalism, and some are listed in the two sections 'Elections' and 'Civil Service' above. On religious freedom, see W. S. Holdsworth, 'The State and Religious Nonconformity: An Historical Retrospect', *Law Quarterly Review*, 36 (1920), and the following detailed studies: W. L. Arnstein, *The Bradlaugh Case: A Study in Late Victorian Opinion and Politics* (1965); D. W. Bebbington, *The Nonconformist Conscience: Chapel and Politics 1870–1914* (1982); U. R. Q. Henriques, *Religious Toleration in England 1787–1833* (1961) and her article 'The Jewish Emancipation Controversy in Nineteenth-Century Britain', *Past and Present* (July 1968); and the two books by G. I. T. Machin *The Catholic Question in English Politics 1820 to 1830* (1964) and *Politics and the Churches in Great Britain 1832 to 1868* (1977).

On freedom and privacy of the person, see P. McHugh, *Prostitution and Victorian Social Reform* (1980); J. R. Walkowitz, *Prostitution and Victorian Society: Women, Class, and the State* (1980); P. McCandless, 'Liberty and Lunacy: The Victorians and Wrongful Confinement', *Journal of Social History* (Spring 1978); R. M. MacLeod, 'Law, Medicine and Public Opinion: The Resistance to Compulsory Health Legislation 1870–1907', *Public Law* (1967); and B. Porter's three books *The Refugee Question in Mid-Victorian Politics* (1979), *The Origins of the Vigilant State: The London Metropolitan Police Special Branch before the First World War* (1987), and *Plots and Paranoia: A History of Political Espionage in Britain 1790–1988* (1989).

On pacifism and opposition to conscription, see R. J. Q. Adams and P. P. Poirier, *The Conscription Controversy in Great Britain 1900–1918* (1987); M. Ceadel, *Pacifism in Britain 1914–1945: The Defining of a Faith* (1980); T. C. Kennedy, 'Public Opinion and the Conscientious Objector 1915–19', *Journal of British Studies* (May 1973); S. Koss (ed.), *The Anatomy of an Anti-war Movement* (1973); J. Rae, *Conscience and Politics: The British Government and the Conscientious Objector to Military Service 1916–19* (1970); N. Stammers, *Civil Liberties in Britain during the Second World War: A Political Study* (1983).

On civil liberties issues after 1914, see G. D. Anderson, *Fascists, Communists and the National Government: Civil Liberties in Great Britain 1931–1937* (1983); J. Morgan, *Conflict and Order: The Police and Labour Disputes in England and Wales 1900–1939* (Oxford, 1987). K. D. Ewing and C. A. Gearty, *Freedom under Thatcher: Civil Liberties in Modern Britain* (1990) covers useful territory, but is highly tendentious.

# A British Political Calendar 1860–1995

| Year | Monarchy (imperial events in small capitals, diplomatic in bold, ceremonial in italic) | Parliament | The State |
|---|---|---|---|
| 1861 | Death of Prince Albert | Public Accounts Committee established | |
| 1863 | *Prince of Wales marries Princess Alexandra of Denmark* | | |
| 1865 | | | |
| 1866 | *Queen Victoria opens parliament in person (again in 1867, 1871, 1876, 1877, 1880, 1886)* | | Exchequer and Audit Departments Act establishes office of Comptroller and Auditor-General |
| 1867 | Reform Act ends the requirement that parliament dissolve at the monarch's death | Reform Act ends the requirement that ministers submit themselves for re-election when moving from one official post to another | |
| 1868 | | Disraeli sets the precedent of a government resigning on electoral defeat before meeting the House | |
| 1869 | Queen Victoria mediates between Church of England and House of Lords on Irish Church disestablishment | | First number of the *Civilian* (magazine of the civil service) published |

| Political Parties and Elections (elections in capitals) | Interest and Pressure Groups | Civil Liberties | Year |
|---|---|---|---|
| J. S. Mill's *Representative Government* recommends Hare's scheme for proportional representation. Liberal Chief Whip establishes Liberal Registration Association (Liberal Party's central organization) | | Paper duty abolished | 1861 |
| | | | 1863 |
| GENERAL ELECTION | National Reform League founded to promote franchise extension | | 1865 |
| Movement for women's suffrage launched | First women's suffrage societies founded | | 1866 |
| Second Reform Act extends franchise to many working men, and its minority-representation clause introduces six three-member constituencies. Disraeli founds National Union of Conservative and Constitutional Associations | | First parliamentary debate on women's suffrage | 1867 |
| GENERAL ELECTION | Trade Union Congress founded at Manchester | | 1868 |
| | Josephine Butler launches her campaign against state-regulated prostitution (Contagious Diseases Acts suspended 1883, repealed 1886). National Education League founded at Birmingham to promote universal compulsory (obtained 1880) and free (obtained 1891) elementary education. Charity Organization Society (later Family Welfare Association) founded to co-ordinate charity | J. S. Mill's *The Subjection of Women* (written 1861) published. Anglican Church in Ireland disestablished | 1869 |

| Year | Monarchy (imperial events in small capitals, diplomatic in bold, ceremonial in italic) | Parliament | The State |
|------|------|------|------|
| 1870 | Prince of Wales involved in unsavoury divorce proceedings | | Civil service gains its first women employees when telegraph system transferred to the Post Office; henceforth entrance appointments to permanent posts in all civil-service branches except the Foreign Office made only by examination |
| 1871 | Royal warrant abolishes purchase of army commissions | | Local Government Board set up to co-ordinate central direction of public health, poor law, and sanitary services; Sir John Simon its chief medical officer |
| 1872 | 27 Feb.: *Thanksgiving for Prince of Wales's recovery from serious illness.* Queen Victoria rejects Gladstone's suggestion that Prince of Wales should reside in Dublin for five months a year as her representative | | |
| 1873 | | | |
| 1874 | Queen Victoria virtually initiates the (anti-ritualist) Public Worship Regulation Act. *Wedding of Queen Victoria's second son, the Duke of Edinburgh.* Nov.: *Prince and Princess of Wales visit Birmingham, and are received by Joseph Chamberlain as mayor* | General election produces Alexander Macdonald and Thomas Burt as the first working-men MPs | Playfair Commission appointed; it recommends standardized fourfold job grading throughout the civil service. The consequent 1876 reorganization replaces the 'writer' category by standardizing the lower division and the boy clerks throughout the home civil service |
| 1875–6 | PRINCE OF WALES'S INDIAN TOUR | | Public Health Act consolidates major health legislation and constitutes the basis for all later developments. Sale of Food and Drugs Act gives power to appoint public analysts (compulsory from 1879) |
| 1876 | ROYAL TITLES ACT MAKES QUEEN VICTORIA EMPRESS OF INDIA. Bulgarian Atrocities agitation finally alienates Queen Victoria from Gladstone | | |
| 1877 | Queen Victoria visits Disraeli's home at Hughenden (hitherto only two royal visits to PMs' homes: Peel's and Melbourne's) | | |

| Political Parties and Elections (elections in capitals) | Interest and Pressure Groups | Civil Liberties | Year |
|---|---|---|---|
| Conservative Central Office established, J. E. Gorst Principal Agent | | | 1870 |
| | H. A. Bruce's government Licensing Bill fails because opposed both by drink interest and by prohibitionists | University Tests Act abolishes tests for entering Oxford and Cambridge | 1871 |
| National Union head office and Conservative Central Office housed under the same roof. Ballot Act | | | 1872 |
| Nov.: Home Rule League founded | | | 1873 |
| GENERAL ELECTION | | | 1874 |
| | Frances Power Cobbe founds Anti-Vivisection Society | | 1875–6 |
| | Bulgarian Atrocities agitation launched | | 1876 |
| | National Liberal Federation founded at Birmingham to co-ordinate reforming activity behind the Liberal Party. Malthusian League founded to promote birth control. | Bradlaugh–Besant trial (for publishing a birth-control pamphlet) publicizes birth-control methods | 1877 |

| Year | Monarchy (imperial events in small capitals, diplomatic in bold, ceremonial in italic) | Parliament | The State |
|---|---|---|---|
| 1879 | | | |
| 1880 | Queen Victoria forced to accept Gladstone as PM after first sending for Hartington. Queen Victoria uses Dilke's earlier republicanism as a reason for excluding him from the cabinet | Bradlaugh, atheist leader, prevented from affirming instead of swearing on the Bible (allowed to take his seat 1886) | |
| 1881 | | 2 Feb.: Speaker Brand closes debate on Coercion Bill after forty-one hours of obstruction, and puts the motion to the House | |
| 1882 | Roderick Maclean fires at Queen Victoria at Windsor | First two House of Commons standing committees (for trade and legal matters) set up; they soon lapse, but are revived 1888 | |
| 1883 | Queen Victoria's influence ensures Randall Davidson succeeds Wellesley as Dean of Windsor | | |
| 1884 | Queen Victoria mediates between House of Commons and House of Lords on Franchise Bill. Prince of Wales becomes a member of the Royal Commission on Housing | | Civil servants required to resign when standing for parliament |
| 1885 | *Prince of Wales tours Ireland* | 24 Jan.: House of Commons chamber badly damaged by Irish terrorist dynamite | Scottish Office established. Royal commission on the Housing of the Working Classes |
| 1886 | *Queen Victoria visits Liverpool international exhibition of navigation, commerce, and industry.* 4 May: QUEEN VICTORIA OPENS COLONIAL AND INDIAN EXHIBITION AT SOUTH KENSINGTON | | Charles Booth begins his *Life and Labour of the People in London* (completed 1903) |

| Political Parties and Elections (elections in capitals) | Interest and Pressure Groups | Civil Liberties | Year |
|---|---|---|---|
| | William Morris's Society for the Preservation of Ancient Buildings formed (to protect buildings against savage 'restoration') | | |
| (−1880) Gladstone's Midlothian campaigns | | | 1879 |
| GENERAL ELECTION | | Elementary education becomes compulsory | 1880 |
| | | T. H. Green's lecture *Liberal Legislation and Freedom of Contract*. Married Women's Property Act | 1881 |
| | | Lawsuit *Beatty* v. *Gillbanks* upholds Salvation Army's right of public meeting against disruption by the 'Skeleton Army' | 1882 |
| Primrose League founded. Corrupt Practices Act the first really effective legislation against electoral corruption. Fixes a maximum limit on candidates' election expenses and increases the penalties | | Contagious Diseases Acts (allowing inspection of women suspected of being prostitutes) suspended (repealed, 1886) | 1883 |
| Third Reform Act enfranchises many agricultural labourers. Fabian Society founded | Fabian Society founded to promote the gradual acceptance of socialism. National Society for the Prevention of Cruelty to Children founded | Mrs Weldon sues Dr Forbes Winslow for wrongful confinement in an asylum, and Lunacy Act (1890) tightens restrictions on procedure for certification | 1884 |
| GENERAL ELECTION | | | 1885 |
| GENERAL ELECTION (Lord Randolph Churchill attacks Gladstone's campaign as 'plebiscitary'). Liberal Unionist Association (under Hartington) and National Radical Union (under Chamberlain) organize Liberal opposition to home rule (merge 1889) | | Atheist leader Charles Bradlaugh allowed to take his seat in parliament after several attempts at excluding him were rebutted by his being re-elected | 1886 |

| Year | Monarchy (imperial events in small capitals, diplomatic in bold, ceremonial in italic) | Parliament | The State |
|------|------|------|------|
| 1887 | Mar.: *Queen Victoria visits Birmingham to lay foundation-stone for new law courts.* *Golden Jubilee (21 June: Westminster Abbey thanksgiving service)* | | |
| 1888 | | | |
| 1889 | **Visit of Shah of Persia.** *Spithead review* | | Ministry of Agriculture and Fisheries established. Official Secrets Act makes it a crime for a civil servant wrongfully to communicate information obtained in the course of duty (further extended 1911, 1920). *Fabian Essays in Socialism* published |
| 1890 | | | Consolidating Housing of the Working Classes Act extends the powers of local authorities to clear slums and build houses. Ridley report recommends reorganizing the civil-service divisions into First and Second divisions; this leads to consolidation of the Second Division as an all-service class |
| 1891 | | | Elementary education becomes free |
| 1892 | Prince of Wales (aged 51) at last gains access to the complete range of state papers | | |
| 1893 | *Queen Victoria vetoes proposal for the future George V and Queen Mary to visit Ireland* | | |

| Political Parties and Elections (elections in capitals) | Interest and Pressure Groups | Civil Liberties | Year |
|---|---|---|---|
| | | | 1887 |
| Women's Liberal Federation founded. Liberal Unionist Women's Association founded | National Federation of Property Owners and Ratepayers founded | Oaths Act permits an atheist to become an MP on affirming oath of allegiance. Lloyd George launched on his political career by championing the nonconformist who resists the refusal by the rector of Llanfrothen to bury his daughter in his churchyard | 1888 |
| | Fur and Feather Group (later Royal Society for the Protection of Birds) founded in Manchester; 556,000 members by 1989 | | 1889 |
| | | | 1890 |
| | Liberal Party adopts Newcastle Programme to co-ordinate the separate demands of progressive cause groups | | 1891 |
| GENERAL ELECTION | | | 1892 |
| Independent Labour Party founded at Bradford | Society for Checking the Abuses of Public Advertising formed. National Free Labour Association founded to promote strike-breaking and thus limit trade-union power. Independent Labour Party founded at Bradford | | 1893 |

| Year | Monarchy (imperial events in small capitals, diplomatic in bold, ceremonial in italic) | Parliament | The State |
|------|------|------|------|
| 1894 | Queen Victoria sends for Rosebery as PM without asking Gladstone (who would have favoured Spencer) | | |
| 1895 | | | |
| 1897 | *Diamond jubilee* | | Workmen's Compensation Act makes compensation for death or injury a charge upon industry |
| 1899 | | | Seebohm Rowntree's first survey of York (published as *Poverty* in 1901). Ministry of Education established (Department under Privy Council from 1856) |
| 1900 | *Duke of York visits Ireland* | | |
| 1901 | PRINCE AND PRINCESS OF WALES GO ON EMPIRE TOUR, ON JOSEPH CHAMBERLAIN'S INITIATIVE. (22 Jan.) Accession of Edward VII. 1 Feb.: *Funeral of Queen Victoria.* Demise of the Crown Act abolishes the requirement that government posts be resigned on the monarch's death | | |
| 1902 | 25 June: *Edward VII's coronation* | | |
| 1903 | Edward VII's state visit to Paris (his first foreign tour as King) helps pave the way for the 1904 Entente | | |
| 1904 | | | Report of Committee on Physical Deterioration published |

| Political Parties and Elections (elections in capitals) | Interest and Pressure Groups | Civil Liberties | Year |
|---|---|---|---|
| | | | 1894 |
| GENERAL ELECTION | National Trust founded | | 1895 |
| | Royal Automobile Club founded | | 1897 |
| | | | 1899 |
| GENERAL ELECTION<br>ILP, Social Democratic Federation, Fabians, and trade unions collaborate to form the Labour Representation Committee (becomes Labour Party in 1906) | | | 1900 |
| | | | 1901 |
| | | | 1902 |
| MacDonald–Gladstone electoral pact between LRC and Liberal Party. | Women's Social and Political Union founded as an offshoot of the Labour Party (but later goes independent and militant) to promote votes for women.<br>Tariff Reform League founded to promote protection (imperial tariff introduced in 1932).<br>Institute of Directors established | Poor Prisoners' Defence Act, the first Act making provision for legal aid (extended 1930) | 1903 |
| | Lincolnshire Farmers' Union set up (four years later, National Farmers' Union) | Aliens Act reduces freedom of immigration | 1904 |

| Year | Monarchy (imperial events in small capitals, diplomatic in bold, ceremonial in italic) | Parliament | The State |
|------|------|------|------|
| 1905 | | | Unemployed Workmen Act allows local authorities to subsidize charitable public-works schemes from the rates and organize them through 'distress committees' which can establish labour exchanges and arrange emigration |
| 1906 | Edward VII fails to mediate successfully between the Archbishop of Canterbury and the PM in controversy on the Education Bill, and again in 1908 | | Education (Provision of Meals) Act empowers local authorities to subsidize school meals, recovering cost from parents where possible |
| 1907 | | Number of legislative standing committees raised to four, but now deprived of subject specification and labelled alphabetically | Education (Administrative Provisions) Act establishes the schools health service. Welsh Department of the Board of Education set up in Wales |
| 1908 | (June) Edward VII makes a state visit to the Tsar, the only visit ever paid by a British monarch to Russia | | Old-age pensions introduced, non-contributory until 1925. Children Act introduces, among other things, juvenile courts. Miners obtain the eight-hour day, one of the earliest limitations on adult male working hours. Trade Boards Act sets up boards to establish minimum wages in specified trades |
| 1909 | Edward VII's state visit to Berlin Oct.: Edward VII fails to get Balfour and Lansdowne to restrain Tory peers from throwing out Lloyd George's budget. Dec.: Edward VII tells Asquith he requires a second election before he can agree to coerce the House of Lords through creating peers | | Royal commission on the poor laws (appointed 1905) reports. Labour exchanges established to foster labour mobility. People's Budget. Beveridge's *Unemployment: A Problem of Industry*. Housing and Town Planning Act forbids the building of back-to-back houses |
| 1910 | 6 May: Accession of George V. 17 May: *Funeral of Edward VII.* 16 Nov.: George V reluctantly gives secret guarantee that he will create enough peers after a second election | | |
| 1911 | 22 June: *George V's coronation.* July: *Royal visit to Dublin.* 13 July: *Prince of Wales invested at Carnarvon.* | Parliament Act provides that House of Lords cannot block money bills, and that any other bill passed by House | Lloyd George's National Insurance Act introduces a national system of insurance against ill health, |

| Political Parties and Elections (elections in capitals) | Interest and Pressure Groups | Civil Liberties | Year |
|---|---|---|---|
| | Automobile Association founded | | 1905 |
| GENERAL ELECTION. One-quarter of the nation's cars (36,000) mobilized for election purposes. LRC becomes the Labour Party | | | 1906 |
| | | | 1907 |
| Miners' Federation of Great Britain affiliates to the Labour Party | Women's National Anti-Suffrage League founded (admits men from 1910) to oppose votes for women | | 1908 |
| Osborne judgement renders trade-union fund-raising for political purposes illegal | | | 1909 |
| Jan.: GENERAL ELECTION. (highest turn-out in twentieth century: 87 per cent). Dec.: GENERAL ELECTION | | | 1910 |
| Parliament Act reduces maximum House of Commons term from seven years to five | National Insurance Act incorporates several British Medical Association demands | Official Secrets Act extends restrictions, and so weights prosecution more strongly against the accused than the Act of 1889 (extended 1920) | 1911 |

| Year | Monarchy (imperial events in small capitals, diplomatic in bold, ceremonial in italic) | Parliament | The State |
|------|------|------|------|
| | 12 Dec.: GEORGE V'S CORONATION DURBAR AT DELHI | of Commons in three successive sessions and rejected by House of Lords must become law, and that the maximum term of the House of Commons fall from seven years to five | unemployment, etc. for certain trades, with contributions from employed, employer, and the state (initially covers 2,250,000 for unemployment insurance) |
| 1912 | | Select Committee on Estimates appointed to ensure better Treasury supervision of public expenditure (lapsed 1914; re-established 1921; replaced by Expenditure Committee 1971) | Launching of the national insurance scheme greatly extends the civil service's welfare role and draws for administrative talent on several ministries |
| 1913 | | | |
| 1914 | George V first monarch to present the FA cup. **State visit to France.** July: George V accepts Asquith's suggestion of a conference, chaired by the Speaker, of leading politicians at Buckingham Palace to seek settlement of the Irish question, and opens it in person | | |
| 1915 | 24 Aug.: Unsuccessful Buckingham Palace conference between political leaders on compulsory military service, George V present throughout. The King's (wartime total abstinence) pledge | | Rent control introduced to prevent war profiteering. June: Ministry of Munitions established |
| 1916 | | | National insurance extended to munitions workers Ministry of Labour established; takes over administration of labour exchanges, trade boards, and unemployment insurance Feb.: Ministry of Blockade established Dec.: Lloyd George sets up the five-member war cabinet, with its own secretariat (originally the secretariat of the Committee of Imperial Defence) Dec.: Ministries of Food, Labour, and Shipping, and Department of National Service established |

| Political Parties and Elections (elections in capitals) | Interest and Pressure Groups | Civil Liberties | Year |
|---|---|---|---|
| Liberal Unionist Party merges with Conservative Party | | Board of Censors established, and on 1 Jan. 1913 begins categorizing films as suitable for different types of audience | 1912 |
| Liberal government reverses Osborne judgement and requires trade unionists unwilling to contribute to the political levy to contract out | Pilgrimage of non-militant suffragists from National Union of Women's Suffrage Societies converges on London | 'Cat and Mouse Act' allows rearrest of self-starved prisoners to complete their sentence | 1913 |
| | Union of Democratic Control founded to promote open diplomacy | Defence of the Realm Acts extend government powers of requisition etc. in wartime (further Acts in 1915 and 1916). First Aliens Restriction Act (subsequent Acts require internment of aliens of military age and repatriation of others) | 1914 |
| | 10 Mar.: Lloyd George and trade-union leaders make dilution agreement at the Treasury meeting | | 1915 |
| | Government helps create the Federation of British Industries | Conscription first introduced into Britain | 1916 |

| Year | Monarchy (imperial events in small capitals, diplomatic in bold, ceremonial in italic) | Parliament | The State |
|------|------|------|------|
| | | | Dec.: Department of Scientific and Industrial Research established |
| 1917 | **George V abandons his German titles and name (henceforth the royal family calls itself the House of Windsor).** *Royal tour of industrial areas in the north of England helps to moderate discontent* | | Jan.: Food Production Department established. Mar.: Department of National Service becomes a Ministry. Autumn: Department of Overseas Trade established. Aug.: Ministry of Reconstruction established |
| 1918 | Buckingham Palace first appoints a full-time salaried press secretary (discontinued thereafter only between 1931 and 1944) | | Jan.: Air Ministry set up (first Air Board appointed May 1916). Mar.: Ministry of Information established (disbanded Nov.). Haldane committee on machinery of government reports. Maternity and Child Welfare Act allows local authorities to set up 'home help' schemes for pregnant mothers |
| 1919 | | The four standing committees increased to six in a reorganization of the committees aiming to accelerate post-war reconstruction. Lady Astor the first woman to take her seat. Re-election of Ministers Act abolishes the need to re-elect MPs on accepting office within nine months of a general election (re-election requirement abolished altogether 1926) | Ministry of Health established to co-ordinate all government health services with Sir George Newman as Chief Medical Officer till 1935. Addison's Housing and Town Planning Act requires local authorities to make good their deficiencies of housing and provides Treasury subsidy, thus establishing the basis of social policy on housing. Whitley Council henceforth represents both employers and employees within the civil service in negotiation about pay and conditions. Treasury institutes common salary scales throughout the civil service for administrative staff below the level of deputy secretary. Welsh Board of Health established in Cardiff. Mar.–May: Ministries of Blockade and National Service and Food Production Department disbanded. June: Ministry of Reconstruction disbanded. |

| Political Parties and Elections (elections in capitals) | Interest and Pressure Groups | Civil Liberties | Year |
| --- | --- | --- | --- |
| | National Federation of Women's Institutes founded | | 1917 |
| Labour Party's new constitution gives it a constituency branch structure for the first time, thus superseding ILP and trades councils as the main form of local Labour Party effort<br>Fourth Reform Act enfranchises most women over 30, introduces adult male suffrage, and requires all election polls to be held on the same day<br>GENERAL ELECTION dominated by Lloyd George | 27 Feb.: National Industrial Conference to bring employers and trade unionists together | | 1918 |
| | National Confederation of Employers' Organizations founded to operate in the political sphere (British Employers' Confederation from 1934; amalgamates with Federation of British Industries in 1965 to form Confederation of British Industry).<br>League of Nations Union founded to promote internationalism | Police Act makes it a crime to cause disaffection in the police force, and creates the Police Federation as an alternative to trade-union police representation | 1919 |

| Year | Monarchy (imperial events in small capitals, diplomatic in bold, ceremonial in italic) | Parliament | The State |
|------|------|------|------|
| | | | July: Ministry of Health established, and assumes all the powers of the Local Government Board. |
| | | | July: University Grants Committee appointed. |
| | | | 4 Sept.: Treasury minute officially recognizes the Permanent Secretary of the Treasury as Head of the Civil Service as part of major reorganization of Treasury structure. |
| | | | Nov.: Lloyd George reverts to full peacetime cabinet of twenty ministers |
| 1920 | | S. and B. Webb's *Constitution for a Socialist Commonwealth of Great Britain* suggests duplicated legislative assemblies: 'political' for public order, foreign policy, etc., and 'social' for welfare. | Unemployment insurance extended to all manual workers (except in agriculture and domestic service) and to lower-paid non-manual workers; 11 million workers now covered. |
| | | Government of Ireland Act sets up Stormont parliament | Welsh Department of Agriculture established at Aberystwyth. |
| | | | 12 Mar.: Treasury circular says PM's consent needed for appointment of top civil servants. |
| | | | 22 July: Order in Council empowers Treasury to make regulations 'for controlling the conduct of His Majesty's Civil Establishments'. |
| | | | Sept.: Ministry of Transport established |
| 1921 | Duke of York (later George VI) promotes his first boys' camp. | | Order in Council creates 'Treasury' classes of civil servant common to most departments. |
| | 22 June: George V opens the new parliament of Northern Ireland and makes conciliatory speech helping to foster Anglo-Irish settlement. | | Apr.: Ministries of Munitions, Food, and Shipping disbanded. |
| | **State visit to Belgium** | | From May: Various powers transferred to the governments of southern and Northern Ireland |
| 1922 | | | Geddes committee recommends, among other things, abolition of the Ministry of Labour (unsuccessfully). |
| | | | Apr.: Various functions transferred to the Irish Provisional Government |

| Political Parties and Elections (elections in capitals) | Interest and Pressure Groups | Civil Liberties | Year |
|---|---|---|---|
| Communist Party of Great Britain founded | | Welsh Church disestablished | 1920 |
| | Howard Association and Penal Reform League amalgamate to form the Howard League for Penal Reform. British Legion founded to help ex-servicemen and their dependants. Jan.: Lord Rothermere founds Anti-Waste League through his *Sunday Pictorial*; it wins three by-elections during the year | | 1921 |
| GENERAL ELECTION | | | 1922 |

| Year | Monarchy (imperial events in small capitals, diplomatic in bold, ceremonial in italic) | Parliament | The State |
|------|------|------|------|
| 1923 | **State visit to Italy.** 26 Apr.: *Much popular interest aroused by wedding of Duke of York, later George VI* | | |
| 1924 | | | Wheatley's Act introduces a long-term programme for council-house building and increases subsidies. Apr.: Irish Office abolished, residual functions relating to Irish Free State transferred to Colonial Office (in 1926 to Dominions Office) |
| 1925 | | | Widows and Orphans Pensions Act ties old-age pensions to the national insurance system, and widows and orphans of insured persons to receive pensions as of right. July: Dominions Office established |
| 1926 | | | Guardians (Default) Act enables the Minister of Health to appoint his own nominees to poor-law boards where expenditure is considered excessive |
| 1927 | | | Trade Disputes Act bans civil-service unions from political affiliation |
| 1928 | | | |
| 1929 | | | Local Government Act abolishes poor-law guardians and transfers their duties to county councils and county borough councils. Local Government Act abolishes the poor-law boards and transfers their duties to the local authorities |
| 1930 | | Winston Churchill's Romanes lecture suggests creating a House of Industry to deal with social and industrial problems | Economic Advisory Council grows out of the Committee of Civil Research set up in June 1925 (the Council's descendants— the Central Statistical Office and the Economic Section of the |

| Political Parties and Elections (elections in capitals) | Interest and Pressure Groups | Civil Liberties | Year |
|---|---|---|---|
| GENERAL ELECTION | | | 1923 |
| GENERAL ELECTION; for the first time, the three party leaders broadcast political speeches | Protectionist Empire Industries Association founded | Guardianship of Infants Act vests guardianship of infant children in parents jointly, the courts adjudicating in the event of conflict | 1924 |
| Conservative Party first employs travelling cinema vans. Welsh Nationalist Party founded | | | 1925 |
| Re-election of Ministers Act removes the need for ministers to seek re-election on accepting office | Conservation societies amalgamate to form Council for Rural Amenities (now Council for the Preservation of Rural England) | | 1926 |
| Trade Disputes Act substitutes contracting in for contracting out of the trade unions' political levy; Labour Party membership falls from 3,238,939 to 2,025,139 within a year | | | 1927 |
| National Party of Scotland founded (Scottish National Party from 1933). Franchise equalized as between men and women | Mond-Turner talks between trade unions and employers | Suppression of *The Well of Loneliness*, Miss Radclyffe Hall's novel on lesbianism | 1928 |
| GENERAL ELECTION. Lloyd George's 'yellow book' elaborates Liberal scheme for conquering unemployment | National Smoke Abatement Society formed (later National Society for Clean Air). National Federation of Townswomen's Guilds grows out of the descendant of the non-militant advocates of women's suffrage | Lord Chief Justice Hewart's attack on creeping bureaucracy, *The New Despotism*, published | 1929 |
| | 18 Feb.: Beaverbrook's campaign for imperial protection launched as the United Empire Party. National Birth Control Association founded to integrate several independent | | 1930 |

| Year | Monarchy (imperial events in small capitals, diplomatic in bold, ceremonial in italic) | Parliament | The State |
|------|------|------|------|
| | | | Cabinet Office— grow out of it in Jan. 1941) |
| 1931 | George V prominent in ensuring that Labour minority government is succeeded by a National Government coalition. Civil list reduced by £50,000 for as long as the economic crisis lasts | | |
| 1932 | George V's first Christmas radio broadcast | | 29 Feb.: Import Duties Act establishes Import Duties Advisory Council (Board of Trade assumes its duties 1939). 25 Apr.: Exchange Equalisation Fund established to smooth variations in exchange-rates |
| 1933 | | | Children and Young Persons Act extends the protection provided in 1908, especially for children in care |
| 1934 | | | July: Unemployment Assistance Board established, and assumes responsibility for the able-bodied unemployed from the local Public Assistance Committees. 21 Dec.: Special Areas (Development and Improvement) Act recognizes problems of the distressed areas and appoints two commissioners (extended 1936 and 1937) |
| 1935 | *Silver jubilee* | | |
| 1936 | 20 Jan.: Death of George V; Accession of Edward VIII. 28 Jan.: *George V's funeral.* 10 Dec.: Edward VIII abdicates. 11 Dec.: Accession of George VI | | Seebohm Rowntree's second survey of York, published as *Poverty and Progress* in 1941. Mar.: Sir Thomas Inskip appointed Minister for Co-ordination of Defence, and a joint planning staff set up |

| Political Parties and Elections (elections in capitals) | Interest and Pressure Groups | Civil Liberties | Year |
|---|---|---|---|
| | birth-control groups (Family Planning Association from 1939) | | |
| Feb.: Mosley founds the New Party, renamed British Union of Fascists in 1932. GENERAL ELECTION. Oct.: Liberal National Party founded to support Liberal members of the National Government (National Liberal Party from 1948, merged with Conservatives 1966). National Labour Party founded for supporters of Ramsay MacDonald in the National Government (wound up in 1945). | | | 1931 |
| Labour Party conference disaffiliates the Independent Labour Party | | | 1932 |
| | India Defence League resists devolution proposals, but these enacted by the India Act (1935). East Fulham by-election demonstrates pacifist strength | | 1933 |
| | British Iron and Steel Federation formed. Peace Pledge Union founded. National Council for Civil Liberties formed | National Council for Civil Liberties founded. Incitement to Disaffection Act, though much curtailed by opposition in the course of enactment, extends government powers to protect the armed services against disaffection | 1934 |
| GENERAL ELECTION. Radio broadcasts help mould the issues discussed at public meetings, which attract reduced numbers | Peace Ballot | | 1935 |
| Gallup poll successfully predicts Roosevelt's 1936 victory | Jarrow March of the unemployed. Abortion Law Reform Association formed | Public Order Act prohibits political uniforms and empowers the police to forbid political processions | 1936 |

| Year | Monarchy (imperial events in small capitals, diplomatic in bold, ceremonial in italic) | Parliament | The State |
|------|------|------|------|
| 1937 | 12 May: *George VI's coronation* | | |
| 1938 | | | Harold Macmillan's *The Middle Way* published |
| 1939 | **June: George VI visits USA.** George VI resumes the Christmas radio broadcasts | | Aug.: Ministry of Supply established. Sept.: Ministries of Home Security, Information, Economic Warfare, and Food established. 4 Sept.: Exchange control imposed. Oct.: Ministry of Shipping established |
| 1940 | 9 and 13 Sept.: Buckingham Palace bombed. George VI visits Coventry directly after major bombing raids | | Treasury loses its central role in handling the economy, supplanted by new agencies of economic planning (from which the Economic Section of the Cabinet Secretariat emerges in 1941). Ernest Bevin, Minister of Labour and National Service, takes factory inspectorate from the Home Office. May: Churchill combines premiership with acting as Minister of Defence. May: Ministry of Aircraft Production established. Oct.: Office of Works becomes a new Ministry of Works and Buildings |
| 1941 | | 10 May: Bomb destroys House of Commons chamber | Determination of Needs Act abandons household means test as a test of personal need. Apr.: Budget for the first time acknowledges government's responsibility for planning the economy as a whole. |

| Political Parties and Elections (elections in capitals) | Interest and Pressure Groups | Civil Liberties | Year |
| --- | --- | --- | --- |
| British Institute of Public Opinion founded to introduce the opinion poll to Britain.<br>Labour Party conference increases constituency representatives on NEC from five to seven, and requires them, the trade-union representatives, and the representatives of the socialist societies to be elected separately by their respective conference delegates | | | 1937 |
| | National Marriage Guidance Council founded.<br>Women's Voluntary Services founded | | 1938 |
| | National Citizens' Advice Bureaux formed | Peacetime conscription introduced for the first time.<br>Emergency Powers (Defence) Act enables government to arrest and detain suspected persons, requisition property, enter and search premises, etc. (extended 1940) | 1939 |
| | National Old People's Welfare Council founded (Age Concern from 1971) | Massive internment of Austrians and Germans in the Isle of Man and elsewhere | 1940 |
| | | | 1941 |

| Year | Monarchy (imperial events in small capitals, diplomatic in bold, ceremonial in italic) | Parliament | The State |
|------|------|------|------|
|  |  |  | May: Ministry of Shipping combines with Ministry of Transport to form Ministry of War Transport |
| 1942 |  |  | Beveridge report on social insurance and allied services. July: Ministry of Production established. June: Ministry of Fuel and Power established |
| 1943 | George VI visits the troops in North Africa |  | Treasury recovers its central role in economic policy when Anderson succeeds Kingsley Wood as Chancellor of the Exchequer. Foreign Secretary recommends amalgamating the Foreign Office, and the consular, diplomatic, and commercial-diplomatic services. Feb.: Ministry of Town and Country Planning established. Nov.: Minister of Reconstruction appointed (post abolished May 1945) |
| 1944 | George VI visits British troops in Italy | Select Committee on Statutory Instruments set up (replaced by joint Lords–Commons committee 1973) | Government white paper on social insurance issued. Ministry of Education created. Assheton committee on training of civil servants report leads to Training and Education Division being set up in the Treasury (in 1945) to supervise the training and education of all civil servants. Barlow committee recommends modified entrance examination catering for civil servants whose education the war had interrupted; this leads to adoption of the 'country-house method', retained when normal open competition resumed in 1948. Nov.: Ministry of National Insurance established |
| 1945 |  |  | Family Allowance Act passed by the coalition government (allowances being paid to over 4 million children by the end of 1946). Apr.: Ministry of Civil Aviation established. May: Ministries of Economic Warfare and Home Security dissolved. |

| Political Parties and Elections (elections in capitals) | Interest and Pressure Groups | Civil Liberties | Year |
|---|---|---|---|
| | Aims of Industry founded (anti-nationalization) | | 1942 |
| | | | 1943 |
| | | | 1944 |
| GENERAL ELECTION. Political broadcasts heard by 45 per cent of the population. Twenty-five new seats created by subdividing the largest constituencies (number of MPs rises from 615 to 640) | United Nations Association founded | | 1945 |

| Year | Monarchy (imperial events in small capitals, diplomatic in bold, ceremonial in italic) | Parliament | The State |
|------|------|------|------|
| | | | Summer: Ministries of Production and Economic Warfare disbanded |
| 1946 | | | National Health Service Act (comes into force 1948). National Insurance Act. Marriage bar removed from women civil servants. Civil-service unions allowed to resume party affiliation. Bank of England and civil aviation nationalized. Mar.: Ministry of Information disbanded, its role being assumed by Central Office of Information. Apr.: Ministry of Aircraft Production merged into Ministry of Supply; Department of Overseas Trade disbanded. Dec.: Service ministries merge into a single Ministry of Defence with a seat in the cabinet (heads of service ministries have no seat in the cabinet) |
| 1947 | ROYAL TOUR OF SOUTH AFRICA. 15 Aug.: GEORGE VI CEASES TO BE EMPEROR OF INDIA. 20 Nov.: *Princess Elizabeth marries Philip Mountbatten* | | Aug.: India Office disbanded, and relations with India and Pakistan transferred to Commonwealth Relations Office Sept.: Cripps appointed Minister for Economic Affairs; takes his planning staff with him when appointed Chancellor of the Exchequer in Nov. |
| 1948 | 26 Apr.: *George VI and Queen Elizabeth's silver wedding* | 700-year record established by fifty-hour sitting through two consecutive nights, discussing objections to nationalization of iron and steel | National Assistance Act abolishes remnants of the poor-law system and creates the National Assistance Board. Railways and road haulage nationalized. National Assistance Act greatly enhances central government's welfare role at the expense of local authorities. Sir Ernest Gowers's *Plain Words* (written at the invitation of Sir Edward Bridges, then head of the civil service) published to guide new entrants to the civil service on writing simple English. |

| Political Parties and Elections (elections in capitals) | Interest and Pressure Groups | Civil Liberties | Year |
|---|---|---|---|
| Attlee government reverses the Trade Disputes Act (1927) provision that trade unionists wishing to contribute to the political levy should contract in; Labour Party membership rises within the year from 2,500,000 to 4,400,000. Lord Woolton appointed chairman of the Conservative Party organization | National Association for Mental Health founded (from 1973, Mind) | | 1946 |
| Maxwell-Fyfe report on Conservative Party organization. First Nuffield election study (by McCallum and Readman, on 1945) published Town and Country Planning Act severely limits use of posters at elections thereafter | Government sets up British Travel and Holidays Association to foster tourist trade. Government committee (appointed by President of Board of Trade in 1945) leads to British Institute of Management being established. Hayek establishes the Mont Pelerin Society | Peacetime conscription resumes, imposing eighteen months' military service | 1947 |
| Conservative Research Department set up. Labour government's Representation of the People Act reduces number of MPs to 625, prescribes routine redistribution of population between constituency boundaries within the life of each parliament, abolishes the plural (business and university) vote, and prescribes one registered party car per 2,500 electors in boroughs and one per 1,500 in other constituencies (Tories remove the limitation in 1958) | Feb.: Voluntary incomes policy launched (ends Oct. 1950) | | 1948 |

| Year | Monarchy (imperial events in small capitals, diplomatic in bold, ceremonial in italic) | Parliament | The State |
|------|------|------|------|
| | | | Mar.: Attlee government bans Communists and Fascists from 'work . . . vital to the security of the State'. |
| | | | Nov.: Board of Trade 'bonfire' of controls |
| 1949 | | Parliament Act reduces House of Lords delaying-powers to two sessions and one year | |
| 1950 | | Rebuilt House of Commons chamber completed; first meeting there 26 Oct. | Iron and steel nationalized (denationalized 1953, renationalized 1967, privatized 1988). |
| | | | Seebohm Rowntree's third survey of York, published as *Poverty and the Welfare State* 1951 |
| 1951 | **Princess Elizabeth and Prince Philip visit USA** | Select Committee on Nationalized Industries established temporarily (permanent from 1956) | July: Ministry of Materials established (disbanded 1954) to meet needs created by Korean War |

| Political Parties and Elections (elections in capitals) | Interest and Pressure Groups | Civil Liberties | Year |
|---|---|---|---|
| House of Commons (Redistribution of Seats) Act institutes mechanism for regularly revising constituency boundaries through four Permanent Boundary Commissioners— for England, Scotland, Wales, and Northern Ireland —at minimum once every three years, maximum once in seven (revised 1958 to ten-year minimum, fifteen-year maximum) | | Legal Aid and Advice Act greatly extends legal-aid provision | 1949 |
| GENERAL ELECTION. Postal ballots first available: 470,000 cast, mostly for the Conservatives; these were sufficient to decide the result in ten constituencies—but for the postal vote, Labour would have won a majority of twenty-six instead of six. Annual target of 300,000 houses built per year voted into the Conservative Party programme by the party conference. 23 Feb.: First TV report of general election results | Aims of Industry mounts 'Mr Cube' campaign against nationalization | | 1950 |
| GENERAL ELECTION. Television (three fifteen-minute broadcasts) first used by party leaders during an election campaign. 742,605 postal votes cast (threefold increase on 1950), and (assuming a 6 : 4 distribution to the Conservatives) produce Conservative victory in ten seats. London Conservatives especially active in switching their constituency workers from safe to marginal seats. David Butler's *British General Election of 1951* first uses the term 'psephology' | | UK ratifies European Convention on Human Rights (1950), which comes into force in 1953 | 1951 |

| Year | Monarchy (imperial events in small capitals, diplomatic in bold, ceremonial in italic) | Parliament | The State |
|------|------|------|------|
| 1952 | 6 Feb.: Death of George VI; Accession of Elizabeth II | | 'Positive vetting' introduced for civil servants in specially secret work |
| 1953 | 24 Mar. *Death of Queen Mary, followed by lying-in-state*, 2 June: *Coronation of Elizabeth II* | | Aug.: Ministries of Pensions and National Insurance amalgamated. Sept.: Cabinet's Economic Secretariat moves to Treasury. Oct.: Ministry of Civil Aviation merges with Ministry of Transport to form Ministry of Transport and Civil Aviation. Nov.: Economic Section placed under Treasury |
| 1954 | ROYAL VISIT TO AUSTRALIA | | Crichel Down case exposes arrogant civil-service handling of the public; Minister of Agriculture (Sir Thomas Dugdale) resigns |
| 1955 | | | Apr.: Ministry of Food merged into Ministry of Agriculture and Fisheries to form Ministry of Agriculture, Fisheries and Food |
| 1956 | | | 1 Sept.: Norman Brook and Roger Makins are made joint Permanent Secretaries to Treasury, Brook (Secretary of the Cabinet) responsible mainly to the PM, Makins |

| Political Parties and Elections (elections in capitals) | Interest and Pressure Groups | Civil Liberties | Year |
|---|---|---|---|
| | | | 1952 |
| | Samaritans founded.<br>June: National Television Council set up to resist pressure (promoted by the Popular Television Association) for commercial television, but defeated 1954 | General Council of the Press established to uphold freedom of the press, (renamed Press Council in 1963, when its role was enlarged to consider complaints about press conduct) | 1953 |
| | | Television Act sets up Independent Television Authority | 1954 |
| GENERAL ELECTION<br>First routine redistribution of population between constituencies causes much restiveness (hence Redistribution of Seats Act 1958 reduces such redistribution to fifteen-year intervals).<br>For the first time in British history, every seat is contested.<br>33 per cent of electorate watch at least one TV party broadcast, 57 per cent hear at least one party sound broadcast.<br>Some candidates (mostly Conservatives) project the national party political television broadcasts at their meetings to serve as texts for subsequent discussion.<br>526,904 postal votes cast (2 per cent of the total).<br>Gallup poll shows that 6 per cent of the electorate claim to have been taken to vote in party cars.<br>Wilson report very critical of Labour Party organization | National Campaign for the Abolition of Capital Punishment founded (hanging abolished 1965).<br>Antony Fisher (Buxted Chickens) founds Institute for Economic Affairs.<br>Commercial TV launched after contest between the (victorious) Popular Television Association and the (defeated) National Television Council.<br>22 Sept.: first commercial television broadcast | | 1955 |
| | | | 1956 |

| Year | Monarchy (imperial events in small capitals, diplomatic in bold, ceremonial in italic) | Parliament | The State |
|------|------|------|------|
| | | | mainly to the Chancellor of the Exchequer |
| 1957 | **Queen Elizabeth's first state visit to France.** 14 Oct.: Queen's first TV broadcast 25 Dec.: Queen's first TV Christmas broadeast | | 12 Aug.: Council on Prices, Productivity, and Incomes set up (disbanded 1961) |
| 1958 | 21 Mar.: *Last presentation of débutantes at court* | Life Peerages Act | Public Records Act introduces the 'fifty-year rule', opening to the public most government records fifty years after their creation |
| 1959 | | | |
| 1960 | 6 May: *Princess Margaret's wedding gets estimated world audience of 300 million* | | |
| 1961 | ROYAL TOUR OF INDIA | | 20 July: Plowden committee on public expenditure reports; Treasury responds by reorganizing itself in 1962 along functional rather than departmental lines, and dividing itself into management and economic–financial sides |
| 1962 | | | 7 Mar.: First meeting of National Economic Development Council. 26 July: National Incomes Commission announced |

| Political Parties and Elections (elections in capitals) | Interest and Pressure Groups | Civil Liberties | Year |
|---|---|---|---|
| | Consumers' Association launched; *Which?* founded. Civic Trust founded. | | 1957 |
| ITV reportage of Rochdale by-election in March breaks down BBC inhibitions on political reporting | Campaign for Nuclear Disarmament founded; first Aldermaston march | | 1958 |
| GENERAL ELECTION. Morgan Phillips organizes daily press conference for the Labour Party during election campaign. Twelve party political broadcasts on TV, eighteen on radio. 61 per cent of electorate (over 20 million) watch at least one party TV broadcast. 27 per cent of electorate hear at least one party radio broadcast. Labour's 'Television and Radio Operations Room' run by Benn's committee. Four of the nine national daily newspapers publish poll results at least weekly. Party leaders now timing their speeches so as to get into late-evening TV news programmes. Both parties now making special efforts to boost support in marginal seats | | Obscene Publications Act (extended 1964) strengthens police power to suppress pornography | 1959 |
| | | | 1960 |
| | National Economic Development Council set up to co-ordinate government, employers, and trade unions | R. v. *Penguin Books Ltd* (publication of *Lady Chatterley's Lover*) | 1961 |
| Conservatives sponsor a private poll after the Orpington by-election | | | 1962 |

| Year | Monarchy (imperial events in small capitals, diplomatic in bold, ceremonial in italic) | Parliament | The State |
|---|---|---|---|
| 1963 | ROYAL TOUR OF AUSTRALIA AND NEW ZEALAND | Peerage Act enables peers to disclaim their peerages | Centre for Administrative Studies set up to train young civil servants in relevant disciplines. Greater London Council created to manage the area previously covered by the London County Council, together with its surrounding area |
| 1964 | | | Ministry of Technology established (merged with Ministry of Aviation Feb. 1967, Ministry of Power 1969, when it also took in large parts of the Board of Trade and the Department of Economic Affairs). Apr.: Service ministries abolished and all service departments' functions transferred to Ministry of Defence. Apr. Functions of Ministry of Education and Office of Minister for Science transferred to a new Department of Education and Science under a Secretary of State. 16 Oct.: Department of Economic Affairs set up under George Brown |
| 1965 | ROYAL VISIT TO AFRICA. | Conservative Party adopts formal procedures for enabling its MPs to elect its leader (implemented to change the leader in 1975 and 1990) | 17 Mar.: Aubrey Jones appointed chairman of Prices and Incomes Board (first report 23 Aug. 1966). 16 Sept.: DEA publishes National Plan for 25 per cent growth by 1970 |
| 1966 | | 24 Nov.: Proposal to televise House of Commons on an experimental basis for a limited period rejected by 131 votes to 130 | Race Relations Board established. Colonial Office absorbed into Commonwealth Relations Office. National Assistance Board and Ministry of Pensions and National Insurance merge to form Ministry of Social Security. 25 Jan.: Industrial Reorganization Corporation established to improve industrial efficiency |

| Political Parties and Elections (elections in capitals) | Interest and Pressure Groups | Civil Liberties | Year |
| --- | --- | --- | --- |
| May: Labour Party launches major advertising campaign | Mary Whitehouse co-founds Clean Up TV Campaign, which in 1965 becomes National Viewers' and Listeners' Association (Protection of Children Act 1978, Indecent Displays Act 1981, Video Recordings Act 1984) | | 1963 |
| Early in the year: Conservatives launch 10,000-interview NOP survey. GENERAL ELECTION. BBC1 and radio broadcast *Election Forum* shortly before the election, in which party leaders answer questions sent in by listeners and viewers | Child Poverty Action Group founded | | 1964 |
| Conservative MPs elect Heath leader of the Conservative Party by the new procedure | | Race Relations Act sets up Race Relations Board | 1965 |
| National Front created by merger between League of Empire Loyalists and British National Party. 85 per cent of electorate claim to have seen one or more party TV broadcast. Soon after March Conservatives outline the 70+ 'critical seats' on which to focus their effort. GENERAL ELECTION | Employers' organizations (including Federation of British Industries) merge to form Confederation of British Industry. July–Dec.: Pay freeze, eased 1967–8, strengthened Apr. 1968, ends June 1970 Dec.: Shelter founded to combat homelessness | | 1966 |

| Year | Monarchy (imperial events in small capitals, diplomatic in bold, ceremonial in italic) | Parliament | The State |
|------|------|------|------|
| 1967 | | | Parliamentary Commissioner for Administration ('Ombudsman') created.<br>First government 'green paper' issued.<br>Public Records Act subjects most public documents to the 'thirty-year rule', whereby they are normally made publicly available thirty years after they were created |
| 1968 | **Royal tour of South America** | Apr.–May: House of Commons experiment with sound broadcasting of debates for four weeks (further experiment summer 1975) | Commonwealth Relations Office merges with Foreign Office to become FCO.<br>Civil Service Department (abolished 1981) takes over the Treasury's role of managing the civil service.<br>Ministry of Social Security merges with Ministry of Health into DHSS.<br>26 June: Fulton report on the civil service published; government accepts its main recommendations |
| 1969 | 1 July: *Prince of Wales invested at Carnarvon.*<br>21 June: Royal family participate in the TV film 'Royal Family' | Labour and Conservative backbenchers defeat proposals for Lords reform | |
| 1970 | ROYAL VISIT TO AUSTRALIA | Jan.: First white paper on projected expenditure to be followed by a parliamentary debate | Ministries of Transport, Public Building and Works, and Housing and Local Government merged to form Department of the Environment (transport hived off into separate ministry 1976).<br>Civil Service College founded |

| Political Parties and Elections (elections in capitals) | Interest and Pressure Groups | Civil Liberties | Year |
|---|---|---|---|
| | Society for the Protection of Unborn Children (from 1970, Life) founded. Committee for Homosexual Law Reform (from 1970, Campaign for Homosexual Equality) founded | Breathalyser test introduced (184,000 tests in Great Britain by 1980) | 1967 |
| | | Race Relations Act extends the 1965 Race Relations Act and sets up Community Relations Commission to improve race relations | 1968 |
| Representation of the People Act lowers franchise age from 21 to 18 and allows mention of a parliamentary candidate's party on the ballot sheet. Second routine redistribution of population between constituencies but Labour government controversially delays implementation until local government reform | Government helps create the Women's National Commission (superseding Women's Consultative Council set up in 1962 for EEC purposes), to give government wider access to the views of women's organizations Women's Liberation Workshop founded. Anti-apartheid movement begins boycotting Barclays Bank, which succumbs to student pressure in 1986 and sells off its South African interests | | 1969 |
| GENERAL ELECTION. Harold Wilson rules out 'confrontation programmes' on TV during election campaign. At least two-thirds of Labour-held marginals receive 'mutual aid' within the Conservative Party machine. Opinion polls come in for much criticism for failing to predict the election result | Friends of the Earth founded in London First Gay Pride festival | Equal Pay Act requires that terms of employment should apply equally to both sexes, and makes provision for extending equal pay for equal work | 1970 |

| Year | Monarchy (imperial events in small capitals, diplomatic in bold, ceremonial in italic) | Parliament | The State |
|---|---|---|---|
| 1971 | **Second royal visit to France** | | `In response to the Fulton Report, 210,000 civil servants from the administrative, clerical, and executive grades merge into a single administrative group |
| 1972 | May: Queen visits the dying Duke of Windsor (formerly Edward VIII). *Queen Elizabeth II's silver wedding celebrations (thanksgiving service at Westminster Abbey followed by walkabout in the City).* 12 Oct.: Students insult the Queen during her visit to Stirling University | 30 Mar.: Stormont parliament suspended. 26 Oct.: House of Commons rejects a proposal to televise its proceedings for an experimental period by a majority of twenty-six | Local Government Act (implemented 1974) introduces the first full-scale reorganization of local government structure in England and Wales since 1889, creating a top tier of metropolitan counties in the six conurbations and forty-seven non-metropolitan counties elsewhere |
| 1973 | Mark Phillips and Princess Anne give a ninety-minute interview to the press before their wedding 14 Nov. | First National Health Service Commissioners (Ombudsmen) appointed under National Health Reorganization Act. Select Committee on Statutory Instruments (founded 1944) amalgamated with House of Lords Special Orders Committee to form Joint Committee on Statutory Instruments | |
| 1974 | 20 Mar.: Attempt to kidnap Princess Anne in the Mall. 13 June: Prince Charles's maiden speech in House of Lords (in debate on sport and leisure); his second speech, on opportunities for young people, on 25 June 1975 | Select Committee on EEC Secondary Legislation appointed. Commissioners (Ombudsmen) for Local Administration appointed under Local Government Act | Department of Energy hived off from Department of Trade and Industry. DTI breaks up into separate ministries for energy, industry, trade, and prices/consumer protection (trade and industry remerge to reform DTI in 1983) |

| Political Parties and Elections (elections in capitals) | Interest and Pressure Groups | Civil Liberties | Year |
| --- | --- | --- | --- |
| Ian Paisley forms the Democratic Unionist Party | Action on Smoking and Health (ASH) founded. Campaign for Real Ale (CAMRA) founded. Greenpeace founded. Industrial Relations Act (subsequently rendered inoperative by trade-union hostility). 6 Mar.: First national demonstration of Women's Liberation Movement in London. 8 June: Upper Clyde Shipyards liquidation followed by work-in | The three editors of *Oz* magazine found guilty on four obscenity charges in the longest obscenity trial so far held in British history. 9 Aug.: Internment without trial begins in Northern Ireland | 1971 |
| | Band of Mercy reorganizes as the Animal Liberation Front. Public schools set up Independent Schools Information Service (changed name from 'public' to 'independent' in 1973). People Party founded, soon renamed Ecology Party, then (from 1985) Green Party. Nov. 1972–Jan. 1973: Ninety-day statutory wages and prices standstill following failure of tripartite talks on a voluntary policy | | 1972 |
| | 1 Apr.: phase two of statutory Prices and Incomes Policy. Nov. 1973–Feb. 1974: Phase III of statutory Prices and Incomes Policy. 13 Dec.: Three-day week announced to save electricity | Northern Ireland (Emergency Provisions) Act extends powers of the authorities to counter terrorism (amended 1975). May: Physical assault on Prof. H. J. Eysenck, when lecturing on race at London School of Economics to the Social Science Society. June: Sussex students prevent Prof. Samuel Huntington from lecturing on the role of the military in US foreign policy. July: Lord Windlesham appointed cabinet minister in charge of government support for voluntary societies | 1973 |
| Feb.: GENERAL ELECTION. Successful Liberal election campaign run from Barnstaple, and Liberals get 19.3 per cent of the votes cast (over 6 million). Labour Party installs facilities to record and play back all TV broadcasts in the campaign. | Mar.–July: Labour Party's 'social contract' with the trade unions. Sir Keith Joseph founds Centre for Policy Studies (pioneer of 'Thatcherism'). | Prevention of Terrorism (Temporary Provisions) Act seeks to curb urban guerrillas by extending police powers beyond the Public Order Act (1936) | 1974 |

| Year | Monarchy (imperial events in small capitals, diplomatic in bold, ceremonial in italic) | Parliament | The State |
|------|------|------|------|
| 1975 | | Home Committee's recommendations for enabling Conservative MPs to challenge an existing leader are implemented; on first ballot Thatcher gets more votes than Heath, and wins on second ballot.<br>5 June: First referendum (not binding on parliament) on EEC membership; yes votes win 67.2 per cent.<br>5 June: First register of MPs' interests published | National Enterprise Board set up, modelled on the Italian Institute for Industrial Reconstruction.<br>Legal action retrospectively justifies Crossman for publishing his diaries as a cabinet minister in the Wilson governments |
| 1976 | | 12 June: Liberal Party Special Assembly at Manchester settles procedure whereby all party members can choose a new leader from the candidates proposed by Liberal MPs; Steel elected. | |

| Political Parties and Elections (elections in capitals) | Interest and Pressure Groups | Civil Liberties | Year |
|---|---|---|---|
| For the first time, Labour Party sponsors during the election daily polls on the salience of election issues.<br>BBC *Election Call* programme at 9 a.m. gets 9,000 calls and 1 million listeners.<br>Walkabouts now more common than public meetings during the campaign; Heath concentrates his in the marginal seats.<br>Of candidates asked which is the most useful campaign activity, 14 per cent say public meetings, 43 per cent publicity, 55 per cent canvassing.<br>Oct.: GENERAL ELECTION.<br>This the election producing the highest number of valid postal votes cast to date (870,000) | | | |
| 11 Feb.: Conservative MPs elect Mrs Thatcher Conservative leader. | National Association for Freedom founded to resist collectivist threats to liberty.<br>11 July: Phase I of compulsory (not statutory) pay policy announced (ends July 1976) | Sex Discrimination Act outlaws discrimination on grounds of sex in all aspects of employment, education, etc. and establishes the Equal Opportunities Commission.<br>Children Act provides that where the wishes of parent and child conflict, parents' views should be considered, but more weight should be given to the welfare of the child.<br>Twenty-one die and 184 badly injured in Birmingham pub bombings, leading to Prevention of Terrorism (Temporary Provisions) Bill, superseded in 1976 by a new Act which has since been annually renewed | 1975 |
| Houghton committee recommends funding of political parties from public revenue | Healey, Chancellor of the Exchequer, publicly bargains with trade unions on tax changes in budget (phase 2 of compulsory pay policy Aug. 1976–July 1977) | Prevention of Terrorism (Temporary Provisions) Act extends further the Act of 1974.<br>Race Relations Act outlaws discrimination in employment and education, and makes it an offence to stir up hatred; replaces Race Relations and Community Relations commissions by Commission for Racial Equality | 1976 |

| Year | Monarchy (imperial events in small capitals, diplomatic in bold, ceremonial in italic) | Parliament | The State |
|---|---|---|---|
| 1977 | 7 June: *Elizabeth II's silver jubilee (royal walkabout after service in St Paul's)* *Princess Anne's visit to Northern Ireland in March precedes Queen's jubilee visit there amidst intensive security precautions* | Labour Party Conference carries total abolition of the House of Lords by 6,248,000 votes to 91,000 | Central Policy Review Staff report wants to cut expenditure on diplomatic service so as to accord better with Britain's reduced world standing |
| 1978 | Revd Graham Leonard (Bishop of Truro) says Princess Margaret (recently holidaying in Mustique) should retire from public life | 3 Apr.: Regular sound broadcasting of parliament begins. July: 161 votes for and 181 against televising House of Commons debates | |
| 1979 | 21 June: Prince Charles the first member of the royal family to address a trade-union assembly (Iron and Steel Trades Federation's annual conference). Aug.: Earl Mountbatten assassinated. 5 Sept.: *State funeral for Earl Mountbatten.* QUEEN ELIZABETH VISITS SOUTHERN AFRICA | 1 Mar.: Referenda on devolved assemblies in Edinburgh and Cardiff; 32.9 per cent vote 'yes', 30.8 per cent 'no', 36.3 per cent do not vote. 7 June: First direct elections to EEC parliament. BBC drops regular broadcasting of PM's question-time on the ground that its confrontational mood does not represent parliament's work fairly. | Sir Derek Rayner, a director of Marks and Spencer, forms a unit to advise Thatcher on civil-service efficiency (departs 1982, leaving Clive Priestley to run the efficiency unit). Price Commission (created 1973) abolished. Heseltine introduces his Management Information System to decentralize management and monitor expenditure (made general throughout the civil service in 1982 under the Financial Management Initiative). 24 Oct.: Exchange controls abolished |
| 1980 | *Queen Mother's eightieth birthday celebrations (procession from Buckingham Palace to St Paul's)* | 30 Jan.: Speaker's casting vote resolves tied vote of 201–201 in favour of televising House of Commons debates. No action taken. Revised system of twelve select committees introduced to match government departments (as recommended by Select Committee on Procedure in 1978). Labour Party Conference carries mandatory reselection of parliamentary candidates | |
| 1981 | 29 July: *Wedding of Prince Charles and Lady Diana Spencer* | | Twenty-one-week strike by civil servants severely delays government receipt of tax revenue. |

| Political Parties and Elections (elections in capitals) | Interest and Pressure Groups | Civil Liberties | Year |
|---|---|---|---|
| 23 Mar.: Lib-Lab pact saves government in confidence vote | CBI's first national conference (at Brighton, Nov.) begins CBI's competition with the TUC for publicity. 15 July: Healey announces phase III of incomes policy. Three university teachers, based at St Andrews, found the Adam Smith Institute | European Court of Human Rights condemns British army interrogation techniques in Northern Ireland | 1977 |
| | | | 1978 |
| GENERAL ELECTION. David Steel's Liberal 'battle-bus' Political parties extensively exploit local radio. Mrs Thatcher refuses Callaghan's challenge to TV debate. Both parties now holding morning press conferences. More nation-wide opinion polls than in any previous general election (twenty-eight nation-wide polls and seven panel surveys) All mass-circulation papers except the *Mirror* publish results of their own opinion polls. Conservatives guided by poll evidence on where to place their advertisements so as best to capture their 'target' (i.e. convertable) voters | 'Winter of discontent': public employees' 'day of action' is followed by widespread strikes for the next six weeks. Ecology Party fights fifty-three seats and wins 41,869 votes in general election. Nov.: British Leyland employees, balloted by company Chairman Michael Edwardes, endorse by 87 per cent the restructuring package the trade unions had opposed; convener 'Red Robbo' dismissed at Longbridge | 23 Oct.: Howe announces abolition of remaining exchange controls | 1979 |
| Labour Party conference votes for mandatory reselection of MPs | Terence Beckett (Director-General CBI) retreats the next day from his threat at CBI conference of a 'bare-knuckled fight' between CBI and the government on economic policy, after interview with Mrs Thatcher | | 1980 |
| 24 Jan.: Labour Party's Wembley conference carries new procedure for choosing the party leader: 30 per cent | | | 1981 |

| Year | Monarchy (imperial events in small capitals, diplomatic in bold, ceremonial in italic) | Parliament | The State |
|---|---|---|---|
| | | | Feb.: 52 per cent equity in British Aerospace sold off |
| 1982 | Elizabeth II receives the Pope at Buckingham Palace | | |
| 1983 | | | Sarah Tisdall prosecuted for passing to the *Guardian* documents relating to the locating of cruise missiles in Britain. |
| | | | 22 Dec.: Trade unions' selective disruption leads government to ban trade unions from GCHQ Cheltenham |
| 1984 | 30 May: Prince Charles's vigorous attack on modern architecture (designs for the National Gallery 'a monstrous carbuncle on the face of a much-loved and elegant friend') | Televising House of Lords begins on experimental basis, continued July 1985, authorized as permanent May 1986 | July: Clive Ponting (Ministry of Defence) secretly briefs Tam Dalyell on Falklands tactics (resigned from civil service Feb. 1985). |
| | | | 28 Nov.: Government sells off 33 per cent of British Telecom |
| 1985 | 3 Sept.: Princess Anne the first senior member of the royal family to appear in a radio phone-in | 20 Nov.: House of Commons rejects motion to televise its debates by 275 to 263 | Local Government Act abolishes GLC and the six Metropolitan County Councils and redistributes their functions to boroughs and some joint authorities |
| | | | Government launches attempt to ban publication of Wright's *Spycatcher* (government finally defeated 1988) |
| 1986 | 23 July: *Prince Andrew marries Sarah Ferguson.* | | Dec.: Government sells off British Gas |
| | 17 Sept.: 13,500,000 people watch the first of two ITN television programmes on the public and private life of the Prince and Princess of Wales (sixth of the 'top ten' TV ratings on all channels) | | |

| Political Parties and Elections (elections in capitals) | Interest and Pressure Groups | Civil Liberties | Year |
|---|---|---|---|
| PLP, 30 per cent CLPs, 40 per cent trade unions.<br>25 Jan.: The 'gang of four' forms the Council for Social Democracy<br>26 Mar.: SDP launched | | | |
| 25 Mar.: Roy Jenkins wins Hillhead by-election for SDP | | Pope John Paul II the first pope to visit the UK | 1982 |
| GENERAL ELECTION.<br>First general election in which the parties make serious use of computers; SDP the only party using a computer to keep a central record of all its members.<br>Conservatives' central computer is used to run the most sophisticated direct-mailing operation in British politics to date (500,000 letters sent to named individuals who have been identified as potential Conservative voters, in sixty marginal constituencies).<br>First general election in which all three national parties systematically use private polls | | | 1983 |
| | 5 Jan.: Press conference chaired by Des Wilson launches coalition of twenty-five pressure groups and voluntary bodies to push for open government in Britain.<br>8 Mar.: Miners' year-long strike begins (miners vote to end strike on 3 Mar. 1985) | 25 Jan.: Howe announces GCHQ staff henceforth cannot be members of trade unions, only of government-approved departmental staff association. Trade unions boycott NEDC but return for the meeting of 5 Dec. | 1984 |
| Representation of the People Act raises level of deposit paid from £150 (established in 1918) to £500, enfranchises British citizens who have resided abroad for up to five years, and allows holiday-makers to claim postal vote | | | 1985 |
| | 14 Apr.: Sunday Trading Bill defeated on second reading by 296 to 282 | | 1986 |

| Year | Monarchy (imperial events in small capitals, diplomatic in bold, ceremonial in italic) | Parliament | The State |
|---|---|---|---|
| 1987 | QUEEN'S INTERVENTION FAILS TO FRUSTRATE COUP IN FIJI | | Feb.: Government sells off British Airways |
| 1988 | 28 Oct.: Prince of Wales's controversial TV programme 'A Vision of Britain' attacks modern architects | 9 Feb.: House of Commons votes by 318 to 264 for its proceedings to be televised (eight-month experiment begins Nov. 1989; House agrees it should be permanent 1990) | (Feb.): Government accepts recommendations of the Efficiency Unit's report on 'The Next Steps' for devolving much civil service activity to semi-autonomous agencies<br>July: DHSS split up into separate departments for health and social security, each represented in cabinet<br>Dec.: Government sells off British Steel |
| 1989 | Separation of Princess Royal from Captain Mark Phillips publicly announced | | Dec.: Government sells off regional water companies |
| 1990 | 27 June: *Queen Mother's ninetieth birthday parade* | Nov.: Conservative backbenchers oust Mrs Thatcher in leadership ballot | (Dec.) Government sells off electricity distribution companies |
| 1991 | | | 23 Mar.: John Major first uses the phrase 'citizen's charter' in speech at Southport (white paper launches it on 23 July).<br>Mar.: Government sells off National Power and PowerGen.<br>July: Cabinet Office has machinery in place to implement Citizen's Charter, designed to apply market-style incentives to ensure responsiveness to the consumer in the areas remaining under government management |

| Political Parties and Elections (elections in capitals) | Interest and Pressure Groups | Civil Liberties | Year |
|---|---|---|---|
| GENERAL ELECTION. Computers enable parties to target their propaganda increasingly on selected groups of voters. Vodaphones first enable journalists to dictate their copy while party leaders are speaking | Green Party fights 133 seats and wins 89,753 votes in general election. STOPP (Society of Teachers Opposed to Physical Punishment) gets corporal punishment outlawed from state schools, and dissolves in 1988 | | 1987 |
| SDP votes to merge with Liberals; the merged party calls itself the Social and Liberal Democrats (SLD); Owenites within the SDP continue to go it alone, leaving the centre parties divided | Institute for Public Policy Research founded Sept.: TUC boycott leads Norman Fowler to end CBI–TUC–government structure for employment and training. Sept.: Thatcher's 'green' speech to Royal Society | 19 Oct.: Home Secretary Hurd bans IRA from radio and TV (ban lifted 1994) | 1988 |
| | 9 Jan.: TUC's automatic right to nominate trade-union representatives to NEDC challenged when government nominates Eric Hammond. 6 Apr.: Dock Labour Scheme ended. Dec.: Labour Party abandons its commitment to the closed shop. 8 Dec.: On Thatcher's invitation Jonathon Porritt, Director of Friends of the Earth, visits her for discussion at 10 Downing Street | | 1989 |
| 3 June: SDP winds up | 23 Apr.: Society for the Protection of Unborn Children sends life-sized plastic models of a 20-week-old foetus to all MPs for debate on embryo research | 30 Mar.: anti-poll tax riots in Trafalgar Square (308 arrested, 300 injured) | 1990 |
| | Nov.: On John Major's invitation, Sir Ian McKellen visits 10 Downing Street to discuss gay rights | | 1991 |

| Year | Monarchy (imperial events in small capitals, diplomatic in bold, ceremonial in italic) | Parliament | The State |
|---|---|---|---|
| 1992 | 6 Feb.: BBC film 'Elizabeth R' on the Queen's personality and activities in 1991. 19 Mar.: Duke and Duchess of York's impending divorce announced 7 June: *Sunday Times* publishes first extract from Andrew Morton's *Diana: Her True Story* 20 Nov.: Fire at Windsor Castle | Betty Boothroyd elected first woman Speaker | 5 May: *Hansard* first provides a full list of cabinet committees. July: William Waldegrave announces government cost-cutting through policy of 'market testing' civil-service functions. |
| 1993 | Queen decides to allow her personal wealth to be taxed | | 16 July: Stella Rimington, Director-General of MI5, gives press conference; thirty-six-page guide to the security service published. 1 Oct.: Pauline Neville-Jones, chairman of Joint Intelligence Committee, gives press conference; twenty-eight-page guide to central intelligence machinery published Nov.: Head of MI6 gives press conference *without* photographs |
| 1994 | 29 June: Jonathan Dimbleby interviews Prince of Wales in ITV documentary 'Charles: the Private Man, the Public Role' Jonathan Dimbleby's *The Prince of Wales* published | | 24 Mar.: Full cost and extent of MI5, MI6, and GCHQ published for the first time. Apr.: Minutes of monthly meetings between Chancellor of the Exchequer and Governor of the Bank of England henceforth to be published. 12 June: Stella Rimington gives Dimbleby lecture (televised) on the security services. 19 Oct.: Far-reaching cuts in Treasury announced (one-third of its senior policy-making posts to go) |
| 1995 | 20 Mar.: THE QUEEN ADDRESSES THE SOUTH AFRICAN PARLIAMENT **31 May: Prince of Wales dines at Dublin Castle (first formal royal visit to southern Ireland since 1911)** 20 Nov.: Princess of Wales interviewed on Panorama | Parliament's Intelligence and Security Committee meets for the first time | Department of Employment abolished, its responsibilities dispersed |

| Political Parties and Elections (elections in capitals) | Interest and Pressure Groups | Civil Liberties | Year |
|---|---|---|---|
| GENERAL ELECTION | NEDC abolished<br>8 Sept.: Howard Davies becomes first Director-General of the CBI to address the TUC | | 1992 |
| 29 Sept.: John Smith persuades Labour Party Conference to introduce one member one vote | July: John Smith becomes first Labour leader to address the CBI's annual conference. | | 1993 |
| | TUC committee structure ceases to mirror government departments.<br>July: David Hunt, Employment Secretary, attends TUC | | 1994 |
| 29 Apr: Labour Party Conference votes to remove Clause 4 from its constitution<br><br>4 July: John Major re-elected Conservative leader on first ballot | 16 Aug.: John Redwood launches Conservative 2000 Foundation | | 1995 |

# Index of Persons

*Note*: Page references in **bold** are the most important for the heading under which they appear. As most of this book concerns the period before 1974, place names are assigned to counties as they were before that date.

# General Index